"HOME COMFORT" COOK BOOK

Containing
A General Course of Instruction
In the Art of

Home Cooking and Canning

Including

1000 Modern Recipes
And Valuable Formulae

★ ★ ★ ★ ★

Also

Many Pages of Interesting and Valuable
Information of Special Character
and of Much Interest to the
General Household

★ ★ ★ ★ ★

REVISED EDITION
Compiled and Published for Presentation
To Purchasers of

"HOME COMFORT" FAMILY RANGES

By the

Wrought Iron Range Company
ST. LOUIS, U. S. A.

Established 1864   Capital $1,000,000

NOTE—This Book is not for sale at Book Stores; however, the Company will be pleased to forward
a copy to any address upon receipt of cost of Postage and Mailing—10 cents.

FOREWORD

For over Seventy Years the "HOME COMFORT" Family Range has been manufactured by this Company and sold direct to the American home. For over Seventy Years, the "HOME COMFORT" Cook Book has been published and distributed as a friend and aid to the housekeeper, until more than a Million Copies have found their way into as many welcoming hands— hands of our contented "HOME COMFORT" Range Users.

This Revised Addition has been compiled, at the cost of much time and expense, with the especial view to its being of the greatest possible help to the busy housewife. To those who delight in having at their finger-tips a compendium of reliable recipes, this book will find great favor; while, to those who have young daughters to instruct in the Art and Mastery of Cooking, it will prove to be an invaluable aid. If it accomplishes its special mission, this Company will be very happy. This book is therefore,

DEDICATED TO
The Greatest of all Institutions
"THE AMERICAN HOUSEWIFE"

BY THE

Wrought Iron Range Company
of ST. LOUIS

INTRODUCTORY

The WROUGHT IRON RANGE COMPANY, whose Home Office and Manufacturing Plant are at **St. Louis, Mo.,** are manufacturers and sole, direct distributers of the famous "HOME COMFORT" FAMILY RANGE. The Company was founded in 1864. Today, its Operating Capital is $1,000,000 fully paid.

The "HOME COMFORT" RANGE has been on the market since the founding of this Company over Seventy Years ago. More than a Million have been placed in American Homes. There are thousands of "HOME COMFORT" RANGES in daily use today that have been in constant service for 20, 30 and even 40 years. There is no other Family Range built in the world that can show a better record of performance and durability. That is why the name "HOME COMFORT" has been a familiar household term throughout America for the past half-century.

The "HOME COMFORT" SALES ORGANIZATION is known in practically every county of every state in the Union. Today, this large force of trained and efficient Salesmen is working daily throughout the country—calling **directly** at the Home. These men are not "Agents," but are regularly employed "Traveling Salesmen" paid by the Company to sell "HOME COMFORT" RANGES and **nothing else.** They are under the general supervision of the Home Office and the direct supervision of its Division Superintendents, whose duty it is to see that the policies of the Company are carried out, and that the interests of the Customer are properly served. Many of these Superintendents and Salesmen have been selling "HOME COMFORT" RANGES for 20 to 30 years, and several of them have been with this Company 40 to 45 years. Honesty and Integrity have always been the first consideration in employing our Salesmen, and this Company takes much pride in commending them as honorable, courteous gentlemen.

The "HOME COMFORT" SELLING PLAN has broadcasted **real comfort** into more than a million American Homes by its simple and time proven method. Experience of over Seventy Years has taught us that the most satisfactory means of securing the confidence and friendship of the public is through personal solicitation—through actual contact with the customer. The shortest possible route to an understanding between two parties entering into a sale, is when they are face-to-face. Experience has also proved that the average buyer of a manufactured article much prefers to purchase **direct** from the manufacturer; and, furthermore, that a **satisfied customer,** who has become acquainted with this Company and its Product through personal contact with one of its representative salesmen, is the best and most highly prized investment we can make.

Our Method of Solicitation is fundamentally simple: Our salesman visits a particular county or locality at consistent periods, calling upon "HOME COMFORT" users and all their neighbors who should own a "HOME COMFORT" RANGE. Through the medium of a small "Model"—a Miniature Reproduction of the full sized "HOME COMFORT" RANGE—our salesmen demonstrate and explain its many superior, strictly "HOME COMFORT" features of construction and operation, and takes orders for early carload shipment to the nearest central shipping point.

The Company's Guarantee, in the form of a regular printed "Warrant," which has the **moral** and **financial strength** of this Company behind it, is given to each customer.

IMPORTANT

At various times it has been reported to us that men posing as representatives of the Wrought Iron Range Company have solicited repair business from our customers.

The Wrought Iron Range Company has no repair men or agents selling repairs whatsoever, but carries out all such business with its customers by mail through the home office in St. Louis.

The information given in this Cook Book is from sources which are believed to be reliable. However, the Company does not guarantee any recipe, formula or other information herein set forth, nor assume any responsibility for its correctness or accuracy.

WROUGHT IRON RANGE COMPANY.

WROUGHT IRON RANGE COMPANY
5661 NATURAL BRIDGE AVE.
ST. LOUIS, MO.
CAPITAL $1,000,000.00

REGISTERED TRADE MARK
USED FOR
HALF CENTURY

ON THE PRODUCTS
OF THE
WROUGHT IRON RANGE COMPANY

EMBLEM OF THE
CULVER MILITARY ACADEMY
CULVER INDIANA

FOUNDED AND ENDOWED
BY OWNERS OF
WROUGHT IRON RANGE COMPANY

TO THE PROSPECTIVE BUYER:

Ranges and Stoves are manufactured in countless varieties ranging into the hundreds, with a wide variance in design, construction and price. To the prospective buyer, who wishes to own a really good Kitchen Range, this "confusion of makes" often presents a most perplexing problem, and results in a mistaken selection.

Some Purchasers simply want "just something to cook upon", wholly disregarding the character and durability of the device. Other Purchasers desire a flashily ornamented article for the sake of appearance alone, forgetting everything else. Many Purchasers consider nothing but Price, and put their good money into an inferior range just because it is cheap.

The "MAKESHIFT" Stove, the mere "something to cook upon", is always a source of continual aggravation, and, in proportion to its short life, costs immeasurably more than A Good Range.

The "GAUDY" Range or Stove, carrying an unnecessary mass of polished metal trimmings and covers, invariably hides under its shoddy coverings many deficiencies in material, construction and workmanship, and means constant work and worry. Selected as a "Thing of Beauty", it soon becomes a "Thing of Toil".

The "PENNY WISE" Range, the one flaunting a low price-tag, because of its short life and the cost of repeatedly burnt-out parts, results in an expensive experience that holds many regrets, and causes a keen sense of being "pound foolish".

The "REAL RANGE" sought after by careful and conservative buyers, and the ultimate choice of the great majority, must embody Efficiency, Simplicity and Durability -- the essentials of True Economy. It must be built upon scientific principles, and must generate and distribute a quick, even heat with the least amount of fuel. It must be simple in operation and not overburdened with excess trimmings. It must be quality through and through, and withstand any amount of usage for an indefinite period without frequent repair bills. Then, when we add Beauty and Symmetry, we have found the "perfect range".

This "PERFECT RANGE" is described in detail on the pages immediately following -- please turn them and read -- and farther over you will find many interesting "Comments" from some of our "Home Comfort" Range users.

Yours truly,

WROUGHT IRON RANGE COMPANY

"HOME COMFORT" VICTORIES

Three Gold Medals and One Silver Medal
World's Industrial and Cotton Centennial Exposition, New Orleans.

Highest Awards
Nebraska State Board of Agriculture.

Diploma
Alabama State Agricultural Society, Montgomery.

Awards
Chattahoochee Valley Exposition, Columbus, Ga.

Highest Awards
St. Louis Agricultural and Mechanical Association Fair.

Gold Medal and Six Diplomas Awarded
World's Columbian Exposition, Chicago.

Highest Awards
Western Fair Exposition, London, Canada.

Six Gold Medals and Diplomas
California Midwinter Exposition, San Francisco.

Silver Medal
Industrial Exhibition, Toronto, Canada.

Grand Prize
Louisiana Purchase Exposition, St. Louis, Mo.

The Wrought Iron Range Company have received awards on all their exhibits, for distinguished merits in their goods, as follows:

For hotel and family ranges made of wrought steel and malleable iron; for the practical introduction of malleable iron in the manufacture of ranges, which gives increased strength with lightness and durability; especially for the manner of securing, supporting and strengthening the malleable iron range tops, effectually preventing warping and cracking.

For excellence of design and finish; first-class material and good workmanship throughout.

For an excellent and attractive exhibit of hotel and family ranges and appliances for hotel or restaurant use, including a broiler, sand oven, steam and carving table, and a set of urns.

For improvement in the construction of boilers, with broad apron in front.

Combination of a steam table with a carving table, convenience and design.

These awards they may justly be proud of, as they were given after the sharpest and most persistent competition on the part of other prominent and reliable range and stove manufacturers from other cities, in this as well as foreign countries.

OUR FIRST FACTORY
1864

Above is shown the Home of the "HOME COMFOR
circular insert above) we have been compelled, by the g
double the existing factory capacity at five different periods
Ten Acres of Floor Space, and is the "Largest Single Ra
construction throughout, is absolutely fire-proof, and is of the
is amply supplied with all the shipping and other facilities of r

Iron Range Company—St. Louis, Mo.

ange.   Starting in 1864 in our First Factory (shown in the
g popularity of the "HOME COMFORT", to more than
that time.   Today Our Manufacturing Plant covers nearly
'lant in the World".   This plant is of modern re-inforced
ight factory" type.   It is situated on 11½ acres of ground, and
industry.

World's Columbian Exposition in com-
memoration of the four-hundredth
Anniversary of the Landing of
Columbus 1492-1893.

World's Columbian Exposition in com
memoration of the four-hundredth
Anniversary of the Landing of
Columbus 1492-1893.

Industrial Exhibition Association
of Toronto.

California Mid-Winter International
Exposition,
San Francisco

Industrial Exhibition Association
of Toronto.

St. Louis Agricultural and Mechanical
Association

St. Louis Agricultural and Mechanical
Association

The World's Industrial and Cotton
Centennial Exposition.
New Orleans 1884-85.

The World's Industrial and Cotton
Centennial Exposition.
New Orleans 1884-85.

Louisiana Purchase Exposition
St. Louis 1904.

California Mid-Winter International
Exposition,
San Francisco

Louisiana Purchase Exposition
St. Louis 1904.

Louisiana Purchase Exposition
St. Louis 1904.

Louisiana Purchase Exposition
St. Louis 1904.

MODEL "CB"

RANGE		OVEN	
Top Cooking Surface	34"x28"	Height	14½"
Height of Range	33"	Width	18¼"
Extreme Height of Range	62"	Depth	21¼"
Extreme Width of Range	55"		

APPROXIMATE SHIPPING WEIGHT,
520 Pounds

HOME COMFORT "STAR" FEATURES

★ STURDY, RUGGED CONSTRUCTION.

★ MODERN, TRIM APPEARANCE.

★ GLEAMING VERLUC ENAMEL INSIDE AND OUT
   Excepting cooking-top and oven.

★ ADAPTIVENESS OF COLOR to any kitchen.

★ DRAFT CONTROL, effecting:
   Rapid heating.
   Even baking.
   Economy of fuel.

★ "FULL FLOATING" SIX-HOLE COOKING-TOP:
   Malleable Iron.
   Unrestricted expansion.
   Greater durability.

★ DUPLEX GRATES; for coal or wood.

★ ABUNDANT SUPPLY OF HOT-WATER from—
   Waterback, or
   Reversible reservoir.

★ ELECTRICALLY WELDED, ARCH-REINFORCED OVEN.
   Rounded corners.
   Extra heavy bottom, hammer hardened.
   Adjustable oven-door spring.
   Heat-Indicator.

★ LOWER WARMING CLOSET.

★ MANTLE WARMING CLOSET.

★ ASBESTOS INSULATED FLUES.

The "HOME COMFORT" Range

The Wrought Iron Range Company is entering its seventieth year of range making by introducing its latest and finest product, The New "HOME COMFORT."

This Range, the result of careful experimentation and planning, represents the acme of quality, craftsmanship and durability. From the sturdy, clean-cut appearance of the range as a whole to its most minute detail every effort has been expended by our engineers to build the utmost in a labor-saving, practicable range without marring in any manner its pleasing design and finish. Accordingly, a gleaming coat of Verluc Vitrified Enamel covers the entire range body, shelf and reservoir, a few small castings excepted, which for beauty are given a velvety nickel finish to set the range off.

The color of the range is Jersey Gray blended with Sage Green. All door frames are Dove Tan in color and surround soft Ivory tone panels. The complete range presents a harmonious ensemble of a warm, clean, neutral color tone which is pleasing and adaptable to any kitchen color scheme.

Attention must be called to the fact that vitrified enamel is a form of glass and, therefore, cannot be guaranteed against cracking or injury from any outside force. The glass surface provides an easily cleaned, sanitary and beautiful finish that will protect the underlying steel indefinitely, unless abused.

The new Full Floating Top, moulded from highest grade electrically annealed malleable iron to prevent cracking from over-heating or sudden temperature changes, allows free expansion in all directions and yet is kept firmly locked in place to the range body.

In keeping with this progressive range is the innovation of the electrically-welded oven. Welding does away with all projecting nuts, bolts and rivets, which are not only unsightly but are apt to cause trouble and expense by rusting out. And, too, welding has been proved to be stronger, tougher and more lasting than bolts or rivets. The hygienic cleanliness of this oven must not be overlooked, for all crevices and dirt-catching cracks which heretofore have necessitated great care and attention to keep clean, have been eliminated. The result is a rounded and smooth-surfaced oven interior, easily cleaned.

The experience of seventy years range building combined with modern engineering and dependable workmanship presents to you

THE NEW "HOME COMFORT" RANGE.

Evolution of the "Home Comfort" Range

This series of illustrations shows the evolution, or progressive development, of the "Home Comfort" Range, beginning with the "Farmer" Cook Stove, the first stove manufactured and sold direct to the home by the founders of the Wrought Iron Range Company in 1864.

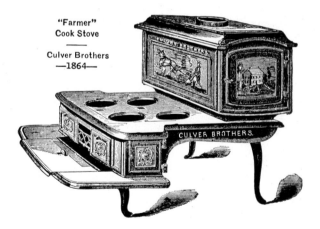

"Farmer"
Cook Stove
—
Culver Brothers
—1864—

With this modest beginning, came the building of the "Home Comfort"— **the First Family "Range" ever manufactured.** With the adoption of Malleable Iron in its construction, this "Range" became the **First "Malleable Iron" Range ever built.** Then followed a half-century of further "Home Comfort" development as shown in the following progressive illustrations, leading up to the present beautiful Enameled Master-Model of today.

Evolution of the "Home Comfort" Range

Original "Home Comfort"
First Range manufactured.
All castings made of grey iron.
—1870—

"A"
First Malleable Iron Range
Automatic swing oven
door, slide draft and
extension shelf.
—1885—

Original "Range"
With First Mantel-Shelf.
—1872—

"I"
First drop shelf Oven
Door. Grapevine
finish.—1886—

New Style Oven, Draft
Door; Improved Mantel-Shelf.
—1880—

"C"
First Reservoir
with two pipe
waterback.
—1888—

Evolution of the "Home Comfort" Range

"C-I"
First polished Iron
Range. Closet
shelf and sifting
dump grate.
—1890—

No. 64
First Roller Door
closet shelf.
—1891—

No. 65
Range and Oven
three inches
larger.
—1892—

No. 66
First six-hole
Range. Four 8"
and two 7" lids.
—1893—

No. 96
First one-hole
pocket water back.
—1896—

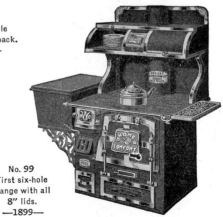

No. 99
First six-hole
Range with all
8" lids.
—1899—

Evolution of the "Home Comfort" Range

No. 1900
First nickel plated
Range. Pouch
feed fire door and
pressed steel en-
ameled reservoir.
—1900—

No. 1905
First heavy body,
square oven door
Range. Teapot
brackets; corner
tubes; new open
shelf bracket.
—1905—

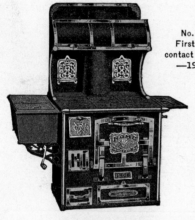

No. 1906
First pocket
contact reservoir.
—1906—

No. 1910
First flat contact reservoir
enameled. Extension
shelf with towel rack.
—1910—

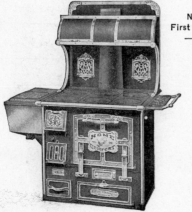

No. 1915
First square oven.
—1915—

No. 1918
First side door warm-
ing closet. First
sanitary legs.
—1918—

Evolution of the "Home Comfort" Range

No. 1922
First spring balanced oven door. New design polished doors and frames.
—1922—

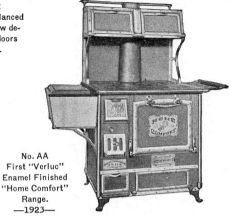

No. AA
First "Verluc" Enamel Finished "Home Comfort" Range.
—1923—

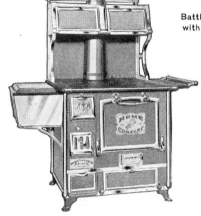

No. AB
Battleship Grey Enamel with nickel trimmings.
—1924—

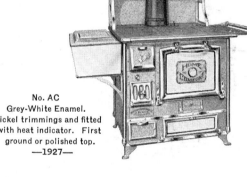

No. AC
Grey-White Enamel. Nickel trimmings and fitted with heat indicator. First ground or polished top.
—1927—

No. AE
Fitted with contact water heater on both right and left side of Range. Full Grey-White Enamel Finish.
—1927—

No. A1
Grey-White Enamel. Steel encased reservoir. Fitted with towel rack and adjustable draft door.
—1928—

Evolution of the "Home Comfort" Range

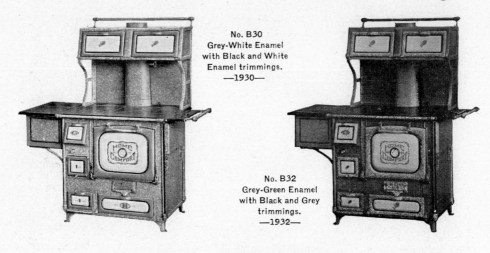

No. B30
Grey-White Enamel
with Black and White
Enamel trimmings.
—1930—

No. B32
Grey-Green Enamel
with Black and Grey
trimmings.
—1932—

No. CA
Jersey grey enamel
with dove tan
frames and fittings.
—1933—

WROUGHT IRON RANGE CO.

ST. LOUIS, MO.

SECTIONAL PARTS OF THE "HOME COMFORT" RANGE

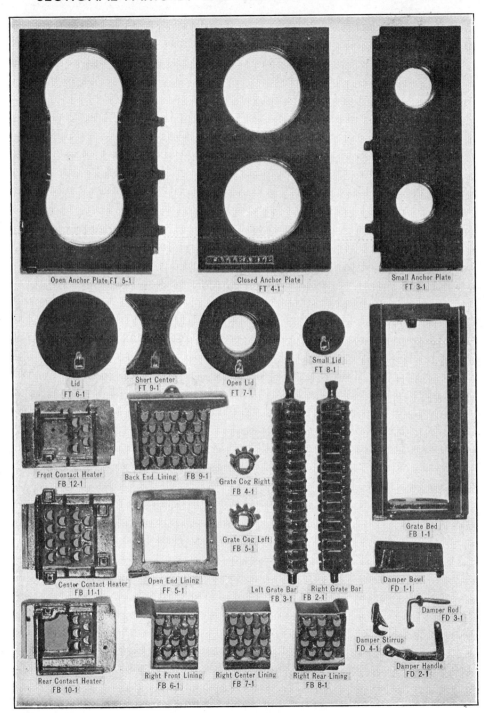

Open Anchor Plate FT 5-1

Closed Anchor Plate
FT 4-1

Small Anchor Plate
FT 3-1

Lid
FT 6-1

Short Center
FT 9-1

Open Lid
FT 7-1

Small Lid
FT 8-1

Front Contact Heater
FB 12-1

Back End Lining   FB 9-1

Grate Cog Right
FB 4-1

Grate Cog Left
FB 5-1

Grate Bed
FB 1-1

Center Contact Heater
FB 11-1

Open End Lining
FF 5-1

Left Grate Bar
FB 3-1

Right Grate Bar
FB 2-1

Damper Bowl
FD 1-1

Damper Rod
FD 3-1

Damper Stirrup
FD 4-1

Rear Contact Heater
FB 10-1

Right Front Lining
FB 6-1

Right Center Lining
FB 7-1

Right Rear Lining
FB 8-1

Damper Handle
FD 2-1

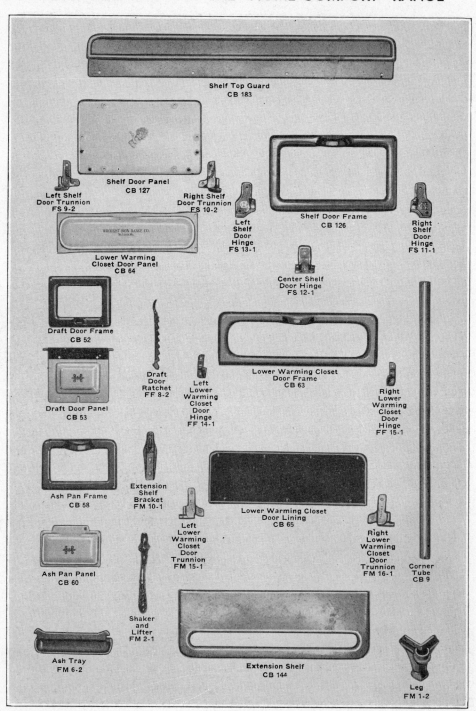

Shelf Top Guard
CB 183

Shelf Door Panel
CB 127

Left Shelf
Door Trunnion
FS 9-2

Right Shelf
Door Trunnion
FS 10-2

Left
Shelf
Door
Hinge
FS 13-1

Shelf Door Frame
CB 126

Right
Shelf
Door
Hinge
FS 11-1

Lower Warming
Closet Door Panel
CB 64

Center Shelf
Door Hinge
FS 12-1

Draft Door Frame
CB 52

Draft
Door
Ratchet
FF 8-2

Left
Lower
Warming
Closet
Door
Hinge
FF 14-1

Lower Warming Closet
Door Frame
CB 63

Right
Lower
Warming
Closet
Door
Hinge
FF 15-1

Draft Door Panel
CB 53

Ash Pan Frame
CB 58

Extension
Shelf
Bracket
FM 10-1

Lower Warming Closet
Door Lining
CB 65

Left
Lower
Warming
Closet
Door
Trunnion
FM 15-1

Right
Lower
Warming
Closet
Door
Trunnion
FM 16-1

Corner
Tube
CB 9

Ash Pan Panel
CB 60

Shaker
and
Lifter
FM 2-1

Ash Tray
FM 6-2

Extension Shelf
CB 144

Leg
FM 1-2

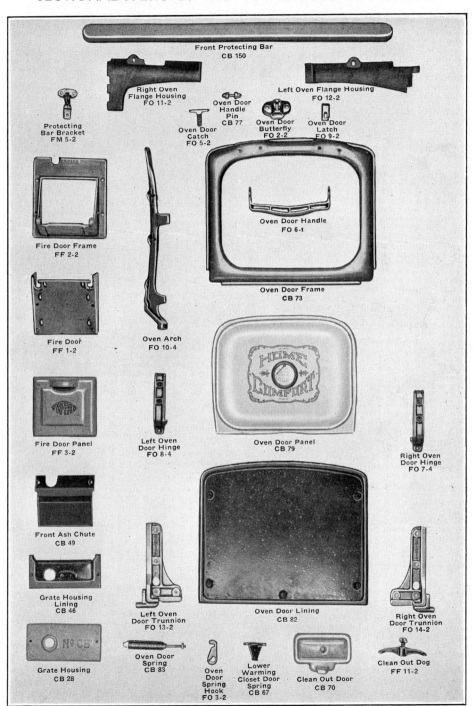

Front Protecting Bar
CB 150

Right Oven
Flange Housing
FO 11-2

Left Oven Flange Housing
FO 12-2

Oven Door
Handle
Pin
CB 77

Oven Door
Butterfly
FO 2-2

Oven Door
Latch
FO 9-2

Protecting
Bar Bracket
FM 5-2

Oven Door
Catch
FO 5-2

Fire Door Frame
FF 2-2

Oven Door Handle
FO 6-1

Oven Door Frame
CB 73

Fire Door
FF 1-2

Oven Arch
FO 10-4

Fire Door Panel
FF 3-2

Left Oven
Door Hinge
FO 8-4

Oven Door Panel
CB 79

Right Oven
Door Hinge
FO 7-4

Front Ash Chute
CB 49

Grate Housing
Lining
CB 46

Left Oven
Door Trunnion
FO 13-2

Oven Door Lining
CB 82

Right Oven
Door Trunnion
FO 14-2

Grate Housing
CB 28

Oven Door
Spring
CB 83

Oven
Door
Spring
Hook
FO 3-2

Lower
Warming
Closet Door
Spring
CB 67

Clean Out Door
CB 70

Clean Out Dog
FF 11-2

Details of Construction

BODY OF RANGE—The range body is constructed of high grade enameling steel, properly formed and sized in presses exerting approximately one million pounds pressure which insures a perfect fit to each part. These individual parts are joined together by modern electrical welding machines—bolts or rivets being used only where welding is impractical. Verluc vitrified enamel covers the range body steel both inside and out, providing protection against rust or corrosion. Asbestos is used in the flue passages as a protection against intense heat and also to serve as an insulator to minimize heat loss through side walls of the range.

By means of processes recently developed in our plant, the new "Home Comfort" range presents the many advantages of a carefully designed flue passage with joints which approach air-tightness more nearly than any range heretofore built to our knowledge. A careful scrutiny of the interior of the new "Home Comfort" will reveal to even the casual observer the correct design, the expert engineering and the careful workmanship which has produced this range to meet the exacting requirements of a company that has been in the family range business for seventy years.

TOP COOKING SURFACES—Probably the most perplexing problem of building ranges is that of the range top, for here we must combine rugged and durable construction with well finished appearance; and while the top must fit tightly to the range it must be free to move in any direction in order to allow for the normal expansion and contraction that takes place with extreme change in temperature. The top of the "Home Comfort" Range is the result of many years experimenting and presents to our customers the first "Full Floating Top," featuring close fitting joints yet free to expand with heat in any direction. The castings are made of Malleable Iron to insure longer life and prevent cracking from over heating or contact with cold water. The top consists of four plates:

Back Rail—Extending across the back of the top.
Open Anchor—With 2 eight-inch lids and short center.
Closed Anchor—With 2 eight-inch lids.
Small Anchor—With 2 small lids.

The Back Rail is bolted securely to the range body as there is no probability of the necessity of i's removal by the customer.

To remove any Anchor Plates the customer has only to follow this simple procedure:
First: Remove bolt in rear of Closed Anchor Plate.
Second: **Slide** Closed Anchor Plate toward **front** of range until it unlocks.
Third: Lift off Closed Anchor Plate.
Fourth: Remove bolt holding down Mantle Shelf Bracket on Anchor Plate you wish to remove.
Fifth: **Slide** Anchor Plate toward **center** of range until it unlocks.
Sixth: Lift off Anchor Plate.

To replace top the above proceedings should be reversed.

All the plates and lids of this top are reinforced underneath by ribs, or bridge work, and each top is individually machined and the top surface ground by specially designed grinding equipment. These tops have been tried and tested and represent the combined experience and engineering ability of three generations of range building.

DETACHABLE EXTENSION SHELF—Finished with Enameled Towel-Rack. The Extension Shelf is a serviceable addition to the Top Cooking-Surface.

PROTECTING BAR—Enameled Steel Bar. Extends completely across front of Range-Top and is a protection for clothes.

FIRE BOX—Ample Capacity; Readily Accessible and Easily Cleaned. Flanged **Fire-Door** at front: Drop-hopper Type; Securely Hinged to Enamel Iron Frame, and easily opened; Forms Fire-Box Extension for extra-length fuel. **Fire-Walls**, or **Linings**, are sectional—allowing for expansion and contraction—with raised designs of "horseshoe" or "cup" shape on their inner, or "fire" sides—deposit of ashes on these lugs insulate and add life to linings. Diamond-shaped lugs on back, or reverse side, of linings provide space, or "air-cushion"—protects Oven and adds life to linings.

GRATE BED—One-piece; Strong and Durable; Forms permanent support to Fire-Box Linings. Fitted with Duplex, Revolving Grate-Bars, interlocked by protected "cog," easily controlled from front of Range. Grate-Bars cannot get out of adjustment; easily removed and replaced if necessary. Adjustable to burn, equally well, Hard or Soft Coal, Wood, or Other Fuel.

CONTACT WATER HEATERS—Form entire length of fire box on the left and Same Space on the Right-hand side of Range. Outer side of each Heater being exposed and slightly extended to form a perfect contact with the side of tank, the flanges of both Heaters being insulated with Asbestos and neither affected by the removal of reservoir.

RESERVOIR—Of ample capacity and heated by direct contact on either side of the range. The reservoir itself is made of pure copper, nickel-plated to afford easier cleaning and better appearance. This copper body is enclosed in an enameled steel casing. The cover is provided with a large opening to facilitate filling reservoir or removing water. The hinges of lid are of Monel Metal and are applied with Monel Metal rivets to prevent any rust or corrosion. As in all other parts of the range quality has been the watch-word and has been insisted upon by "Home Comfort" designers to the most minute detail of construction.

The complete reservoir is supported in position on either side of the range by a hinged reservoir shelf, which, when not in use, closes up over the contact heater as a protective cover.

Two reservoirs for hard or soft water can be used at the same time; or a pressure water back can be used in fire-box together with a right hand reservoir.

PRESSURE WATER BACK—For Pressure Water System. A Water-back can be substituted in place of the left-hand Reservoir Contact Heater.

DRAFT CONTROL—These words mean more in the new "Home Comfort" than the mere opening and closing of a draft door or damper. "Draft" is the only operating power in a range, and it is a power that, for years, has defied the attempts of engineers to harness it to definite rules and formulas. Realizing its great importance our Research Engineers have made an exhaustive study of "Draft;" ranges have been built with "windows" at strategic locations for observation, instruments have measured volumes and velocities of gases through the flue passages, and the flow has been studied to eliminate eddies and back currents in the range. The result of this work is that the owner of a "Home Comfort" will have:

      1. A quick heating oven with evenly distributed heat.

      2. Closer control of oven temperature.

      3. Economy of fuel.

The draft of your range may be regulated by a combination of two general means—above and below the fire. For the first a damper is provided in the flue section just below the mantle shelf and for the second there is the draft door on front of the range below the fire box. The Direct-Damper Control located at back of range top, and easily reached from the front of the range, should be opened (handle pushed back) when fire is lighted and until the chimney has had time enough to become warm. Then close (pull handle forward) and force the flame and hot gases around the oven.

BACK FLUE—Made in One-piece, Formed, Heavy Special Enamel Steel; Enameled Inside and Out. Lined with Asbestos Board thoroughly riveted to Inside. Wide Flanges all around securely welded to Range-body.

OVEN—This is one of the most important parts of a cooking range and yet in many instances it conceals hidden economies of material and workmanship by which the builder has attempted to "save money." The attention of the "Home Comfort" purchaser is directed to the following outstanding features of his oven:

      1. Extra heavy copper bearing steel used throughout.

      2. Electrically welded seams, joining top, sides and bottom.

      3. Expansion joints at front and rear.

      4. Rounded corners to facilitate cleaning.

      5. No stove putty used in its construction.

6. No bolts or rivets in bottom to work loose and catch on edges of utensils or cleaning rags.

7. Bottom made of 12 gauge steel (approximately one-eighth inch thick) and reinforced by two "L" section girders welded in place across oven bottom.

8. Top arched for added strength—and further reinforced by heavy "Oven Arch" Malleable Iron casting securely bolted in place with lock washers across oven top.

9. Oven door with extra heavy frame, fitted with steel lining, panel and oven heat-indicator, all enameled and assembled in a manner to provide pleasing appearance and easy cleaning.

10. Adjustable oven door spring which may be easily reached and the amount of tension changed by tightening or loosening thumb screw.

11. Twin latches on oven door.

12. Oven door set into range front, providing better fit around door.

The "Home Comfort" challenges comparison of its large, thoroughly engineered and carefully constructed oven with that of any range built. No expense has been spared to put into your range the wholesome quality typical of "Home Comfort" ranges since 1864 and upon which, as a foundation, this Company was built and has endured.

FLUE BOTTOM—One of the greatest essentials to The Perfect Oven, is a thorough and equal distribution of Heat. This is accomplished by directing the heat entirely over the Arched Top of the Oven, down the right-hand Side, under the entire Bottom around a baffle-plate, into the Flue Base—thus completing a circuit entirely and uniformly heating all surfaces. This heating-chamber, therefore, becomes a veritable "Flue"—and must be substantial. This Flue-Bottom is made of extra-heavy steel, flanged all around. Enameled both sides, and securely welded to Body of Range. Baffle-plate securely welded to Flue-Bottom.

SOOT DOOR—Located just beneath the oven door and fitted with a positive and simple locking device. To open, for removal of soot, unscrew knob (turn to left) until door is loose. Then slip to left or right until unlocked and remove from range. When replacing be sure that the locking bar ends are inside of range body before tightening knob.

LOWER WARMING CLOSET—Under the Oven, between Flue-Bottom and Range Bottom, forms available warming space adaptable to many uses. Fitted with Enameled Drop-shelf Door and Panel.

ASH PAN—Formed of Heavy Steel, finished with Enameled Front, Convex Handle with Enameled Panel-insert. Pan has Folding Riveted Bail-Handle with Scoop End to take up any loose ashes in Range Bottom upon replacing. Removable Ash-Tray below Pan. Capacity of Ash-Pan is fixed as the maximum accumulation of ashes for ideal results.

RANGE BOTTOM—Made of Heavy Special Enamel Steel. Both Sides Enameled; Formed with wide flanges all around, and securely welded to Range Body; also welded to flange of heavy Steel Cross-Section between Ash-Box and Lower Warming-Closet. Gives added rigidity to Range.

LEGS—Of graceful, pleasing design; Enameled. Gives access to space beneath Range for cleaning, and allows for ventilation.

MANTLE-SHELF WARMING-CLOSET—Spacious. Two-Door Compartment of Special Design. Enameled inside and out; Drop-shelf doors are attached to Enameled Front-Frames mounted upon and securely bolted to open enameled shelf-brackets, and to heavy, enameled splash-back extending entirely across back of Range-Top affording sufficient space above Top Cooking-Surface, and giving exceptional rigidity. Top and bottom of closet, around base-pipe, reinforced and strengthened by special raised stamped collar, adding "finish" and rigidity. Top forms flat shelf, "flush" for easy removal of dishes. Closet is heated from radiation from base-pipe passing through it, and from top cooking-surface. Entire warming-closet, in design and finish, is in pleasing conformity with general appearance of range, and saves many steps in preparing a meal.

Pressure Water Heater

OUR PRESSURE WATER HEATER is designed for a Continuous System of Water Supply, and is easily installed in the "Home Comfort" Range, by substituting it in place of the Left-Hand Contact Reservoir Heater.

THE PRESSURE BOILER should be set as near the Range as practical. See that it is fitted inside with a one-half inch galvanized Cold Water Supply Pipe extending within 6 or 12 inches of the bottom of the tank.

You will have trouble heating water without this extension pipe inside of the pressure boiler. Or, trouble if you reverse the connections.

A Pressure Tank should always stand alongside of, or be elevated above the range.

CONNECTIONS: Connect the Cold Water Pipe from the bottom of the Tank to the bottom-hole in the Water Heater. Then connect the Hot Water Pipe from the top hole in the Water Heater to the hole in the side of the Tank. Or, if a Pressure Tank, you may plug this side hole up, and make the connections to the Hot Water (not Cold Water) discharge pipe, leading off from the top of the Pressure Tank.

Either method of connecting to Pressure Tank is practical. These connections should be made with Unions—to be easily removed when necessary for cleaning. Underneath the Pressure Tank, there should be installed in your pipe connections, a Tee fitted with a plug, stop-cock, or faucet to permit ready flushing or draining of the Tank for any purpose.

CAUTION—Do not build a fire in the Range until the System is filled up with water; otherwise, you will crack the Water Front. Or, if there is a possibility of the Water Front or Pipe Connections being frozen, look out for an explosion.

In freezing weather, keep a fire in the Range, or, drain the Water System.

Rumbling noises in the Water Front or Tank are invariably caused by improper connections or poor water circulation.

In time, hard water forms deposits in the connections and Water Front, and, if not cleaned out occasionally, will stop the water circulation, and cause the Water Heater to "burn out," or break. These Lime Deposits prevent free water circulation —consequently reduces the volume of Hot Water. Once a week **DRAIN** 3 to 5 gallons of Water from Bottom of your Pressure Tank, to flush it out.

If using Open Tank, or Barrel, never draw off the water lower than the top of the Water Front.

When burning coal it is not advisable to have the fire box over about 2/3 full. A greater amount of coal is unnecessary and results only in choking the fire and a waste of fuel.

Directions for Properly Setting Up and Operating
"HOME COMFORT" Ranges

Any "HOME COMFORT" Range set up in the open with only three joints of straight pipe, will bake and do all kinds of cooking to perfection.

Such expressions as "My stove will not draw;" "fills with soot;" "will not burn;" "will not bake on the bottom,"—are invariably the result of poor fuel or defective chimney flue.

The best chimney flue is a clean, straight one, not less than 9 inches in diameter, without defective joints and built higher than any other point of the house or obstructions. Should not have an Arch over its top, nor be used for any other purpose; if there are any other openings, they should be tightly closed. Whenever possible, smoke pipe from Range should include at least One Elbow to prevent rain falling direct into Range. When two or more Joints of Pipe are used from the Elbow to the chimney, the smoke pipe should have a rise of $\frac{1}{2}$ inch, or more, to the joint. Sometimes smoke pipe is carelessly pushed too far into chimney flue, shutting off draft.

No. 1. Before starting a fire always see that the fire-box and ash pan are clean. Lay the fire with dry kindling or other fuel. Open *direct damper* by pushing back damper rod on the right side of base-pipe. Open *draft door* underneath the fire door, or pull the ash pan slightly forward. Light the fire, and after it is well started pull the damper forward, closing it. The direct damper should remain open *ONLY* when starting fire.

No. 2. The oven door should be closed tight and the oven thoroughly heated before attempting to bake. The length of time required for perfect baking is governed entirely by conditions, which can be ascertained after a few trials.

The correct operation of drafts will insure quick service, abundance of heat and economy in fuel. (The opening or closing of the fire door or the draft door, ash pan, lids or damper in pipe—if any—will serve this purpose.)

No. 3. At least once a week scrape accumulated soot and ashes out of the soot door directly underneath the oven. This requires little time—improves baking and protects the range.

Empty the ash pan at least once a day. Cold air circulation underneath the grate and back of fire linings, as provided for in "HOME COMFORT" Ranges, will preserve them indefinitely—provided ashes are not allowed to accumulate, which will reflect heat to them causing serious injury and preventing proper draft to Range.

No. 4. Protect the Range from Dampness. Openings, if any, in roof or around smoke pipe should be closed.

In extreme cold weather we advise the Reservoir being emptied at night, to prevent injury by freezing.

These directions, if followed, insure perfect operation and preservation of "HOME COMFORT" Ranges.

For your information: The life of your Range (like any other household or farm equipment) depends on the care you give it.

Keep your Range in a dry place, free of soot and ashes to prevent a formation of creosote, and wipe off the top and other parts liable to rust with a dry oiled cloth after every meal.

Chimney Construction

Until recent years there were very few Chimney Builders, or even Architects, who knew anything about the Science of Drafts or the requirements of a chimney.

The average brick mason throws up a pile of brick and mortar full of pockets and offsets, and calls it a "chimney." The name is a misnomer. So, in the interest of the afflicted we give below for your guidance such information as our SIXTY odd years experience now suggests:

The first and foremost purpose of a chimney is to produce a draft that will cause sufficient combustion to carry off the resulting smoke. Many unsatisfactory cooking and heating plants, and much excessive fuel consumption are due to improperly constructed chimneys—which are the rule rather than the exception.

As constructed, a range or stove has no more draft than a steam boiler has without a stack or chimney. *The chimney furnishes the draft.* However, one often hears such expressions as—

"My stove will not draw;"
"It fills up with soot;"
"The fire will not burn;"
"The oven will not bake on the bottom."

Such complaints will never end until the *cause* is removed—and the *cause*, nine times out of ten, is a *poor flue.*

If it were possible for the manufacturer to furnish a flue with each stove or range sold, there would be no such thing as a stove or range that did not do its work satisfactorily.

The National Board of Fire Underwriter's Report shows that a larger number of fires are caused by *defective chimney construction* than anything else.

The Most Common Faults in Construction and Care of Chimneys

1st—**The use of unsuitable materials**—Clay sewer pipe—hollow building blocks, or unprotected concrete should never be used.

2nd—**The improper laying of brick.** Brick should *never* be laid on edge. Linings should be used in all brick chimneys where the walls are less than 8 inches thick.

3rd—**The lack of proper support for chimneys.** No chimney should be carried on any timber-construction of the building, and where it rests upon the ground sufficient masonry foundation should be provided to prevent settling.

4th—Building inflammable material into chimney or against it without proper insulation.

5th—Failure to keep flue free of soot and joints in brick work properly pointed.

A "leaky flue" is the most frequent cause of draft troubles, high fuel bills and destructive fires.

To Test Chimney for Leaks

First drive out cold air by burning paper. Then throw a wet blanket over top of flue and start smudge fire in range.

The Draft in a chimney depends entirely upon the flue. The better the flue, the more satisfactory and efficient will be the operation of your cooking apparatus. The strength or intensity of the draft is dependent mainly upon the size and height of the chimney flue. A chimney may be high enough, yet have an area too small to carry the volume of smoke. On the other hand, the size may be sufficient, but the chimney too low to produce a draft. Either fault—or a combination of the two—will result in unsatisfactory service.

A straight, round Flue not less than 9 inches in diameter on the inside and built higher than the house or other obstructions will furnish the necessary draft for family stove or range.

See figure number 1 and number 2.

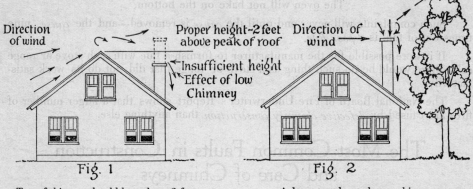

Fig. 1

Top of chimney should be at least 2 feet above top of peak of roof

Fig. 2

A large tree located near chimney may deflect wind currents down the chimney and interfere with drafts

The minimum height of a chimney for family stove or range should not be less than 35 feet above the fire pot—the higher the better. Some authorities contend that any flue under 40 feet in height will produce an erratic draft—good some days and poor others.

Chimney Connections

Many fires are caused by more than One opening in the flue. This should never be permitted as sparks may enter the flue at one opening and pass out into the house at the other. Not only is there risk of fires from 2 openings, but this is one cause of unsatisfactory draft.

When two stoves are connected to the same flue—if the fire is hotter in one than the other (which is invariably the case) then the one with the smaller fire will have practically no draft. Whenever a stove or range is connected to a chimney with an open fire place, then by all means either brick up fire place, or see that the opening is closed up with an air-tight screen when same is not in use.

It is very important that proper care be taken in making stove pipe connections with chimney and that all openings around pipe are closed up tight. Where two or more joints of pipe are used from the elbow to chimney, the smoke pipe should have a rise of from ½ to 1-inch to the joint.

See that stove pipe is properly anchored to the chimney and that it does not extend too far into flue.

See figure number 3 and number 4.

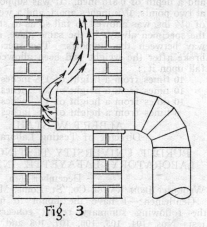

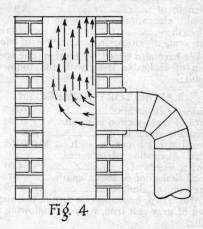

| Fig. 3 Shows wrong connection—producing interference and a poor draft. | Fig. 4 Correct connection—a good draft and free passage for smoke and gases. |

If a smoke pipe must be carried through a wooden partition the woodwork should be protected by a galvanized iron ventilating thimble at least 12 inches larger than smoke pipe. Smoke pipes should not pass through floors, closets, or enter a chimney in a garret.

Your chimney should be thoroughly cleaned of soot and examined for misplaced brick, defective joints and leaks at least once a year.

"Home Comfort" Materials

Laboratory Tests

PURDUE UNIVERSITY,
LAFAYETTE, IND.
PRESIDENT'S ROOM
December 16th.

Wrought Iron Range Co., St. Louis, Mo.

Gentlemen:—This is to certify that we have this day tested for you, by tension, one specimen of gray cast iron, with the following result:

LABORATORY NUMBER 104

Diameter in inches	0.365
Area of cross-section in sq. in...	0.105
Breaking strain in lbs	3,110
Tensil strength per sq. inch.	29,619 lbs.
Total elongation determined for length of	3.9 in.
Total elongation of above length	.02 in.
Per cent. of elogation	$^{51}/_{100}$ of one %

We have also tested, by tension, one specimen of malleable iron, with the following result:

LABORATORY NUMBER 107

Diameter in inches	0.365
Area of cross-section in sq. in	0.105
Breaking strain in lbs	4,200
Tensil strength per sq. inch	40,000 lbs.
Total elongation determined of a length of	4.06 in.
Total elongation of above length	.07 "
Per cent. of elongation	$1^{96}/_{100}$%

Also tested, by transverse strain, one specimen of gray cast iron, with the following result:

LABORATORY NUMBER 105

Distance between supports	6½ in.
Breadth of specimen	0.385 "
Depth of specimen	0.385 "
Total deflection of centre at moment of fracture	0.096 "
Breaking strain	500 lbs.

And, by transverse strain, one specimen of malleable iron, with the following result:

LABORATORY NUMBER 108

Distance between supports	6½ in.
Breadth of specimen	0.385 "
Depth of specimen	0.385 "
Total deflection of centre at moment of fracture	2.902 "
Breaking strain	610 lbs.

And have tested one specimen of gray cast iron in the following manner:

LABORATORY NUMBER 106

The specimen had a bredth of 0.760 inch, and a depth of 0.310 inch. It was supported at two points $1^9/_{16}$ inches apart, and a weight of 6½ lbs. was allowed to fall so as to strike the specimen always in the same place, midway between the supports. The specimen broke after the weight had been allowed to fall on it:

10 times from a height of 1½ inches
2 times from a height of 3 inches

Also tested one specimen of malleable iron in the following manner:

LABORATORY NUMBER 109

The specimen had a breadth of 0.755 inch, and a depth of 0.315 inch. It was supported at two points, $1^9/_{16}$ inches apart, and a weight of 6½ lbs. was allowed to fall so as to strike the specimen always in the same place, midway between the supports. The specimen broke after the weight had been allowed to fall upon it::

10 times from a height of 1½ inches
10 times from a height of 3 inches
10 times from a height of 4½ inches
6 times from a height of 6 inches

ALBERT W. STAHL,
Director of Testing Laboratory

PURDUE UNIVERSITY TESTING
LABORATORY, LAFAYETTE, IND.

December 16th.

Wrought Iron Range Co., St. Louis, Mo.

Gentlemen:—I have the honor to make the following summary report concerning tests Nos. 104, 105, 106, 107, 108 and 109, made this day by me for you on specimens of gray cast iron and of malleable iron castings. These tests were made in precisely the same manner and with precisely the same care on both kinds of iron, and their results leave no doubt of the decided superiority of the malleable iron in every respect.

In the first place, its tensile strength is 40,000 pounds per square inch, while that of the cast iron is only 29,619 pounds. In other words, the malleable iron has 1.35 times as great a tensile strength as the cast iron. Its percentage of elongation is 3.84 times as great as that of cast iron. Its superior tensile strength, combined with its greater elongation, show it to be very much the tougher metal of the two. When tested by transverse strain, its strength was found to be 1.22 times as great as that of the cast

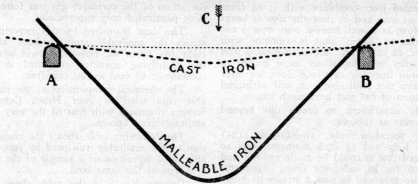

C

CAST IRON

A   B

MALLEABLE IRON

Heavy dotted line shows shape of *cast* iron specimen just before fracture.
Black line shows shape of *malleable* iron specimen just before fracture.
A B are the supports; arrow at C shows direction of pressure.

iron, while its total deflection before breaking was 30.23 times as great as that of the cast iron. The total deflections of the two specimens before breaking are very instructive as to their toughness and ductility. The great disproportion in the amount of bending of the two metals is clearly shown in the two following sketches, drawn accurately half the size of the originals:

In withstanding shock, the malleable iron also shows its superiority. The same number of blows that caused the fracture of the cast iron produced absolutely no perceptible effect on the malleable; it was only on the application of more numerous and more violent blows that the latter finally broke. In this connection, it is important to note that the cast iron broke suddenly, without previous warning, while the malleable iron withstood several blows after it had shown signs of incipient fracture. Again I desire to call your attention to the greater toughness of the malleable iron, as shown by this test, and its consequent superiority for all purposes where it is to be subjected to accidental blows and rough usage.

If the specimens sent me are fair samples of the two materials actually employed, there is but one conclusion that can be drawn from these tests, taken separately or collectively; and that is, that for the purposes for which you are using it, your malleable iron is very greatly superior to the cast iron.

Very respectfully,
ALBERT W. STAHL, M. E.
Director of Testing Laboratory.

J. N. HURTY, M. D., Analytical Chemist,
INDIANAPOLIS, IND.
Indianapolis, Jan 2,
Wrought Iron Range Co., St. Louis, Mo.

Gentlemen—I beg to make the following report on the adaptability and worth of malleable iron for range fabrication, as determined by chemical and mechanical tests.

Malleable iron is intermediate between cast and wrought iron in those qualities and properties most generally useful. It is soft, elastic and ductile; is most difficult to melt; and, compared with cast iron, is very slow to enter into chemical combinations. Its tenacity is enormous.

Cast iron is hard, brittle, melted with comparative ease, and combines with oxygen, sulphur, etc., with much more ease than malleable iron.

FIRST EXPERIMENT

Made to determine the relative melting points.

Two pieces of iron, one malleable, the other cast, were placed side by side in a clean reverberatory furnace, thus exposing both to the same heat. Within one minute's time the piece of cast iron commenced to melt, losing its sharp corners and edges, and in two minutes had entirely melted.

The piece of malleable iron did not lose its corners and edges for twelve minutes, and was not entirely melted until full twenty-five minutes had passed.

The resistance of the malleable iron on this count is twelve and one-half (12½) times greater than cast.

SECOND EXPERIMENT

Made to determine the relative power to withstand continuous heat.

Cast iron "burns" easily. This is evidenced by the warping, sealing and cracking of stove-tops and fire-backs. This so-called "burning" is simply oxidation, that is, the oxygen of the air coming in contact with the heated iron combines with it to form oxide of iron and in time the iron is burnt up. Now, as is well known, *pure iron* is not so prone to "burn," that is, combine with oxygen, as cast iron; and as malleable iron approaches in composition more nearly to *pure iron* than any cast iron does, we infer therefore that malleable iron will withstand the action of fire and heat much longer.

My experiment to prove this beyond doubt was as follows:

A porcelain tube, twenty-four (24) inches long and ⅝ inch diameter, was so arranged that it could be made red-hot and held so for an indefinite time. Apparatus was also arranged to pass a stream of moist oxygen through the tube while heated. Into the tube was placed a piece of cast iron ¼ inch in diameter and one inch long, weighing 223.4 grains. The tube being made red-hot, the stream of oxygen was made to pass slowly through; these conditions being maintained for thirty (30) minutes.

The tube was allowed to cool and the piece of iron examined, and was found—after removing the iron oxide (rust)—to weigh 191.49 grains, showing a loss of 14.28 per cent.

A similar piece of malleable iron—of the same size—but weighing 220.8 grains—was submitted to the same test, and was found to weigh, after the experiment, 211.4 grains, showing a loss of 4.26 per cent.

The comparative resistance then is as one (1) to three and three-tenths (3.3)=1 to 3.3.

THIRD EXPERIMENT

This experiment was made to determine the comparative power of resistance of the two kinds of iron, to chemicals; making plain thereby which iron would withstand the sulphur gases and other destroying agencies formed in the combustion of coal.

A piece of cast iron ⅛ inch square and ½ inch long was submitted to the action of sulphuric acid gas in the same manner and way as in the oxygen experiment. Sulphurous acid gas used because it is the gas formed by the combustion of coal containing sulphur.

A piece of malleable iron of the same size and shape was treated in like manner as the cast iron.

The two pieces, after the same treatment, appeared very different. The piece of cast iron was very nearly destroyed, being rendered so brittle that very light hammering easily reduced it to small pieces.

The piece of malleable iron withstood the test admirably; for, upon examination,

the action of the corrosive gas was found to have penetrated only superficially.

The data furnished by this experiment shows the malleable iron to have about eight (8) times the resisting power against the destroying agencies generated in the combustion of coal as has cast iron.

The chemical composition of the malleable iron used in your Home Comfort Ranges compares with that of the very best malleable iron known.

The following table shows the composition of the malleable iron used by you, and also the composition of a sample of the very best iron of the same kind.

Column No. 1 in this table shows the composition of Range Casting, and column No. 2 shows the composition of first quality malleable iron.

W. I. R. CO.

	No. 1	No. 2
Silicon	.699 per cent	.719 per cent
Phosphorus	.207 per cent	.204 per cent
Manganese	.267 per cent	.270 per cent
Sulphur	.033 per cent	.036 per cent
Carbon	1.840 per cent	1.842 per cent

J. N. HURTY,
Analytical Chemist.

Summary of Experiments Showing the Superiority of Malleable Over Cast Iron

On every count malleable iron has been found superior to cast. Its mechanical superiority is very great and its resisting power against the destroying action of fire and the oxygen of the air, also the chemical compounds generated in the combustion of coal, is far above cast iron.

The table submitted shows the above facts very plainly. By reference to the column headed "malleable" one can readily see how many times better it is than cast iron on each count given.

CHEMICAL	Cast	Malleable
Comparative melting point	1	12½
Comparative resistance to fire	1	3.6
Comparative resistance to sulphur gases	1	8

MECHANICAL		
Tensil strength	1	1.35
Elongation	1	3.84
Transverse strength	1	1.22
Deflection	1	30.23
Resistance to shock	1	10

J. N. HURTY,
Analyst

The "Home Comfort" Kitchen

The most essential things in a kitchen are convenience, good light, ventilation, and, above all, attractiveness by cleanliness and order.

Considering the time spent by the housewife in the kitchen, the entire household should lend their aid to her in keeping it in such a manner—lightening her labor and brightening her three-times-daily task in the kitchen.

Commendation and agreeableness will bring about many a change in the diet.

WEIGHTS AND MEASURES

Standard Weight

27 1/3	grains	1 dram
16	drams	1 ounce
16	ounces	1 pound

Standard Measure

4	gills	1 pint
2	pints	1 quart
4	quarts	1 gallon

Kitchen Measure

60	drops	1 teaspoon
3	teaspoons	1 tablespoon
4	tablespoons	¼ cup
8	tablespoons	½ cup
16	tablespoons	1 cup
½	cup	1 gill
2	cups	1 pint
4	cups	1 quart
16	cups	1 gallon

Kitchen Weights

1	teaspoon Water (or Milk)	1/6 oz.
1	tablespoon Water (or Milk)	½ oz.
1	cup Water (or Milk)	8 ozs.

2	cups Water (or Milk)	1 lb.
2	tablespoons Shortening	1 oz.
2	tabelspoons Salt	1 oz.
2	tablespoons Sugar	1 oz.
4	tablespoons Flour	1 oz.
5	tablespoons Nuts (chopped)	1 oz.
1	square Chocolate	1 oz.
2	cups Butter	1 lb.
2	cups Shortening	1 lb.
2	cups Sugar (Gran.)	1 lb.
2 2/3	cups Sugar (Pow'd.)	1 lb.
2 2/3	cups Sugar (Brown)	1 lb.
3½	cups Sugar (Conf.)	1 lb.
4	cups Bread-crumbs	1 lb.
4	cups Flour (White)	1 lb.
4½	cups Flour (Graham)	1 lb.
3 7/8	cups Whole-wheat Flour	1 lb.
2 2/3	cups Cornmeal	1 lb.
4 1/3	cups Ryemeal	1 lb.
2 2/3	cups Oatmeal	1 lb.
5	cups Rolled Oats	1 lb.
2 1/3	cups Beans (Dry)	1 lb.
1 7/8	cups Rice	1 lb.
2	cups Raisins (Packed)	1 lb.
4	cups Currants	1 lb.
4 1/3	cups Coffee (Liquid)	1 lb.
9	medium Eggs	1 lb.

Use Level Measurements in All Recipes in This Book.

Correct measurement is one of the secrets of success in cooking. All materials are measured level by filling the spoon or cup more than full and leveling with a table knife.

Select a measuring cup that holds exactly half a pint. Ordinary coffee, or tea cups vary in size, and cannot be depended upon for correct measurement unless tested. A standard measuring cup of tin, aluminum, or glass, showing half, quarter, third, and two-third measurements is the best, and can be had at a very small cost.

Dry ingredients, such as flour, meal and sugar, are sifted lightly into the measure, then leveled. Shortening materials, like butter, lard, or vegetable fat, are packed into the measure and leveled.

To measure: A full-spoon, fill the spoon heaping, then level with a knife; a half-spoon, fill the spoon and level, then divide in half lengthwise; a quarter-spoon, divide a half-spoon crosswise.

Time Required for Cooking

Meats, Fowl and Fish

Baking or Roasting—

Beef Ribs, or loin, rare, per lb.	8 to 10 min.
Beef Ribs, or loin, well done, per lb.	12 to 16 min.
Beef Ribs, rolled, rare, per lb.	12 to 15 min.
Beef Ribs, rolled, well done, per lb.	15 to 18 min.
Beef Fillet, rare, per lb.	20 to 30 min.
Beef Fillet, well done, per lb.	50 to 60 min.
Pork, well done, per lb.	18 to 20 min.
Mutton Leg, well done, per lb.	12 to .. min.
Mutton Shoulder, stuffed, per lb.	15 to 25 min.
Lamb, well done, per lb.	15 to 20 min.
Veal, well done, per lb.	18 to 22 min.
Venison, rare, per lb.	9 to 10 min.
Ham	4 to 6 hrs.
Turkey, 8 to 10 pounds	3 hrs.
Chicken, 4 to 5 pounds	1 hr.
Goose, 8 to 10 pounds	2½ hrs.
Duck, domestic	1 to 1¼ hrs.
Duck, wild	20 to 30 min.
Fish, 3 to 4 pounds	25 to 30 min.
Fish, small	20 to 30 min.

Boiling—

Beef, fresh	4 to 6 hrs.
Beef, corned	4 to 8 hrs.
Beef Tongue	3 to 4 hrs.
Ham, 10 to 15 pounds	4 to 6 hrs.
Meats, braised	3 to 5 hrs.
Turkey, per pound	15 to 18 min.
Chicken, 3 to 4 pounds	1 to 1½ hrs.
Fish, 2 to 5 pounds	30 to 45 min.
Halibut, thick piece, per lb.	14 to 15 min.
Salmon, thick piece, per lb.	10 to 15 min.
Codfish, per lb.	5 to 6 min.
Clams and Oysters	3 to 55 min.
Lobster	25 to 30 min.

Broiling—

Steak, 1 inch thick	4 to 10 min.
Steak, 1½ inches thick	8 to 12 min.
Veal Chops	5 to 10 min.
Lamb Chops	6 to 11 min.
Chicken, Spring	18 to 20 min.
Quail	7 to 9 min.
Squabs	10 to 12 min.
Fish, White	15 to 20 min.
Fish, slices or steaks	12 to 15 min.
Liver	4 to 5 min.

Frying—

Croquettes	1 to 1½ min.
Fish, small and smelts	3 to 5 min.
Fish Balls	1 to 1½ min.

Vegetables

Baking—

Beans, Boston or New York	1 to 2 hrs.
Cauliflower	15 to 20 min.
Potatoes, White, with jackets	40 to 60 min.
Potatoes, Sweet, with jackets	45 to 60 min.
Squash	30 to 45 min.

Boiling and Stewing—

Asparagus	20 to 30 min.
Beans, string	1 to 2 hrs.
Beets, new	50 to 60 min.
Brusselsprouts	15 to 20 min.
Cabbage	15 to 20 min.
Carrots	50 to 60 min.
Cauliflower	20 to 30 min.
Celery	1½ to 2 hrs.
Corn	12 to 20 min.
Onions	45 to 60 min.
Parsnips	30 to 45 min.
Peas	30 to 60 min.
Potatoes, White	20 to 30 min.
Potatoes, Sweet	15 to 25 min.
Rice	20 to 30 min.
Spinach	15 to 20 min.
Squash	30 to 45 min.
Turnips	30 to 45 min.
Tomatoes	15 to 20 min.

Bread, Cakes, Pastry

Baking—

Bread, White Loaf	40 to 60 min.
Bread, Graham Loaf	35 to 45 min.
Bread, Boston Brown, steamed	3 hrs.
Bread, Whole-wheat Loaf	40 to 50 min.
Rolls, Yeast	10 to 30 min.
Biscuits, Yeast	10 to 20 min.
Biscuits, Baking-powder	12 to 15 min.
Muffins, Yeast	25 to 30 min.
Muffins, Baking-powder	20 to 25 min.
Popovers	28 to 30 min.
Pies, Fruit	20 to 30 min.
Tarts	15 to 20 min.
Patties	15 to 25 min.
Gems	25 to 30 min.
Cookies	8 to 10 min.
Ginger-bread	20 to 30 min.
Cake, layer	20 to 30 min.
Cake, loaf	40 to 60 min.
Cake, Fruit	2 to 3 hrs.
Cake, Sponge	45 to 60 min.
Cakes, small	15 to 25 min.
Pudding, Bread	45 to 60 min.
Pudding, Batter	35 to 45 min.
Pudding, steamed	1 to 3 hrs.
Custard	20 to 25 min.
Scalloped Dishes	15 to 20 min.

Terms Used in Cooking

The following terms will be frequently referred to in "Home Comfort'" Recipes. Becoming familiar with these terms is quite important, as a misunderstanding of the method of mixing or cooking may result in failure.

Methods of Mixing

Stirring—Simply the blending of ingredients by moving, or rotating a spoon, knife, or paddle, round and round, in circles from the sides of the vessel to the center.

Beating—To incorporate all the air possible into a mixture to make it "light" or "puffy." With a wire or other beater held vertically, strike the mixture with long strokes, cutting through each time.—Churning.

Whipping—Another form of "beating" used for certain materials, such as eggs or cream. If a stiff, or close texture is desired, place the material in a large cup, or bowl, using a rotary (Dover) beater; if a looser texture is wanted, place the material in a large flat dish, using a large fork, or flat wire whisk, being careful to whip only in one direction.

Folding—To combine two or more mixtures without losing the air already "beaten" into one or more of them. With a wide knife, cut through the mixture to the bottom of the dish, folding one portion back over the other, and repeating until properly mixed.

Cutting-In—To combine two or more ingredients which should be only partially mixed for best results. With a case-knife in each hand and used much like a knife and fork, cut the ingredients into fine particles until mixed as desired.

Working—The opposite of "cutting-in;" employed when a mixture is to be thoroughly combined to stiffen the texture or drive out the air. This is done entirely with the hands, and is ordinarily called "kneading."

Blanching—To remove the skins from the meats of Almonds or other nuts. Pour boiling water over the nutmeats, allowing them to stand for a few minutes; drain; cover with cold water—and the skins are easily removed by pressure of the fingers.

Caramelizing—Melting sugar without the addition of water or other liquid. Put the sugar into a shallow granite saucepan; place on the hot cooking surface of the range, and stir constantly until the sugar is melted; pour at once into mixture to be flavored.

Creaming—Reducing to the consistency of thick cream. As for butter, or shortening, in cake and pastry, this is done by allowing the material to take on "room-temperature" (about 70° F.) and thoroughly stirring, or beating to a uniform consistency.

Methods of Cooking

Roasting—The basic—the oldest—method of cooking, from which practically all the other methods have been derived. It consists of the direct application of even heat, intensively at first, say for the first ten minutes, that the outside may be quickly seared in order to retain the juices; then allowing to cook more slowly, frequently turning, so that all sides may be cooked uniformly. There are two methods of roasting: direct and indirect.

In *direct* roasting the meat or fowl is exposed directly to the fire, upon the correct management of which greatly depends success. The fire should be kept clear, bright, brisk, and steady. Cooking too quickly all the time tends to toughen the roast. Frequent *basting*—about every ten minutes—together with steady, slow cooking makes the meat more tender since it helps to retain the juices and flavor, preventing dryness by carrying the heat and moisture into the interior. The proper time for direct roasting, if the fire has been kept bright and even, will be found to be about fifteen minutes per pound, with twenty minutes added, for beef or mutton; and about twenty minutes per pound, with thirty minutes added, for veal or pork.

In *indirect* roasting, instead of being exposed directly to the fire, the roast is placed in the oven of the range, and is usually referred to as *oven-roasting*. This method of roasting is now employed almost altogether for small roasts, since by this method the roast loses less of its weight. Like *direct* roasting, the excellence depends greatly upon the amount and quality of basting. The time for cooking greatly varies for various meats, for cooking greatly varies for various meats, and depends upon the amount and regularity to the good judgement and management of the cook.

Broiling—A modification of roasting, but applied altogether to thinly sliced meats. Like roasting, there are two methods: *direct* and *indirect*. Direct broiling, called *grill-*

ing, is done by placing the meat slices upon an open grill, or gridiron, directly over the fire. The fire must be clear, intensely hot, and high in the grate. The grill must be hot and lightly "greased" to prevent sticking. The meat should be turned often so the outer surfaces will be well done, while inside is but delicately cooked. Indirect, or pan-broiling, is done on the cooking surface of the range, and by using a heavy pan, skillet, or griddle, instead of the open grille, as in direct broiling. The same precautions as in direct broiling should be observed.

Baking—As applied to meats, baking is a modification of oven-roasting, the essential difference being that the "roasting" is done only after the meat or fowl has been partially boiled—called *parboiling,* and the cooking completed in the oven, the same precautions being followed as in oven-roasting. Proper regulation of the heat, and frequent basting are essential to success. As applied to vegetables and fruit, baking is simply roasting whole. As applied to bread, pastry, etc., the term is familiar.

Boiling—Another modification of primitive roasting, the difference being that the heat is applied through the medium of boiling water. In fresh meats—called *pot-roasts* —sear, or harden the outer side by plunging into boiling water; do not allow it to remain at this high heat very long, not more than five minutes, but allow it to finish cooking by simmering for the required period. The pot should be but slightly larger than the meat, and only sufficient water to cover it used; but, the meat should be kept completely covered while cooking and precaution taken not to allow the water to entirely boil away. In salt meats, the outer surface should not be closed by plunging into boiling water, but should be immersed in cold or lightly warm water and allowed to come to the boiling point, held there for about five minutes, then dropped back to simmering. Very salt meats should be soaked in cold water before boiling. Vegetables should be boiled in slightly salted water or with salt meats.

Stewing—A modification of boiling, employed principally for small or cheaper cuts of meat, especially when it is to be served with its juices, or gravy. The best plan is to make a suitable gravy, and after the ingredients are well blended, lay the meat into it, allow it to boil for about two minutes, then complete the cooking by simmering. The time required for stewing greatly depends upon the quality of the meat—one and a half to two hours is usually necessary.

Steaming—Cooking by steam—a method necessary for certain foods. Accomplished without special equipment by placing a small quantity of water in the bottom of a boiling-pot and resting the food to be steamed upon a framework of wire (a perforated tin can inverted and resting on the bottom will do very well) above the water. Covered and set to boil, the steam fills the pot and supplies the moist heat with an even temperature.

Over Hot Water—Indirectly applying heat to the article to be cooked through the medium of hot water. A double boiler commonly called a "rice-cooker" is most useful for this purpose. In melting certain ingredients, a dish set into a shallow pan containing hot water accomplishes the purpose for low temperatures.

Frying—Perhaps the most used of cooking methods, and one of the easiest to do well, and also badly. Proper frying is of the greatest importance to the household. Two methods are in practice—deep and shallow frying. *Deep-fat* frying—far superior to *shallow* frying—is done in a deep pan or kettle, of hot fat, such as lard, vegetable fat, or butter, referred to in "HOME COMFORT" Recipes as cooking fat. The kettle—a graniteware stew-kettle is ideal—should be kept for this purpose, and provided with a woven wire frying-basket, or tray, suspended into the kettle to within about an inch of the bottom. The fat should be hot —just under the *smoking point*—before placing the articles to be fried into it. Drop them in one or two at a time to allow the fat to regain its temperature after being slightly cooled by their cold surface. Use plenty of fat, always sufficient to cover the articles, for there is very little waste, and no real economy in using too little, since by this method the surface of the articles are quickly crisp, the cooking fat does not penetrate far, nor does the fat absorb the juices or odor of the food to any great extent. For this reason the fat can be repeatedly used for practically *all frying* by straining out the particles of food after each cooking, and clarifying. To clarify completely, strain through a cloth while warm, *not hot,* and and fry a few pieces of potatoes in it. For the same reason always fry potatoes last when preparing a meal, especially after frying such articles as fish, croquettes, etc. *Shallow Frying*—called Sauteing—is familiar to every cook. It is merely frying in a small quantity of fat, just enough to cover one side, only, of the article, which must be turned and re-turned until done. This method is best suited for salt or smoked meats in thin slices. Fresh meats in the form of steaks and chops may be fried by this method, but are much better when broiled.

Braising—The combining of meats and vegetables in such a way that all the flavors of both are retained and deliciously blended. This is accomplished by combining the two methods, broiling and stewing, with the difference that the heat is applied both above and below. In olden times, this was done with a hearth-oven; today, perfect braising is done in the range oven, since the proper heat may be maintained on all sides. Oven-braising is best done in an earthenware pot provided with a cover—*en Casserole*. The French method, which is considered the most excellent, is to line the pot with strips of bacon, and upon this place the chosen vegetables cut to suitable size. Upon this place the meat, and moisten with a small quantity of soup-stock or gravy, cover and place in the oven, which should be kept at a moderate even heat. Frequent basting aids the cooking and greatly improves the blending of the flavors. In braising with delicate meats such as fowls, and fillets, it is best to cover them with buttered paper to protect their surface from the more intense heat of the cover. In serving, take out the meat separately; remove the fat from the vegetables; then remove the gravy, which is strained, reduced and blended with a selected sauce.

Poaching—Applied to the method of quickly cooking some foods by placing them for a few minutes in boiling water—egg.s being a familiar example.

En Casserole—Cooking in a glazed earthenware utensil. Quite often, when the cooking has been done in what is known as a Casserole, the food is served to the table in the same receptacle.

Basting—Process of dipping up the juices in which meat or fowl is being cooked. This is best done with a long-handled spoon or ladle, and usually at periods of about ten minutes apart.

Larding—A method of combining the flavors of meats, such as flavoring veal or liver with salt, or smoked pork. Cut the pork fat into large threads of about one-fourth inch square, and two to four inches long, and thread them into a larding-needle —a large sacking-needle will do—taking stitches into the meat to be "larded," distributing them over the surface desired.

Marinating—A method similar to "pickling" designed to improve the flavor of meats. The meat is placed in a mixture of acids, oils, and spices, and allowed to soak for a short time, or until it has become saturated, either partially or wholly, with the blended flavors. Marinating with cooking oil makes meat more tender.

Shirring—Breaking into a dish with cream or crumbs, or both, and cooking in the oven, or in hot water—eggs being a familiar example.

Scalloping—Originated from a method of cooking oysters in scalloped shells. Preparing with crumbs of bread or cracker, seasoning well, and baking in the oven, usually *en casserole*.

"HOME COMFORT" RECIPES

Like all other sciences, cooking is governed by well defined "rules of practice"—by tried and proven formulae called *recipes*. In each group or classification, there are what are termed *basic* recipes from which a wide range of other recipes have been derived. For example there are two basic recipes in the "cake" group; cakes *with* and *without* butter or shortening. From these two recipes, a wide variety of different cakes may be made by adding or leaving out certain ingredients or quantities, or by the manner of baking. A young cook, especially, should begin with these basic recipes, master them, and become proficient in plain wholesome cooking before undertaking their derivations.

THE SECRET OF GOOD COOKING

The Secret of Good Cooking is: First, be a critical judge—know *excellent* cooking from *poor* cooking; Second, find a fascination in the *science,* and become thoroughly familiar with "what, and what not to do;" Third, find a genuine pleasure in the practice—mastering the basic recipes and the operation and control of your Range—and above all, "THINK."

ADVICE TO YOUNG COOKS

A convenient place for everything, and everything kept in its proper place is one of the big secrets in saving steps in preparing a meal. A small table, kept clear of everything except the particular material and utensils being used, is most indispensable to any cook. Before commencing to cook, look up the chosen recipe and study it thoroughly. On a slip of paper make a memorandum of the required materials and the quantities called for, and collect the necessary materials and utensils to be used. All quantities, liquid and dry, should be measured or weighed exact, for careful attention to details is one of the most important secrets of success in cooking. Young girls, especially, who are just learning to cook, should follow these instructions and not trust too much to luck and memory. "Luck" in cooking is "knowing how" and being sure quantities, temperatures, and methods of handling and mixing are right, and, above all, the proper handling of the Range, which must come from actual practice. Use good, dry fuel; keep the reservoir supplied with fresh, clean water; see that the oven heat is at proper temperature for the particular food you are preparing before placing it in the oven; see that the oven is kept properly regulated while cooking; prove to your own satisfaction that the big secret in all cooking is in "knowing exactly how." A century ago, no cook was considered proficient under thirty years of age; today, thousands of girls have become fine cooks at eighteen or twenty.

Be Sure to Use Level Measurements in All Recipes

See Weights and Measurements—Page 35

Bread and Bread Making

Bread is divided into two general classifications: *Yeast Bread,* and *Quick Bread.* In their plain form, these constitute basic recipes, from which many plain and fancy variations are made by the interchanging of materials, or by the form of the finished product.

Bread is composed of flour (used in its general term), salt, shortening, liquid, and a rising agent.

For plain, white bread, flour from Spring wheat—called Bread Flour—is best. While usually spoken of as "white flour," it has a slightly cream tinge, but produces a fine, practically white loaf.

Shortening gives to bread a tender texture, rendering it not only more palatable, but more readily digestible; therefore, a small amount is used in all the better breads.

Water, as the liquid in bread, is in universal use, for not only is it cheaper, but bread will hold its moisture longer if made with water. Milk, however, is more nutritious, since it contains practically all the food values; also, milk gives bread a more spongy texture. A half-and-half mixture of the two liquids is often used.

The purpose of a "rising agent" in bread (also most cake, and some pastries) is to render the product light and porous, making it more palatable and digestible. Flour, shortening, and liquid, form an elastic paste which may be formed into a multitude of small air-cells by laboriously beating air into it; when heated, the air expands the cell-walls, rendering the product porous. "Rising agents," such as yeast, baking powder, or soda with sour milk or molasses, take the place of the air process by forming gas (carbonic-acid gas—the same as in "soda water"), which, when heated, expands and inflates the cells, causing the bread to "rise." The cell walls are then baked in this condition and retain their shape and volume.

Besides perfecting the taste of bread, *salt* strengthens the elasticity of the dough, and also aids in holding the moisture and keeping it fresh.

Yeast is composed of living cells or plant life. Provided with moisture, warmth and the food on which it thrives, such as the flours of grains, the yeast plant will grow and multiply; but, robbed of these, the living plant will remain in a state of rest awaiting the proper conditions. Yeast, as in general use, is of three kinds: *Liquid,* or simple yeast; *Compressed,* or fresh compact; and *Dry Cake,* or foam. The two latter are the ordinary forms of commercial yeast, or a collection of yeast plants in a state of rest, and may be obtained at almost any grocer.

Some general rules to be observed in making Yeast Bread:—

In preparing yeast for bread, cold or luke-warm water should always be used, as extremely hot or boiling water will "kill" the yeast plant.

Yeast should first be softened in a small quantity of water, and this stirred into the bulk of the liquid.

Always add the flour to the liquid, remembering that the liquid determines the quantity of the dough, while the amount of flour determines the texture or quality.

Bread may be mixed at night, covered with a cloth, and set on the top of the warm reservoir of your range to rise; by morning, the fermentation should be complete, and soon made ready for early baking.

Bread should be mixed in a bowl of earthenware or crockery, as it holds the warmth more evenly. Since dough is too heavy for *beating,* it should be mixed with a stiff mixing knife, or spatula.

It is necessary to knead bread twice—*before* and *after* the first rising—the first, to thoroughly distribute the ingredients; the second to break up the larger air cells and make firm.

Do not hurry the second rising—let it be slow and natural; this will result in a finer texture.

It is best to bake bread in small loaves, as this gives a larger proportion of crust, thus giving it a higher food value.

It is necessary in baking bread, to "kill" the yeast plant quickly and thoroughly, since it has accomplished its work of supplying the necessary gas, and must be prevented from further spreading. This is done by placing in a very hot oven for a few moments, and the baking completed in a moderate oven.

The term "Quick Bread" is here used to cover that classification in which baking powder, or other similar rising agent, is used instead of Yeast, and from the fact that the principal object is the saving of both *time* and *energy* in the making of it. Many of the same general rules applying to Yeast Bread may also be applied to Quick Bread, since the principles of mixing and baking are the same. Detailed instructions will be found contain in each particular "Home Comfort" recipe.

Home-Made Yeast

Simple Yeast—Make a thin batter of flour and luke-warm water; let it stand in a warm place until it ferments and is full of bubbles. Two cups of this liquid yeast is equal to one cup of old yeast.—Yeast is good when foamy and full of beads, has a brisk pungent odor, and has snap and vim; it is bad when it has an acid odor, is watery, and has a thin film on top.

Liquid Yeast—Early in the day, boil one ounce of best hops in two quarts of water for thirty minutes; strain and let the liquid cool to the warmth of new milk; put it in an earthen crock or bowl, and add four tablespoons each of salt and brown sugar; now, beat up two cups flour with part of the liquid and add to remainder, mixing well together and set aside in a warm place for three days; then, add one cup smooth, mashed, boiled potatoes, keep near the range in a warm place, and stir frequently until it is well fermented; place in a sterilized, wide-mouthed jug, or glass fruit jar, seal tightly, and keep in a cool place for use. It should thus keep well for two months and be improved with age. Use same quantity as of other yeast, but always shake the jug or jar well before pouring out

Dry Yeast Cake—To a quantity of Liquid Yeast add enough sifted flour to make a thick batter, stir in one teaspoon salt and set to rise; when risen, stir in sifted and dried corn-meal enough to form a thick mush; set in warm place and let rise again; knead well and roll out on a board to about one-half inch thickness, and cut into cakes one and one-half inches square, or with two-inch round cutter; dry slowly and thoroughly in the lower warming closet of the range; keep in cool, dry place for use; will keep fresh for six months. To use, dissolve one cake in a cup of luke-warm water.

Compressed Yeast—Fresh compact yeast is cheaper than home-made yeast, and saves both time and trouble when it is convenient to obtain it. Almost all grocers keep it— be sure it is fresh. The following recipe for Yeast Bread provides for progressive baking, starting with a single cake of yeast, or one cup good home-made liquid yeast.

Yeast Bread

Dissolve one yeast cake in one cup luke-warm water; add three-fourths cup smooth, mashed, boiled potatoes, one-half cup sugar, one-half teaspoon salt, and four cups cold water; set on reservoir or other warm place of about seventy-five degrees temperature over night. On following morning, pour off two cups of this yeast liquid into a sterilized jar, cover tightly, and set aside in a cool place for next baking. To the remainder, add one-third cup sugar, one and one-half tablespoons salt, and two tablespoons shortening; mix. Place sufficient flour in a large mixing bowl, gradually add yeast liquid and work into good stiff dough, kneading until elastic; put into clean, dry, slightly greased, warm bowl, and set to rise again—do not hurry it on this second rising, but let it take its natural time. Form into loaves, kneading each lightly, place into greased loaf baking tins to half fill them, cover and let them rise to twice their size or until light; brush tops with melted butter or sweet milk, place in very hot oven for five minutes, lower oven-heat to moderate, and bake about one hour, keeping the oven-heat even

When you want to bake again, start with the two cups left-over yeast instead of the yeast cake and warm water; as before, save two cups of liquid yeast for next baking.— This recipe never fails when properly handled, and may be used for rolls as well as bread.

Two-Hour Bread

Dissolve two cakes compressed yeast and one tablespoon sugar in one cup warm water. Sift a quantity of flour into mixing bowl, and place in center two tablespoons shortening and one tablespoon salt; add a mixture of two cups milk and one cup water, luke-warm; add yeast and mix to soft dough, handling slowly and carefully; turn onto floured board; wash, dry and grease bowl; shape dough into ball and place it back in the bowl and set in a moderately warm place to rise; in one hour, it should have risen, when it may be lightly kneaded and formed into loaves or rolls; set pans in warm place for about one hour to properly rise, brush tops with melted butter; bake in a moderate oven thirty to thirty-five minutes.

Corn Yeast Bread

Dissolve one cake compressed yeast in one-fourth cup luke-warm water; mix two cups each corn-meal and wheat flour, and add enough warm water to make a stiff batter; combine yeast and batter and set in warm place to become light; scald eight cups good corn-meal with boiling water, and when cooled to temperature of the rising sponge, combine the two, and add four cups flour, two cups smoothly mashed boiled sweet potatoes and two teaspoons salt; add just enough water and milk to work into dough that will not stick to board, knead well, form into ball, place in clean lightly greased warm bowl and set to rise; when light, press down, form into loaves, put into greased baking pans, let rise to double its bulk; bake in moderate oven.

Corn Yeast Rolls

When baking Corn Yeast Bread, form part of finished dough into rolls and bake in the usual way.

Raisin Nut Bread

Raisins should be added to yeast bread at time of molding into loaves. Divide dough into loaf portions, roll each out lightly while kneading, cover surface with seedless raisins, roll up like a jelly-roll, pinch ends firmly together, and place in greased loaf baking pans; let rise until light, brush, and bake. Raisins added in this way will not discolor the bread, and will be evenly distributed through the loaf. Nuts, or raisins and nuts combined, are used in this manner.

Self-Rising Bread

In the evening of day before baking, set the leaven by pouring a cup of boiling milk over one-half cup corn-meal, cover, and set in a warm place to rise; next morning, pour one cup sweet milk into an earthenware bowl, crock, or pitcher; add one-half teaspoon salt, one tablespoon sugar, and mix in four cups flour and enough boiling water to make a stiff batter; then, add leaven which thins yeast to proper consistency; place bowl in a pot of warm water, cover, and keep warm—this yeast should rise in an hour; when sufficiently risen, add two cups

warm water, one teaspoon salt, one-half cup shortening, place in center of five pints sifted flour, and mix into a dough that can be well kneaded—not too stiff, but elastic; form into ball, grease surface lightly, place in warm, clean bowl, cover, and set in warm place to rise; when well risen, knead, form into loaves, let rise, and bake one hour in moderate oven.—This method has been misnamed "Salt Rising."

Self-Rising Rolls

Take part of the bread dough, work a little more sugar into it and make into small rolls; put into greased pans and set in a warm place until risen to top of pan; bake in a hotter oven than for bread.

Whole Wheat Bread

Dissolve one cake compressed yeast in one-fourth cup luke-warm water. Mix one and one-fourth cups each of milk and boiling water; add two tablespoons shortening, two tablespoons sugar, and two teaspoons salt; mix well, add yeast liquid and three and one-half cups whole wheat flour; mix to stiff batter, set in warm place and let rise until light; work in enough more flour to make a soft dough, knead, and mold into two loaves, place in greased loaf pans, and let rise again until double in bulk; brush over with melted butter or sweet milk; bake in moderate oven about one and a half hours.

Cinnamon Rolls

Dissolve one cake compressed yeast in one-fourth cup warm water, add one cup scalded milk and one and a half cups flour, mix batter and set in warm place to rise; when light, add one-fourth cup sugar, one-fourth cup shortening, two beaten egg yolks, one teaspoon salt and enough flour to form dough; work together and knead until smooth and elastic; cover closely and set in warm place to rise to double in bulk; turn onto floured board, roll out in a sheet, spread with four tablespoons soft butter or shortening, sprinkle with a little sugar and cinnamon, and roll up as a jelly roll and cut into sections an inch or more in thickness; put two or three tablespoons butter or shortening in an eight by ten baking pan, and distribute over this about three-fourths cup brown sugar; lay the rolls in sidewise or flat, and set aside to rise or become light; bake in a moderate oven and turn out top side down on a cloth to cool; bottoms will be found to be glazed with sugar Makes about eighteen rolls.

It is necessary in baking bread, to "kill" the yeast plant quickly and thoroughly, since it has accomplished its work of supplying the necessary gas, and must be prevented from further spreading. This is done by placing in a very hot oven for a few moments, and the baking completed in a moderate oven.

The term "Quick Bread" is here used to cover that classification in which baking powder, or other similar rising agent, is used instead of Yeast, and from the fact that the principal object is the saving of both *time* and *energy* in the making of it. Many of the same general rules applying to Yeast Bread may also be applied to Quick Bread, since the principles of mixing and baking are the same. Detailed instructions will be found contain in each particular "Home Comfort" recipe.

Home-Made Yeast

Simple Yeast—Make a thin batter of flour and luke-warm water; let it stand in a warm place until it ferments and is full of bubbles. Two cups of this liquid yeast is equal to one cup of old yeast.—Yeast is good when foamy and full of beads, has a brisk pungent odor, and has snap and vim; it is bad when it has an acid odor, is watery, and has a thin film on top.

Liquid Yeast—Early in the day, boil one ounce of best hops in two quarts of water for thirty minutes; strain and let the liquid cool to the warmth of new milk; put it in an earthen crock or bowl, and add four tablespoons each of salt and brown sugar; now, beat up two cups flour with part of the liquid and add to remainder, mixing well together and set aside in a warm place for three days; then, add one cup smooth, mashed, boiled potatoes, keep near the range in a warm place, and stir frequently until it is well fermented; place in a sterilized, wide-mouthed jug, or glass fruit jar, seal tightly, and keep in a cool place for use. It should thus keep well for two months and be improved with age. Use same quantity as of other yeast, but always shake the jug or jar well before pouring out

Dry Yeast Cake—To a quantity of Liquid Yeast add enough sifted flour to make a thick batter, stir in one teaspoon salt and set to rise; when risen, stir in sifted and dried corn-meal enough to form a thick mush; set in warm place and let rise again; knead well and roll out on a board to about one-half inch thickness, and cut into cakes one and one-half inches square, or with two-inch round cutter; dry slowly and thoroughly in the lower warming closet of the range; keep in cool, dry place for use; will keep fresh for six months. To use, dissolve one cake in a cup of luke-warm water.

Compressed Yeast—Fresh compact yeast is cheaper than home-made yeast, and saves both time and trouble when it is convenient to obtain it. Almost all grocers keep it— be sure it is fresh. The following recipe for Yeast Bread provides for progressive baking, starting with a single cake of yeast, or one cup good home-made liquid yeast.

Yeast Bread

Dissolve one yeast cake in one cup luke-warm water; add three-fourths cup smooth, mashed, boiled potatoes, one-half cup sugar, one-half teaspoon salt, and four cups cold water; set on reservoir or other warm place of about seventy-five degrees temperature over night. On following morning, pour off two cups of this yeast liquid into a sterilized jar, cover tightly, and set aside in a cool place for next baking. To the remainder, add one-third cup sugar, one and one-half tablespoons salt, and two tablespoons shortening; mix. Place sufficient flour in a large mixing bowl, gradually add yeast liquid and work into good stiff dough, kneading until elastic; put into clean, dry, slightly greased, warm bowl, and set to rise again—do not hurry it on this second rising, but let it take its natural time. Form into loaves, kneading each lightly, place into greased loaf baking tins to half fill them, cover and let them rise to twice their size or until light; brush tops with melted butter or sweet milk, place in very hot oven for five minutes, lower oven-heat to moderate, and bake about one hour, keeping the oven-heat even

When you want to bake again, start with the two cups left-over yeast instead of the yeast cake and warm water; as before, save two cups of liquid yeast for next baking.— This recipe never fails when properly handled, and may be used for rolls as well as bread.

Two-Hour Bread

Dissolve two cakes compressed yeast and one tablespoon sugar in one cup warm water. Sift a quantity of flour into mixing bowl, and place in center two tablespoons shortening and one tablespoon salt; add a mixture of two cups milk and one cup water, luke-warm; add yeast and mix to soft dough, handling slowly and carefully; turn onto floured board; wash, dry and grease bowl; shape dough into ball and place it back in the bowl and set in a moderately warm place wrap in clean cloth to cool. Slice cross-section to serve.—Whole-wheat flour may be substituted for graham flour; rye meal or oatmeal may be substituted for wheat flour; additional molasses may be substituted for brown sugar, or vice-versa; but, if strong molasses is used, leave out two or three tablespoonfuls. Five teaspoons good baking powder and one and a third cups sweet milk may be substituted for the buttermilk and soda. One-half cup seedless raisins may be mixed with ingredients if desired.

Quick Loaf Bread

4 cups flour 1 teaspoon salt
7 teaspoons baking powd. 1 cold potato
1 tablespoon sugar Milk or water

Sift well together flour, baking powder, sugar and salt, and into these rub one medium sized potato; add enough milk and mix smoothly into a good, stiff batter; place in a well greased loaf baking pan and smooth top over with a buttered knife; stand pan in warm place about a half hour, then bake in moderate oven about one hour; when baked, moisten top crust with damp cloth, remove from pan, wrap and allow to cool.

Graham Bread

Measure and sift together: Four cups Graham flour, one cup wheat flour, two teaspoons baking powder, one teaspoon salt, one-half cup sugar, and two teaspoons soda; add one-half cup melted shortening and three cups buttermilk; mix thoroughly, turn into two greased loaf pans, smooth with knife dipped in cold water, and bake in moderate oven about fifty minutes.

Rich Graham Bread

Measure and sift together: Three cups Graham flour, three cups wheat flour, eight teaspoons baking powder, and two teaspoons salt; to three cups water and milk mixed, add two beaten eggs, two tablespoons melted shortening, and four tablespoons molasses or sugar; stir liquids into dry mixture and beat well; add enough more milk if necessary to make a drop batter; pour into two greased loaf pans, smooth with wet knife, and bake in moderate oven about one hour.

Corn Lightbread

Early in the morning, take one pint boiling water and stir in slowly enough meal to make a thick mush; put in a teaspoon of salt and cook five minutes, then add four pints cold water; stir in enough meal to make it very thick and set in a warm place to rise. When it has risen sufficiently, add two eggs, one and a half cups of molasses

or brown sugar, and one to one and a half cups flour; pour into well greased baking pan; set in warm oven until it begins to rise, then bake fast in hot oven until browned; lower oven-heat to moderate and bake slowly three to four hours.

Corn Bread

1 cup cornmeal 4 tablespoons sugar
2 cups flour 5 teaspoons baking powd.
½ cup shortening 1 teaspoon salt
1½ cups sweet milk 2 eggs, separated

Cream shortening and sugar together, and add egg yolks beaten light with a teaspoon cold water; sift together corn meal, flour, baking powder, and salt, and add alternately with milk to egg mixture; beat in egg whites; pour in greased bread pan and bake in moderate oven twenty to twenty-five minutes or until done.

Doughnuts

Sift and measure two and a half cups flour, add three-fourths teaspoon salt, one-half teaspoon nutmeg, and two teaspoons baking powder, sift together to mix well; cream two and a half tablespoons shortening with one-half cup sugar and two beaten eggs, and mix; add one-half cup milk alternately with flour to egg mixture to form a soft dough that can be handled· roll out, cut with doughnut cutter and fry in deep fat hot enough to turn bread crumb a golden brown in one minute, or test with a bit of the dough.—Sufficient for thirty doughnuts.

Yeast Doughnuts

Dissolve one cake yeast in one-fourth cup luke-warm water; scald and cool one cup milk, add yeast liquid, one-half teaspoon salt, and enough flour to form a drop batter; set in warm place to rise. Cream four tablespoons shortening with one cup sugar; add two beaten eggs, one teaspoon salt, one teaspoon nutmeg; add yeast with enough flour to form a stiff dough, and set to rise again; when risen, roll into small balls, or pat into sheet and cut with doughnut cutter; fry in hot deep cooking fat until brown and done.—Makes about six dozen.

Crullers

Cream four tablespoons shortening, and gradually add one cup sugar and two well-beaten eggs; sift together three cups flour, one-half teaspoon salt and three teaspoons baking powder; add half dry ingredients to shortening mixture, then add slightly more than half a cup milk and remaining dry ingredients to form soft dough; roll out on floured board to about a half inch thick;

cut into half-inch strips four to six inches long, roll round in hands and twist in form of twist tobacco; fry in hot deep fat, drain and dust with powdered sugar.

Biscuit Making

The ingredients alone are not what make the best biscuits, altho the quality of the materials used has much to do with it. The preparation—the mixing, handling and baking—is what really makes good biscuits.

Be sure to have all materials and utensils before you: A clean, well-dredged flour board; roller and cutter absolutely clean and dry; pans greased; and, above all, have range fire properly regulated so the oven heat will be just right and ready when the biscuits are prepared.

Biscuits should not be packed closely together in the pans, but should be so separated that they do not touch. They are improved if brushed with sweet milk or melted butter before placing in the oven, thus giving the biscuits an even brown on top.

Biscuit recipes calling for two cups flour will make about twelve medium sized biscuits—double recipes for larger quantity.

Biscuits

2 cups flour
4 teaspoons baking powd.
½ teaspoon salt
2 tablespoons shortening
¾ cup milk, about

Sift flour, baking powder and salt together two or three times; add shortening, half butter and half other fat, and lightly rub in with finger-tips; add milk, or half milk and half water, slowly until mixture becomes a soft dough; turn out on floured board and roll, or pat, out lightly to about one-half to three-quarters inch thick; cut out with biscuit cutter and set rounds in shallow lightly greased baking pan and sufficiently spaced from each other; brush tops with melted butter, and bake in hot oven fifteen to twenty minutes.

Drop Biscuits

To recipe for Biscuits, add a little more milk to make a stiff batter; drop by spoonfuls on greased pan or baking sheet, or into muffin tins; bake in hot oven.

Buttermilk Biscuits

2 cups flour
1 cup buttermilk
½ teaspoon soda
½ teaspoon baking powd.
½ teaspoon salt
2 tablespoons shortening

Sift flour, salt and baking powder together into a mixing bowl, add shortening and rub it lightly into them; add soda to buttermilk and stir thoroughly until it effervesces, then add to flour, gradually working it into a stiff dough; turn onto floured board and knead lightly until smooth; roll out slightly more than a quarter-inch thick, cut out biscuits, and bake on greased pan in hot oven twelve to fifteen minutes.

Beaten Biscuits

2 cups flour
½ teaspoon salt
2 tablespoons butter
⅔ cup milk, about

Sift flour and salt well together; cut in or rub in butter lightly; mix in enough milk, which should be ice cold, to make a stiff dough; knead until smooth and easily handled; turn out on a floured board and beat with rolling-pin until air-cells, or blisters, appear; cut out with small biscuit cutter, prick well with the prongs of a fork, and place on greased pan; set aside in refrigerator or other cool place for about one hour; bake in moderate oven for about thirty minutes.—Shortening may be substituted for butter if a little more salt is used; biscuits may be made richer by doubling amount of butter or shortening. It is not hard beating, but the regularity of the motion that counts.

Tea Biscuits

2 cups flour
3 teaspoons baking powd.
½ teaspoon salt
2 tablespoons shortening
½ cup water
1 tablespoon sugar
1 egg

Sift flour, salt, baking powder and sugar together; add water and beaten egg to shortening, and mix with dry ingredients to make soft dough; turn out on floured board, and roll out to about half-inch thickness; cut out with small biscuit cutter; bake on greased pan in moderate oven about twenty-five minutes.

The "HOME COMFORT" Oven has been recognized for half a century as a Perfect Baker. Master the control of your oven-heat and there will be no room for failure.

Griddle Cakes and Waffles

Few dishes, if any, can compare with good, wholesome, hot griddle cakes or waffles, especially for breakfast—but they should be really *good*, since the common variety of heavy, flat, greasy "pancake" is far too often the direct cause of serious digestive disorder.

Griddle cakes, particularly "wheat cakes," should be light, not too thin, and properly cooked without excess of cooking-fat. An iron "griddle" or a polished sheet of steel thick enough to hold an even heat should be used for best results. This should be but lightly greased, just enough to prevent the cakes from sticking, and the heat should be kept just under the smoking point. The proper *turning* point is detected by the air bubbles arising to the surface of the batter as it is cooking.

Waffles are cooked in a regulation "waffle iron," instead of on a griddle, and the same general rules apply as for griddle cakes. Professional cooks use the simple method of providing a small cup or bowl of melted cooking-fat, and apply it to the waffle and griddle iron with a small brush kept for that purpose. The finished waffle should be of rich golden brown in color, and served while hot and crisp.

Chef's Wheat Cakes

2 cups flour	1 teaspoon sugar
1 cup milk	½ teaspoon fine salt
1 tablespoon butter	2 eggs, separated
3 teaspoons baking powd.	

Sift well together flour, baking powder, sugar and salt; add beaten egg yolks, melted butter and milk; beat to smoothness and stir in well beaten egg whites; bake on lightly greased hot griddle, turning but once. Batter can best be handled if poured from a small pitcher, allowing the batter to spread to size of a saucer.

Buckwheat Cakes

½ cup buckwheat flour	1 cup cold water
½ cup wheat flour	¼ cup milk
3 teaspoons baking powd.	1 tablespoon melted
¾ teaspoon salt	shortening

Sift well together flours, baking powder, salt and sugar; add melted shortening to milk and water and mix with dry ingredients, beating to a smooth batter; bake on hot, slightly greased griddle; turn but once.

Real Southern Griddle Cakes

1¾ cups flour	½ teaspoon salt
1½ cups milk	3 teaspoons baking powd.
2 tablespoons shortening	2 eggs

Sift together flour, salt and baking powder; slightly beat eggs and add, with milk, to dry ingredients; add melted shortening and beat well to smooth batter; bake at once on lightly greased hot griddle, spreading to size of plate bottom.

Southern Corn Cakes

1½ cups corn meal	1 tablespoon molasses
1½ cups boiling water	½ cup flour
¾ cup milk	2 teaspoons baking powd.
1 tablespoon shortening	1 teaspoon salt

Sift together flour, baking powder and salt; scald corn meal in boiling water, and add milk, shortening and molasses; mix dry ingredients with meal mixture well, and beat until smooth batter; bake on hot, slightly greased griddle, turning cakes but once.

Whole Wheat Cakes

2 cups whole wheat flour	molasses
4 teaspoons baking powd.	1 tablespoon melted
½ teaspoon salt	butter
1¾ cups milk	2 eggs, beaten
1 teaspoon sugar or	

Sift together flour, baking powder, and salt; mix milk, beaten eggs, melted butter and sweetening, and combine with dry materials; beat well to mix; bake on slightly greased hot griddle; turn but once.

Graham Wheat Cakes may also be made by above recipe by using one cup wheat flour and one-half cup graham flour in place of whole wheat flour; batter should be a little thinner than for plain wheat cakes.

Rice Griddle Cakes

1 cup cooked rice	1 cup flour
1 cup milk	2 teaspoons baking powd.
1 tablespoon butter	1 egg, beaten
1 teaspoon salt	

Mix rice, milk, butter, well beaten egg, and salt; gradually add and stir in flour and baking powder, sifted well together; mix well; bake on hot, slightly greased griddle, turning but once.

Plantation Pancakes

2 cups sifted flour	1 teaspoon soda
2 cups sour milk	¼ teaspoon salt

Sift together flour, soda and salt; gradually add and stir into milk, beating to a good stiff batter; drop in large spoonfuls on hot, greased griddle or frying pan, and bake.

French Pancakes

1 cup flour	2 cups milk
2 teaspoons baking powd.	½ cup cream
½ teaspoon salt	2 eggs, beaten
1 tablespoon sugar	jam and powd. sugar

Sift well together flour, baking powder and salt; beat together eggs, sugar, milk and cream; mix and beat until smooth; melt a little butter in frying pan and pour in enough batter to cover bottom of pan; cook over hot range-top; turn but once and brown both sides; spread with jam or jelly, and roll up like a jelly-roll; sprinkle with powdered sugar and serve while hot.

Fritter Batter

1 cup flour	powder
⅔ cup milk	¼ teaspoon salt
1½ teaspoons baking	1 egg

Add milk to beaten egg; add baking powder, salt and flour sifted together; beat to smooth batter. Used for fruit fritters, and as a batter covering for fried oysters, chops, eggplant, etc., referred to in subsequent recipes.

Waffles

1¾ cups sweet milk	3 teaspoons baking powd.
2 cups flour, about	½ teaspoon salt
½ cup melted butter	2 eggs, separated

Beat egg yolks, and add milk; add flour to make a stiff batter; add melted butter, or other shortening, and salt; add baking powder; fold in stiffly beaten egg whites; bake in well greased hot waffle iron until brown; serve hot with butter and syrup. Will make six large waffles. One or two tablespoons sugar may be added if waffles are preferred slightly sweetened.

Buttermilk Waffles

2 cups flour	2 tablespoons shortening
1 teaspoon soda	1 cup buttermilk
¼ teaspoon salt	2 eggs, separated

Sift flour, soda and salt well together; add beaten egg yolks to half a cup of the buttermilk to make a good pouring batter; beat and fold in egg whites last.

Yeast Waffles

1 cake yeast	1 tablespoon shortening
¼ cup warm water	1 teaspoon salt
1¾ cups milk, scalded	2 eggs, separated.
2 cups flour	

To the scalded milk, add salt and melted shortening; when cooled to lukewarm, add yeast dissolved in warm water, then add flour; beat well and set in warm place to rise about one and a half hours; just before baking, stir in beaten egg yolks and fold-in well beaten egg whites; bake in hot waffle iron and serve hot. By using one-fourth cake yeast, mixture may be made up and set to rise overnight, ready for an early breakfast.

Dixie Corn Waffles

½ cup white corn meal	4 teaspoons baking powd.
1½ cups boiling water	1½ teaspoons salt
1½ cups sweet milk	4 tablespoons shortening
3 cups flour	2 eggs, separated
3 tablespoons sugar	

Cook corn meal in boiling water twenty minutes; add milk; add flour, sugar baking powder and salt sifted well together; add egg yolks and melted shortening; beat well and fold in stiffly beaten egg whites; bake at once.

Rice Waffles

¾ cup cooked rice, cold	4 teaspoons baking powd.
1½ cups milk	¼ teaspoon salt
1¾ cups flour	2 teaspoons butter
2 tablespoons sugar	1 egg, separated

Sift together flour, sugar, baking powder and salt; add rice and work in with fingertips; add milk, egg yolk and butter; beat well and fold-in stiffly beaten egg whites.

Cocoanut Waffles

3 cups flour	2 tablespoons sugar
2 cups milk	½ teaspoon salt
1 cup shredded cocoanut	4 teaspoons butter
4 teaspoons baking powd.	2 eggs, beaten

Sift well together all dry ingredients; add eggs, milk, melted butter and cocoanut, and beat well; cook in hot, well greased waffle iron and serve with syrup or honey.

Biscuit Waffles

Make batter as for Drop Biscuits—see recipe—and cook in hot, well-greased waffle iron; serve with syrup or honey, jelly or jam; also served in form of shortcakes with various fruit fillings and vegetables, such as peas, creamed asparagus, etc.

Waffleized Cakes

Any of the stiff cake batter, such as Drop Cakes, Brownies, etc., may readily be cooked in waffle irons and when served in form of sandwiches with fillings of sugar-butter, icings, fruit jellies and jams, or ice cream, are most delicious. Try Waffleized Chocolate Brownies with ice cream.

Ice Cream Cones

Ice Cream Cones are baked in specially shaped baking irons made on the principle of waffle irons; it is not likely that these will be found in the average household, but the idea of the cone may be converted into an ice cream sandwich made from regular cone batter.

Cone Batter—1 cup granulated sugar, 4 cups fine pastry flour, enough water to form a good drop batter, and vanilla extract to flavor; bake in ordinary waffle irons, and form into a sandwich with ice cream between.

Cereals and Cereal Products

From such cereals as corn, wheat, oats, rye, barley, and rice, many wholesome and healthful dishes may be prepared, either from the natural grains or from products derived from them by special preparation The starch of such grains, served in some form, comprises an important part of our daily diet, without which our foods would not be well balanced and our system denied proper nutrition. In the form of natural cereals, this may be supplied in a manner readily digestible, and among the recipes that follow, will be found many that are wholesome and tempting even to the invalid.

Simple rules govern the plain and proper cooking of all starchy grains. They should never be slowly cooked and rendered to a mushy mass, but should be kept practically whole and separate, at the same time be *well cooked*. After sufficiently washing the cereal, such as barley or rice, or a cereal product such as macaroni or spaghetti, drop into *rapidly boiling salted water,* and keep boiling furiously for the length of time required to render tender and well cooked. If cereal grain, drain into a colander and place into the heated oven for a very few minutes to evaporate some of the surface moisture and allow the grains to separate. If macaroni, or like product, drain into a colander and pour cold water over it until particles are sufficiently separated. Special treatments are included in various recipes.

Breakfast Foods

Under the name of "Breakfast Foods," a number of cereals have been placed on the market in sealed packages. Most of these are completely prepared and cooked at the factory, and require only to be served in the home.

Children's Porridge

For each cup of milk, use 2 level tablespoons of any coarse cereal such as rice, corn-meal, cracked wheat, oatmeal or barley, and 2 level tablespoons any sweetening, such as any sugar, syrup, honey, or molasses; flavor with nutmeg, cinnamon or any spice, and season with salt. Put flavored and seasoned milk in double boiler, or if large amount is being prepared, put in kettle; add cereal and sweetening and cook about 1 hour without covering. When made with more milk, or thinner, makes a delicious sauce for stewed fruits. When made with honey or molasses, flavoring may be omitted. A little butter may be added just before removing from fire if desired.

Oatmeal

Put 4½ cups water and 1 teaspoon salt in top section of double boiler, set directly over fire and bring to boiling point; pour 1 cup oatmeal slowly into water while constantly stirring, and cook 5 minutes; assemble double boiler and continue cooking without stirring for 30 minutes to an hour, as for corn-meal mush. May be cooked in evening and prepared quickly for breakfast by adding a little water and re-heating.

Rolled Oats

Put 2½ cups water and 1 teaspoon salt in a granite or porcelain lined sauce pan and bring to boiling point; when boiling, slowly add and stir in 1 cup rolled oats; let boil steadily for twenty minutes or more over even heat, constantly stirring to prevent burning; drain off surplus water and set back on range to drive off excess moisture. Some rolled oats require less time for cooking, since they art partly cooked at factory.

Corn-Meal Mush

Put 3½ cups water and 1 teaspoon salt in top section of double boiler, set directly on range and bring to boiling point; pour 1 cup corn-meal slowly into water while constantly stirring, and cook 3 minutes; have water hot in lower section of boiler, put top section of boiler in place, and cook the mush 30 minutes and longer if convenient; serve warm or cold with milk or cream, or put in molds for slicing and frying.—If no double boiler is at hand, use a stew pan and set it in a larger pan of hot water. Mush may be cooked for 2 to 3 hours, and is improved with each minute of cooking.

Mush With Cheese

Make corn-meal mush with coarse, or yellow meal; for each cup of meal used, allow ½ cup grated cheese, stirring it into the mush during the last few minutes of cooking; fry cold slices in deep fat with, or without, coating with beaten egg and fine bread crumbs.

Baked Mush

When corn-meal mush is partly cooked, pour into greased baking pan to not more than 2 inch thickness; bake in oven until brown.

Buttermilk Mush

Make a corn-meal mush with buttermilk as the liquid, allowing 6 cups buttermilk and 1 teaspoon salt for each cup corn-meal; this is said to closely resemble cottage cheese in flavor; serve cold with cream.

Hominy

Wash hominy thoroughly in one or two waters, put in pan and cover twice its depth with cold water; bring slowly to boiling point and let it simmer—if large, 6 hours; if small or broken, 2 hours; as water evaporates, add hot water; serve with cream, fry in butter, or serve plain with boiled dinner. Hominy Flakes and Hominy Grits may be cooked like corn-meal mush, but require cooking about two hours.

Hominy Balls

Form cooked and cooled hominy into small balls about the size of a walnut with dampened hands; roll in fine, soft bread crumbs, dip into a mixture of a beaten egg and 3 tablespoons milk; roll again in crumbs, and fry in hot deep fat until browned; serve in place of potatoes. Any of the forms of hominy may be used. Farina may be used in the same way.

Hominy and Cheese

Have hot, 2 cups cooked hominy; melt 3 tablespoons butter or other cooking fat; add 3 tablespoons flour, season with salt and paprika, stir and cook until puffy; add 1½ cups milk and bring to boiling while stirring; add and stir in 1 to 2 cups grated cheese; butter a baking dish and put alternate layers of hominy and cheese mixture until all of the hominy is used, having the cheese mixture on top; mix about one-half cup fine cracker or pastry crumbs with 2 tablespoons melted butter, season with salt, and spread over top; put in hot oven and bake until crumbs are nicely browned.

Rice

Rice should not be put into a double boiler and cooked slowly into a pasty mass; but, after cleansing it, throw it into plenty of rapidly boiling salted water and keep it boiling furiously for twenty-five or thirty minutes without stirring; drain into a colander and set it into the oven for a few minutes, just long enough to drive off the excess surface moisture; it is then ready to serve, or to be made up into special dishes.— The Chinese use an iron kettle, and at least a gallon of water to a cup of rice.

Serve Chinese style, without sweetening but salted to taste, in place of bread; always serve in this style with chop suey and other Chinese dishes.

Serve with sugar and milk or cream; a little butter is an improvement.

Serve with raisins, figs, dates, sugar and cream.

Serve on individual plates; press rice into a teacup or other buttered mold, and turn out on plate or shallow dish.

Rice Croquettes

Cook 1 cup well washed rice. Whip into the hot rice, 4 tablespoons each butter and sugar, and season with salt; when partly cooled, add 2 well beaten egg yolks; moisten with enough milk to cause it to hold its form when molded with hands; mold into balls or cakes, dip in beaten egg, roll in fine bread crumbs or cracker meal, and fry in either deep or shallow fat; serve hot.

Spanish Rice

Cook 1 cup well washed rice. In a pan, fry 3 slices of bacon, remove, and put into the hot bacon fat, 1 medium sized onion and 1 large green pepper, both finely chopped; fry until browned, add 1 cup tomatoes, season with salt and paprika or chili powder, add cooked rice and mix well; put into hot oven to drive off some of the surplus moisture; serve. Bacon may be cut up into the rice or strips laid on top as preferred. Nice *en casserole.*

Barley

Barley is cooked like rice; it may be served as a breakfast food with cream and sugar, or in any of the ways rice is served; it is a fine addition to many soups.

Cracked Wheat

Soak cracked wheat over night in cold water, allowing a quart of water for each cup of wheat; cook as directed for oatmeal, and have thoroughly done; serve with cream and sugar.

Macaroni and Spaghetti

Both macaroni and spaghetti should always be boiled before proceeding to make them up into the many appetizing dishes in which they are included. Have a stew-pan or kettle well filled with rapidly boiling water, to which salt—in the proportion of 1 teaspoon salt to each quart of water—has been added. For some dishes, it is essential that the sticks be cooked in full length rather than broken into short pieces, in which case, the sticks should be lowered into the boiling water endwise, since they quickly soften and become flexible and will settle into the water. Let the macaroni or spaghetti boil continuously for twenty to thirty minutes, in which time it should double in size; do not cover pan. If strands or pieces are desired separated and without pastiness, drain in a colander, then pour cold water over it to wash the surface; it is then ready to reheat and include in the desired dish. Add the cooking water to the soup stock.

If to be served plain, reheat, season with salt, pepper and butter, adding whatever else you desire.

Vermicelli is spaghetti made in thread-like strips or sticks.

Macaroni and Cheese

Cook 6 ounces macaroni in boiling salt water until tender, drain and cut into convenient lengths; melt 3 tablespoons butter, add 3 tablespoons flour and blend together until smooth; add 1½ cups milk gradually, constantly stirring until mixture boils; add ½ teaspoon salt, ¼ teaspoon pepper, cook for 3 minutes, stir in ½ cup grated cheese, and add the macaroni; serve.

Or: Put in a baking dish or casserole, sprinkle with additional grated cheese, and bake in moderate oven until a golden brown. —A few strips of bacon, placed on top a few minutes before baking is complete, is a good addition. Serve *en casserole*.

Or: Butter bottom and sides of baking dish, put in layer of the macaroni, sprinkle with grated cheese, dot with bits of butter and season with salt, pepper, paprika and dry mustard; fill dish with alternate layers of macaroni and cheese and seasoning; pour over contents, one cup rich milk; bake in hot oven until crust is formed; serve *en casserole*.

Spaghetti Italianne

Cook 6 ounces full length spaghetti in boiling salt water ten minutes; drain, add sauce, put into a double boiler to avoid scorching, and cook until spaghetti is tender and has absorbed most of the moisture; serve with grated cheese in separate dish to be sprinkled on each individual portion if desired.

Sauce: Melt 2 tablespoons fried bacon fat, add 2 tablespoons flour and cook and blend until browned; add 1½ cups strained stewed or canned tomato pulp, constantly stirring until it boils; add ¼ teaspoon each salt and pepper; add 3 tablespoons minced cooked ham.

Shell Macaroni

Macaroni manufactured in the form of shells, stars, and other designs, is prepared in the same manner as the tubular form, and may be served with favorite, well seasoned gravies or sauces. Don't forget to treat with cold water to separate the shells.

Noodles

Noodles may be prepared in either freshly made or in dried form. They may be used in soups entirely or as accompaniment; or, they may be made up in various dishes, and as a substitute for macaroni, spaghetti or vermicelli.

To each egg used, add ¼ teaspoon salt, and beat until smooth and well mixed; add fine flour sifted in a little at a time until fairly stiff dough is formed; turn on floured board and knead thoroughly until dough is elastic; roll out into a sheet as thin as possible, and roll sheet up quite tightly like a jelly-roll; with a sharp knife slice the roll cross-wise in thickness desired for the width of the noodles, and unroll into narrow strips; these may be spread in a warm dry place and slowly dried and kept for future use, or used at once without further treatment except cooking.

Or: To each egg used, add ¼ teaspoon salt, and water up to 1 tablespoon; beat all together smoothly; proceed as above. These are not quite so rich but are more economical than as above recipe.

Noodles may be cut into strips of ⅛ to ¾ inches wide; cut into squares of about 1 inch; squares may be rolled before drying to represent sea-shells; or, forms may be cut with small, special or fancy noodle-cutters.

Soups and Chowders

Soups may be classified as being either "clear" or "thick"—the latter containing vegetables, cream, starch, or other thickening materials. They may also be classified as those *with* or *without* meat—these being usually named from their predominating vegetable or flavor.

Soups afford a valuable means of utilizing, at small cost, the rich nutrition to be extracted from the bones, joints, cheaper cuts, and trimmings of meats, as well as the rich juices of meats and vegetables left over from boiling, that are often discarded and wasted. The economical housewife will use these rich extracts by converting them into "stock," from which she may, on short notice, prepare any of a wide variety of good, wholesome soups.

The proper handling of "stock" is the basic essential of all good soups, and this is covered by a few well defined general rules:

Beef, veal, and poultry are meats best adapted to the making of good soup-stock, and may be used separately or in combination. Mutton and lamb also may be used, but sparingly, owing to their strong flavor.

Stock should contain, in combination: The gelatine from bones, gristle, and tendonous portions; the savory extracts from the meats; a certain amount of fat; and, the acid salts and alkaline from fresh meats. Care must be taken to avoid any material of doubtful purity and freshness.

A stock-pot may be kept on the back of the range-top, in which such bits of bone or meat may be accumulated through the day. These are then turned into stock while fresh— all meat and bones must be cut or broken into small pieces.

Cold water, with a little salt added, should always be used in extracting the juices from the meats. Hot water quickly hardens the outer albumen, thus preventing the extraction of the essential juices, while *cold water* readily dissolves this albumen, as well as other juices, and the salt—not too much—aids in their extraction.

The stock-pot, with cold water and materials, is placed in position and allowed to *slowly* reach the boiling-point, and is then set back to simmer until the juices are sufficiently extracted.

In cold weather, left-over vegetables may safely be added to the stock-pot; but, in warm weather, these are inclined to sour, and should always be freshly cooked and added to stock when soup is made.

Floating fats and solids should be skimmed off before the stock is set aside or allowed to cool; or, before cooling, the stock should be strained off into a clean vessel. Do not leave it in the stock-pot over night.

Stock may be used the following day, or may be kept for several days by placing in a glass fruit-jar and kept in a cool place.

If all nourishment has not been extracted from the meats, they may be used in a second stock, but it will usually be necessary to add some fresh materials to bring up to full strength. Bones, especially, may be used in second stock.

Left-over soups may be strained, and the liquid included in the next stock.

In hot weather, left-over stock should be brought to the boiling-point every day, and poured into a clean vessel to prevent souring.

When clear soups—as consommé—are required, the floating film of excess fat may be removed by passing absorbent, or blotting paper lightly over the surface.

Soups should not be allowed to boil again, after the addition of such thickening materials as eggs, milk, or starch.

Soups and broths of fish may be made either from the whole fish, or from stock made from the bones, skins and trimmings of white fish. These should be broken into small bits and the stock well strained. As the flavor is stronger, and the juices more easily extracted than of domestic meats, a somewhat larger proportion of water should be used.

Chowder is, in reality, a thickened soup closely approaching the stew; however, the term is generally accepted as applying to such dishes made from various vegetables, fish and seafoods. By following the recipes, anyone may make perfect chowders; however, a wide range of variation is permissible and one must be governed by the materials at hand.

Pastry in Soups

Noodles, Macaroni and Vermicelli are always nice additions to almost any soup. By boiling these products in any kind of good soup stock, Noodle Soup, Vermicelli Soup, etc., is made in the plain form; however, many variations will suggest themselves. Macaroni is especially adapted to beef and vegetable soups. Vermicelli is a valuable addition to chicken soup, or clear, rich soup of any kind that is served in the smaller quantities. These pastries should, in most cases, be swelled by standing in luke-warm water for a time before putting into the soup. See Chapter "Cereals and Cereal Products."

Beef Extract

Score, or cut, a piece of round steak in all directions, and salt very lightly; put it into a double boiler, over boiling water, and extract the juice. Should always be made fresh for each meal when served to babies or invalids. Feed babies 1 teaspoon fresh extract once a week at the beginning of the 9th month on 1 tablespoon mashed potatoes, increasing the amount during the month, until at the beginning of the 10th month 1 tablespoon is being given.

Consomme

From 1 quart good strong soup stock, skim all fat from the surface; put in a stew pan, and add the white and clean shell of 1 egg beaten thoroughly with 1 tablespoon cold water; place over fire and heat gradually, constantly stirring to prevent egg from sticking to the pan; boil gently until egg rises to surface in thick white scum and stock becomes clear under the egg; remove egg, and filter stock through a folded napkin or cloth laid on a colander, but do not move or squeeze it through, allowing it to pass through naturally; season with salt and serve while hot.

Beef Bouillon

Finely chop 2 pounds lean beef, removing all fat and gristle; put in soup kettle, cover with 1 quart cold water, add ½ teaspoon celery seed or some chopped celery, 1 bay leaf, a sprig of parsley, and a small onion sliced; cover closely and set on back of range 2 hours; strain, place over fire and simmer gently 4 hours; strain, return to kettle, season with salt and pepper; beat 1 egg-white with ½ cup cold water until thoroughly mixed, adding egg shell after washing and mashing it; add egg mixture to boiling bouillon and boil furiously 10 minutes; remove and strain through flannel bag; salt to taste. Color with caramel if desired; serve.

Care should be taken not to include any of the egg yolk, as it prevents bouillon from being perfectly clear.

Chicken-Gumbo Soup

Joint a young chicken and brown in equal parts of lard and butter; simmer in 2 quarts water until tender, remove all bones, cut the meat in smaller pieces and return to broth after skimming off all the grease; add 1 cup okra, which has been sliced, floured and fried; add 2 chopped onions, 2 to 6 sliced medium tomatoes, 1 cup diced celery, and season with salt, pepper, and a little sugar; cook slowly for 30 minutes, add 2 cups milk or cream in which 1 tablespoon corn-starch has been smoothly mixed; bring just to the scalding point; remove and serve.

Chicken-Tomato Soup

Joint a half grown chicken, and boil 30 minutes in 4 quarts water; add 2 large tomatoes, sliced, or 1 cup canned or stewed tomatoes; add 1 cup boiled rice or barley, and, just before removing from fire, add 1 cup milk and cream, 2 tablespoons butter, season with salt and pepper; serve.

Fish Soup

Clean, wash and dry 1 pound any white fish, and cut into small pieces or flake; put into pan or kettle with 1 pint each milk and water; add 1 cup finely chopped mixed vegetables, such as carrots, onions, celery, etc., with a little chopped parsley and a small bit of any herbs desired; simmer for 30 minutes, strain off liquor; melt 2 tablespoons butter or clear fat in a pan and smoothly mix in 2 tablespoons flour, then add fish liquor and stir until it boils; set from over fire and let it cool slightly, and add 2 egg yolks beaten with ½ cup cream, straining it into the cooled soup; reheat it to almost boiling point, but do not let it boil; season with salt and pepper, add a few drops of lemon juice if convenient, and a little finely chopped parsley; serve with croutons.

Green Turtle Soup

Behead and bleed turtle; dismember and clean well; separate legs, neck and other coarser portions of meat, dip in boiling water, remove skin, and cut into small pieces; remove fine, delicate inside meat also cut, and the green fat; rinse in cold water and put all together in kettle, adding 1 or 2 onions, such sweet herbs as desired, pepper and salt, and about 2 quarts cold water; stew continuously, but very slowly, for 5 hours or more; strain off the liquid through a colander, then pick out a quantity of finer meat and bits of the fat, and add to the soup; add 2 or 3 finely chopped hard-boiled eggs, or the turtle eggs, if there are any; add the juice of a lemon and about ½ cup well flavored wine; thicken with browned flour; reheat; serve.

Or: The coarser meat may be boiled separately with rice, any chosen vegetables, and seasonings, strained if preferred, and added to the finer meat and fat stewed in 2 quarts water for 1 hour, and thickened with browned flour; add eggs, lemon juice and wine.

Green Turtle meat may be purchased like canned fish, lobster, and other sea-food.

Mock Turtle Soup

Let someone besides yourself clean a calf-head, removing brains and tongue whole, the meat from the bone, and chopping the bone into several pieces; put all to soak separately in salt-water for several minutes to bleach; use brain and tongue for separate dishes, turning meat and bone into soup.

Put a stock kettle with about 1 gallon cold water and the bone, head-meat, tongue, half a bunch of parsley, half a stalk of celery, one large bay leaf, three cloves, half an inch of a stick of cinnamon, six whole allspice, six peppercorns, half of a large carrot, and one turnip. When the tongue is tender take out, to be served as a separate dish. Leave in the flesh for about two hours, when it will be perfectly tender. Let the bones, etc., simmer for six hours, then strain and put stock away until the next day.

At the same time that the calf's head is cooking in one vessel, make a stock in another, with a small beef or veal soup bone, and any scraps of poultry (it would be improved with a chicken added; and one might take this opportunity to have a boiled chicken for dinner, cooking it in the stock); put into two or three quarts of water, and simmer until reduced to a pint.

The next day remove fat and settlings from the two stocks.

Put into a two-quart pan 2 tablespoons butter and when it bubbles stir in an ounce of ham, cut in strips, and 2 tablespoons of flour, stirring it constantly until it gets quite brown; pour the reduced stock over it, mix well, and strain it.

Now, to half a pound of calf's head cut into dice add one quart of calf's-head stock boiling hot, the pint of reduced and thickened stock, and the juice of half a lemon. When it is about to boil set it to one side and skim it very carefully. Add the head-meat cut in dice, and two hard-boiled eggs cut in dice, and salt; serve.

To clean the calf-head: Cut from between the ears to the nose, touching the bone, then cutting close to it, take off all the flesh. Turn over the head, cut open the jaw bone from underneath, and take out the tongue whole. Turn the head back again, crack the top of the skull between the ears, and take out the brains whole; they should be saved for a separate dish.

Creole Soup

Drop ¼ cup washed rice in 3 cups boiling water and boil 30 minutes. Fry ½ cup chopped onion in 2 tablespoons bacon grease until tender but not brown; add 2 cups tomato pulp, stew 10 minutes, and rub through strainer into rice and water; season with salt, sugar and paprika or chili to taste; add 1 chopped green pepper or a tablespoon finely chopped parsley if desired; serve with crackers.

Mexican Soup

Make a stock with a small soup-bone and some fat or from the water in which beef has boiled by adding trimmings or scraps of meat and poultry; to 2 quarts of stock, add 1 each, sliced, large onion, large tomato, small turnip, small carrot, and salt to taste; simmer for 5 or 6 hours, frequently skimming; about 30 minutes before soup is done, stir thoroughly and add 1 tablespoon chili powder; strain through a sieve; serve.

Ox-Tail Soup

Cleanse and cut 1 ox-tail into joints, put into stew kettle, cover with salted cold water, par-boil, strain off liquid or stock; have ready ½ cup finely chopped bacon or ham, and 2 each onions, carrots, small turnips and single stalks of celery, all finely sliced or chopped; now, dry each ox-tail joint, roll them in flour, and put into a stew pan containing 4 tablespoons hot cooking fat; add bacon and chopped vegetables, and fry all together until brown; add the strained ox-tail stock, 12 whole peppers, 2 cloves, any herbs desired, and season with salt if necessary; bring whole to boiling point, skim well, cover with lid, and simmer for about 3½ or 4 hours; strain, remove excess fat, return to kettle, add 1 tablespoon corn-starch beaten into a little milk or wine, stir and cook a few moments; put in some of the smaller joints of ox-tail; serve.—Larger joints may be served in brown gravy as meat.

Split Pea Soup

Wash 1 cup split peas and soak overnight in cold water; boil with 2 quarts water and a marrow bone; adding, after it reaches

— 54 —

a vigorous boil, 1 chopped onion; boil about 3 hours, strain and return to kettle, grate and add 1 turnip and 1 carrot, and season with salt and pepper; let it come to a boil and serve with croutons.

Onion Soup

Cook 2 cups fine chopped onions in 2 tablespoons bacon grease or butter in a covered sauce pan; shake pan to keep from browning and cook until tender; add 4 cups vegetable or rice stock; boil about 5 minutes, and season with salt, white pepper, and paprika or chili powder; add finely chopped parsley or green pepper if desired.

Mushroom Soup

Wash 1 cup mushrooms through several cold waters and slice thinly, without peeling, into sections running with the gills, not across them; put one cup each milk and stock from boiled chicken in a double boiler, and when hot, add mushrooms and ½ teaspoon salt; cook slowly 5 or 6 minutes until tender, then stir in 1 tablespoon corn-starch beaten into ¼ cup cold water; cook several minutes and add 1 lightly beaten egg yolk; when serving, drop a small piece of butter and a few croutons in each individual plate of soup.

Croutons: Dry bread cut into shape of dice, and toasted to a golden brown in oven; or, they may be fried to crispness in butter.

Mid-Summer Soup

Make a blended stock from the liquids in which the vegetables of your dinner have been boiled; peas, beans, tomatoes, spinach, cauliflower, cabbage, and even macaroni, spaghetti, noodles, rice. Put in a pot with an onion and some parsley, and cook until onion is well cooked; season to taste, and add lightly beaten egg; add flour or corn-starch to suitably thicken if desired; serve at once

Cream of Soups

Practically any Cream of Soups may be made from the following foundation sauce, simply by the addition of the dominating fish or vegetable and slight variations in the method of combining.

Sauce: Scald 3 cups milk in a double boiler, and thicken with 3 tablespoons each of melted butter and flour worked smoothly together; add prepared vegetable or fish, and mix; thin to consistency of cream with 2 cups, more or less, boiling water; season with salt and white pepper to taste; add any herbs, spice, or other seasonings desired; serve with croutons. Six plates.

If flavor of onion is desired, add 2 tablespoons grated onion to milk before thickening, and cook about 10 minutes before proceeding.

Cream of Potato Soup—Follow sauce recipe and add to the thickened milk; 2 cups smoothly mashed boiled potatoes with any lumps removed; add 1 or 2 teaspoons finely chopped parsley just before serving.

Cream of Corn Soup—Follow sauce recipe and add to thickened milk: 2 cups canned or stewed green-corn, mashed and rubbed through a coarse sieve; add boiling water and cook 15 to 20 minutes, then proceed.

Cream of Pea Soup—Follow sauce recipe and add to thickened milk: 2 cups canned or boiled green peas, mashed and rubbed through colander; add boiling water and cook 3 to 5 minutes; proceed.

Cream of Vegetable Soup — Follow sauce recipe, flavoring with onion as above, and add to thickened milk: 1 cup smoothly mashed potatoes and 1 cup mixed, carrot, turnip and celery; pare and chop vegetables, boil until tender, and mash with fork or masher to a paste; add to sauce; add boiling water and cook 10 minutes; proceed.

Cream of Celery Soup—Follow sauce recipe and add to thickened milk: 2 cups chopped celery boiled until tender and pressed through a sieve; add boiling water and cook 5 minutes; proceed.

Cream of Tomato Soup—Follow sauce recipe and add to thickened milk: 2 cups canned or stewed tomatoes, measured after rubbing through a colander or sieve and stewed slowly for 20 minutes in 1½ cups water; 2 tablespoons grated onion and 1 to 2 tablespoons sugar; thin with just enough boiling water and proceed.

Cream of Fish Soup—Follow sauce recipe and add to thickened milk: 2 cups flaked boiled fish that has been rubbed through a sieve; thin, and proceed.

Puree of Peas

Soak 1 cup dry or split peas in cold water overnight; drain, put in 2 quarts cold water and boil for 3 hours, cooking slowly and adding water while cooking, so as to have 3 pints when done; rub through a sieve to make smooth, then return to the kettle, season with salt and pepper; add 2 tablespoons butter and 1 tablespoon flour stirred to smoothness with a little cold water and a tablespoon sugar; add 1 cup milk, or ½ cup rich cream just before serving; serve with croutons.

Puree of Vegetables

Prepare 2 potatoes, 1 tomato, 1 onion, 1 carrot, and put all together in soup kettle; add 1 quart water and as soon as boiling, add 2 tablespoons rice; boil about 1 hour until vegetables are tender, adding boiling water occasionally to replace evaporization; when vegetables are tender, press all through a sieve and return to kettle; mix 2 table-spoons corn-starch with a little milk and add to puree; add remainder of 1 pint milk, stir until it boils, season with salt and pepper and add 2 tablespoons butter; serve with croutons.

Puree of Chestnuts

Remove shell from 5 dozen chestnuts, put in boiling water to soften inner scale and remove it; boil kernels until tender and rub through a coarse sieve; add this puree to 4 or 5 cups good chicken stock which has been seasoned and combined with 2 cups hot rich milk or cream; add 2 tablespoons butter, season with salt and pepper to suit taste, and a little paprika or nutmeg if desired; serve with croutons.

Puree of Clams

Mash about 30 clams, press through a colander or coarse sieve, and heat in a deep pan; blend 1 tablespoon each flour and melted butter, mix with ½ cup cream, and stir into 4 cups milk already heated in double boiler; mix dressing with clams, which should not be cooked, only heated. Serve to six.

Potato Chowder

Peel and cut into dice shape, 6 medium sized potatoes, or about 3 cups; cut into small bits, ¼ pound or about 4 cubic inches, bacon or salt pork, and prepare a tablespoon finely chopped onion; put meat into hot frying pan, then add onion and fry together until a light brown; put a layer of potatoes into a saucepan, sprinkle on a layer of meat and onion, salt and pepper to taste, and, if liked, a little finely chopped parsley; build layers alternately until all are used; add 2 cups water, cover closely and let simmer twenty minutes, then add 2 cups milk and 1 tablespoon each flour and melted butter worked together; stir carefully to avoid breaking up the potato cubes, until chowder boils; serve with crackers.

Corn Chowder

Follow Potato Chowder recipe, and add 2 cups fresh green-corn with the potatoes; or, add 2 cups cooked or canned corn with the milk.

Vegetable Chowder

Follow Potato Chowder recipe, and add 2 cups, altogether, of one or more vegetables finely chopped; add by same rule as corn chowder.

Fish Chowder

Follow Potato Chowder recipe, and add 1 to 2 cups, depending upon strength of flavor, of flaked fish; if fresh fish, parboil, flake, and add with potatoes; if salt fish, such as cod, etc., is used, flake or shred, and soak out the salt in luke-warm water before adding; if canned fish, use the liquid, adding only enough water to make the 2 cups required; use all milk instead of part water if desired; or, the last cup of milk added may be sweet cream; broken crackers, softened in a little milk, may be added just before last boiling.—Also see "Fish."

Clam Chowder

Follow Potato Chowder recipe, adding 2 cups chopped parboiled clams in layers with potatoes when putting into saucepan; and adding 1 cup each water and clam juice for first boiling; just before serving, add to suitably thicken, broken crackers softened in a little milk.

To prepare clams: If fresh, wash about two dozen clams perfectly clean and boil in a kettle until they open easily; remove clams and separate meat from the juice; or, open clams and boil in their own juice 3 minutes, separate meat from juice, chop meat and strain liquid. If canned, separate meat from liquid, chop and strain as above.

Oyster Stew

Put 1 quart fresh oysters in a strainer placed over a stew pan, and strain off the liquor; pour over the oysters ¾ cup cold water, letting it run into the liquor; carefully pick over the oysters, removing any bits of shell; heat liquor to boiling point and skim thoroughly; add 4 cups milk and 1 cup cream, and when it boils, add 1 tablespoon each flour and butter rubbed together, and mix to smoothness; season with salt and pepper to taste; keep hot until ready to serve; now, just before carrying to table, bring liquid to boiling point, remove from over fire to prevent further boiling, and pour in the oysters, and when they have cooked enough to be plump and the edges begin to curl, serve.—If all milk and no cream has been used, double the amount of butter. Never allow milk to reach a boil after putting in the oysters, as they will be toughened, and the quality of the stew spoiled. Serve with oyster crackers.

Salads and Salad Dressings

Salads provide a palatable form for the serving of a wide variety of raw food demanded by our systems. Most of us get enough raw food in the summer-time, when fruit and vegetables are abundant, but in winter, many of us cease eating raw food almost entirely. This is a serious mistake—eat some raw food every day and you will avoid many winter ills.

When fresh vegetables and fruits are not abundant or available, such foods as dried fruits of all kinds and nuts should not be overlooked; dried dates, figs and other fruit; oranges and apples in their natural state; all nuts, including cocoanuts; raw vegetables, such as cabbage, upon which science has come to place much importance—most, or all, of these are available to practically every household through the winter, and may be combined into a variety of fine, wholesome salads.

Salad dressings, while primarily meant as decorative, or to improve the flavor by blending with the salad, have, if properly made, certain food values of their own. Many of these may be kept fresh for some time and kept on hand for daily use.

Simple Salads

Those in which a single vegetable, fruit or meat is served with a "dressing," either with or without a "garnish" or decoration.

The tender leaves of Lettuce, Endive, Chickory, Water Cress and Young Mustard make excellent salads when served with salt, pepper, and a salad-oil or salad-dressing.

Crisp, tender Celery cut into small sections; quartered or sliced Tomato; sliced green Cucumber soaked in good vinegar; hard-boiled Egg, sliced, quartered or diced; Fish, either canned, or baked, flaked or diced —any one of these, when served on a nice crisp lettuce leaf with Mayonnaise or other salad dressing and garnished make a most excellent, simple salad.

Other vegetable salads are: Cold cooked Asparagus-tips; Cold Kidney Beans; Cold boiled Peas; or Candied Yams may be served as above.

Such fruits as: Apples, either ripe, stewed, canned, or even apple-sauce; halves of firm canned Pears; sliced or crushed ripe or canned Pineapple; split Banana; Oranges, sectioned or sliced; canned Cherries or Plums, drained; cold or left-over stewed dried Fruits, such as Apples, Peaches, Apricots, Pears, Figs, or Prunes; any one of these form a nice simple salad when served on lettuce leaves with Mayonnaise or other favorite dressing, and garnished with grated cheese and nuts.

Garnishes: Sliced or diced hard-boiled Egg; Sprigs of Parsley; Celery sprigs or leaves; Grated Cheese; Shredded Cocoanut; Ground Nuts of any kind; Slice of Lemon; Strips of green Sweet Pepper.

Combination Salads

Most any combination of cold cooked meats, raw and cold cooked vegetables, fruits, nuts, and cheese make attractive salad dishes when nicely arranged on lettuce leaves in salad plates, and served with a favorite salad dressing and garnished. Meats and large fruits and vegetables should be sliced, diced or cut into small pieces or strips; small fruits and vegetables may be included whole or halved. Here are a few well blended combinations:

Lettuce, Green Onions, Radishes; vegetable dressing or mayonnaise.

Green Cucumbers, White Onions, Radishes; vegetable dressing or mayonnaise.

Raw Cabbage, Ripe Apple, Celery; mayonnaise.

Head-lettuce, Water-cress, Mustard leaves, Radishes, Cucumber; vegetable dressing; with or without mayonnaise.

Ripe Tomato, Celery, hard-boiled Egg; any dressing.

Celery, Nuts, Olives or Pickles; any dressing.

String Beans, Radishes, Celery, Olives or Pickles; French dressing.

Asparagus-tips, Cauliflower, Young Carrots; choice dressing.

Beets, Celery, Onion, Ripe Tomatoes; or in tomato baskets; any dressing.

Cauliflower, Beets, Peas, Boiled Egg or Grated Cheese; mayonnaise.

Cold Meats, Celery, Bread-crumbs, and pickles, Olives or green peppers; grind together and moisten with salad dressing, season.

Minced Ham; Cheese, Pimiento; favorite dressing.

Cheese, Pimiento, Olives or Pickles.

Cottage Cheese, Green Pepper, Nuts; mayonnaise or variation.

Ripe Apples, Bananas, quartered Marshmallows; mayonnaise.

Cantaloupe, Celery, Nut-meats; mayonnaise.

Dates, Figs, Cheese and Nuts; lemon juice; mayonnaise.

Canned Apricots or Peaches in halves, quartered Cherries, Nuts; mayonnaise, fruit jelly.

Any dried or canned Fruit; quartered Marshmallows, Nuts; fruit jelly, mayonnaise.

Ripe or canned Fruit. Cheese, Pimiento; mayonnaise or fruit dressing.

Stewed Prunes or Figs, sliced Orange, Nut-meats; mayonnaise or fruit dressing.

Swelled Seedless Raisins, Ripe Apple, Celery; mayonnaise or fruit dressing.

Fancy Salads

Stuffed Peppers—Select sweet green peppers of uniform size; place them in boiling water and let stand for fifteen to twenty minutes; split in half lengthwise, remove seeds; fill each half with any salad containing meat, or those with a combination of vegetables that blend with the green pepper; serve to table on a nicely folded napkin placed on a table plate, or serve each on individual salad plate lined with lettuce or a white paper doily; garnish with celery.

Tomato Baskets—Select well ripened, medium sized tomatoes, one for each person being served; scald with boiling water, and slip off the skins; with a sharp knife, take a slice off the stem end, and with a spoon or thin knife take out the central core and seeds; stuff with any of the plain combination, or special salads that blend with the ripe tomato flavor; set upright on lettuce leaf or bare salad plates, or several on large serving plate; form a handle for each with an arched strip of green sweet-pepper; serve with, or without, mayonnaise or other salad dressing; garnish if desired.

Tomato Surprise—Prepare tomatoes as for Tomato Baskets; stuff with salad and dressing, but instead of the basket handle, replace the stem end slice; or, leave skins on tomatoes and do not slice stem end entirely off, but leave it hinged with a bit of the skin; garnish with a nice well washed tomato leaf, or leave a bit of stem and a nice leaf attached when selecting the tomatoes.

Orange Peel Cups—Cut oranges in half, scoop out pulp with a spoon, and set in cold place to stiffen; fill with a fruit salad made with the orange, nuts, and choice of dressing; serve on lettuce leaves. If oranges are large, cups may be cut lower or smaller.

Fruit Stars—Salads containing orange, grape-fruit, peaches, or even ripe apples may be well served in this design. On fine, crisp lettuce leaf, place five sections of orange or grape-fruit, or five of each, the orange on top the grape-fruit section, with ends together at center of plate and sections radially. In the center and between the sections, place the other fruits and nuts composing the salad in artistic arrangement. Serve the salad dressing in a side dish.

Flower Salads—Slice hard-boiled eggs lengthwise into six equal sections; mix yolks with mustard, salt and paprika, and remold into balls. On crisp lettuce leaves, place a yolk ball and arrange white sections around it in form of a daisy; sprigs of parsley may be used to add color.

Arrange sections of fruit in much the same manner as for Fruit Stars; form a center for the flower from chopped dates or figs and nuts; form stems and leaves from green sweet pepper, serve on lettuce leaf, plain plate or a paper doily in contrasting color.

Birthday Salad

Place a thick round slice of canned pineapple on a lettuce leaf on each plate for base of candle stick; cut a banana in half crosswise, and stand a half endwise in the center of the pineapple ring to form the candle; place a half or whole cherry on top for the flame; form a handle of a strip of lemon or orange peel, or sweet green pepper. Also a nice Christmas salad, when garnished with a sprig of holly. A few shreds of cocoanut may be used to give the effect of dripping tallow. Whipped cream or thickened salad dressing may be piped around pineapple.

SALAD SPECIALS

Chicken Salad

2 cups chicken, diced	Salt and pepper
2 cups celery, chopped	Salad dressing
2 hard-boiled eggs, sliced	

Chill boiled or roast chicken, and cut into small dice or cubes; add and mix coarsely chopped celery; eggs may be chopped finely and mixed, or they may be sliced and placed on top; season with salt and pepper to taste; chill until ready to serve. Serve on lettuce leaves with mayonnaise or other choice dressing; garnish with sliced olives,

radishes, capers, pickles, or other relish.—
Some prefer to run salad through meat chopper and moisten with a bit of favorite salad dressing; this method is much preferred for sandwiches.

Meat Salad

3 cups chopped meat	½ cup melted butter
6 eggs, hard boiled	2 tablespoons chili powder
1 onion, medium	
1 bunch celery	1 teaspoon English mustard
1 bunch parsley	

Chop veal, pork or fowl very fine and boil until tender; add chili powder and boil fifteen minutes longer; finely chop onion, celery and parsley and mix in the mustard with them; drain meat and mix with the vegetables; add and mix thoroughly melted butter, or mayonnaise. Serve on lettuce or in tomato baskets with slice of lemon; garnish with slices of egg.—Egg may be chopped and mixed with salad if preferred. Left-over cold meats may be used by chopping and boiling with chili powder as above. As much meat as desired may be used.

Flaked Fish Salad

1 cup flaked fish	1 teaspoon celery seed
1 egg, hard boiled	⅛ teaspoon cayenne pepper
2 medium potatoes, boiled	
1 small cucumber pickle	Mayonnaise

Fish may be canned salmon, tuna fish, or other fish flakes; or, bake any available fish, chill, and separate into small flakes. Cut potatoes, egg and pickle into small cubes or pieces; add fish flakes, celery seed and pepper, and enough mayonnaise to hold salad together. Serve on lettuce leaves, with a garnish of small cubes of beet or strips, rings, or squares of green pepper or pimiento; mayonnaise over top.—Baked fish may be easily picked into small flakes with the prongs of a silver fork.—See Flaked Fish.

Potato Salad

6 large potatoes	1 teaspoon salt
1 large onion	1 teaspoon celery salt
½ cup vinegar	½ teaspoon white pepper
3 tablespoons bacon grease	½ tablespoon flour

Boil potatoes, peel, chill, slice; finely chop onion; mix. Mix vinegar, bacon grease and seasonings; heat to boiling and thicken with flour; pour over potatoes and onion, mix and cool. Serve on lettuce leaves; or garnish with sprigs of parsley.—Variations: Add one-half to one cup chopped marshmallows to above. Use potatoes, onion and vinegar, and add true or mustard mayonnaise in place of regular dressing. To either combination, add a few chopped nut meats. Addition of chopped apple is relished by some. Try other combinations with materials at hand.

Fresh Fruit Salad

6 ripe peaches, diced	1 slice watermelon
6 large plums, diced	1 orange, diced
6 cherries, halved	1½ cups raspberries
½ cantalope, sliced	

Mix all together; serve ice-cold in individual salad dishes, with mayonnaise, or Thousand Island Dressing. Other similar fruits may be substituted. Canned fruits may be served in the same manner.

Dried Fruit Salad

2 cups large dried peaches	¼ cup chopped figs
½ cup chopped nut meats	Mayonnaise

Wash peaches, soak several hours, stew in same water until tender. Select large peach halves for each person and roll in finely chopped or ground nut-meats; mix remainder of chopped nuts with figs and fill center of peaches. Serve on lettuce leaves and top with mayonnaise.—Dried apricots may be used instead of peaches. Small fruit, such as grapes, raisins or cherries, may be added if desired.

Cherry Salad

1 cup canned cherries	1 teaspoon grated horseradish
1 cup chopped celery	
1 cup chopped peanuts	Mustard-Mayonnaise
1 cup cream, whipped	

Mix stoned cherries, chopped celery and peanuts with mustard mayonnaise to suit taste; serve on lettuce leaves, with sweetened whipped cream and sprinkled with just a little horseradish; or, may be served in plain salad dishes, or in half-orange rinds.—Will serve six persons.

SALAD DRESSINGS

True Mayonnaise

Mayonnaise is doubtless the most popular of all the well known salad dressings, being not only one of the most delicious, but universally liked, and the base from which many of the other well known dressings are made.

There are so many dressings and sauces called by, and sold under, the name of mayonnaise that it is well to understand that the real, true, legitimate mayonnaise is nothing but oil, raw egg yolks, vinegar, salt and seasoning. It is of a rich cream color, and about the consistency of whipped cream.

With a little practice and patience, mayonnaise is easily made in any kitchen, even in considerable quantity. For the amateur, two egg yolks are easier to work with than one—the problem being to beat oil into them, and season the whole with a bit of vinegar, salt and paprika. After a little practice, you will be able to beat up a quart of mayonnaise in practically no time, using not more than one or, at most, two egg yolks and a quart of oil. While pure olive oil is best, any good, well refined salad oil such as corn product oil, or even peanut oil, may be used. Beating is much easier done with a rotary, or Dover beater, altho it may be done with a wire whisk, or even a common fork.

All ingredients should be of the same temperature—cold is considered the safest. Try the following proportions and use inexpensive oil until you learn:

2 egg yolks
½ cup oil
2 teaspoons vinegar
⅛ teaspoon salt
⅛ teaspoon paprika

Put egg yolks, salt and paprika into a deep soup plate if using a whisk, or in a deep bowl if using the Dover beater; beat them until they have lightened up considerably in color; now, add some of the oil, drop by drop, beating it in rapidly; after several tablespoons have been worked in, the oil may be added by the half-spoonfuls, and then by spoonfuls—altho the dressing may break a little, beating will bring it together again; add vinegar by drops when dressing threatens to become too stiff, adding all the remaining vinegar at the end of the process. Some famous chefs add a little boiling water at the end to finish and keep it from oiling.

While learning, take your time, do not hurry, as haste means failure. When put in sterile glass jars and kept fairly well covered, true mayonnaise will keep fresh for many weeks.

Mock Mayonnaise

1 cup milk
4 tablespoons butter
3 eggs
1 teaspoon salt
1 tablespoon flour
1 tablespoon sugar
¼ teaspoon cayenne pepper
½ cup vinegar

Put milk and butter in a pan on back of range-top to warm. Beat eggs, and add salt, flour, sugar and pepper; mix well and strain into the milk; set pan in a hotter place on range, and add vinegar slowly, stirring constantly; when thick, remove from range, and beat a few minutes to a smooth cream. Put in glass jar and dressing will keep fresh for several weeks in a cool place.—This dressing does not equal True Mayonnaise, but may, in emergency, be used as a substitute, either alone or in other dressing recipes.

Mustard Mayonnaise

Mix a little prepared mustard with hot water; gradually beat this into a quantity of True Mayonnaise until blended to suit taste.

Thousand Island Dressing

1 cup true mayonnaise
½ cup chili sauce
1 teaspoon grated onion
1 tablespoon each any 3 of following, finely chopped:
chives, olives, pickles, pimento, green pepper, canned sweet pepper pickled beet, young onion, pickled green tomato

Beat chili sauce into mayonnaise and add grated onion; mix three finely chopped ingredients selected, and thoroughly mix into the chili-mayonnaise. When placed in a covered glass jar it will keep fresh for many days.—A substitute for chili sauce may be made by cooking down one cup canned tomato fine pulp and juice to half quantity, along with an onion and a green sweet pepper; but let it cool to the same temperature of the mayonnaise before combining the two.—If dressing is desired stiffer, beat in a small quantity of whipped cream to thicken. Some chefs add a little chili powder, or paprika; some add a pinch of salt; others add various native herbs finely chopped or ground.

French Dressing

1 cup salad oil
6 tablespoons vinegar
1 teaspoon salt
2 teaspoons sugar
¼ teaspoon paprika

Olive oil, or corn oil may be used; also, either vinegar or lemon juice. Mix dry ingredients, add oil and vinegar, and beat until thick or lightly creamy.—May be made in larger quantities and kept in a bottle; shake as used.

American Club Dressing

1 cup French dressing
1 cup chili sauce
2 teaspoons Worcestershire Sauce
2 teaspoons grated white onion

Mix ingredients thoroughly; ready to serve. Half above quantity is sufficient for small meal.

Tartare Sauce

1 cup true mayonnaise
2 tablespoons olives
2 tablespoons capers
2 tablespoons gherkins
1 tablespoon parsley
1 teaspoon onion juice

Fine chop olives, capers, gherkins and parsley; mix thoroughly, and fold into mayonnaise; add onion juice; serve cold.—Substitutions, if necessary: Pickled green tomatoes for olives; nasturtium pods, or pickled green beans for capers; sour pickles for gherkins; fine mixed pickles for olives, capers and gherkins; however, recipe as given is superior. Just a sprinkle of cayenne pepper may be added if desired.

White Cream Sauce

1 cup sweet milk
2 tablespoons butter
2 tablespoons flour
¼ teaspoon salt
Pepper to taste

Melt butter and make into a paste with flour; add salt and pepper; lastly, gradually add milk and beat until smooth and creamy.

Relishes and Sauces

Usually served with the coarser foods, are various condiments intended to make them either more palatable or attractively tempting—or both. Such condiments include a wide variety of spices and flavorings, mostly made from barks, berries, buds, roots and seeds. With these condiments, many savory combinations are prepared which are commonly known as *relishes,* many of which give to meat courses most dilectible and well blended flavors. *Sauces* of fruits are also often used in this manner as appetizers and to improve the taste of many meat dishes.

Recipes covering the ordinary basic preparation of such condiments and their combinations, are here given, with the idea that many of them may not only be grown in the home garden, but may also be prepared for use in the average household kitchen.

Herbs for Winter

Herbs for flavoring and seasoning, such as mint, sage, savory, thyme, marjoram, or other sweet herbs, may be gathered and dried for winter use. Gather the mature plants in their season, pick over carefully and discard poor branches or sprigs, wash and shake off water; wrap or tie in cheese cloth and place in a warm, dry place such as the lower warming-closet of the range; when dry pick off all the leaves and stem-tops, and place at once in sealed dry glass jars until needed; when wanted, rub into fine powder and sift. —See list of domestic herbs under "Kitchen Garden."

Kitchen Bouquet

The "bouquet" of herbs used for flavoring soups, etc., and often referred to in recipes, consists of the following: A sprig each of parsley, savory and thyme, a small leaf of sage, and a bay leaf, bunched and tied together. This will season 1 gallon of soup cooked for 1 hour, and many other dishes in comparison.

Celery Salt

Celery Salt may be purchased at most any grocers, or may be made at home. Save celery tops in season, put them in a warm dry place and allow to dry until crisp and brittle; crush to a fine powder and mix with an equal amount of fine salt; bottle to keep dry.—Celery leaves thus dried and stored in glass jars may be used to flavor soups, stews and salads when celery is scarce.

Currie Powder

Currie Powder may be purchased at most grocers, or may be compounded from ingredients obtainable at the druggists. Take one ounce each of mustard, pepper and ginger, three ounces each of coriander seed and tumeric, half ounce of cardamons, and one-quarter ounce each of cayenne pepper, cinnamon and cumin seed; grind together in a mortar, or have druggist do it for you, sift and keep in tightly corked bottle. Used for salad dressings and relishes.

Currie Sauce

Chop one large slice onion very finely and fry in one tablespoon butter until brown; add one tablespoon flour and one teaspoon currie powder and stir about one minute; add one cup meat stock, and season with salt and pepper to taste; simmer about five minutes, strain and serve. Excellent with broiled or shallow fried meat, fowl or fish.

Prepared Horseradish

Grate well cleaned horseradish root until very finely shredded; put in glass jars, filling them to within an inch of the top; add enough vinegar to thoroughly saturate and cover; seal and set aside to thoroughly digest.

Prepared Mustard

Gradually stir 2 cups good white cider vinegar into 1 cup very finely pulverized mustard seed; add ½ teaspoon pulverized cloves, and bring mixture to complete boil over moderate heat; add ½ teaspoon pulverized sugar, and let mixture boil up again; take off, and beat well until entirely smooth; if too thick, thin with a little cold vinegar while beating; pour into glasses or jars, and if too thin plunge a red-hot iron rod into each, until rod cools, to drive off excess moisture. Spiced or flavored mustards may also be prepared in this manner, by using spiced vinegar, tarragon vinegar, celery vinegar, horseradish vinegar, etc., instead of the plain vinegar.

Spanish Chili Mustard

Mix together three tablespoons ground white mustard, one tablespoon sugar, one egg, one cup vinegar, and three tablespoons chili powder. Set bowl or pan in cold water, boil for ten minutes, stirring constantly until thick, and cool. When cold, add a tablespoon of olive or salad oil, and bottle.

Worcestershire Sauce

An almost undetectable imitation of the original Worcestershire Sauce may be made as follows:

To 5 cups good cider vinegar, add: 1 level teaspoon each, all in finely powdered form, cloves, black pepper, cayenne, Jamaica ginger, paprika, chili powder and pimiento, 2 tablespoons currie powder, 5 tablespoons each of the table salt and grated shallots; mix all together, and add 2 cups sherry wine substitute; simmer whole about 1 hour, strain, let stand in stone or glass jar a week, strain again, and put in corked bottles; straining out the coarser particles is all that is necessary.

Cold Slaw

2 cups chopped cabbage	½ teaspoon salt
½ cup cider vinegar	1 tablespoon celery seed

Cut, or mince, white tender cabbage until almost a pulp—it may be ground in meat chopper if quantity justifies; mix in enough vinegar to suit taste; season with salt and celery seed to suit taste, or, use celery salt instead, if desired. A little black pepper may be added if desired.

Cabbage Relish

Chop very finely, one medium head of cabbage and two red peppers; add four teaspoons each of mustard seed and celery seed; to one quart cider vinegar, add a little sugar to suit taste, and bring to a boil; mix liquid and vegetables; let cool. Will fill three pint glass jars; ready to use when cool.

Chili Relish

Put five pounds washed green tomatoes in a chopping bowl, sprinkle with one cup salt, and chop fine; as green water rises, pour it off; when chopped very fine, lift out by handfuls, squeeze out juice, and place in a granite cooking vessel. Chop three pounds white, tender cabbage, and add 3 pounds fine chopped white onions and thoroughly mix; add three tablespoons each of ground white mustard seed and ground allspice, four tablespoons chili powder, one cup fine sugar, and one quart good cider vinegar. Add to tomatoes and cook slowly for three-quarters hour, add four tablespoons more of chili powder, and finish cooking for fifteen minutes longer, and set to cool. When cold, seal in sterilized glass jars.—Keeps well in any climate, and is a delicious relish for meats, fish, oysters and other seafoods.

Mexican Relish

Chop together and grind very finely in a meat grinder: Four nice green tomatoes, two large green sweet peppers, one medium sized onion, and a little horseradish. Put into a jar and cover with boiling vinegar, to which has been added one teaspoon salt, one tablespoon pulverized mustard, and two tablespoons chili powder.

Raisin Relish

Put one cup sugar in one-half cup water and one-half cup vinegar; tie one teaspoon whole cloves and a two-inch stick of cinnamon in a piece of cloth, and drop into liquid; then boil until sugar is dissolved; add two cups seeded or seedless raisins and cook very slowly until most of the syrup has been absorbed; seal in sterilized glasses. Served with meats.

Cranberry Relish

Cut two cups cranberries in halves and wash in a colander to remove seeds; wash one orange and one lemon, and slice them very thinly, then cut into small pieces; mix cranberries, orange and lemon, together with two cups seeded or seedless raisins, two cups brown sugar, one-half cup vinegar, one teaspoon each of cinnamon and nutmeg, and one-half teaspoon cloves; cook very slowly until thick; pour into sterilized glasses and seal. Serve with meats.

Cranberry Mold

4 cups cranberries	2½ cups sugar
1 cup water	

Cook cranberries in water until berries are tender; strain; add sugar and stir until dissolved, but do not allow to boil; turn into glass or chinaware mold which has been wet with cold water, and set aside to become firm; serve cold.—Small individual molds may be used if preferred, such as tea cups, glasses or fancy molds, but do not use metalware of any kind, except aluminum.

Cranberry-Sauce

1 quart cranberries	2 cups sugar
2 cups boiling water	

Boil sugar and water together for five minutes; skim; add cranberries and cook, without stirring, until clear and transparent—five minutes is usually long enough to cook. If strained sauce is desired: Cook cranberries in water until tender, press through strainer, add sugar and finish cooking until clear.

One-Day Pickles

Prepare a pickling mixture by adding to each cup of vinegar you desire to use, one tablespoon each of fine salt and pulverized table mustard; put this mixture into a glass fruit jar or jars, or a stone crock. Select medium sized cucumbers; wash and dry them thoroughly, as the secret of this process lies in their being absolutely dry when dropped into the mixture; put in a sufficient quantity to be well covered, cover jar tightly. They are ready for use the following day. By replenishing cucumbers as pickles are used, a progressive supply is assured at any time during the summer.

Ripe Tomato Pickle

Scald one-half peck ripe tomatoes, remove skins, slice, remove seeds, leaving solid portion, and drain for six hours; chop and add two large onions. Mix two finely chopped red peppers, without seeds, one cup each of salt, brown sugar, mixed mustard seed, two tablespoons each of celery seed and black pepper, one teaspoon each of cloves, cinnamon and mace, and one quart good cider vinegar. Mix seasoning well with tomatoes; put in glass jars.—Another cup of sugar may be added if desired sweeter.

Celery Vinegar

Prepared like Tarragon and other herb vinegars, except two ounces of celery seed are used with each half-gallon of vinegar. Cayenne pepper seed may also be used in the same manner and proportion. Both vinegars are an excellent addition to fish and other seafood sauces.

Chervil Vinegar

Half fill a bottle or glass fruit jar with either fresh or dry chervil leaves, and fill to top with good cider vinegar; heat gently by placing bottle or jar in warm water, which is then brought to boiling point; remove from range; cool, cork, and let stand two weeks, when it is ready for use. Used extensively by French cooks in fish sauces and salad dressings, a few drops being sufficient.

Tarragon Vinegar

At blossom time, put two ounces of Tarragon leaves and blossoms in a half-gallon fruit jar, and fill with sharp cider vinegar; let stand ten days, strain off and bottle. Sweet basil, thyme, sage, marjoram, savory, or mint may also be used in the same proportions, or half quantity may be used. These vinegars will be found most welcome the year around for adding piquent flavor to meat and salad dressings, and one will be well repaid for the time and trouble in preparing them.

White Sauce for Meats

For each pint of sauce: Melt 4 tablespoons butter, or substitute, in a pan, stir in 4 tablespoons sifted flour, and heat; when it bubbles, add gradually 2 cups milk, while stirring constantly; cook 5 minutes, and season with 1 teaspoon salt and ¼ teaspoon white or black pepper.

If further seasoning is desired, add any one of the following:

Dry Mustard	2	teaspoons
Curry Powder	1	tablespoon
Horseradish	1	"
Capers, chopped	2	"
Worcestershire Sauce	2	"
Onion grated or juice	3	"
Celery, seed or extract	3	"
Salad Dressing	3	"
Tomato Catsup	4	"
Green Pepper, chopped	5	"
Pimiento, chopped	6	"
Olives, chopped	6	"
Cheese, grated	1	cup

Chili Sauce

Boil together two dozen ripe tomatoes, three small green peppers or a half teaspoonful of cayenne pepper, 1 onion cut fine, half a cup of sugar. Boil until thick; add 2 cups of chili vinegar; then strain the whole; set back on the fire and add a tablespoonful of salt, and a teaspoonful each of ginger, allspice, cloves and cinnamon; boil all five minutes; remove and seal in glass bottles.

Green Tomato Sauce

Peel and stew green tomatoes until they become a soft, smooth mass; to a gallon of tomatoes, add five cups vinegar, three cups sugar, one cup onions finely chopped, one tablespoon each salt, pepper, allspice, and pulverized mustard. Boil all slowly until thoroughly mixed; bottle while hot; seal.

Mustard Catsup

Prepare a mixture of one quart good vinegar, one pound light brown sugar, one-quarter pound fine salt, one ounce black pepper, one ounce allspice, one-half ounce cloves, one-half pound finely pulverized table mustard, two red peppers. Wash and dry one peck choice ripe tomatoes, bake in the oven until quite soft, drain off water, and pass the pulp through a colander. Combine pulp and liquid mixture, boil one and one-half hours, stirring constantly; bottle and cork.

Meats and Meat Specials

When properly cooked, meat becomes one of the most readily digestible of foods; but, when improperly cooked, it is perhaps the most difficult to assimilate. *Good cooking* can make any meat tender, juicy and nutritious; *bad cooking* can make any meat tough, destroy its nutritive value, and render it impossible of digestion, leaving illness and trouble in its wake.

The *secret* to proper cooking of meats, therefore, is to retain its natural juices, reserving to it their full flavors and nutrition, and neither allowing them to escape nor become over-cooked. This applies whether the method is frying, broiling, baking, boiling, or roasting. (Refer to "Methods of Cooking" on another page.) The exception is in the cooking of some meats, as salted, or cured, meats; those for soup-making or stewing; or those for blending as in braising—when the object is to extract a part, or all, of the juices, instead of retaining them altogether.

To accomplish this result, two basic rules must be observed. The natural juices of meat are albuminous in character and, when meat is cut some of these juices escape, forming a thin film on the outer surface. Like the albumen of eggs, this coating may be quickly coagulated, or hardened, by the sudden application of high heat (searing), whether from boiling water, direct fire, or heated oven. On the other hand, this coating may be quickly dissolved and dissipated by contact with cold water, allowing the juices to be extracted.

Since all meats should be cooked by a *moderate heat* for the length of time required according to the degree of tenderness (see table "Time Required for Cooking"), the above basic rules are applied thus: When meat is cooked with the intention of retaining its natural juices—as for joints or fowl—its surface should be "seared" by the application of *high heat* at the beginning, and the temperature *lowered to moderate* to complete cooking; but, when meat is cooked with the intention of extracting a part or all of its natural juices—as for soups or stews—it should be started at *low heat* at the beginning, and the temperature *raised to moderate* to complete cooking. In both cases, the *cooking temperature* should be just right to properly *set* the juices, care being taken not to harden or over-cook them.

With this basic principle in mind, and a knowledge of the proper control of the heat of the range, young cooks should soon master the art of preparing juicy, wholesome, perfectly cooked meats.

Sirloin Steak

Broil the steak—see table: "Time Required for Cooking"; season with butter, salt and pepper, and a dash of paprika. Peel about four bananas for each steak, slice lengthwise and fry in butter 5 minutes; serve over top of steak.

Flank Steak

Score the steak on both sides in criss-cross fashion with a sharp knife; sprinkle well with pepper and salt, and fresh chopped mint if the flavor is liked; pour over it enough vinegar to soak in well during 30 minutes; drain, shake off the mint, and broil.

Stuffed Flank Steak

Score 2 flank steaks on both sides in criss-cross fashion with a sharp knife. Make a dressing with 2 cups bread crumbs mixed with 1 minced onion and moistened with a little boiling water and seasoned with ½ teaspoon poultry seasoning; spread dressing on one flank steak, place the other steak on top and tie together securely; put in 2½ table-spoons hot butter and sear both outer sides of steak well, then place it in a casserole or baking dish, add 1 cup boiling water, cover, and cook slowly in oven until tender —about 2½ hours.

Filet Mignon

Procure about 2½ pounds fine, tender fillet, or tenderloin, of beef; trim it nicely all around, and cut into 6 equal, small fillets; with the side of a cleaver, flatten them slightly and equally; place them on a plate and season lightly and evenly with salt and pepper; heat 2 tablespoons butter in frying pan, put in the fillets, and saute 4 minutes on each side for "medium"; prepare 6 bread croutons by cutting sliced bread into rounds about the size of the fillets and frying crisp and brown in butter; on individual plates, place a bed of tartare sauce, or similar thick dressing, upon which place a fillet, and crown this with a crouton; garnish with 2 or 3 small prepared mushrooms, if desired; serve as hot as possible.—Fillets cut from tender veal round are also prepared into *filets mignons.*

Rolled Steak

Large cut round steak; prepare a dressing of bread crumbs moistened with ½ cup butter and a very little water, adding 1 finely chopped onion; place dressing on lightly salted steak, roll up compactly and tie the ends or fasten with skewers; dredge with flour, cover top with small pieces of butter; put in baking pan, and brown in hot oven; add 1 cup water, cover, bake in moderate oven in about 1 hour; carve across to serve.

Swiss Steak

Salt and pepper a thick round steak, and pound in as much flour as it will take; put in hot frying pan and brown good on both sides; add boiling water until steak is covered, put in hot oven and cook in about 1½ hours.

German Steak

Large, thick round steak; put in a deep pan, dredge with flour; cover with layer of slices of potato, season with salt and pepper; cover this with a layer of tomatoes, salt, pepper, and flour; on top, place a few slices bacon; fill pan about half with water, cover, cook slowly in moderate oven about 4 hours.

Beef Roly-Poly

Cut 2½ pounds round steak into 8 or 9 square pieces, brush each with beaten egg, and season; roll each piece up tightly and fasten with skewer or tie; lay them in baking pan, cover with strips of bacon, add 1 cup each water and tomato juice; put in hot oven, sear, reduce heat and cook slowly for 2 hours; thicken gravy and serve with rolls.

Curried Beef

Cut 2½ pounds round steak into two-inch pieces, roll in 5 tablespoons siften flour and set flour remaining aside; sprinkle with 1 teaspoon currie powder—see index. Cook 2 medium onions, sliced, in bacon fat or drippings, then brown the meat in it; add rest of flour, then 2 cups water to which ½ cup tomato juice, or catsup, has been added, and let it come to boil; put in casserole or baking dish, cover, and bake 2½ hours in slow oven; when ready to serve, add 1 tablespoon vinegar and 2 tablespoons grape jelly.

Savory Brown Stew

Cut 1 pound tender lean beef into about 1 inch cubes; put 2 ounces suet in stew pan, shake it over hot range-top until rendered, and remove cracklings; dust meat with flour and put it into hot fat, shaking until each piece is seared on all sides; add 1 tablespoon flour and 2 cups good stock, or 1 cup each water and milk; stir until boiling and add 1 teaspoon browning, a teaspoon salt, a slice of onion, and pepper to season; cover, and push pan over gentle heat, and stew slowly for 1 hour.

Dumplings: Mix 2 cups sifted flour, ¼ teaspoon salt, and 2 teaspoons baking powder; moisten with milk to make a dough; roll quickly into walnut-sized balls, drop them over top of stew, cover pan and stew 12 minutes; dish dumplings around edge of serving plate, put stew in center, and dust with finely chopped parsley; serve.

Braised Beef

Sear a 2 pound chuck roast on all sides in roasting pan in hot oven; add ½ cup sliced onions, and 1 cup boiling water, ½ tablespoon salt, cover pan, lower heat to moderate, and roast 1 hour. Then add 1½ cup diced carrots, ¼ cup diced celery, 6 to 8 potatoes sliced small, and 1 cup boiling water; cover, and roast 1 hour more. Serve on platter, with vegetables around meat; thicken and season liquid in pan for gravy.

Fillet of Beef

Lard well with pork fat—see "Methods of Cooking"—and dredge with flour, salt and pepper; turn thin end of fillet back to make it even thickness, and tie or skewer it in place; place in shallow pan without water, and place in hot oven; for a 2 or 3 pound steak, roast about ½ hour; serve with mushroom sauce, tomato sauce, or with sliced tomatoes as garnish.

Dutch Pot Roast

Cut in pieces, as for stew, 4 pounds rump, shank or chuck beef, roll in flour to thoroughly cover, and brown in 2 tablespoons hot bacon fat or drippings. Place in a kettle with 2 cups stewed tomatoes, 1 cup chopped carrots, ¾ cup chopped celery, 1 finely chopped Spanish onion, and 2 green peppers cut in strips; season with 2 teaspoons salt, and add 2 cups water; cover, and cook on top of range slowly about 3½ hours. Thicken the gravy left with a little flour made into a paste with cold water, let bubble a few minutes; serve.

Rump Roast

Put the meat in a roasting pan, sear in a hot oven; lower heat to moderate, add 3 tablespoons cooking fat and ½ cup water; cover, and roast for 2 hours, remove cover and brown for 30 minutes; potatoes may be added ½ hour before cover is removed for browning.

Hamberger Roast

Put through meat-grinder, 2 pounds nice lean beef from the round; regrind 2 or 3 times, working in 1 teaspoon grated onion, 1 tablespoon finely chopped parsley, one-third cup fine soft bread crumbs, 1 teaspoon salt, and ¼ teaspoon pepper; mix thoroughly with 1 egg, beaten light, and about 3 tablespoons butter or other fat; form into a nice even loaf or roll, set into a greased baking pan, and bake about a half hour, basting several times with hot fat; when meat is done, drain fat from pan, add a half-cup boiling water, and let simmer until browned meat-juices in pan are absorbed; heat about 3 tablespoons of fat, blend with it 3 tablespoons flour, season with ½ teaspoon salt, and ¼ teaspoon pepper, then add 1 cup finely strained tomato pulp, and the liquid in the baking pan; cook and stir until boiling, then add a tablespoon catsup and ¾ cup boiled and rinsed macaroni—see macaroni recipe; when very hot, sprinkle with ½ cup grated cheese; place meat loaf on serving platter and the macaroni dressing around it; garnish meat with sprigs of parsley or any other desirable garnish.

Italian Style Beef

Sear 2½ pounds shank meat in hot frying pan; place in casserole with 1½ cups water, cover, and bake in oven 1½ hours; add 2 small onions and 1 carrot, both sliced, ¼ cup diced turnip, and 1 teaspoon salt; cook 1½ hours more, replenishing water if necessary; put meat on platter, and thicken the liquor with flour, add ¼ cup catsup and 1 teaspoon mustard, pour over meat when portions are served.

Beef Loaf

Chop 2 pounds chuck or round and ¼ pound salt pork in meat chopper; combine with 1 cup bread crumbs, 1 tablespoon chopped parsley, season to suit taste, and 1 slightly beaten egg; mix well and pack solidly into greased loaf bread pan; bake in moderate oven 45 minutes to 1 hour; serve in slices or cubes.

Corned Beef

Rinse the corned beef in cold water, tie it in shape, put in kettle and cover with cold water; heat to boiling point, move it from directly over fire, and simmer until tender—about 30 minutes to the pound.

With Cabbage: Half hour before meat is done, add cabbage cut up; serve with the corned beef; include a red pepper pod if desired.

With mixed vegetables: If boiled dinner is desired, add potatoes, turnips, carrots, and onions 1 hour before meat is done, and cabbage a half-hour later; after vegetables are added, the whole should be cooked just a little faster than the simmering point, as in corned beef alone.

Corned Beef Hash

Brown 2 medium onions with 2 tablespoons butter in a saucepan; add 2 cups cooked, well chopped corned beef, and 2 cups hashed cooked potatoes; moisten with ½ cup broth, or water and butter; season with pepper and nutmeg, stir well, and cook 15 minutes; serve with 5 or 6 poached eggs on top; garnish with a little finely chopped parsley.

Or: Make the hash as above; and let cool; just before serving, mold with the hands into individual portions, and saute in hot butter, or substitute, until browned; place a freshly poached egg on each portion and serve.

Or: Make the hash as above, put in a lightly buttered baking dish, sprinkle over with bread crumbs, moisten with about 1 tablespoon melted butter, and bake in oven 15 minutes, or until a good brown color; serve.

Or: Form a border around a baking dish with mashed potatoes, and set in hot oven for 2 minutes; then, fill in center with hot corned beef hash; sprinkle with finely chopped parsley, and serve.

Creamed Chipped Beef

Put finely chipped dried beef in suitable dish, cover with water and set to back of range, allowing it to soak and swell to its original size before drying; allow the water to become hot but do not let it boil; when softened, pour off water, and pour over beef a cup of cream, or milk and butter as substitute, and season with pepper; bring to boiling point, and thicken with about 1 tablespoon flour mixed with a little milk; serve on fresh toast.

Veal Cutlets

Trim and flatten veal chops, or cutlets, nicely; cook and serve in any style in which pork chops are prepared, except, when frying or broiling, allow about 2 minutes longer on each side.

Or: Prepare cutlets, season well with salt and pepper, dip them in beaten egg, then in finely grated cheese, and finally in fresh bread crumbs; flatten them, put in frying pan with butter or other cooking fat, and fry 5 minutes on each side; serve with or without sauce.

Or: Prepare and fry as above, omitting the cheese, and serve with a rich tomato sauce on the side.

Or: Prepare mock cutlets by grinding very finely nice lean veal and finally grinding into it fresh veal suet, allowing 1 ounce of suet to each pound lean veal; season with salt, pepper, and nutmeg; add ¼ cup good cream, ½ chopped shallot, and 1 raw egg for each pound lean veal, and mix all together; shape into form of chops, cover with bread crumbs, and fry in butter 4 minutes on each side; serve with any kind of sauce on the side.

Breast of Veal

Trim nicely about 3 pounds of the breast of veal; make a few incisions on the top, and tie it firmly together; lay it in a deep frying pan, with a piece of pork-skin cut up, a carrot, and a cut-up onion; cover with buttered paper, and when it begins to color after about 5 minutes, moisten it with about 2 cups water or good broth; baste frequently and cook 1 hour; dish up on a platter, strain the sauce over it; garnish with a few fried croutons; serve with stuffed head-lettuce, stuffed artichokes, stuffed tomatoes, or similar salad.

Fricassee of Veal

Cut a choice slice of veal steak into cutlets for serving, roll in flour, put in 3 or 4 tablespoons hot cooking fat in frying pan, and saute brown, first on one side and then on the other; remove meat to casserole; pour hot water or clear stock into the pan, then pour liquid into casserole; season with salt and pepper, cover, and cook in moderate oven an hour or more; add tomato sauce, or thicken the sauce in which it was cooked if desired; serve *en casserole*.

Or: Saute the prepared cutlets in melted butter; cover, without removing from pan, with boiling water, and cook slowly until meat is tender; make a gravy by melting 4 tablespoons butter or substitute, add 4 tablespoons flour, and brown; add 4 cups of water in which the veal was cooked, and season with salt, pepper, onion juice and lemon juice; add ¼ cup cream and 2 tablespoons butter just before serving; serve veal in center of hot platter, and surround with the hot sauce; garnish with parsley.

Veal Croquettes

Melt 1 tablespoon butter and work in thoroughly 1 tablespoon flour; add 1 cup milk and cook until thick; stir in 2 cups finely ground veal, cook a minute, and let cool; form into croquettes, roll in cracker crumbs, egg, cracker crumbs again, and fry in hot deep fat.

Liver and Bacon

Slice and trim nice calf's liver, put on a dish and season with salt and pepper; add about 1 tablespoon cooking oil, covering all surfaces of slices by rolling it in the oil; broil 4 minutes on each side; arrange slices on a hot serving dish, and place on each a crisp slice of broiled bacon; serve over this, if desired, a sauce made by blending 2 tablespoons good butter with 1 teaspoon very finely chopped parsley and juice of ½ lemon, and seasoning with a very little nutmeg.

Stewed Liver

Trim, wash, and cut about 1 pound fresh calf's liver into 2-inch cubes; prepare a browned sauce by adding 1½ tablespoons flour to 1 tablespoon melted butter and cook slowly until properly browned, then add salt and pepper to season, and 2 cups water, cooking to consistency of good cream; pour boiling water over the liver cubes and immediately drain, drop them into the brown sauce, and cook slowly about 12 minutes; do not allow them to cook rapidly nor too long; serve.—Nice with mushrooms; just before serving, drop in some mushrooms that have been fried in butter or other fat.

Calf's Brains

To Prepare: Place fresh brains in cold water, letting them rest until the outside membrane becomes softened, then peel off the skin, removing all of it between the lobes; put them in fresh water, and when ready for use, carefully drain.

Brains in Butter Sauce: Put prepared calf's brains in a pan, and cover with fresh water; add 2 tablespoons salt, and about ½ cup good vinegar, 1 medium carrot sliced, a few whole peppers, and a bit of thyme and bay-leaf, or other favorite herbs; boil 5 minutes, drain well, and cut each brain in half; dress them on a hot plate with a garnish of parsley, and serve with regulation white sauce—see index—to which add an extra tablespoon butter and the juice of a lemon.

Fried Brains: Prepare for cooking as above; parboil 5 to 10 minutes; drain well on a napkin or other soft cloth; cut into serving portions, dip in milk, then into a mixture of flour and cracker-crumbs, roll them in a colander to remove surplus crumbs; drop into hot deep cooking fat, and fry for 5 minutes; serve either with or without tartare sauce.

Brains and Eggs: Prepare for cooking as above; par-boil 5 to 10 minutes, drain on a napkin, and sprinkle lightly with flour; break brains up with 3 or 4 eggs to the set of brains in a bowl; put into hot shallow fat, and fry until eggs are set to suit taste; serve.

Baked Beef Brains: Prepare brains of grown beef same as above for cooking; put in pan with water to cover, and simmer at back of range for 1 hour; drain, rub with flour and salt, and lay in baking dish with about 1 cup cold water; lay over top a few bits of butter, and bake in moderate oven about 1 hour, frequently basting; serve with mushroom, onion, or other white sauce—see index.

Sweetbreads

To Prepare: Clean and neatly trim sweetbreads; soak for 3 hours in 3 different fresh waters—1 hour in each water—with a teaspoon salt in each water for each pair sweetbreads; drain, place them in cold water and bring to boiling point, then drain again, freshen them with cold water, cover with a napkin, and set aside until ready to use.

Fried Sweetbreads: Prepare as above; after freshening, drain on soft napkin, cut into serving portions, dip in milk, then into a mixture of flour and cracker-crumbs; roll them in a colander carefully to remove surplus crumbs; drop into hot deep cooking fat, and fry until a golden brown; serve with or without tartare sauce.

Sweetbread Ramekins: Prepare as above, but after bringing to boiling point, par-boil 20 minutes, then cut into small pieces; season rich white sauce with paprika and a little lemon juice, and add sweetbreads; put into buttered individual baking cups, or ramekins, cover with buttered bread crumbs, and bake in hot oven until brown.

Sweetbread Patties: Prepare, par-boil, and cut into small pieces as for ramekins; mix with plain rich white sauce and put into pastry pattie shells; serve hot.

Sweetbread on Toast: Prepare exactly as for patties, except serve hot over toast.

Veal Loaf

To each pound finely chopped cold roast veal, add: ½ pound sausage meat, 2 tablespoons butter, or cooking fat, ¼ cup bread crumbs, and 1 egg; mix or grind together well, season with salt and pepper, and moisten with about ½ cup good stock, or the gravy in which the meat was cooked; form into a loaf, or short thick roll, brush over with beaten egg, and roll in bread crumbs; bake as for hamberger roast—see recipe.

Pork Chops

Trim and flatten the pork chops nicely, then salt and pepper them about 1 hour before cooking; heat 2 tablespoons butter in frying pan, put in chops, and saute 6 minutes on each side; remove chops to hot platter, skim off surface fat from butter, and make into gravy with flour and milk, or add ½ cup some broth, let it come to boil, and strain over chops; serve with apple-sauce.

Or: Prepare chops as above, except add to the seasoning, ½ teaspoon good cooking oil for each chop, roll in well; broil 6 minutes on each side, arrange on hot dish, and spread over them 2 tablespoons creamed butter mixed with 1 tablespoon very finely chopped parsley, and juice of ½ lemon, seasoned with a little nutmeg, this quantity being sufficient for 6 chops.—Broiled Chops.

Or: Prepare chops as above, except dip in beaten egg, roll in flour or bread crumbs, and saute in hot butter or cooking fat 6 minutes on each side; remove chops to warm platter; make a gravy in the pan by adding a little milk, and serve separately.—These are "Breaded Pork Chops."

Arabian Chops

Sear half-dozen pork chops on both sides in hot frying pan, then place them in casserole; cover them with sliced tomatoes, a little thinly sliced onion, and a bit of minced green pepper; add 3 cups hot water, cover, and bake in moderate oven 2½ hours.

Chop Pot Pie

Trim required number of pork chops, and prepare with seasoning of salt and pepper; put in a stew pan, cover with cold water and let come quickly to boiling point; boil 5 minutes, then allow to simmer until chops are tender; have ready drop-dumpling dough; pour off enough of the broth to expose the top surface of the chops, and place the dumpling dough, by scraping from a tablespoon onto the meat above the broth; cover and cook undisturbed for about fifteen minutes, or until dumplings are thoroughly cooked throughout; meantime, thicken the broth removed from pan into a gravy; serve hot, arranging the chops on a hot platter, the dumplings around them, and the gravy poured over the whole.—Veal and lamb chops may be prepared in the same manner.

Pork Chop Fricassee

Substitute nicely trimmed pork chops for the veal cutlets in the recipe: "Fricassee of Veal."

Pork Tenderloin

Neatly trim full-sized pork tenderloins, and split in two lengthwise without detaching the halves; season about 1 hour before cooking, then put them in pan with a tablespoon hot butter, and saute six minutes on each side; arrange on a hot serving dish, then skim the fat from the surface of the gravy and thicken with flour and thin with milk into cream gravy and serve over the tenderloins; or: Add a little clear vegetable stock to the frying-butter, and strain over the meat; garnish with any sauce or dressing desired.

Tenderloin De Luxe

Wipe large pork tenderloin with damp cloth and trim edges; slit lengthwise and fill with regulation poultry dressing seasoned with chopped apple, onion and sage; sew up or tie, rub all over with salt and pepper to season, place in greased baking dish; add a little water and bacon fat, roast in hot oven 45 minutes, basting often.

Savory Spareribs

Roast spareribs 1 hour; season them; place small whole potatoes or quartered large ones, and quartered cooking apples on top of roast, and bake another hour.

Stuffed Spareribs

With a cleaver, crack side of spareribs crosswise in two places; spread with dressing as used in Tenderloin de Luxe—see recipe—fold ribs over dressing and secure with skewer; place in roasting pan with ½ cup water, cover, and roast at least 30 minutes to the pound, in a moderate oven; season after the first hour of cooking.

Pork Hearts En Casserole

Slice the hearts thin, and across the grain of the meat; roll them in flour, fry with a little chopped onion in hot bacon fat; place in casserole with 1 cup water or stock; add any desired herbs and a chopped pimiento; season with salt and pepper; cover, and cook about 2 hours in moderate oven; when almost done, drop biscuit dough over the meat, and bake until brown and done through.

Pork Pot Roast

Sear fresh pork shoulder butt, or similar roast, in hot fat in roasting pot; add 1 cup water, cook 1 hour; add 1 cup sliced or diced carrots, ½ cup wedge-shaped parsnips, and a small red cabbage or brussel sprouts; cook together until vegetables are done, then remove them; cut pork into slices, arrange down center of serving platter, surrounding the meat with the vegetables.

Roast Shoulder of Pork

Wipe fresh pork shoulder well with damp cloth; rub it with cooking fat, or shortening, and dredge with flour; put in roasting pan without water, and roast 30 minutes in hot oven; lower oven heat and continue roasting until tender—allowing about 30 minutes for each pound of meat; turn from side to side frequently, and baste about every 20 minutes, unless using a self baster.

Roast Loin of Pork

Season well with salt and pepper, place pork loin in hot oven and sear well; lower oven heat and roast 25 minutes to the pound of meat; as there is sufficient fat, no water is required; the gravy is very rich, so remove some of the fat before making it.

Roast Young Pig

Dress a young pig about six weeks old, and thoroughly wash it inside and out; then rinse it in still another water with a teaspoon soda dissolved in it, thoroughly rinse the inside, and with a dry clean kitchen towel dry the inside well and salt sufficiently; prepare regular well seasoned bread dressing as for poultry, stuff the inside of the pig until it is plump and of natural size, then sew it up, fold the legs under it and tie them; place the youngster in a roaster or baking pan in a kneeling posture in ½ cup cold water, completely cover all around with well buttered paper, put it in a moderate oven, and let it roast for at least 2 hours, and longer if necessary; baste frequently while cooking, with its own gravy, and if, by chance, the skin at any time becomes dry and begins to smoke, rub it over with a clean cloth dipped in melted butter, or provide a fresh buttered-paper covering; see to it, of course, that the buttered side is next to the pig; when done and delicately browned evenly, remove it to a hot platter, untie the legs, put a sprig of parsley, a nut, or a small apple in the mouth, garnish with a wreath of parsley, or, if at Christmas-time, holly around the neck, and a bed of garnish all around; make a good thick sauce with some of the gravy in the pan, and serve separately in a gravy-dish; also provide good apple-sauce. To carve: Cut off the head, slit down the back, take off the hams and shoulders, then separate the ribs, exposing the dressing.

Pork Sausage De Luxe

Fry and serve: on slices of pineapple; with apple rings delicately browned in butter; with fried bananas; with sweet potatoes; bore a hole in potatoes and stuff with sausage and bake; with broiled tomatoes; roll small cakes or links in biscuit dough and bake them; put in egg omelet just before turning it; serve with hot waffles and syrup.

Baked Ham

Scrub ham thoroughly, score skin in several places with sharp knife, and fill scores with cloves; put in very hot oven for 30 minutes, uncovered; mix 3 tablespoons sugar and 3 tablespoons vinegar, pour over ham, cover, and bake according to size of ham—see "Time Required for Cooking."

Or: Rub a thick slice of ham with mustard, place in casserole or baking dish, and cover with milk; bake 1 hour in moderate oven; when done, remove ham to serving dish, and thicken milk with flour and serve as gravy.

Baked Shoulder

Scrub cured pork shoulder, cover with cold water, and bring to boil; add 1 cup sliced onions, ¾ cup diced celery, and a tablespoon mixed whole spices; move over to reduce heat, and simmer about 3 hours or until tender; remove shoulder from liquor, skin it, dust the fat with brown sugar and bread crumbs, place it in a roasting pan with ½ cup of the liquor, 2 tablespoons vinegar, and ¼ cup brown sugar; bake in oven ½ hour, basting with its liquor.

Creamed Salt Pork

Freshen a piece of salt pork in cold water and dry surface; chop or grind meat, put in frying pan and slowly fry out; pour off some of the grease if too much, blend the remaining meat and grease with flour, and bring to creamy consistence with milk; season with pepper, and also salt if necessary; serve on toast; may also be served with corn-bread or potatoes.

Or: Salt pork may be sliced, freshened, and fried like bacon; remove meat to platter, make the gravy as above, and serve either over the meat or in separate dish.—Sliced bacon may be prepared in the same manner.

Salt Pork Fritters

Slice and freshen salt pork, or use bacon, and cover with thick Fritter Batter—see recipe for batter; fry in hot deep fat; serve with apple-sauce or jelly.

To freshen salt pork, slice and soak over-night in equal quantities of water and milk, using either skimmed, sour, or buttermilk; rinse in fresh water until the water runs clear; dry between soft cloths, and fry.

Roast Lamb

Leg of Lamb, or other roasts of this delicious meat, should be first properly prepared; see that every bit of "fell," or thin oily under-skin, is removed and the roast wiped thoroughly with a damp cloth, as this is the secret of removing "that wooly taste." Put roast in uncovered pan in very hot oven until thoroughly seared; then reduce the temperature, cover, and unless using a self-baster frequently baste with the natural fat that drips from the meat, but do not add any water, stock or other fat; roast about 15 minutes per pound of meat, seasoning with salt after the first half-hour of roasting; serve with mint sauce; lamb should always be served either hot or cold, never merely warm.

Lamb Stew

Cut breast of lamb in small pieces, and put in stew kettle with enough water to cover, salt, and a few slices of onion; cook slowly 1 hour, then add diced potatoes, allowing 2 cups to each 1 cup meat, 1 cup tomatoes, and stew 1 hour more; thicken with flour, allowing 1 tablespoon flour to each 1 cup liquid; if desired with dumplings, drop them in the boiling liquid before adding thickening, then cook 12 minutes without removing lid.

Lamb Chops En Casserole

Fry as many lamb chops as desired in a hot pan without adding other fat, until partially cooked on both sides; grease the casserole and put in it 2 cups canned peas, 1 diced carrot, 1½ cups diced potatoes; season with salt and pepper; lay the chops on top, and pour over whole the lamb fat in the pan made into a gravy with butter or bacon fat added, thickened with flour and thinned with about 1 cup hot water; bake in moderate oven about 1½ hours.

Breaded Lamb Chops

Dip lamb chops in a milk and egg mixture, roll in bread crumbs, and fry in hot deep fat; use 2 tablespoons milk and a little salt to each beaten egg.

Or: Cut each chop in two, removing the bone; dip in thick fritter batter—see recipe—and fry few pieces at a time.

Curried Lamb

Prepare 3 cups diced cooked lamb; make a sauce of 3 tablespoons flour, 4 tablespoons melted butter, and 2 cups milk; add 1 or 2 teaspoons curry powder, season with 1 teaspoon salt, add diced lamb, and heat thoroughly; just before serving, add 1 well beaten egg; serve on bed of hot rice, and garnish with slices of hard-boiled egg.

Lamb Patties

Dice or cut 2 or 3 cups cold roast lamb; make a white sauce by melting 4 tablespoons butter or substitute, adding 4 tablespoons flour and cooking until it bubbles, stirring in 2 cups milk slowly to avoid lumping; season sauce and add chopped meat; serve very hot in pastry patty shells—see recipe—made day before, with currant or other tart jelly on top.

Hash

To each cup chopped cold cooked fresh meat, add 2 cups chopped cold boiled potatoes, and mix; season with salt and pepper; moisten with water, milk or stock; for each cup hash, melt 1 tablespoon cooking fat in frying pan, put in hash, and stew for about twenty minutes, occasionally shaking pan to prevent sticking; may be moistened to suit; if onions or celery are used, finely chop required amount with potatoes. Baked in a baking dish with a crust of pastry on top, hash may be converted into hash pie.

Spanish Hash

Combine 2 cups chopped boiled potatoes, 1 cup chopped any kind cold fresh meats, 1 cup tomato pulp, 2 chopped small onions, 1 chopped pimiento, season with salt and paprika; mix with 1 beaten egg, and add ½ teaspoon Worcestershire Sauce; put in baking dish, spread ½ cup fine bread crumbs over top; bake in moderate oven forty minutes.

Stews

Any left-over meat may be made into delicious stew, if carefully prepared and well seasoned. The meat should be cut in small pieces and slowly heated in good gravy, or, if no gravy has been left over, use good stock, or melted fat, and make one; or, white sauce may be used; add chopped potatoes and any other left-over vegetables desired. For Irish Stew, use mutton, carrots, potatoes, and onions. For Spanish Stew, use any meat, green or red peppers, tomatoes, and season with paprika or chili; for Hungarian Goulash, use beef, carrots, onions and tomatoes; for Mock Chicken, use veal and pork mixed, and peas.

Meat Pies

Prepare any well seasoned stew, pour into a baking dish and cover with pastry crust; bake until brown in moderate oven.—Crust should be perforated slightly, or made in strips, or biscuit rounds of pastry laid closely together.

Pickled Pig's Feet

Cut off the horny parts of feet and toes, scrape clean and wash thoroughly, singe off the stray hairs, place in a kettle with plenty of water, boil, skim, pour off water and add fresh, and boil until the bones will pull out easily; do not bone, but pack in a stone jar with pepper and salt sprinkled between each layer; cover with good cider vinegar. When wanted for the table take out a sufficient quantity, put in a hot skillet, add more vinegar, salt and pepper if needed, boil until thoroughly heated, stir in a smooth thickening of flour and water, and boil until flour is cooked; serve hot as a nice breakfast dish. Or, when the feet have boiled until perfectly tender, remove the bones and pack in stone jar as above; slice down cold, when wanted for use. Let the liquor in which the feet are boiled stand over night; in the morning remove the fat and prepare and preserve for use.

Head Cheese

Having thoroughly cleaned a hog's or pig's head, split it in two, take out the eyes and the brain; clean the ears, throw scalding water over the head and ears, then scrape them well; when very clean, put in a kettle with water to cover it, and set it over a rather quick fire; skim it as any scum rises; when boiled so that the flesh leaves the bones take it from the water with a skimmer into a large wooden bowl or tray; then take out every particle of bone, chop the meat fine, season to taste with salt and pepper (a little pounded sage may be added), spread a cloth over the colander, put the meat in, fold cloth closely over it, lay a weight on it so that it may press the whole surface equally (if it be lean use a heavy weight, if fat, a lighter one); when cold take off weight, remove from colander and place in crock. Some add vinegar in proportion of one pint to a gallon crock. Clarify the fat from the cloth, colander and liquor of the pot and use for frying.

Dutch Scrapple

Boil fresh lean pork on the bone until meat is tender and may be easily removed; grind or chop very finely, avoiding fat. Remove all fat and bone from broth, cool and measure; to each quart of broth, allow 1 cup corn-meal, and cook into mush; add about one pound ground meat, salt and pulverized sage to season; turn into bread pan or other flat mold and cool. To serve, slice and fry in deep fat as for fried mush.

Beef, meat of pig's head, and trimmings may also be used in same way.

Mexican Tamales

Select large, clean corn-shucks, and trim ends to leave them 6 or 7 inches long; open them up, wash, let them soak in water until flexible, and sort them to have 2½ inches or more in width.

In a pot, boil equal quantities of fresh beef and pork with a bone, covering well with salted water; cook until tender, remove the meat and grind very fine. In a frying pan, melt some butter or other fat, add a few slices of onion, removing them as soon as the juice has been extracted; add ground meat, stirring constantly, fry for five minutes, then add enough broth in which the meat was boiled to thoroughly cover; mix and add seasoning of salt, cayenne, and chili powder to taste; continue stirring and cook ten minutes; then add enough flour to thicken sufficiently to mold mixture with hands; remove from pan to dish and cool.

Strain remaining broth in which meat was boiled into a pan; add this liquid to coarse corn-meal to form a thick dough or mush; for each cup of meal used, now add 3 or 4 tablespoons hot tallow rendered from beef suet; season with salt and mix well; finally add enough more broth to make a workable dough.

Form the tamales: spread out a corn-shuck, and place in the center a layer of dough 4 inches long and 1½ inches wide, and ⅛ inch in thickness; lengthwise in center of dough, spread a teaspoon of the meat, roll up the whole like a cigarette, and gather each end, tying it with a strip of well soaked shuck like a bag. Place endwise in a strainer, place over hot water, cover with a cloth, and steam about one hour; always serve hot. Tamales may be made larger by rolling larger quantity in two or three sections of shucks placed side by side with edges overlapping by nearly half the width. —One pound of meat will make about fifty small tamales. Chicken Tamales may be made in the same manner by using chicken meat alone or in combination.

Chop Suey

Chop Suey, originated in China, has been one of the most favored dishes with the Chinese people for several centuries. Introduced by Chinese cooks, it has found so much favor with American appetites that elaborate Chop Suey "Joints" have, in recent years, become permanent eating places in practically all of the larger cities. Many American cooks have affected dishes under the name of "Chop Suey," some of which are passable imitations, but the majority of them should, by all means, be called by some such name as "Celery Salad," or "Excusable Hash."

Here is the Genuine Chinese Recipe:

Ingredients: 1 pound lean cooked pork, sliced and cut into dice shaped pieces; 1 full stalk celery, cut up like the meat, making about 4 cups; 1 cup Chinese dried mushrooms, soaked in water and cut in small pieces; 2 cups dry onions, cut in small strips or pieces; white pepper and salt; Chinese Sauce; lard.

Method: Bring 1 tablespoon lard in a hot skillet almost to boiling point; add diced meat and cook about 15 minutes; add chopped celery and onion, and cook 5 minutes longer; moisten with boiling water and let steam 5 minutes under cover; add mushrooms, salt and white pepper to season; add 2 tablespoons Chinese Sauce, stir well, replace the lid and steam 10 minutes longer; serve hot, with rice cooked Chinese style. Serve four.

Substitutions: Chicken meat may be substituted for pork, making Chicken Chop Suey, the real favorite of the Chinese. Many Chinese cooks use veal or beef tenderloin, or veal and pork together, for the meat. Chinese Sauce may be purchased at Chinese stores in the largest cities, and sometimes from the nearest Chinese laundryman or cook; however, if not obtainable, Worcestershire Sauce or Challenge Sauce, obtainable at any grocer's, makes a good American substitute. Mushrooms, fresh or canned, may replace the foreign dried ones. Chinese cooks sometimes substitute Chinese or bamboo sprouts for the mushrooms, or use some of both; a fair substitute for Chinese sprouts is tender sprouts or shoots from beans, which have been kept dampened and in a warm place.

When served as above, it is known on the menu as Chinese Chop Suey; however, many prefer it with an excess of rich brown gravy made as follows: To 1 cup of the broth or juice left in skillet, add 2 tablespoons flour and 1 tablespoon Chinese Sauce, stir until smooth and pour over the Chop Suey; serve in deep chowder bowls.

Barbacue

Barbacued Meats are merely roasted meats basted and cooked in a special sauce or "dope." Treat any oven-roasted meat by preparing the "dope," and frequently and thoroughly moistening the roast with it while cooking, by means of a clean cloth wraped around the end of a stick.

Barbacue "Dope."—2 cups vinegar, ½ cup butter, ¼ cup bacon-drippings, ¼ cup catsup, 1½ teaspoons cayenne, 1 teaspoon finely ground mixed spices, onion or garlic to taste. Mix all together and boil until thoroughly blended; keep warm while using.

Poultry and Game

Poultry and Game are to be primarily classified as Meat, and their proper cooking is governed by the general instructions given under "Methods of Cooking" and "Meats and Meat Specials"; however, they require a somewhat more delicate treatment than the more mature or coarser joints and cuts, and, as a rule, a much longer time for proper cooking—see "Time Required for Cooking."

In preparing poultry and wildfowl for cooking, there is little variation from the regular methods employed with coarser meats. Cooking authorities do not agree as to the proper method; however, some cookery "experts" contending that poultry should never be wet or washed before cooking, holding that it has a tendency to make the skin and flesh soft and sodden. This is not only poor advice, but surely a weak reason for the practice, for one of the first and most important principles in *all* cookery is *absolute cleanliness*.

In dressing all poultry and fowl for whatever method of cooking, after carefully removing all pin-feathers, and thoroughly singeing, a *good cook* will use many clear, cold waters—washing and rewashing until absolutely clean, using a small quantity of soda in the last rinsing water. She will not allow the bird to remain in the water while dressing, but will accomplish the washing by frequent dipping and splashing in order that the water may not remain long enough to penetrate the tissues. After sufficient washing, the bird must be immediately dried by the use of a soft, clean cloth, merely *blotting* the surface lightly, inside and out, instead of roughly wiping. Lightly sprinkling with salt and allowing to remain for a few moments rolled up in a dry clean cloth, will insure a sufficiently dry, unshrunken bird ideal for even roasting or baking.

Dressings for Roast Fowl

Bread Dressing—Soak 3 cups stale bread crumbs in cold water until wet throughout, then squeeze out all the water until crumbs are light and flaky; moisten with ½ cup melted butter, or butter and cooking fat mixed; season with salt, pepper, sage, and any desired herbs to taste.—Add chopped onion if desired.

Apple Dressing—To Bread Dressing recipe, add: 1½ cups chopped apples.

Oyster Dressing—2 cups bread crumbs, 1 cup drained canned oysters; moisten with ½ cup milk and 3 tablespoons melted butter; season with salt and pepper.

Potato Dressing—2 cups mashed potatoes, 1 cup bread crumbs; moisten with ½ cup melted butter, or fat; season with salt and pepper; add 1½ cups seeded raisins.

Chestnut Dressing—Shell and blanche about 2 dozen large chestnuts, cook in boiling water until tender, drain, press through a sieve, and measure 1 cup; add 2 cups bread crumbs; moisten with ½ to 2-3 cup melted butter, or fat; season with salt and pepper and herbs.—Excellent for stuffing loin of veal, flank steak, or pork tenderloins, which are then roasted or baked in the usual way.

Roast Turkey

After properly plucking, dressing and cleansing, prepare for the roasting pan; cut off some of the neck if too long, and tie the skin over it; prepare a dressing of double the quantity in the bread dressing recipe, stuff the crop, and then the body, carefully stitching up the openings; tie or skewer the wings and legs in folded position and close to body; rub over with soft butter, sprinkle with salt and pepper, and dredge with flour; place on rack in dripping pan, pour in 1 or 2 cups water, and set in hot oven for 30 minutes; then, reduce heat of oven to moderate, and finish roasting in about 20 minutes to the pound; baste frequently while roasting; if any portion should seem to be browning too rapidly, protect it by pinning a piece of buttered paper over it; turn frequently, that all portions may be evenly baked and browned; when pierced with a fork, and the juice runs out perfectly clear, the roast is done; serve up on hot platter; stew the giblets separately until tender, remove them and chop fine, thicken the gravy in which they were stewed with flour and butter rubbed together, return the chopped giblets, and serve in gravy dish on the side. Serve with cranberry sauce.

Roast Chicken

Prepare the bird for the oven, following directions given under Roast Turkey; put on rack in dripping pan, but pour in 2 cups water with 2 tablespoons butter, adding 2 teaspoons salt and 1 teaspoon pepper; put into hot oven, baste frequently, and let it roast quickly, without scorching, allowing about 20 minutes for each pound of bird; just before roasting is finished, add 2 tablespoons butter to water in pan, and when it melts, baste with it, dredge bird with flour, baste once again, and let it finish browning; serve up fowl on hot platter. Having stewed the giblets, thicken the gravy in the baking pan with sufficient browned flour and butter —after skimming off the surface fat—and add the finely chopped giblets; or, bake the giblets in the dripping pan during the latter part of the roasting. Serve gravy separately, and provide cranberry, or other tart sauce.

Roast Capon

Select a capon weighing about 10 pounds; dress and follow instructions of roast turkey and roast chicken.

Roast Goose

The goose should be young, not more than 8 months old, and the fatter, the more tender and juicy the meat. Prepare it for cooking—reserving the giblets to be stewed separately—and stuff fowl with *bread dressing,* using double quantity called for in recipe, and seasoning strongly; do not stuff too full, and sew up opening firmly to keep flavor in and cooking fat out; tie legs and wings in folded position; put into baking pan with at least 2 cups salted water—a little vinegar or lemon juice added will shorten the time of cooking—and bake in a moderate oven for 2 hours or more until tender; baste frequently, adding a little more water as required, and turning the fowl often, that sides and back will be evenly and nicely browned; if skin should seem to be drying out or browning too rapidly, brush over with melted butter, or cover well with a well buttered paper. When done, remove to hot platter, pour off the liquid and fat, and to the brown gravy remaining in the pan add the chopped, tender giblets, and the water in which they were stewed; thicken with a little flour and butter rubbed well together, bring to boiling point; serve.

Or: Prepare as above, stuffing with *Apple Dressing.*

Roast Duck

Tame—Dress and prepare for the oven exactly as Roast Goose, except: Unless duck is unusually fat, it should be either larded with salt pork, or the basting liquid made rich with fat or butter, and basted more frequently; dredge with flour and seasoning, place on wire rack in drip pan or baking pan, and set in hot oven for first 10 minutes if young, 30 minutes if old, then reduce oven heat to moderate and roast 15 to 20 minutes longer for young, and 30 to 50 minutes longer for old, according to size; baste frequently after reducing heat; if browning too rapidly cover with buttered paper; serve with giblet gravy as Roast Goose.

Wild—Prepare and roast exactly the same as Tame Duck, except: Since most wild ducks have the flavor of fish, it is best before stuffing to par-boil them with a small peeled carrot, placed inside each fowl, to remove the fish taste; remove carrot, stuff with a well seasoned dressing; proceed as above.

Canvas-Back—This "King of Birds," unlike other duck, needs little or none of the usual flavorings to make it perfect, as the meat has an exceedingly delicious flavor all its own; pluck, dress, and singe; truss the head under the wing, place on rack of baking or dripping pan, and roast quickly in hot oven in 30 minutes, while basting often; do not stuff, but season with salt and pepper when done, and serve on hot dish, and with the rich gravy that has been extracted in the roasting; the breast alone is usually eaten.

Roast Guinea Hen

Dress and truss like chicken; cover breast with thin slices of bacon; bake in roaster, basting frequently until tender; remove bacon, brown, and dish up on hot platter; make white sauce with 2 tablespoons of the fat in roaster, 2 tablespoons flour, and 2 cups scalded milk or cream, seasoned with salt, pepper, and just a very little nutmeg; garnish fowl with parsley, serve sauce separately and potato croquettes or balls fried in deep fat.

Barbecued Fowls

(See "Barbacued Meats")

Mock Roast Fowl

Cook 2 cups breadcrumbs in 2 cups water for few minutes, then add about 6 finely chopped hard-boiled eggs; mix; remove from fire and add 2 cups finely chopped black walnut meats, and 2 cups boiled rice; mix well, add 3 slightly beaten eggs, 1 tablespoon grated onion, and season with salt, pepper, nutmeg, and sage or other herbs desired. With the above mixture, mold, with the hands, the body of the bird; using a piece of raw macaroni for the bones, form legs and stick into place; likewise the wings, formed in folded position, are stuck to sides; brush over with melted butter, and bake in moderate oven 1 hour; serve with apple or cranberry sauce.

Fried Chicken

Clean and dress young chicken, passing through several fresh waters; disjoint into: 2 thighs, 2 drumsticks, 2 wings, 2 to 3 pieces of breast, 2 to 3 pieces of back—neck, liver and gizzard may be included if desired, but must be carefully prepared and the gall discarded; rinse thoroughly, put on plate, cover with napkin, and set in cool place over night, or several hours before frying; when ready to fry, wipe off surplus salt, sprinkle with a little pepper, dredge thoroughly with flour; have ready a frying pan with 1 cup or more very hot frying fat, enough to make pan at least half-full after chicken is put in; put in chicken and brown quickly and evenly on all sides; reduce heat and fry slowly under cover, turning as required, until each piece is tender, plump, and evenly cooked; dress on hot platter, and make a white sauce with a little of the frying fat left in pan, 1 tablespoon flour and 1 cup milk, cooking to proper thickness; and season with salt and pepper to taste; serve separately.

Or: Follow above recipe, except: Dredge pieces in flour, dip in beaten egg, roll in cracker crumbs; fry in hot deep fat, or saute.

Or: *Make fritter batter*—see recipe—dry each piece of salted chicken, dip in the batter, and fry as above, using plenty of fat.

Or: (Italian Style) Make fritter batter and mix into it: Finely chopped tomatoes, small onion, minced parsley, salt and pepper; dip pieces of chicken into it, and fry in plenty of butter in thick bottomed pan, first rubbing the sides and bottom of pan with a clove of garlic; serve with tomato sauce, or with corn-croquettes.

Or: (Parisian Style) Prepare springers for frying; dry well and put into frying pan with 2 tablespoons hot butter; season with salt and pepper, and saute over brisk heat 5 minutes on each side; moisten with ½ cup tarragon vinegar—see index—and 1 cup hot water and butter, or fresh vegetable stock; cook 20 minutes, drain on napkin, serve on hot platter; decorate with large fried croutons cut in heart shape.

Or: (Matured Fowls) Dress, cleanse, and cut into joints exactly as young chicken; wash quickly, and drop into kettle or pot with enough rapidly boiling water to cover; boil 5 minutes, reduce heat and let simmer until tender, usually 2 to 3 hours for a 1-year-old bird; when tender, drain on napkin, season, dredge with flour, and fry same as young chicken; serve with mashed potatoes, thick gravy, and Southern Corn-cakes.

Broiled Chicken

Dress and prepare nice, young broilers as for roasting, except: Instead of trussing, split thru the back lengthwise, and lay the chicken open; turn over on flat surface and press down the breast without breaking the bone; cut the tendons under each wing and lay them out flat; cut sinews under second joint of legs, and lay them out flat also; season evenly with salt and pepper, and lay inside down on gridiron; place iron over a direct fire of clear, slow coals, place a tin and light weight on the bird to hold it flat; broil about 10 minutes, turn, and likewise broil the other side; keep fire even underneath and do not allow any part to scorch or over-cook; place on hot plate with 1 or 2 tablespoons butter and a little hot water, brush the butter over the entire chicken; garnish with a little parsley, serve with poached eggs separately;—if chicken is half or wholly matured, steam it about 1 hour, then broil.

Oven-Broiled Chicken

Dress and prepare nice, young broilers; cut neatly through both back and breast, dividing lengthwise in 2 halves; dry them thoroughly with cloth, season with salt and pepper, cover them thoroughly with plenty of butter, put in shallow pan in moderate oven, and slowly broil until tender, basting frequently in the butter, adding more if necessary; serve as other broiled chicken.

Fricassee of Chicken

Dress and cut up 1 or 2 young chickens as for frying, and put them in a stew pan with just enough cold water to cover; cover pan closely, set to heat ve-y slowly, then stew for an hour or more, or until meat is tender—the older the chicken, the longer the time required; when tender, season with salt and pepper, 2 or 3 tablespoons butter, and other desired flavorings, such as celery or herbs; thicken with 2 tablespoons flour mixed with a little milk to a smooth paste; add 2 beaten eggs; let come to a full boil and immediately remove. Dress on hot platter by placing the trimmings and inner pieces of the chicken in the center with the two breast pieces on top, and arranging the other pieces around the platter; over the whole, pour the sauce, and sprinkle with a little parsley.

Or: Browned Fricassee may be made by first browning about 4 tablespoons butter, or substitute, in a pan; put in the pieces of chicken and stir until each piece is nicely browned; add 2 tablespoons flour and 2 cups boiling water, and stir until it boils, then season with about 1 teaspoon salt; simmer, or stew slowly until tender, then add about 1 teaspoon onion juice and a little black pepper; serve as above.

Chicken Pot Pie

Dress a chicken or fowl, and separate into joints; put into stewing kettle, cover with cold water, and heat quickly to boiling point; boil 5 minutes, then gently simmer until chicken is tender; have ready *drop dumpling* dough; dip off enough of the broth to expose the top of the chicken, and place the dumpling dough, by scraping from a tablespoon, onto the meat above the broth; cover, and cook undisturbed for about 15 minutes, or until dumplings are thoroughly cooked throughout; thicken the broth removed, into gravy; serve hot, arranging the chicken on a platter, placing the dumplings around it, and the gravy poured over the whole.

Or: Proceed as above, and when the chicken is tender, remove the pieces to a baking dish; thicken the broth with ¼ cup flour, ½ teaspoon salt, and pepper to season, with enough cold milk to make a smooth paste; pour enough of gravy into baking dish to nearly cover chicken, reserving rest to serve separately; put drop dumplings on chicken by spoonfuls, cover and bake about 25 minutes in moderate oven.

Drop Dumplings

Sift together: 2 cups pre-sifted flour, 4 teaspoons baking powder, and ½ teaspoon salt; rub or cut in 2 tablespoons shortening; mix ½ cup milk with 1 egg, beaten light, and use as liquid in making the dough; after all of the liquid is used, add enough more milk to make soft dough; drop in pot pies by tablespoonfuls.

Chicken a la King

Melt 4 tablespoons butter, add 4 tablespoons finely chopped green peppers and cook until peppers are soft; add 1 tablespoon flour mixed with 1 teaspoon salt, and stir until well blended; add 2 cups milk and stir until smooth; add 2 cups diced cooked chicken, 2 tablespoons chopped red pimientos, and ½ cup canned, or cooked, mushroom cut into bits; mix; serve on toast or in pattie shells.—Canned or baked fish may be used instead of the chicken in the same manner.

Chicken, Creole Style

Prepare chicken as for frying; salt; boil until meat separates from bone; 1 hour before serving, put fried meat fat in pan, add 1 finely cut onion, a bit of garlic, and cook, but do not let brown; add 2 cups tomatoes, season with pepper, cloves, cinnamon, mace, chopped parsley, and chili powder; cook 15 minutes, then add to chicken; thicken with a little corn-starch, and serve with rice.—Chicken meat may be chopped or diced if desired. Other seasonings, such as chopped green pepper, horseradish, lemon juice; in fact, any combination of rich seasoning may be used according to material at hand.

Chicken with Oysters

Prepare and fry two young chickens, and make a thick white sauce with the fat in which they were fried; to this, add liquor from 1 quart fresh oysters; cook a few minutes, add oysters, stir and when edges begin to curl, remove from heat; serve chicken on hot platter with oyster-sauce over it.

Or: Fill the inside of a young chicken with oysters and sew up; place in a gallon stew kettle or pail, and cover tightly; place kettle in a pot of boiling water, and boil 1½ hours; remove bird, and thicken the gravy that has been cooked out of it with flour and milk paste, season with salt, pepper, and more oysters; serve sauce separately or over chicken.—Other dressing may be substituted for the oysters.

Chicken of Maryland

Select plump young fryers; dress; cleanse, cut into joints; dry; ; salt and pepper; dredge with flour; dip in beaten egg diluted with a little milk; roll in soft bread crumbs; put in lightly greased baking pan and put in hot oven; as soon as pieces begin to harden a little on outside, baste with 6 or 8 tablespoons melted butter, or other fat, amply salted; baste every 5 minutes thereafter until baking is complete, or about 30 minutes; when tender, arrange on hot serving dish, and make a white sauce, using about half the basting fat; pour over chicken; serve.

Left-Over Roast Fowl

Cut all the meat from the bones of chicken, turkey, etc., left from dinner; put the bones in a pan covered with water; stew about half an hour, until the goodness is cooked out; take out the bones; add the cold gravy left, the stuffing cut into small pieces, a little cold rice, if you have it, then the chicken. Season with a little salt and pepper, and stew ten minutes. This can be served on toast if desired.

Other Dishes of Fowl
(See "Sandwiches and Cold Meats.")

Canapes for Game

Specially prepared toast on which roast small game and birds are served, holding them as placed on the serving plate: Cut slices of stale loaf bread about 1½ inches thick, either cross-section or lengthwise according to the size of the bird; trim neatly all around into an oblong shape, then cut out some of the center to form a recess in which the back of the bird may rest; butter well, lay on baking sheet or tin, put in hot oven and let toast to an even golden brown; ready for serving.

Quails and Partridges

Roast—Dress and prepare as any other bird for roasting, handling them carefully and delicately; truss them, and lay a thin layer of larding fat on the breast of each; lay them in roasting pan, spreading a little butter on each, and moisten with ½ cup water; season with salt and pepper; roast in a brisk oven—18 minutes for quails and 25 minutes for partridges—basting frequently; untruss, and dress each bird upon a canape, and garnish with parsley or cresses; strain gravy in bowl and serve separately.—May be served with other choice sauces if desired.

Braised—Prepare as above; season, lard, and spread with butter; put into frying pan with a piece of pork rind, ½ carrot and ½ onion, both chopped or thinly sliced, and any herbs desired; saute to a nice golden brown, then moisten with ½ cup water, and place in oven and cook 20 minutes; serve with celery sauce.

Broiled—Prepare for cooking, and split each bird through the back without separating the halves; spread on a plate and season each with salt and pepper, and brush all over with salad oil, breaking leg joints to flatten them out; put to broil over moderate fire, and broil 6 minutes for quail, 7 minutes for partridges, on each side; serve on toast with butter sauce.

Or: Prepare and broil exactly as in *Oven Broiled Chicken.*

Fried—Dress quail, split each lengthwise into separate halves, and proceed exactly as for *Fried Chicken,* removing from pan just as soon as cooked through.

Roast Pigeons

Dress and cleanse pigeons, ready for roasting. In each, place a lump of butter the size of a pigeon egg, which has been rolled in finely chopped parsley, pepper, and salt; place them in roasting pan, dust with flour, and baste with a little hot butter, while roasting in hot oven about 20 minutes; serve on hot dish with creamed asparagus, a garnish of parsley sprigs, and butter sauce.

Broth Stewed Pigeons

Unless pigeons are quite young they are better braised or stewed in broth than cooked in any other manner. In fact, it is always the best way of cooking them. Tie them in shape; place slices of bacon at the bottom of a stewpan; lay in the pigeons side by side, all their breasts uppermost; add a slice of carrot, an onion with a clove stuck in, a teaspoon of sugar, and some parsley, and pour over enough stock to cover them. If you have no stock use boiling water. Now put some thin slices of bacon over the tops of the pigeons; cover them as closely as possible, adding boiling water or stock when necessary. Let them simmer until they are very tender. Serve each pigeon on a thin slice of buttered toast with a border of spinach, or make little nests of spinach on pieces of toast, putting a pigeon into each nest.

Squabs

Broiled on Toast—Dry-pluck, singe, draw, cut off necks, wipe neatly, and truss fine, large squabs; split them without detaching halves, lay them on a dish, and season each with ½ teaspoon salt and a little pepper evenly sprinkled on, and cover each well with a teaspoon salad oil; broil 6 minutes on each side; arrange each squab on two pieces of toast, and serve with buttersauce made by blending 2 tablespoons butter, 1 teaspoon finely chopped parsley, juice of ½ lemon, and a little grated nutmeg; serve sauce on top and garnish with a slice of broiled bacon if desired.

Roasted, plain—Prepare fine, small squabs as above; do not split them, but truss as you would a chicken; place them in a roasting pan, sprinkle with a little salt, and spread ½ teaspoon butter over each; put pan into brisk oven and roast 12 minutes; remove, untruss, dress on a hot dish, placing each bird on a canape of golden brown toast; garnish as desired; skim fat from gravy and make into a white sauce, serving it separately.

Blackbird Pie

Dress and cleanse well, a dozen blackbirds as you would pigeons; split each in half, put them into stew pan with plenty of water and bring to boiling point; skim off rising scum, then add salt and pepper to season, some minced parsley, a chopped onion and about 3 whole cloves; add about 1 cup diced salt pork, and boil until tender; thicken broth with browned flour and boil up; add 2 tablespoons butter, mix and remove from fire; cool; add 2 cups diced potatoes; grease baking dish, and put in alternate layers of birds and potatoes, moistening well each layers with some of the rich broth; cover with rich pastry crust, with slit, or openings in top, and bake in oven until cooked and browned. Or: Baking dish may be both lined and covered with pastry.—Other small game birds, such as quail, snipe, wild pigeons, etc., may be cooked in same way.

Snowbirds

Dress and clean birds exactly as for roast fowl; stuff each with an oyster, put them into a buttered baking dish, and add a small dice of boiled salt pork for each bird, and a few thin slices of raw potatoes; add 1 cup oyster juice and 1 tablespoon butter for each 6 birds; season with salt and pepper, cover with pastry crust, and bake in moderate oven.

Or: Dress birds as above; hang by wires or strings before an open fire-place or open fire-box door, and roast; roll in salted and peppered butter; serve to kiddies on toast.

Rabbits and Hares

Fried—Unless very tender, rabbits and hares, after being dressed and cleansed, should be put into boiling water and parboiled 10 minutes before being cut into joints for frying; then disjoint and proceed in any style as for fried chicken.

Fricassee—Prepare as for *Fricassee of Chicken,* except: After cutting into joints,

put in salt and water to cover, and soak about ½ hour before proceeding.

Roast—Skin, dress, wash well with cold waters, and rinse finally with luke-warm water; or, if not absolutely taintless inside, rub inside with vinegar, then proceed with the luke-warm water until all taint of vinegar is removed; stuff with *Dressing for Roast Fowl,* and sew up, truss legs, roast ½ to ¾ hour, or until tender and well browned, basting often with butter; just before taking from oven, dredge with flour, baste, and give final quick browning; after removing, pour off the clear surplus gravy, leaving the brown drippings, to which add 2 tablespoons flour, brown, add 2 cups boiling water, season with salt and pepper, let boil up; serve separately; provide currant jelly.

Barbecued—Proceed as with *Roast Rabbit,* except: Do not stuff with dressing; baste entirely with prepared *Barbecue Sauce* —see "Barbecued Meats"; keep roast thoroughly saturated with the sauce throughout the roasting; or, proceed as for *Barbecued Meats.*

Pot Pie—Cut rabbit into smallest joints and proceed as for *Black Bird Pie,* except: Scatter through it slices of hard-boiled eggs; make crust of puff paste; cover with paper if it browns too quickly.

Broiled—Dress rabbit, and split in half lengthwise; flatten out the halves, and proceed as for *Broiled Chicken.*—Some cooks wrap them in well buttered paper before placing them on the griddle.

Squirrels

Squirrels may be served in any of the styles in which Chicken or Rabbit is prepared.

The regulation of your oven-heat is one of the big secrets in both roasting and baking. The oven-door of the "HOME COMFORT" is readily adjustable by means of the "handle" to gradually and properly cool an over-heated oven. In hot weather, if you object to the heat escaping into the room, the lowering of the oven-heat may be accomplished by placing a pan of water in the oven until its temperature is just right.

Fish and Seafoods

Fresh Fish

Fried—Scale, clean out, wash, and wipe dry; season with salt and pepper, and roll in corn-meal; fry in deep fat, or at least enough to cover well; guard against over-cooking, or burning.

Or: Dry, dip in milk, roll in flour; fry.

Or: Dry, dip in beaten egg, roll in bread crumbs; fry.

Or: Dry, dip in milk, roll in flour and cracker-crumbs; fry.

If fish are small, fry whole; if large, such as halibut, channel-cat, etc., cut cross-section into steaks; or, if flat, cut in small sections, or slice off boneless fillets. Serve plain or with tartare sauce.

Broiled—Prepare fish steaks, dry, season with salt and pepper, and roll in a little salad or cooking oil; place on broiler, opened and flattened out, and broil about 10 minutes on the split side and 1 minute on the skin side; or, if not spread, 8 to 10 minutes on each side, according to the thickness; serve hot with butter sauce.

Broiled—Sew up well-cleaned fish tightly in cloth; put in deep pot and cover with cold water containing 1 tablespoon each of salt and vinegar, or lemon juice; after bringing to boiling point, boil about 15 minutes to the pound of fish; remove cloth covering; serve on hot plate with white cream sauce.

Baked — Soak well-cleaned fish in slightly salted cold water 1 hour before cooking; bake from 30 minutes to 1 hour, according to size, on griddle in baking or dripping pan containing a little hot water; just before taking up, butter well and brown evenly; serve with brown sauce made from the drippings, or with tartare sauce.

Planked—Prepare fish as for broiling; heat clean, smooth plank, brush with melted fat or drippings, and dust with salt and pepper; place fish, skin side down, doubling thin part to prevent it burning; have oven hot, put in plank, and cook 20 minutes, then, reduce oven heat to moderate, and cook 10 to 20 minutes longer; serve with seasoned melted butter over it; garnish with mashed potato rosettes, parsley, and lemon slices, on the plank.

Stuffed—A choice method of preparing bass, croppie, trout, and similar fish. Clean and dress the fish in the usual way; stuff well with force meat made from a smaller fish of the same variety, and prepared as follows: Separate the flesh from all skin and bones; grind or pound the meat in a mortar, or grind very fine in a meat grinder; mix to a paste with egg whites, allowing whites in proportion to 3 to each pound of fish meat; season with salt, pepper, and nutmeg; fill the fish with this and sew up, just before placing in baking dish or pan; bake with or without vegetables and herbs.

Salt Fish

To Prepare for Cooking—Soak salt fish, such as cod, mackerel, etc., in cold water at least 12 hours, changing water as often as possible; spread fish open in large pan, with the skin side up, thus preventing the salt from penetrating further into the flesh; finally rinse in fresh water, and put on range in kettle of cold water; bring it almost to boiling point, but do not let it boil and thus harden; remove, drain well, and it is then ready for cooking after the manner of fresh fish.

Cod-fish Cakes—Prepare about 3 pounds salt cod for cooking, as above; after draining, pick out any bones, and add about 5 medium, well washed, thinly sliced potatoes, ½ cup cold water, cook over moderate heat about 20 minutes, then add 1 tablespoon butter; remove from fire, season with a little white pepper, and with a potato-masher, mash all together in the pan; transfer to a dish and cool; make into cakes, or balls, dust well with a little flour, and drop into hot deep frying fat; fry to a nice brown color, lift out with a skimmer very gently, and serve on folded napkin on hot plate; garnish with parsley.

Finnan Haddie—Select large finnan haddie, and prepare for cooking as above; after draining, sprinkle over with salt and pepper to properly season, and lay out in large baking pan; pour over it 2 cups milk, and dot top, or inner, surface over well with dabs of butter; place in oven—not too hot—until butter is melted and milk hot; serve on hot platter with the milk poured over it.

Salt Mackerel—Prepare for cooking as above, then broil same as fresh fish, seasoning well with pepper and butter; serve with slice of lemon.

Flaked Fish

Fish Flakes—To Prepare: Cook fresh fish of the larger variety, such as cod, halibut, haddock, haddie, salmon, tuna, lake white fish, etc., until tender enough that the flesh may be readily broken or flaked into small bits; remove all bones and skin, and p..k the flesh into small flakes with forks; these flakes may then be prepared in a number of ways.—They may also be purchased in cans.

Plain—Put prepared fish flakes in small pan or cup, set in a larger pan of boiling water and let flakes become hot...... for each cup of fish flakes melt 4 tablespoons butter in ½ cup boiling water, season with pepper and salt to taste, and thoroughly mix with hot fish; serve with boiled or baked potatoes.

Creamed—For each cup fish flakes, make a white cream sauce with 2 tablespoons each of melted butter and flour, 1 teaspoon pepper, and 1 cup milk or cream; mix thoroughly with fish flakes, and season with salt to taste; spread thickly on buttered toast, which may then be cut in rounds with biscuit cutter if desired for effective dish, and sprinkled with grated cheese or crumbled hard-boiled egg yolks; or, place a poached egg upon each; may also be served with croutons and hot baked potatoes.

Scalloped—For each cup fish flakes, melt 1½ tablespoons butter, and when bubbling, add 1½ tablespoons flour, ½ teaspoon salt, and 2 tablespoons, more or less as desired, finely chopped green pepper; mix with fish flakes, and turn into baking dish; cover with ½ cup cracker crumbs, mixed with ¼ cup grated cheese, and moistened with 1 tablespoon melted butter; bake in hot oven until brown on top.

Crusted—Prepare *creamed fish flakes* as above, and pour into a shallow baking dish; split 3 hard-boiled eggs lengthwise, arrange halves on the creamed fish, and press down lightly, cover with a goodly layer of bread crumbs and cheese, and place a slice of bacon over each of the eggs; bake in hot oven until bacon is cooked and the top a golden brown; serve on plates garnished with parsley and slice of lemon, or *en casserole.*

Curried—For each cup fish flakes: Cook 1 tablespoon finely chopped onion in 2 tablespoons butter until soft and yellow; add 2 tablespoons each of flour and currie powder, ¼ teaspoon paprika, and stir until frothy; then, add 1 cup milk and stir until boiling; add fish flakes; serve hot with hot boiled rice.

Mayonnaised—Mix with each cup fish flakes: 4 boiled potatoes, 2 hard-boiled eggs, and 3 small cucumber pickles, all cut into cubes or dice; sprinkle with ½ teaspoon celery seed, ⅛ teaspoon cayenne, salt to taste, 1 cup true mayonnaise; mix well and serve; may be ablso served like salads.

Casserolettes—Partly fill individual baking dishes, or custard cups, with Creamed Fish Flakes, break an egg into each, season, cover with buttered bread crumbs, and bake.

Cutlets—Prepare a seasoning and binding mixture as follows: To 3 tablespoons butter, add ½ tablespoon finely chopped onion, 2 tablespoons finely chopped red or green pepper, and cook five minutes; add 5 tablespoons flour, and stir well until blended; then gradually add 1 cup half-and-half, milk and cream, stirring constantly; bring to boiling point, then add 2 cups fish flakes, or more if necessary, mixing well to the consistency of croquettes; season with salt and paprika to taste, and spread on a lightly buttered plate to cool; shape into serving portions, or cutlets, of equal size, flour, dip in egg, cover with bread or cracker crumbs, and fry in hot deep fat; garnish as desired, and serve with or without tartare sauce, or other dressing.

Balls or Cakes—Mix thoroughly, equal measures of fish flakes and fine mashed boiled potatoes, season with salt and pepper, and add 1 beaten egg for each 2 cups of mixture; mix into a stiff drop batter consistency; shape rounding spoonfuls into balls or cakes, and fry in hot deep fat until a golden brown, crisp and well cooked; either fry in bacon fat, or serve a slice of bacon with each ball or cake.

Patties—Prepare Creamed Fish Flakes and serve hot in pastry Pattie Shells.

Stew—Prepare exactly as Creamed Fish Flakes, except: Add an excess of scalded milk, or about 1 quart instead of 1 cup. Shredded cod-fish is excellent prepared in this way.

Frog-Legs

To Prepare—Select fine, fresh bullfrogs, reserve only the legs; skin them carefully, leaving the legs in pairs; cut off claws, and place in fresh cold water until ready to use.

Fried—Put frog-legs in a bowl, and marinate them with 1 tablespoon each of vinegar and salad oil, seasoned with salt and pepper; take out legs, dip them in frying-batter, and plunge them, one at a time, into hot deep frying fat; fry 5 minutes, lift out and drain them on soft paper or cloth; dress them on a hot dish, on a folded napkin, garnish with parsley sprigs, and serve with tartare or other sauce.

Broiled—Select good-sized legs, marinate them as for frying, using either vinegar or lemon juice; drain, place them on broiler, and broil 4 minutes on each side; dress on hot plate with butter-sauce; serve while hot.

Paris Style—Saute 8 or 10 pair fresh frog-legs in 2 tablespoons butter, seasoning with salt and pepper; and add 2 tablespoons light wine; cover, and cook briskly for 5 minutes; then, add 1 cup Hollandaise sauce, 1 tablespoon finely chopped parsley, and a little lemon juice; mix well 2 minutes, but do not boil again; serve on hot dish.

Or: After proceeding and cooking 5 minutes as above: Add a little green pepper and 1 freshly peeled tomato, finely chopped together; cook 10 minutes longer, and dress on hot dish.

Oysters

Fried—Wash and drain fresh oysters; season with salt and pepper, roll in flour, dip in beaten egg, roll in cracker or bread crumbs; roll off surplus crumbs in colander; press each flat into original shape; drop into hot deep fat, and fry to a golden brown; drain well, and garnish with slice of lemon and parsley; serve with crackers, celery, or cold slaw, and catsup.

Broiled—Roll fresh oysters in half bread and half cracker crumbs, press flat with hands; place on broiler and broil 2 minutes on each side; salt them lightly, and serve 4 oysters on each piece of toast, brush with melted butter.

Scalloped—Grease baking dish and cover bottom with 1 cup bread crumbs; on these, carefully arrange 2 dozen drained oysters, season with salt and pepper, and cover with another cup bread crumbs; moisten with ¼ cup milk, and spread with 2 tablespoons butter; bake in hot oven 20 minutes. —Canned cove oysters may also be prepared in this manner.

Creamed—Prepare a white sauce with 1 tablespoon each butter and flour; ¾ cup milk, and season with salt and pepper; while hot, drop in 2 dozen or more oysters and cook about 1 minute, or until edges begin to curl, then remove immediately; serve on toast with Worcestershire Sauce on side.

Patties—Prepare Creamed Oysters as above, and serve in pastry pattie shells—see recipe.

Cocktail—Serve raw fresh oysters in sherbet glasses; season well with salt, pepper, a very little cayenne, and a teaspoon catsup on top; provide Worcestershire and

tobasco sauce on side; should be served ice cold. Serve with crackers.

Loaf—Select a loaf of day-old bread baked in single-loaf pan; cut out the top crust about a half-inch from edge all around, and lay it aside for a lid; scoop out most of the crumb, leaving about a three-fourths inch wall on sides and bottom; use this crust for the baking pan, filling it with alternate layers of oysters seasoned with salt and pepper, and breadcrumbs moistened with a little of the oyster liquor, or milk; when filled, replace the top-crust lid, and set in moderate oven 15 to 20 minutes; serve in slices.

Clams

The best way to cook clams, according to the coast people, is to put a gallon measure of clams in an iron pot with 1 quart of water, and set to boil; boil up vigorously 3 times, and drain; remove the white meat from clams, dip in melted butter and serve on hot plate.

Roast in Shell—Roast in pan over fire, or in hot oven; or, at a "Clam Bake," on hot stones; when they open, empty the juice into a pan, add the clams, and season with butter, pepper, and a very little salt.

Scalloped—Prepare white clam meat as above; in a baking dish, put alternate layers of clams, seasoned with salt and pepper, and bread crumbs moistened with the natural clam liquor; spread ½ cup cracker crumbs mixed with 2 tablespoons melted butter on top, and bake in oven.—The clam liquor may be replaced with tomato sauce.

Fried—Drain select boiled clams, prepare and fry in the same manner as oysters.

Forcemeat—Fry a finely chopped onion in 2 tablespoons butter to a golden brown; add and mix 1 tablespoon flour, moisten with 1 cup good white stock, or boiling water; stir well and constantly until it thickens, then season with salt, pepper, cayenne, and any desired herbs and table sauces at hand, seasoning it very highly; stir well and add the meat of 24 clams finely chopped —finely chopped mushrooms may be added if desired—cook in saucepan for 30 minutes, remove from over fire and cool.

Stuffed—Prepare 6 good-sized clam shells, and see that they are very clean; refill them with forcemeat, above, filling them amply full and flattening each with hand; sprinkle with fresh bread crumbs, smooth with knife and moisten with melted butter; place them on baking sheet and brown in oven; serve on folded napkin on very hot dish; garnish with parsley.

Lobsters

Boiled—Select fresh, medium-sized lobster; the male is best for boiling, as the flesh is firmer, and he may be distinguished by his brighter red color and narrower tail; have ready a kettle or pot of heavily salted boiling water; plunge the live lobster into it and let it boil 20 minutes, more or less, according to size, but avoid cooking too long, as it will render it hard; remove from water, let it drain, and wipe dry; break off the large claws and separate the tail from the body; take body from its shell, leaving the stomach, remove small fingers and wooly gills, which should be discarded; also discard the craw, near the neck and usually containing sand; save green fat, and, if a female, the coral; break body-shell through middle, and pick out all the meat from the joints; slit tail lengthwise underneath with scissors, take out meat, then draw flesh back on upper end, and pull off and discard intestinal cord; crack large claws and extract the meat; serve with slices of lemon, and well seasoned sauces and condiments, or prepare into other dishes.—Or: Purchase canned lobster, already prepared.

Croquettes—Boil and prepare meat of two medium sized lobsters. Prepare a binding mixture: Melt 4 tablespoons butter, and when bubbling, add ¼ teaspoon each salt and paprika; add ½ cup flour and blend well; add 1 cup milk, stir constantly, and bring to point of boiling, then move to back of range, and add 1 well beaten egg; add 1 teaspoon lemon juice; add the prepared lobsters, reserving the meat of the 4 claws for garnish; heat while well back on range, then set aside and let cool; form into croquettes, roll in bread crumbs, dip in egg beaten with a little cold water, roll in crumbs again, and fry in hot deep fat; 8 croquettes.

Salad—Cut meat of one boiled lobster in small pieces; add desired amount of celery also diced; mix or arrange; serve on lettuce leaves with mayonnaise.

On Toast—To 2 slightly beaten eggs, add: 1 teaspoon salt, ¼ teaspoon paprika, and 1 cup milk all beaten together; melt 1 tablespoon butter in frying pan, put in lobster mixture, and stir and scramble until set as for scrambled eggs; serve on toast.

Newburg—Stir prepared meat of one boiled lobster into 2 tablespoons hot butter; when lobster is thoroughly heated, add ½ teaspoon salt, ¼ teaspoon paprika, a little nutmeg, and 1 tablespoon lemon juice; stir until well mixed; add 1 cup cream in which has been mixed 3 beaten egg yolks; serve on toast.

Spanish—Cook ¼ cup rice—see recipe; cut meat of one boiled lobster in small slices; in 2 tablespoons butter or bacon drippings, cook until softened and yellow, 1 small onion and ½ green pepper, both chopped fine; add 3 tablspoons flour and ½ teaspoon each salt and paprika; cook until frothy, then add 1 cup strained tomato juice, and stir until boiling; set over hot water, and lightly mix-in the rice and lobster.

Fricassee—Cut meat of two boiled lobsters into small pieces, and put, together with the green fat and some coral, into frying pan; season with salt, pepper, and 1 teaspoon Worcestershire Sauce; add 1 cup water, ½ cup rich milk, and 2 tablespoons butter; simmer until liquid is of a rich redish color; when ready to serve, add and stir in ¾ cup white cream sauce made in the usual way—formerly one teaspoon sherry wine was added.

Crabs

Boiled—Crabs should be boiled and prepared in the same manner as lobsters, but they require but a little more than half the time for proper cooking—10 to 15 minutes; remove lower part, and pick the choice meat from the shell and claws.

Deviled—Boil and mince the meat of a dozen fresh crabs; put into bowl and mix with an equal quantity of bread crumbs; cream ½ cup butter, and mix well into it ½ tablespoon powdered mustard; add, portion at a time, the meat-and-crumb mixture, mixing well and moistening with about 2 tablespoons cream; add more bread crumbs if necessary to make a workable mixture; season with salt and a little cayenne to taste; have ready, six well cleaned crab shells, fill them with the mixture, sprinkle bread crumbs over each, distribute a little butter on top of each, and brown them quickly in hot oven.

Stuffed—Prepare exactly as for deviled crabs, except: season meat and crumb mixture with salt, pepper, and sufficient butter, only; fill shells and brown in hot oven. A crab shell will hold the prepared meat of two crabs.

Croquettes—Prepare mixture as for stuffed crabs, moisten with rich milk or cream, and stiffen the mixture, if too soft, with more bread or cracker crumbs, and binding the whole with beaten egg; dredge with flour, dip in beaten egg, cover with bread or cracker crumbs, and fry in hot deep fat.

Eggs and Cheese

How to Judge Eggs

In shaking an egg, if it makes a sound it is not a good egg, and should be rejected. The water test consists in putting them in water deep enough to cover; the "good eggs" will lie flat at the bottom while the "bad eggs" will stand upright, like many other unsound things in the world. The candling process consists in looking through the egg at a light, or holding it between you and the sun. If it shows up clear and spotless, so that the yolk can be perceived, it is good; otherwise it is not.

Boiled Eggs

Eggs should always be dropped into water that is boiling—not before water has reached boiling point. Time for boiling eggs:

Soft Boiled—3 to 3½ minutes.
Medium Boiled—3½ to 4 minutes.
Hard Boiled—4 to 5 minutes.
Dry Hard Boiled—10 to 20 minutes.

Poached Eggs

Have frying pan filled about one inch deep with boiling salted water, allowing a half teaspoon salt to each four cups water put in. Break each egg separately in a small dish and carefully slip it into the water, which should completely cover the egg; when white is firm and a white film covers top of egg, carefully lift out; serve on buttered toast, and season with salt, pepper and butter.

Scrambled Eggs

Break eggs into a deep dish, beat slightly with a fork to mix; have a tablespoon or more fat in a hot frying pan and just under the smoking point; pour in eggs, stir briskly with prongs of fork, and the moment eggs begin to thicken, remove pan from fire and let the hot grease do the cooking while still stirring; remove to serving plate just when desired consistency; season with salt and pepper.—Fat from fried ham and bacon is excellent and usually requires no further seasoning.

Puffed Eggs

Proceed as with Poached Eggs, except cook them in cooking fat instead of water; the eggs will become quite puffy by this poach-frying process; have plenty of hot fat.

Shirred Eggs

Butter small stone-ware dishes, break one egg into each, being careful not to break the yolks; season each with a little butter and salt, and sprinkle over each a little grated cheese or fine bread crumbs, which may be mixed with a little chili powder or paprika; bake in oven until thoroughly set. Left-over yolks from baking may be prepared in similar manner.

Stuffed Eggs

Cut hard-boiled eggs in half cross-section; remove yolks and mash; to each four egg yolks, add 2 tablespoons grated cheese. 1 teaspoon vinegar, ¼ teaspoon mustard, and season with salt and cayenne pepper; add enough melted butter to make a thick paste that can be molded, mold into balls size of yolk and refill white sections; serve with or without cream sauce.

Creamed Eggs

Finely chop 3 hard boiled eggs. Make a cream sauce with 1 tablespoon each of butter and flour, 1 cup milk, and salt and pepper to season; mix eggs into sauce and serve on toast; arrange toast on platter and pour creamed eggs over it. Sauce may also be used with Stuffed Eggs. Garnish with parsley.

Egg Croquettes

Chop 3 hard-boiled eggs and mix with ¼ cup finely chopped ham, a sprinkle of chopped parsley, and salt, pepper and nutmeg to season; melt a tablespoon butter and stir in a tablespoon flour, add 6 tablespoons milk and boil three minutes while constantly stirring; to this, add egg and ham mixture; cool, divide into four croquettes, brush with an egg beaten with a tablespoon water, roll in fine bread crumbs, fry in hot deep fat, until light brown.

Spanish Eggs

Slice 3 or 4 hard-boiled eggs; cook 2 cups tomatoes and rub through strainer; melt 2 tablespoons butter and work 3 tablespoons flour and ½ teaspoon salt smoothly into it; add tomato pulp and bring to boiling point while constantly stirring; add 2 tablespoons finely chopped onion and 2 tablespoons chopped green pepper; add sliced eggs and cook until eggs are thoroughly heated; add 3 tablespoons mayonnaise or salad dressing; serve.—Mixed pickles may be used in place of green pepper.

Plain Omelet

For each omelet, beat 3 eggs with 3 tablespoons milk until combined, and season with salt and pepper; have a teaspoon melted butter or fat in hot frying pan; pour in eggs and gently shake pan to spread mixture to size and distribute thin portion while cooking; when all has set and browned on bottom; fold over and serve on hot plate.

Ham Omelet

Prepare eggs as for plain omelet and stir in desired proportion chopped or minced cooked ham; fry and serve as plain omelet.— Other meats or even shellfish may be prepared the same way; chopped onion added is relished by some.

Pear Omelet

Prepare eggs as for plain omelet and cook; just as top is becoming well set, lay a half canned pear on one-half of omelet and fold other half over it.—Other fruits may be used in same way.

Onion Omelet

Mix finely chopped onion with egg and milk mixture for plain omelet, and proceed to cook and turn.

Mexican Omelet

Prepare mixture for plain omelet and cook; just before folding over, sprinkle with chili powder or paprika.

Cheese Omelet

Prepare mixture for plain omelet and cook; just before folding over, thickly sprinkle grated cheese in center.

Spanish Omelet

Prepare and cook plain omelet; serve with a sauce made by frying a finely chopped onion several minutes in butter, and adding 1 tablespoon flour and ½ teaspoon salt mixed, 1 tablespoon chili powder, 1 cup canned tomatoes, 1 finely chopped green pepper, and salt to season; boil ten minutes, pour over omelet, roll, and serve while hot.

Corn Omelet

Take well-filled ears of sweet corn, and with a linen cloth remove all the silks between the rows of kernels. Cut the kernels down the center, being careful not to loosen them from the cob, and then take out the pulp by pressing downward with a knife. To three tablespoonfuls of the green corn pulp add the well-beaten yolks of three eggs and a little salt. Beat the whites of the eggs to a stiff froth, and mix with the corn and the yolks, and pour into a hot frying pan with a little butter; cover immediately and set it where it will cook, but not burn. When set, fold over the omelet and serve on a hot dish immediately.

Omelette Souffle

Take 10 eggs and separate the yolks from the whites; then take a cup of rich cream, put it in a small pan that has been inside another with boiling water in it; when the cream comes to a boil, take the 5 yolks of eggs, beat them up and mix them in the cream, with powdered sugar to taste, and 3 or 4 drops of extract of vanilla; mix until it slightly stiffens and then take off; whip up the whites of eggs to a light, dry foam; sprinkling in a brimming teaspoonful of cornstarch, which will prevent it from falling; take about ¼ part of the yolks and mix with the foam; then take the rest of the yolks, place them on the center of the dish, with the whites all around; place in the oven to brown, then serve.

Pickled Eggs

Have the eggs hard-boiled, and after removing the shells, put them in pickled blood-beet juice until the whites become colored, cut lengthwise and serve as a relish.

Egg Foo Yong

Beat 5 eggs, and mix with them ½ cup shredded green onions, ½ cup finely chopped bacon, ham, or cold roast meat of any sort, ¼ cup chopped mushrooms, and 2 cups shredded celery; mix to a molding consistency, divide into 6 portions and mold in flat, round form; fry in shallow pan of hot cooking fat; serve with a well seasoned gravy.—The Chinese use bamboo sprouts instead of celery.

Eggs with Cheese

Break 6 eggs in mixing bowl; in another bowl, mix 2 tablespoons grated cheese, 1½ tablespoons butter, 1 teaspoon grated onion or juice, and ½ teaspoon salt; put mixture in hot pan and stir until cheese is melted; slowly pour hot mixture over eggs; stirring until eggs are cooked; add a little finely chopped parsley and serve hot.—A half teaspoon chili powder may be added to melting mixture to give it a Spanish twang.

Cheese Soup

Put in a double boiler: 3 cups milk thickened with 1½ cups flour; cook thoroughly, stirring frequently; when ready to serve, add 1 cup grated cheese, and salt and paprika to season.

Cheese Croquettes

Make a sauce by working smoothly, 4 tablespoons flour into 3 tablespoons melted butter, and adding ¾ cup milk; add 2 egg yolks and mix well; add ½ cup grated cheese, removing from fire when cheese is melted; fold in 1 cup additional cheese cut in small bits, and salt and pepper to season; turn into shallow pan to cool; when cold, cut into squares, dip into beaten egg, cover with cracker or fine bread crumbs, and fry in deep fat.

Cottage Cheese Loaf

A wide variety of fine cheese loaves made by combining cheese with finely ground baked beans or peas, or green vegetables such as spinach, chard, etc., make a good substitute for meat.

Make into a loaf, or roll, 1 cup cottage cheese, 2 cups kidney or other beans finely ground, season to taste with salt, and mix in enough bread crumbs to make the mixture stiff enough to form into shape; bake in a moderate oven, basting with a mixture of butter and water. Season with chopped onions stewed in butter-water if desired. Commercial cheese, finely ground, may be used. Loaf may also be made by substituting for the beans, an equal amount of spinach parboiled ten minutes, drained, cooked with the butter until tender, and finely chopped. Also makes a fine stuffing for meats, by adding eggs or additional seasonings.

This recipe should form a base for many nutritious loaves made from materials at hand.

Cheese Souffle

Melt 2 tablespoons butter and stir in 2 tablespoons flour until smoothly mixed; add 1 cup milk and cook until thickens; add ¼ teaspoon salt and cayenne to taste; set to back on range-top and add 2 well-beaten egg yolks and 1 cup grated cheese; when cool, add the 2 egg whites stiffly beaten, turn into buttered baking dish and bake about thirty minutes in moderate oven; serve in six portions.

Cheese Wafers

Spread grated cheese on thin crackers or tart pastry and heat in oven until cheese is melted; serve with salads, soups, or tea.

Cheese Straws

Prepare puff paste, using finely grated cheese between the layers instead of shortening called for in puff paste recipe; leave paste as thin as possible on last rolling out, cut into quarter inch strips or straws, lay them on slightly floured baking sheet and bake in a moderate oven until crisp, but do not let them brown in the least; keep in dry, moisture-proof place and serve cold, piling them nicely on a glass dish. Straws may be slightly twisted before baking if desired.

Golden Buck

Boil 1 cup milk in a saucepan; add 2 cups grated cheese, ½ teaspoon salt, ¼ teaspoon mustard, and cayenne to season; stir until cheese is melted; prepare 6 pieces of buttered toast and 6 poached eggs; cover each piece of toast with cheese mixture, place a poached egg on top of each, salt and pepper to season; serve while hot.

English Golden Buck

Soak 1 cup stale bread crumbs in 1½ cups milk five minutes; put in double boiler, and when hot, add 1 beaten egg and ½ teaspoon salt; cook until it thickens, remove boiler from over fire, add ½ cup grated cheese and stir until it melts; stir in 2 or 3 tablespoons mayonnaise or salad dressing; serve hot on either toast or crackers.

Welsh Rarebit

Melt 2 tablespoons butter and thoroughly and smoothly stir in 2 tablespoons flour; add 1 cup milk, season with salt, mustard and cayenne to taste; boil until thickened, occasionally stirring; add ½ pound cream cheese cut in bits, and stir constantly until cheese is melted and mixture is smooth; add 1 slightly beaten egg and continue cooking until egg is blended with the sauce, being careful not to let mixture boil after cheese is added; serve to four persons over crackers, or bread toasted on one side only, pouring the rarebit on the untoasted side.

American Rarebit

In a double boiler melt 2 tablespoons butter, stir in 1 tablespoon flour until smooth, and add juice of 1 onion, with salt and cayenne pepper to season; add 1 pound cream cheese cut into bits, and when melted add 1 small commercial can or 1 cup tomato soup and stir in well; add 1 slightly beaten egg, and continue cooking and stirring until egg is blended and mixture is about the consistency of drop batter or thick cream; serve hot on crackers or toast.

Sandwiches and Cold Meats

For parties, picnics, luncheons, or even a light, but fairly substantial meal, the sandwich is a great favorite since it offers a tempting and delicious medium for the serving of a countless variety of left-overs, cold meats, fruits, vegetables, and combinations. Any of the meat salads make choice sandwiches, and when delicately and temptingly served, will add to the reputation of the hostess.

All sandwiches should be so prepared that every particle is edible. The crust of the bread, while highly nutritious, is usually discarded for appearance sake, leaving the slices in squares, rectangles or triangles, and usually trimmed after the sandwich is completed. First trimmed to a full square, they may be cut across to form rectangles or smaller squares, or cut diagonally to form large or small triangles.

For plain sandwiches, when a considerable number must be prepared and the sandwiches small, the slices of bread should be not more than an eighth to a quarter inch in thickness, and are best if lightly buttered before trimming the crust.

Doubtless the most delicious sandwiches are those made with toasted white bread lightly buttered; however, it is quite a task to prepare these if any considerable quantity is required. For these, the bread should be sliced about half-inch thick, trimmed to a square and *quickly* toasted to a delicate golden brown on a *hot* toaster, care being taken not to leave the toast brittle and hard, but fresh and moist inside. Toast sandwiches should be served while fresh and warm.

Cold meats may be advantageously served in a wide variety of ways for light luncheons, aside from sandwiches. Many choice and neatly served dishes are covered by the recipes in this section.

Tea Sandwich

Mince three or four slices of tender chicken breast, and chop finely two tablespoons pecan meats; mix with a tablespoon or more of mustard-mayonnaise; spread on thin slice of bread and cover with another lightly buttered, for each sandwich; trim in delicate or fancy shapes; serve with tea.

Peanut Butter Sandwich

Make a thin paste with peanut butter and thick cream that will spread easily and smoothly, seasoned with a little salt; put on thin slices of fresh bread of fine texture, roll up slices and tie with small ribbon.

Cheese Date Sandwich

Cream together dry cottage cheese and fresh sweet cream until easy to spread and entirely smooth; spread on each slice of nut bread, and put together in pairs with finely chopped dates, figs, or other fruit between.

Pimiento Cheese Sandwich

Put ½ cup diced cream cheese in double boiler, add 3 tablespoons milk with ½ teaspoon cornstarch beaten into it, 1 tablespoon butter, stir and cook until smooth and add salt and paprika to taste; add ½ can red pimientos chopped in small pieces and mix thoroughly; spread between buttered slices of bread, either white, graham, or whole wheat.

Surprise Sandwich

Prepare ample slices of buttered white bread; fill between slices with two or three slices of fried bacon and cover this with banana thinly sliced lengthwise; with or without mayonnaise. Makes a fine luncheon sandwich. Ripe, mellow apple may be substituted for banana.

Toast Cheese Sandwich

Slice and toast fresh bread on hot toaster; do not allow it to lose its moisture, have it crisp on outside, but moist and fresh inside; place thinly sliced cream cheese between buttered slices while warm, allowing the cheese to slightly soften; spread cheese with mayonnaise if preferred; serve while warm.

Luncheon Sandwich

Prepare three slices of buttered toast for each sandwich; place lettuce leaf and sliced boiled ham between two slices, and on top, sliced cream or swiss cheese and mayonnaise, covering with third piece of toast; slice sandwich diagonally across, and serve on small plate. Other meats, or meat and sliced vegetable combinations may be made up in this way; they should always be served while warm, with coffee or tea; nice when served on the lettuce leaf and garnished with a nice slice of tomato with mayonnaise laid on top.

Tutti Frutti Sandwich

Prepare a filling by putting one cup dates, and one-half cup each of seedless raisins, dried figs, and walnut meats through a food chopper or grinder, and moistening with the juice of one orange; spread between slices of buttered bread. This filling with the nut meats left out, may be kept indefinitely in sterilized glasses for future or emergency use.

Maple Butter Sandwich

Prepare a filling by creaming one cup light brown sugar with one or two tablespoons butter and further reducing to an easily spreading mixture with thin simple syrup, and flavoring with maple flavoring; or use maple syrup instead of simple syrup and flavoring. Try this on the kiddies.

Fried Cheese Sandwich

Prepare slices of bread, butter each piece and put together with thinly sliced cream cheese; just before serving, turn the buttered sides of the bread outward, leaving the cheese inside; fry first one side of the assembled sandwich, then the other in hot frying pan. Serve while warm.

Club Sandwiches

Club sandwiches are made of a combination of two or more meats, with or without a vegetable; many various combinations may be devised with materials at hand. As an example, try this one by a nationally known chef:

Toast two slices sandwich bread on both sides, and spread over each a mixture of equal parts of prepared mustard and butter; cover one piece with thinly sliced chicken, lay on two short slices broiled bacon and a nice slice of tomato spread with mayonnaise and a leaf of lettuce; cover with second slice of toast. May be made with plain bread, or tomato and mayonnaise may be served on top.

Sandwich Fillings

Many Plain and Combination Salads, recipes for which will be found under heading "Salads and Salad Dressings" when finely ground or formed into a paste with a Salad Dressing, make fine sandwiches.

Whites of hard-boiled eggs finely chopped and mixed with the crumbled yolks and Mayonnaise or favorite salad dressing.

Chopped stuffed olives, mixed with Mayonnaise or Mustard Dressing.

Peanut Butter, or ground nuts, such as roasted peanuts, blanched almonds or walnut meats, mixed with Mayonnaise or other salad dressing.

Mushrooms, washed, peeled and thoroughly dried, and fried in butter twenty minutes; season with salt and pepper, chop very fine and mix with Mayonnaise.

Dates and nuts put through grinder or chopper, and moistened with favorite salad dressing.

Chopped hard-boiled eggs and stuffed olives, allowing six olives to each egg, moistened with Mayonnaise or Salad Dressing.

Chopped cold cooked chicken and finely chopped celery, allowing a half cup celery pulp to each cup ground chicken, mixed and moistened well with salad dressing.

Peeled and thinly sliced tomatoes, seasoned with salt and pepper and spread with Mayonnaise or other dressing.

Finely chopped red pimiento and walnut meats, added to creamed cheese and salad dressing.

Flaked or ground salmon and thick chili sauce, allowing a half cup chili to a cup of salmon moistened with salad dressing.

Sardines, with skin and bones removed, mashed to paste, and finely chopped hard-boiled eggs, allowing one egg to each can sardines, mixed with salad dressing to moisten.

Finely flaked tuna fish mixed with drained chopped pickle or relish and moistened with salad dressing.

Grated or creamed cheese mixed with Mayonnaise or salad dressing, and sprinkled with paprika.

Thinly sliced peeled cucumbers spread with salad dressing and seasoned with salt and pepper if desired; should be served while fresh and crisp.

Flaked fish mixed with chopped cucumbers carefully drained, seasoned and mixed with salad dressing.

Baked beans mashed and mixed with salad dressing.

Preserved ginger, chopped nuts, lemon juice, moistened with syrup from ginger.

Chopped figs, dates, raisins, or drained canned fruits, made into paste with marshmallow cream.

Cream cheese softened with milk or cream mixed with finely chopped or ground dates, and seasoned with a little salt.

Chopped, crisp, broiled bacon mixed with finely chopped dates in equal proportion, and moistened with Mayonnaise.

Brown or white sugar creamed with butter and flavored with maple syrup, to moisten.

Finely ground ham, or a mixture of any left-over meats, seasoned with ground or chopped onion, pickle, olives, green pepper, any or all of them, and moistened with mayonnaise.

Any tasteful combination that may be made into form of an easily spreading paste, makes good sandwiches.

Cold Meats

Sliced cold meats, as beef, veal, pork, ham and chicken, are familiar dishes in every home; served with potato or other salad, they are nice when served in combination by placing small portions of two or more on individual plates with the salad; cheese may be added to the plate to complete the combination of assorted cold meats. Boiled beef tongue in thin slices also is a nice addition to the plate. Cold meats may also be prepared in a number of tempting ways, such as sandwiches, croquettes and salads and served for luncheon or light supper. They may also be prepared in the form of Rissoles, Timbales, Patties, and Shortcakes.

Rissoles

Roll plain pastry as for pie crust and cut into rounds with a large biscuit cutter. Mince cold beef, lamb, pork, chicken or turkey, season with salt and pepper, moisten with stock, broth, or gravy to hold the meat together; place a spoonful meat mixture on each pastry round, fold, moisten the edges lightly and pinch together all around to close completely so that not a particle of mixture will escape; dip each in beaten egg and drop in hot deep frying fat and brown; or, bake in a hot oven twenty minutes. If chicken is used, they are called Chicken Rissoles, etc. A combination of cold, ground meats may be used; fish may also be used.

Timbales

Heat 2 tablespoons butter or other fat; add ¼ cup dry bread crumbs and 2/3 cup milk and cook 5 minutes, stirring constantly; add 1 cup cold cooked ground meat or flaked fish, 2 slightly beaten eggs, salt and pepper to season, and any other seasonings, such as onion juice, nutmeg, chopped herbs, etc.; turn into well greased molds or baking cups, filling each one-half to three-fourths full, set cups in pan of hot water, set in moderate oven and bake about twenty minutes; turn onto hot plates and serve with choice of sauce or salad dressing. Timbales from cold cooked vegetables may be made by substituting a cup of the vegetable or vegetables for the meat or fish.

Croquettes

Dice, chop or grind 1½ cups any cold cooked left-over meat or fowl. Melt ¼ cup butter or cooking fat, add ½ cup flour, ½ teaspoon salt, ¼ teaspoon black pepper, and stir until mixture bubbles; add 1 cup stock, broth, or milk and full ¼ cup cream, stir and bring to boiling point; add 1 well-beaten egg, cook and stir without letting it boil, until mixture tends to pull away from sides of pan; add the chopped meat, mix, and turn onto a plate to cool; when cold, shape into balls, cakes, or cones, roll in fine bread crumbs, cover with a mixture of 1 slightly beaten egg and ¼ cup milk, and roll again in crumbs; drop each into hot deep frying fat—that will brown a soft bread crumb in forty seconds—brown, and drain on soft paper; serve with creamed cauliflower, asparagus tips, green peas.

Patties

Prepare Pattie Shells by recipe under heading of Pies and Pastry. Prepare any cold cooked meat, fowl or fish, by dicing or flaking, mix with cream sauce, season to taste, fill pattie shells, and serve with vegetables, same as croquettes.

Shortcakes

Cold or left-over boiled chicken and broth in which it cooked; melt ¼ cup butter or cooking fat, add ¼ cup flour, ½ teaspoon salt, ¼ teaspoon pepper, and cook while stirring until smoothly combined; add 2 cups chicken broth and continue cooking while stirring until boiling; add 2 cups chopped, or diced, chicken meat and mix. Prepare biscuit dough, roll out slightly thicker than usual and cut with a three-inch round cutter; bake biscuits, and when cooled, split with knife; form each into an individual shortcake with the chicken mixture between halves and on top. Any boiled meats or fish may be substituted for chicken.

Vegetables and Garden Fruit

While boiling does not preserve the juices of vegetables so well as steaming, it is, nevertheless, the method in universal use, since it requires much less cooking-time. In the boiling of most vegetables, "soft" water should never be used, as it materially softens the fibres, tears down the cells, and allows practically all the food values to escape. "Hard" water, on the other hand, strengthens the cell walls and retains a desirable firmness of the vegetable, preserving its food value to the maximum. Since soda tends to soften water, a small amount—about a teaspoonful to the quart—may be used in the water for parboiling such fibrous vegetables as matured turnips, parsnips, or celery, and such dried vegetables as beans and peas, in order to render the fibers tender; but, after this has been accomplished, the vegetables should be carefully rinsed before proceeding with the regular boiling, which should be finished in hard water. Salt added to the water hardens it to a limited degree and raises the boiling point, making this a desirable process in regular boiling, since by the regulation of the use of both salt and soda any vegetable may be made tender, at the same time kept firm and nutritious.

Root vegetables and tubers should be cooked in a vessel provided with a cover, while those classified as "greens" should always be cooked in an open vessel. Vegetables should be set to cook in a small amount of boiling water, which should be kept replenished as it evaporates, enough to cover—color, as well as flavor and nutrition are thus retained to maximum. Strongly flavored vegetables, such as cabbage and onions, may be boiled in a greater amount of water to lessen the strength, if desired.

Do not peel such vegetables as potatoes, turnips, parsnips and carrots in very warm water, even in cold weather, nor allow them to set on the range for a time before boiling. Potatoes, particularly, may thus be spoiled before cooking, and cannot be restored to proper condition—the damage is done. Young potatoes, parsnips, and carrots should always be "scraped," not "peeled." Young vegetables should never be allowed to boil too long. Tomatoes and beets are readily peeled by scalding—the thin skin may then be slipped off without trouble.

Tuber and root vegetables, especially potatoes, should *not* be pared several hours before cooking, and allowed to stand; but, if prepared for even a short time before cooking, they should always be kept submerged in cold water until time for cooking, to prevent discoloration. After they are cooked, they should be immediately drained to prevent them from absorbing the water and becoming soft and unwholesome. Potatoes, especially, should immediately be salted to render them dry and mealy, allowing them to more readily absorb further seasoning, if added.

It is a mistake to shell fresh peas and allow them to stand overnight, but, after being shelled, they should be kept in a covered dish, as they become toughened when exposed to the air for a short time.

Citrous Fruits are a classification of such vegetable-fruits as citron, cantaloupes, and melons. Special preparations of these fruits will be found in the subsequent recipes.

Artichokes

The artichoke is eaten much the same as asparagus. Remove outer leaves until the edible base of leaves appears tender and meaty. This portion grows sweeter and sweeter until you reach the tender heart, which is most delicious.

Fried Artichokes

Select small, tender artichokes not larger than an inch and a half in diameter. Remove enough outer leaves until light-colored leaves appear, cut tips, quarter the artichokes lengthwise. Dip in beaten egg which has been seasoned with salt and pepper. Roll in flour; fry in pan with butter, cooking very slowly.—Artichokes larger in size may be fried by first parboiling in salt-water for 30 minutes; trim off outer leaves, cut top off fully an inch, quarter, and fry.

Stuffed Artichokes

Six boiled artichokes; cut off the stem end, making the bottom flat so that they will stand on the dish, and one-half inch off the top leaves. Remove leaves from the center of the artichokes. Fill with the following stuffing: Rub frying pan with onion or garlic; melt 4 tablespoons butter, and in it fry 3 cups breadcrumbs lightly; add ¾ cup tomato pulp, and season with salt and paprika; mix well and fill centers of the artichokes; sprinkle with grated cheese, and bake 20 minutes in moderate oven; serve with a strip of bacon or a slice of tomato on top each; or, decorate with mayonnaise or other salad dressing.

Boiled Artichokes

American Style:

Soak in cold salt-water not less than five minutes; drain, place compactly in pot and cook slowly in boiling salt-water until tender; keep pot covered.

Italian Style:

Cut off stem, making the bottom flat, and ½ inch off the top of the artichoke; place one clove garlic deep in the center of each, placing artichokes upright and compact in pot; salt, pepper, and pour a teaspoonful of olive oil in the center of each; keep one inch of water in pot; steam until tender. Can be served with or without salad dressing.

Jerusalem Artichokes—Wash and scrape the tubers, placing them immediately in cold water containing a little vinegar to prevent discoloration; when all are thus prepared, rinse them in cold water and place in a salted mixture of one-third water and two-thirds milk, boiling hot; leave off cover and boil quickly until tender when pierced; when done, lift out onto a hot dish; make white cream sauce, to which add a beaten egg and a little lemon juice; pour over artichokes, sprinkle with finely chopped parsley; serve.

Asparagus

Boil 2 cups asparagus tips in salted water 15 minutes, then drain; meantime, make a cream sauce by boiling 1 cup milk in a double boiler, then pour part of it over 2 eggs, beaten lightly, and adding this to rest of milk in boiler, stirring vigorously throughout process until sauce begins to thicken; add 1 teaspoon butter, season with pepper, and remove; arrange asparagus on toast, and pour sauce over it; or, cut asparagus in small lengths, mix with sauce, and serve in pastry patties.

Or: Cook asparagus as above, and serve with a sauce of 3 tablespoons melted butter, seasoned with a little lemon juice, red pepper and salt to taste; serve on toast or croutons.

Or: Wash asparagus, tie in bunches, and boil until tender; arrange on warm plates or on toast; serve with sauce as above, or with thick cream tomato sauce.

Boston Baked Beans

Boil 1 pint small white or navy beans in ½ gallon water for 1 hour; pour water off, turn beans into a larger pan, pour plenty of cold water over them and wash thoroughly, repeating this rinsing until the skins of the beans have all been washed off and dis-

carded; place beans in a half-gallon stone jar, or baking dish, and cover with water; season with salt to taste and 1 tablespoon maple syrup or molasses, and place in the center in one piece, or on top in slices, fat pork or bacon; bake in a moderate oven about 1 hour, keeping covered tightly, but inspect occasionally and add more water if getting too dry; if preferred, the moistening liquid in the baking may be a thin, rich tomato sauce.

Or:

Take beans not too old, and without imperfection,
Immerse in cold water to stand through a night;
Then boil in a moderate way, 'till inspection
Shall find them to touch and taste tender and right.
Now transfer for baking, your condiments adding—
Don't leave out the pork! Such omission were strange—
And last, to conclude the important proceeding,
Let them bake slow and sure in a "Home Comfort" Range.

New York Baked Beans

Prepared exactly the same as Boston Baked Beans, omitting both the pork and tomato sauce; season with salt, pepper, mustard and syrup; serve with or without tomato catsup on the side.

Bean Croquettes

Select and prepare beans exactly as for Boston Baked Beans, boiling and washing until all the skins are removed, reboiling if necessary, and until beans are very tender; drain and press through a colander; make a binding sauce by rubbing together 1 tablespoon each flour and butter, or shortening, cook in ½ cup cream until almost boiling, then add two beaten egg yolks; stir over fire for a minute, and add the bean pulp; season with salt and pepper to taste, 1 teaspoon onion juice, and 1 tablespoon chopped parsley; when cool, form into croquettes, flour, dip into beaten egg, roll in bread or cracker crumbs, and fry in hot deep frying fat; serve with or without tomato sauce.

Green Beans

"String" the beans by breaking off each end of the pod in turn, removing the string along the edges in the process; break or cut into short lengths, let them soak a few moments and rinse well in cold water; put in a stew pan with just enough cold water to cover, and let them boil 1 hour, more or less, according to age and tenderness; when tender, allow the water to boil down until only a rich juice remains; season with salt, pepper, and butter or other fat or drippings.

Fried Green Beans

Prepare and cook string beans as above and drain completely; dredge well with flour; for each 2 cups beans, chop 3 tablespoons bacon; fry bacon 3 minutes, add beans and fry 10 minutes; if flavor is relished, tomato sauce may be added just before removing from range.

Kidney Beans

Wash shelled beans thoroughly; cover with boiling water well above the beans, and boil until tender, allow nearly all the water to boil away; season with butter, salt and pepper; serve.

Or: If beans are dried, let them stand in cold water over night and proceed as above, adding ⅛ teaspoon soda to each 2 cups beans while boiling; an onion may also be added while boiling, if desired, but should be removed before serving.

Lima or Butter Beans

Prepared exactly as kidney beans; after boiling, they may be drained, mixed with tomato or other sauce, put into a baking dish, covered with thin slices of bacon, and baked until bacon is crisp and brown; or served plain.—Other varieties of beans used as summer vegetables are also prepared in the same manner.

Beets

Wash beets, cover with water and boil until well cooked; drain and remove skins; slice into a sauce pan; add a dressing made by seasoning 1 cup vinegar with 1 tablespoon mixed butter and sugar, and salt and pepper to taste, adding 1 tablespoon cornstarch; boil all together until thick.

Baked Beets—Beets retain their sweet, delicate flavor much better when baked than boiled; wash and dry beets well, put into baking pan and bake in moderate oven until tender; turn or roll them frequently while baking with a knife to avoid pricking them and allowing juice to escape; when done, peel, slice, and serve with salt, pepper, and butter on each.

Brussels Sprouts

Wash brussels sprouts, remove any wilted leaves and soak in cold salted water 15 minutes; drain and boil until tender; drain again; season with bacon drippings or butter, pepper and salt to taste; or, mix with tomato sauce enough to season to suit.

Carrots

Wash and scrape carrots, and slice thinly; cover with boiling water and boil until tender; drain, and mix with white cream sauce seasoned to taste.

Or: Cut carrots into dice shape, and boil as above; fry for a few minutes in butter or bacon drippings seasoned with salt and pepper, until carrots have absorbed a part of seasoning; serve.

Fritters—Select young carrots, wash and carefully scrape them; slit them in half lengthwise, and boil until tender in salted water; drain, dry, and dip them in *fritter batter,* and fry in hot deep frying fat; serve hot.

Cabbage

Boiled Cabbage—Remove tough outer leaves of cabbage, cut the white tender head into eighths or quarters, according to size, and cut out the tough, hard stalk; wash thoroughly and carefully, inspecting for insects; place in cold water for about 30 minutes; drain, cover with boiling, well salted water, and boil until sufficiently tender, but no longer; a pod of red pepper may be put into the boiling water; drain, and season with butter or bacon drippings, salt and pepper to taste.

Creamed Cabbage—Prepare solid white head of new cabbage as above, boiling about 30 minutes; drain, and serve over it a regular white cream sauce of butter, flour, and milk.

Or: Prepare and cook as above, and set aside until perfectly cold; chop fine, and add 2 beaten eggs, 1 tablespoon butter, salt, pepper, and 3 tablespoons milk or cream; mix all together and bake in dish until browned; serve hot.

Or: Cut up tender head of cabbage as for slaw; put in saucepan, and cover with ½ cup water; cover tightly to confine steam, and set to boil; watch closely, replenish water when necessary, and steam until tender; season with 1 or 2 tablespoons butter, salt and pepper to taste; a little vinegar may be added if desired.

Fried Cabbage—Prepare exactly as for steamed cabbage above; do not season, but let cool; put in frying pan with 2 tablespoons butter or drippings, put in cabbage and fry until light brown, then add 2 tablespoons vinegar.

Baked Cabbage—Trim down and wash well, a solid white head of cabbage; with a sharp knife, cut off the top cross-section, and hollow out the head, leaving a thick shell; cut up the heart that was removed, and put in a frying pan with a little cooking fat, a chopped or sliced onion, and some dry breadcrumbs that have been soaked in water and squeezed dry; cook until cabbage is tender, and turn into a bowl; add 2 eggs, cayenne and salt to taste; stuff this mixture into the cabbage shell and place the top on; tie whole up in a clean cloth and boil; when tender, remove cloth, place in a baking dish or pan, put butter on top, brown in oven,— Ground meats may be added to the mixture.

Cabbage Special—Turn a cabbage-head stalk end down, and slice off upper end for a cover. Scoop out inside of cabbage until half inch in thickness. Make small patties of one pound hamburger and pack them closely in the bottom of cabbage. Pare and wash 3 potatoes and cut in small squares. Cut up 3 stalks of celery, 1 onion, and 1 carrot in small dices. Put the vegetables all together in the cabbage and sprinkle with salt. When cabbage is full, replace cover and tie firmly with string. Cover with water and boil about 1 hour and 15 minutes. Put on a platter, remove strings and serve with butter. A large-sized cabbage will serve six persons.

Cauliflower

Wash and pick over head of cauliflower, and put in a deep pan with stem ends down; cover with boiling water, and boil 35 minutes; drain, sprinkle with seasoning of salt and pepper, and add white cream sauce; serve.

Or: Boil and drain; season with salt, pepper, and grated cheese; pour a little melted butter over it, and set in moderate oven 5 minutes; serve with or without tomato sauce.

Or: Boil and drain, then separate into flowerlets; make a white cream sauce; scallop with alternate layers of cauliflower and sauce in a baking dish, seasoning each layer with salt and pepper; put a layer of cracker crumbs on top, moisten it with melted butter, and bake until top has browned.

Celery

Wash and cut celery in small pieces, and boil in water to cover until tender; drain; prepare white cream sauce; scallop with alternate layers of cooked celery and sauce, and cover with a top layer of buttered bread crumbs, using 1 tablespoon melted butter for each ½ cup crumbs; bake a few minutes until properly browned.

Corn

Boiled on Cob—Husk selected green corn, trim and remove all silks; drop into boiling fresh water to cover, and boil 5 minutes; remove, place on folded napkin on platter, fold napkin over ends, serve while warm.

Boiled in Husks—Select green corn, and cut off stalk rather closely, stripping off the outside husks; now turn down, one at a time, rest of the husks as if about to pull them off, exposing the corn; remove all silks and bad grains if any; replace husks smoothly in order, and tie the ends together with string; put in kettle of boiling water to well cover, and boil from 20 to 30 minutes; when done, dip each ear in cold water and the husks may then be easily removed. —Corn boiled in this way is much sweeter and the flavor improved.

Roasted—Prepare as above, lay on shelf in moderate oven and roast until browned and tender. Or, place before open fire without husking; by the time the green husks are parched and seared, the corn will have cooked.

Stewed—Prepare green corn as for boiling, but, with a sharp knife, cut the corn from the cobs, which are then scraped to remove the remaining hearts; put in saucepan with just enough water to prevent burning, and boil about 20 minutes; add 1 cup milk or cream, 1 tablespoon butter, and season with salt and pepper; boil 10 minutes, and serve.—One or two short cobs boiled with the corn improves the flavor. Equal parts of corn and stewed tomatoes are sometimes prepared in this manner.

Fried—Prepare green corn as for boiling, and fry in just enough butter to prevent sticking, stirring frequently to evenly brown; season with salt and pepper, and add a little rich cream if desired, but only after it is removed from fire.

Fritters—Drain stewed corn, and to each 2 cups corn add 2 beaten eggs and 1 cup flour in which is well mixed ½ teaspoon salt and 1 teaspoon baking powder; mold into fritters and fry in hot deep fat; serve while hot with the following sauce: Put together 1½ cups sugar, 1 cup water, and 1 teaspoon butter, let come to boil, then add 1 tablespoon cornstarch; cook until thick, then add 1 teaspoon vanilla; fry in deep hot fat; serve hot.

Eggplant

Fried—Peel eggplant, slice cross-section about a quarter-inch thick; sprinkle with salt and pepper, dip in beaten egg, roll in bread or cracker crumbs, and fry in shallow fat, browning both sides; or, season and dip in fritter batter, and saute, or fry in hot deep fat.

Stuffed—Cut eggplant in halves, and scoop out the inside, leaving shells above a half-inch thick; chop portion taken out and put in saucepan, add 1 small finely chopped onion, ½ cup any cooked meat finely chopped, 1 beaten egg, season with salt and pepper, and divide between and stuff eggplant shells; sprinkle tops with fine soft bread crumbs, and put a bit of butter on each; put in baking dish with a little water or stock, and bake in moderate oven about 15 minutes.—Other ingredients such as tomatoes, green peppers, etc., may be added to forcemeat if desired.

En Casserole—Put slices of eggplant in baking dish, or casserole, alternate them with slices of tomato, onion or garlic, strips of green pepper, etc., and season with salt, pepper, and any other seasoning desired; moisten with a few tablespoons butter or other cooking fat or oil; bake in a slow moderate oven until eggplant is tender.

Broiled—Slice eggplant about ½ inch thick; place on dish, season with salt and pepper, and roll in a tablespoon cooking or salad oil to cover surface; lay slices on broiler and broil 5 minutes on each side; arrange on hot dish, and serve with mayonnaise or other favorite dressing.

Endive

Wash through several waters and cleanse thoroughly, separated leaves of endive; remove the green portions; put into boiling salted water for 10 minutes, then drain free of all water; put into stewpan with any good broth, allowing 1 cup broth for each 3 heads endive, add a little salt and sugar, and stew 5 minutes, or until endive is perfectly tender; thicken with a little butter and flour, and add a little lemon juice; let boil up and serve.

Kohlrabi

Remove stems, peel globe and cut into small pieces; put into boiling water salted with 1 teaspoon salt to the quart, and cook until tender, about 30 to 35 minutes.

Leek

Cleanse, and cut leek in about two-inch lengths and place them in cold water for 30 to 40 minutes to become crisp; drain, and boil in salted water to cover about 30 minutes, or until tender; drain; rinse in cold water, and drain again; make a plain white cream sauce, using 1 tablespoon each of melted butter and flour, and ½ cup milk for each bunch of leek cooked; season with salt and pepper, and then add 1 tablespoon melted butter for each ½ cup sauce, pour over leek and serve hot.

Lentils

Wash lentils well, then cover with cold water and let soak 4 or 5 hours; drain, and put into boiling salted water, add a little herbs, such as bay leaf, parsley, etc., salt and pepper, and powdered mace to season, and cook until tender; in a frying pan, saute a finely chopped onion in 3 tablespoons butter or fat, add 1 cup lentils, 1 cup cooked rice, an additional tablespoon butter, mix and heat well; serve on hot dish with 1½ cups spiced tomato sauce.

Or: Prepare lentils, and soak in milk about 12 hours; fry a small onion in 3 tablespoons butter or fat until lightly brown, add 1 teaspoon currie powder, ½ cup each milk and water, and salt and pepper to season; add ½ to 1 cup lentils, and simmer for 2 hours; add 1 tablespoon lemon juice just before serving; serve with boiled rice.

Lettuce

Wash and trim lettuce heads, and put into a saucepan with 1 sliced onion, 1 tablespoon butter or fat, 2 or 3 teaspoons chopped parsley, and salt and pepper to season; add a little water, and simmer for about 2 hours; when water has almost boiled away, remove onion and parsley; serve lettuce in dish and dress with melted buttter while hot.

Mushrooms

Wash well, and cleanse button mushrooms with a soft damp cloth, such as flannel, lightly rubbing them until they are white; they are then ready to cook, and may be prepared exactly as oysters, and cooked or used in any of the ways called for under oyster recipes.

Okras

Select 2 dozen medium sized, sound okras; wash them well in cold water, drain thoroughly, and pare both ends; put into a saucepan of boiling salted water, and cook 15 minutes; lift them out with a skimmer, and drain on cloth or soft paper; they are then ready to be used in soup, salads, for frying, etc.

Creole Saute—Prepare okras as above; in a frying pan, put 2 tablespoons good butter, 1 medium, minced onion, and 1 medium minced green pepper; place over fire and saute 6 minutes until of golden color, then add 2 raw, peeled tomatoes finely cut in bits, and 3 tablespoons chili sauce highly flavored; season with salt, pepper, and a little garlic; add okras, cover, and cook slowly for 15 minutes; turn into a hot deep dish, sprinkle with a little chopped parsley; serve.

Truffles

Select fine truffles, and wash them through several waters, using a soft brush to remove every particle of sand or grit; wrap each truffle in buttered paper, and bake in a hot oven 15 minutes; remove paper, wipe truffles, and serve on folded napkin on a hot plate.

Or: Prepare in the same manner as mushrooms, as an accompaniment to meat, poultry, game or fish.

Onions

To Peel Onions—Hold them under water in a deep pan while peeling, and they will not effect the eyes.

Fried—Peel, slice and fry them in equal parts of butter and cooking fat or drippings; cover pan until partly soft, then remove cover and brown; season with salt and pepper.

Stewed—Peel and cook in boiling salted water until tender; remove to dish with skimmer, and serve over them white cream sauce as for asparagus or cauliflower.

Or: Boil and drain; add a cup of milk, 2 tablespoons butter, 1 tablespoon flour, stir until creamy, season with salt and pepper, let boil up; serve.

Boiled—Select white onions for boiling; peel and trim the ends, put them in a stewpan of cold water and set them to scald about 2 minutes; drain, then cover with slightly salted cold water, and boil until tender, or 30 to 40 minutes; when tender, drain quite dry, and serve over them a seasoning of salt, pepper and melted butter; serve hot.

Baked—Wash medium sized Spanish onions, but do not peel; place in pan of slightly salted cold water and boil about 1 hour, replenishing water with boiling water when necessary; drain, blot with a soft cloth to dry them; roll each in buttered paper, twisting the ends; bake in slow oven about 1 hour until cooked through; peel, place in baking dish, and return to oven to slightly brown, basting them with butter for about 15 minutes; season with salt and pepper; add a little melted butter over each; serve.

Stuffed—Boil medium sized Spanish onions as for baking, drain and cool a little; with a sharp knife, cut the center out of each to form a thick shell; chop the centers removed, and to each 4 onions, add 1 tablespoon finely chopped cooked ham, 1½ tablespoons bread crumbs, 1 tablespoon butter, 1 tablespoon cream, 1 beaten egg, and season with salt, pepper, paprika or chili powder, and a little chopped parsley; mix together into a forcemeat, and peel and stuff the onion shells; sprinkle each with buttered breadcrumbs, place in baking dish, and bake in moderate oven about 1 hour.

Oyster-Plant

Oyster-plant (Salsify) should be washed, scraped, and plunged quickly into cold water containing a little vinegar to prevent it oxydizing or turning dark; when well washed and acidulated, cut into 2-inch pieces, boil in plenty of water, adding a little salt and vinegar, and about 2 tablespoons flour mixed to paste with water; after 40 minutes, or as soon as they will bend under light pressure, they are done; lift them out, drain them well, and serve with white cream sauce.

Or: Prepare and cook as above, but after draining them, place in frying pan with white cream sauce to which a little nutmeg has been added, thinning and enriching with about ½ cup sweet cream; season further with salt and pepper if necessary, and heat all together 5 minutes; serve hot in deep dish.

Or: Prepare and cook as above, but after draining them, place on a dish, season with salt, pepper and vinegar; dip in fritter batter, and fry in hot deep fat 5 minutes, keeping the pieces separated with a spoon; lift out with skimmer, drain on a cloth; sprinkle with a little salt, and serve on a folded napkin on a hot dish.

Parsnips

Boiled—Wash, scrape, and split in half; put into boiling salted water, and boil until tender—2 to 3 hours, according to size; dry on cloth, and serve with melted butter and seasoning to taste, either as boiled, or mashed like potatoes; or, serve with white cream sauce.—They may also be prepared as above, parboiled, or steamed 1 hour and baked with or without meat.

Stewed—Prepare them for cooking, and slice about a half-inch thick; put in stewpan with just enough boiling salted water to cook them; add a little butter, and salt and pepper to season; cover closely and stew them until soft, carefully watching them to prevent burning, replenishing water boiled away; serve with boiled meat or salt fish.

Creamed—Boil until tender, scrape and slice lengthwise; put in a pan with 2 tablespoons butter, and season with a little salt, pepper, and finely chopped parsley; shake pan until mixture boils; lift out parsnips and dress on a plate and set in warming-closet; stir 1 teaspoon flour into 3 tablespoons milk or cream, add this to the sauce in the pan, and let it boil up while stirring; pour over parsnips; serve.

Fritters—Boil parsnips as above, season, and mash them like potatoes; work into them a beaten egg, and enough flour to form a soft dough; drop spoonfuls into hot bacon drippings, and fry to a delicate brown on both sides.

Peas

Shell green peas and wash in cold water; drain; and put into just enough boiling water to cover them; boil 20 to 30 minutes, depending upon the age, until tender, allowing the water to boil away until just enough remains to keep them from burning; then season with salt—not before, as the salt will toughen them—pepper, and add butter sufficiently to enrichen the reduced liquor; serve hot.—If flavors are liked, a little mint may be added to the boiling water and removed before serving; also a little lemon juice may be added to the buttered liquor.

Or: Brown a sliced or chopped onion in 1 tablespoon butter or drippings in a frying pan; add ½ teaspoon flour and 2 tablespoons finely chopped cooked ham; stir well and add 2 cups cooked peas, 1 tablespoon water or good stock, a small sprinkle of sugar and nutmeg; season with salt and pepper to taste, simmer about 10 minutes, mixing well; serve.

Potatoes

Fried—Peel raw potatoes, wash in cold water, slice very thinly crosswise, quickly rinse, and dry or drain on soft cloth; have ready in frying pan, a tablespoon each of butter and other fresh fat quite hot; put in enough potatoes to well cover bottom of pan, and when boiling hot again, season with salt and pepper; cover closely and let cook in the steam until partly done; then remove lid and cook to golden brown, moving the slices to evenly color.

Or: Slice cold boiled potatoes and fry as above.—*American Fried.*

Or: Prepare as above, slicing lengthwise into strips, season with salt and pepper, and drop into hot deep fat; cook until tender and delicately browned.—*French Fried.*

Or: Prepare as above, but slice lengthwise a quarter-inch thick, then cut these slices into quarter-inch strips; keep under cold water until wanted, then dry on cloth, salt and pepper, and drop into very hot deep frying fat; cook until nearly done, lift out with a skimmer and drain them; let the fat boil up again, and drop the potatoes back into it and fry until done; this operation makes them light and puffy.—*Fillet of Potatoes.*

Potato Chips—Prepare as for frying, but slice cross-section to wafer thickness or shavings; dry and drop into real hot deep frying fat, and fry to crispness, keeping them stirred about and separated; drain, lightly dust with salt and pepper, and keep in dry, warm place.

Steamed—Put potatoes in cold water as peeled; put in a steamer over pan of boiling water, or hang in wire basket in kettle containing boiling water; steam them 20 to 40 minutes, or until soft and well cooked; season, and serve.

Boiled—Wash potatoes, and without peeling, drop them in well-salted boiling water until well cooked throughout.

Or: Peel and slice about a quarter-inch thick, put them into rapidly boiling salted water; they should be well cooked in about 10 minutes; drain, cut up or dice, season with salt, pepper and butter, or cream them in the regular way.—Cold boiled potatoes are prepared in a number of ways as Salads or with Cold Meats.

Baked—Prepare potatoes with or without the jackets on; do not put into an intensively hot oven, but bake moderately and gradually, turning the potatoes from time to time to evenly bake and prevent burning on one side; keep them slightly separated while baking.

Stuffed—Cut rather large baked potatoes in half lengthwise without breaking the skins; scoop out the inside and mash; season with salt, pepper, butter and a little chopped parsley; mix well and refill the potato skins, moisten tops with a few drops of milk, sprinkle with paprika, and brown in oven.

Mashed—Boil, mash, and season nice white potatoes, and mound in center of large plate; place over top a dressing of ½ cup cream stiffly beaten, to which add and mix ½ cup grated cheese, 1 teaspoon melted butter, seasoned with salt, pepper, and cayenne or paprika; put in a very hot oven and quickly and nicely brown; serve.

Puffed—Boil and mash nice white potatoes, and measures 3 cups; add enough of 1 cup milk to nicely cream; add 2 beaten egg yolks, 3½ tablespoons butter, and season with salt and pepper; beat well, and fold in the stiffly beaten whites of the eggs; mound lightly on a buttered baking dish, and bake until puffed and browned nicely.

Pumpkin

Remove seeds and rind from ripe, rich-colored pumpkin, and cut up into small pieces; put into large pot or pan with a very little water, and let it cook slowly on top of range until tender; then, move from directly over fire-box, and let it simmer about half a day until excess moisture is driven off and pumpkin reduced to a deep red color; cool and press through a colander.

Or: Cut pumpkin in fair sized pieces without removing the rind from them; put these in baking pans and set in a slow oven, and bake until soft; take them out, cool a little, and scrape all the baked pulp from the shells; run through a colander.

Spinach

Wash carefully picked spinach through several waters until perfectly free from insects, sand, etc.; put into kettle and add from ½ to 1 cup boiling water, just enough to cover bottom of kettle well; if spinach is real young and tender, no water is necessary, the juice being sufficient. Boil 15 to 25 minutes or until tender; drain completely, chop finely, drain off excess juice, season with salt, pepper and butter; set pan over fire for a few moments, stirring constantly, to reheat and drive off a little of the moisture; serve in warm dish and garnish with slices of hard-boiled egg.—Spinach should not be cooked long enough to lose its bright green color.

Or: Cook spinach as above, drain, chop, and season; measure spinach and set aside an equal measure of rich tomato sauce of pulp of stewed tomatoes; melt 1 or 2 tablespoons butter in a stewpan and blend with it an equal measure of flour; add the tomato sauce of pulp, and bring to boiling point while constantly stirring; add spinach, boil 5 minutes; serve.

Note—Other greens are cooked in the same manner as spinach. Many cooks prefer to wash the greens in strongly salted water, but if this is done, they should be thoroughly rinsed before cooking, as cooking in salt-water tends to toughen the fibres.

Sweet Potatoes

Sweet Potatoes, or Southern Yams, may be boiled, steamed, or baked like white potatoes, and are generally cooked in this way with the jackets on; cold cooked sweet potatoes may be sliced, or split and fried same as white potatoes; parboiled, peeled, then baked in oven until browned, basting with butter or fresh-meat drippings, is another popular way of cooking them.

Glazed or Candied—Wash six medium sized sweet potatoes, put into boiling salted water, and parboil 10 minutes; drain, scrape off skins, split each in half lengthwise, and lay in well buttered pan. Make a syrup: boil ½ cup sugar and 4 tablespoons water 3 minutes, and add 1 tablespoon butter; brush potatoes with this syrup, place the pan on the rack in a moderate oven, and bake until browned, about 35 minutes, basting twice with remaining syrup.

Puffed—Southern Style—Select medium, well rounded, evenly sized sweet potatoes, or yams; bake perfectly done in oven, and let cool; split each in half lengthwise, and carefully scoop out the potatoes with a spoon, reserving the shells; mash the potato removed, and moisten with butter and sweet cream to consistency of mashed white potatoes; season with salt, pepper, and a little wine or fruit juice; refill the shells, brush tops with butter, and brown 5 minutes in oven.

Puffed—Proceed exactly as for Southern Style, but add egg yolks and whites in the manner called for in Puffed White Potato recipe.

Tomatoes

To Peel—Dip ripe tomatoes in boiling hot water for 3 minutes; the thin outer skin can then be peeled, or stripped off with ease.

Stewed—Remove skins, slice them into a graniteware stew-pan, set over fire, and let them stew in their own juice about 20 minutes; add a little butter, season with salt and pepper, and continue the stewing for another 15 minutes.—They may be thickened with soft breadcrumbs; or, sweetened with a little sugar if desired; or, a chopped onion may be added if flavor is liked; or, mixed with green corn, or other vegetables in combination.

Baked—Wash ripe tomatoes, and take a slice off the stem end; cut out the central core and remove soft seed-pulp; stuff with buttered bread crumbs seasoned with salt and pepper; sprinkle more crumbs on top with a little butter on each, and bake in hot oven about 30 minutes.

Scalloped—Drain stewed tomatoes; cover bottom of greased baking dish with some of the pulp, adding a little butter dotted over them, season with a sprinkle of salt and pepper, and sprinkle a generous layer of breadcrumbs; repeat this until dish is nearly filled; moisten with some of the tomato juice, cover with another layer of crumbs, lightly buttered; bake in moderate oven 20 minutes.

Grilled—Wipe ripe tomatoes with damp cloth, and brush each with melted cooking fat; place on a grill-pan before a clear fire and cook 8 to 10 minutes.

Fried Green—Slice nice, solid green tomatoes; season, and fry exactly like eggplant; serve with catsup and crackers.

Turnips

Turnips are boiled either with or without meat, and require about 40 to 60 minutes to cook, depending upon size and age; they may also be mashed like potatoes, or stewed like parsnips.

Or: Pare and trim to pear-shape, small white turnips of equal size; parboil them 5 minutes, then drain them; butter the bottom of a deep frying pan; arrange the turnips upright and slightly separated, sprinkle with 1 cup powdered sugar for each dozen turnips, and saute them to a light golden color; moisten with 1 tablespoon butter in 1 cup hot water, and add a little salt to season; a small piece of stick cinnamon may also be added if desired; cut out a piece of well buttered paper to fit the pan nicely, and place over top to cover turnips; set in moderate oven about 20 minutes; when cooked, lift off paper, place turnips on hot dish, and reduce the gravy to a glaze for six minutes, then add ¼ cup boiling water to loosen the hardened glaze from the pan, remove the cinnamon, and pour the glaze over turnips; serve at once.

Cake and Cake Making

Anyone should learn to make perfect cake. Besides the use of good materials, concentration and accuracy are most essential, and above all, the perfect control of your range oven should be mastered.

Cake is divided into two distinct classes: *Butter Cake* and *Sponge Cake*—with and without shortening. In their plain form, they constitute *basic recipes,* from which many variations are had by adding, or withholding, of ingredients, varying proportions, manner of mixing, time of baking, etc.

Cake is composed of flour, shortening, sweetening, a rising agent, liquid, eggs and flavoring. The use of the best and freshest materials is essential in fine cake making.

A fine, white flour made from winter wheat, called *Cake Flour,* is best. It should be free from mold, and have a faintly pure, fresh odor; also, when a small quantity is pressed in the palm of the hand, it should "hold together," carrying the imprint of the lines of the hand. Such flour gives the cake a delicate, desirable texture.

Flour should always be perfectly dry, and should be sifted before measuring. When used with baking powder, it should be sifted again after the powder has been added. Flour should always be stirred lightly into a cake mixture; i. e., sifted in, and stirred into the mixture a little at a time.

Bread flour may, if necessary, be used as a substitute for cake flour by removing a tablespoon from each cupful called for in the recipe; being heavier and coarser than cake flour, it makes coarser cake.

Potato flour is best for Sponge Cake, but when used as a substitute for wheat flour, only half the quantity called for in the wheat flour recipe should be used.

None but the best Baking Powder, as a rising agent, should be used in cake making—the cheaper powders are usually made from cheap and inferior materials.

Butter is the universal shortening used in the finest cake; however, very good results are had with *vegetable shortening,* especially that made from the oil of nuts—and it is cheaper.

Sweetening for cake is in the form of sugar, syrup, or molasses. Finely granulated sugar makes the finest cake; coarsely granulated sugar makes a coarse-grained cake; powdered or confectioners sugar makes a dry cake.

Creaming of butter, or shortening, is more easily done when the material is at "room temperature"—about 70 degrees Fahrenheit. First, the butter should be well creamed, then the sugar thoroughly creamed into it—this saves about half the work. Time and effort are also saved by using a crockery bowl and a large slitted wooden spoon for creaming and mixing.

Temperature of ingredients being mixed is an important item in good cake making. In cold weather, rinse the mixing bowl in hot water, being cautious to thoroughly dry it before placing the materials into it. The sugar should be warmed to about the temperature of the creamed butter before adding it. One of the big secrets in mixing cake materials is to have them all about the same temperature, unless otherwise directed by the recipe.

None but the finest fresh eggs should be used in cake making. Weak, watery, or undersized eggs are the cause of many failures, and should be avoided.

Whites and yolks of eggs should always be beaten separately, unless otherwise directed by the recipe, care being taken to thoroughly clean the beater when transferring it from one to the other—an egg beater should always be clean and absolutely dry before using.

If whites of eggs are desired dry and of close texture, a rotary (Dover) beater should be used; if moist and of loose texture—commonly termed "frothy"—they should be "whipped" with a woven wire whisk.

Yolks of eggs should always, unless otherwise directed by the recipe, be beaten with a rotary beater.

When eggs and sugar are to be beaten *together* as for some cake, this is best done "over hot water," care being taken to remove immediately when beating is complete.

In all cake baking, the proper regulation of the oven-heat is of most vital importance to success; therefore, study the control of your oven, as well as the effect of various temperatures.

One frequent cause of failure is the sudden jarring of the cake at certain periods of the baking process. The oven door should be opened and closed carefully—open it as often as necessary for the regulation of the heat, or for observing the progress—but do not jar the cake, or open the door for the first fifteen or twenty minutes of baking.

The oven-heat should never be above "moderate" when the cake mixture is placed into it. The air, or gas, in the mixture should be given a chance to be heated and expand before the process of cooking begins—otherwise the cake will be flat and heavy.

Never move, or jar, a cake during the first or last quarter of the period required for baking. In the second or third quarter, it may be moved or turned around if necessary, without serious results. Divide the time required for the particular cake into four quarters, and guard the above rule carefully.

After the cake has risen—in moderate heat—stronger heat should be applied during the second quarter, to give a firm, well baked texture; the browning should be done in the third quarter. For the fourth quarter, the oven-heat may be gradually lessened, as the baking is practically complete. During this last period, the cake will settle firmly and lose its surface moisture, and settle away from the sides of the pan.

Butter Cake should be baked in a greased pan—lining the pan with buttered paper is best. Sponge Cake is usually baked in an ungreased pan—this helps to hold up the cell walls by adhering to the sides—and the cake should not be removed immediately from the pan, but should be turned upside down and the cake allowed to dry and partially cool in this position before removing with a thin knife.

Cake should not be hurried, but the oven-heat should be steady and slow, or slightly moderate; if a very light cake rises too quickly, the result is that it bakes rapidly on the sides and is sunken in the center.

White Butter Cake
(Basic Recipe)

1½ cups sugar	1 cup milk	½ teaspoon salt
½ cup butter	3 teaspoons baking	1 teaspoon flavoring
3 cups flour	powder	3 egg whites

Thoroughly cream the butter, then gradually add the sugar, beating to a smooth mixture. Sift and measure the flour, add baking powder and salt, and re-sift two or three times to completely and evenly mix. With a wire whisk, beat the egg-whites until light and fairly stiff.—Into the sugar-butter, stir in alternately the milk and the flour; add the flavoring extract, and vigorously beat whole to a smooth mixture. Now, carefully "fold in" the beaten egg-whites, handling lightly to prevent tearing down the air-cells that have been beaten into them.

If for *loaf cake,* use a square baking pan about eight inches square and two inches deep; or round pan about nine inches in diameter and two to two and a half inches deep; or a standard round, center-tube cake pan of medium size.

If for *layer cake,* use two shallow cake pans about seven inches square; or two small deep pie tins—dividing the mixture evenly between them.

Baking: Butter the pan, or pans, and dust with fine flour, shaking out the flour that does not adhere; fit well-buttered paper into the pans; pour in the cake mixture, spreading evenly. *Have ready a moderate oven*—one in which white paper will turn a light brown in five minutes; place the cakes in the oven, and do not disturb for the first five or six minutes; now, increase the heat for the next ten or twelve minutes, or until the top begins to turn a delicate golden brown—necessary inspection or careful turning of the pans will not disturb the baking during this period—do not allow to brown too quickly; then, diminish the heat for the next five or six minutes, or until the cake is completely baked; do not jar or disturb it during this period, at the end of which time the cake will be found to have slightly pulled away from the sides of the pan. Turn out on a board covered with cloth, and remove the paper.—Double recipe for large cake; or three large layers.

Golden Butter Cake

Follow the "Basic Recipe" except: Beat the *yolks* of the eggs and mix with the creamed sugar-butter—leaving out the whites entirely (use them for icing). The use of golden yellow butter will improve the color.

Marble Cake

Prepare White Butter Cake mixture, and divide equally into two bowls; leave one plain; to the other half of mixture, stir in 3 ounces (3 squares) of melted bitter chocolate, 1/3 teaspoon soda, and 1 teaspoon ground spice—two parts cinnamon and one part ground cloves is good. Put a large spoonful of the white into the baking pan, then one of the brown mixture, alternating until all is in; do not stir, but smooth over the top, and bake. Decorate with icing, fruits, or nuts if desired

Chocolate Cake

Prepare and bake White Butter Cake in two medium, or three smaller, layers; fill and cover with Chocolate icing.

Cocoanut Cake

Prepare and bake White or Golden Butter Cake in two medium, or three smaller, layers; fill and cover with Cocoanut Icing; or with Cocoanut-Marshmallow Icing.

Baltimore Cake

Prepare and bake White Butter Cake in layers; make a filling of Boiled Icing, into which mix a half-cup each of finely chopped raisins, figs, and nut meats; cover with boiled icing; decorate if desired.

Sun-Set Cake

Prepare mixture for White Butter Cake; divide mixture into four parts and in separate bowls; tint one part pink with coloring or fruit juice; tint another part blue; another yellow; and leave one plain. In successive rotation, place a spoonful of each at a time in the prepared baking pan; with a fork, stir once or twice to slightly mix the colors. Bake in round or square loaf; cover with Boiled Icing or Divinity Icing.

Orange Cake

Prepare and bake White or Golden Butter Cake in layers; divide one large orange into its sections, cut these sections in half, distribute over the bottom layer of cake, and cover with choice of plain white filling or icing; cover top and sides with the same icing.

California Cake

Prepare and bake White Butter Cake in two layers: Fill between layers with fig or other fruit Paste filling; cover top with Boiled Icing.

Tropical Cake

Prepare and bake White, or Golden, Butter Cake in layers: Fill with your choice of Fruit Paste Filling, to which add an equal quantity of chopped nut meats. Cover with Boiled Icing and decorate with candied fruits and nut meats.

Caramel Cake

Prepare and bake White Butter Cake in two layers: Fill between layers and cover top with Caramel Icing.

Snow-Flake Cake

Follow the White Butter Cake recipe except: Use 5 egg whites instead of 3, and leave out one teaspoon of baking powder.

Marshmallow Cake

Prepare and bake White Butter Cake in layers: Fill between layers and cover with Marshmallow Icing.

Cocoanut Marshmallow Cake

Prepare and bake White Butter Cake in layers: Fill between layers and cover with Cocoanut-Marshmallow Icing.

Pineapple Cake

Prepare and bake White or Golden Butter Cake in layers. Put layers together and finish top with Pineapple Icing.

Jelly Cake

Prepare and bake White or Golden Butter Cake in layers: Spread Apple, Currant, Berry, or other jelly between layers; cover top with Sea Foam Icing, or sprinkle with powdered sugar.

Hickory Nut Cake

Prepare and bake White Butter Cake in layers: Put together with Divinity Icing, to which has been added one cup finely chopped hickory-nut kernels. The nut kernels may be put into the cake if desired, and the cake baked in loaf; plain or nut icing may be used.

Black and White Cake

May be made in several ways: Plain White Layer Cake put together with dark filling; or, Dark Layer Cake put together with white filling; or, Marble Cake mixtures baked in separate layers and put together with white icing on dark layer and dark icing on the white layer—any of these furnish a variation.

Maple Syrup Cake

½ cup sugar	2 teaspoons baking
¼ cup butter	powder
2¼ cups flour (about)	⅔ teaspoons soda
1 cup maple syrup	2 eggs
½ cup hot milk	

Cream the butter, and gradually cream-in the sugar; beat the eggs without separating, and add to the sugar-butter mixture; add maple syrup and stir in; sift and measure the flour, add baking powder and soda, and sift again; add flour and hot milk alternately, a little at a time, and completely mix. Bake in a round center-tube pan, and cover with Maple Icing II.

Molasses Cake

½ cup brown sugar	powder
½ cup butter	½ teaspoon salt
½ cup molasses	¼ teaspoon soda
½ cup milk	1 teaspoon mixed spices
2 cups flour	1 egg
3 teaspoons baking	

Cream butter, and gradually cream in the sugar; add molasses and beaten egg, and mix; sift and measure flour, add baking powder, salt, soda and spices, and re-sift together; add flour and milk alternately and mix well; bake in well greased shallow pan in a moderate oven—baking time about 40 to 45 minutes. Serve while yet warm. Ice if desired.

Grandma's Pound Cake

As baked in the "Home Comfort" Range fifty years ago:

2 cups sugar (1 lb.)	4 cups flour (1 lb.)
2 cups butter (1 lb.)	10 eggs (1 lb.)

Beat the yolks and whites of the eggs separately; cream the butter, and cream the sugar into it; add the egg yolks and mix well; add the stiff egg whites alternately with the flour; long beating of air into this mixture is the success of this cake; Grandma always beat the mixture with her hand in a large wooden mixing-bowl, since it was less tiresome. Put in the oven when you can bear your hand on the bottom, and gradually increase the oven heat to moderate; bake two hours.—A half-pound cake may be successfully made with half the quantities.

Southern Ginger Bread

1½ cups New Orleans	½ cup boiling water
molasses	1 teaspoon soda
3 cups flour	2 teaspoons ginger
¼ cup butter	1 teaspoon salt

Sift and measure flour, add soda, ginger and salt, and re-sift; add hot water to molasses; combine these two mixtures; add the butter; beat thoroughly to form smooth batter; pour in greased pan and bake in moderate oven for half an hour. Top with boiled icing if desired.

Rich Spice Cake

2 cups light brown sugar	2 teaspoons cinnamon
1 cup sour milk	1 teaspoon ground cloves
2 cups flour, about	1 teaspoon ground
1 cup seeded raisins	allspice
2 egg whites	½ teaspoon grated
3 egg yolks	nutmeg
½ cup melted shortening	1 teaspoon soda

Sift and measure flour, add all the spices and soda, re-sift; cream the melted shortening and sugar; add the well beaten egg yolks; add flour mixture gradually, alternating with the sour milk, to make a stiff smooth batter; fold-in the stiffly beaten egg whites; dust the raisins with fine flour, and stir into the mixture, sufficiently to distribute them throughout the batter. Bake in two layers. Put layers together with soft Maple or Caramel Icing, with a desirable quantity of coarsely chopped nut meats in the filling. Or: Bake in loaf, and serve cuts with caramel or cream sauce, or whipped cream.

Devil Food Cake

½ cup butter	2 teaspoons baking
1 cup sugar	powder
3 egg yolks	¼ teaspoon ground
¾ cup sugar	cloves
½ cup milk	½ teaspoon cinnamon
1¾ cups flour	1 teaspoon flavoring
2 sqs. bitter chocolate	3 egg whites

Cream the butter and add the cup of sugar; beat the egg yolks, add the ¾ cup of sugar; beat the two mixtures together. Melt the chocolate and add to the mixture; sift baking powder with the flour three times, add with the spices and thoroughly mix; add the milk and the flavoring, and mix; fold-in the stiffly beaten egg whites. Bake in two thick layers, and put together with choice of icing.—Divinity Icing recommended.

College Fudge Cake

2 squares bitter chocolate	1¾ cups flour
½ cup hot water	1½ teaspoons baking
1 cup sugar	powder
¼ cup butter	1 teaspoon vanilla
1 cup sugar	1 teaspoon soda
¼ teaspoon salt	½ cup boiling water
1 egg yolk	

Put the chocolate and hot water in a saucepan and cook and stir about three minutes until thick and glossy; remove from fire, add the egg yolk beaten, butter, sugar and salt; stir in the flour sifted with the baking powder, and add vanilla; at the last, stir in the boiling water in which the soda is dissolved; beat until smooth, pour into a shallow pan; bake in a moderate oven about thirty minutes. Cover with Chocolate Fudge Icing.

White Fruit Cake

1 cup gran. sugar	8 egg whites
1 cup butter	1 cup chopped citron
2 cups flour	1 teaspoon baking powd.
1 cup blanched almonds	¼ teaspoon salt
1 cup grated cocoanut	1 teaspoon flavoring

Cream the butter and cream-in the sugar gradually; sift and measure the flour, add baking powder and salt, and re-sift two or three times; add flour slowly to first mixture and beat in thoroughly; dredge the finely chopped nuts and fruits with sifted flour, add and stir into the mixture, then add flavoring extract; fold-in lightly the well beaten egg whites. Bake in center-tube loaf cake pan, in a moderate oven for about two hours.—Recipe may be doubled for large cake, and baking extended to about three hours; follow baking precautions as with the Christmas Fruit Cake.

Christmas Fruit Cake

2 cups light brown sugar	1 cup chopped nuts
1 cup molasses	3 eggs
1 cup butter	1 teaspoon mixed spices
5 cups flour	1 teaspoon cinnamon
1 cup strong coffee	1 teaspoon grated nutmeg
1 cup seedless raisins	2 teaspoons baking powd.
½ cup currants	¼ teaspoon soda
1 cup chopped dates	½ teaspoon salt
1 cup chopped figs	3 teaspoons vanilla
½ cup chopped citron	Filling and icing

Cream the butter and gradually cream-in the sugar; add the well beaten egg yolks and molasses, thoroughly mixing. Sift and measure 3 cups of the flour, add spices, cinnamon, nutmeg, baking powder, soda and salt to flour and re-sift twice. Into the first mixture, stir in portions of the flour and liquid coffee alternately until all are well mixed; add vanilla, and fold-in the well beaten egg whites. Now, sift and measure the remaining 2 cups flour, and thoroughly mix it with the well chopped fruits and nut meats; add these to the cake mixture the last thing before pouring into the pans. Bake in three equal layers; line pans with three or four thicknesses of brown paper with well buttered surface; place in a moderate oven for about one hour, then cover the pans with a double thickness of the brown paper, reduce the oven-heat slightly, and allow to bake for two or three hours longer, or until done.

When cooled, put cake together with the following special filling: Double the recipe for Caramel Icing and add one cup of finely chopped nut meats. Cover and decorate with white Ornamental Icing— Walnut or pecan halves, and small candies may also be used with pleasing effect; small natural holly sprigs with candy "hot drops" for holly berries, also make a nice decoration; a candy, or even a paper Santa Claus may be used with effect—and many other decorations will suggest themselves.

If desired, this cake may readily be baked in a single loaf, in which case, a large center tube baking pan should be used. Half the given quantities may be used for a smaller cake.

Tropical Ginger Cake

½ cup sugar	2 cups shredded cocoanut
½ cup butter	1 teaspoon soda
½ cup molasses	1 teaspoon ginger
1½ cups flour	1 teaspoon cinnamon
½ cup cold water	¼ teaspoon salt
2 eggs	

Cream butter and cream-in the sugar gradually; add the unbeaten eggs, and beat all together thoroughly; stir soda into the molasses and add to first mixture; sift and measure the flour, add the spices and salt, and re-sift, beating them into the mixture part at a time and alternating with parts of the cold water until all are mixed; lastly, stir in the shredded cocoanut. Pour in a well-greased paper lined pan, and bake in a moderate oven about 35 minutes. Top with icing if desired, or serve plain as gingerbread.

Blackberry Jam Cake

2 cups sugar	6 eggs
1 cup butter	2 teaspoons soda
½ cup sour cream	1 teaspoon cinnamon
4 cups flour	1 teaspoon nutmeg
2 cups jam	Filling and icing

Cream butter and cream-in sugar; add jam and mix; add beaten egg yolks and spices and mix; sift and measure flour, and re-sift with soda added; stir in alternately the flour and sour cream or milk; fold in well-beaten egg whites. Bake in two layers and put together with choice of soft icing. —Other jams or preserves may be substituted and the cake named after the one used.

Apple-Sauce Cake

1½ cups applesauce	1 cup seeded raisins
1 cup sugar	2 teaspoons soda
½ cup butter	1 teaspoon cinnamon
2 cups flour	1 teaspoon spice

Do not sweeten the apple-sauce, but let cool, strain, add the soda and beat until light and puffy; cream butter and sugar; warm the beaten sauce, add the butter mixture, and beat until creamy; add the cinnamon and spice; thoroughly stir in the flour a little at a time; dredge raisins with flour and stir into mixture before pouring into well-greased and paper-lined pans. Bake in two layers and put together with White or Marshmallow Icing; or, in loaf. Bake in moderate oven.

Birthday Cakes

The favorite cake of the one for whose birthday it is meant is usually chosen. This may be either a loaf or a layer cake, but in any event, it is always completely covered, sides and top, with thick, smooth icing and handsomely decorated with Ornamental Icings and small wax candles, one to represent each year of age. The ornamentation may be chosen designs of flowers, leaves, vines, roses, carnations, daisies, etc., are easily formed of colored ornamental icing to meet the taste of the one being honored. See "Ornamenting Cakes" under "Cake Icing and Fillings."

Gold Medal Sponge Cake
(Basic Recipe)

1 cup sugar	¼ teaspoon salt
1 cup flour	½ lemon, rind and juice
6 eggs	2 tablespoons water

Sift and measure the flour, sprinkle in the salt, re-sift and have ready. Grate the lemon-rind, mix into the sugar, and stand this by also. Extract the lemon-juice—not less than one tablespoon—add to the water and also have ready. Beat the egg-yolks until thick and lemon colored—done best with a Dover beater; then, with a slitted wooden spoon, carefully and gradually beat in the sugar and lemon-rind; slowly add and stir in the water and lemon-juice. With a wire whisk, whip the egg-whites until light and fairly stiff; now "fold" a part of the whites into the sugar mixture, then "fold" in part of the flour and salt, repeating alternately until all are nicely incorporated—do not beat or stir the completed mixture, but immediately pour into an ungreased baking pan.

Have the oven-heat just below *moderate,* and set the cake to bake. Time: about one hour. Do not disturb during the first quarter-hour, at the end of which the cake should begin to rise; at the end of a half-hour, it should have its full height and begin to brown; then the heat should be slightly increased—by closing the oven-door tightly—during the next quarter-hour, or until the browning is complete; during the last quarter, the oven-heat should be slightly diminished to complete baking on the inside without over-baking the outside—inspect frequently, but do not move or jar during this last period. When done, turn the pan upside-down on a board without removing the cake, and let it gradually and completely cool in this position to preserve the texture. To serve, do not cut with a knife, but sever with the prong of a pair of table-forks.

Velvet Sponge Cake

2 cups sugar	1 cup boiling milk
1½ cups flour	3 teaspoons baking powd.
6 egg yolks	¼ teaspoon salt
4 egg whites	

Sift and measure flour, add baking powder and salt, re-sift twice; beat egg yolks, add sugar and beat about fifteen minutes; add and mix beaten egg whites, add, a little at a time, the hot milk and the flour mixture alternately, beating to smoothness.

Bake in loaf or layers, following the baking instructions given under Gold Medal Sponge Cake. Use the two egg whites that were left out for icing or filling.

Angel Food Cake

11 egg whites	1 teaspoon cream tartar
1 cup flour	2 teaspoons vanilla
1¼ cups sugar	¼ teaspoon salt

Add salt to egg whites, and beat with a flat wire wisk; when foamy, add cream of tartar and continue beating until fairly stiff; fold in the sugar a spoonful at a time; add the vanilla extract; fold in the flour, which has been sifted, measured, and re-sifted, also a little at a time—stir as little as possible to mix well. May be baked either as loaf cake, or in two layers and put together with icing. If loaf cake, it is best to bake in a round, removable bottom, center-tube baking tin. Whichever the pan selected, it should be ungreased as for Sponge Cake, and baking should be done in a very slow oven, slightly increasing the heat just before baking is complete—baking time, about 50 or 60 minutes. Invert the pan as for Sponge Cake, and allow to cool about an hour before removing. Quantity sufficient for large cake—half quantity may be used for small one with equal success.

Sponge Jelly Roll

Prepare mixture for either Gold Medal or Velvet Sponge Cake; Line a large shallow pan with well-greased paper, pour in sufficient mixture to make a sheet about ¾ inch thick, or slightly less when baked. Follow instructions in Gold Medal Sponge Cake recipe as to regulation of oven heat. When baked, turn out onto a damp cloth, remove paper, and trim edges; spread with choice of fruit jelly, beaten to an easily spreading consistency. Place to cool.

Standard Jelly Roll

1 cup flour	3 tablespoons cold water
1 cup sugar	1 teaspoon baking powd.
3 eggs	½ teaspoon fine salt

Gradually beat the sugar into the eggs until quite thick; have ready the flour, baking powder and salt sifted together; add the cold water to the beaten mixture; sift in the flour, gradually stirring into the mixture to form a perfect batter. Line a shallow pan with greased paper, and pour in the batter evenly; bake in a quick oven for about twenty minutes. Turn out onto a cloth or paper sprinkled with sugar; tear off the greased paper, spread with fruit jelly beaten to an easily spreading consistency; roll up quickly and set to cool.

Strawberry Sponge Cake

Bake Gold Medal Sponge Cake in a sheet as for Jelly Roll, but about one inch thick; when cooled, cut into equal squares of about three inches. Prepare a sufficient quantity of strawberries by cutting in half and adding a half cup sugar to each two cups berries—more if desired. Arrange squares in pairs and put together with berries between layers and on top; decorate top with whipped cream if desired.

Nut Sponge Cake

To recipe for either Gold Medal or Velvet Sponge Cake, add one-half cup finely ground nut meats mixed with the flour. Grated cocoanut may also be used in this manner, the cake taking its name for the nuts used.

Special Sponge Cakes

Sponge Cake may be made in any of the forms and combinations as given under Butter Cake, since it can, when baked in layers, be put together with any of the standard icings and fillings. However, remember that the method of mixing and baking Sponge Cake is distinctive, and the instructions given in the Basic Recipe should be followed.

Crumb Cake

½ cup sugar   3 eggs
¼ cup chopped nuts   ¼ teaspoon baking powd.
½ cup seedless raisins   1 teaspoon vanilla
¼ cup cracker meal

Separate eggs; beat yolks, add sugar, beat creamy; add and stir in cracker meal, baking powder, nuts and raisins; carefully fold in stiffly beaten egg whites. Bake in moderate oven 15 minutes. When cool, cover with jam sprinkled with finely chopped nuts; serve portions decorated with sweetened whipped cream.

ICINGS AND FILLINGS

Divinity Icing

2 egg whites   1 tablespoon white corn
2 cups gran. sugar   syrup
1 cup water

Dissolve sugar in water before letting it come to a boil; add corn syrup, and let boil until syrup forms a soft ball when dropped in cold water; take out half the syrup at this stage, and gradually beat it into stiffly beaten egg whites, until cold; let the remainder of the syrup boil until it spins a heavy thread when dropped from spoon, then beat it also into the icing, beating until thick enough to spread.—Quantity sufficient for icing and filling of eight-inch two-layer cake.

The above is a *basic-recipe,* from which many combinations may be made. The secret of success is in the proper cooking and handling, and a certain amount of patience is required, so do not be discouraged if the first attempt is not perfect, for after a trial or two, you will be able to judge the proper density of the second syrup.

Marshmallow Icing

16 Marshmallows   Divinity Icing

Chop the marshmallows in a bowl; prepare Divinity Icing by recipe, adding the marshmallows just before adding the second syrup; add the hot thickened syrup, and beat to creamy smoothness; use about one-third for filling, the remainder for icing.

Cocoanut Icing

1 cup Shredded Cocoanut   ½ Divinity Icing

Spread the icing over top and sides of cake; sprinkle with the cocoanut.

Cocoanut Marshmallow Icing

2 cups Shredded Cocoanut   Marshmallow Icing

Prepare Marshmallow Icing; stir in half the cocoanut and spread immediately; sprinkle remaining half of cocoanut over icing.

Pineapple Icing

½ cup crushed Pineapple   ½ Marshmallow Icing

Prepare Marshmallow Icing; remove two-thirds of the mixture to another bowl; and set over hot water to keep warm until needed; beat the remaining third until it will hold its shape; drain the crushed pineapple and add it to the icing; use as a filler between layers of cake; remove remainder of icing, and beat it until it holds its shape; ice the top and sides of cake.

Tutti Frutti Icing

Prepare Divinity Icing, adding other ingredients as soon as second syrup is well mixed in; beat until creamy and add flavoring; use as both filler and icing for medium sized cake.

Divinity Icing   1 tablespoon chopped nuts
¼ cup chopped cherries   1 tablespoon shredded
¼ cup chopped seeded   citron
    raisins   1 teaspoon mixed flavor

Chocolate Icing

Divinity Icing   2 sqs. bitter chocolate

Prepare Divinity Icing, beating in the chocolate which has been melted over hot water, before adding second syrup; a little more chocolate may be added if desired richer.

Coffee Icing

Divinity Icing   3 tablespoons strong
    coffee

Prepare Divinity Icing, beating in the cold coffee, then add second syrup, which should be cooked a little harder than usual.

7-Minute Icing

1 egg white (unbeaten)   3 tablespoons cold water
⅞ cup gran. sugar   ½ teaspoon flavoring

Place the egg-white, sugar and water in the top of a double boiler; place into bottom section of boiling water, and beat with a Dover beater for 7 minutes; add flavoring during the last 2 minutes of beating. (To measure ⅞ cup, level cup and take out 2 level tablespoonfuls).

Boiled Icing

1 cup gran. sugar   ½ teaspoon flavoring
½ cup water   1 egg-white

Boil sugar and water without stirring until syrup spins a fine thread when lifted on a spoon; pour very slowly over the stiffly beaten egg-white and beat until smooth; add flavoring and beat in; allow to stand a few minutes before spreading.

Sea-Foam Icing

1 cup brown sugar   1 egg white
⅓ cup water   1 teaspoon baking powder

Boil sugar and water without stirring until syrup spins a fine thread; pour very slowly over stiffly beaten egg-white and whip until smooth; add flavoring if desired; lastly, whip in the baking powder until icing foams; use as filling and icing.

Nougat Icing

2½ cups sugar   1½ teaspoons flavoring
1 cup light corn syrup   2 oz. bitter chocolate
½ cup water   (2 sqs.)
2 egg whites

Cook together sugar, corn syrup and water until syrup spins a fine thread; pour the hot syrup gradually into the well beaten egg-whites, constantly beating while adding; add flavoring and beat until well mixed; melt the chocolate over hot water, and slowly add and mix with a final beating.—If desired plain, leave out the chocolate, using only the flavoring which may be vanilla, orange, lemon, maple, or any other extract desired.

Chocolate Fudge Icing

2 cups sugar   1 tablespoon butter
¾ cup milk   4 oz. bitter chocolate

Place all ingredients in a saucepan; mix well and cook until a small amount dropped into cold water will form a very soft ball. Allow to cool and then beat until thick enough to spread on the cake. Eight tablespoons of Cocoa may be substituted for the chocolate. Equal parts of light brown and granulated sugar may be used. One teaspoon vanilla while beating is an improvement.

Caramel Icing

2 cups light brown sugar   1 tablespoon butter
1 cup cream   1 teaspoon vanilla

Cook the sugar and cream in a saucepan

until it forms a soft ball when dropped in cold water; add butter and flavoring; remove from the fire and beat until it is grainy and of right consistency to spread.

Honey Icing

½ cup strained honey   1 egg white
1 tablespoon corn syrup

With the water boiling vigorously in a double boiler, place the ingredients in the upper part and constantly beat with a Dover beater for seven minutes. Spread while warm, finishing the surface smoothly with a buttered knife to prevent sticking.

Maple Icing I

1 cup maple sugar   1 tablespoon white corn
½ cup water   syrup
1 egg white

Boil maple sugar, corn syrup and water without stirring until syrup spins a thread; pour gradually over the stiffly beaten egg-white and whip until smooth; spread at once.

Maple Icing II

1 cup maple syrup   2 egg whites

Boil syrup without stirring until it spins a fine thread; pour gradually over the stiffly beaten egg-whites and whip with a wire whisk until smooth and stiff enough to spread.

Butter Scotch Icing

2 cups light corn   ½ cup butter
syrup   ½ cup milk

Boil the ingredients together until it forms a soft ball when dropped into cold water; cool slightly, without stirring, and pour and spread on cake while yet warm.

Cream Filling

½ cup sugar   1 teaspoon butter
1 cup milk   ⅛ teaspoon salt
2 tablespoons cornstarch   ½ teaspoon vanilla
2 eggs

Heat the milk, bringing it to the boiling point; beat the eggs and mix into them the sugar, cornstarch and salt; pour the scalded milk into this mixture gradually, and add the butter; cook in a double boiler, constantly stirring until thick and smooth; stir in the flavoring; spread on cake.—4 egg-yolks may be substituted for the 2 eggs.

Chocolate Cream Filling

Prepare the plain Cream Filling as above, adding 2 extra tablespoons of sugar; and melting 1½ ounces (1½ sqs.) bitter chocolate in the scalding milk.

Fruit Paste Filling

1 cup dried fruit   2 tablespoons sugar, or
¼ cup water   sweeten to taste

Chop finely and measure choice of dried fruit—may be either figs, dates, raisins, prunes, peaches, apricots, pears, or apples; add water and sugar, and let boil to an easily spreading paste; when slightly cooled, spread between cake layers.

Molasses Filling

½ cup New Orleans molasses	2 tablespoons milk
1 egg yolk	½ teaspoon vanilla

Mix well the egg yolk and milk, and stir into the molasses; cook in a double boiler, constantly stirring until it thickens; stir in the flavoring, and allow to slightly cool before spreading.—If desired, two squares of chocolate, melted over hot water, may be added to the molasses.

"Home Comfort" Special Filling

1 cup brown sugar	1 cup pecan meats
1 cup sour cream	3 egg yolks

Put sugar, cream, and beaten egg yolks into double boiler and cook until thick, adding a little flour mixed to a paste in a little milk if necessary to properly thicken; add finely chopped pecan meats; mix well and spread between layers.—The juice of 1 lemon and 1 cup sweet cream may be substituted for sour cream.—Cover with Divinity Icing.

Ornamenting Cakes

The ornamenting or decorating of cakes by means of forming the icing into fancy designs is a matter of individual taste and workmanship, rather than a set science. Such designs as borders, ribbons, bows, loop, flowers, rosettes, etc., are readily formed with *Ornamental Icing* pressed through the fancy tips of *pastry bags,* which may be secured at almost any hardware store, dealer in cooking equipment, or from the larger mail-order houses. An emergency bag may be formed of paper rolled into a cone shape and fastened with pins or sewed, leaving a small opening at the apex; place the icing in the cone, fold the open end to close it, dampen the point so the icing will flow smoothly, then, while squeezing the upper part of the cone, "write" the design upon the cake which has already been covered with icing. A little practice will point the way.

Ornamental Icing I

1¾ cups confectioner's sugar	⅛ teaspoon cream of tartar
2 egg whites	1 teaspoon flavoring

Have bowl and beater cold, and the eggs and sugar the same temperature; add 2 tablespoons of sugar to the egg whites and beat for 3 or 4 minutes; add another like quantity of sugar and beat the same length of time, continuing this process until about half the sugar has been beaten into it; mix the cream of tartar with the remaining sugar, and continue the beating while adding a tablespoon of sugar at a time, thoroughly beating between each addition—this being most important—until the icing may be cleanly sliced with a knife. Add the flavoring during the last two minutes of beating If lemon juice is used instead of the cream of tartar, add the juice gradually as the mixture thickens. This icing will dry very quickly, therefore, it should remain in the bowl covered with a damp cloth held snuggly with a plate until ready for use.—½ teaspoon lemon juice, ½ teaspoon baking powder may be substituted for cream of tartar if necessary. Quantity is sufficient for decorating a medium-sized cake upon which one of the other icings has been spread. If for complete icing and ornamentation, or for a large or elaborately decorated cake, the quantities may be doubled.

Ornamental Icing II

1½ cups granulated sugar	2 egg whites
	1 teaspoon baking powd.
½ cup water	1 teaspoon flavoring

Boil sugar and water without stirring until syrup spins a fine thread; pour very slowly over the stiffly beaten egg whites, and beat until smooth; add flavoring and baking powder and beat in well; place the bowl in hot water, and continue the beating until icing is smooth and slightly grates on the bottom of the bowl; it is then ready to use. Quantity sufficient as in No. 1.

Coloring Icings

Pink—Juice of strawberry, cherry cranberry or currant.

Blue—Juice of blackberry, blueberry, elderberry or raspberry.

Purple—Grape, or mix pink and blue.

Brown—Chocolate, cocoa, or coffee.

Yellow — Grated orange rind cut with lemon juice, or egg-yolk.

Green—Juice from spinach.

Coloring should be added with, or in place of, the flavoring in the icing.

SMALL CAKES
Vanilla Wafers

1 cup sugar	1 egg
½ cup butter	2 teaspoons baking powd.
1½ cups flour	½ teaspoon salt
½ cup milk	½ teaspoon vanilla

Cream the butter and gradually cream the sugar into it; add the well beaten egg and mix; sift and measure flour, add salt and baking powder, re-sift and stir into egg mixture alternately with the milk, little at a time; add vanilla and let the mixture chill. Roll out on a floured board to about ¼ inch thickness; cut; sprinkle top with sugar; bake

in a strong moderate oven about 15 minutes.
—Quantity, about three dozen cookies.

Cocoanut Vanilla Wafers

Prepare and cut, ready to bake, recipe for Vanilla Wafers; lightly brush the tops with slightly beaten egg; and sprinkle on ¾ cup grated or shredded cocoanut; bake in hot oven about 15 minutes.

Chocolate Wafers

1 cup sugar	2 oz. chocolate (2 sqs.)
½ cup butter	2 tablespoons milk
2 cups flour	½ teaspoon soda
1 egg	¼ teaspoon salt

Cream the butter and sugar; add melted chocolate, then the milk and the well beaten egg and mix. Sift and measure flour, add soda and salt and resift; gradually add flour to sugar-butter mixture thoroughly mixing. Roll out on floured board and cut with small round cutter, place on buttered baking tins and bake from eight to ten minutes in moderate oven. May be put together in pairs with Boiled Icing between them. Sufficient for about four dozen single wafers.

Cocoanut Chocolate Wafers

1 cup sugar	2 oz. bitter chocolate
½ cup butter	2 eggs
1 cup flour	1 teaspoon baking powd.
1 cup shredded cocoanut	½ teaspoon salt
½ cup chopped nuts	½ teaspoon vanilla

Cream butter and gradually cream-in sugar; add well beaten eggs and mix; stir in the melted chocolate, chopped nuts, cocoanut, and vanilla; sift and measure flour, add baking powder and salt, resift and add a little at a time constantly stirring. Drop from a teaspoon on a greased pan or buttered paper sheet. Bake in moderate oven for 12 to 15 minutes. Mound top with cocoanut-marshmallow icing if desired.

Dixie Molasses Wafers

1 cup New Orleans molasses	3 cups flour
	3 teaspoons ginger
½ cup butter and shortening	3 teaspoons soda
	1½ teaspoons salt

Bring molasses to a boil; add butter and shortening; add ginger and salt; add soda dissolved in a little milk; mix well, and add flour, stirring in gradually. Roll mixture out thinly on floured board, and cut in small shapes as desired. Bake in moderate oven.

Ginger Snaps

1 cup brown sugar	½ cup hot water
1 cup molasses	1 teaspoon ginger
½ cup shortening	1 teaspoon soda
6 cups flour	1 teaspoon salt

Thoroughly cream the shortening, which may be butter, or butter and other shortening mixed; into this, gradually beat in the sugar and molasses; add salt and ginger; dissolve soda in the hot water and stir in;

add flour and knead well. Roll thin, cut to shape and bake in moderate oven on greased tins. Let cool without removing from pans. —Recipe may be doubled for larger quantity. If desired they may be baked on greased heavy paper laid on bottom of pan; by sliding the paper onto a table or board, pan may be used while snaps are cooling.

Maple Ginger Snaps

Substitute in Ginger Snap Recipe: 2 cups gran. sugar instead of brown sugar; 1 cup maple syrup instead of molasses; use cold water instead of hot water.

School Boy Jumbles

2 cups sugar	3 tablespoons cold water
1 cup butter	1 teaspoon vanilla
4 cups flour	1 teaspoon almond extract
4 eggs	
3 teaspoons baking powd.	

Cream butter and thoroughly cream in sugar; gradually add eggs well beaten, and liquid; add flavoring extracts; sift and measure flour, add baking powder, re-sift, and gradually stir into mixture to form light dough. Roll out lightly on a floured board, cut with doughnut cutter or in odd shapes, sprinkle top with white or colored sugar, and lay on well buttered tins. Bake in moderate oven a few minutes until light brown. Sufficient for about six dozen cookies. Placed in a stone jar, they will keep fresh for three or four weeks.

School Girl Jumbles

Prepare and bake as for School Boy Jumbles; but cut out in more dainty shapes, as squares, diamonds, crescents, etc., and decorate with colored or cocoanut marshmallow icing. Some may be dipped in melted sweet milk chocolate and decorated with nut meats, or put together in pairs with icing between and then dipped.

Chocolate Macaroons

3 oz. bitter chocolate	3 egg whites
2 cups pulverized sugar	

Beat egg whites with wire whisk until light; melt chocolate over hot water and beat-in beaten egg whites until thoroughly mixed; add sugar gradually and work into a thick paste; place on a lightly floured or starched board, and roll down to about a quarter inch thickness; cut with a small round cutter; lightly butter baking tins and dust with flour, starch or powdered sugar; place in the rounds of paste and bake in a moderately hot oven until a delicate brown. Serve cold.

Nut Paste Macaroons

2 cups nut meats	4 tablespoons flour
1 cup pulverized sugar	Almond extract
2 egg whites	

Beat egg whites with a wire whisk until light; beat flour into eggs gradually; sift and measure sugar and add spoonful at a time, constantly beating into the mixture to form a thin paste; add the almond extract to flavor; add nut meats ground to a fine paste or powder and work to a thick paste. Place paste on a lightly floured or starched board, roll out to about a quarter inch thickness, and cut with a small round cutter. Place on buttered paper on flour—dusted, greased tins and bake in a moderate oven until a delicate brown.—Nuts used may be hickory nuts, walnuts, pecans, blanched almonds, peanut butter, or almond paste.

Lady Fingers

¾ cup powdered sugar	½ teaspoon baking powd.
1 cup flour	¼ teaspoon salt
4 eggs separated	½ teaspoon flavoring

Sift and measure flour, add baking powder and salt and re-sift twice. Beat egg yolks until thick, add sugar and beat until lemon colored; add flavoring and flour, mixing smoothly. Beat egg whites until stiff and fold them into the mixture. Drop on buttered tin in finger-length strips and dust with powdered sugar. Bake about 12 minutes in moderate oven. When cool, join together in pairs with icing between; or, use for Charlotte Russe.

Raisin Drop Cakes

1 cup sugar	1 cup seeded raisins
¼ cup butter	3 teaspoons baking powd.
1¾ cups flour	1 egg
⅔ cup milk	1 teaspoon vanilla

Cream butter and cream-in the sugar gradually; slowly add and mix the well beaten egg, and then the milk; sift and measure flour, add baking powder, re-sift and add to mixture while stirring; add raisins which have been washed, drained, and slightly dredged with flour; add vanilla and mix well. Drop on well greased tins or baking sheet, and bake in a hot oven about 15 or 20 minutes. Cover with icing if desired.

Fruit Drop Cakes

⅔ cup sugar	1 egg
1¾ cups flour	¼ teaspoon cinnamon
1 cup rich milk	¼ teaspoon vanilla
3 tablespoons butter	½ cup chopped nuts
2 tablespoons baking powder	½ cup chopped figs and dates

Sift and measure flour, add baking powder and cinnamon, re-sift; cream butter and cream-in gradually the sugar, to which add the well beaten egg; into this mixture, stir in the flour and milk alternately until thoroughly mixed; add vanilla; stir in the chopped fruits and nuts; drop spoonful at a time on a well greased baking sheet or tin, and bake in a moderate oven.

Oatmeal Drop Cakes

1¼ cups sugar	5 tablespoons milk
1 cup shortening	2 teaspoons cinnamon
1 cup raisins or dates	¼ teaspoon soda
2 cups rolled oats	2 eggs
1 cup flour	

Cream shortening, which may be butter, vegetable shortening or a mixture of both, and cream sugar into it; if shortening is used, add a little salt to taste; add beaten eggs, chopped raisins, dates or figs; add rolled oats mixed with flour; add cinnamon, soda and milk and mix thoroughly into fairly stiff batter; drop by teaspoonfuls on well greased pan or baking sheet, spacing well to allow spreading; bake fifteen minutes in moderate oven.

Honey Drop Cakes

½ cup strained honey	1 egg
¼ cup gran. sugar	1½ teaspoon baking
⅓ cup butter	powder
1½ cups flour	½ teaspoon lemon juice

Cream butter and gradually cream-in sugar; add the beaten egg yolk, honey and lemon juice, and mix well; sift and measure flour, add baking powder, and re-sift, and mix thoroughly with first mixture; fold in the well beaten egg whites. Drop on well greased tins or baking sheet, and bake in hot oven about 10 to 15 minutes. Decorate with Honey Icing if desired.

Molasses Drop Cakes

½ cup molasses	1½ teaspoons baking pdr.
¼ cup sugar	¼ teaspoon soda
¼ cup melted butter	1 teaspoon cinnamon
¼ cup boiling water	½ teaspoon nutmeg
1½ cups flour	½ teaspoon spice
½ cup bread crumbs	¼ teaspoon salt

Mix molasses, sugar, boiling water and melted butter in the order named; sift and measure flour, add baking powder, soda, salt and spices, re-sift, and thoroughly stir into first mixture; add bread crumbs and mix to stiff batter. Drop spoonfuls on well greased tin, or baking sheet, and bake for 10 to 12 minutes in a moderate oven. Recipe may be doubled for larger quantity.

Ginger Drop Cakes

1 cup brown sugar	2 eggs
1 cup molasses	1 tablespoon ginger
1 cup shortening	1 teaspoon soda
4½ cups flour	¼ teaspoon salt
1 cup hot water	

Cream shortening, butter, or butter and shortening mixed, and gradually beat-in sugar, molasses, and beaten eggs; add salt and ginger; dissolve soda in the hot water; add flour and water alternately to form a good stiff batter; beat well. Drop spoonfuls on well greased tins or paper, separating sufficiently to allow for spreading; bake in moderate oven about twenty minutes.

Golden Cup Cakes

Prepare mixture for Golden Butter Cake and bake in gem or muffin pans. Top with a spoonful of boiled icing if desired.

Cocoanut Cup Cakes

1 cup sugar	2 tablespoons butter
2 cups flour	2 teaspoons baking powd.
1 cup sour cream	½ teaspoon soda
1 cup shredded cocoanut	¼ teaspoon salt
1 egg	1 teaspoon vanilla

Cream the butter and gradually add and cream-in the sugar; add and mix thoroughly the well beaten egg; sift and measure the flour, add baking powder, salt and soda, and re-sift; add flour and sour cream alternately to the sugar-butter; add flavoring and cocoanut and beat until thoroughly mixed. Bake in muffin pans in a moderate oven about 25 minutes Cover with Cocoanut Icing.

Cocoanut Fruit Bars

1 cup sugar	2 eggs
1 cup flour	1 teaspoon baking powd.
1 cup shredded cocoanut	¼ teaspoon salt
1 cup chopped fruit	Flavoring

Beat egg yolks, add sugar and beat until creamy; sift and measure flour, add baking powder and salt, re-sift, then add cocoanut and chopped fruit (which may be figs, dates, stewed prunes, or dried persimmons seeded); beat egg whites stiff; add alternately a little at a time and stir in thoroughly, first the flour mixture, then the egg whites. Pour and spread in a small shallow buttered tin, and bake in a moderate oven about 30 minutes. Remove from pan and cut into desired strips or bars, and roll in powdered sugar.

Cocoanut Dainties

2 cups gran. sugar	4 egg whites
1 cup shredded cocoanut	1 teaspoon vanilla

Beat the egg whites until entirely stiff and dry; add gradually the sugar and beat until mixture is quite firm; add vanilla. Drop in heaping teaspoons on ungreased tins, sprinkle thickly with cocoanut and bake in a slow oven until dry and a delicate brown.

Chocolate Nut Brownies

2 cups sugar	4 eggs
1 cup butter	2 oz. chocolate
1 cup flour	1 teaspoon vanilla
1 cup nut meats	

Cream butter and cream-in sugar; set aside one of the egg whites for icing, and beat the remainder of the eggs, and add to the creamed sugar-butter; add melted chocolate and blend well; gradually stir in the flour; add broken nut meats and mix thoroughly, adding the vanilla while beating. Bake in a sheet about ¾ inches thick and cut in strips when cooled. Quick oven about 15 minutes. Cover with boiled icing.

Molasses Brownies

Same as for Chocolate Nut Brownies, except replace one cup of the sugar with one cup molasses, which should be mixed into the creamed sugar-butter; omit the chocolate; use choice of flavor.

Molasses Squares

½ cup sugar	1½ cups nut meats
½ cup butter	¼ teaspoon salt
½ cup molasses	1 teaspoon vanilla
1½ cups flour	3 eggs

Cream butter and gradually cream-in sugar, add the well beaten eggs, then the molasses; sift and measure flour, add salt and re-sift; stir in flour gradually, and add vanilla; drop in the chopped nuts a little at a time and mix throughout the batter. Pour about three-quarters inch thick in a well greased shallow pan and bake in a moderate oven about 30 minutes. When cooled, cut into about two-inch squares. Cover with icing if desired. This is a form of cake-candy.

Fancy Cream Cakelets

1 cup gran. sugar	3 egg whites
½ cup butter	3 teaspoons baking powd.
⅔ cup milk	¼ teaspoon salt
2 cups flour	1 teaspoon vanilla

Cream butter and cream-in sugar, adding gradually and beating until very light; add milk, constantly beating; add flavoring; sift and measure flour, add baking powder and salt, re-sift, and stir into first mixture; fold in well beaten egg whites. Pour into a shallow well greased cake pan and bake in a hot oven about 10 to 15 minutes. When cooled, cut into small squares, diamonds, crescents, or other shapes, and top with colored cocoanut, marshmallow or other icing. Cakes should be about an inch or less in height when baked.

Fancy Golden Cakelets

1 cup gran. sugar	3 egg yolks
½ cup butter	2 teaspoons baking powd.
½ cup milk	¼ teaspoon salt
2 cups flour	1 teaspoon lemon extract

Prepare cake mixture as for Cream Cakelets, except: Use above quantities; beat the egg yolks with 3 teaspoons of the milk, and add yolks before adding the flour. ½ lemon rind, grated and cut with ½ teaspoon lemon juice may be substituted for the lemon extract; flavoring may also be vanilla if desired. Bake and decorate as with Cream Cakelets.

Fancy Chocolate Cakelets

Prepare mixture for either Cream or Golden Cakelets except: use vanilla flavoring, and add 4 oz. melted bitter chocolate to recipe, or 2 oz. melted chocolate to half the batter of either. Decorate to suit.

Pies and Pastries

Among the classifications of our foods, Pastry is one of the easiest to make *properly*, and also, the easiest to make *badly*. Starch and fats are the source of muscular nourishment and energy, and when the flour and shortening in pastry are *properly* combined and baked, it is highly nutritious and readily digestible by even the more delicate systems; but, when *improperly* mixed and *badly* baked into a hard or soggy substance that can scarcely be called "food," it invites digestive disorders, and the result is *failure* on the part of the cook, and *imprudence* on the part of those who eat it. Anyone should be able to make good pastry.

Pastry is composed of flour, fat (shortening), liquid, and salt. There are three kinds of pastry—forming *basic recipes,* from which a wide variety of fancy pastries may be made by slight variations in the method of handling—these are *plain, flake, and puff* pastries.

For *plain* pastry, the flour and shortening are mixed evenly throughout by "cutting-in" with two knives. For *flake* pastry, part of the shortening is folded into the mixture of flour and liquid. "Puff" or "French" pastries are sometimes considered variations of *flake* pastry, but are of a different texture, produced by both the variation of ingredients and the method of combining.

The detailed manipulation of these three general classes of pastries will be found in their respective *basic recipes,* but there are a number of general rules by which good pastry makers are guided.

"Pastry Flour"—which is made from best Winter wheat—should be used, as it is lighter and absorbs but a small amount of liquid as compared with ;"bread flour."

Too much flour makes pastry tough; too much shortening, and not enough liquid, makes it dry and crumbly; too much liquid makes it heavy and soggy.

The amount of shortening, for best results, should not be less than one-half the weight of the flour used for plain and flake pastries; equal weights of flour and shortening for most puff-pastries.

The liquid (water or milk) renders pastry mixtures smooth and pliable. Just enough liquid should be added to prevent the mixture from sticking to the bowl, for at this point, the flour has absorbed the necessary amount.

Pastry dough should be stiff and elastic, but not porous or spongy. It should be mixed to a consistency that allows it to roll into a compact ball that will not stick to the bowl, nor will crumble and fall apart—in this form, the paste will be found to "clean the bowl."

If too much liquid has been added to prevent "cleaning the bowl," then "cut into" three or four tablespoons of flour, a tablespoon of shortening, and add this—a little at a time—until stickiness is overcome.

Pastry is made "light" by the presence and expansion of air in the dough when it is placed into the hot oven. All ingredients should be mixed when cold—warm shortening or liquid prevents the proper incorporation of air in the mixture, and makes the pastry heavy and flat. Handling with the warm hands has much the same effect; therefore, it is best to use the "cutting-in" or "folding-in" method of mixing. (Refer to "Methods of Mixing").

The texture of pastry is improved by placing the dough in a closely covered crock, or bowl, and allowed to stand in a cool place for a few hours before forming.

The molding-board on which pastry is rolled or formed should be sprinkled lightly with fine flour—sticking prevents the proper handling which should be delicately done. Some expert pastry makers cover their molding-board with a light canvas cloth—and cover the rolling-pin with cotton "stockinette"—since the pastry can, in this way, be handled with less flour. Always roll pastry with a light, even motion, for best results, rolling in but one direction; too heavy or too much rolling presses out the air needed to make the pastry light.

Pastry in thin layers is inclined to shrink after rolling-out; lift lightly into place—do not stretch tightly—allowing for slight shrinkage. When two layers of pastry are to be combined at the edges—as in double-crust pies—the edge of the lower crust should be lightly dampened with cold water to make them more readily combine. Crimp together all around with the prongs of a fork.

Shell pastry which is to contain a cooked filling—as for single-crust pies and cup pastries—is baked before the filling is placed into it. If for raw or uncooked filling such as custard, the shell and filling are cooked at the same time. The pastry is lightly placed in the pan in the usual manner, but is trimmed about an inch away from the rim of the pan, and this margin is folded back over the edge, and scalloped, or fluted, with the fingers, to form a rigid rim around the inside of the crust.

It is necessary, in making shell and flat pastries, to provide for the escape of excess air while baking, thus preventing bubbles; after the paste is placed in the tin, puncture at regular spacing with the prongs of a fork. Top crusts of pies should always contain a few perforations with the point of a knife to allow escape of any steam or vapor.

Pies should never be allowed to set after being assembled, but should be placed in the hot oven at once. For this reason, always have the oven prepared before putting the pie together. For the same reason, the upper-crust paste should be rolled out and ready to put in place before the filling is placed in the lower crust.

Avoid underbaking of all pastry, as it will be heavy and rendered less digestible.

Proper baking of pastries depends upon the careful attention given it. Always place pastry to bake on the lower oven-shelf with strong heat from below. See that the direct-damper is closed and that the flue around and under the oven is kept practically free from soot, and your range will faithfully perform its duty, and add its share to your reputation as baker of fine pastries.

Plain Pastry
(Basic Recipe)

No. 1—Quantity for one nine-inch pie shell; double for two shells.

1 cup sifted pastry flour   4½ tablespoons   Cold water to moisten
½ teaspoon fine salt   shortening

No. 2—Quantity for one nine-inch double crust, or two lower.

2 cups sifted pastry flour   8 tablespoons   Cold water to moisten
¾ teaspoon fine salt   shortening

Have all ingredients of the same temperature.

Add salt to flour and resift; add shortening and "cut in" with two knives until mixture has appearance of coarse meal; add water, spoonful at a time while mixing with a knife or spatula into a stiff paste—just when the paste rolls into a ball and cleans the bowl of flour and paste, enough water has been added. Lightly transfer paste to a slightly floured board; do not knead, but with floured fingers form quickly and lightly into dough; roll out lightly from the center outward, spreading into desired thickness.

If *bread flour* is to be used, remove 1 tablespoon from each cup called for in pastry flour recipe.

When No. 1 is to be used for extremely juicy fillings, leave out ½ tablespoon of shortening. All measurements are level.

When No. 2 is used, divide the dough in half and roll out each crust separately.

Flake Pastry

Plain Pastry No. 2   4 tablespoons shortening, creamed

For upper crust of pies: Roll out one-half No. 2 dough on lightly floured board to a quarter-inch thickness and in rectangular shape about three times as long as broad; with the point of a knife, cover exactly two-thirds of the surface with little dots, or dabs, of the creamed shortening, each about the size of a pea. and placed about an inch apart; lightly dust the dotted portion with fine flour, fold the undotted third over the floured surface, and fold the remaining third back over this, thus making three layers; with a quick pressure of the rolling-pin, close the loose edge; turn the board with an open end of the folded dough toward you, and in the same way close both these open ends in order to shut in the air between the layers; in like manner press the layers gently together in three or four places across the dough in the same direction to distribute the imprisoned air; now roll out lightly into another rectangle a quarter inch thick; dot, flour, fold, close, and roll out as before; repeat this operation until half of creamed shortening has been used, and bring to desired thickness and shape on the last rolling out.—The remaining half of plain dough may then be used for lower crust, or may be worked with the remaining half of creamed shortening as above.

For tarts, cup pastries, **or** little pies: The entire quantity may be handled at **one** operation.

Puff Pastry

Puff Pastry should be attempted only when materials may be kept under *cold* conditions, since its success depends very greatly upon an even, low temperature in handling. A little patience and practice will be required to master the art of making perfect puff pastes, but the time and patience required will be well rewarded.

1 cup butter   2 cups pastry flour   ½ teaspoon salt   Cold water

Place butter in cold water and work until it is smooth and pliable; if necessary, change water frequently to keep it as cold as possible; cool the hands in cold water before beginning. When sufficiently pliable, roll or press the butter into a square sheet about a quarter inch in thickness; wrap in a cold damp cloth and set aside until needed. It is important that, throughout the process, the butter be kept at a temperature to be pliable, yet firm.

From the flour, salt and sufficient cold water form a paste and knead to an elastic dough as in plain pastry—no shortening is used in the paste—and set aside for a few minutes in a cold place to bring it to the temperature of the butter.

Place dough on a floured board, and roll out into a rectangular sheet slightly more than twice in width and three times in length the size of the square of butter, and slightly less than half-inch in thickness.

Place the square of butter on one corner of the sheet of dough, leaving a slight margin of dough at the two corners, or outside edges; now fold the dough lengthwise into a double thickness, enclosing the butter in one end of the strip; press the long edges together with the rolling-pin, and, likewise, close the open edges at the butter end; now fold the third of the strip containing the butter back over the dough evenly, then fold the opposite end of the strip up over the butter section; this brings the dough to a square form, and of 6 layers, with the sheet of butter in the center.

Turn the dough-board so the pressed-together edge of the dough is nearest to you, and roll out the folded dough into another sheet of the same size and thickness as the first one on which the butter was placed—being careful to keep the edges of the folded dough even, and the butter in place.

Now, fold the sheet of dough in exactly the same manner as at first, forming six layers as before, keeping the edges even; turn as before, and roll again into a rectangular sheet. Repeat this folding, turning, rolling process at least six times, setting the dough in a cool place for about ten-minute periods between each rolling-out to restore the elasticity of the dough and the firmness of the butter. On last rolling out, bring to desired thickness and shape, ready for cutting out forms.

"Home Comfort" Special

1 Paste Pie Shell   1 tablespoon vinegar
1 cup gran. sugar   1 teaspoon cinnamon
1 cup buttermilk   1 teaspoon allspice
1 cup chopped raisins   2 egg yolks
1 tablespoon flour   Meringue

Soak seeded raisins a few minutes in hot water, drain, chop finely and measure; beat egg yolks to smoothness, add sugar, buttermilk, vinegar and spices; beat flour to smoothness in a little milk and add to mixture, beating until all ingredients are thoroughly blended; lastly, stir in the chopped raisins. Pour in paste shell and bake; cover with meringue made with the two egg whites and two tablespoons sugar, and brown in oven.

Apple Pie

1 Paste Double Crust   2 tablespoons flour
2 cups sliced apples   4 tablespoons butter
1 cup sugar   ½ teaspoon cinnamon
3 tablespoons water

Prepare bottom crust and fill with tart cooking apples sliced very thinly, and sprinkle sugar over them; add water; distribute butter in small lumps over surface; sprinkle with flour and then the cinnamon; adjust top crust paste, well perforated. Bake in moderate oven.—If preferred, top crust may be made of latticed strips of paste.

Apple Cream Pie

1 Paste Pie Shell   ¾ cup milk
1 cup grated apple   ½ teaspoon nutmeg
½ cup sugar   2 eggs, separated

Beat egg yolks, and slowly beat sugar into them; add milk, grated appel and nutmeg, mixing well; lastly, stir in well-beaten egg whites. Fill paste shell and bake for ten minutes in hot oven, reduce temperature to moderate and finish baking. Serve with or without sweetened whipped cream.

Apricot Pie

1 Paste Pie Shell	¾ cup bread crumbs
1 cup canned apricots	3 tablespoons sugar
½ cup apricot juice	2 egg yolks
1 cup rich milk	Meringue

Drain canned or cooked apricots, cut into slices and measure; scald the milk; prepare fine bread crumbs; to the beaten egg yolks, add sugar and apricot juice; when milk is half cooled, add and stir in the egg mixture; add and mix bread crumbs; add apricots and mix all together well. Pour mixture into prepared paste shell and bake about 45 minutes in a moderate oven; remove, cover with meringue made with the two egg whites and two tablespoons sugar, return to oven and brown top.

Banana Cream Pie

1 Baked Pie Shell	1 large banana
1 Cream Pie Filling	Meringue

Prepare Cream Pie Filling and place in Baked Shell; cover surface of filling with thin slices of banana; cover with meringue and brown.

Blueberry Meringue Pie

1 Paste Pie Shell	1 tablespoon lemon juice
⅔ cup sugar	¼ teaspoon salt
2 cups cooked blueberries	2 egg yolks
3 tablespoons flour	Meringue

Beat egg yolks and add cooked or canned blueberries and lemon juice; to the sugar add flour and salt and mix well; combine the two mixtures and blend them. Place in prepared deep pie shell, and bake in a moderate oven about thirty minutes; remove, spread with meringue made with the two egg whites beaten with two tablespoons sugar; return to oven for about fifteen minutes until backing is complete and meringue browned.

Buttermilk Pie

1 Paste Pie Shell	½ tablespoon butter
⅔ cup sugar	1 teaspoon lemon extract
1 cup buttermilk	2 egg yolks
1 tablespoon flour	Meringue

To beaten egg yolks, add buttermilk, sugar and butter; mix well; beat flour into a little sweet milk and add to mixture; add lemon flavoring; pour into prepared paste shell and bake as for Custard Pie; when baked, spread with meringue made of the two egg whites and two tablespoons sugar; return to oven and brown top; cool before serving.

Butterscotch Pie

1 Baked Pie Shell	3 tablespoons melted
1½ cups brown sugar	butter
1½ cups boiling water	¼ teaspoon salt
¼ cup cornstarch	¾ teaspoon vanilla
¼ cup cold water	3 egg yolks
2 tablespoons gran. sugar	Meringue

Carmelize the granulated sugar; add brown sugar and boiling water and cook for about five minutes; beat cornstarch into the cold water and add to mixture; add salt; continue cooking and stirring until mixture thickens; then add butter, cool slightly, and add beaten egg yolks and vanilla. Pour into baked pie shell, cover with meringue made with the three egg whites and three tablespoons sugar; brown top in oven.

Butter Meringue Pie

1 Paste Pie Shell	2 tablespoons flour
¾ cup sugar	½ teaspoon vanilla
¼ cup butter	2 eggs, separated
½ cup rich milk	Meringue

Cream butter and sugar, add flour beaten into a little of the milk; add remaining milk and lightly beaten egg yolks, mix thoroughly and add flavoring. Pour into prepared paste shell, set in hot oven to quickly bake crust, reduce heat to moderate and cook until filling is custard-like; remove, cover with meringue made with the egg whites and two tablespoons sugar; return to oven and brown top; serve cool.

Chess Pie

1 Paste Pie Shell	1 tablespoon corn-meal
1 cup gran. sugar	½ teaspoon lemon extract
¼ cup butter	2 egg yolks
½ cup sweet cream	Meringue

Lightly beat egg yolks to smoothness; cream sugar with butter, and add to yolks; mix corn-meal into cream and add to mixture; add flavoring and stir to smoothness. Pour into paste shell and bake in a moderate oven; remove, add meringue of two egg whites and two tablespoons sugar; return to oven and brown top.

Chocolate Pie

1 Baked Pie Shell	1½ cups milk
1½ oz. chocolate	2 teaspoons butter
(1½ sq.)	1 teaspoon vanilla
½ cup sugar	2 egg yolks
¼ cup cornstarch	Meringue

Shave and melt chocolate; add cornstarch beaten into a little of the milk, sugar, remaining milk, and mix; add lightly beaten egg yolks and butter; place in double boiler and cook until thick, constantly stirring. Pour into baked crust and cover with meringue made from the two egg whites stiffly beaten with two tablespoons granulated sugar. Brown top in oven and serve cold.—Three or four tablespoons cocoa may be substituted for chocolate if necessary. If a richer chocolate flavor is desired and more is added, more milk should also be used.

Chocolate Cream Pie

1 Baked Pie Shell	2 tablespoons chocolate
1 Cream Pie Filling	Meringue

Follow Cream Pie Recipe and stir in the melted chocolate as soon as the mixed ingredients have become warm.

Cocoanut Butterscotch Pie

1 Baked Pie Shell	1 cup grated cocoanut
1 Butterscotch Filling	Meringue

Prepare as for Butterscotch Pie, thoroughly stirring in cocoanut after adding egg yolks. Sprinkle meringue with shredded cocoanut if desired.

Cocoanut Cream Pie

1 Baked Pie Shell   ¾ cup shredded cocoanut
1 Cream Pie Filling   Meringue

Follow recipe for Cream Pie, adding ½ cup finely shredded cocoanut to filling while cooking; bake as for Cream Pie, spread meringue and sprinkle top with the remaining cocoanut and brown in oven.

Cocoanut Custard Pie

1 Paste Pie Shell   1 cup grated cocoanut
1 Custard Filling

Follow Custard Pie Recipe, adding the cocoanut after the milk has been stirred in, and leaving out one of the eggs.

Cranberry Raisin Pie

1 Paste Double Crust   1 cup seedless raisins
1 cup sugar   3 tablespoons flour
2 cups cranberries

Select, wash and measure perfect cranberries; mix sugar, flour and salt with raisins; add and mix cranberries; fill prepared lower crust and adjust top crust. Set into hot oven for about ten minutes, reduce heat to moderate and bake a half hour longer.—Two tablespoons cornstarch may be substituted for flour.

Cream Pie

1 Baked Pie Shell   1½ tablespoons flour
⅔ cup gran. sugar   1 teaspoon vanilla
1 cup sweet milk   2 egg yolks
1 tablespoon butter   Meringue

Beat egg yolks lightly and stir in sugar; add milk and butter; beat flour into ¼ cup milk or water to smoothness, and stir into mixture; place in a double boiler and cook over hot water until quite thick. Pour into baked shell; cover with meringue made from the two egg whites stiffly beaten, into which beat two tablespoons sugar; place in oven and allow top of meringue to become a delicate brown.

Custard Pie

1 Paste Pie Shell   ½ teaspoon salt
3 eggs   1 teaspoon vanilla
¾ cup sugar   ½ teaspoon nutmeg
2 cups rich milk

Beat eggs, add sugar and salt, and beat again; scald milk and add slowly, stirring thoroughly; add vanilla at last; pour into deep pastry shell and place in a moderately hot oven, lowering the temperature to moderate after a few minutes so as not to allow the custard to overcook. When a knife stuck into the center comes out dry, baking is completed. Sprinkle with nutmeg and cool before serving.—If a thicker pie is desired, prepare a deeper shell and add another egg and a half-cup milk to recipe.

Date Cream Pie

1 Baked Pie Shell   1 cup chopped dates
1 Cream Pie Filling   Meringue

Follow recipe for Cream Pie, adding the seeded and coarsely chopped dates to the cream mixture two minutes before removing from the double boiler; bake as for Cream Pie.—Top may be sprinkled with shredded cocoanut if desired, making a Cocoanut-Date Cream Pie. Raisins may also be substituted for dates.

Dried Peach Pie

1 Paste Double Crust   1½ cups water
¾ cup gran. sugar   1 tablespoon butter
2 cups dried peaches

Soak dried peaches in water for several hours, or over-night, and cook slowly without sugar until tender; dredge prepared paste lower crust with flour, put in layer of peaches, sprinkle generously with sugar; alternate peaches and sugar until crust is filled; distribute butter over top layer; adjust top crust and join around rim with moistened edges; dredge top lightly with flour and bake in moderate oven until well browned.—Latticed strips of pastry may be substituted for top crust.

Dried Peach Cream Pie

1 Paste Pie Shell   2 tablespoons lemon juice
½ cup gran. sugar   1 teaspoon vanilla
1 cup rich milk   2 egg yolks
1½ cups dried peach pulp   Meringue
2 tablespoons flour

Strain and measure pulp of stewed dried peaches; mix flour into milk and cream, put into double boiler and cook until thick; beat egg yolks, beat in sugar, and add peach pulp, lemon juice and flavoring; pour this last mixture slowly into cream and cook about five minutes. Pour into paste shell and bake; remove from oven, spread with meringue made with the two egg whites and two tablespoons sugar; return to oven and brown lightly.

Dried Apricot Pie

Follow either of the Dried Peach Pie Recipes, using dried apricots and increasing the quantity of sugar to balance the flavor.

Fig Meringue Pie

1 Baked Pie Shell   ⅛ teaspoon salt
1½ cups chopped figs   2 egg yolks
1½ cups boiling water   Meringue
2 tablespoons sugar

Bring water to boiling point and add figs finely chopped, and let cook about 30 minutes until tender; beat egg yolks and beat in sugar and salt, then mix with figs and allow to cook a little longer until eggs are set while constantly stirring. Turn into baked shell and spread with meringue made with the two egg whites and two to four tablespoons sugar beaten into them. Cook in slow oven about 20 minutes.

Fresh Berry Pies

Select and wash a pie pan full of ripe, fresh berries; mix sugar to sweeten, and cornstarch or flour to thicken; fill lower crust and adjust top crust; bake ten minutes in hot oven, reduce the heat to moderate, and cook about thirty minutes longer, or until done.—For blackberries, raspberries, blueberries, or loganberries, use ¾ cup sugar and 1 tablespoon cornstarch or two tablespoons flour for each pie. For cherries, gooseberries, cranberries, or currants, use twice the above quantities.

Grape Pie

1 Paste Double Crust	2 tablespoons flour
1 cup seeded grapes	1 tablespoon butter
1 cup sugar	1 egg

Seed grapes by pressing pulp from skins, placing each in separate containers; press pulps through a colander to remove seeds; then combine pulp and skins and measure. Beat egg and gradually beat sugar into it; add butter and flour and stir well together; add grapes and mix well. Prepare and fill deep lower crust, adjust top crust paste and bake in moderate oven.

Lemon Cream Pie

1 Baked Pie Shell	1 medium lemon, juice
1 cup gran. sugar	2 egg yolks
1½ cups boiling water	Meringue
5 tablespoons flour	

Measure sifted flour, add sugar and resift to mix; add egg yolks and mix; add lemon juice and mix; add some of the grated lemon rind to juice if desired; add boiling water and cook in a double boiler, stirring constantly until sugar is dissolved and mixture is smooth and desired thickness; pour into baked crust, cover with meringue made with the two egg whites stiffly beaten with two tablespoons sugar beaten into them; set in oven and brown.

New England Date Pie

1 Paste Pie Shell	½ teaspoon salt
¾ cup sugar	¼ teaspoon nutmeg
1 cup sour cream	1 teaspoon cinnamon
1 cup chopped dates	½ teaspoon mixed spices
½ cup shredded cocoanut	2 eggs
1 tablespoon bread crumbs	

Beat eggs to smoothness, and add sugar, sour cream, crumbs, salt and spices, mixing thoroughly; stir in the coarsely chopped dates; pour in paste shell and sprinkle top with the cocoanut; bake in a hot oven for ten minutes, reduce the oven heat to moderate for about thirty minutes longer, or until well baked.

Orange Pie

1 Baked Pie Shell	1 tablespoon lemon juice
1 cup sugar	2 tablespoons butter
⅓ cup flour	¼ teaspoon salt
1 cup orange juice	3 egg yolks
1 grated orange rind	Meringue

To sugar, flour, salt and grated orange rind, add the orange and lemon juices and cook in double boiler until thickened to suit; two minutes before removing, add lightly beaten egg yolks and butter and mix to smoothness. Pour into baked deep pie shell, cover with meringue made with the egg whites and three tablespoons sugar and brown top in moderate oven.

Peach Cream Pie

1 Paste Pie Shell	2 tablespoons flour
1 cup canned peaches	½ teaspoon nutmeg
1 cup thin cream	Whipped Cream
2 tablespoons sugar	

Drain canned peaches, or fresh peaches cooked as for canning, slice, and measure; combine sugar and flour, and beat them well with the cream slowly added; arrange slices to thickly cover and practically fill the prepared paste pie shell, pour over this the cream mixture, sprinkle with finely grated nutmeg, and bake in quick oven about 20 to 25 minutes. Serve warm with whipped cream.

Pear Cream Pie

1 Baked Pie Shell	3 tablespoons flour
2 cups canned pears	¼ teaspoon cloves
1 cup pear juice	Whipped Cream
2½ teaspoons sugar	

Drain canned pears, or fresh pears cooked as for canning, and lay thickly into baked pie shell. Combine sugar, flour, cloves and pear juice in a pan, by cooking three or four minutes to produce a fairly thick sauce; pour sauce over layer of pears; serve with whipped cream.—If preferred, may be covered with meringue and browned in oven, instead of whipped cream.

Pineapple Cream Pie

1 Baked Pie Shell	2 tablespoons cornstarch
½ cup gran. sugar	⅛ teaspoon salt
1½ cups milk	½ teaspoon vanilla
1 cup grated pineapple	2 egg yolks
1 tablespoon butter	Meringue

Mix sugar, salt and corn-starch; bring milk to boiling point, remove and add slowly, mixing with dry ingredients; place in top of double boiler and cook until thick and corn-starch is thoroughly cooked—about 40 minutes. Beat egg yolks to smoothness, pour on the cooked mixture and mix; return to double boiler and cook about 3 minutes to thicken the egg yolks; cool and add well drained crushed or grated pineapple; add vanilla. Pour into baked shell, cover with meringue made with two egg whites and two tablespoons sugar; brown quickly in oven.—Four tablespoons flour may be substituted for two tablespoons corn-starch.

Pineapple Cocoanut Pie

1 Baked Pie Shall	½ cup shredded cocoanut
1 Pineapple Pie Filling	Meringue

, Prepare Pineapple Pie Filling, adding shredded cocoanut at time of adding pineapple.

Plum Cream Pie

1 Baked Pie Shell	1 cup seeded raisins
1½ cups canned plums	Whipped Cream
¾ cup fruit jam	

Drain plums, remove stones, and measure; steam raisins until full and tender, then allow to cool; mix raisins and fruit jam, which may be grape, plum, fig, or peach; spread raisin and jam mixture into baked shell, and fill with the plums; bake in slow oven for about ten minutes to drive out excess moisture. Serve with whipped cream on top.—Meringue may be used instead if desired.

Prune Pie

1 Paste Pie Shell	½ lemon, rind and juice
1 cup gran. sugar	1 egg
2 cups stewed prunes	Meringue
1 tablespoon butter	

Remove seeds from unsweetened stewed prunes, and measure; add beaten egg yolks, sugar, and butter; grate lemon rind, add the juice and stir into the mixture; mix all ingredients well, spread into paste shell and bake in a moderate oven; remove, cover with meringue of two egg whites and two tablespoons sugar, return to oven and brown.

Pumpkin Pie

1 Paste Pie Shell	1 tablespoon butter
1 cup cooked pumpkin	¼ teaspoon cinnamon
¾ cup sugar	¼ teaspoon allspice
½ cup rich milk	2 eggs

Cook and strain pumpkin; using the measure of fine pulp; place in a bowl and thin with half the milk; mix in lightly beaten eggs and melted butter; mix spices with sugar and thoroughly stir these into the mixture; add enough of the remaining half of the milk to reduce to batter-like mixture; pour into prepared paste shell and set into hot oven for about fifteen minutes, or until shell has baked, then reduce heat to moderate and bake for about 45 minutes longer, or until filling has cooked and browned.—A tablespoon of corn-syrup added with the sugar gives the filling a little more firmness, and is an improvement when the pie is used for school lunches.

Pumpkin Meringue Pie

1 Paste Pie Shell	Meringue
1 Pumpkin Pie Filling	

Prepare filling as for Pumpkin Pie, except: separate eggs, using yolks only, and add a little more milk if necessary to properly thin mixture; allow pie to bake but not to brown on top; remove from oven, spread with meringue made with the two egg whites and two tablespoons sugar; return to oven and brown top of meringue.—If preferred, makes as for Pumpkin Pie, using additional egg whites for meringue.

Rhubarb Pie

1 Paste Double Crust	1 tablespoon flour
2 cups fresh rhubarb	¼ teaspoon salt

Trim and peel fresh rhubarb stems, cut into small pieces and measure; put rhubarb into deep paste lower crust, cover with sugar, flour or corn starch, and salt; adjust top crust; bake in hot oven about thirty minutes.

Raisin Pie

1 Paste Double Crust	3 tablespoons flour
1¼ cups seeded raisins	¼ teaspoon salt
1¼ cups boiling water	½ lemon, rind and juice
½ cup sugar	1 egg

Cook raisins in the boiling water until tender, replenishing water as it boils away; mix sugar, salt and flour, gradually stir in with raisins, boiling and stirring until thick; add lemon juice and grated rind; lightly beat egg and stir in just before removing. Pour into prepared lower crust, dredged with a little flour, dampen around edge and adjust top crust; bake in moderate oven.—Two tablespoons corn-starch may be substituted for flour.

Rich Fig Pie

1 Paste Double Crust	½ lemon, juice and rind
1½ cups chopped figs	1 teaspoon butter
1 cup gran. sugar	

Steam sun-dried figs in a colander for about 15 minutes until soft; chop very finely or grind in a meat chopper. Add sugar, lemon juice and grated lemon rind; add water to sufficiently moisten and cook slowly until clear and jelly-like—keep sufficiently moistened to prevent scorching. Turn into prepared bottom crust, adjust perforated top crust or latticed strips of pastry as preferred; bake in moderately hot oven.

Southern Molasses Pie

1 Paste Pie Shell	½ tablespoon butter
1 cup New Orleans molasses	¼ teaspoon salt
	2 eggs

Boil molasses and butter a few minutes; break eggs into a bowl, add salt, and beat until well mixed; pour molasses over eggs and stir very briskly. Pour into paste shell and bake. Top with meringue if desired.

Squash Pie

1 Paste Pie Shell	½ teaspoon nutmeg
1 cup cooked squash	½ teaspoon ginger
¾ cup gran. sugar	½ teaspoon flavoring
2 cups milk	2 eggs
½ teaspoon salt	

Beat eggs and add milk and sugar; mash and strain cooked squash and add salt and spices; mix together the two mixtures, blending well. Fill deep pie shell and bake in a moderate oven.

Sunkist Lemon Pie

1 Baked Pie Shell	½ tablespoon butter
1 cup gran. sugar	⅛ teaspoon salt
3 tablespoons flour	1 lemon, juice and rind
4 tablespoons cornstarch	3 egg yolks
1½ cups boiling water	Meringue

Mix sugar, flour, corn-starch and salt in top of double boiler; add boiling water slowly and stir; cook on range-top until boiling point is reached; assemble the double boiler and allow to cook over hot water for 20 minutes, occasionally stirring; mix grated lemon rind and juice with egg yolks beaten to smoothness, and add to mixture in double boiler; add butter, stir, and cook about 2 minutes. Cool and spread into baked shell; cover with meringue made with the three egg whites and three tablespoons sugar; bake six or eight minutes in a moderate oven.

Sweet Potato Custard Pie

1 Paste Pie Shell	1 cup sweet milk
½ cup sugar	½ teaspoon nutmeg
½ cup mashed sweet potatoes	2 eggs

Boil and finely mash the potatoes and measure; add sugar, lightly beaten eggs, and milk; beat to a smooth mixture; pour into paste shell and bake as for Custard Pie, sprinkle top with nutmeg; serve after cooling.—Egg whites may be left out and used in meringue if desired.

Tarts and Tartlets

Tarts, proper, are a conversion of ordinary pies, the difference being that tarts are much richer, consequently the portions served are smaller. Either plain or flake pastry is used for most tarts, a small round, or square, shallow baking tin being lined with crust and baked as for pies.

Tartlets are small or individual tarts, and are often served under the name of French Pastry. They are of puff paste in various plain and fancy forms, baked and filled with a rich filling, and decorated according to taste.

Fillings for tarts and tartlets may be of any thick, rich jams, preserves, jellies, marmalades, conserves, or similar preparation of fruits.

Tartlets should be cut with a knife or cutter dipped in cold water; the edges will thus be greatly improved in the baking.

New England Tart

Prepare and bake a crust of plain or flake paste as for pie. Use 2 cups cold dry apple-sauce, or fresh apple-sauce cooked with as little water as possible; press through a sieve before measuring; add 2 cups cream, 3 beaten egg yolks, and mix, adding ½ teaspoon each of nutmeg and salt; add 1 cup sugar, more or less, to properly sweeten; spread in paste shell, and bake filling in moderate oven; when partially cooled, cover with meringue made of the 3 egg whites and granulated sugar, and brown top in oven. Filling may also be used in tartlet shells, made from the left over paste.

Marlborough Tart

Line a deep pie pan or dish with plain or flake pastry; to 2 well beaten eggs, add 2 cups grated apple; mix; add ½ lemon, juice and grated rind, and 1 cup granulated sugar; mix; add 1 cup seeded raisins and 2 tablespoons melted butter; mix well and turn into the pastry; cover top with strips of pastry arranged lattice fashion, then finish with a strip of pastry around the rim; put in hot oven, reduce heat to moderate after fifteen minutes, and bake until crust is baked and center of tart is firm. May be made in individual sizes in muffin tin if preferred.

Plain Tartlets

Prepare plain or flake pastry, roll out to about ¼ inch thickness, cut out in biscuit rounds or in squares the size of a cracker, puncture with prongs of a fork, place on slightly greased baking sheet or tin; bake in oven as for pie crust. Spread with any desired filling or icing.

Or: Cut out in 3 or 4 inch squares, fold each of the four corners over the center, moistening corners to cause them to stay in place; bake.

Banbury Tartlets

Prepare flake pastry, roll out to ¼ inch thickness or slightly more; cut in 4 inch squares, place a spoonful filling in center of each square, fold over in triangular shape, moisten edges with cold water and press edges firmly together; bake in hot oven.—Closed Shell.

French Tartlets

Prepare puff pastry; line tartlets or muffin tins with pastry, and bake in hot oven, as for Quick Pattie Shells. Other small baking pans of oval or other fancy shapes may also be used to good effect. Regular Pattie Shells—see recipe—are also widely used for fancy tartlets.—Open Shell.

Special Tartlet Fillings

Raisins—Cook 1½ cups seeded raisins in an equal measure of boiling water until plump and tender; mix 1 tablespoon flour with ½ cup sugar, and add to raisins; continue cooking and stirring until thick; remove from fire, add ½ lemon juice and grated rind, and 1 tablespoon butter; cool and fill open tartlet shells.

Cheese—Mix until smooth, 1 cup cottage cheese and ½ cup sugar; add 2 beaten eggs, ½ cup milk, 1 lemon, juice and grated rind, 1 tablespoon butter, and 1 cup seeded raisins; cook until of jam-like thickness; remove from fire, cool, and fill open tartlet shells.

Raisin-Nut—Cream 5 tablespoons butter and ½ cup sugar; add 1 egg and beat all together well, then add second egg, beating thoroughly also; add 1 cup seeded raisins, ½ cup chopped nuts and ½ teaspoon vanilla; pour into pastry lined tartlet pans, bake in hot oven five minutes, then reduce heat to moderate until firm in center.

Sliced Peach—Slice firm canned peaches, and cut into fine strips of short length; drain, and distribute into 8 to 12 pastry lined tartlet tins; cream ¼ cup butter with ¼ cup sugar, add 1 beaten egg, 1 tablespoon peach juice, and ½ cup flour sifted with ¼ teaspoon baking powder; add grated lemon rind or extract to flavor; beat well and pour over peaches in prepared shells; bake in moderate oven 15 to 20 minutes, sprinkle with sugar; cool.

Pineapple—Mix 6 tablespoons powdered sugar with each cup well drained and finely grated pineapple; fill baked pattie or tartlet shells; top with a bit of meringue if desired. Other cooked or canned fruits may be prepared in the same way by regulating the amount of sugar to taste. Try dry applesauce.

Fruit-Cocoanut — Prepare pastry lined tartlet tins; put in each, a half canned peach, apricot, or a tablespoon of jam or conserve; mix 1 cup shredded cocoanut, ½ cup sugar, ¼ cup milk, 1 beaten egg, 1 tablespoon melted butter, and ¼ teaspoon salt; beat to a smooth paste, and fill shells; bake in hot oven about twenty minutes.

Fig-Nut — Chop dried figs into small pieces and measure 1 cup; barely cover with water, add ½ teaspoon maple or other flavoring; and cook gently for 25 to 30 minutes; add 1 tablespoon sugar and cook 5 to 10 minutes longer, remove from fire and allow to cool; when cooled, add ½ cup chopped nut meats, 1 teaspoon lemon juice, and the yolks of 2 eggs, mixing well; pour into pastry lined tartlet tins and bake in hot oven; cover each with a meringue made of the 2 egg whites and 2 tablespoons sugar; brown in oven; cool.

Peach Souffle—Wash, soak and cook dried peaches until nearly all the water has evaporated, then mash and rub through a coarse strainer; to each cup peach pulp, mix ¼ cup sugar, heat to boiling point, and slowly poud over 1 well-beaten egg white and beat well together; fill baked tartlet shells, top with whipped cream; serve.

Any preserves, marmalade, jelly, conserve or jam makes rich tartlet fillings, and when served with fresh whipped cream, makes one of the richest of desserts. They may be used with equal success in any form of tartlet pastry.

Cream Puffs

| 1 cup flour | 1 cup hot water |
| ½ cup butter | 3 eggs |

Melt the butter in the hot water; while boiling, beat in the flour; remove from range and stir in the eggs, one at a time, without beating; drop on slightly buttered tins quickly and bake in the oven handling very carefully. For Filling:

1 cup milk	3 tablespoons Sugar
1 egg	Vanilla to flavor.
2 tablespoons flour	

Mix sugar and flour, add slightly beaten egg and stir into this gradually the scalded milk. Cook about 15 minutes in a double boiler, stirring constantly until thickened; cool slightly and flavor.

Open a side of each puff with the point of a table knife, and fill with the cream.

Chocolate Eclairs

Prepare paste as for Cream Puff; drop on buttered tins in strips one by five inches and bake; slit and fill with Cream Filling as for Puffs, or whipped cream; cover top with Chocolate Icing.

Patty Shells

Prepare Puff Paste and leave about a half-inch in thickness on last rolling-out. With a small round biscuit cutter, cut out an even number of rounds, dipping the cutter in hot water each time before cutting. From half of these, cut a one-inch round out of the center leaving them in the form of rings, as for doughnuts. With a broad knife, or spatula, carefully set the rounds onto a paper lined tin, moisten their edges with cold water, and set the rings in place on top the rounds. Set tin in a cold place—on ice if possible—and let chill for about twenty or thirty minutes. Set into hot oven and allow shells to rise to their full height, reduce the heat to moderate, and bake about twenty to twenty-five minutes, or until they just begin to brown; protect with paper if necessary to prevent browning before baking is complete. —Using a cutter with fluted edge makes patties a little more ornamental.

Quick Patty Shells

Prepare Plain or Flake Pastry; roll out to thickness of pie crust. Cut out rounds of ample size, and form on the outside of muffin, or similar, pans. Bake in a hot oven on inverted pans, until lightly browned; remove carefully from tins, set upright on a baking tin, and return to the oven for about 5 minutes to complete baking, and brown inside.

Desserts and Frozen Ices

Cornstarch Blanc Mange

4 cups milk   1 teaspoon vanilla
1 cup sugar   4 eggs
½ cup cornstarch Whipped cream
½ teaspoon salt

Mix sugar, corn-starch and salt; stir them into a smooth paste with a half-cup of the milk; pour the remaining milk into a double boiler, and bring to boiling point; add starch-paste to hot milk, constantly stirring; add slightly beaten eggs, and cook, while stirring, until rather thick; remove from range, add vanilla; pour into cold, wet molds or cups, and cool; turn out on dessert plates and serve with whipped cream, or vanilla sauce.—Any or all of the eggs may be omitted if necessary, but it is much richer and better with them; or, for purely white blanc mange, whites alone may be used.

Chocolate Blanc Mange

To Corn-Starch Blanc Mange, add:

2 oz. chocolate (2 sqs.)
Whipped Cream

Prepare Corn-Starch Blanc Mange by recipe; shave chocolate into boiler at time of adding other ingredients to hot milk; cook; add eggs and vanilla; mold and cool; serve with whipped cream.

Cherry Blanc Mange

To Corn-Starch Blanc Mange, add:

2 cups cherries   Whipped Cream
½ cup water

Prepare Corn-Starch Blanc Mange by recipe except: take out a quarter-cup of the sugar, and add this to cherries and water after cherries have been stewed until tender; boil a few minutes longer, and drain cherries; place a few cherries in bottom of wet molds and fill about one-third with blanc mange; dust cherries with corn-starch, and add a layer to each mold, then fill with blanc mange, and cool; turn into dessert dishes, and serve with the cherry syrup, which may be slightly thickened with a little corn-starch; top with whipped cream.—Canned, or preserved, cherries may also be used. Berries may be substituted for cherries if desired, and may be used either fresh or cooked. Rich cream, sweetened and flavored, may be substituted for whipped cream.

Fruit Blanc Mange

Cooked dried fruit   Favorite sauce

To Corn-Starch Blanc Mange, add:

Prepare Corn-Starch Blanc Mange by recipe; fruit may be fresh or dried peaches, pears, apricots, figs, prunes, or other fruit; stew fruit until tender and sweeten to taste; take fruit from syrup, dry the surface of each piece and place a few pieces in each mold, which has been first dipped in cold water; pour blanc mange over fruit to cover; cool, turn into dessert dishes or glasses; serve with slightly thickened syrup of the fruit, or other favorite sauce.

Canned fruit may be used in the same way. Canned pineapple is excellent; ripe oranges and bananas also may be used without cooking.

Strawberry Bavarian Cream

1½ cups heavy cream   ¼ cup cold water
½ cup gran. sugar   1 tablespoon gelatine
1 cup strawberries   1 tablespoon lemon juice

Reduce strawberries to pulpy juice, and measure; whip cream until stiff; soak gelatine in cold water for few minutes, then set cup in hot water and warm until gelatine is completely dissolved; strain into berry juice and pulp, to which lemon juice has been added; stir in sugar and when it has dissolved, set bowl into pan of cold water, and stir until mixture begins to thicken; add and fold-in whipped cream; turn into mold, which has first been dipped in cold water; chill.—Mold may be lined with fresh strawberry halves before pouring; may be further garnished with whole berries arranged around plate with clean berry leaves; a few berries on top add to appearance. Canned berries of any variety my be used instead of the fresh strawberries, the cream taking name from the berry used.—Granulated Gelatine may be had at grocers.

Charlotte Russe

1 doz. Lady Fingers   1 tablespoon sugar
1 cup cream, whipped ¼ cup cherries

Prepare and bake Lady Fingers by recipe given under "Small Cakes." When cool and crisp, split each Lady Finger lengthwise, and line dessert glasses with a few sections, standing them on end around the glass. Whip cream to stiffness and beat in sugar to sweeten; fill cake lined glasses with whipped cream, and place a nice canned or preserved cherry on top.—As sold at bakeries, powdered sugar is used, and they are made in special paper cups.

Chocolate Charlotte—To Plain Charlotte Russe cream, add melted chocolate, or cocoa, to taste and color. Top with white cream.

Mocha Charlotte—Flavor plain Charlotte Russe with one tablespoon strong liquid coffee; three-fourths cup seedless raisins may also be added to cream if desired.

Maple Charlotte—Flavor plain Charlotte Russe with maple flavoring to suit taste; black walnut meats improve the taste.

Bavarian Charlotte—Prepare cream as for Bavarian Cream and mold in cake-lined glasses; strips or crisp left-over sponge cake may be used instead of Lady Fingers if desired·

Fruit Charlotte — Crushed berries or other fruit may be mixed with the whipped cream to give desired color and taste.

Cream Charlotte—Prepare cream as for Cream Pie; fill cake-lined glasses as for Charlotte Russe. Sliced bananas may also be used for Banana Cream Pie.

Marshmallow Charlotte—Fill cake-lined glasses with Marshmallow Whip, recipe for which will be found in this section.

Snowdrift

1 cup sugar	¼ teaspoon salt
2 cups water	1 lemon—juice
3 tablespoons cornstarch	3 eggs, separated

Bring sugar and water to the boiling point; add corn-starch, salt and lemon-juice; boil ten minutes. Remove from range and add stiffly beaten egg whites, by spoonfuls, constantly beating. Pour into wet molds, and cool· When cooled, turn into sherbet glasses, and serve with whipped cream, or with custard sauce made from the egg yolks.

Marshmallow Whip

2 doz. marshmallows	1 cup cream, whipped
2 cups fruit juice	1 tablespoon sugar

With a sharp, dampened knife, cut marshmallows into quarters or eights, place them in a bowl, and cover with fruit juice, which may be cherry, berry, grape, or any other juice; let stand until marshmallows have absorbed as much of the juice as desired; whip cream until stiff and whip in sugar to sweeten to taste; mix marshmallows and whipped cream; serve in sherbet glasses with a cherry or berry on top.

Date Souffle

2 cups chopped dates	1 tablespoon flour
½ cup gran. sugar	1 teaspoon baking powd.
1 cup nut meats	2 eggs
1 tablespoon milk	Whipped Cream

Wipe one pound dates with wet cloth, remove seeds, chop finely and measure. Beat eggs until light, add sugar and milk; mix flour and baking powder, and add to mixture; add chopped nut meats and dates, mixing into smooth batter. Pour in greased shallow square cake tin and bake in moderate oven as for cake. Cool, cut into six or eight squares; serve with sweetened whipped cream or vanilla sauce.

Mrs. McGee's Date Loaf

3 cups sugar	1 cup nut meats
1 cup milk	Lump of butter
1 pkg. dates	Vanilla

Mix milk and sugar in saucepan; remove seeds from dates, add to mixture and boil slowly to a soft ball stage. Remove from fire, add butter and beat until cool, add flavoring and nuts. Wring a cloth out of cold water, pour mixture on one side and roll. Slice when cold.

Peach Meringue

3 egg whites	1 teaspoon vinegar
1 cup sugar	Sliced peaches
1 teaspoon vanilla	

Beat the egg whites stiff and dry; add sugar gradually and beat in well; add vanilla, then the vinegar, and beat in. Bake in two 8 or 9 inch shallow, well buttered tins, in a moderate oven until crisp. Fill between layers and cover top with finely stripped, or thinly sliced, peaches—fresh or canned—and top whole with whipped cream

Angel Shortcake

Angel Food Cake   Sweet Whipped Cream

Serve slices of Angel Food Cake on pie-plates; pile stiffly whipped cream, sweetened to taste, on each piece; decorate with a cherry if desired, and garnish with two or three cherry leaves.

Boston Cream Pie

¾ cup sugar	1½ teaspoons baking
1 cup flour	powder
½ cup boiling milk	⅛ teaspoon salt
2 eggs	½ teaspoon vanilla

Sift and measure flour, add baking powder, sugar and salt, and re-sift together three or four times; beat egg yolks to lemon colored cream, beat egg whites stiff, then mix the yolks into the whites; gradually fold the flour mixture into the eggs; add hot milk very slowly, constantly mixing; add vanilla. Bake in a deep layer cake pan in a moderate oven about 35 minutes. When cool, split the layer with a long knife, and put together with stiff Cream Filling—see Icings. Serve cold. Sufficient for six or eight persons

Washington Cream Pie

Prepare and bake cake as for Boston Cream Pie above Put together with Chocolate Cream Filling—see Icings.

Panama Cream Pie

Prepare and bake cake and cook filling as for Boston Cream Pie. Spread bottom layer with bananas thinly sliced in cross-section, and spread with filling; place on the top layer, and dust with powdered sugar.

Fruit Shortcakes

While strawberries are the most popular fruit for shortcakes, many other fresh fruits such as blackberries, raspberries, loganberries, peaches, oranges and bananas, as well as stewed and canned fruit, and even stewed rhubarb, make most delicious shortcakes.

Pastry Shortcake

Either thinly rolled plain pastry or more thickly rolled flake pastry make delicious old-fashioned shortcake; roll out pastry and cut out large rounds about 3 or 4 inches across; allow two for each individual served; bake as for tartlets in hot oven and keep fresh and dry in warming-closet; have fruit prepared and put the shortcakes together just before serving; whipped cream on top makes a nice addition.

Biscuit Shortcake

Make dough as for biscuits, adding a little more shortening to the biscuit recipe; a little sugar may also be added if desired. Cut out in large rounds and bake in pan so separated that they do not touch; split and lightly butter each and put together the individual shortcake with the two halves.

Rich Shortcake

Prepare and bake cake as for Boston Cream Pie; when cool enough, split cake horizontally with a long knife, butter sections, and put together with crushed and sweetened fruit in the usual way; whipped cream may be added between layers and on top as desired; decorate top with designs made of the whole fruit.

Cottage Pudding

½ cup sugar	⅛ teaspoon salt
½ cup milk	2 teaspoons butter
1 cup flour	1 egg
2 teaspoons baking powd.	

Sift and measure flour, add sugar, baking powder and salt, and re-sift to mix; add beaten egg, milk and melted butter; beat well to smooth batter; pour in greased shallow pan and bake about 20 minutes in hot oven. Serve with choice of sauce.

Cabinet Pudding

½ cup sugar	1 teaspoon nutmeg
1½ cups milk, scalded	2 eggs
1 cup seeded raisins	Left-over Cake
1 teaspoon vanilla	

Cut dry cake into slices, then into three or four inch strips; in a buttered baking dish, place a layer of cake strips, then a layer of raisins, another each of cake and raisins, and a cake layer on top. To the beaten eggs, add sugar, hot milk and vanilla in the order named and mix well; pour this over cake and raisins, sprinkle with the nutmeg. Place dish in a pan of hot water, and bake in a moderate oven until firm in center. Serve with vanilla, orange or other sauce.

Royal Bread Pudding

2 cups bread crumbs	1 tablespoon lemon juice
4 cups milk	4 eggs separated
1 cup sugar	Jelly or preserves
2 tablespoons butter	

Cream butter and sugar, and add beaten egg yolks; add milk, bread crumbs, and lemon juice; mix well, pour into a greased baking pan, and bake in moderate oven. Spread top with jelly or preserves, and cover with stiffly beaten egg whites, sweetened and flavored to taste, while arranging in dessert dishes.

Orange Bread Pudding

Prepare Royal Bread Pudding using grated rinds and juice of four oranges, instead of jelly or preserves; add rind and juice with lemon juice in the recipe. Cover with Orange Foam Sauce and brown as for meringue.

Cocoanut Bread Pudding

Prepare as for Orange Bread Pudding, adding one cup shredded cocoanut to mixture before baking; sprinkle meringue with cocoanut and brown.

Rice Pudding

½ cup rice	3 tablespoons sugar
3 cups water	¾ teaspoon salt
2 cups rich milk	3 teaspoons butter

Wash rice quickly in one or two waters and drain; mix ingredients except butter, and pour into a well buttered baking pan or dish; bake two and one half hours in a very slow oven; stir every fifteen minutes for first hour to prevent rice from settling, adding the butter at time of last stirring. Serve with sweet cream, flavored as desired, or with nutmeg.

Pineapple Rice Pudding

1 Rice Pudding Mixture   ½ cup seedless raisins
3 cups crushed pineapple   ¼ cup sugar, additional

Prepare Rice Pudding mixture, using the additional quarter-cup sugar; add well drained, crushed pineapple and raisins just before pouring into baking pan; proceed as directed in Rice Pudding recipe. Serve hot with hard sauce.—Other crushed fruits may be substituted for pineapple.

Raisin Rice Pudding

1 Rice Pudding Mixture 2½ cups seedless raisins

Prepare Rice Pudding mixture, and add raisins just before pouring into baking pan; proceed as directed in Rice Pudding recipe. Serve hot with hard sauce.

Tapioca Pudding

¼ cup pearl tapioca   ⅛ teaspoon salt
¾ cup rich milk   ½ teaspoon vanilla
1¼ cups water   2 eggs, separated
3 tablespoons sugar

Cover tapioca with cold water and soak for about one hour; drain, and transfer to double boiler; add water and milk, and cook until tapioca is transparent; mix sugar, salt, and slightly beaten egg yolks; slowly pour on these the tapioca mixture, return to double boiler and cook until it thickens; remove from range and lightly fold in the stiffly beaten egg whites; add vanilla and chill.—Serve six.

Creole Molasses Pudding

1 cup New Orleans   1 cup seeded raisins
   molasses   ½ cup citron
½ cup hot water   1 teaspoon soda
2 cups flour   2 eggs

Beat eggs until light; add soda to hot water and add this to molasses, mixing well, then add beaten eggs; beat flour into mixture; chop raisins, roll in flour, and stir into mixture with finely chopped citron. Pour into muslin steaming-bag and steam two hours. Serve with choice of sauce.

Cherry Pudding

1 cup canned cherries   1 cup cherry syrup
2 cups milk   1 tablespoon sugar
2 egg yolks   1 tablespoon cornstarch
1 tablespoon cornstarch   2 egg whites, beaten
¼ teaspoon salt   2 teaspoons sugar
1 teaspoon vanilla   Whipped Cream

Drain and measure cherries, and set to one side until needed.

Custard: Beat corn-starch in a little of the milk, and add to remaining milk; beat egg yolks, add salt, and add to milk; put into double boiler and cook to a thick custard; add vanilla; cool.

Syrup: Bring cherry syrup to boiling point, add sugar, and thicken with the corn starch; let cool.

Top: Beat egg whites until quite stiff, and sweeten to taste. Prepare a sufficient quantity of whipped cream.

To serve: Just before serving, add drained cherries to custard and mix; place a portion of custard on each dessert dish, with beaten egg whites on top of custard; decorated with a cherry in center; pour prepared syrup around this, and cover syrup with a border of whipped cream.

Cranberry Pudding

2 cups cranberries   1 teaspoon cream tartar
1 cup sugar   ¾ teaspoon soda
½ cup milk   ¼ teaspoon salt
2 cups flour   2 egg yolks
3 tablespoons butter

Coarsely chop and measure the cranberries. Sift and measure flour, add cream of tartar, soda and salt; re-sift. Cream butter and cream sugar into it; beat egg yolks and beat into sugar-butter; add milk and stir; add flour mixture and beat to batter; add chopped cranberries. Turn into baking dish and cook in a moderately hot oven about 45 minutes. Serve hot with favorite sauce.

Dried Apple Pudding

1 cup dried apples   ½ teaspoon cinnamon
2½ cups flour   ¼ teaspoon cloves
½ cup molasses   1 tablespoon butter
½ cup buttermilk   1 egg
1 teaspoon soda

Soak dried apples over-night and chop finely. Beat eggs and stir in buttermilk and molasses, to which the butter and soda have been added. Sift and measure flour, add spices and re-sift to mix well. Gradually add and mix flour into first mixture; pour into a greased baking pan and bake in a moderate oven. Serve with choice of liquid sauce.

Dixie Plum Pudding

1 cup bown sugar   1 cup broken nut meats
1 cup New Orleans   4 cups flour
   molasses   2 teaspoons soda
¾ cup buttermilk   2 teaspoons cinnamon
4 cups seedless raisins   2 teaspoons nutmeg
1 cup chopped dates   1 teaspoon cloves
1 cup currants   4 eggs

Beat eggs until light; mix soda into buttermilk, add eggs and molasses and mix; mix together, flour sugar and spices, run through sifter, and add to first mixture, beating in thoroughly; add nut meats; flour the raisins, dates and currants, and mix in with final stirring, making a thick, smooth batter. Prepare pudding for boiling: grease a cloth on top side and pour batter in the center, quickly gather up edges and tie to form a bag, leaving enough room for the pudding to swell; dredge outside of bag with flour, and drop into a kettle of rapidly boiling water to cover pudding; keep water briskly boiling for four hours; keep water replaced with more boiling water as it boils away; do not allow it to stop boiling in the kettle. Serve with choice of sauce.

Floating Island

1 layer sponge cake	Raspberry jam
4 cups rich cream	Sugar to sweeten
Currant jelly	

Bake a layer of sponge cake to about one inch thickness; when cooled, cut into squares, or rounds of about two inches and spread each with rasberry jam. Into two cups of the cream, stir sufficient currant jelly to give it a rich pink color, and enough sugar to generously sweeten. Beat the remaining two cups cream until quite stiff and add sugar to sweeten. Into individual sherbet or dessert dishes, pour some of the pink cream, drop a square of the cake and jam in center, and cover with the whipped cream; decorate with a preserved cherry if desired, and serve.—Other jelly or jam may be substituted. .

Apple Fritters

Slice firm apples crosswise into one-fourth inch slices; cut into rounds with biscuit cutter; sprinkle with powdered sugar, and moisten with lemon juice; allow to stand ten minutes, dry one or two at a time on a napkin, and dip into fritter batter, being careful to cover; drop into deep fat and fry a light brown; roll in powdered sugar and serve with a hard sauce.—Pineapple or Orange Fritters may be made in the same manner. Any canned whole or halved fruits may be drained from their syrup, dried, and made into fritters; chopped fruits may be mixed with the batter which is then dripped into frying fat by spoonfuls. Fritters are usually served with a sauce made with the juice or syrup of the fruit used.

Chef's Hard Sauce

2 cups powdered sugar	1 tablespoon cream
2 tablespoons butter	½ teaspoon vanilla

Cream butter and gradually add and cream in half of powdered sugar; add and thoroughly mix cream, and beat in remainder of powdered sugar; add vanilla or other flavoring.

Vanilla Cream Sauce

½ cup gran. sugar	1½ tablespoons flour
1 cup boiling water	1 teaspoon vanilla
1 tablespoon butter	

Mix flour into sugar and gradually add boiling water, constantly stirring. Boil five minutes, remove from range, and stir in butter and vanilla.

Seafoam Nog Sauce

1 cup sugar	1 teaspoon flavoring
½ cup butter	1 egg white
½ cup boiling water	

Cream butter and cream in sugar; beat egg white stiff and dry; thoroughly fold-in egg white and sugar-butter; beat in flavoring; just before serving, add boiling water and beat until foamy.—Nog taste may be added by flavoring with Berry Vinegar—recipe found under "Beverages."

Dixie Creole Sauce

1 cup New Orleans	2 lemons—juice
2 tablespoons butter	

Boil molasses and butter for five minutes; remove from range; add lemon juice and mix.

Orange Foam Sauce

1 orange—rind and juice	⅛ teaspoon salt
½ lemon—juice	2 egg whites
¾ cup sugar	

Beat egg whites, adding salt, to stiffness; gradually add and beat in sugar; add and beat in sugar; add grated orange rind and juices. Serve with cottage pudding or as meringue for liquid sauces.

Orange Syrup Sauce

1 cup orange juice	1 lemon, juice
1 cup gran. sugar	½ lemon rind, grated
1 teaspoon orange rind	

Stir all ingredients together in saucepan, and boil fifteen minutes; remove from range, skim and, strain, and cool before serving.—Sealed in sterile glass jar, will keep well for some time, ready for immediate use. Splendid syrup for Ice Cream Sundae, or puddings. May be used in connection with Orange Foam Sauce.

Fig Syrup Sauce

½ cup stewed fig syrup	2 tablespoons flour
1 cup hot water	3 tablespoons lemon juice
2 tablespoons brown sugar	1 tablespoon butter

Add enough hot water to fig syrup to make one and one-half cups; add this slowly to sugar and flour mixed, bring to a boil, constantly stirring, and boil for about five minutes. Keep mixture hot in a double boiler until ready to serve; just before serving, add lemon juice and butter and beat until thoroughly mixed.—Prune sauce may be made same way.

FROZEN ICES

Handling the Freezer—See that freezer-can, cover and dasher are thoroughly scalded and rinsed with cold water before using; also that they are well washed and dried immediately after using.

It is best not to have freezer more than three-fourths full of mixture at beginning.

Rock, or crystal, salt is better for mixing with the crushed ice than finer salt. After freezer is emptied, let salt settle to bottom of bucket, drain off water and spread salt on a board to dry, that it may be used again.

One part salt to three parts crushed ice is the proper mixture for freezing.

Fill in around can with ice and salt to within about one inch of the top of can. As ice melts, drain off water and replenish with ice and salt.

Before removing can cover, always wipe off the salt, dash with a bit of clean water and wipe thoroughly, especially around the edge of the cover.

The hole in the side of the bucket should be corked when packing the freezer with ice.

Packing should be done with one part salt to four parts ice. pack dry ice over top of can, and cover the freezer with a heavy blanket and set in cool place.

In replacing can cover before packing, place a clean paper over top of can and replace cover tightly; also cork the dasher hole in top of cover.

Vanilla Ice Cream

4 cups fresh milk	3 tablespoons milk
1½ cups rich cream	¼ teaspoon salt
½ cup gran. sugar	2 teaspoons vanilla
¼ cup sugar, extra	1 egg
3 tablespoons flour	

Scald the fresh milk in a double boiler. Mix the ½ cup sugar, flour and salt, and sift; moisten with the 3 tablespoons cold milk, add 1 cup of the scalded milk and mix; then add to remaining hot milk; cook thirty minutes. Beat egg to lightness and beat in the quarter cup sugar; mix beaten egg and cooked mixture and set to cool. Beat cream a few minutes and when mixture is entirely cold, add beaten cream and vanilla; mix well and FREEZE.—Makes one-half gallon.

Chocolate Ice Cream

To Vanilla Ice Cream Mixture add:

2 oz. chocolate (2 sqs.)	3 tablespoons hot water
¼ cup gran. sugar	

Prepare Vanilla Ice Cream Mixture as directed, except leave out one tablespoon of the flour, and add the additional quarter-cup sugar. Melt chocolate in the hot water and add to the cream mixture just before setting it to cool; then, proceed as for Vanilla.

Tutti-Frutti Ice Cream

To Vanilla Ice Cream Mixture, add:

2 cups fruit pulp	Sugar to sweeten
1 cup fruit juice	

Soak finely crushed fruit pulp in fruit juice and sweeten to taste. When Vanilla Cream is nearly frozen, add pulp and juice; finish freezing.

For regulation Tutti-Frutti, a mixture of seedless raisins, candied pineapple and cherries is used with orange juice, or the juice from the cherries; however, other available fruits may well be substituted.

Strawberry Ice Cream

To Vanilla Ice Cream Mixture, add:

3 cups crushed straw- berries	Sugar to sweeten

When Vanilla cream is frozen to a stiff mush, add crushed, fresh strawberries, and finish freezing. Other berries may be used in the same manner; or, cherries, peaches or oranges, prepared with their natural juices may be used alone or in combination, the cream taking its name from the fruit used.

Neapolitan Ice Cream

Usually in the form of brick ice cream in three layers, but may be served from separate containers by preparing and freezing Chocolate, Vanilla, and Strawberry Ice Cream separately in three layers, which may be molded in a cup or small desert dish in the order named, and turned upon a serving plate. As each of the first two are frozen, transfer to tin pails packed in ice, cover tightly and pack over top.

Caramel Nut Ice Cream

⅔ cup gran. sugar	1½ teaspoons vanilla
⅓ cup sugar	⅛ teaspoon salt
2 cups milk	⅔ cup chopped walnuts
1 cup rich cream	3 egg yolks

Put first part of sugar into a granite saucepan, and place pan on hot part of range; stir until melted and the color of maple syrup; chop, or grind, nuts very finely, mix with the caramelized sugar and turn into well buttered pan to cool; when cooled, pound or grind into powder and pass through a sieve; beat egg yolks, add the one-third cup sugar, milk and salt; add and mix in caramelized sugar-nut powder, vanilla and cream. Mix and freeze.

Orange Sherbet

1½ cups gran. sugar	1½ cups orange juice
2 cups boiling water	1½ cups lemon juice
2 cups rich cream	2 egg whites
2 grated orange rinds	

Dissolve sugar in boiling water; add grated orange rind, lemon and orange juice; pour into freezer and freeze until mushy. Beat cream until thick, and beat egg whites until stiff; add these to mixture in freezer and finish freezing; pack.

Lemon Milk Sherbet

| 7 cups fresh milk | 4 lemons, juice |
| 1 cup gran. sugar | 1 cup gran. sugar |

Dissolve first cup sugar in milk and freeze to thickness of cream; mix lemon juice with other cup of sugar, add this to freezing mixture, stir it in, and finish freezing; pack.

Grape Sherbet

| 2 cups grape juice | 4 cups milk |
| 1 cup sugar | |

Warm the grape juice and dissolve the sugar in it; add to the milk, which should be ice cold; freeze at once. Sherbet will have a delicate purple tint.

Cranberry Sherbet

6 cups cranberries	2 tablespoons flour
4 cups water	2 lemons—juice
2 cups sugar	1 orange—rind and juice
2 cups boiling water	

Boil cranberries and water ten minutes; strain through sieve. Mix flour with sugar, add boiling water and boil, while stirring, until smooth. Combine the two mixtures, adding more sugar if desired to suit taste; cool; add lemon juice and grated rind and juice of orange. Freeze; serve in sherbet glasses with roast fowl. Fifteen portions.

Fruit Ice

2 cups gran. sugar	1 cup fruit juice
2 tablespoons flour	2 cups fruit pulp
2 cups hot water	2 lemons—juice

Mix sugar and flour well together; add to boiling water and boil until flour is well cooked and sugar dissolved; add and mix fruit juice and lemon juice; run drained fruit through a meat chopper, measure and add to mixture; cool, freeze.—Fruit may be peaches, apricots, pineapple, cherries, grapes, or other canned or cooked fruits. Quantity: One-half gallon.

Lemon Ice

| 6 cups water | 1 cup lemon juice |
| 2½ cups sugar | |

Bring sugar and water to boil and let boil five minutes; add lemon juice; cool and strain into freezer; pack freezer with three parts ice to one part salt, and let stand for about five minutes, then freeze until stiff. Remove dasher, pack mixture down into freezer, and drain off salt water; re-pack freezer with four parts ice to one part salt, and stand by until needed.

Orange Ice

2 cups gran. sugar	½ cup lemon juice
4 cups water	¼ grated orange rind
2 cups orange juice	

Boil sugar, water and grated orange rind five minutes; cool and add orange and lemon juices; strain and freeze.—Follow directions for Lemon Ice.

"Home Comfort" Freeze

3 oranges—juice	3 cups sugar
3 lemons—juice	3 cups water
3 bananas—mashed	

Mix thoroughly and freeze. Serve like ice or sherbet.

Peach Parfait

1 cup gran. sugar	1 cup crushed peaches
1 cup water	1 tablespoon lemon juice
2 cups cream	3 eggs

Bring sugar and water to boil, and let boil five minutes; beat eggs until light and gradually add syrup to them; put into double boiler and cook until eggs thicken mixture, or about three minutes; chill. Whip the cream well and add to mixture; add crushed peaches and lemon juice; mix thoroughly. Pour into mold, or pail, and securely pack in equal parts of cracked ice and salt for about four hours. Serve in sherbet dishes. —Such fruits as strawberries, raspberries, pineapple, etc., may be substituted for peaches if desired. Lemon juice may be omitted if necessary. By caramelizing the sugar and adding the water boiling hot, the parfait may be given a caramel flavor.

Mocha Mousse

1 cup sugar	1 teaspoon gelatin
½ cup water	½ teaspoon vanilla
1 cup coffee	3 egg yolks
1 cup cream, whipped	

Set granulated gelatin to soften in two tablespoons cold water. Boil sugar and water five minutes, pour onto beaten egg yolks, and cook in double boiler until cream-like; dissolve the soaked gelatin in the strong boiling coffee, and when cooled, add the cooked mixture, whipped cream and vanilla. Pour into a mold and pack in equal parts of crushed ice and salt for about three hours. Serve in dessert dishes.

Frozen Pudding

3 cups milk	1 tablespoon cornstarch
1 cup sugar	3 eggs
1 cup chopped fruits	

Heat milk in a double boiler. Mix cornstarch with a little cold milk and add to beaten egg; add sugar and a small pinch of salt; mix well. Add this mixture to the hot milk and stir until it thickens; set aside to thoroughly cool. Chop the fruit, or fruits, in a meat chopper, and add to cooled mixture. Put in freezer and freeze, but not too stiff; pack into a mold if desired, or leave in the freezer, and pack well with ice and salt until ready to serve. Any of the dry fruits, or even nuts, in a well-blended combination will do, available material and taste being the guide.

Beverages and Cold Drinks

Coffee

In general use, there are two methods of making good coffee: *direct boiling* and *filtering* or percolating. With either method, the use of pure and strictly fresh water is absolutely necessary for best results, and no water should be used that has once been boiled and cooled.

Boiled Coffee—(4 cups) Beat half an egg white with 3 tablespoons cold water, add ¾ cup ground coffee, and stir until coffee is well moistened; put into scalded coffee-pot and add 1 quart fresh water that has just been brought to a boil; boil vigorously for five minutes, add ¼ cup cold water, and set aside for three minutes to settle; serve.

Many noted cooks boil the coffee in an open pan or kettle, and pass it through a strainer into the serving pot, enabling them to omit the egg, and yet serve good, clear coffee.

Filtered Coffee—In this method, very finely ground or pulverized coffee is suspended in a strainer in the top of the coffee-pot, and the boiling water filtered through it. This method is the principle on which the large coffee urns used in restaurants and large kitchens are made, and is the one recommended by the National Association of Coffee Roasters as the best, even for the household.

Prepare the filter by placing over an open china tea-pot or ordinary coffee-pot, a clean, wet, old linen napkin, or a new square of medium weight unbleached muslin, letting it sag at the center, forming a bag—the cloth may be sewed to a strong wire ring made to fit the top of the pot.

(4 cups) Have fresh water boiling vigorously; put 4 heaping tablespoons finely pulverized coffee into the wet bag adjusted to pot; pour the boiling water over the coffee slowly enough to allow it to go through until slightly more than 4 cups are used; remove bag; serve.

Never permit the bag to get dry; wash it out immediately and keep it in a jar of cold water, which should be changed every day; every effort should be made to keep the bag sweet and clean, as the least souring ruins the coffee—this is most important.

This method is far superior to direct boiling, especially for the cheaper grades of coffee.

Coffee-pots made on this principle may be had on the market. Another pot made on the same principle, but which requires less manipulation, but a longer time in which to make the coffee, is a patented article called a "Percolator."

A combination of the two methods is employed by placing finely pulverized coffee in a cloth bag with a string attached, and suspending it in water boiling in the coffee-pot; remove bag; serve.

Tea

Like coffee, tea is ta its best when made with *freshly boiled fresh water;* therefore, do not use water that has been once boiled and cooled, but have fresh water (spring water is best, filtered water next) and let it just reach the point of vigorous boiling, and use.

Teas are of varying strength, but for the average, 1 teaspoon dry green tea is used with each tea-cup of boiling water; scald tea-pot or other rustproof vessel, put in proper quantity of dry tea, cover and let stand in the moisture one minute; add proper quantity of boiling water, cover closely, set in hot warming closet, and let it steep five to ten minutes; strain off into hot tea-pot; serve. —Most healthful without milk.

Iced Tea

Usually relished in much weaker form than hot tea. Make tea of regular strength or stronger if desired; let it thoroughly cool; place portion in large glasses, weaken to suit individual taste with cold water, put in broken ice; serve with small slice of lemon on side. Sweetened to individual taste.

Iced Coffee

Place an ample amount of ice in a pitcher or in individual glasses, and slowly pour over it either cold, warm or even hot coffee; serve like iced tea. Care should be taken in pouring hot coffee into glasses; the glass should not be cold, but ice should be placed in it just before pouring the coffee, which should be poured on the ice, thus cooling it before it touches the glass.

Breakfast Cocoa

Mix 4 teaspoons powdered cocoa and 2 tablespoons sugar in a cup; have water boiling; heat cocoa pot by filling with hot water for a few minutes; heat 2 cups milk by standing container in hot water for a few minutes; have 2 cups water boiling hot, and with a half cup of it, dissolve the cocoa and sugar; pour into the warmed cocoa pot, add remainder of boiling water, the hot milk, and ½ teaspoon salt; mix and serve at once with or without cream. Makes four cups.

Or: Make as above, using 3 cups milk and 1 cup boiling water.

Hot Chocolate

Melt 1½ squares bitter chocolate in pan over hot water; add 4 tablespoons sugar, ½ teaspoon salt and, gradually, 1 cup boiling water; stir until smooth, then place pan directly over fire and boil one minute; have ready and add, 3 cups scalded milk; beat about two minutes with an egg beater just before serving; serve hot with a spoon of whipped cream or one square of marshmallow. Makes four cups.

Or: Make as Breakfast Cocoa recipe, using 3 tablespoons cocoa, 4 tablespoons sugar, 3 cups milk, 1 cup boiling water, and ½ teaspoon salt.

Orangeade

Make a syrup: boil 1 cup sugar in 2 cups water ten minutes, and add 1/3 cup orange juice; cool. To serve: dilute with ice water to suit taste or pour over cracked ice.

Or: Boil grated yellow rind of 1 orange with 1 cup water and 1/3 cup sugar for five minutes; strain syrup and add to juice of 4 oranges and 1 lemon, and 3 cups additional water. Serve with crushed ice and garnish with a quarter slice of orange. Six large glasses, or twelve punch glasses.

Lemonade

To the juice of each large lemon, add 2 tablespoons granulated sugar and 1 cup cold water, then further sweeten to individual taste. Serve ice-cold.

Fruit Lemonades

To Lemonade made from juice of three lemons, add 1 cup any berry, grape, pineapple, prune, or other fruit juice; or 1 cup crushed fruit pulp. Adding 1 cup ginger ale also makes a choice drink. Serve ice cold.

Bazaar Fruit Punch

Make a syrup; boil 2 cups granulated sugar in 1 cup water ten minutes; add 1 cup cold tea, 2 cups strawberry or other berry syrup, juice of 5 oranges and 5 lemons, 1 can grated pineapple and juice; cover and let stand thirty minutes to an hour; strain, and add ice-cold water to make one and one-half gallons; just before serving, add a block

of ice to punch bowl, and add 1 cup maraschino, or similar, cherries; improved if 1 quart of carbonated—Selzer—water is added at last minute. Will serve fifty punch glasses. Double recipe for a hundred persons.

Grape Punch

To 2 cups grape juice add 4 cups cold water, 1 cup sugar, and the juice of 3 large lemons and 2 oranges; mix. Serve ice-cold. Six large glasses, or twelve punch glasses. Flavor with mint if desired.

Cranberry Punch

Cover cranberries with water, and boil until tender; strain and measure juice; add sugar in proportion of 1 cup sugar to 4 cups juice, and let come to a boil; add juices of other fruits to taste. Serve ice-cold.

Rhubarb Punch

Cut rhubarb in pieces to measure 1 quart, and cook with 1 quart water until plant is soft; strain through double thickness cheese cloth, and add ¼ cup each orange and lemon juice, and 1½ cups syrup made by gently cooking eight minutes, without stirring, 1 cup each sugar and water. Add carbonated water if desired. Serve ice-cold. Twelve medium glasses, or twenty-four punch glasses A few grains of salt is considered an improvement by some.

Grape Juice

To 10 pounds of grapes use 3 pounds of sugar.

Wash grapes, put in kettle, cook slowly and stir constantly to prevent them sticking to kettle. Strain and return to fire, add the sugar and let it come to boil, remove and pour into bottles and seal. A portion of this added to ice water makes a very delightful and healthful drink.

Society Punch

Mix 3 cups sugar and 4 cups water and boil for 5 minutes. Chill and add 4 cups syrup drained from crushed or grated Hawaiian pineapple, the juice from 8 oranges and 4 cups ice water. Add 4 oranges sliced very thin without removing rind, 2 cups crushed or grated pineapple from which syrup has been drained and ½ cup maraschino cherries. Pour over a block of ice in a punch bowl. This will serve 25 persons.

Hawaiian Punch

Prepare 4 cups of strong tea and while it is hot add 1½ cups sugar, stir until it dissolves and chill. Add 4 cups syrup drained from crushed or grated Hawaiian pineapple,

½ cup lemon juice and 6 cups water. Chop 1 cup mint leaves and mix with ½ cup powdered sugar, put in bottom of the punch bowl with several pieces of ice and pour the punch over them. This will serve 25 persons.

Waikiki Punch

Mix 2 cups syrup drained from crushed or grated Hawaiian pineapple, 2 cups ice water and 2 cups grape juice. Serve with crushed ice.

Pineapple Orangeade

To 3 cups of orange juice (about 1 dozen oranges) add 2 cups syrup drained from crushed or grated Hawaiian pineapple and 1 cup ice water. Serve in glasses set in individual bowls of crushed ice.

Pineappleade

Mix 1 cup water and ½ cup sugar, boil ten minutes and chill; add 3 cups ice water, 2 cups of syrup drained from crushed or grated Hawaiian pineapple and ½ cup lemon juice.

Pineapple Egg Nog

For each individual glass, beat 1 egg yolk slightly, add ⅛ teaspoon salt, ½ teaspoon powdered sugar, and ½ cup syrup drained from canned crushed or grated Hawaiian pineapple; add ½ of a stiffly beaten egg white, mix, and pour into glass; heap remainder of egg white on top and sprinkle with nutmeg.

Pineapple Julep

Chop fresh mint leaves to make ¼ cup, add ½ cup powdered sugar, and rub well together; add 3 cups syrup drained from canned crushed or grated Hawaiian pineapple, ¼ cup lime or lemon juice, and 3 cups ice water; allow to stand in cold place at least one hour; serve in glasses with a cube of ice in each, and garnish with a sprig of mint.

Strawberry Syrup

Take fine ripe strawberries, crush them in a cloth, and press the juice from them; to each pint of it, put a pint of simple syrup, boil gently for 1 hour, then let it become cold, and bottle it; cork and seal it. When served, reduce it to taste with water, set on ice, and serve in small tumblers half filled.

Berry and Fruit Vinegars

Along with the canning of the summer fruits, a few simple vinegars may be prepared from berries, which will prove a foundation for much refreshment during the year. All that is necessary to serve these vinegars is to add cold water in quantity to suit taste, and serve like lemonade.

Blackberry Vinegar — Wash and pick over a quantity of berries; mash berries to a pulp in a stoneware jar; add good cider vinegar to cover pulp, cover jar with a thin clean cloth, stand it in sun during the day, and set in the cellar or other cool place during the night. The next morning, strain; wash and crush the same amount of fresh berries, and over this fresh pulp pour the strained juice; set in the sun again during the day and in cool place at night. The third day, strain again; to each quart of juice allow one pint water and five pounds of granulated sugar. Heat mixture slowly until it reaches boiling point; skim, let it boil a minute, strain and bottle in sterilized bottles, and seal airtight to prevent fermentation.

Raspberry Vinegar — Put two quarts raspberries in a stone jar and cover berries with one quart of good clear cider vinegar; cover closely and stand aside for two days. At the end of that time, mash the berries well and strain off the liquid. Pour liquid over one quart of fresh berries, cover and set aside for another two days. Mash berries, strain, and allow one pound of sugar to each pint of juice; add sugar to juice and cook gently for five or ten minutes; skim, strain, bottle and cork airtight.

Black Currant Vinegar — Put four pounds ripe currants into a stoneware jar and cover with three pints good cider vinegar; cover, and let stand three days, stirring occasionally; squeeze and strain the fruit. Measure juice and set aside one pound of sugar for each pint of liquid; boil juice for ten minutes, add sugar, and boil twenty minutes longer; skim, strain, bottle and cork airtight.

Pineapple Vinegar — Peel and slice nice ripe pineapples into a stone jar, and cover with good cider vinegar; cover closely and stand aside for three to four days; mash pulp and strain off liquid which should be clear; add five pounds sugar to each three quarts juice; boil about ten minutes, skimming until entirely free from rising sediment; remove from range, cool, put into sterile bottles and cork. Serve about a tablespoon of such Vinegar stirred into a glass of ice cold water. Vinegar of most highly flavored fruits may be made in like manner.

Candy and Candy Making

Plain Fondant

4 cups gran. sugar   1/16 teaspoon cream
1 cup cold water   tartar

Stir sugar into water, cover pan and set aside for a half hour; on the point of the teaspoon measure cream tartar about the size of a navy bean, and add to sugar and water. Set pan on hot range top and bring quickly to a boil, stirring constantly; at this point, stop stirring; take a damp cloth and carefully wipe the crystals from the sides of the pan, being cautious not to touch the boiling syrup or jar the pan—this precaution aids to prevent graining of mixture. After cooking a few minutes, begin testing small amounts in cold water; when it has reached the stage where it can be gathered up into a soft ball that will retain any shape it is pressed into, remove from range at once; pour mixture very carefully into a wide ungreased pan and set aside in a cool place until cool enough to handle; while still warm, gather into a mass and work vigorously with a large spoon until too thick to stir; then gather quickly into a ball and knead with the hands as you would dough; place in a clean bowl, cover with a plate and set aside a few hours before using. In its finished form, the fondant should look much like lard when broken, soften enough to readily form or cup with a knife, about as firm as hard butter, and when placed in mouth, it should melt away, leaving no grain or crystals whatever.

This fondant is used for cream chocolate centers, or for a wide variety of plain and fancy bonbons. It may be kept in a mass for many days under cover in a cool place and worked into candy after bringing it again to room temperature.—If it develops that fondant has been cooked too much and has a tendency to dry out. moisture may be restored by placing a dampened cloth over dish and setting aside until fondant has absorbed sufficient moisture. Avoid attempting to make this fondant on a rainy day.

Chocolate Creams

2 cups gran. sugar   ⅛ teaspoon soda
1 cup sweet milk   1 cake bitter chocolate
1 tablespoon butter   1 teaspoon paraffine

Mix sugar, milk, butter and soda; cook while stirring, until small amount of mixture, when dropped into cold water, will form a soft ball; remove, pour into a platter and allow to cool to a merely warm mass; while yet warm, beat without stopping until it forms a fairly stiff cream; shape into pieces in any form desired, place on a well buttered plate and set in a cold place to harden. Melt the chocolate in a deep bowl over hot water; add and stir in the paraffine. Place a well buttered paper on a flat surface to receive the finished chocolates. With two forks, drop each cream into the melted chocolate, and place them on the buttered paper to cool.—The amount of paraffine determines the smoothness of the coating; add just enough to make the coating smooth and easy to work.

Cherry Cocktails

Prepare Cream Fondant and Chocolate coating as for Chocolate Creams: When forming the cream center, form the cream around a maraschino cherry—any good, whole, preserved cherry may well be substituted—and proceed to cool and coat with the chocolate.

Fancy Bon Bons

Bon Bons are made from Cream Fondant. Prepare the fondant in its completed or dough form; plain bon bons are then made by forming the fondant into small shapes such as squares, rounds, ovals, oblongs, or any other form desired. A half pecan or walnut may be placed on each (adding to appearance and taste. They may also be flavored with vanilla, lemon, maple, mint, wintergreen, or other flavoring by working the fruit or extract flavoring into the fondant while being kneaded. Fruit coloring may also be added in the same way, thus giving a wide range of choice variations.

Cream Caramels

1 cup gran. sugar   ¾ cup rich milk
1 cup brown sugar   2 tablespoons butter
½ cup light corn syrup   1 teaspoon vanilla

Put sugar and milk into a saucepan and set to back of range-top until sugar is well dissolved; add syrup, place over fire and let come to a boil; continue boiling slowly until syrup forms a firm ball when tested in cold water; add butter and vanilla, mixing well. Pour into a large shallow square cake tin, well buttered, and set to cool; just before entirely cold, transfer from pan to a well-buttered paper sheet cut into small squares with a sharp knife point dipped in hot water; caramels may be wrapped in buttered tissue paper if desired.

Chocolate Caramels

1 cup brown sugar	4 tablespoons butter
2 cups molasses	4 oz. bitter chocolate
1 cup rich milk	1 teaspoon vanilla

Melt butter and chocolate; add sugar, molasses and milk; cook until consistency of a soft caramel when tested in cold water; pour into buttered square pan and, when half cold, cut into squares, or oblongs.—Nuts may be added immediately on removing from range, if desired.

"Home Comfort" Cream

First part:

1½ cups gran. sugar	3 egg whites
½ cup water	

Second part:

3 cups gran. sugar	½ cup hot water
1 cup light corn syrup	1 cup almond kernels

Place sugar and water of first part in one pan, and sugar, syrup, and water of second part in another. Beat the egg whites until very light and stiff set first part to boil, and when it is cooked to form a thread, gradually add and beat into the egg whites without stopping; set second part to boil as you remove the first part syrup, and when syrup forms a hard ball when tested in cold water, pour over the beaten egg and syrup mixture gradually and briskly beat well. Stir in the almond kernels to distribute well through mixture; pour in a well-buttered paper-lined cake pan and let cool and harden; remove pan and paper; slice in any form desired.

French Nougat

1 cup strained honey	¼ teaspoon salt
1 cup brown sugar	1 teaspoon flavoring
½ cup light cream	¼ teaspoon cream tartar
1 tablespoon butter	

Melt butter in a saucepan, and add honey, sugar, cream and salt; place pan over a slow fire and stir until all are dissolved and well mixed; add cream tartar; boil until small amount dropped in cold water forms a hard ball; remove from fire and stir in the flavoring extract—lemon preferred; pour into a shallow, well-buttered pan and mark into squares or oblongs before entirely cool; when sufficiently cooled, remove from pan and cut into portions; wrap in waxed paper if desired to facilitate handling. One-half cup chopped nuts may be added during final beating, just before pouring.

Divinity Fudge

1 cup gran. sugar	1 cup corn syrup
1 cup water	2 egg whites
1 cup brown sugar	1 teaspoon flavoring

Cook white sugar and water until syrup, tested in cold water, is crisp; in separate pan, cook brown sugar and corn syrup until crisp in cold water; have egg whites beaten to lightness; add gradually and beat in the white syrup; then, add and beat in the brown syrup, beating until very stiff. Flavor. Pour, or spread, in a buttered pan to about three-quarters inch thickness; when half cold, cut into squares.—Granulated sugar may be used instead of the brown sugar in second syrup.

Variations: Vanilla—use white sugar and vanilla extract; Lemon—white sugar and lemon extract; Maple—brown sugar and maple flavoring, or use maple syrup instead of water in first syrup; Caramel—caramelize white sugar in first syrup before adding the water; Cherry—use one cup juice from canned cherries instead of water and use white sugar in second syrup; Chocolate—add two squares melted chocolate to second syrup and flavor with vanilla; Nut—add one-half to three-quarter cup broken nut-meats during final beating; Fruit—add choice of chopped fruit instead of nuts.

Cream Fudge

2 cups gran. sugar	1 tablespoon butter
1 cup rich milk	

Put milk and sugar into a saucepan, and set to boil; cook until syrup forms a soft ball when tested in cold water; add butter, take from fire, and beat steadily to a thick cream; pour into a well-buttered square pan, and when nearly cool, cut into small squares with a buttered knife.

Cocoanut Cream Fudge

Follow recipe for Cream Fudge; add 1 cup finely shredded cocoanut during last half of beating; flavor with 1 teaspoon vanilla.

Marshmallow Cream Fudge

Follow recipe for Cream Fudge; add 10 average marshmallows beaten to a cream; mix during last half of beating.

Fruit Cream Fudge

Follow recipe for Cream Fudge; add 1 cup finely chopped or ground dates, figs and nutmeats while beating.

Chocolate Cream Fudge

Follow recipe for Cream Fudge; add 2 ounces (2 squares) bitter chocolate to milk and sugar in beginning, melting chocolate first.

Layer Cream Fudge

Prepare and pour into a buttered pan in a shallow layer, any one of the above fudges; pour onto this a layer of different colored or flavored fudge; follow with third layer if desired.—This makes an excellent fudge for parties.

Rich Chocolate Fudge

3 cups brown sugar	¼ cup butter
½ cup rich milk	¼ cake chocolate

Melt chocolate in a pan, and add butter, milk and sugar in order named and boil; when it will form a soft ball when tested in cold water, remove from fire; let cool a little and beat until thick; pour into a buttered shallow pan, cut into small squares and let cool.

Chocolate Nut Fudge

Follow recipe for Rich Chocolate Fudge; add and stir in ¾ cup chopped nut meats just after removing from fire.

Maple Fudge

Follow recipe for Rich Chocolate Fudge except: leave out chocolate; substitute 1 cup maple syrup for 1 cup of the brown sugar; or, use 2½ cups brown sugar and ½ cup shaved maple sugar.

Maple Walnut Fudge

Prepare Maple Fudge; add ½ cup chopped Black Walnuts just after removing from fire, and mix well.

Cocoanut Squares

1 cup rich milk	½ cup shredded cocoanut
2 cups gran. sugar	

Put sugar and milk into pan and set on range; when it has come to a boil, add cocoanut and cook without stirring until it will form a very soft ball in cold water; remove from range, and when nearly cold, stir briskly until thick; pour quickly into well buttered pan or dish; cut into desired squares or bars.

Cocoanut Snowballs

1 cup shredded cocoanut	1 teaspoon vanilla
4 cups powdered sugar	1 egg white
4 tablespoons water	

Beat egg white to stiffness and beat in sugar, adding a tablespoon of water alternately with each cup of powdered sugar; add vanilla; add and fold in cocoanut until thoroughly mixed and stiff; mold into one-inch balls, lay on buttered paper and set in cool place to harden.

Cocoanut Macaroons

⅔ cup sugar	⅓ cup water
½ lb. shredded cocoanut	3 egg whites

Boil sugar and water to syrup until it forms a soft ball in cold water; remove from fire and stir in the cocoanut; add by degrees the well-beaten egg whites and mix thoroughly. Drop on well-buttered tins and bake slowly until slightly browned.

Cocoanut Surprise

Prepare Cream Caramel, and while yet warm, form into small balls with an almond kernel in the center; roll in loose shredded cocoanut to thoroughly cover outside of balls.

Mexican Pinoche

2 cups brown sugar	2 cups pecan halves
1 cup rich milk	6 tablespoons butter

Mix sugar and milk; boil until a small amount dropped into cold water forms a soft ball; add butter and nut meats; stir well while warm and drop, by large spoonfuls onto a buttered plate or tin; set to cool. —Fewer nuts may be used if desired; walnuts or hickory-nuts may be used.

Maple Pinoche

1½ cups gran. sugar	2 tablespoons butter
1½ cups maple sugar	1 cup nut meats
1 cup rich milk	

Dissolve maple sugar in milk, add granulated sugar and butter; boil while constantly stirring, until small amount will form a soft ball when dropped in cold water; remove and beat until creamy; add and stir in nutmeats; pour onto buttered tin or plate as for Mexican Pinoche.—Nuts may be omitted if desired; black walnuts are first choice.

Hawaiian Pinoche

1 cup gran. sugar	1 tablespoon butter
½ cup brown sugar	½ teaspoon vanilla
¼ cup cream	½ cup broken nut meats
½ grated pineapple	

Cook sugars, cream and grated Hawaiian Pineapple until a soft ball forms when a little is dropped in cold water. Remove from range, add butter and beat until creamy; add vanilla and nutmeats; drop by spoonfuls onto buttered plate, and cool.

California Pinoche

1 cup brown sugar	½ cup chopped nuts
1 cup gran. sugar	½ cup seedless raisins
½ cup rich milk	2 teaspoons vanilla

Stir sugars into milk until dissolved and boil until syrup forms soft ball when dropped in cold water; add raisins, nuts and flavoring; beat until creamy, and pour into a buttered shallow pan; when cool, cut into squares; or, drop onto buttered paper or tin, as for Mexican Pinoche.

Molasses Kisses

2 cups molasses	1 teaspoon vinegar
¼ cup butter	

Melt butter in kettle; add molasses and when it has begun to boil, stir constantly, frequently testing by dropping a small amount into cold water; when it thus becomes brittle, add the vinegar and remove from fire; pour into a buttered plate or pan. When sufficiently cooled, pull until a golden color; pull out into a rope about three-fourths inch in diameter; cut with large shears into one inch lengths; wrap separately in buttered tissue paper if desired.—New Orleans molasses preferred.

Molasses Caramels

2 cups New Orleans molasses
½ cup rich milk
3 tablespoons butter
¼ teaspoon vanilla

Cook as for Molasses Kisses, except add vanilla just after removing from fire; pour into well-buttered, square, shallow tin; when sufficiently cooled, mark off and cut into small squares with a knife dipped into hot water; finish cooling; wrap in buttered paper if desired.

Butter Scotch

1 cup gran. sugar
¼ cup corn syrup
¼ cup hot water
2 tablespoons butter
2 tablespoons lemon juice

Put sugar, syrup and hot water in a saucepan and bring to boil; add butter and lemon juice, and continue boiling slowly until brittle when dropped into cold water; pour into well-buttered shallow, square tin, or plate, dent into small squares when slightly cooled; break squares apart when entirely cold.

Butter Chips

1 cup sugar
½ cup milk
4 tablespoons butter
¼ teaspoon salt
½ teaspoon vanilla

Put milk and sugar into saucepan and set on range to boil; when syrup forms a soft ball in cold water, add butter, remove from range and beat steadily to thin cream; drop from teaspoon point onto buttered tin or paper to cool.

Marshmallows

1 box Knox's gelatine
4 cups gran. sugar
½ cup powdered sugar
½ cup cornstarch
2½ cups water
1 teaspoon vanilla

Cover granulated sugar with one cup water, cover pan and set aside for 30 minutes. Soak gelatine in 12 tablespoons water. Put sugar and water on range and cook until it threads; pour syrup over soaked gelatine, thoroughly mix and add vanilla to taste; beat briskly and thoroughly for about 30 minutes; dust dough-board and rolling-pin with cornstarch or powdered sugar, and roll the mass out to about one-inch thickness; cut into one-inch squares and roll in the half cups of powdered sugar and cornstarch mixed and sifted together.—The gelatine may be had at any grocer's.

Marshmallows II

½ pound gum arabic
½ pound fine sugar
1 pint water
½ cup powdered sugar
½ cup corn-starch
Vanilla to flavor
4 egg whites

Dissolve gum arabic in the pint of water; strain and add the fine sugar; place on range, stir constantly and bring to a boil; continue stirring until syrup is the consistency of honey; gradually add and stir in the well-beaten egg whites; continue stirring until mixture is somewhat thin and will not adhere to finger; flavor with vanilla. Pour about one inch thick into a square pan which has been dusted with cornstarch. When cool, cut into one-inch squares and roll in powdered sugar and cornstarch mixed and sifted together.—Gum arabic may be had at any druggist's.

Stuffed Dates

Wipe large, well-formed dates with a damp cloth; with a sharp knife, slit one side the full length, remove the seed. Fill the dates with any one of a variety of fillings:

Half a pecan meat in each date.
Quarter of a walnut meat in each.
Peanuts, or peanut-butter in each.
Almond halves, or almond paste.
Candied orange peel, or citron.
Candied cherries or other fruit.
Rolls of cream fondant the size of the removed seed.
Strips of marshmallow or fudge.

After filling the seed-pit of each date, close and roll in granulated sugar.

Taffy

2 cups gran. sugar
1 cup water
1 tablespoon butter
1 tablespoon vinegar

Place all ingredients in a pan and cook without stirring until small amount of mixture hardens when dropped in cold water. Pour onto a well buttered, or greased, plate and allow it to cool enough to handle. Pull until white, form into a flat strip about two inches wide, and cut off into lengths with clean sissors; wrap in buttered tissue paper if desired.—One teaspoon cream tartar may be substituted for vinegar, and is an improvement.

Candied Popcorn

1½ cups sugar
3 tablespoons water
1 tablespoon butter
3 quarts popped corn

Cook sugar, water and butter into a syrup until it spins a long thread when tested in cold water; have ready select popcorn with burnt and hard grains removed; pour syrup over corn while continually stirring; stir until candied, and grains separate.—Same quantity of maple syrup may be substituted for the sugar if desired.

Popcorn Briques

2 gal. popped corn	1 cup corn syrup
2 cups salted peanuts	1 tablespoon butter
1 cup brown sugar	1 tablespoon vinegar

Boil sugar, syrup and butter together until it becomes brittle when tested in cold water, then add vinegar and remove; have popped corn ready with all hard grains removed; scatter the peanuts over top of corn and gradually but quickly pour the syrup over them and briskly stir until the peanuts are well mixed in and the corn coated; while warm, form into briques, using a well dampened box butter-mold or some such form for molding—form into balls if preferred—and keep in dry place at "room-temperature" to keep them fresh and crisp. Puffed rice or wheat may be used in place of corn. Any syrup will answer, but dark corn syrup is best.

Peanut Brittle

1 cup New Orleans molasses	½ cup melted butter
	1 cup peanuts

Cook molasses and butter until well cooked; add and stir in the peanuts, which may be either fresh or roasted; continue boiling until candy is brittle when tested in cold water. Pour into shallow, well-buttered pan, cut into squares or bars, and cool.

Peanut Puff

Make a syrup according to the Popcorn Brique recipe, adding an extra tablespoon vinegar and a teaspoon soda just before removing from fire, and stirring until puffy; stir in desired quantity of peanuts; cool.

Glacé Fruits and Nuts

1 cup gran. sugar	2 tablespoons hot water
1 cup corn syrup	

Put ingredients into top section of double boiler and set over fire; boil slowly until syrup becomes hard and brittle instantly when dropped into cold water. Assemble double boiler with hot water in bottom section to keep mixture warm while dipping; dip in fruit or nuts, one at a time with a clean hat-pin, and lay on oiled or buttered paper to harden.—Whole ripe apples, stuck on a small round stick, such as meat-skew and dipped in the glace, has become popular with the children.

Glacé Peanut Brittle

To left-over Glace after dipping, add a little butter in the proportion of 1 tablespoonful for the full recipe; pour the warm glace over shelled peanuts in proportion of 1 cup peanuts to the full recipe.—Glace may be thinned by adding a little boiling water, a teaspoonful at a time, if desired.

"HOME COMFORT" PLEASURES

"Home Comfort" Recipes have been compiled with much care and in anticipation of the many pleasurable hours they will provide for those who are the recipients of this book. Your "Home Comfort" Range is a piece of beautiful and useful furniture, and you are sure to find a facination in preparing upon it these choice viands and will be rewarded by the compliments and favor of those to whom you serve—this is only one of the many supreme "Home Comfort" pleasures.

Canning and Preserving

Success in canning fruits and vegetables depends upon absolute sterilization, and too much care and attention to this important detail cannot be given by the home canner. With the proper sterilization of every utensil, implement and container, together with proper and perfect sealing, there need be no failure.

Have all jars, covers and rings in perfect condition. Examine each jar and cover to see that there are no defects in them; inspect closely each cover and rim, making sure that they form a perfectly even contact all around and are not chipped or dented. Use none but fresh, elastic rubber rings; it is poor economy to use rings that have been used before, or unused ones that are a year or more old—this is most important, for thousands of jars of fruits and vegetables are lost each year through the use of old rings alone.

With the foregoing precautions attended to, the next step is to properly cleanse and sterilize them: Wash jars and covers thoroughly, rinse well and drain. Have two pans with some cold water in them; put some of the jars in one, laying them on their sides, and in the other place some of the covers; place the pans on the range, bring to boiling point and allow to boil at least 10 minutes before removing them just before putting in the prepared fruit of vegetables. Have another pan of boiling water, and in this emerse dipper, cup, spoon, funnel, skimmer, etc., being used, for a few minutes to sterilize them.

Have at hand some absolutely clean clothes with which to handle the sterilized jars and covers, since perfect sterilization is the object in view. With a broad skimmer, lift out the hot jar, drain free from water, and set it in a shallow pan to be immediately filled according to the method of canning being used. Canning should always be done in a kitchen as free as possible from dust, since spores or yeast plants carried by contaminated air is often the cause of spoilage although the sterilization has been carefully carried out. The utmost care should also be taken to see that all flies are excluded from the kitchen.

Methods of Canning

In the several methods of canning in use, the principle in all of them is the same. It is that of preparing the product by cooking or sterilization in such a way as to exclude or kill all spores, yeast-plants and bacteria that cause fruits and vegetables to ferment and spoil. The next step is to seal them in sterilized cans or jars *absolutely airtight*, so these micro-organisms cannot enter the product after it is canned. These are the simple fundamental rules upon which all canning is based.

Of the several methods, two of the most successful are, because of common equipment, open to the home-canner. These are what are known as the "open-kettle" and the "can-cooked" methods. In the first, which is universally employed for fruits and preserves, the cooking is done in the preserving kettle before being placed in the cans; in the second, which is extensively used for vegetables and other foods, as well as some fruits, all or part of the cooking is done after being placed in the can.

Open-Kettle Method—Prepare the fruit according to variety. Cook the fruit in its own juice, in fruit syrup or simple syrup just enough to render it tender and digestible—no longer; if water is used at all, as in the case of some of the larger, dryer fruits, use just as little as possible, otherwise the rich natural flavor of the fruit will be destroyed by too much dilution; the syrup method ot canning is far superior to others, and gives a product with all its richness preserved. Sterilize the jars according to directions above and have them hot and ready when the fruit is cooked; fill the hot jar with boiling fruit and syrup, run a sterilized silver knife blade around the inside to release all air-pockets or bubbles, and fill to overflowing with the boiling syrup; wipe top of jar carefully with a perfectly clean cloth, dipped in boiling water; dip a new, fresh sealing-ring, or rubber, in boiling water and adjust to the jar; adjust and fasten the hot sterilized cover tightly; invert the jar and place it way from draft to cool; when cooled, if screw caps are used, tighten them again thoroughly, since the cooling has slightly contracted both jar and cap; wipe jar with damp cloth; label; store in a dark, cool place.

Can-Cooked Method—Prepare the fruit according to variety the same as for the open kettle; also, prepare a sufficient quantity of hot simple syrup of proper density. Fill the hot sterilized jar with the uncooked fruit and add enough syrup to fill jar solidly to within a quarter inch of the opening; run a sterilized silver knife blade around the inside; then, proceed to cook by one of the two following methods:

1—Oven Cooking—Provide a sheet of asbestos large enough to practically cover the bottom of the range-oven—such sheets may be had at most plumbing establishments or hardware stores. If asbestos is not obtainable, provide a large pan and fill with about two inches of hot water. Place the filled, open jars in the moderately heated oven, upon the asbestos, or in the pan of water; cook for the length of time required for the particular fruit—see separate recipes—remove from oven and fill to top with boiling syrup; seal, employing the same precautions as in open-kettle method.

2—Boiler Cooking—Provide a wash-boiler or large lard-stand, and fit into the bottom a latticed wooden rack for the jars to rest upon, thus preventing them from touching the bottom; fill the boiler with warm water to about four inches above the rack; put the filled jars into the boiler, separating them by a latticed, wooden frame, or by weaving around and between them a small cotton rope, to prevent them from touching or hitting together when the water boils; cover the boiler, bring the water to boiling point and cook for the required time counting from this period; when cooked, draw boiler back from over fire, take off cover, and when steam has passed off, lift out each jar, set it in a pan of boiling water, fill with syrup to top, wipe, and properly seal; set away from draft to cool, employing the same precautions as in the open-kettle method.

Note—It is absolutely essential in all canning, that the fruit or vegetable shall be heated throughout to boiling temperature.

Selecting the Fruit

One of the first and most important steps to successful canning is the selection of the fruit. The best time to can any fruit is just before it has fully ripened, for although fully ripe fruit has developed its highest stage of flavor, it has also reached the stage where fermentation begins, which is not favorable to successful canning. Also, in the case of jelly making, overripe fruit has lost most of its strength of pectin bodies and their jelly-making qualities. Therefore, select only sound fruit that is fully developed, but just a bit under full-ripe for best results.

Preparing the Fruit

First of all, fruit should be well washed before paring, not for the sake of cleanliness alone, but millions of contaminating bacteria will thus be washed away. Quinces should be rubbed with a coarse cloth before washing; small fruits that are to be seeded should be washed before the seeding is done; berries should usually be washed before being stemmed by quickly washing in a colander and draining in a sieve.

Peaches, apricots and plums are best skinned like tomatoes, by scalding or blanching. Place the fruit in a wire basket, lower it into boiling water for about three minutes, then dip into cold water for a moment—the skins are then easily removed. Such fruits as apples, pears, quinces, etc., should be pared with a silver knife, if possible, to prevent discoloring.

Only enough fruit as can be cooked while it retains its color and freshness should be prepared at a time, and the sugar or syrup, measuring bowls, kettle, jars, etc., should be in readiness when the fruit is prepared. If being can-cooked, the fruit should be placed in the sterilized jars as each piece is prepared, and immediately covered with the syrup.

When canning or preserving some whole, unseeded fruits, as cherries, plums, crab-apples, etc., all or some of the short stems may be left on, as it tends to improve the flavor.

If seeds are to be removed from berries, as for marmalades, etc., this is best done by pressing the pulp through a fine sieve that will hold back the seeds. Strawberries should not be hulled with the fingers—a simple metal huller may be purchased for a few cents.

When placing halves of such fruits as peaches, apricots, pears, etc., in the jars in either method, the rounds should be turned upward with the pieces overlapping, and the blossom ends turned toward the glass sides or light.

Simple Syrups for Canning

The use of sugar in the canning of fruits is not essential to its preservation, but it is used exclusively for improving the flavor, and usually included at the time of canning in the form of prepared syrups. These syrups are used in varying consistencies, depending upon the fruit to be sweetened, and are made with varying proportions of sugar and water. When the measure of sugar is large and the water small, the syrup is said to be heavy; when the proportion of water is large and the sugar small, the syrup is said to be light.

There are several methods of measuring the proportion of sugar or density of syrups, the most accurate of which is the standard syrup gauge; but, careful measuring is quite satisfactory in canning, since the syrup need not be boiled long enough to evaporate the water and thereby change the density. As a guide, the following densities are given.

The sugar is first dissolved completely in boiling hot water that has just been removed from the fire; it is then put back, brought to the boiling point and boiled for 1 minute without stirring.

Density	Sugar	Water
40°	4 parts	1 part
36°	3 "	1 "
32°	2 "	1 "
28°	2 "	1½ parts
24°	1 part	1 part
17°	1 "	1½ parts
14°	1 "	2 "

For preserving berries, cherries, blue plums, etc.—Syrup 40°.

For preserving peaches, plums, quinces, currants, etc.—Syrup 28° to 36°.

For canning acid fruits, such as apples, gooseberries, blue plums, grapes, etc.—Syrup 24°.

For canning peaches, pears, cherries, sweet plums, berries, etc.—Syrup 14° to 17°.

For jelly making, syrup of 25° density made by using the fruit juice instead of water, has been found to be right for combining the sugar and pectin bodies, causing the juice to properly jell—this is about the density of 24° syrup boiled for 3 minutes.

Apples—If it becomes necessary to can apples to save the last of the winter storage, they may be prepared in any manner as for the table by the open kettle method. Remember that all fruit must reach boiling temperature, be put into hot sterilized jars, and sealed while hot.

Apple Juice—When canning apples reserve the sound parings and cores; add a few quartered apples, cover with water and cook about 30 minutes; strain through the jelly-bag, re-heat the juice to boiling, and seal in hot sterilized jars. This juice may then be kept on hand for emergency jelly making, for cooking purposes, or for frozen deserts.

Apricots—Prepare and can exactly the same as peaches.

Blackberries—Pick over, wash and drain 6 qts. fresh blackberries; measure 1 qt. sugar. Put 1 qt. of the berries in preserving kettle, heat slowly and, with a wooden vegetable masher, crush the berries into pulp to release the juice; strain through a cheese-cloth, return the juice to the kettle, add the sugar and stir until dissolved; then bring it to boiling point and when it has boiled 1 minute add the remaining 5 qts. berries, bring up to boiling again and boil 10 minutes; fill jars and seal as directed.

Blueberries—Pick over, wash, and drain 6 qts. blueberries; put ½ pt. water, the berries and 1 pt. sugar in the preserving kettle; heat gradually to boiling point, and boil 15 minutes; fill sterilized jars and seal as directed.

Cherries—Wash, stem and measure 6 qts. cherries, cautiously saving the juice if they are seeded; put 3 pts. sugar and ½ pt. water in the preserving kettle, slowly heat and stir until sugar is dissolved; add cherries and juice; bring to boiling point, and boil 10 minutes, skimming carefully; fill sterilized jars, put a well washed cherry leaf in each, fill with syrup, and seal as previously directed.

Crabapples—Prepare simple syrup of about 20° density, allowing 1½ qts. sugar to 2 qts water for each 6 qts crabapples; wash the apples and rub the blossom ends well; have the syrup in the preserving kettle, drop the fruit into it and cook gently until tender, which will require from 25 to 50 minutes, according to the degree of ripeness and variety of the apples

Cranberries—Sort and wash select, sound cranberries; can with or without cooking, exactly as directed for rhubarb and green gooseberries.

Currants—Can exactly the same as blackberries, except use twice the amount of sugar.

Damson Plums—Wash and stem the fruit, and without skinning, proceed exactly as for sweet plums, but cook 7 to 8 minutes instead of 5.

Fruit in Grape Juice—Prepare apples, pears, plums, or any other fruit for canning; put 6 qts. grape juice in preserving kettle, and boil it until it is reduced to 4 qts.; put in the prepared fruit so long as it is covered well with the juice, and boil gently until the fruit is tender; fill sterilized jars and seal according to previous directions.

Gooseberries—Wash and prepare 6 qts. green gooseberries; in the preserving kettle, prepare simple syrup of 36° density using 3 pts. sugar to 1 pt. water; put in the gooseberries and cook gently 15 minutes; fill jars and seal as directed. For ripe gooseberries, proceed exactly as above, use half the quantity of water and put in berries as soon as sugar is dissolved.

Or: Can green gooseberries without cooking same as rhubarb and cranberries.

Grapes—Pick over and wash grapes thoroughly; to each 6 qts. grapes, allow 1 qt. sugar and ¼ pt. water. Press the pulps out of the skins and put into separate vessels; rub the pulps through a sieve that is just fine enough to keep back the seeds, put the seedless pulp into the preserving kettle and add the skins to it; add the water, bring to boiling point and add sugar, which may be more or less than the above quantity, according to the tartness of the grapes; boil 15 minutes; fill sterilized jars and seal as previously directed

Peaches—Prepare a simple syrup of 14° density, according to instructions above, allowing 1 pt. sugar to 2 pts. water for each 4 qts. prepared peaches after boiling 1 minute, skim and set syrup kettle back on range to keep hot, just under the boiling point, but not boil. Wash, skin, halve and seed just enough peaches at a time to make a layer in the bottom of the preserving kettle; cover them with some of the hot syrup; bring to boiling point, skim carefully, and boil 10 minutes or until easily pierced with a silver fork; fill hot sterilized jars with peaches and fill to overflowing with the hot fruit syrup; allowing about 1 cup syrup to each quart of fruit; seal as directed.—Peaches and similar fruit may also be canned by the can-cooked method by following directions previously given.

Pears—Wash, pare, halve and core pears, then proceed exactly the same as with peaches.

Plums—Wash and prepare 8 qts. plums, with or without skins removed; prepare simple syrup of 40° density, using 4 pts. sugar to 1 pt. water for the above quantity, keeping it heated around the boiling point in the preserving kettle; put in 2 qts. of the plums at a time, cook for 5 minutes, fill jars, fill up with syrup, and seal as previously directed.—It may be necessary to add a little more syrup at the last, depending upon how much fruit has been put into the jars. For easily skinning plums, see directions for preparing fruit. Plums may be canned in syrup of much lighter density, since the amount of sugar has nothing to do with their preservation, but canned as above, depending upon their natural sweetness, the tartar varieties will be found to be rich and delicious. Plums and quinces are better preserved than canned.

Quinces—Wipe, wash, pare, core and quarter fruit; prepare simple syrup of 32° density, using 2 qts. sugar to 1 qt. water for each 4 qts. prepared quinces; parboil fruit in clear water until tender, skim it out and drain; meantime, let the syrup re-boil 20 minutes; put half the fruit in preserving kettle and cover with half the syrup; cook gently for 25 minutes, fill sterilized jars and seal as previously directed.—Parings, cores and the parboiling water may be combined and made into jelly.

Or: prepare fruit as above and put 4 qts. into preserving kettle and cover well with cold water; heat gradually and cook gently until tender—as each piece becomes tender enough to be easily pierced with a silver fork, take it out and drain on a platter; when all are out, strain the liquid through a cheesecloth, put 2 qts. of it and 1½ qts. sugar into the preserving kettle, heat and stir until sugar dissolves, then skim; put in the cooked fruit and boil gently for 20 minutes; fill jars and seal as directed.

Raspberries—Follow the quantities and directions given for blackberries.

Or. Heat, crush, and strain the juice from 3 qts. currants; to this add 6 qts. raspberries and 3 pts. sugar; cook, fill jars and seal as directed for blackberries.

Rhubarb—Select young tender rhubarb, wash, pare and cut into about 2 inch lengths; without cooking, pack into sterilized jars, fill with cold water that has been boiled and strained; let stand 10 minutes, drain off the water and replace it with more water of the same kind to overflowing; place on sterilized rings and covers and seal tightly.

Or: Prepare the rhubarb, and cook exactly as directed for green gooseberries.

Strawberries—In canning strawberries, they should never be spoiled by cooking in water. Prepare a light simple syrup of 17°

to 24° density and keep hot just under the boiling point; prepare the strawberries, washing all sand and dust through a colander, drain and have ready; put 5 or 6 cups of the hot syrup into the preserving kettle, put in a quart of berries, giving the kettle a shake to submerge all the berries; bring to the boiling point, and as soon as the syrup has boiled up a moment, quickly skim out the berries, fill the hot sterilized jar, fill to overflowing with boiling syrup, seal, invert, and cool. Put in a little more syrup, add another quart of berries and repeat.—About 1 qt. of syrup to the gallon of strawberries will be required

Vegetable Canning

Success in canning vegetables, like fruit, depends entirely upon the proper selection, preparation, sterilization and sealing of the product. Remember that the fundamental object is to destroy the ever present bacteria and its spores and to prevent them from entering the product after sterilization; no step of the process may be overlooked and success attained. While there are several methods of canning vegetables, the one most successful and best adapted to kitchen canning, known as the Sterilization Process, is here given. A little patience and practice may be needed, but with proper precaution and attention to details, there need be no failure.

In the canning of vegetables by this method, much importance should be given to the selections of the can or jar to be used. In practice, it has been found that the most practical jar is that of the wide-mouth glass type, fitted with glass cover held by a stout wire, lever-action, spring clamp which is attached to the neck. The following directions and recipes are for this type of jar in pint and quart sizes. With jars at hand, carefully inspect them, fit with fresh rubber rings, and thoroughly sterilize them according to previous instructions at the beginning of this chapter.

Under the can-cooked method for fruit will be found direction for converting a common wash-boiler into an ideal canning steamer. With the steamer, or cooker, in readiness, the vegetables may be prepared according to their particular recipes and carried through the process next described.

Sterilization Process

Select and prepare vegetables according to the subsequent recipes given for their proper canning. Put the prepared vegetables into hot sterilized jars, filling each to within about an inch of the top; fill up the jar to top with hot fresh water that has just been boiled, passing it through a strainer and being particular that the water penetrates through the vegetables to the bottom of the jar; adjust sterilized ring and cover, and place the wire in position over the top, but do not clamp down the lever at the side—leave it in upward position.

Place the filled jars upon the rack, or false bottom, in the steamer, being careful to separate them sufficiently to prevent them from touching or hitting together when the water boils; pour into the steamer enough hot water to extend about half-way the height of the jars; adjust the cover of the boiler and set to boil. Boil steadily and gently for 1 hour, keeping the boiler cover in place during the period; then set boiler back on range, remove cover and allow steam to escape; when cool enough, lift out the jars, press down the spring clamp to tighten, wipe, and set aside to cool away from wind or draft.

The following day, put the jars back into the steamer with cold water instead of hot, release the clamp lever, bring to boiling point; boil 1 hour as before, tighten clamps while hot, wipe, and set aside as before.

On the third day, repeat the process; wipe, cool, label and set aside.

In a day or two, the jars should be tested. To do this, release the clamp and move wire from over top; now, carefully lift up each jar by the glass lid or cover alone—if the top comes off, the sterilization is not complete and fermentation or decomposition has set in; but, if the weight of the jar may be lifted by the top, tighten down the clamp and store as perfectly sealed.

Beans—Lima, kidney and similar varieties of shelled beans should be gathered in the early morning and kept in a freshened state until shelled; after shelling, they should be immediately placed in the jars and carried through the sterilization process as directed. —Before shelling, all pods that have begun to harden should be discarded.

Stringbeans should be gathered while the dew is still on them and canned while still crisp and fresh; select only young, tender beans, string them and break into short lengths; pack at once into the jars, add a teaspoon of salt to each quart jar after the water has been added, and carry through the sterilization process as directed.

Beets—Select young beets, wash them, trim off tops, and boil them in plenty of water for about 1½ hours or until well cooked; dip them in cold water, skin and slice them; put into jars and fill to top with the hot water in which they were boiled passed through a strainer; cover and pass through the sterilization process as described.—By using half water and half vinegar, they are converted into pickled beets, to which a little sugar and spices or herbs may also be added if desired.

Carrots—Carrots should be canned early in the season when they are young before they have become stringy and strong; prepare them exactly as you would for the table, put them into hot sterilized jars and carry through the sterilization process as directed.

Cauliflower—Prepare choice cauliflower as for the table, fill jars and carry through the sterilization process as directed.

Corn—Select choice ears of sweet, green corn, carefully gathering those with full, well-developed grains at the stage just before they begin to harden; at this stage, the corn will be at its best in richness and sugar contents. Do not allow it to wait—since the sugar strength diminishes very rapidly after being pulled from the stalk—but, within the hour that it is gathered, have it prepared and in the jars. Husk, brush off silks with a stiff brush, and shave off the grains with a sharp knife; pack immediately in jars and carry through the sterilization process as directed. When testing, if any jars are discarded, do not try to save them, but empty and put the jars through the process again with new corn.

Eggplant—Pare and slice eggplant as for cooking; drop into boiling water and boil gently for about 20 minutes; pack in jars and carry through the sterilization process as directed. May be used like fresh eggplant.

Kohlrabi—Prepare and cook as for the table—see index—pack in sterilized jars, and carry through the sterilization process as directed.

Okra—(Gumbo) Select young, tender pods, wash them and cut them in 3 or 4 pieces; fill jars and pass through the sterilizing as directed. For soups or stews.

Parsnips—Prepare and can according to directions given for carrots.

Peas—Gather choice pods of green peas in the early morning, shell them, fill jars and carry through the sterilization process as described. It is important that they should be just off the vines and not allowed to remain in the air longer than necessary after being shelled; to avoid this, drop them in cold water as they are shelled, then drain and put into the hot jars.

Pumpkin—Prepare and cook the pumpkin exactly as for the table; pack solidly in sterilized jars, filling to overflowing with the liquor or boiling water; cover and carry through the sterilization process as directed, but steam for 1½ hours during each of the 3 periods instead of 1 hour; mashed vegetables, being solidly packed, require a longer time for the heat to penetrate to the center of the jar.—Pumpkin may also be pared and cut into cubes, then put directly into the jars and carried through the sterilization process with success.

Spinach—Prepare and cook the spinach as for the tables, pack sterilized jars and carry through the sterilization process as previously directed.

Succotash—As prepared by canners, succotash is a combination of green corn and lima beans. It is rather more difficult to can than the ingredients separate, but the sterilizing in 1½ hour periods instead of 1 hour as directed, little difficulty should be encountered. Use the same precautions in gathering and preparing as for corn and beans.

Summer Squash—Canned exactly like pumpkin—follow the pumpkin recipe.

Tomatoes—Blanch or skin the tomatoes in the usual way, and cook them to your liking; however, they are best when cooked in as little water as possible. Like other fruit, the open-kettle method is best adapted to their canning; put the boiling tomatoes into hot sterilized Mason or other jars, seal and invert until cool, using all the precaution previously given for this method. Special care should be taken not to touch the inside of cover and ring with the fingers after they are sterilized.

Turnips—While not ordinarily canned, it may become necessary to save turnips, as well as pumpkins, squash, etc., that are not keeping well in storage. Cook turnips until tender, place in jars and carry through the sterilization process as directed.

Jams and Marmalades

Jams are primarily preserves reduced to pulp form; marmalades are jams with seeds and most of the moisture removed, and cooked "low" into a semi-jellied state. The term "conserve" is used for jams or marmalades made from a combination of fruits.

The best fruits for jams and marmalades are berries, cherries, grapes, currants, some varieties of plums, apples, quinces, oranges and lemon.

In making jams and marmalades, it is essential that no water be added to the more juicy fruits, such as cherries, grapes, berries, etc.; and, to the dryer fruits, such as apples, peaches, etc., add only enough water to barely cover the bottom of the pan or kettle in which they are cooked—even then, it is better to use juice of some other fruit, such as currants, or, for apples, sweet cider.

When the more juicy fruits are used, rinse or moisten the inside of the kettle with cold water; for other fruits, cover the bottom with water or fruit juice; put the prepared fruit in the kettle in light layers, sprinkling each layer generously with the sugar before adding another. For jam, cook the fruit until soft, reduce it to a pulpy mass and continue cooking gently until just enough of the moisture has been evaporated. For marmalades, gently stew the larger fruits at slow heat until tender, reduce to pulp and pass through a sieve; reduce smaller fruits to pulp uncooked and pass through a sieve to remove seeds; then, proceed to cook according to the time required in the subsequent recipes, or until a little of the juice will jell when dropped on a cold plate.

While the amount of sugar used naturally varies with the fruit, the basic allowance for jams is 1 pt. sugar to each qt. of fruit pulp, while for marmalades it is 1½ to 2 pts. sugar to each qt. of fruit.

Jellies

Jelly can be made from the natural juices of practically any acid fruit by the addition of sugar, and boiling until the density of the fruit syrup is 25° when tested with a standard syrup gauge. The uncertainties of jelly making in the average household are due, principally, to the fact that this degree of density of the fruit-syrup must be gauged, or judged by experience and off-hand judgment alone.

Such common complaints as "My jelly refuses to jell," or "My jelly is turning to sugar" may be evaded by bearing the above fact in mind and following a few well-known rules of practice in the selection of the fruit, preparing the juice, and reducing the fruit-syrup to the proper density.

For jelly-making, select only tart, or acid, fruits in their newly ripened or near-ripened stage. These may be divided into two classes:

1—Large, firm fruits, such as apples, peaches, quinces, etc. These require the addition of moisture to draw out the flavoring and the pectic acid that combines with the sugar, causing the juice to jell, and to produce a juice of sufficient volume and richness. The amount of water added, however, varies with the fruit; apples, for instance, usually requiring 4 qts. of water to 8 qts. of sliced fruit, which, after boiling until tender and straining without pressing, produces just 3 qts. of strained juice—if there is more than this amount, it should be cooked down to that quantity. Such fruits as peaches, containing a liberal amount of natural juice, require less water, the average requiring 3 to 3½ qts. of water to produce 3 qts. juice from 8 qts. of prepared fruit. Such semi-juicy fruit as plums require the addition of only 1 pt. of water to each 1 gallon fruit, which should be slightly under-ripe when used for jelly.

2—Small, soft fruits, such as currants, berries, cherries, grapes, etc. These do not require the addition of moisture, or water, since they are rich in natural juice. They should, therefore, never be gathered just after a rain, or, after gathering, should not be allowed to stand in water, but should be quickly washed in a colander and drained, since they will readily absorb too much moisture. Except grapes, these juicy fruits are best for jelly when just ripening—grapes should be gathered half-ripe, or half of them newly ripe and half of them green. To extract the juice, some of the fruit is crushed in the bottom of the preserving kettle, some whole fruit added and cooked in its own juice until tender and the juices released; it is then crushed, or "jammed," and the juice strained ready for the jelly kettle.

In separating or straining the juice from the pulp, it is best to strain it through cheese-cloth without squeezing or pressing. If the cheese-cloth is doubled, or a thin muslin bag used, the juice will be quite clear; and, if a flannel or felt bag is used, the juice will be very clear.

The amount of sugar added to the fruit-juice depends upon the density or thickness of the juice before it is added. When the fruit contains quite a little natural sugar, its juice, after boiling, naturally is of slightly higher density. By referring to the Table of Syrup Densities given at the beginning of this chapter, it will be noted that syrup made from equal parts water and sugar and boiled 3 minutes is of approximately 25° density; therefore, if the fruit-juice is of the density of water, the rule of equal parts of sugar and juice may be followed out; but, if the juice is heavier than water, the sugar should be slightly less than an equal part.—Damsons, for instance, requires but little more than ½ part of sugar to 1 part of fruit-juice. *Sugar should always be heated in the oven before adding it to the fruit-juice.*

Measure the fruit-juice into the preserving kettle, add the proper amount of sugar and set it on the range. Heat gradually, gently stirring ntil all the sugar is dissolved; if grains of sugar settle on the sides of the kettle above the juice, they should be washed down with a wet cloth as in candy-making. Bring the juice to the boiling point and let it boil-up just 1 minute, then draw the kettle back from the fire and skim carefully and well; set it over the fire again, let it boil-up 1 minute, draw it back and skim again; repeat this operation for the third time, thus giving the fruit-syrup a total of 3 minutes boiling; pour into hot sterilized glasses, set them away from a draft or wind, cover with a pane of glass, and do not disturb until cool and "set;" seal and label.

Unless the new "patent" top glasses are used, the very best method of sealing jelly glasses is by the use of good parchment or heavy writing paper; cut paper disks to exactly fit the inside of the glass at the surface of the jelly or marmalade; dip the disk in brandy or similar liquor and adjust it flatly upon the surface of the jelly; then, cut another similar disk for the top of the glass, allowing an inch margin all around, brush one side with egg-white, adjust it over the top of the glass snugly, folding the margin down and sticking it tightly to the sides; brush over the outer surface of the paper with egg-white, thus giving it a double coat.—The presence of the brandy prevents mold, while the airtight paper cover prevents the escape of the vapor and retains the natural moisture. When parafine is used, as some prefer, the deposit on the top of the jelly should be at least one-fourth inch thick to prevent it from cracking.

Note—Crystalization, or "sugaring" of jellies is due to two causes: *first,* failure to completely dissolve the sugar in the fruit-juice before boiling; *second,* over-cooking of the fruit-syrup. By following the above method carefully, these causes will be eliminated.

Special Recipes

Apple Butter—Wash apples, cut in quarters without peeling or coreing, but removing all inferior places; to 5 gallons cut apples, add 6½ pounds sugar, and allow to stand over-night; add about 1 tablespoon whole starannis, or cloves, ½ stick cinnamon, broken, and cook over a moderate heat, covered and do not open until done; do not add water, as the juice of the apples is sufficient; may be cooked in a 50-pound lard can, with the lid weighted down; when done, press through a colander, and seal in sterilized jars.

Apple Chutney—Pare, core and slice two and a half pounds of tart apples and place them in the kettle with a pint of vinegar and a pound of brown sugar. Cook the apples until they are reduced to a pulp, then add three-quarters of a pound of seeded raisins, two ounces of salt, a half ounce of mustard seed, a half ounce of ground ginger, a quarter ounce of peeled and minced garlic and half teaspoonful of cayenne pepper. Mix these ingredients well, then cover and stir them daily thoroughly for one week. Then place them in jars or bottles, cover and cork them and store them in a cool place.

Apple Jellies—When tart, juicy apples of good flavor are selected for jelly making, the fruit is usually rich enough in pectin bodies that the juice may be greatly diluted and still make a fair quality of jelly. The best apple jelly is made when the juice is extracted with the addition of just enough water to cover the bottom of the kettle; jellies weaker in flavor may be made, however, by adding ½ pt. water to each lb. of prepared apples, and adding 1 lb. sugar and the juice of 1 lemon to each pt. of strained juice; but a larger quantity of jelly may be made from a given quantity of apples.

Apple Jam—Select sound apples of the same kind, pare, core and slice them; for each pound of sliced apples, allow ¾ lb. sugar, and the rind and half the juice of a lemon; put the apples in a baking dish or jar with the bottom covered with water, placing the fruit in layers and sprinkling each layer with sufficient sugar, the grated lemon rind and juice; cover vessel closely, set in shallow pan of water and slowly cook in a moderate oven until the fruit is tender and of sufficient dryness; put into sterilized jars.

Apple Marmalade—Prepare apples in quarters, mix 2 lbs. in a light jar with 4 oz. sugar and 1 oz. butter; cook until soft in a pan of boiling water or in a temperate oven; pass through a fine sieve and store in sterilized jars.

Apple and Blackberry Jam — Sliced apples, 4 pts.; blackberries, 2 qts.; sugar, 4½ pts. Put prepared blackberries into a crock, or stew-jar, with 1 pt. of the sugar, cover, and set aside for 12 hours or more, then place jar in the oven, which should be only slightly warm at first, and bently stew until the juice is extracted; put the thinly sliced apples in the preserving kettle, add the strained berry-juice, then the rest of the sugar, and boil gently 45 to 50 minutes; put into sterilized jars and closely cover.

Apricot Jam—Skin, or blanch, apricots, halve them and remove the seeds; weigh the apricots and allow an equal weight of sugar; put them in a dish or stone jar in layers with sugar sprinkled between, cover, and set aside to digest for at least 12 hours; crack the seeds, remove the kernels and blanch them; put fruit, kernels and sugar in the preserving kettle, simmer gently and keep skimmed; as the pieces of apricots become clear, take them out and put into sterilized jars, and when all are filled, cover with some of the syrup and seed kernels; seal airtight.

Barberry Jelly—Barberry jelly is made exactly as blackberry jelly; however, particular precaution must be taken with barberries, for the principal causes of failure lies in using berries that are not freshly gathered, or are over-ripe. Use freshly picked, just-ripe barberries and success will be more frequent.

Blue Plum Conserve — Wash, dry, and cut up two dozen large California blue plums, removing the seed; put plums in a preserving kettle, and cover with four and a half pounds granulated sugar; add juice of four oranges; then grind up pulp and peel of the oranges and add them also; add one and one-half pounds of seeded raisins, put on

range, bring to boil and let boil thirty minutes; put into sterilized jelly glasses and seal.

California Conserve — Dip two dozen large peaches in boiling water for one minute, then plunge into cold water, drain, peel off the skins, cut into quarters; finely chop two pounds seeded raisins and two cups walnut or other nutmeats; wash six oranges, cut without peeling into small pieces; mix above ingredients, measure, and allow an equal amount of sugar; cook all together very slowly, stirring and frequently until thick. Pour into sterilized jelly glasses and seal.

Cider Pear Sauce—Pare, quarter and core nice sweet pears, put 4 qts. of the prepared fruit in the preserving kettle, and cover with 5 pts. boiled cider; place the kettle upon an iron ring placed on the hot range-top so it will prevent scorching the fruit; cook slowly 2 to 3 hours or until the fruit is tender, stirring very carefully to prevent breaking up the fruit too much; seal in sterilized jars.—Apples may be prepared in the same way. If fruit is tart, sugar may be added to suit, usually 1 cup to each pt. of cider being sufficient.

Cider, Boiled—Put sweet cider into an open preserving kettle, not to exceed two-thirds full; boil until reduced to one-half; keeping it skimmed while boiling; store in stone or glass jug.

Crabapple Jelly—Wash and halve crabapples, weigh them, put them in the preserving kettle, and for each pound of fruit, add 1 pt. water, 1 clove, and ginger root the size of a pea; also, weight and set aside 1 lb. sugar for each 4 lbs. fruit; cook fruit very slowly until tender, then strain well without pressing; put liquid in clean kettle, boil until jelly sets when tested on a cold plate, put into sterilized glasses and cover well when cold.

Cranberry Butter—Cook 3 qts. washed and selected cranberries in 1 pt. water until skins of fruit are all broken; separate pulp by pressing through a sieve; return pulp to range and cook until quite thick; add 1 qt. sugar and cook over gentle heat 30 minutes, constantly stirring; cool slightly; pour into sterilized jars and cover closely.

Cranberry Jelly—Cook 2 qts. washed and selected cranberries in 1 qt. water until fruit is tender; mash and strain through a jelly bag; measure the juice and allow ¾ pint of sugar for each 1 pt. juice; heat together until sugar is dissolved, but do not boil; put into sterilized glasses, cool and cover.

Cumquat Preserves — Without peeling them, halve and seed cumquats; weigh the fruit and set aside an equal weight of sugar; cook the fruit until perfectly tender, being careful that the pieces are not broken, allowing 1 cup water to each lb. comquats; skim out the fruit; add a little water to the liquid to restore it to its original volume of 1 cup to the lb. of fruit or sugar, adding the juice of ½ lemon to each cup of liquid; dissolve the sugar in the heated liquid, boil about 5 minutes and skim; add the cumquats and gently simmer until the fruit is clear or transparent; skim out the fruit into sterilized jars, reduce the syrup to preserve thickness and pour over the fruit; cover closely or seal tight.

Currant Bar-Le-Duc—Select a quantity of large ripe currants and wash; with the point of a sharp paring knife, open each currant, and squeeze out the pulp, keeping pulp and skins separate. To each cup of pulp add one-half cup water, put into a preserving kettle and cook until very soft; then rub through a fine sieve; to this pulp and juice add the skins, cook twenty minutes and add sugar measure for measure; return to range, bring to a boil, skim carefully, and test as for jelly. When it has reached the stage of jell, pour into small glasses, cool, and cover.—Gooseberries may be prepared in the same manner.

Gooseberry and Currant Jam—Head and tail 6 lbs. red gooseberries, put them into preserving kettle and allow them to stand near the fire until some of the juice is extracted; put over fire, bring to boiling point, and when they have boiled 10 minutes, gradually add 4 lbs. granulated sugar; add the strained juice of ½ pt. red currants and boil until the jam sets when tested on a cold plate; pour into sterilized jars, cover tightly and keep in cool, dry place.—Skim constantly while boiling, and stir well during last few minutes of cooking. Requires about 2 hours.

Grape Marmalade—Wash and pick over ripe grapes and separate pulps from the skins, placing them in separate bowls; boil the pulps until easily pressed through a sieve to discard the seeds; weigh the skins and allow an equal weight of sugar; mix the juicy pulp, skins and sugar in the preserving kettle and cook 25 minutes after reaching the boiling point; put into sterilized glasses and cover closely.

Grapefruit Marmalade—Make exactly as Orange Marmalade, using ½ lemon to each Grapefruit.

Hawaiian Jam—Wash six pounds Concord grapes, separate hulls from pulp, cook pulp fifteen minutes and press through a sieve to remove seeds; add pulp to skins, add five pounds sugar, one pound seeded raisins, the juice and chipped rinds of four large oranges; boil twenty minutes, mixing well; five minutes before removing from range, stir in one cup chopped English walnuts or other nutmeats; put in jars or glasses.

Jellied Figs—Soak two tablespoons gelatine in ¼ cup cold water; drain stewed or canned whole figs, and cut each in half; if there is not 1½ cups of syrup, add enough water to complete measure and bring to boiling point, then add the softened gelatine and stir until it has dissolved; add three tablespoons lemon juice to syrup, and pour over prepared figs; ½ cup broken nutmeats may be mixed with syrup if desired; set aside to cool place until firm, serve with cream.

Orange Marmalade—Peel 12 oranges, remove all white skin and slice thin, removing any seeds; slice 2 lemons thinly with rind on; put together in a jar, cover with 11 pts. cold water, cover and let stand 24 hours; put into preserving kettle and boil steadily 3 hours; add 7 pts. sugar, mix well, and boil 1 hour more; put hot sterilized glasses, cool and cover.—Makes about 18 regular glasses.

Orange Peel, Candied—When making orange marmalade, wipe the oranges with a damp cloth and quarter the peel with a sharp knife, then carefully remove it. Put the peel of 6 oranges in the preserving kettle, cover with cold water, bring to boiling point and cook slowly until soft; drain, remove the white portions using the bowl of a spoon; cut yellow portions into strips, using scissors. Boil 1 cup sugar in ½ cup water until it threads; place the strips of peel in the syrup and cook 5 minutes; drain and coat peel with fine granulated sugar.—Useful in candy making, cake decorating, tarts, etc

Peach Jelly—Blanch and skin the peaches, quarter them, removing the stones; remove the kernels from half the stones, and blanch and skin them also; put all together in the preserving kettle with just enough cold water to cover them; stir often and cook until fruit is very tender, then strain through the jelly-bag; to each 1 pt. juice, allow the juice of 1 lemon and 1 pt. sugar; follow instructions for cooking jellies, but boil up in 4 periods of 5 minutes each; put into sterilized glasses, cool and cover.

Pear Chips—Peel and core sound, ripe pears and cut into small pieces or slices; to each 5 lbs. pear chips, allow 2½ lbs. sugar and 2 oz. ground ginger; mix all together in a stone jar and stand aside overnight; next morning, wash and dry 2½ lemons, slice them cross-section, remove the seeds and cut the slices in half or quarter; add lemons to pears, mix well in the preserving kettle or set the stone jar in boiling water in the oven, and cook very slowly and gently for 3 hours; put into sterilized jars and seal.

Persimmon Preserves — Select large, firm, ripe persimmons, cover with cold water and allow to stand 12 hours; drain, stew in enough water to cover until tender; drain and place them on platters to cool and become firm. Make a syrup of 32° density—see "Simple Syrups for Canning"—using 1 cup sugar to ½ cup water for each 1 qt. persimmons; when syrup reaches boiling point, put in the persimmons, restore the boiling point, and boil 10 minutes; skim out the fruit onto the platters and set in the sun to become firm; add the rind and juice of ½ lemon to each qt. syrup and boil until quite a little thicker; put persimmons into hot sterilized jars and cover with the syrup; seal.

Pineapple Marmalade—Peel, core and slice pineapples, and grate them to fineness; put into preserving kettle with sugar, allow 14 oz.—or 4 tablespoons less than 1 pt.—of sugar to each lb. pulp; boil gently until thick and clear; put into sterilized jars or glasses, cover with paper disk dipped in brandy, and seal airtight.

Plum Butter — Cook plums slowly and press the pulp through a colander, cooking in just enough water to prevent the fruit from scorching; to each quart of plum pulp, add 2 cups of strained honey, or 1 cup each of honey and sugar, heating the pulp to the boiling point before adding the honey and sugar; cook until the consistency of apple butter.

Pumpkin Chips — Prepare small, sweet pumpkin in pared strips as for cooking, but cut into crosswise slices instead of large pieces; allow equal weights of pumpkin and sugar, and ¼ cup lemon juice to each lb. of sugar; put pumpkin and sugar into preserving kettle in alternate layers, pour the lemon juice over the whole, cover and stand aside for 24 hours; shred the lemon peel and add to the pumpkin with 1 oz. ginger to each lb. of pumpkin; add ½ pt. cold water for each 3 lbs. sugar used; boil until pumpkin is tender, then pour into an earthenware jar or crock, cover and let it remain a few days; finally, pour off the syrup into the kettle, boil until reduced and thickened, then pour, while hot, over the pumpkin which may be stored in hot sterilized jars if preferred; cover closely.

Quince Marmalade—Wash, quarter, and remove seed from five large quinces, but do not peel; cover with boiling water, and cook until very tender, drain, and rub through a colander or coarse strainer; measure, and add half the quantity of sugar as quince pulp; add one cup seeded or seedless raisins, and cook slowly until thick; pour into sterilized glasses and seal. Double quantity may be as easily made.

Raspberry and Currant Jelly—Make the same as with the separate fruits, using equal measures of currants and raspberries.

Rhubarb Jam—Remove outer skin of rhubarb as for cooking and cut into short pieces; weigh it and allow an equal measure of sugar; put them together in the preserving kettle, add ½ teaspoon ground ginger and the grated ½ lemon rind; set beside the fire and let it come slowly to boiling point; stir occasionally and boil until the jam sets when tested on cold plate; fill sterilized jars and cover closely. Requires 1 to 1½ hours, depending upon the age of the rhubarb.

Rhubarb Conserve—Prepare rhubarb as for jam; for 7 pounds, rhubarb, allow 5 pounds sugar, 3 oranges and 1 lb. seeded or seedless raisins; wash, dry and slice oranges, remove seeds and cut slices in half; mix all together in the preserving kettle and when the bottom is covered with the juices, cook same as for rhubarb jam.

Strawberry Jelly—To each 5 qts. of strawberries, add 1 qt. red currants and proceed according to instructions under "Jellies," except: let the fruit-syrup boil up for 5 minutes each period, instead of 1 minute.

Strawberry Preserves — For preserves, select only sound, dry (not watery) strawberries that have just ripened, rejecting all others; stem the berries and wash them through a colander and drain quickly; put 5 cups of berries and 4 cups of sugar in the preserving kettle and add ½ cup cold water; bring to boiling point and boil briskly for 30 minutes; put into sterilized jars; will keep without tightly sealing.—Do not try to cook a larger quantity than above at one time in one kettle, if a *quantity* is to be preserved, have 3 kettles and put the above quantity in each, then start them boiling 10 minutes apart; they will then rotate in 10 minute periods and the work will be progressive and of the same quality.

Tomato Jam—Take ripe tomatoes, peel and take out the seeds; put into a preserving kettle with one-half pound sugar to each pound of prepared tomato; boil two lemons soft, and pound them fine. Take out the pips and add to the tomato; boil slowly, mashing to a smooth mass. When smooth, and thick, put into jars or tumblers.

Tomato Marmalade — Blanch, skin and cut in halves or quarters, 3½ lbs. ripe tomatoes; peel 3 lemons, remove all the white skin from the fruit and slice thinly. Make thin syrup with 4 lbs. sugar and 1 cup water, add the tomatoes and lemons and bring to boiling point; stir and skim often and boil until it jells when tested on a cold plate; put into hot sterilized glasses, cool, and closely cover.

Tomatoe Preserves — Peel the tomatoes and to each pound add a pound of sugar and let stand overnight. Take the tomatoes out of the sugar and boil the syrup, removing the scum. Put in the tomatoes and boil gently twenty minutes; remove the fruit and boil unil the syrup thickens. On cooling put the fruit into jars and pour the syrup over. The round, yellow variety of tomato should be used and as soon as ripe.

Apple Pickle — Take ripe, hard, sweet apples. Peel evenly, and if the apples are perfect leave them whole, otherwise cut in quarters. To a peck of apples take about two quarts of vinegar and four pounds of sugar, half an ounce of mace, half an ounce of cloves and the same amount of allspice, all unground, one teaspoonful of mustard seed, a few pepper grains and a little salt. Heat the vinegar and sugar together till it boils, skin well, put the spices into a thin muslin bag and add to the vinegar, then put in the apples. Place over the fire, and stew slowly until the apples are soft. Then take out the apples, let the vinegar boil down and pour it over the fruit; cover and put away.

Cabbage Pickle — Cut a sound cabbage into quarters, spread it on a large flat platter or dish and sprinkle thickly with salt; set it in a cool place for twenty-four hours and cover with cold vinegar for twelve hours. Prepare a pickle by seasoning enough vinegar to cover the cabbage with equal quantities of mace, all-pice, cinnamon and black pepper, a cup of sugar to every gallon of vinegar, and a teaspoon of celery seed to every pint. Pack the cabbage in a stone jar; boil the vinegar and spices five minutes and pour on hot. Cover and set away in a cool, dry place. It will be good in a month. A few slices of bet root improves the color.

Beet Sweet-Pickle — Select even-sized young beets and boil them as usual until they are tender, then skin them under cold water, trim them and set them aside. Put into the preserve kettle, three pints of vinegar and 1½ pts. of sugar. Add a generous spice-bag and let the mixture boil for 20 minutes. Skim it, then add the beets and cook the mass until it is reheated. Put the beets into

jars, pour the hot syrup over them and seal them.

Cauliflower Pickle — Wash and separate choice heads of cauliflower into sprays of flowerlets; weigh them and provide an equal weight of small white shallots; prepare a brine sufficient to cover the cauliflower sprays by adding 4 oz. salt to each quart water, boiling 10 minutes and setting aside to become cold; cover sprays with the cold brine and allow to remain 3 days, then drain well; peel shallots and place in alternate layers with the cauliflower sprays in wide-mouthed bottles or jars, sprinkling each layer with a little allspice, a few pepper corns and a bit of mace; measure and set aside enough vinegar to cover or fill the jars; mix to a paste 1 level teaspoon black pepper and 1 tablespoon each of tumeric, currie powder, ground mustard, salt, lemon juice and lime juice and add to each quart of vinegar by gradually thinning the paste with the vinegar; pour this seasoned vinegar over the sprays and shallots in the jars and seal closely; do not disturb for 4 weeks.

Cherry Pickle — Select sound, freshly ripened and freshly gathered Kentish cherries; leave the short stems attached; wash and drain them and measure enough vinegar to cover them when placed in the jars; boil the vinegar and to each pint add ½ lb. sugar and cayenne to taste, skim well, boil a few minutes longer and pour into a stone jar to cool; when cold add a few drops of carmine fruit coloring and fill sterilized jars in which the cherries have been loosely packed; seal.

Chili Sauce — 1 — Blanch and cook 1 peck ripe tomatoes and run the pulp through a sieve; meantime, stew ½ gallon sliced onions until tender and grind in food chopper when cool; mix and add ¾ cup salt, 1 teaspoon celery-salt, ⅛ teaspoon cayenne, 1 qt. good vinegar, and ½ cup or more sugar according to taste; in a bit of cloth, tie a teaspoon each of cloves and nutmeg and suspend it into the sauce; gently cook to desired thickness; put into sterilized bottles and cork tightly.

2 — Blanch and chop 30 large ripe tomatoes, finely chop 8 medium onions, mix and cook in 2 qts. good vinegar; add 8 tablespoons brown sugar, 6 tablespoons salt and 12 chopped green peppers; cook down to 1 gallon; store in sterilized jars.

Chow-Chow — Two large cauliflowers, two quarts green peppers, three quarts green tomatoes, three quarts green cucumbers, three quarts small onions. Slice about half an inch thick. Sprinkle with salt, alternate with layers of tomatoes and onions and cucumbers. Boil the cauliflower about five minutes; set overnight; then strain all well and free from water. After this place in jars and make the seasoning as follows: One pound mustard seed, one-half pound whole allspice, one-half pound whole black pepper, one pint beef brine, one gallon vinegar, one-half stick curry powder. Boil hard for fifteen minutes, then pour over the vegetables. If too thick add vinegar. Mix the mustard with vinegar. Put the spices in a bag closely tied. Mustard and spices must boil together in a vinegar.

Or: One peck of green tomatoes, half peck stringbeans, quarter peck small white onions, quarter pint green and red peppers mixed, two large heads cabbage, four teaspoon white mustard seed, two of white black cloves, two of celery seed, two of allspice, one small box yellow mustard, one pound brown sugar, one ounce of tumeric; slice the tomatoes and let stand overnight in the brine.

Cucumber Preserved—Pare and thinly slice sound, green cucumbers, sprinkle well with salt and allow them to stand overnight; drain and pack the slices closely in jars, sprinkling well with salt again; seal airtight with paper coated on both sides with egg-white; when wanted, wash in cold water and serve with vinegar, pepper and salad oil.

Dill Pickles—Wash select large green cucumbers and place them in brine that is strong enough to float an egg; weigh them below the surface of the liquid and let them remain for four days. Wash again, and place them in a porcelain preserving kettle, cover with cold water and put on range; bring to a boil and cook for five or six minutes; rinse again and pack into a sufficiently large crock, sprinkling plenty of dill seed between each layer of cucumbers; cover again with a strong brine, to which add about one-half cup of cooking oil to prevent mould. Cover crock with a cloth and a plate or wooden cover, after weighing pickles below surface.

Mixed Pickles—Peel 1 gal. green tomatoes and chop finely together with 1 gallon cabbage, 1 gallon small onions, 6 dozen cucumbers, 2 green peppers and 1 pt. salt; mix, and let drain overnight in a cloth bag; add ½ oz. tumeric powder; 1 teaspoon nutmeg, 6 tablespoons ground mustard, 4 cups sugar and 1 gal. good vinegar; boil all together for 1 hour and seal in sterilized jars.—Sugar may be omitted when preferred sour.

Mustard Pickles—Put cucumbers in brine (strong enough to float an egg) for twelve hours, then wipe and pack in quart bottles. In each quart put one tablespoon black pepper, one and one-half tablespoons celery seed, one and one-half tablespoons Colemans Mustard, three tablespoons salad oil, fill up with vinegar and seal. Ready for use in two weeks.

Mustard Pickles, Mixed—Mix 2 qts. small white shallots, 2 qts. chopped green tomatoes, 2 qts. gherkin pickles and 2 heads of cauliflower separated into flowerlets or sprays; cover well with weak brine and allow to stand overnight. Make a pickling liquid; mix together 1½ tablespoons tumeric powder, 1 scant cup flower, 1 large cup sugar and 6 tablespoons powdered mustard; moisten with a little vinegar to a paste, then add to 2 qts. good cider vinegar and stir in well; bring to boiling and pour over the pickles packed in sterilized jars; seal.

Mushrooms, Pickled—Wash, dry and peel 1 qt. button mushrooms and cut off the tops of the stalks; sprinkle them with a little salt, place them in a stewpan; shake the pan over the fire until the liquid begins to flow from them, then set back on the range a little and allow to remain warm until most of the moisture has evaporated; then add 1 qt. vinegar to which has ben added ginger, peppercorns, mace and salt to suit; bring to boiling point, simmer 10 minutes and put into jars; cover closely.

Onions, Pickled—Gather onions when dry and ripe, carefully remove the outer skins, then, with a silver knife, remove another layer or two leaving the onion white and clear; as fast as onions are thus prepared, put them into very dry jars and cover them with cold vinegar to which has been added allspice and whole black pepper, in the proportion of 1 teaspoon each to each pint of vinegar; seal airtight and put in a dry place; ready for use after two weeks.

Piccalilli—Cut one peck of gren tomatoes and six onions in thin slices, and with one teacupful of salt, pack in layers of tomatoes, onions and salt and let stand overnight. In the morning pour off the liquid that has formed, add four green peppers and chop all fine. Put the the whole in a porcelain-lined kettle with a pint of vinegar and a tablespoonful each of cloves, cinnamon and white mustard seed. Cook until soft and sweetened to taste.

Peper Hash—Finely chop 3 heads cabbage and 6 red peppers; mix together with 4 tablespoons each of celery and mustard seeds, and a little salt; boil 3 quarts good cider vinegar, adding sugar to suit taste; mix all together. When cool, it is ready to use. Makes 5 quarts.

Spanish Pickle—Make a brine of 1 cup salt to each 1 gal. water; in this brine, soak separately in 3 crocks; 1 gal, cucumbers, 1 gal. green tomatoes, 2 doz. large onions, all evenly sliced and measured, soak overnight, drain and mix. Make a pickling liquid of following: 1 gal. vinegar, 1½ lbs. brown sugar, 2 red peppers, 1 oz. tumeric, 1 oz. white ginger, 1 oz. horseradish, 1 oz. celery seed, 4 oz. dry mustard, 4 tablespoons flour, boil together until well blended. Meantime, heat the mixed vegetables, being cautious to keep under the boiling point for about 20 minutes; put into pickle jar, cover with the hot pickling liquid and cool; weight down and cover closely.

Spiced Peaches—Scald and skin 4 lbs. sound ripe peaches. Tie in a small bag the following spices: 1 tablespoon each cloves and cinnamon, 1 teaspon ginger and ⅛ teaspoon cayenne. Dissolve 3 lbs. brown sugar in 1 cup cider vinegar, bring to boiling point, adding 1 teaspoon salt; put in the peaches and the spice bag, restore to boiling point and cook until peaches are sufficiently tender, then pour into a stone crock or jar. On every day for week drain off the syrup, reheat it to boiling point and pour back over peaches.—All kinds of fruit may be spiced by this method.

Spliced Pears—Boil together for fifteen minutes one pint of cider vinegar, one and three-fourth pounds of granulated sugar. Tie in a small piece of cheese cloth half a dozen whole cloves, one dozen whole allspice, one teaspoon of ground cinnamon, ¼ teaspoon of ground mace, and a small piece of ginger root. Put with vinegar and sugar and boil. Select a fine, large pears, pare and remove the stems, put into the vinegar and let all boil gently until the pears look clear; then drain off the vinegar, put the pears into jars, reheat the vinegar and pour over the pears. Seal and use as a sweet pickle. This is a delicious pickle is properly and carefully done.

Stuffed Peppers—Select large, firm sweet peppers. Place in a large stoneware jar and cover with a brine made by mixing one cup salt with one gallon cold water. Soak the peppers for twenty-four hours. Remove from the brine, rinse in fresh water and carefully cut a circle from the top of each pepper. Remove seeds and white membrane and soak the peppers in fresh water for two hours. Drain and stuff with cabbage and pepper relish, allowing about two quarts of the mixture to 18 peppers. Do not stuff too tightly. Place the tops on the peppers and fasten with toothpicks or string. Pack in a deep stoneware jar and cover with spiced vinegar made by scalding one-half cup grated horseradish, two tablespoons

pulverized mustard, two tablespoons of celery seed, one cup sugar, one tablespoon salt and one-half ounce stick cinnamon with two quarts of vinegar; strain.

Sweet Pickles—Peaches, cherries, damsons, pears, or any kind of firm fruit may be used: to 7 lbs. of fruit, use 3 lbs. sugar, 1 qt. cider vinegar, 1 oz. cinnamon, ½ oz. cloves; bring the vinegar, sugar and spices to boiling point and pour over fruit in a crock or earthenware bowl; 24 hours later, drain off the liquid, bring it to boiling point again and pour back over fruit; on the third day, put all in the preserving kettle together, bring to boiling, gently simmer a few minutes and put into sterilized jars and seal.

Tomato Sweet Pickle—Evenly slice 4 qts. green tomatoes and 4 medium onions; place in an earthenware jar in alternate layers, use about ½ cup salt and sprinkle it well over each layer; weight down and stand aside overnight; next morning, drain well and rinse with cold water and drain again; place in the crock again in layers, use 2 to 4 cups brown sugar according to taste, and sprinkle this generously between the layers, at the same time add to each layer a sprinkling of mixed spices composed of 1 tablespoon each of ground cloves, mustard and cinnamon and ¼ teaspoon cayenne; add 4 cups water and 2 cups good cider vinegar; boil until a thick syrup forms; put in preserve jars and cover closely.

Tomato Catsup—Scald, peel and core a peck of sound, ripe tomatoes. Mash as if for stewing. Season with a tablespoon of ground black pepper, half a teaspoon of red pepper, one tablespoon each of cloves, allspice and mace, and three large onions cut very fine, with salt to taste. Put all in porcelain-lined kettle to boil, and when the tomatoes are thoroughly cooked; rub the catsup through a sieve to get out the seeds and pieces of spice. After straining, return to the kettle and let it boil until thick as cream. Set aside and when cold put into pint bottles, filling each to within half an inch of the cork, and pouring in on top of each a teaspoonful of salad oil. The bottles should be kept in a cool, dry place, resting on their sides.

Watermelon-Rind, Pickled—To each qt. of the best vinegar add three lbs. of the best brown sugar, four ounces of stick cinnamon and two ounces of cloves. Bruise the spices, tie in a muslin bag and boil with the vinegar for five minutes. Then pour over the rind, letting it stand twenty-four hours. Remove the liquid and after heating it, pour it over the rind again and let stand another twenty-four hours, after which boil all together for a short time.

"Home Comfort" Hints

Kitchen Hints

Don't be afraid to try again if you fail again and again; success is the result of perseverance and application.

A little boiling water added to an omelette as it thickens will prevent it being tough.

Open canned fruit an hour or two before it is needed for use. It is far richer when the oxygen is thus restored to it.

Almonds are blanched by scalding them with boiling water.

To keep cookies from burning on the bottom turn the baking pan upside down and bake on the bottom of the pan and you will never do any other way.

Put a handful or two of tissue paper, torn into shreds, in the bottom of the cookie jar. This allows the air to pass through, keeping the cookies crisp and good.

If the top of a cake is sprinkled with flour as soon as it is turned from the pan the icing will spread more easily and will not be so likely to run. Before the cake is iced most of the flour should be wiped off.

Ginger cookies mixed with cold coffee instead of milk have a delicious taste.

In order to have potatoes always white, the kettle in which they are cooked should never be used for any other purpose.

A currycomb makes an excellent fish scraper.

Hot milk added to potatoes when mashing them will keep them from being soggy or heavy.

When making a steamed or boiled pudding, put a pleat in the cloth at the top to allow for the pudding to swell.

A pinch of soda stirred into milk that is to be boiled will keep it from curdling.

Heavy cakes are often the result of using damp fruit. After washing, currants and raisins should be left in a colander in a slightly warm place for twenty-four hours.

Before baking potatoes, peel them and rub with butter or bacon. The outside, when baked, will be a delicate brown, which can be eaten with the rest of the potato.

If roasted potatoes are burst with a fork they will be found much lighter and more digestable than if cut with a knife.

Pumpkins should be kept in a dry part of the cellar, apples in a moderately dry part; turnips should be kept in a damp part of the cellar.

To cut hard-boiled eggs in smooth slices dip the knife in water.

An oven door should never be slammed when anything is baking.

When cooking lima beans, rice, etc., it is very provoking when they foam and sputter onto a clean stove. Drop into the kettle a small lump of butter and there will be no boiling over.

Do not use newspapers to wrap about anything eatable.

By stewing some rhubarb in aluminumware pans and kettles, they may be cleaned and brightened — there yet remains to be manufactured, a polish that will do the work better.

To keep icing soft, add a pinch of baking soda to the whites of the eggs before beating them, then beat and proceed in the usual way.

To keep a cake fresh for several weeks take it from the oven, and while still hot, pack it completely in brown sugar.

If soup is too salty, add slices of raw potatoes and boil a few minutes until saltiness is reduced to taste. The potatoes may then be used in many ways.

Save all liquids from mustard or spiced pickles and use them in salad dressings or for mixing with meat for sandwiches.

Save the liquor from pickled peaches, etc.—it may be used in places where wine was formerly used, such as mince pies, sauces, etc.

In cooking vegetables, cover those that grow under the ground, as turnips, onions, etc.; leave uncovered those that grow above the ground.

When cream will not whip, add the white of an egg, both being chilled to same temperature; it will then whip quite readily.

To improve the flavor of boiled corned beef, add a small onion, a few cloves, a pinch of ginger, and a bay leaf.

To keep vegetables fresh and cool, place them in a deep pan or dish with cold water to half cover them; over them spread a folded wet napkin, allowing the corners to dip into the water; place on window or other place where cool air can reach them.

Dry lettuce leaves by blotting with soft paper, patting them carefully to prevent brusing.

After boiling salt beef, leave two or three carrots in the liquid until cool; these absorb the salt and the liquor may be turned into soup.

Instead of wasting skimmed milk, make it into cottage cheese.

If syrup returns to sugar, re-heat, add a small piece of butter making a sugar butter; use on hot cakes instead of syrup.

By placing a rubber fruit ring under a dish that is being placed on ice, the ring will stick to both ice and dish, thus preventing it from slipping.

A little baking soda added to boiling syrup will prevent it from crystalizing; a little vinegar likewise will prevent syrup from returning to sugar.

Save all the grease not suited for cooking and turn it into soap by the use of lye.

Small scraps of soap tied into a cloth or bag is excellent for cleaning bathtubs, graniteware, etc.

Broken bits of licorice sprinkled about pantry shelves will, it is said, banish red ants. Borax is also useful, the crystal and not the powder being preferred.

The lid of a teapot should always be left so that the air may get in. This prevents mustiness. The same rule, of course, applies to a coffee pot.

When an oven is too hot for the proper baking of what is in it put a basin of cold water inside. As the water becomes hot add more cold water and in this way keep the oven at the desired temperature.

A double layer of brown paper on the pantry shelf and kitchen table covered with oilcloth will enable the oilcloth to last longer.

Use a little ammonia in the dish water when washing glassware. It will make it sparkle like cut glass.

It is said that if a small piece of camphor be placed in a silver chest the silver will not become discolored.

Baking tins are easily kept smooth if scoured with Bon Ami and then washed after they have been used.

Have in your kitchen a cheap office stool to sit on when ironing or washing dishes, this will prevent backache and tired feet.

An equal mixture of turpentine and linseed oil will remove the white marks from furniture caused by water.

A solution of soda and water applied with a whisk broom kept for the purpose will remove the brown streaks in bathroom bowls made by sediment in the dripping water; if the spots do not come off readily, let the solution stand a few minutes, and it will rub off very easily.

Bore a hole through the broom handle and slip a string through it so you can hang it up.

A panful of lime kept in the cupboard with your jams and preserves will prevent moulding.

When a tea or coffee pot has become stained inside, fill with cold water, add a teaspoonful of soda. If set upon the stove and boiled for three-quarters of an hour, the inside will become as bright and clean as new.

After broiling or frying, wipe off the fat that has spattered on the range with an old newspaper, thus keep the top free from dirt and grease.

A very important point in washing cut glass is to avoid sudden changes from extreme heat to extreme cold and vice-verse. A pitcher or tumbler which has been filled with ice water, a tray that has been used for ice cream, if plunged at once into hot water, will be apt to crack. Use tepid water and the risk of breakage is avoided.

Rats and mice can be driven away by putting potash into holes or where they are likely to go.

Sour milk added to the water with which oilcloth or linoleum is washed, gives it a luster like new. In fact any kind of milk is good.

To remove grease from wood floors, sand is much better than soap for this purpose. If the floor is dirty mix a little chloride of lime with the sand. You will need plenty of warm water.

Restore stale crackers by placing them in a warm oven for a few minutes.

Stale bread may be refreshed by slicing and wrapping first in a dry cloth, then in a moist towel around it and the whole placed in a covered jar or breadbox.

To warm over biscuits, rolls, muffins, etc., sprinkle lightly with water, place them in a pan and set this pan in another containing a little hot water; place in oven until just right.

To retard the melting of ice in the icebox, cover the top of it with wet paper.

In the emergency of illness, when no refrigerator is at hand and ice is not regularly kept, a block of ice may be best kept by placing it in a stone crock of sufficient size after wrapping the ice in wet newspapers; the jar should then be thoroughly surrounded with feather pillows; it will keep in this manner several days.

In a custard recipe calling for several eggs, some of the eggs may be left out by substituting for each egg omitted one-half tablespoon corn-starch.

To prevent milk from scorching when scalding, rinse the pan in water to moisten it before putting in the milk.

To freshen shredded cocoanut, soak it in sweet milk a few minutes before using it.

Sugar in fried cakes, fritters, etc., should always be added to the milk—this prevents the cakes from absorbing the fat in the frying.

When filling gem or muffin pans, leave one of the small sections empty and fill it half with water—the gems will then never scorch.

In making fruit pies, the sugar should not be put on top, but between two layers of the fruit—sugar next to the top crust toughens it.

When fruit ferments, re-heat it, add a little sugar and make it up into pies or tarts.

When jellies ferment, re-heat or melt, add a little sugar and water, then thicken with corn-starch for sauce.

When making sandwiches, cut the bread loaf lengthwise instead of crosswise—it saves much of the waste and aids in making fancy sandwiches.

"Spinach may be the broom of the stomach, but Sauerkraut is the vacuum-cleaner."—Dr. Brokaw.

Meat should be placed in the refrigerator, but not against the ice. Ice always draws out the flavor of any meat pressed against it.

To prevent corn cakes and bread from having a raw taste, mix the meal with milk a few hours before baking the bread. When ready to bake it add the salt, egg, a spoonful of flour and last of all the soda, or if sweet milk be used, add baking powder.

If the milk to be used in making baked or boiled custard is first scalded and cooled before using, the custard will be smoother.

It is always better to handle oysters with a fork as contact with the hands may make them tough.

Add one drop of vanilla and beat well just before serving chocolate, and notice the improved delicacy of flavor. The longer chocolate simmers the better it is.

After scaling fish and picking ducks, geese, etc., did you ever try rubbing them well with a damp cloth dipped in corn meal? Try it; you will be surprised to see how nicely it cleans them.

Fish may be scaled much easier by dipping them into scalding water for a moment.

The white of an egg dropped into a kettle of soup will gather to it all impurities. Remove it when it curdles.

When cleansing rice, wash it twice in warm water, which is said to be more effective in removing starch than several washings in cold water.

A tablespoonful of sugar added to the water for basting roast beef will give a rich brown color as well as a fine flavor.

In making sponge cake, if you desire it to be yellow, use cold water, hot water makes it much whiter.

Fold the whipped whites of eggs into any mixture rather than stir them in, as the latter method breaks the air cell.

Milk and butter should be kept in closely covered vessels, as they readily absorb flavor and odor from other articles.

Dishes which are to be frozen need an extra amount of sweetening.

A lump of sugar put in to boil with green vegetables will preserve their color and improve their flavor, especially that of peas.

A piece of charcoal placed upon the shelves of the refrigerator will absorb any unpleasant odors and keep it sweet smelling.

When soaking beans a tiny pinch of soda in the water will be an improvement.

If you spill grease upon a hot stove, cover the spot at once with a thick layer of ashes; this will absorb the grease, so you will not be offended by its odor while burning, and a little later you can brush away the ashes, and none of the grease will remain.

To remove the odor of onions from a knife dip it into cold water, then dry and polish it. Hot water tends to set the odor of onions both on the knife and the hands, and for this reason should be avoided.

To clean a fishy frying pan fill it with cold water and place on the fire to boil. When boiling, put a red hot ember in, then wash in usual way.

Cane-seated chair bottoms that have sagged may be made as tight as ever by washing them with hot water and leaving to dry in the open air.

To clean the frying pan after frying, pour off the hot lard and wipe the pan with clean paper until all sediment is removed. It can then be easily washed.

A few stalks of rhubarb cut up and boiled in a tea kettle full of water will soften the deposit of lime so that it may be all scraped away.

Discolored china baking dishes can be made as clean as when new by rubbing them with whiting.

Clean the keys of the piano with a soft cloth dampened with alcohol, and wipe quickly with a clean, dry cloth.

The mixing pan can be quickly cleaned if a little boiling water is poured into it for a few minutes and a close cover put over. The steam softens the dried dough so that it will readily wash off.

Tinware may quickly be cleaned by rubbing it with a damp cloth, dipped in soda. Rub briskly and wipe dry.

Do not put pans and kettles partly filled with water on the stove to soak, as it only makes them more difficult to clean. Fill them with cold water and soak away from the heat.

By mixing enough flour of sulphur with a pint of water to give a golden tinge, and in this boiling three bruised onions, you can renovate your gilt picture frames.

Equal parts of water and skimmed milk, warm, will remove fly-specks from varnished woodwork or furniture, and make it look fresh.

Loose knife handles are easily mended. Take the handle off, mix together three parts resin and one of brick dust. Nearly fill the handle with this, heat the steel beyond the blade till nearly red hot, insert in the handle, and press down into place. It will be as firm as when new.

To wash a glass from which milk has been poured, plunge first into cold water before putting it into warm. The same rule holds good with egg cups or spoons from which eggs have been eaten.

To prevent wooden bowls from cracking immerse them in cold water; then set over the fire, bring to the boiling point and let boil an hour, and don't take them out until the water has gradually cooled.

A little washing soda mixed in the blacklead will remove all grease and give grates and stoves an excellent polish.

To take anything hot from the back of the oven, have a stiff wire with a hook at the end.

Rub the range daily with a soft cloth moistened with a few drops of deodorized kerosene; this should keep it clean.

The odor that clings so persistently to a utensil in which fish or onions have been fried may be dispelled by placing in hot oven for ten or fifteen minutes after washing and drying.

Hot Sour Milk will brighten silverware.

Lemon juice added to milk until it curds and then bound upon parts swollen with rheumatism will sometimes bring relief and reduce the swelling.

Lemon juice and salt will remove iron rust.

A hot lemonade will cure or greatly relieve a cold.

Wash fruit stained hands in lemon juice to remove stains.

For all salads containing fruits or fish, lemon juice is much nicer than vinegar.

To keep lemons fresh a long time invert over them a glass or earthenware dish that fits closely.

A few drops of lemon juice added to the shampoo will help cut the oil on hair that is too greasy.

Grate the rinds of four lemons in half pint of alcohol. Shake frequently and at the end of four weeks you will have a fine lemon extract.

Put half a pound of sugar in a bowl, add grated rind and juice of one lemon and one-half cupful of boiling water. Whip stiff and spread between cake layers.

A platter of cold meat is nicely garnished with slices of lemon.

A slice of lemon in a glass of ice tea will make it "Russian Tea."

Gargle a bad sore throat with strong solution of lemon juice and water.

Bind a cloth soaked in lemon juice on a cut or wound to stop bleeding.

Apply cloth soaked in lemon juice to soft corn for several nights. It can then be pared off.

A strong, unsweetened lemonade, taken before breakfast, will prevent and cure sick headache.

Salt water is preferable for cleaning bamboo furniture, as it prevents it from turning yellow, and is also good for wiping Chinese or Indian matting.

Mixed mustard will keep its color if a pinch of salt be added.

For stings or bites from any kind of insect, apply dampened salt. Bound tightly over the spot, it will relieve, and usually cure very quickly.

To bake potatoes quickly, boil them in salted water for ten minutes, then put in the oven. The boiling water will heat them through so they cook in a short time.

A pinch of salt will make the white of an egg beat quicker, and a pinch of borax in cooked starch will make the clothes stiffer and whiter.

Salt, dissolved in alcohol, will often remove grease spots from clothing when nothing else will.

If a small pinch of salt is added to every gallon of water boiled for drinking purposes, it will not have that flat, insipid taste common to boiled water.

Sprinkled salt on the carpet will collect the dirt quickly and prevent dust from flying all over everything.

A tiny pinch of salt added to coffee before the boiling water is poured on will accentuate the delicious flavor and aroma.

Waste pipes may be cleaned of soap and slime by placing a handful of common salt in the bottom of the basin over night. The salt will gradually melt and the first flush of water in the morning will clear the pipe.

Enameled kitchen ware that has become burned or discolored may be cleaned by rubbing with salt wet with vinegar.

In cooking a tough fowl or meat, one tablespoonful of vinegar in the water will save nearly two hours' boiling.

Vinegar removes lime spots.

Indian meal and vinegar, used on hands when roughened by labor or cold, will heal and soften them.

The mica windows of coal stoves can easily be cleaned with a soft cloth dipped in vinegar and water. This should be done when putting the stove up.

If vinegar is added to prunes when stewing—about three tablespoonfuls to a pound —it will improve the flavor.

When cracked eggs have to be boiled a little vinegar added to the water will prevent the white from boiling out. The acid coagulates albumen and stops the leaks. The

One generous teaspoonful of vinegar added to the water in which whitefish are boiling will be found to improve the flavor very decidedly. It also has tendency to make the flesh firm without thoughtening it.

Boil a little vinegar in frying pans before washing them.

cracks may also be covered with a bit of paper wet with the exuding albumen. Nothing sticks like white of egg and not even boiling water will remove the paper.

The lime deposit which forms in the bottom of a teakettle can be removed by boiling vinegar in the kettle.

A tablespoonful of vinegar in the lard that you fry doughnuts in will prevent them being greasy.

Marks from perfume may be removed from the tops of bureaus and dressers by rubbing with a cloth dipped in kerosene or oil and turpentine.

If one insists on using kerosene as a fire kindler, better pour a pint or so into an old tin pail and stand as many corncobs or pieces of board or kindling in it as the pail will hold overnight. The cobs will be thoroughly saturated by morning and are not so dangerous to use.

After removing all dust, wipe screen doors with kerosene and they will look new, and as long as the odor remains mosquitoes and moth millers will give them a wide berth.

Clean the rollers of the clothes wringer with gasoline and be careful to wipe off all superfluous oil from the cogs and crank that the clothes may not be soiled by the oil that has been on the cogs.

Kerosene will remove the gummy substance which forms on sewing machines.

When using fly paper, it is apt to fall or come in contact with some article of furniture, floor, etc. After removing the paper, apply a generous amount of kerosene to the article of furniture or clothing and it will quickly remove the stickey substance. It does not injure clothing and readily operates. Try this and you will be pleased with results.

A flannel wet with kerosene oil will remove fly specks from brass. Polish with chamois.

A woolen cloth dampened with gasoline will make the dirt disappear as if by magic when used for cleaning porcelain sinks, bath tubs or marble wash-bowls.

Gasoline is a sovereign remedy for bugs. It can be literally poured on the mattress, springs and bed without injuring the most delicate carpet, and every bug will disappear.

Kitchen Garden Hints

Artichoke — Produces large globular heads, thick, succulent scales, the bottom of which is the edible portion. In February or March, sow in hot-bed, transplant to the open in May in rows three or four feet apart in the rows. Should give globes the same year. Seed sown in May and transplanted in June has to be wintered—tie up leaves, then bank with dirt; will mature the second year. Boiled till tender, makes a delicious dish.

Asparagus—Requires little care for its successful cultivation. To secure the choice early stalks, bed should be made of a warm, rich loam, preferably exposed to the south. Manures and fertilizers must be used lavishly to secure the best results. Plants can be easily grown from seed, which should be sown about 12 inches apart and about 3 feet between rows. Furnishes the first green delicacy for the table in the spring.

Beans—Plant about the first of May in rows, placing seeds 2 or 3 inches apart in drills about 2½ inches deep. Rows should be about 2½ feet apart, and the soil slightly hilled, to insure good drainage and keep the beans from touching the ground. Most beans should be picked when about four inches long. Frequent pickings insure a more prolonged bearing season. Avoid jerking the plant, as this frequently disturbs young feeding roots—use the finger-nails to pinch the stem. Do not pick when the bushes are wet, as this often causes blight and rust. For continuous supply, plant every two weeks up to August.

Beets—Seed should be sown the first part of April. The ground should be spaded well and deep, placing rows about 18 inches apart, and the drills 1 inch deep. Cover the seed carefully and firm in the ground by walking over the drills. When seedings appear about 3 inches above the ground, thin out to about four inches apart to give ample room between the bulbs. Successive sowing for continuous supply may be made up to the middle of July.

Brussels Sprouts—The very best winter vegetable, having small knobs or heads along the stem, which may be cooked like cabbage. Planted about the middle of June, and transplanted four to six weeks apart for succession. Same treatment as late cabbage; pinch out tops of stalks when "buttons" are formed.

Cabbage—Sow the early kinds in hotbeds in February and March, and in the open ground in April and May. The late varieties for fall and winter use, sow in May, and transplant from 8th to 25th of July. Plant the early sort 20 inches distant in a row, and 2 feet between the rows; the latest sorts 2½ feet each way. To be well grown, cabbage requires a deep, rich, loamy soil.

Cardoon — Large fleshy-leaved plants, chiefly used as a winter vegetable. The blanched and broad ribs of the inner leaves, when properly cooked, are tender and of an agreeable flavor.

Carrots—April is the time to sow for early use. Sow seed in drills 12 to 15 inches apart, and thin out from 3 to 4 inches in drills, covering seed about ½ inch. For general crop, sow in May, same distance apart as above, but cover seed a little deeper as the sun is stronger. Perfect specimen require a fine pulverized deep soil. Carrots are not appreciated as they should be. Their table qualities are excellent, and as a food for stock they are surpassed by few root crops. They are especially valuable when fed to dairy cows, producing an increased flow of rich milk and imparting a beautiful golden yellow to the butter. Like other root crops, it flourishes best in a well enriched sandy soil deeply tilled, and if plowed the fall before, so much the better.

Celeriac — A Turnip Rooted Celery. Treat seeds and plants same as recommended for celery with the exception that it is customary to set plants in rows a foot apart.

Cauliflower—Start plants in a frame or seed bed, or for early plants start in a hotbed. Transplant as soon as large enough to handle. Set the plants 2 or 3 feet apart each way. One ounce of seed will produce from 3,000 to 4,000 plants.

Celery—The proper time to sow is early in April, transplanting about the first of June. Set in rows 3 feet apart, and about 8 inches between the plants in the row. Keep down all weeds, and as fall approaches, draw earth up to the plants, keeping the stalks well together.

Chicory—Eaten raw or as a salad and is also sometimes cooked like ordinary Endive. To grow good chicory, seed should be sown during April in the open ground, in drills 10 to 12 inches apart, in deep, rich soil. Allow the plants to grow until November, then take up the roots and trim off the leaves up to about 1½ inches from the neck. Then plant in a trench 8 to 12 inches deep, placing the roots upright, about 1½ inches apart.

Collards—A great favorite in the South where they are used extensively for "greens." Culture, similar to cabbage.

Corn Salad—(Fetticus). Sow the seed in early spring at the time of the first sowing of lettuce, and make progressive plantings as often as desired. For very early salads, sow in the fall and by protecting the plants during the winter months with leaves or straw, it can be gathered very early in the spring. If planted in April, it is soon ready for use. Corn Salad is best served in mixtures with other herbs as lettuce, water cress or white mustard.

Corn—(Sweet or Sugar). To serve the finest Sweet Corn, it must be picked in just the right condition, that is, when the skin of the grain breaks at the slightest puncture. It will be of inferior quality if either a few days too old or too young. One pound seed plants 100 hills.

Cress—The refreshing piquancy of the leaves of Cress has caused it to be widely used as an appetizing salad, or for garnishing various dishes. One ounce of seed will sow 200 feet of row.

Cucumber—The first planting should be made in May in hot beds; inverted sods form an excellent medium for both planting on and carrying the young plants to their permanent location, or small paper pots may be used. Such plantings are usually ready for transplanting to the open ground in from three to four weeks. 1 oz. seed—50 hills.

Water Cress—A very hardy plant that can be grown easily in a shallow pond of fresh water, or along the edges of shallow running streams. Seed may be started readily in pans or boxes of very moist earth, and when well started, they may be transplanted to the stream, pond, or spring.

Egg Plant—An early club-shaped, dark purple fruit, 4 to 8 inches long. Preferred by some for slicing and frying. Plant second or third week in May, usually in hills 30 inches by 24 inches. One ounce of seed will average 1000 plants. Enrich hills; give plenty of water; and protect from potato bugs.

Endive—One of the best and most wholesome salads for fall and winter use. Sow in shallow drills in April for early use, or for late use in June or July. When nearly full grown, and before they are fit for the table, they must be bleached. Most widely planted is the "Green Curled."

Horseradish—Should be planted from roots; soil should be very rich. Prepare with vinegar as a relish.

Kale—For spring use, sow in September and protect during Winter with a covering of straw. For fall use, sow in May or June,

covering seed one-half inch deep.

Kohlrabi—This is a very delicious vegetable and is increasing in popularity rapidly; combines the good qualities of the turnip and cabbage, but excels both in edible and productive qualities. Sow in spring in rows 14 inches apart, and thin away the plants to 8 inches. Flesh is white and tender.

Leek—A mild onion-flavored plant, prized as being ideal for soup, etc. Transplant in rows a foot apart and 6 inches between the plants.

Lettuce—Seed should be sown early in the spring and at intervals of 15 days for a succession; sow the seed in shallow drills—being careful to firm the soil well over the seed and thin to 4 inches apart in the row. Two ounces of seed will sow 150 feet of row.

Mushrooms—A highly prized, delicate and delicious garnish or dressing for many meat dishes. Not grown in the open, but is best produced and cultivated in a damp, dark place. Grown from "Spawn" which comes in bricks weighing about 18 or 20 ounces sufficient to plant ten square feet of bed.

Mustard—Should be sown in every garden. It is always in great demand by hotel cooks, as it is used in many ways for greens, salads, etc., and is unsurpassed. Allowed to "seed," it is the source of prepared table mustard. One ounce of seed will sow 40 feet of drill.

Okra—Pods gathered young are very delicious and appetizing; used principally in soups and salads; sow seed in drills one inch deep and three feet apart. When well up, thin out the plants to 1 foot apart.

Onions—Sow in rich, sandy soil, in drills 1 foot apart, as early as possible in the spring; cover with fine soil; when plants are strong enough, thin out to 3 or 4 inches. Have ground thoroughly cultivated, free from weeds and well fertilized. For fine young green onions in a short time after planting, it is advisable to plant Onion Sets instead of seed.

Oyster Plant—(Salsify.)

Parsley—May be sown in hot-beds in February, or later in open ground. Plant in rows 12 to 14 inches apart; thin to 3 or 4 inches apart, or transplant at this distance. Late in autumn, place frames over some of the plants to lengthen out the season for cutting. One ounce will sow 100 feet of drill.

Parsnips—Work the soil very deep and pulverize the surface thoroughly. Sow the seed in early spring, ¾ of an inch deep, in rows 12 to 18 inches apart. As soon as the young plants appear, cultivate and hand weed them, and when 3 inches high, thin to 6 inches apart in the row. Ounce of seed will drill 200 feet of row.

Peas—Plant early, smooth varieties as soon as frost is out of the ground; follow with the early wrinkled sorts in a week or ten days, and make successive plantings every 10 days until the middle of June. Plant 2 or 3 inches deep, in rows 24 inches apart, if to be cultivated by hand. Stake tall varieties. One pound will make 50 feet of drill.

Pepper—Sow in hot-bed in March or April; transplant in open ground when all danger from frost is over, in rows 3 feet apart and two feet apart in the rows. One ounce of seed will produce about 2000 plants. Grow Sweet, Pimiento, Chili, Cayenne, Small Red, and Tobasco for full variety.

Potatoes — For early Potatoes, which mature in 8 to 10 weeks from planting, the soil must be particularly rich. A rich clover sod, manured and broken the year before and planted to corn, beans, or peas, is in best shape for giving a good yield of nice clean potatoes; such rich soil, if available may be transferred to the garden. Furrows 3 to 4 inches deep and 3 feet apart, planted with good sized pieces with not less than 2 or 3 eyes, 15 inches apart in the furrows for early potatoes, and 18 inches apart for late ones. Cover well and drag; cultivate often; spray frequently for protection against insects and blight.

Pumpkins—Plant in April or May, among corn, or in the garden, in hills 8 to 10 feet apart; cultivate as melons.

Radishes—Sow seed as early in the Spring as ground can be well cultivated, in drills, 10 to 12 inches apart; thin out to one inch apart for small, 2 to 4 inches apart for large varieties. Soil should be rich, light and well pulverized. Continue sowing every week or 10 days for continuous supply. Quick growth insures good quality; they mature in from 18 days to 4 or 5 weeks, according to variety. One ounce of seed will drill 100 feet.

Rhubarb—One of the most important and healthful of garden vegetables; this plant is mostly propagated by division of the roots. The best time to set out the plants is in the spring, although it is sometimes done in the autumn with success. Transplant roots in highly manured soil, setting them 4 to 6 feet apart. Do not pull stalks until second year after transplanting.

Salsify—Plant and cultivate same as spinach.

Spinach—A well known source of "greens;" may be planted on any good soil, and its cultivation is simple. Maye be grown both as a spring and an autumn crop, or continuous. One ounce of seed will sow a 50 foot drill row.

Squash — Do not plant until settled weather, as plants are very tender and delicate; same treatment in plant and cultivating as cucumbers, or melons. One ounce small seeded varieties will plant 20 hills.

Swiss Chard—Plant seed as for beets; transplant 12 inches apart in rows 18 inches apart. The root is edible as beets; leaves are among the best early "greens," and may be prepared as spinach, or the stems only, cooked and served as asparagus. Leaves grow to 20 to 24 inches in length.

Turnips—For early, sow seed of the flat varieties in open ground in the spring in drills one foot or more apart, using seed sparingly. Thin to 3 or 4 inches apart. For succession, sow every two weeks until June. For fall and winter, sow in July and August; take up the roots just before winter. and store in cool cellar or pit. One ounce of seed will sow 200 feet of drill.

Basil Sweet—For highly seasoned dishes, soups, etc.

Tomato—Seed should be sown in a hot-bed about the first week in March in drills 5 inches apart and ½ an inch deep. When the plants are about 2 inches high, they should be transplanted to another hot-bed, and planted 4 inches apart, or planted in 4 inch pots, allowing a single plant to the pot. About the 15th of May the plants may be set out in the open ground 3 feet apart. Water freely at the time of transplanting. Sufficient plants for a small garden may be started by sowing in a shallow box or flower pots, and placing it in a sunny window of the room or kitchen. The fruit is very much improved in quality if tied to a trellis or framework. Size and quality are also improved by limiting the number of tomatoes to the plant by pinching some of the buds.

Herbs—For an early use, sow seed in hot-bed in March, or open ground in May, in rows a foot apart. Cover very lightly, and thin out when large enough to 6 or 8 inches in the row. They should be cut on a dry day just before they come into bloom. Tie in bunches and keep where they will dry quickly in the shade. When perfectly dry, wrap them up in paper and store them in a dry place; or rub the leaves to a powder, pack in bottles or jars, and cork tightly, which will preserve them for any period of time.

"Home Comfort" Formulary

Fire Extinguisher

Every household should be equipped to combat a chance blaze at its inception. There are many patented extinguishers for this purpose on the market, but their cost has prevented them from coming into universal use. To fill this gap, a home-made grenade is rceommended and while of utmost simplicity, the following described equipment ranks with the high priced ones: fill ordinary 1 pint thin, flat whiskey flasks with a strong brine of salt and water, using all the salt the water will take up; cork tightly and bind the flasks together in pairs to insure their being broken when thrown into a blaze; place about the house in convenient places for instant use in an emergency.

To extinguish a fire in the chimney, quickly close all the doors and windows in the room to decrease the draft; throw a few handfuls of common salt upon the fire in the range or grate, and the chimney fire will at once be extinguished by the gas evolved by the burning salt.

Government Whitewash

This white-wash, used for many decades on United States Government lighthouses and other weather and wave beaten properties, has withstood the elements for many decades without the ordinary renewing necessary with other whitewashes and paints; the east end of the White House, itself, painted with it stood the test of many years. It will be found an economical method of barn and fence painting, and without an equal.

Take half a bushel of unslacked lime, slack it with boiling water, cover during the process to keep in the steam; strain the liquid through a sieve or fine strainer, and add to it a peck of common salt previously dissolved in warm water; add three pounds of ground rice; boil to a thin, paste and stir in while hot; add half pound of Spanish whiting and one pound of clean glue previously dissolved by soaking in cold water and then hanging over a slow fire in a small pot hung within a larger one filled with water; add five gallons of hot water to the mixture, stir well and let stand a few days, covered from dirt. It should be applied hot, for which purpose it can be kept in a kettle on a portable heater.

Ice

Weight—The correct weight of a block of ice can be closely approximated by application of the following rule: weight equals the number of cubic inches divided by 30; thus, a block 10x10x15 equals 1500 cu. in. divided by 30 equals 50 pounds, the correct weight.

Keeping Without an Ice-House—Select a dry, shady spot, make a platform of lattice work of sufficient size and cover it with a thick layer of moss or leaves and sawdust; upon this build a pyramid of ice which should be sawed in squares and packed closely together with any chance space between the blocks filled with fine sawdust; when completed, cover the whole with a thick layer of earth packed well; a ditch should surround the pack to carry away the water.

Keeping Fresh Meat

When ice is not available, fresh beef and other butcher's meat may be kept nice and fresh for a week or two in summer by emersing it in buttermilk and placing in a cool cellar; when wanted, rinse it well in cold water and dry; it will be nice and fresh; bones and fat need not be removed if properly handled.

Lard Making

Preparing the Fat—Too much importance cannot be given to cleanliness in lard making and handling, if the product is to be white and pure. After the fresh fat is freed from all fleshy and discolored matter, it is then cut into small pieces, and washed through several waters until the water runs clear. See that nothing but the freshest of clean fat goes into the rendering kettle.

To Preserve—Lard may be kept sweet and fresh, even in the warmest weather by adding to the rendering or remelting kettle, a handful slippery elm bark. No salt or further preparation is necessary for this purpose. Tins, crocks, or jars, in which lard is placed should always be thoroughly sterilized before filling.

To Prepare for Market—Lard intended for the market should be bleached to be of first quality. This is best done by cutting the cold lard into small pieces about half the size of an egg, and then allowing it to stand in cold water for half an hour; then, wash through 5 or 6 successive waters, working it with the hands; drain well, working out all the water possible, remelt over a boiling water bath, and strain through fine linen; if necessary to get rid of all the water, remelt the second time, repeating the process of straining.

Paper Hangers' Paste

Put 1 quart hot water just under the scalding point into a pail; add 1 tablespoon pulverized alum, and dissolve; while beating constantly, sift in enough flour to form a thick batter that can no longer be beaten; now pour in boiling water until the paste begins to cook, then stop pouring, but continue stirring until paste is well cooked or scalded; level the surface and pour on a little cold water to prevent cracking; this will keep for several weeks, or until papering is finished; to use, cut out cakes, place them in the paste bucket, and thin with cold water to proper consistency.

Plumbers' Cement

Melt 1 part black rosin and thoroughly incorporate with it 2 parts fine brick dust to form a sort of sealing-wax; this cement is then run into leaky joints and cracks by applying with a melting heat.

To Restore—Dried out putty may be restored to original condition by crumbling it into an iron kettle or pot, covering with water with a little raw linseed oil added, and letting it boil, stirring well while hot; the putty will absorb the oil; pour off the water, and when cool enough to handle, work like new putty, restoring it to new condition.

Stove Pipes

Cleaning-out—A few pieces of old scrap sheet zinc placed on live coals in the firebox will burn and form a gas that loosens up the soot in the pipe and flue, allowing the draft to carry it out the chimney.

Virginia Cured Hams

After the hams are trimmed and cooled, pack them in a cask or tub very closely dusting the trimmed surfaces slightly with salt; after 2 or 3 days, cover with brine, allowing for each 100 pounds of ham, the following mixture; best coarse salt, 8 lbs. saltpeter, 2 oz. brown sugar, 2 lbs. potash, 1¼ oz. water, 4 gallons. Let the hams remain in this brine for 6 weeks, then take out and drain, dust every part of the flesh or trimmed side with very fine powdered black or white pepper, and hang up to dry, after they dry for several days, expose them to hickory smoke in the customary way. The hams will be ideally soft, deliciously seasoned, and proofed against insects, and will keep until wanted.

Washing Clothes

To wash clothes without rubbing, it is not necessary to buy any of the various so-called labor-saving compounds, since they all work on the same principal—that of dissolving the oils in the fabrics and thus releasing the dirt which is then washed away One of the very best solvents is soap, and soap is at its best as such when it is in the form of strong hot suds.

Shave one-half to two-thirds of an ordinary cake of laundry soap in about one-half gallon water and boil until soap is completely dissolved; pour this into one-half to two-thirds wash-boiler of boiling hot water; put in enough clothes to loosely fill but not pack; it is not necessary to boil them furiously, but keep the temperature to, or a shade under, the boiling point until all the dirt is loosened; have at hand another boiler of hot water, and pass the clothes, one at a time, into it with the stick, agitating it in the water to rinse out most of the suds and then pass the garment through the wringer into the final rinsing water in the usual way.

Wash white clothes first, and if the water has not become too dirty, the colored goods may be put into the same suds which, of course, must be kept hot.

Flannels, woolens, blankets, sweaters, etc., are washed in the same manner as above, but never let them boil—keep the suds just under the boiling point; rinse them through two or three relays of clean, warm water; squeeze them out, but never twist or rub woolen goods as it distorts the fibers.

Silks, and dainty lingerie require a more delicate handling; do not use extremely strong soap and after the soap is dissolved in a little hot water, use just enough to form a good lather in warm water—for silks, use nothing but warm water in which the hands may be comfortably placed; never wring or twist silk goods, but squeeze out the water; do not hang them out to dry, but press out with a warm iron—not hot—until they are dry; all crepe fabric should be lightly stretched while pressing.

Laces, lace curtains, tatting, etc., are washed and handled exactly as silk fabrics.

If you have a clothes-wringer, try folding your sheets, tablecloths or other flat pieces lengthwise to form a strip that will pass through the wringer. If folded smoothly and passed through the wringer wet, it will save more than half the work of ironing.

Sort your clothes and fill your wash-boiler the night before, start your washing before breakfast, and proceed deliberately—not hurriedly—but systematically; the early finish, the beautiful result, and your own untired condition will surprise you.

Ropp's Perpetual Calendar

GOOD FOR THREE CENTURIES

It is not only interesting but often essential to know on what day of the week, births and notable events occurred particularly on matters pertaining to business and law.

To find for instance on what day of the week the 4th of July occurred in 1876 look first for the year 1876, run down that column to July line where you will find the figure 6, which refers to the 6th calendar (column of days) as the one to be used for July, 1876, showing the 4th to have occurred on Tuesday, the 1st on Saturday, etc.

The small figures indicate the calendar for the same month 100 years earlier or later. Thus the small figures 1 and 4 in the angle of 1876 and July show that the first calendar is to be used for July, 1776, and the fourth for 1976.

In Leap years use the bottom lines for January and February.

Copyrighted 1892, by C. Ropp, Jr.

1800 1806	1801 1807	1802 ----	1803 1808	---- 1809	1804 1810	1805 1811
----	1812	1813	1814	1815	----	1816
1817	1818	1819	----	1820	1821	1822
1823	----	1824	1825	1826	1827	----
1828	1829	1830	1831	----	1832	1833
1834	1835	----	1836	1837	1838	1839
----	1840	1841	1842	1843	----	1844
1845	1846	1847	----	1848	1849	1850
1851	----	1852	1853	1854	1855	----
1856	1857	1858	1859	----	1860	1861
1862	1863	----	1864	1865	1866	1867
----	1868	1869	1870	1871	----	1872
1873	1874	1875	----	1876	1877	1878
1879	----	1880	1881	1882	1883	----
1884	1885	1886	1887	----	1888	1889
1890	1891	----	1892	1893	1894	1895
----	1896	1897	1898	1899	1900	----

Calendars (column of days)

Day	1st Cal.	2nd Cal.	3rd Cal.	4th Cal.	5th Cal.	6th Cal.	7th Cal.
1	M	T	W	T	F	S	S
2	T	W	T	F	S	S	M
3	W	T	F	S	S	M	T
4	T	F	S	S	M	T	W
5	F	S	S	M	T	W	T
6	S	S	M	T	W	T	F
7	S	M	T	W	T	F	S
8	M	T	W	T	F	S	S
9	T	W	T	F	S	S	M
10	W	T	F	S	S	M	T
11	T	F	S	S	M	T	W
12	F	S	S	M	T	W	T
13	S	S	M	T	W	T	F
14	S	M	T	W	T	F	S
15	M	T	W	T	F	S	S
16	T	W	T	F	S	S	M
17	W	T	F	S	S	M	T
18	T	F	S	S	M	T	W
19	F	S	S	M	T	W	T
20	S	S	M	T	W	T	F
21	S	M	T	W	T	F	S
22	M	T	W	T	F	S	S
23	T	W	T	F	S	S	M
24	W	T	F	S	S	M	T
25	T	F	S	S	M	T	W
26	F	S	S	M	T	W	T
27	S	S	M	T	W	T	F
28	S	M	T	W	T	F	S
29	M	T	W	T	F	S	S
30	T	W	T	F	S	S	M
31	W	T	F	S	S	M	T

Cent	17	18	19	17	18	19	17	18	19	17	18	19	17	18	19	17	18	19	17	18	19
Jan.	5	3	1	6	4	2	7	5	3	1	6	4	2	7	5	3	1	6	4	2	7
Feb.	1	6	4	2	7	5	3	1	6	4	2	7	5	3	1	6	4	2	7	5	3
Mar.	1	6	4	2	7	5	3	1	6	4	2	7	5	3	1	6	4	2	7	5	3
Apr.	4	2	7	5	3	1	6	4	2	7	5	3	1	6	4	2	7	5	3	1	6
May	6	4	2	7	5	3	1	6	4	2	7	5	3	1	6	4	2	7	5	3	1
June	2	7	5	3	1	6	4	2	7	5	3	1	6	4	2	7	5	3	1	6	4
July	4	2	7	5	3	1	6	4	2	7	5	3	1	6	4	2	7	5	3	1	6
Aug.	7	5	3	1	6	4	2	7	5	3	1	6	4	2	7	5	3	1	6	4	2
Sep.	3	1	6	4	2	7	5	3	1	6	4	2	7	5	3	1	6	4	2	7	5
Oct.	5	3	1	6	4	2	7	5	3	1	6	4	2	7	5	3	1	6	4	2	7
Nov.	1	6	4	2	7	5	3	1	6	4	2	7	5	3	1	6	4	2	7	5	3
Dec.	3	1	6	4	2	7	5	3	1	6	4	2	7	5	3	1	6	4	2	7	5
Jan.	4	2	7	5	3	1	6	4	2	7	5	3	1	6	4	2	7	5	3	1	6
Feb.	7	5	3	1	6	4	2	7	5	3	1	6	4	2	7	5	3	1	6	4	2

The reckoning of time has been a subject under discussion by scientists for many years and has produced many systems for fixing the length of years, months, and weeks. Mohammedan and Julian calendars are still in use in some parts, but the world at large uses the Gregorian or reformed Julian calendar, which was introduced by the bull of Pope Gregory XIII in February, 1852, and adopted in England in 1752. The length of the year of the Gregorian calendar is regulated by the Gregorian rule of intercalation, which is that every year whose number in the common reckoning since Christ is not divisible by 4, as well as every year whose number is divisible by 100 but not by 400, shall have 365 days, and that all other years, namely, those whose numbers are divisible by 400, and those divisible by 4 and not 100, shall have 366 days. The Gregorian year, or the mean length of the years of the Gregorian calendar, is 365 days, 5 hours, 49 minutes, and 12 seconds, and is too long by seconds. The Gregorian rule has sometimes been stated as if the year 4000 and its multiples were to be common years; this however, is not the rule enunciated by Gregory. The Gregorian calendar also regulates the time of Easter, upon which that of the other movable feasts of the church depend; and this it does by establishing a fictitious moon, which is purposely made to depart from the place of the true moon in order to prevent the coincidence of the Christian Paschal feast with that of the Jews.

INTEREST CALCULATIONS

RULE—Multiply the principal by as many one hundredths as there are days, and then divide as follows:

Per cent	3	4	5	6	7	8	9	10	12	15
Divide by	120	90	72	60	52	45	40	36	30	24

EXAMPLES—Interest on $100. for 90 days at 5 per cent.: 100 x .90 = 90.00 divided by 72 = 1.25 (one dollar and 25 cents); on $1. for 30 days at 6 per cent.: 1 x .30 = .30 divided by 60 = .005 (5 mills).

TABLE—Showing the number of days from any date in one month to the same date in any other month.

FROM \ TO	JAN.	FEB.	MCH.	APR.	MAY	JUNE	JULY	AUG.	SEP.	OCT.	NOV.	DEC.
JANUARY	365	31	59	90	120	151	181	212	243	273	304	334
FEBRUARY	334	365	28	59	89	120	150	181	212	242	273	303
MARCH	306	337	365	31	61	92	122	153	184	214	245	275
APRIL	275	306	334	365	30	61	91	122	153	183	214	244
MAY	245	276	304	335	365	31	61	92	123	153	184	214
JUNE	214	245	273	304	334	365	30	61	92	122	153	183
JULY	184	215	243	274	304	335	365	31	62	92	123	153
AUGUST	153	184	212	243	273	304	334	365	31	61	92	122
SEPTEMBER	122	153	181	212	242	273	303	334	365	30	61	91
OCTOBER	92	123	151	182	212	243	273	304	335	365	31	61
NOVEMBER	61	92	120	151	181	212	242	273	304	334	365	30
DECEMBER	31	62	90	121	151	182	212	243	274	304	335	365

EXAMPLE—How many days from May 5th to October 5th? Look for May at left hand and October at the top; in the angle is 153. In leap year add one day if February is included.

MEASURING CORN OR GRAIN IN BIN, CRIB OR WAGON

Table for estimating the capacity of any bin or box, or the amount of heaped bushels of shucked corn-in-ear it contains at any time.

Length (ft.) / Width (ft.)	½	1	2	3	4	5	10	12	14	16	18	24	30
2	6	12	24	36	48	60	120	144	168	192	216	288	360
3	9	18	36	54	72	90	180	216	252	288	324	432	540
4	12	24	48	72	96	120	240	288	336	388	432	576	720
4½	13	27	54	81	108	135	270	324	378	432	486	648	810
5	15	30	60	90	120	150	300	360	420	480	540	720	900
5½	16	33	66	99	132	165	330	396	462	528	594	792	990
6	18	36	72	108	144	180	360	432	504	576	648	864	1080
6½	19	39	78	117	156	195	390	468	546	624	702	936	1170
7	21	42	84	126	168	210	420	504	588	672	756	-1008	1260
7½	22	45	90	135	180	225	450	540	630	720	810	1080	1350
8	24	48	96	144	192	240	480	576	672	768	864	1152	1440
8½	25	51	102	153	204	255	510	612	714	816	918	1224	1530
9	27	54	108	162	216	270	540	648	756	864	972	1296	1620
10	30	60	120	180	240	300	600	720	840	960	1080	1440	1800
12	36	72	144	216	288	360	720	864	1008	1152	1296	1728	2160
14	42	84	168	252	336	420	840	1008	1176	1344	1512	2016	2520
16	48	96	192	288	384	480	960	1152	1344	1536	1728	2304	2880
18	54	108	216	324	432	540	1080	1296	1512	1728	1944	2592	3240
24	72	144	288	432	576	720	1440	1728	2016	2160	2592	3168	4320

To find the capacity of a bin or crib: Find the number in the table above, opposite the width and in the column under the given length; multiply this number by the height and "point off" the right-hand figure;—the result will be the number of heaped bushels of corn the crib will hold. Example:—How many heaped bushels of corn (in ear) will a crib 12 ft. long, 8 ft. wide, and 6 ft. high hold?—In the table above, in the column under "12," and on a line opposite "8," we find "576."

$$576 \times 6 \text{ (height)} = 3456 \text{ or } 345.6 \text{ bu.}$$

To find the amount of corn in crib: Proceed as above, but multiply by the height of the leveled corn instead of the full height of the crib.

To find the amount of "struck" bushels of shelled grain: Find the number of bushels as above, and multiply the answer by 1 4/5 (or add 80%); for instance, the crib, 12x8x6, in the example above will hold 345.6 + 80% = 622 struck bushels of any grain.

To apply table to odd dimensions: Suppose the length of the crib should be 7½ ft. and the width 4 ft.—Method: (7½ = 4 + 3 + ½). On the line opposite the given width (4 ft.) will be found: under "4," 96; under "3," 72; and under "½," 12.

$$96 + 72 + 12 = 180$$

simply multipy 180 by the height and point off the right-hand figure as above example.

Weights and Measures

Troy Weight

24 grains=1 pwt.
20 pwts.=1 ounce.
12 ounces=1 pound.

Used for weighing gold, silver and jewels.

Apothecaries' Weight

20 grains=1 scruple.
3 scruples=1 dram.
8 drams=1 ounce.
12 ounces=1 pound.

The ounce and pound in this are the same as in Troy weight

Avoirdupois Weight

27 11/32 grains=1 dram.
16 drams=1 ounce.
16 ounces=1 pound.
25 lbs=1 quarter.
4 quarters=1 cwt.
2,000 lbs.=1 short ton.
2,240 lbs.= 1 long ton.

Dry Measure

2 pints=1 quart.
8 quarts=1 peck.
4 pecks=1 bushel.
36 bushels=1 chaldron.

Liquid Measure

4 gills=1 pint.
2 pints=1 quart.
4 quarts=1 gallon.
31½ gallons=1 barrel.
2 barrels=1 hogshead.

Time Measure

60 seconds=1 minute.
60 minutes=1 hour.
24 hours=1 day.
7 days=one week.
28, 29, 30 or 31 days=1 calendar month.
(30 days=1 month in computing interest.)
365 days=1 year.
366 days=1 leap year.

Circular Measure

60 seconds=1 minute.
60 minutes=1 degree.
4 quadrants=12 signs, or 360 degrees=1 circle.
30 degrees=1 sign.
90 degrees=1 quadrant.

Long Measure

12 inches=1 foot.
3 feet=1 yard.
5½ yards=1 rod.
40 rods=1 furlong.
8 furlongs=1 sta. mile.
3 miles=1 league.

Cloth Measure

2¼ inches=1 nail.
4 nails=1 quarter.
4 quarters=1 yard.

Mariners' Measure

6 feet=1 fathom.
120 fathoms=1 cable length.
7½ cable lengths=1 mile.
5,280 feet=1 stat. mile.
6,085 feet=1 naut. mile.

Square Measure

144 sq. inches=1 sq. foot.
9 sq. ft.=1 sq. yard.
30¼ sq. yards=1 sq. rod.
40 sq. rods=1 rood.
4 roods=1 acre.
640 acres=1 sq. mile.

Miscellaneous

3 inches=1 palm.
4 inches=1 hand.
6 inches=1 span.
18 inches—1 cubit.
21.8 in.=1 Bible cubit.
2½ ft.=1 military pace.

SURVEYORS' MEASURE

7.92 inches=1 link.
25 links=1 rod.
10 square chains or 160 square rods=1 acre.
640 acres=1 square mile.
36 sq. miles (6 miles sq.)=1 township.
4 rods=1 chain.

CUBIC MEASURE

1,728 cubic in.=1 cub. ft.
27 cubic ft.=1 cubic yd.
2,150.42 cubic inches=1 standard bushel.
231 cubic inches=1 standard gallon.
1 cubic foot=about four-fifths of a bushel.
128 c. ft.=1 cord (wood)
40 cub. ft.=1 ton (shpg.)

METRIC EQUIVALENT
Linear Measure

1 centimeter=0.3937 in.
1 decimeter=3.937 in. =0.328 feet.
1 meter=39.37 in.= 1.0936 yards.
1 in.=254 centimeters.
1 ft.=3.048 decimeters.
1 yard=0.9144 meter.
1 rod=0.5029 dekameter.
1 mile=1.6093 kilometers.
1 dekameter=1.9884 rods
1 kilometer=0.62137 m'e.

Square Measure

1 sq. centimeter= 0.1550 sq. in.
1 sq. decimeter=0.1076 sq. ft.
1 sq. meter 1.196 sq. yd.
1 acre=3.954 sq. rd.
1 hektar=2.47 acres.
1 sq. kilometer=0.386 sq. miles.
1 sq. inch=6452 square centimeters.
1 sq. foot=9.2903 squ'e decimeters.
1 sq. yd.=0.8361 sq. m'r.
1 sq. rd.=0.2529 acre.
1 acre=0.4047 hektar.
1 sq. m.=259 sq. kilometers.

Measure of Volume

1 cu. centimeter= 0.061 cu. in.
1 cu. decimeter= 0.0353 cu. ft.
1 cu. mr.
1 stere
1 liter=
1 dekaliter=
1 hektoliter=2.8375 bu.
1 cu. in.=16.39 cu. centimeters.
1 cu. ft.=28.317 cu. decimeters.
1.308 c. yd. 1 c. yd.=0.7646 c. m.
0.2759 cord. 1 cord=3.624 steres.
0.908 qt. dry. 1 qt. dry=1.101 liters.
1.0567 qt. liq. 1 qt. liq.=0.9463 liter.
2.6417 gl. 1 gal.=0.3785 dekaliter.
.135 pcks. 1 peck=0.881 dekaliter.
1 bu.=0.3524 hektoliter.

Weights

1 gram.=0.03527 ounce.
1 kilogram=2.2046 lbs.
1 metric ton=1.1023 English ton.
1 ounce=28.85 grams.
1 lb.=0.4536 kilogram.
1 English ton=0.9072 metric ton.

APPROXIMATE METRIC EQUIVALENTS.

1 decimeter=4 inches.
1 meter=1.1 yard.
1 kilometer=⅝ of mile.
1 hektar=2½ acres.
1 stere or cu. meter=
¼ of a cord.
1 liter= 1.06 qt. liquid. / 0.9 qt. dry.
1 hektoliter=2⅝ bush.
1 kilogram=2 1/5 lbs.
1 metric ton=2,200 lbs.

To Find the Capacity of a Tank in Gallons

First, find the capacity in cubic inches. For rectangular tanks, multiply the length by width, by the heighth.

For cylinderical tanks, multiply the length by the square of the diameter, by .7854.

For elliptical tanks, multiply the length by the short diameter, by the long diameter, by .0339.

Second, divide the number of cubic inches arrived at above, by 231; the answer will be the capacity in gallons.

Rule for Measuring Hay

First, find the volume in cubic feet by one of the three following methods:

1. Measure over stack with rope. 2. Measure the width of stack. 3. Substract the width of stack from what it measures over. 4. Divide the remainder by "2," 5. Multiply the result thus obtained by the length and width. or:

Find the length, breadth and depth of the hay, in feet, and multiply these three dimensions together.

If stack is circular, find the average circumference in yards and "square" the result; i. e., multiply it by itself; multiply this result by 4x the height of stack in yards; then, point off the two right-hand figures and multiply by "27,"

To find the weight: Divide the volume in cubic feet by—if the hay is on the wagon or newly stored, 540; but if it is well settled in the mow or stack, divide by 512; if baled, divide by 270. The result is the weight in tons.

Capacity of Wells or Cisterns

The following list gives the capacity, or number of gallons a well will hold *per foot of depth*. Simply multiply the number of gallons opposite the given diameter by the number of feet deep. Example: A well 3 ft. in diameter and 20 ft. deep will hold— 53 (gallons per ft.) x 20 (feet deep)=1060 gallons.

2	ft. diameter—	23 gal.	per depth-foot
2½	ft. diameter—	36 gal.	per depth-foot
3	ft. diameter—	53 gal.	per depth-foot
3½	ft. diameter—	72 gal.	per depth-foot
4	ft. diameter—	94 gal.	per depth-foot
4½	ft. diameter—	119 gal.	per depth-foot
5	ft. diameter—	147 gal.	per depth-foot
5½	ft. diameter—	178 gal.	per depth-foot
6	ft. diameter—	211 gal.	per depth-foot
6½	ft. diameter—	248 gal.	per depth-foot
7	ft. diameter—	288 gal.	per depth-foot
7½	ft. diameter—	331 gal.	per depth-foot
8	ft. diameter—	366 gal.	per depth-foot
8½	ft. diameter—	425 gal.	per depth-foot
9	ft. diameter—	477 gal.	per depth-foot
9½	ft. diameter—	531 gal.	per depth-foot
10	ft. diameter—	588 gal.	per depth-foot
10½	ft. diameter—	639 gal.	per depth-foot
11	ft. diameter—	712 gal.	per depth-foot
11½	ft. diameter—	779 gal.	per depth-foot
12	ft. diameter—	848 gal.	per depth-foot

Useful Information for Builders

One thousand shingles, laid four inch to the weather, will cover one hundred square feet of surface and five lbs. of shingle nails will fasten them on.

One-fifth more siding and flooring is needed than the number of square feet of surface to be covered because of the lap in siding and flooring.

One thousand laths will cover 70 yards of surface and 11 pounds of lath nails will nail them on.

Eight bushels of good lime, sixteen bushels of sand and one bushel of hair will make enough good mortar to plaster 100 square yards.

One cord of stone, three bushels of lime and a cubic yard of sand will lay 100 cubic feet of wall.

Cement one bushel, and sand two bushels, will cover 3½ square yards, one inch thick; 4½ square yards ¾ inch thick, and 6¾ square yards ½ inch thick.

One bushel of cement and one bushel of sand will cover 2¼ square yards one inch thick; 3 square yards ¾ inch thick, and 4½ square yards ½ inch thick.

AMOUNT OF PAINT REQUIRED FOR A GIVEN SURFACE

It is impossible to give a rule that will apply in all cases, as the amount varies with the kind and the thickness of the paint, the kind of wood or other material to which it is applied, the age of the surface, etc. The following is an approximate rule: Divide the number of square feet of surface by 200. The result will be the number of gallons of liquid paint required to give two coats: or divide by 18 and the result will be the number of pounds of pure ground white lead required to give three coats.

ROOF ELEVATIONS

By the "pitch" of a roof is meant the relation which the height of the ridge above the level of the roof-plates bears to the span, or the distance between the studs on which the roof rests.

The length of rafters for the most common pitches can be found as follows from any given span:

If ¼ pitch, multiply span by .559 or 7-12 nearly.
If ⅓ pitch, multiply span by .6 or 3-5 nearly.
If ⅜ pitch, multiply span by .625 or 5-8 nearly.
If ½ pitch, multiply span by .71 or 7-10 nearly.
If ⅝ pitch, multiply span by .8 or 4-5 nearly.
If full pitch, multiply span by .1-12 or 1-18 nearly.

To length thus obtained must be added amount of projections of rafters at the eaves.

As rafters must be purchased of even lengths, a few inches more or less on their length will make a difference to the pitch so slight that it cannot be detected by the eye.

Example—To determine the length of rafters for a roof constructed one-half pitch, with a span of 24 ft. —24x.71=17.04; or, practically, just 17 feet. A projection of one foot for eaves makes the length to be purchased 18 feet.

Nails

Below: The first line gives the size (d=penny); the second line, the length in inches; and the third line, the number of nails in a pound.

2d	3d	4d	5d	6d	7d	8d
1	1¼	1½	1¾	2	2¼	2½
557	480	353	232	167	141	101
9d	10d	12d	20d	30d	40d	50d
2¾	3	3½	4	4½	5	5½
72	68	54	34	16	12	10

Brickwork

Bricks vary in size from 7¾ to 8 in. long, 4 to 4¼ in. wide, and 2 to 2½ in. thick; but are usually 8 in. long, 4 in. wide, and 2 in. thick, and contain 64 cubic inches. 27 bricks make 1 cu. ft.

Front bricks are 8¼ in. long, 4½ in. wide, and 2½ in. thick.

Fire bricks are 9½ in. long, 4⅝ in. wide, and 2⅜ in. thick.

To find the number of bricks in a wall: multiply together the length, height and thickness in feet and that product by 20— since 20 common bricks, well laid, equal 1 cubic foot.

For walls 8 in. thick, multiply the length by the heighth, the result being square feet, and multiply this result by 15 to find the number of bricks in the wall.

One and one-eighth barrels of lime and —of a yard of sand will lay 1000 bricks. (One and a quarter barrels of lime and 1 yard of sand will lay 100 feet stone.)

Chimney size	Flue size	Number of bricks for each ft. in height
16x16	8x 8	30
20x20	12x12	30
16x24	8x16	40
20x24	12x16	45

Note: In measuring and estimating masons make no allowance for doors, windows, or corners; however, in some places, it is customary to allow one-half for openings. They measure from outside to outside.

CONVENIENT SEED TABLE

	Weight per Bu.	Quantity to Sow 1 Acre
Alfalfa or Lucerne	60	20 to 30 lbs.
Alsike or Swedish	60	8 to 10 lbs.
Bokhara	60	8 to 10 lbs.
Crimson or Scarlet	60	10 to 15 lbs.
Mammoth or Sapling	60	8 to 10 lbs.
Red	60	6 to 8 lbs.
White	60	3 to 5 lbs.
Cat-Tail (Pearl)	50	8 to 10 lbs.
Common	50	25 to 35 lbs.
German or Golden	50	25 to 35 lbs.
Siberian	50	6 to 8 lbs.
Hungarian	48	25 to 35 lbs.
Awnless Brome	14	28 to 42 lbs.
Bermuda Grass	40	3 to 3½ lbs.
Creeping Brent	14	15 to 20 lbs.
English Perennial Rye	20	30 to 40 lbs.
English Blue	14	20 to 30 lbs.
Italian Rye	20	30 to 40 lbs.
Johnson	25	25 to 30 lbs.
Kentucky Blue (Pasture)	14	20 to 25 lbs.
Kentucky Blue (Lawn)	14	40 to 50 lbs.
Meadow Fescue	14	20 to 30 lbs.
Orchard Grass	14	12 to 15 lbs.
Red Top—in chaff	14	15 to 20 lbs.
Red Top—solid seed	6	to 10 lbs.
Fescue	14	20 to 30 lbs.
Tall Meadow Oat	12	20 to 30 lbs.
Timothy	45	10 to 12 lbs.
Mixture for Pastures	14	30 to 40 lbs.
Mixture for Lawns	14	40 to 50 lbs.
Barley	48	1¼ to 1½ bu.
Beans—Navy	60	1½ to 2 bu.
Beans—Field	60	1½ to 2 bu.
Beans—Soja	60	20 to 30 lbs.
Broom Corn Seed	48	2 to 4 qts.
Buckwheat	52	1 to 1¼ bu.
Cane Seed—for sugar	50	4 to 8 lbs.
Cane Seed—for fodder	50	30 to 50 lbs.
Castor Beans	46	4 to 5 lbs.
Corn—Field	56	4 to 5 qts.
Corn—fodder, broadcast	56	2 bu.
Corn—fodder, drilled	56	1 bu.
Corn, Pop—shelled	60	2 to 4 qts.
Cow Peas	60	1½ to 2 bu.
Flax	56	1 to 1¼ bu.
Hemp	44	
Kaffir Corn—in drills	50	3 to 5 lbs.
Kaffir Corn—broadcast	50	½ to 1 bu.
Oats	32	1½ to 2 bu.
Peas—Field	60	1½ to 2 bu.
Peanuts—in pod	22	2 bu.
Pumpkin, Common Field	30	2 to 3 qts.
Rape, Dwarf Essex	50	5 to 8 lbs.
Rye	56	1 to 1½ bu.
Sunflower	22	2 to 3 lbs.
Teosinte		4 to 6 lbs.
Wheat—Spring or Winter	60	1¼ to 1½ bu.
Vetches—Spring or Winter	60	1 to 1½ bu.

WEIGHT PER BUSHEL OF GRAIN, ETC.

The following Table shows the number of pounds per bushel required, by law or custom, in the sale of articles specified, in the several States of the Union.

STATES	Barley	Buckwheat	Coal	Corn, shelled	Corn Meal	Onions	Oats	Potatoes	Rye	Wheat	Salt	Turnips	Beans, wh.	Clover Seed	Timothy
Maine	48	48		56	50	52	30	60		60		50	64		
New Hamp.				56	50		30	60	56	60			60		
Vermont	48	48					32	60	56	60	70		64	60	42
Mass	48	48		56	50	52	32	60	56	60					
Conn		45		56			32	60	56	60					
New York	48	48		58			32	60	56	60			62	60	44
New Jersey	48	50		56			30	60	56	60			64		
Penna	47	48		56			30	56	56	60	85		62		
Delaware				56					60						
Maryland	48	48		56		57	32	60	56	60	56		62	64	45
Dist. Col.	47	48		56	48	57	32	56	56	60	50	55	62	60	45
Virginia	48	48		56			32	60	56	60		56	60	64	45
West Va.	48	52	80	56	48		32	60	56	60		60	60	60	45
N. C.	48	50		54	46		30		56	60			64		
S. C.	48	56	80	56	50	57	33	60	56	60	50		60	60	
Georgia	40		80	56	48	57	35	56		60	56			60	45
Louisiana	32			56			32		56	60					
Arkansas	48	52	80	56	50	57	32	60	56	60			60	60	45
Tennessee	48	50		56	50	56	32	60	56	60			50		45
Kentucky	48	52		56	50	57	33	56	56	60			60	60	45
Ohio	48	50		56			32	60	56	60			60	60	45
Michigan	48	48	80	56		54	32	60	56	60	56	58	60	60	45
Indiana	48	50	70	56	50	48	32	60	56	60			60	60	
Illinois	48	52		56	48	57	32	60	56	60			60	60	
Wisconsin	48	50		56			32	60	56	60				60	
Minnesota	48	42		56			32	60	56	60				60	
Iowa	48	52		56			57	33	60	56	60		60	60	45
Missouri	48	52		56			57	32	60	56	60		60	60	45
Kansas	50	50		56	50		57	32	60	56	60	50	55	60	45
Nebraska	48	52		56	50	57	34	60	56	60	50	55	60	60	45
California	50	40		52			32		54	60					
Oregon	46	42		56			36	60	56	60			60		

SUITABLE DISTANCE FOR PLANTING

Apples—Standard	25 to 35 ft. apart each way
Apples—Dwarf (bushes)	10 ft. apart each way
Pears—Standard	10 to 20 ft. apart each way
Pears—Dwarf	10 ft. apart each way
Cherries—Standard	18 to 20 ft. apart each way
Cherries—Dukes and Morrellos	16 to 18 ft. apart each way
Plums—Standard	16 to 20 ft. apart each way
Peaches	16 to 18 ft. apart each way
Apricots	16 to 18 ft. apart each way
Nectarines	16 to 18 ft. apart each way
Quinces	10 to 12 ft. apart each way
Currants	3 to 4 ft. apart each way
Gooseberries	3 to 4 ft. apart each way
Raspberries	3 to 5 ft. apart each way
Blackberries	6 to 7 ft. apart each way
Grapes	8 to 12 ft. apart each way

To estimate the number of plants required for an acre, at any given distance, multiply the distance between the rows by the distance between the plants, which will give the number of square feet allotted to each plant, and divide the number of square feet in an acre (43,560) by this number. The quotient will be the number of plants required.

NUMBER OF SHRUBS OR PLANTS FOR AN ACRE

Distance Apart	No. of Plants	Distance Apart	No. of Plants	Distance Apart	No. of Plants
3 x3 in.	696,960	4 x4 ft.	2,722	13x13 ft.	257
4 x4 in.	392,040	4½x4½ ft.	2,151	14x14 ft.	222
6 x6 in.	174,240	5 x1 ft.	8,712	15x15 ft.	193
9 x9 in.	77,440	5 x2 ft.	4,356	16x16 ft.	170
1 x1 ft.	43,560	5 x3 ft.	2,904	16½x16½ ft.	160
1½x1½ ft.	19,360	5 x4 ft.	2,178	17x17 ft.	150
2 x1 ft.	21,780	5 x5 ft.	1,742	18x18 ft.	134
2 x2 ft.	10,890	5½x5½ ft.	1,417	19x19 ft.	120
2½x2½ ft.	6,960	6 x6 ft.	1,210	20x20 ft.	108
3 x1 ft.	14,520	6½x6½ ft.	1,031	25x25 ft.	69
3 x2 ft.	7,260	7 x7 ft.	881	30x30 ft.	48
3 x3 ft.	4,840	8 x8 ft.	680	33x33 ft.	40
3½x3½ ft.	3,555	9 x9 ft.	537	40x40 ft.	27
4 x1 ft.	10,890	10 x10 ft.	435	50x50 ft.	17
4 x2 ft.	5,445	11 x11 ft.	360	60x60 ft.	12
4 x3 ft.	3,630	12 x12 ft.	302	66x66 ft.	10

USEFUL MULTIPLIERS

Inches	×	0.08333	= feet
Inches	×	0.02778	= yards
Inches	×	0.00001578	= miles
Square inches	×	0.00695	= square feet
Square inches	×	0.0007716	= square yards
Cubic inches	×	0.00058	= cubic feet
Cubic inches	×	0.0000214	= cubic yards
Cubic inches	×	0.004329	= gallons (U. S.)
Feet	×	0.3334	= yards
Feet	×	0.00019	= miles
Square feet	×	144.	= square inches
Square feet	×	1.1112	= square yards
Cubic feet	×	1728.	= cubic inches
Cubic feet	×	0.03704	= cubic yards
Cubic feet	×	7.48	= gallons
Yards	×	36.	= inches
Yards	×	3.	= feet
Yards	×	0.0005681	= miles
Square yards	×	1296.	= square inches
Square yards	×	9.	= square feet
Cubic yards	×	46656.	= cubic inches
Cubic yards	×	27.	= cubic feet
Miles	×	63336.	= inches
Miles	×	5280.	= feet
Miles	×	1760.	= yards
Avoir. ounces	×	0.0625	= pounds
Avoir. ounces	×	0.00003125	= tons
Avoir. pounds	×	16.	= ounces
Avoir. pounds	×	0.001	= hundredweight
Avoir. pounds	×	0.0005	= tons
Avoir. tons	×	32000.	= ounces
Avoir. tons	×	2000.	= pounds
Gallons (U. S.)	×	8.33	= pounds
Gallons (U. S.)	×	0.13368	= cubic feet
Gallons (U. S.)	×	231.	= cubic inches
Gallons (U. S.)	×	3.78	= liters
Cubic feet water	×	62.425	= pounds
Cubic feet water	×	7.48	= gallons
Cubic feet water	×	0.028	= tons
Cubic feet ice	×	57.2	= pounds
Cubic inches water	×	0.036024	= pounds
Cubic inches water	×	0.004329	= gallons
Cubic inches water	×	0.576384	= ounces
Pounds water	×	27.681	= cubic inches
Pounds water	×	0.01602	= cubic feet
Pounds water	×	0.083	= gallons
Tons water	×	268.80	= gallons
Tons water	×	35.90	= cubic feet
Circumference of circle	=	diameter × 3.1416	
Circumference of circle	=	radius × 6.283185	
Area of circle	=	square of radius × 3.1416	
Area of circle	=	square of diameter × .7854	
Area of circle	=	square of circumference × .07958	
Area of circle	=	½ circumference × ½ diameter	
Diameter of circle	=	circumference × .31831	
Radius of circle	=	circumference × .159155	
Side of inscribed square	=	circumference × .225	
Side of inscribed square	=	diameter × .7071	
Side of an equal square	=	circumference × .282	
Side of an equal square	=	diameter × .8861	
Side of inscribed triangle	=	diameter × .86	
Area of a triangle	=	base × ½ altitude	
Surface area of a sphere	=	circumference × diameter	
Surface area of a sphere	=	square of diameter × 3.1416	
Surface area of a sphere	=	square of circumference × .5236	
Volume of a sphere	=	surface × ⅙ diameter	
Volume of a sphere	=	cube of radius × 4.1888	
Volume of a sphere	=	cube of diameter × .5236	
Volume of a sphere	=	cube of circumference × .016887	
Side of an inscribed cube	=	radius of sphere × 1.1547	
Surface of inscribed cube	=	area of its side × 6	
Volume of a cone	=	area of its base × ⅓ altitude	

Damp Cellars

To eliminate the habitual dampness of cellars, potato houses, etc., obtain from any druggist one pound calcium chloride and divide the package into three or four fruit cans; leave the cans open and place them in unmolested positions in the cellar; the moisture in the air will be attracted to and accumulated by the chloride; when the water accumulated covers the chloride, do not discard it, but place the cans over a strong fire and evaporate the contents of the can to dryness; the chloride will re-crystalize and the cans may be placed back in the cellar.

Moldy cellars may be eliminated with a little care and attention; if the cellar walls have a tendency to develop mold, prepare a quantity of unslacked lime finely pulverized, which is then blown onto the walls dampened sufficiently to cause the lime to stick; the lime slacks upon contact with the water and kills mold plant, entirely eliminating it, and if the cellar is kept dry, it will not return; care should be taken to blow the lime into every crack and crevice to insure a thorough job; allow the lime to remain a day or so, then wash the walls removing it and air the cellar well, warming it with several hot stones to drive out the moisture.

Water Paint

Slack a quantity of lime in a tub covered to keep in steam; when slacked, pass through a fine screen or sieve; to each 6 parts this lime, add 1 part finely powdered rock salt and 4 parts water; boil all together and skim well; to each 2½ gallons this liquid, add ½ pound powdered alum, ¼ pound powdered green copperas, then, very slowly, 6 ounces powdered caustic potash add 2 pounds very fine sand; mix thoroughly and add coloring ingredients to suit; for stone color, add 1 pound ocher to 2 gallons of paint; durable as slate, and renders stone and brick practically waterproof.

Oil Water Paint

Boil together, 14 lbs. Silicate of Soda (Water Glass), 45° density, Beaume, and 2½ gallons water; while boiling, sift in 3½ lbs. dark rosin pounded to a powder, stirring continuously, and continue the boiling until all the rosin is dissolved; strain through a canvas; mix this liquid with an equal quantity of boiled linseed oil when cooled.

Waterproof Paint

Dissolve ½ pound thinly shaved cheap brown soap in 1 quart water over fire until a smooth liquid; skim, and add 3 quarts boiled linseed oil and ½ ounce blue vitriol; remove from fire, and add 1 quart turpentine and any coloring ingredients to suit; mix thoroughly and strain well; thin with turpentine for use.—Suitable for tents, tarpaulins, etc.

Comments and References

Just a few letters from the many thousands we have received together with a few names and addresses of users of Enameled "HOME COMFORT" Ranges selected at random from our Sales Register.

ALABAMA

WILL HAVE NO OTHER
Andalusia, November 10th.
Wrought Iron Range Co., St. Louis, Mo.
Gentlemen:—
Six years ago I bought a "Home Comfort" Range and it has remained in good condition under constant use. I never expect to use anything but a "Home Comfort".

Mrs. J. F. Carson

USER FOR 50 YEARS
Florala, December 1st.
Wrought Iron Range Co., St. Louis, Mo.
Gentlemen:—
We have used your "Home Comfort" Ranges for the past 50 years, having used two in that time. We have constantly used the one we now have for the past 26 years for we bought it in 1899, and to my best belief, it is good for at least 5 years yet. When I do replace it, it will certainly be with another "Home Comfort", for it is the best range made and uses so much less fuel than the ordinary kind.

J. J. Barnes, Farmer

30 YEARS—SAME PIPE
Florala, December 3rd.
Wrought Iron Range Co., St. Louis, Mo.
Gentlemen:—
We used a "Home Comfort" Range for over 30 years and discarded it for a small ordinary stove, which is in no way satisfactory. We are using some of the same pipe that came with our "Home Comfort" on this new stove, and can certainly recommend "Home Comfort" material as the best. Could we have had the opportunity to replace our old range with a new "Home Comfort" at the time we were forced to buy, I would never have bought anything else.

Bill Watkins

SHE ENJOYS COOKING NOW
West Butler, August 28th.
Wrought Iron Range Co., St. Louis, Mo.
Gentlemen:—
We are well pleased with the "Home Comfort" Range, and think no other can beat it. Wife enjoys cooking—and I enjoy eating—much better since we have had it. We would not take twice the price for it and do without it.

L. E. Hearn

WILL NOT PART WITH IT
Guntersville, October 1st.
Wrought Iron Range Co., St. Louis, Mo.
Gentlemen:—
We like our "Home Comfort" Range just fine and would not part with it at all.

J. N. Feemster

BEST IN THE WORLD
Union Grove, December 22nd.
Wrought Iron Range Co., St. Louis, Mo.
Gentlemen:—
Our "Home Comfort" Range, which we have had in daily use for over 25 years, has always given perfect satisfaction. I believe it is the best range in the world.

W. L. Hughes

LIKE MEMBER OF FAMILY
Skinnerton, November 15th.
Wrought Iron Range Co., St. Louis, Mo.
Gentlemen:—
We have found the "Home Comfort" Range satisfactory for the 35 years we have used one. I am now 88 years old, nevertheless I was glad to have the opportunity, about 90 days ago, to purchase a new Model "AB." It is giving the same satisfaction and service the old model did, except, I find it uses much less fuel. When our old range was removed, I felt like one of the family had left us. No one makes a mistake when they buy a "Home Comfort" Range.

W. M. Snowden

WORDS CANNOT EXPRESS IT
Blocton, September 10th.
Wrought Iron Range Co., St. Louis, Mo.
Gentlemen:—
My "Home Comfort" Range is the best stove I have ever seen and I am so well pleased with it that I would not take what I paid for it. Words cannot express my thanks for it.

Jim Hill

IT COOKS PERFECTLY
Andalusia, November 12th.
Wrought Iron Range Co., St. Louis, Mo.
Gentlemen:—
Our new Enameled "Home Comfort" Range is proving that it is a real comfort and satisfaction. It cooks perfectly and uses so little wood.

F. A. Harton

WITH VERY LITTLE FUEL
Arab, December 22nd.
Wrought Iron Range Co., St. Louis, Mo.
Gentlemen:—
I bought one of your "Home Comfort" Ranges in 1921 and we have always been well pleased with it. It cooks with very little wood and there could not be a better baker made.

W. O. Traylor

MOST PERFECT RANGE
Belleville, November 26th.
Wrought Iron Range Co., St. Louis, Mo.
Gentlemen:—
We have used our "Home Comfort" Range for 20 years and it has always given perfect satisfaction in every respect. My mother, Mrs. J. W. Gaston, of Repton, has used her "Home Comfort" for 28 years and it is now in good condition. We are today giving your salesman our order for our latest Model "AB" Enameled Range for we earnestly believe it to be the most perfectly constructed range for all modern conveniences that can be built.

C. C. Gaston, Merchant

WANTS ANOTHER ONE
Trinity, August 1st.
Wrought Iron Range Co., St. Louis, Mo.
Gentlemen:—
I want to buy another "Home Comfort" Range. I bought one from your wagon 27 years ago which we are still using, but I want a new one.

Chas. Emens

FINDS US RELIABLE

Marion, February 1st.

WROUGHT IRON RANGE CO., St. Louis, Mo.

Gentlemen:—

This certifies that I have a "HOME COMFORT" Range that I have been using 23 years and always have found satisfactory in every way. I looked the new "HOME COMFORT" Range over and decided to buy one because it had so many improvements added to the 1899 range like the one I am using now. I have found the Wrought Iron Range Co. to be a straight and reliable company to do business with as their goods always prove to be as recommended. The "HOME COMFORT" is worth 100 cents on the dollar.

L. M. NICHOLS

F. O. Bryars	Atmore	J. C. Coker	Evergreen	M. Joy	Magargel	Alex Stevens	Peterman
E. M. Willisma	Axis	W. A. Stephens	Ensley	Chas. Lee	Millry	A. R. Agee	Perdue Hill
Ben Bodwin	Atmore	L. Williams	Escatawpa	Robert Weeks		W. M. Cooper	Rabun
B. Johnson	Andalusia	W. H. Hasty	Excel		Magnolia Springs	W. Gruk	Robertsdale
Prince Crook	Bromley	L. Winberg	Fairhope	W. H. McNaught		M. C. Heaton	Range
C. C. Hires	Barnwell	W. T. Wall	Foley		Muscogee	W. L. Reeves	Repton
L. J. Hull	Bay Minette	G. B. Beech	Foley	L. P. Dickson		W. M. Long	Range
Eli Stevens	Bon Secour	W. J. Runyon	Fruitdale		Montgomery	A. K. Graham	Stockton
Wesley Bishop	Boonville	E. M. Deer	Franklin	Jim Stalworth	Monroe	D. Miller	Stapleton
R. J. May	Bessemer	Jack Kelly	Flomation	E. L. Smith	Monroeville	E. L. Malone	Seminole
C. G. Ross	Boaz	S. McGrue	Freemanville	C. Clayton	Mt. Vernon	Sam Dubose	Summerdale
M. T. Dorman		Sarah Brown	Falco	Ed. Sherls	McIntosh	C. A. Huff	Silver Hill
	Bayou Labatre	M. C. Kimbrough		C. B. Moore	McCullough	J. W. Hardee	Skinnerton
J. T. Tedder	Burbanks		Gilbertown	W. H. Gilly	McDavid	A. J. Lowery	Semmes
J. S. Alford	Brewton	W. I. Hanks	Goodway	J. M. Black	Natchez	D. O. Hall	Tensaw
A. J. Green	Castlebury	L. Meaner	Gulf Crest	Wm. Decatur	Navco	J. L. Williams	Tibbie
J. A. Lowery	Chariton	Sam Lawson	Grand Bay	B. M. Byres	Nokomis	S. J. Miller	Theodore
C. O'Cain	Coden	Henry Sledge	Hurricane	R. C. Brown	Owassa	A. J. Snow	Uriah
Richard Byrd	Citronelle	I. C. Rowell	Hixon	J. F. Floyd	Opileka	C. B. Turner	
J. J. Lewis	Chunchula	E. Baas	Jones Mills	R. R. Smith	Oak Grove		Vinegar Bend
T. E. Spivey	Canoe	J. H. Phillips	Little River	J. S. Howard	Perdido	W. H. Tew	Whistler
Jessie Stapleton	Dephane	C. A. Nimmo	Laxley	A. C. Nelson	Point Clear	W. H. Howell	Wilmer
Sam Anderson	Drewry	M. W. James	Local	W. R. Abbott		W. P. Myers	Whistler
Paul Haupt	Elberta	F. W. Cannon	Mercia		Perdidi Beach	G. W. Bell	Wallace
		T. L. Lloyd	Mexboro	Wm. Cox	Perkinstown		

ARKANSAS

IS PLEASED IN EVERY WAY

Bald Knob, July 3rd.

WROUGHT IRON RANGE CO., St. Louis, Mo.

Gentlemen:—

We have one of your Enameled "HOME COMFORT" Ranges and have found it to be all you represent them to be; a perfect baker and heater, a wonderful fuel saver, rigid and durable, and far superior to any range or stove we have ever used. We are pleased with it in every way.

T. P. LASSITER

A REAL HOME COMFORT

Williford, December 27th.

WROUGHT IRON RANGE CO., St. Louis, Mo.

Gentlemen:—

I have found my new Enameled "HOME COMFORT" Range all your salesman represented it to be. It bakes perfectly and is so easy to keep clean. Every woman should have a "HOME COMFORT" and know what real home comfort is.

MRS. SARAH LADD

AFTER 40 YEARS' EXPERIENCE

Mountain Home, September 29th.

WROUGHT IRON RANGE CO., St. Louis, Mo.

Gentlemen:—

We purchased a "HOME COMFORT" Range from one of your traveling salesmen in 1885, and this Range has been in constant use all this time. Sixteen years of this time, we used the Range in a hotel, during which it was kept hot almost day and night. We have recently purchased one of your Latest Model Enameled "HOME COMFORT" Ranges, altho our old one is still in fairly good shape. After 40 years' experience with your "HOME COMFORT" Range, I can cheerfully recommend it without a single reservation.

MRS. J. A. CASE

MAKES WORK A PLEASURE

Mountain Home, November 29th.

WROUGHT IRON RANGE CO., St. Louis, Mo.

Gentlemen:—

I have now had my Enameled "HOME COMFORT" Range more than a year and I like it so well that I would not want to part with it. It is all you represent it to be and satisfactory in every way. My kitchen work is not nearly so wearisome as it was with the old cast-iron stoves I have used.

MRS. R. G. RUSSELL

GIVES PERFECT SATISFACTION

Judsonia, July 18th.

WROUGHT IRON RANGE CO., St. Louis, Mo.

Gentlemen:—

I bought my "HOME COMFORT" Range in June, 1924, and find it all you recommended it to be. It is one of your new model Enameled Ranges and is a real piece of furniture. It is so easy to keep bright and clean and all the features are so convenient. It is the best "baker" I have ever used and uses less fuel than any stove I have ever seen. I am perfectly satisfied with it.

MRS. C. R. JONES

THERE'S NO COMPARISON

Hoxie, April 24th.

WROUGHT IRON RANGE CO., St. Louis, Mo.

Gentlemen:—

We have been using one of your "HOME COMFORT" Ranges since April, 1915, and are pleased to say that it gives entire satisfaction. Before buying our "HOME COMFORT," we used one of the best known "retail ranges," but our "HOME COMFORT" heats quicker, bakes and cooks better, and uses much less fuel than it did. I don't regret buying your Range and wish we had installed one long before.

W. C. MADDEN

IS MORE THAN REPRESENTED

Bald Knob, July 17th.
WROUGHT IRON RANGE CO., St. Louis, Mo.
Gentlemen:—
I didn't know that a real range meant so much to the work in a kitchen until we got our new Enameled "HOME COMFORT". It looks like a real piece of furniture and my family wants to cook all the time and I sure do my share of the eating. We have found it exactly as represented, and then some

E. S. COLEMAN

NO MORE "COMMON STOVES"

Kensett, July 10th.
WROUGHT IRON RANGE CO., St. Louis, Mo.
Gentlemen:—
I have had my "HOME COMFORT" Range since June, 1922, and it has always given complete satisfaction. I would not like to think I had to give it up and go back to a common stove. I would not take the price I paid for it and be without it.

MRS. F. W. HALL

IT'S ALWAYS BRIGHT AND CLEAN

Monson, April 10th.
WROUGHT IRON RANGE CO., St. Louis, Mo.
Gentlemen:—
I bought one of your Enameled "HOME COMFORT" Ranges more than a year ago and have found it to be the perfect baker and fuel saver your salesman represented it to be. I would not want to go back to the tedious care of a common stove for my "HOME COMFORT" is always bright and clean and saves so much work and worry.

MRS. ELIZA LINN

COOKS "JUST TO SUIT"

Hoxie, May 1st.
WROUGHT IRON RANGE CO., St. Louis, Mo.
Gentlemen:—
We purchased one of your Enameled "HOME COMFORT" Ranges in May, 1924, and I am pleased to say that it gives entire satisfaction in every way. I don't see how I ever got along with a common stove, but it is easy to understand how anyone can have "good luck" baking in the steel oven of the "HOME COMFORT" for it can be regulated "just to suit." Then, it takes so little fuel to bake with, and the fuel saving and the many conveniences will soon pay for the range.

MRS. R. J. BLACKWELL

IS A REAL FUEL SAVER

Bellfonte, August 31st.
WROUGHT IRON RANGE CO., St. Louis, Mo.
Gentlemen:—
We used a "HOME COMFORT" Range for 20 years, but when we saw your new Enameled Model, we decided to have one; so we disposed of our old one and replaced it with a new one. We think we have one of the very best Ranges in Arkansas for we have found it exactly as represented and entirely satisfactory in every way. I believe, tho, it is a better fuel saver than the older models and bakes perfectly like the old one always did. When you have a "HOME COMFORT" in your kitchen, you don't have to worry about "cook stoves."

W. M. ABNEY

SAVES HALF THE STEPS

Portia, May 1st.
WROUGHT IRON RANGE CO., St. Louis, Mo.
Gentlemen:—
We bought one of your Enameled "HOME COMFORT" Ranges in April, 1924, and am pleased to say that it gives entire satisfaction. I have found it to be exactly as represented by your salesman, but I don't believe he was able to give me half of an idea as to the amount of real work it was going to save me in my kitchen. It seems to me that my steps are reduced by half.

MRS. J. W. HOLLIMAN

HEATS PRESSURE BOILER

Walnut Ridge, April 2nd.
WROUGHT IRON RANGE CO., St. Louis, Mo.
Gentlemen:—
We are now using one of your latest improved Enameled "HOME COMFORT" Ranges recently purchased through your traveling salesman. I have this Range connected to a 40-gallon pressure boiler and it is giving fine satisfaction for it heats the water very quickly. I had the same boiler connected to another range, but it would not do the work. We find your "HOME COMFORT" a perfect baker, a quick heater, and it consumes much less fuel than any other stove or range we have ever used. I will cheerfully answer any inquiry concerning it.

JOE HALL
Ex-Sheriff of Lawrence Co.

HOT WATER ALWAYS HANDY

Bald Knob, July 17th.
WROUGHT IRON RANGE CO., St. Louis, Mo.
Gentlemen:—
I am certainly well pleased with my new Enameled "HOME COMFORT" Range. It consumes about half the fuel my old stove did, and that means my stove-wood work and expense is cut in half. I find it saves just as much work in many other ways: hot water always handy, food keeps warm in the warming-closet and saves steps, and the oven bakes perfectly and quickly.

MRS. SARAH EMEB

GLAD THEY BOUGHT IT

Pocahontas, March 14th.
WROUGHT IRON RANGE CO., St. Louis, Mo.
Gentlemen:—
The Enameled Model "HOME COMFORT" Range I bought from you in January, 1924, was found to be just as represented and has been giving us excellent satisfaction. There could not be a better baker, nor one more economical in fuel. It looks as bright and clean as it did when new. I do not regret the investment when I bought it.

W. C. HUNTER

WON'T TAKE PRICE THEY PAID

Bradford, July 3rd.
WROUGHT IRON RANGE CO., St. Louis, Mo.
Gentlemen:—
We are using one of your Enameled Models of the "HOME COMFORT" Range and have found it to be as represented. It is giving entire satisfaction. It is a fine baker, a great wood saver and has meant a great saving of time and work for my family. We wouldn't take what we gave for it and do without it.

H. H. MOYER

THEY MADE NO MISTAKE

Conway, October 25th.
WROUGHT IRON RANGE CO., St. Louis, Mo.
Gentlemen:—
When I bought our "HOME COMFORT" Range in September, 1924, I thought I was buying the best Range on the market. Now, I'm sure of it, for we have found it to be exactly as you represented it and gives entire satisfaction.

FRED HAHLEN

M. C. Alexander Almond	C. A. Stephens Dexter	A. F. Pierce Leachville	G. W. Melton
G. H. Stanage Alicia	T. P. Martin Diehlstodt	J. A. Davis Little Rock	Running Lake
R. C. Savage Atkins	J. Wooldridge Dalton	J. G. Virges Levy	Albert Blair Red Stripe
A. P. Dalton Anniston	G. E. Lambie Egypt	M. F. Hicks Lonoke	C. P. Piker Russell
G. A. Hester Alexander	G. W. Still Elmo	Jake Bowden Moncttc	E. A. Wallace Success
J. M. Brown Ash Flat	J. B. Butler Eaton	O. O. Tharp Morrillton	M. C. Evans Solgohashia
J. E. Wright Bentonville	M. G. Marshall England	T. C. Moore Monette	E. J. Wilson Sedwick
H. S. Bishop Brookland	W. A. Belew Elnora	T. E. Collins Mayflower	A. H. Warthan
C. T. Bell Barnes	R. C. White Elpaso	Geo. Evans Martinville	Stonewall
J. W. Shipley	W. T. Owens East Prairie	J. H. Morris Morrillton	R. A. Allen Salado
Beech Grove	W. P. Stephens Essex	M. Kissie Many Islands	J. R. Perry Swifton
W. P. Jordan Bono	G. L. Doran Elm Store	L. C. Nael Marmaduke	N. Bilbrey Smithville
J. W. Berry, Brookland	J. E. Hawkins	W. J. Waldrip Magness	W. D. Barber
R. E. Goodwin Beebe	Eleven Points	R. L. Hewlitt McRae	Sulpher Rock
F. M. Faulkner Bucoda	John Bies Fontain	C. M. Rabb Mena	George Moore Scott
M. J. West Batesville	J. C. Nicholson Floral	Taylor McAfee McRae	M. Hicks Sweet Home
H. R. Bridges Black Rock	Ed. Wilcox Greenbrier	J. E. Davis Mablevale	Burton Ingram Scott
R. C. Waters Butlerville	Elvie Cooper Grange	C. O. Ingram Maynard	L. E. Bayer Supply
A. Rodgers Bayouville	A. A. Gilbreath Garner	T. B. Magness Newark	Eugene Smith Searcy
W. M. Johnson Bertrand	J. P. Tryer Hattieville	J. S. Posley Newport	G. G. Forbess Truman
W. R. Biggers Biggers	A. J. Craig Hoxie	Ray Williams	Sam Gates Tie Plant
H. McNabb Brockett	Leonia McCarthy	North Little Rock	G. J. Wharton Vilonia
R. D. Barden Birdell	Harrisburg	J. J. Batta Noland	R. L. Mashburn
Chas. Heuer Benton	T. J. Hill Higginson	J. B. Like Okean	Viney Ridge
B. W. McWherter	G. A. Hicks Hensley	C. S. Hawkins Oil Trough	J. W. Braskett
Bald Knob	A. J. Rogers Hardy	F. M. Hill Oneal	Wolf Bayou
H. H. Moyer Bradford	S. L. Tyer Imboden	Jack Getson Okean	J. M. Scott Wooster
W. O. French Corning	Dudley Waldron Ingram	C. F. Thomas Perry	C. S. Adams Walcott
W. M. Mosley Conway	Rev. D. M. Smith	W. C. Pigue Paragould	C. H. D. Williams
Julia Martain Cushman	Jonesboro	Dr. J. A. Hook	Walnut Corner
S. M. Shelby Charleston	Anton Keller Judsonia	Pleasant Dale	J. K. Jackson Ward
Joe Woodard Crosno	W. S. Sheets Jacksonville	Dr. W. J. Robinson	J. J. Blaylock Wyatt
J. F. McFadden Cabot	Lilburn James Keo	Portia	D. Williams Wrightsville
Wm. Kriegbaum Congo	V. R. Lee Kensett	W. E. Martin Powhatan	J. R. Whitrock
W. M. Watson Datto	J. W. Patterson Leonard	T. H. Pinson Perry	Warm Springs
J. T. Cothran Dela Plaine	P. S. Pierce Lake City	D. F. Kirk Pocahontas	T. G. Garner Williford
A. R. Egnes Desha	J. R. Butler Lafe	T. H. Nelson Rector	J. W. Ray West Point
J. M. Hicks Dorena	Arthur Lee Lauratown	T. A. Jones Rockroad	M. E. Perry Ward
	J. A. Williams Lonooe	M. L. Adams Reyno	

FLORIDA

WORTH THE PRICE
Lakeland, October 15th.

WROUGHT IRON RANGE CO., St. Louis, Mo.
Gentlemen:—
Our "HOME COMFORT" Range is the best we have ever owned or have ever seen. We feel that it is worth all we paid for it and that it is all it is claimed to be.

E. R. STETTLER

RANGE A MASTERPIECE
Pensacola, September 18th.

WROUGHT IRON RANGE CO., St. Louis, Mo.
Gentlemen:—
I have had the pleasure of dealing with your company for many years, and have always found you and your salesmen strictly "on the square." I have just bought one of your new Enameled Model "HOME COMFORT" Ranges because I know

just what your goods are. This is our third "HOME COMFORT" Range. Although our last one is still serviceable, we think your new model such a masterpiece that we must have one. With kindest regards,

L. S. GILMORE
Commissioner, Escambia County

NO BETTER ONE
Florida Lea Groves,
Sarasota, January 23rd.

WROUGHT IRON RANGE CO., St. Louis, Mo.
Gentlemen:—
Our "HOME COMFORT" Range is the best stove we have ever seen, and we do not expect to see a better one. We are delighted with it and the results obtained from its use.

Florida Lea Groves,
J. H. YOHE

John B. Laws Arran	M. J. Hall Chiefland	H. Christian Grove Park	R. F. Merritt Lake Butler
G. W. Wilson Alachua	H. B. Rodgers	H. F. Yates Greenville	C. S. Clyatt Lulu
O. M. McNeill Archer	Cedar Keys	H. C. Wimberley	S. S. Keen Lake City
D. E. Davis	J. C. Barber Concord	Highland	J. T. Perry Live Oak
Bowling Green	Sam Dukes Dukes	D. W. Miller Havana	T. F. Terry Lawtey
Albert Martin Bell	I. P. Armstrong	O. F. Williams	L. H. Hendry Lake Bird
J. James Brooker	Drifton City	High Springs	J. R. Younge Loughridge
W. F. Oatman Bronson	F. R. Shackleford Ebb	F. W. Capell Hawthorne	Sam McGee Lloyd
R. W. Ashmore	W. M. Pinner Eugene	B. B. Harrison	H. D. Carter Maxville
Benhaden	L. B. Shipman Earlton	Hardeetown	L. L. Perry Mayo
B. E. Raysor Citra	B. L. Price Ellzy	R. C. Philpot Inglis	T. L. Ainson Melrose
W. R. Gainey Cross City	D. M. McNair Ft. White	J. Burnett, Jr. Jasper	E. A. Blanton
W. S. Boyd Capitola	A. H. Howard Falmouth	R. M. Cason Jennings	Monticello
C. W. Howard Clara	R. B. Isaac Fairbanks	J. Philmon Jena	Lee Reeves Metcalf
W. A. Kelley Carbur	C. H. Neal Gainsville	J. A. Perryman Lecanto	M. J. Sapp New River

S. A. Hussey Newberry	J. E. Houston	W. B. Hicks St. Marks	C. H. Cox Water Town
J. W. Neisler Ocala	Sopochoppy	H. D. May Theressa	H. C. Powers Wellborn
H. R. High Old Town	G. H. Lander	James Watson Trenton	James Cornell Wanchula
H. Boatright O'Brien	Suwanee Valley	W. C. Tully Tallahassee	H. L. Chancy Wacissa
B. J. Collier Otter Creek	J. A. McKinney Starke	M. R. Mott Vernon	J. F. Britt Williston
J. M. Faulker Perry	C. L. Woods	T. J. Kemp	W. C. Beach Walds
L. E. Mosley Raiford	Stephensville	White Springs	C. C. Brownless
T. B. Bradley Rochelle	R. E. Bailey Shady Grove	J. W. Hernby Wilbur	Woodville
			T. L. Blanton Wilcox

GEORGIA

BACKS UP CONTRACT

Adairsville, November 7th.

WROUGHT IRON RANGE CO., St. Louis, Mo.

Gentlemen:—

I wish to say a word for the "HOME COMFORT" Range. It is all its name implies, and more, for it is truly a "comfort" and a "pleasure" to cook on a "HOME COMFORT"—its baking is perfect. As to the durability of your Range, I cannot say how long they last. Mine has been in constant use for over 14 years, and it looks and cooks just as well as it did at first. I have had a large family to cook for all the time, besides doing all my canning and preserving, which will average about 600 quarts a year. We Southern people serve three hot meals a day. I am still using the pipe that came with my Range, even the pipe joint next to the fire is in perfect condition. I am proud of my Range and am proud of the company that makes it, for I know it puts out good material and backs up every word of its contract.

MRS. C. M. ERWIN

A. F. Wilson Axson	W. R. Wade Dixie	P. G. Hooper Lula	W. H. Purvis Pearson
M. J. Day Ambrose	A. C. McMillian Enigma	J. R. Kinard Lenox	R. H. King Patterson
M. M. Jackson Alapaha	J. A. Davis Greenville	J. O. Hadden Madison	J. C. Howard Quartz
G. W. McClellan Alma	I. S. Mikell	J. J. Crews MacClenny	C. N. Johnson Quitman
S. E. Cowart Adel	Glen St. Mary	T. E. Powers Manning	W. R. Peters Ray City
L. J. Kirkland Broxton	B. Rountree Hahira	Mrs. J. M. Ellison	J. G. Barber Rockingham
A. H. Hendley	W. L. Dye Helen	Mount Airy	R. M. Dickerson
Bannockburn	Rubert Allen "	Hester Davis Mershon	Rabun Gap
H. H. Pittman Blackshear	W. H. Smith Hollywood	W. J. Rawlerson Moniac	D. J. Digger Sanderson
J. B. Brown Bristol	H. C. Burk Harnest	C. T. Waldon Millwood	W. C. Alley Sautee
Ira Lee Beach	W. L. Whiting	W. T. Prescott Manor	J. J. Crumpton Sparks
W. G. Steedley Bristol	Habersham	M. F. Lawson Morven	Timothy Hicks
W. C. White Boston	R. Corbett Homerville	E. D. Connell Naylor	Tallulah Falls
F. G. Fry Clarksville	T. B. Davis Howell	Dr. W. L. Hall Nicholls	M. L. Herndon Valdosta
M. D. Free Cornelia	J. C. Whitfield Homer	A. H. Giddens Nashville	Mrs. R. F. Lineberger
B. H. Bridges Coleman	W. B. Morris Kirkland	R. O. Cobb Olustee	Valdosta
E. E. Sample Cornelia	O. T. Allen Lee	R. H. Hadden	Dan Wall Wilacoochee
J. A. Gunn Demorest	W. R. King Lake Park	Pinetta City	H. A. Jones Whitesburg
R. J. Leavens Douglass	G. J. London	J. H. Sims Ousley	

ILLINOIS

IT'S A LIFETIME RANGE

Macomb, April 6th.

WROUGHT IRON RANGE CO., St. Louis, Mo.

Gentlemen:—

This is to certify that I have used the "HOME COMFORT" Range for 10 years. It has not warped or cracked; I have not paid a cent for repairs. It is the finest baker we ever used. I would not take $150 for it if I could not get another one like it. I had to buy a stove every 5 or 6 years before I got a "HOME COMFORT". I have a lifetime range. Anyone can see it at my home any day, and I cheerfully recommend it. I cannot say too much in favor of the Range.

THOMAS J. PATTERSON

FIRE LINING LASTS

Bushnell, May 18th.

WROUGHT IRON RANGE CO., St. Louis, Mo.

Gentlemen:—

This is to certify that I bought a "HOME COMFORT" Range 6 years ago, and that it has given entire satisfaction. It uses a great deal less fuel than any other stove I ever used, and it has not warped or cracked; the lining and fire walls are as good as new today.

J. M. PELLEY

RESERVOIR IS A TREASURE

Scottsburgh, May 25th.

WROUGHT IRON RANGE CO., St. Louis, Mo.

Gentlemen:—

We have purchased a "HOME COMFORT" Range and are much pleased with it. The reservoir in itself is a treasure, always having hot water at hand. It bakes with less fuel than any stove we ever used.

MR. AND MRS. O. M. MCELVAIN

MEAL WITH SIX STICKS

Dongola, April 26th.

WROUGHT IRON RANGE CO., St. Louis, Mo.

Gentlemen:—

Will say we are certainly proud of our "HOME COMFORT" Range. Wife can cook a meal with 5 or 6 sticks of wood any time. My neighbors bought new ranges of another make both nice lookers, but I hear complaints of them being "wood eaters".

F. DEXTER

PROVED STATEMENT FALSE

Batchtown, September 24th.

WROUGHT IRON RANGE CO., St. Louis, Mo.

Gentlemen:—

We, the undersigned, purchased "HOME COMFORT" Ranges from one of your wagons several years ago. We had been cautioned so much about buying from traveling agents that we had about come to the conclusion we had been humbugged. Several hardware men tried to convince us that they could purchase the same range for a great deal less money (which we found untrue), and tried in several ways to discourage us over our purchase. We are pleased to say that after having used the "HOME COMFORT" Ranges for the past several years, we are highly pleased with them, and would not take double the amount paid for them if we could not procure other HOME COMFORTS" in their stead. We wish to add also, that we found the ranges fully as represented, and would suggest to those who are desirous of purchasing a cooking range of any kind to look into the merits of "HOME COMFORT" Ranges before purchasing.

STEPHEN W. BAILLEY
F. W. FEIDLER

30 YEARS—GOOD AS NEW
Bartelso, March 11th.
WROUGHT IRON RANGE Co., St. Louis, Mo.
Gentlemen:—
This is to certify that I bought a "HOME COMFORT" Range off one of the wagons in 1895, and it has given satisfaction in every respect. It is as good as it was when new. We would not do without a "HOME COMFORT".

NICK EALINGER

OUTLASTS 3 RANGES
Edwardsville, April 21st.
WROUGHT IRON RANGE Co., St. Louis, Mo.
Gentlemen:—
This is to certify that I have a "HOME COMFORT" Range. It has been in use for over 25 years and is still in good order. My neighbors have bought three ranges since I bought this and paid not less than forty dollars each for them. I consider "HOME COMFORT" the cheapest Range.

J. N. STAHTHUT

STANDS HARD USAGE
El Dara, August 17th.
WROUGHT IRON RANGE Co., St. Louis, Mo.
Gentlemen:—
We, each of us, have had a "HOME COMFORT" Range in use for eight years and are pleased to say that they give entire satisfaction. They are a great fuel saver, a good baker and cooker, and a Range that will stand hard usage.

MRS. J. S. DOLBARE
MRS. W. P. PREYOB

RIVALS GAS STOVE IN SUMMER
Bardolph, April 19th.
WROUGHT IRON RANGE Co., St. Louis, Mo.
Gentlemen:—
I have used a "HOME COMFORT" Range for 6 years. It is a No. 1 baker and does not heat the room in summer—more like a gasoline stove; a saving in coal, and is as good as the day I bought it.

J. D. WISSLER

TWELVE TIMES AS GOOD
Jerseyville, June 20th.
WROUGHT IRON RANGE Co., St. Louis, Mo.
Gentlemen:—
I bought of your salesman, off of the wagon 23 years ago, one of your "HOME COMFORT" Ranges and used it on the farm until 2 years ago. When I moved to town, I bought a new range, and left the "HOME COMFORT" on the farm. And the old

"HOME COMFORT" is in better shape today than the range I paid sixty dollars for two years ago. I take great pleasure in indorsing the merits of "HOME COMFORT" Ranges. While it is high in price, in my mind it is the cheapest in the long run. I was born and raised in Jersey County and anyone doubting this statement can address me at Jerseyville, Ill., and I will verify it. I am,

ZED. REDDISH

NOT A CENT FOR REPAIRS
Time, August 10th.
WROUGHT IRON RANGE Co., St. Louis, Mo.
Gentlemen:—
We have in use one of your "HOME COMFORT" Ranges 10 years, and am well pleased with it in equal cannot be found. Our Range is as good as new, and has never cost us a cent for repairs. We would not part with it at any price.

MRS. SAM W. MILLER

NOT A WARP
Crescent City, June 24th.
WROUGHT IRON RANGE Co., St. Louis, Mo.
Gentlemen:—
I have used one of the "HOME COMFORT" Ranges 10 years, and am well pleased with it in every respect. It has never warped or cracked, and with 10 years constant use, we have never had one cent of repairs. As a baker, it cannot be equaled. I can safely recommend this Range to anyone.

MRS. E. M. HARROUN

BAKES WITH TWO STICKS
Fairview, June 3rd.
WROUGHT IRON RANGE Co., St. Louis, Mo.
Gentlemen:—
I have used a "HOME COMFORT" Range and can recommend it as one of the finest bakers we have ever used; also, a great fuel saver. Can do my baking with two sticks of wood; therefore would not part with it for any other range I have ever seen.

MRS. JAMES ALLISON

COOL IN SUMMER
Mt. Sterling, December 26th.
WROUGHT IRON RANGE Co., St. Louis, Mo.
Gentlemen:—
We have been using a "HOME COMFORT" Range for 6 years and we can highly recommend it for quick baking, small consumption of fuel and durability. It does not throw out the heat in summer like an ordinary stove, and is in good order. Anyone needing a range should look into the merits of the "HOME COMFORT" before buying.

MR. AND MRS. W. E. CADY

PLEASED WITH THE SETTLEMENTS
Gilman, June 17th.
WROUGHT IRON RANGE Co., St. Louis, Mo.
Gentlemen:—
We have been using a "HOME COMFORT" Range for 7 years. It is an excellent baker and performs all the duties of a stove perfectly. We are well pleased with it, and, as our neighbors know, have always praised it. Knowing its merits as we do, we would not exchange it for any other make of stove or range now. In behalf of the company, we will say they fulfilled their contracts; and our settlements with them were as pleasant as they could possibly have been with any company.

JAMES SCOTT

T. L. Thoden	Ashmore	Cecil Woolens	Bone Gap	Harvey Bales	Bogota	Isaac Baylor	Clay City
Harry Dukeman	Arcola	H. C. Dampster		L. E. Ogalsbee		B. F. James	Charleston
Alvy Summers	Albion		Bridgeport		Bridgeport	R. L. Beck	Casey
H. E. Jones	Allendale	Earl V. Nash	Browns	Milas Otterson	Benton	L. F. Sanford	Cisne
L. R. Smith	Altamont	Arthur Parr	Bellmont	E. W. Sloan	Baldwin	L. P. Byers	Calhoun
Henry Lacey	Bushton	C. S. Stevens	Birds	J. K. Willis	Casey	Chris Stern	Cowling

Elbert Wright	Chrisman	W. P. Phipps	Janesville	Chas. Canney	Olney	G. W. Decker	Trilla
W. E. Miller	Dietrich	P. H. Wallace	Keensburg	C. C. Shively	Oliver	J. N. Reuther	Teutopolis
H. W. Stoelting	Dennison	E. E. Simpson	Kansas	L. B. Carson	Palestine	E. B. Cross	Tower Hill
R. C. Powers	Dudley	U. S. Wolf	Louisville	T. M. Wilson	Paris	T. L. Vance	Vermillion
Guy Coleman	Etna	Wm. Lyons	Lerna	G. A. Schloz	Pana	H. Cooper	West Union
Walter Matteson		W. L. Rocnot	Loxa	Wm. Folck	Robinson	Earl Hammond	Westfield
	Effingham	Wm. Gibson	Landes	Walter Cokley		Fred Guyer	West York
John Nilson	Edgewood	Fred Streich	Lancaster		Parkersburg	Wm. Alley	Watseka
J. E. Craig	Fairgrange	J. McBride	Lawrenceville	George Hearn	Rinard	L. Loos	West Frankfort
C. Carlson	Flora	Chas. Finks	Lakewood	W. H. Vaughn	Robinson	G. W. Reynolds	
Lewis Martz	Findley	V. J. Moore	Martinsville	Wm. Foltz	Rose Hill		West Salem
A. C. Maxedon	Gays	John Reed	Marshall	Paul White	Redmon	W. W. McCoy	Willowhill
Link Schwartz	Gorham	Peter Morgan	Mattoon	J. L. Rasico		A. W. Naddell	
W. W. Kunce	Gr. Tower	C. N. Price	Mt. Carmel		St. Francisville		West Liberty
Henry Brader	Greenup	W. A. Edwards	Mason	C. E. Baker	Sumner	E. Mason	Wheeler
Chas. Holsapple	Greenup	Fred McClean	Montrose	H. R. Speer	Sigel	Joe Heady	Winterbrowd
V. Athey	Hutsonville	Arlie Craig	Mode	N. N. Robinson	Scotland	Wm. F. Marten	Watson
P. D. King	Hidalgo	John Hundley	Noble	N. F. Helton	Shelbyville	O. T. Cole	Windsor
T. M. Craig	Humer	Clyde Ross	Newton	A. L. Seward	Stewardson	A. N. Holbrook	
F. F. Pulliam	Horace	W. E. Ellis	Neogo	M. G. Buesking	Strasburg		Westervelt
R. J. Roe	Iuka		Orchardsville	James Hoene	Sigel		
J. W. Austin	Johnsonville	A. Geiger	Oblong	R. L. Carter	Sullivan	J. W. Hawkins	Xenia
J. B. Hustin	Jewett	L. S. Sanders	Ohlman	J. E. Hughes	Toledo	Paul Goodin	Yale

INDIANA

THE GOVERNOR'S DAUGHTER

Shanondale, June 1st.

WROUGHT IRON RANGE CO., St. Louis, Mo.

Gentlemen:—

We purchased one of your "HOME COMFORT" Ranges 12 years ago, and are pleased to say it gives entire satisfaction. You can use this certificate in any manner you see proper.

MRS. CHAS. BUTLER
Daughter of Gov. J. A. Mount

BURNED UP THREE CAST STOVES

Sullivan, May 10th.

WROUGHT IRON RANGE CO., St. Louis, Mo.

Gentlemen:—

I have used a "HOME COMFORT" Range for over 10 years, and consider it the best stove on earth. It bakes perfectly and consumes less than half the fuel of other stoves. Before buying a "HOME COMFORT" Range I burned up three cast-iron stoves. I consider it the cheapest stove anyone can buy.

AUSTIN SINCLAIR

HAS NEVER CRACKED

Witt, June 17th.

WROUGHT IRON RANGE CO., St. Louis, Mo.

Gentlemen:—

I have been using a "HOME COMFORT" Range for 24 years, and the top has never cracked or warped. Three years ago I purchased a new range from a hardware dealer. I have now set it aside and am using the old "HOME COMFORT", as it bakes better and does not take half the fuel that the other did. I would advise anyone to buy a "HOME COMFORT".

MRS. ANTHONY WITT

BURNS GREEN WOOD

Vincennes, March 5th.

WROUGHT IRON RANGE CO., St. Louis, Mo.

Gentlemen:—

This is to certify that we bought a "HOME COMFORT" Range, and our experience has proved to us that it is O. K. It does all that was claimed for it by the salesman. We use green wood with perfect satisfaction. It consumes less than half of the fuel that our cast-iron stove did. Would advise anyone needing a range to buy a "HOME COMFORT".

MRS. T. S. PEA

HAS NEVER WARPED

Churubrisco, April 9th.

WROUGHT IRON RANGE CO., St. Louis, Mo.

Gentlemen:—

I have been using a "HOME COMFORT" Range, bought 22 years ago, and it has always given the best of satisfaction, and is a No. 1 baker. It has never warped and seems to be as good as when we bought it. I can surely recommend it.

MRS. MARTIN JACKSON

BURNED COBS FOR NINE YEARS

Oxford, June 24th.

WROUGHT IRON RANGE CO., St. Louis, Mo.

Gentlemen:—

I purchased a "HOME COMFORT" Range 9 years ago, and can cheerfully recommend it to all for economy, durability and convenience. Have burned nothing but cobs constantly for nine years, and my Range is as good today as when purchased.

GEORGE BLIKINS

BURNED GAS DAY AND NIGHT

Ossian, April 7th.

WROUGHT IRON RANGE CO., St. Louis, Mo.

Gentlemen:—

Twenty-six years ago my father, David Stine, bought a "HOME COMFORT" Range from the wagon. There was natural gas burned in this range night and day for 12 years.

We are using this range now, and think it will last us several years yet. They cannot be beat as a baker. Anyone doubting this statement kindly call in person or phone me.

MRS. JOHN F. STINE

THEY BURN COAL

New Harmony, November 4th.

WROUGHT IRON RANGE CO., St. Louis, Mo.

Gentlemen:—

This is to certify that we bought a "HOME COMFORT" Range 11 years ago. It has been in constant use every day since, and is in perfect order today.

We burn coal in our Range most of the time. We know of ranges that have been bought since we bought ours, that have been burned out years ago. Would advise any neighbor needing a Range to buy a "HOME COMFORT". Anyone doubting this statement please call on me.

MRS. M. R. CHARLES

PAID FOR ITSELF

Covington, June 3rd.

WROUGHT IRON RANGE CO., St. Louis, Mo.

Gentlemen:—

This is to certify that we have used a "HOME COMFORT" Range for several years and it has always given perfect satisfaction. We would not take $150.00 for it now if we could not get another like it, for it is a perfect baker, and uses only about one-half of the fuel of an ordinary stove. In summer you can arrange it so that it makes very little more heat than a four-burner gasoline stove. You can also arrange it to warm your room in winter. We consider our stove has paid for itself in the fuel it has saved. We heartily recommend them to all who are thinking of buying a stove.

NEWTON BOORD

GOOD AFTER 20 YEARS

Decature, June 15th.

WROUGHT IRON RANGE CO., St. Louis, Mo.

Gentlemen:—

I have used a "HOME COMFORT" Range 21 years and I believe it will last another 20 years, for it is apparently as good as ever. It bakes well, and doesn't take much fire to do good work. Anyone needing a good, lasting range will not make a mistake in buying a "HOME COMFORT".

MRS. WM. HOLLE

CAN'T MAKE MISTAKE

Newport, April 11th.

WROUGHT IRON RANGE CO., St. Louis, Mo.

Gentlemen:—

I bought a "HOME COMFORT" Range in 1901, and it is in perfect order today. We consider it has paid for itself in the saving of fuel. In summer one can operate it so it does not throw out the heat and, also, in the winter to heat the room. One will not make a mistake by buying a "HOME COMFORT".

MRS. AMANDA HOLLINGSWORTH

BUYS ONE FOR SON

Deck, March 21st.

WROUGHT IRON RANGE CO., St. Louis, Mo.

Gentlemen:—

Having used a "HOME COMFORT" Range for 8 years and find that in every respect it is a comfort to use one. We bought our Range in 1900, and one for our son today. No one can say too much in the praise of your Ranges.

MRS. WALTER SMITH

WOULD NOT EXCHANGE

Merom, May 7th.

WROUGHT IRON RANGE CO., St. Louis, Mo.

Gentlemen:—

We have used a "HOME COMFORT" Range and wish to say that we think it is the best in the market. We would not take the price we paid for our Range and exchange it for any other stove or Range we've ever seen; and, we have been using it for a number of years.

E. F. BENNETT

HONORABLE DEALINGS

Meron, May 7th.

WROUGHT IRON RANGE CO., St. Louis, Mo.

Gentlemen:—

I bought one of your "HOME COMFORT" Ranges several years ago, and it has been in constant use ever since we bought it, and has never cost us one cent for repairs. Thanks to the company for its honorable dealings. I make this statement solely with the object of aiding a worthy enterprise.

MRS. A. WOOD

F. W. Schwab	Aurora	John Oberlate	Dillsboro
Lon Hern	Alert	Ernest Wynne	Deputy
R. P. Ailes	Alpine	Nate Desbro	Dupont
John Rich	Austin	G. H. Sommers	Ewing
E. W. Moore	Bedford	Mrs. Coda Lake	Everton
Ira Embry	Burney	I. F. Bryson	Edinburg
Wm. Shepler	Brownsville	C. A. Carter	
H. Powell	Bentonville		Elizabethtown
Adam Lohrey	Brookville	C. A. Manuel	Freetown
Wm. Jones	Brownstown	Roy Reeve	Falmouth
G. R. Holder	Brooksburg	W. A. Brown	Florence
J. H. Reed	Bedford	D. B. Barnett	Flat Rock
J. R. Cook	Batesville	J. L. Huffman	Falmouth
A. A. Brown	Bennington	Edward Witt	Guildford
Louisa Reed	Brooksburg	J. B. Richardson	
T. Morgan	Brownsville		Glenwood
J. W. Shaw	Columbus	Marshall DeArmond	
H. Murphy	Charlestown		Glenwood
C. Brown	Connersville	J. Percifield	Hartsville
G. Reuss	Cedar Grove	Chas. M. Shoaf	Hope
J. A. Hensley	Cortland	L. A. Smith	Henryville
W. Wolfe	College Corner	Roy Hinson	Harrison
A. G. Kay	Cottage Grove	Chester Gains	Hanover
Fred Tice	Centerville	Alex Hinton	Hayden
		J. L. Henry	Jonesville
		George Seitz	Kennedy

G. T. Fox	Kelso	W. A. Huston	
J. M. Fleetwood	Kurtz		New Philadelphia
H. O. Meyer	Kitchel	H. H. McCliffain	
David Walson	Lexington	George Weis	Osgood
L. E. Chance		A. O. Coffey	Oxford
	Lawrenceburg	Dan Kinnan	Patriot
Charlie Oaks	Letts	John A. Wilson	Rugby
R. L. Beck	Liberty	D. V. Whicker	Rushville
Grant Bravard	Laurel	C. W. Woods	Rising Sun
Frank Moody	Little York	John F. Renn	Sellersburg
John Munk	Memphis	Albert Hahenicht	Sunman
Nathan Hunter	Memphis	H. Brown	Sparksville
Ed. Mullins	Moores Hill	Melvil Owen	Seymour
Henry Lingg	Milton	Hershel Herring	Scipio
Virgal Hall	Medora	John Greve	Spades
Bryan Guyman	Madison	Leo Feller	Sunman
O. G. Austin	Milan	Jos. Mitchell	Scottsburg
R. F. Reister	Morris	Wm. Hein	Terre Haute
Evert Christian	Mays	R. N. Bush	Vallonia
Jess Kemper	Madison	R. Thompson	Vincennes
Van Crawford	Milton	Edd. Weedman	Victoria
James Wells	Metamora	Ray. Oneal	Versailles
Wm. Deringer		Frank Hall	Vevay
	North Vernon	C. D. Miller	Versailles
Wm. D. Gates	Nineveh	E. Brooks	W. Main St.
		J. F. Miller	Yorkville

IOWA

CHEAPEST RANGE TO BUY

Leon City, March 3rd.

WROUGHT IRON RANGE CO., St. Louis, Mo.

Gentlemen:—

My mother bought a "HOME COMFORT" from your salesman over 40 years ago, and it is still in use in Decatur City. We bought our "HOME COMFORT" in 1920, and have always been more than pleased with it in every respect. We consider the "HOME COMFORT" the cheapest range anyone can buy, considering the amount of fuel they save, the time they last, and their wonderful baking qualities. We always recommend the "HOME COMFORT" to our friends, because we know they cannot make a mistake when they buy one.

MR. and MRS. S. W. SEARS

THOROUGHLY CONVINCED

Clarinda, September 3rd.
WROUGHT IRON RANGE CO., St. Louis, Mo.
Gentlemen:—

Our new Enameled "HOME COMFORT" has been given a thorough test and has proved to be all your salesman recommended it to be, and more. We are thoroughly convinced that the "HOME COMFORT" has no equal as a perfect baker, general cooker and quick heater. We consider it the best little investment we have ever made. It is surely beautiful and cooks as good as it looks.

MRS. WILLIE HULSE

A LIFETIME RANGE

Elliote, December 6th
WROUGHT IRON RANGE CO., St. Louis, Mo.
Gentlemen:—

I used a "HOME COMFORT" Range for 35 years and never had to spend a cent for repairs in that time, and the fire-linings were still good when it was discarded. It was a fine baker and very economical on fuel. I am using an inferior range, as your salesmen were not in this county when I decided to buy a new one, and I could not get a "HOME COMFORT." When I buy another range, it will be a "HOME COMFORT."

MRS. A. H. MILLS

BEST EVER MADE

Woolstock, July 13th.
WROUGHT IRON RANGE CO., St. Louis, Mo.
Gentlemen:—

My "HOME COMFORT" Range has already given me 10 years of faithful service. It is in excellent condition, and looks like it will be good for many years to come. It is the best range I have ever used, and I believe the best one ever made.

MRS. ERNEST FRAKES

35 YEARS—STILL IN USE

Modale, November 16th.
WROUGHT IRON RANGE CO., St. Louis, Mo.
Gentlemen:—

I bought a "HOME COMFORT" Range 35 years ago, used it for 30 years, and when I sold it 5 years ago, it was seemingly as good as ever. I never had to put any repairs on it and it is still in use in this town today. I always found it to be everything your salesman represented it to me, and if I were younger and keeping house, I would certainly have another "HOME COMFORT."

MRS. MARGRET HARKER

JUST LIKE A SAVINGS ACCOUNT

Goose Lake, March 7th.
WROUGHT IRON RANGE CO., St. Louis, Mo.
Gentlemen:—

We have been using our "HOME COMFORT" Range since 1917. This is our fourth stove, and I can truthfully say that it is worth more than the other three together. We consider the "HOME COMFORT" like our savings account in the bank—making money for us every day.

PETER M. PAYSON

STILL FIRST CLASS

Ottumwa, March 6th.
WROUGHT IRON RANGE CO., St. Louis, Mo.
Gentlemen:—

My "HOME COMFORT" Range was bought from your salesmen in 1911. It has always been perfectly satisfactory in every way, and is still a splendid baker and in first-class condition. It has always required so little fuel, that we feel this economy has justified its purchase. I would not think of parting with it except for a new "HOME COMFORT."

MRS. G. W. BENDER

KNOWS FROM EXPERIENCE

Albert City, August 10th.
WROUGHT IRON RANGE CO., St. Louis, Mo.
Gentlemen:—

Our folks, having used a "HOME COMFORT" Range for 30 years, we bought one 10 years ago, and have never been sorry that we made the selection. We knew when we bought it that we could not go wrong, and we do not believe that anyone can make a mistake when they install one in their kitchen.

MRS. JOHN HOLTOPP

30 YEARS—A PERFECT BAKER

Bedford, January 15th.
WROUGHT IRON RANGE CO., St. Louis, Mo.
Gentlemen:—

We are using a "HOME COMFORT" Range that we bought from Mrs. Jno. Stuart, whose mother gave it to her over 30 years ago when she started keeping house. The range is as complete today as the day it was bought, and we expect it to last us for several years to come. I do not think there is any range that will compare with the "HOME COMFORT," for ours is still a perfect baker and heater, and requires so little fuel as compared with other stoves and ranges.

A. A. HORNING

COULDN'T ASK MORE

Malvern, October 20th.
WROUGHT IRON RANGE CO., St. Louis, Mo.
Gentlemen:—

We have been using our "HOME COMFORT" Range since 1912 and have found it to be everything it was represented to us. It is a good cooker and heater, a perfect baker, and does everything that could be expected of a cooking range in perfect shape. We have found it does its perfect work on a very small amount of fuel and is quick to heat, ready for cooking or baking. Who could ask more?

MR. and MRS. G. W. SULLIVAN

HE REGRETS NOT BUYING

Woodbine, February 3rd.
WROUGHT IRON RANGE CO., St. Louis, Mo.
Gentlemen:—

We used a "HOME COMFORT" Range over 30 years without needing any repairs except one section of fire-box lining, which was put in after the range had seen 25 years' service. We moved and left the old range behind, thinking we could readily get another one, but found your salesmen would not visit our new locality for about three years, so we bought another range and paid more money for it than a "HOME COMFORT" would cost. We find it is not satisfactory, as it burns twice as much fuel as a "HOME COMFORT" and is not the perfect baker our old range was.

JNO. R. TUPPER

25 YEARS—NO REPAIRS

Blockton, March 19th.
WROUGHT IRON RANGE CO., St. Louis, Mo.
Gentlemen:—

We have used our "HOME COMFORT" Range since 1890, and it has always given the very best satisfaction. It is still in first-class condition and is still a perfect baker and a quick, even heater on very little fuel. We have never had any repairs for it during all this time, and it still has the same pipe that came with it. We have always found it to be everything it was represented to be and more. Anyone doubting this statement of its condition and cooking ability may come and see the range for themselves.

M. W. SIEMILLER and SISTERS

NEVER REGRETTED PURCHASE

Bradgate, August 5th.
WROUGHT IRON RANGE Co., St. Louis, Mo.
Gentlemen:—

We have used our "HOME COMFORT" Range 12 years, and can honestly recommend it as being the best range money can buy. I have never regretted its purchase, for it has been a comfort and convenience to my family—a real saver of labor and fuel.

J. A. BLAKE

OUT-BAKES OTHER RANGES

Nodaway, May 13th.
WROUGHT IRON RANGE Co., St. Louis, Mo.
Gentlemen:—

I have cooked on my "HOME COMFORT" Range for over 29 years and it has always given perfect satisfaction in every way and is still a perfect baker and fuel saver. My daughter has a "retail" range of well-advertised make, but my old "HOME COMFORT" will out-bake her's any time. Anyone wanting a new range cannot buy a better one than the "HOME COMFORT"—I ought to know, for I've seen other ranges come and go, but my "HOME COMFORT" bakes on forever.

MRS. SAM HOLLIS

30 YEARS—BUYS NEW ONE

Muscatine, February 26th.
WROUGHT IRON RANGE Co., St. Louis, Mo.
Gentlemen:—

Having used our first "HOME COMFORT" Range for 30 years, we have been well pleased with it; we could not resist buying one of your New Enamel Models which we have just installed. We find this new model "HOME COMFORT" to be all you represented, and more. I consider we now own the finest range made.

MR. and MRS. M. R. WALTS

NONE CAN COMPARE

Rembrandt, February 27th.
WROUGHT IRON RANGE Co., St. Louis, Mo.
Gentlemen:—

I have had my "HOME COMFORT" Range since 1915, and have never used a range that begins to compare with it for cooking and baking. It is certainly a real comfort, supplying plenty of hot water at all times, and doing its cooking and baking perfectly.

MRS. OLIVER BRANDVOLD

BROWNS BREAD WITHOUT TURNING

Linn Grove, March 11th.
WROUGHT IRON RANGE Co., St. Louis, Mo.
Gentlemen:—

I bought my "HOME COMFORT" Range in 1915, and have always been well pleased with it; for I have found it to be exactly as represented. It is a marvelous baker, the oven heating so evenly that I have never had to take my bread out and turn it, as in other stoves. It is also a wonderful fuel saver. If I ever replace this one it will be with another "HOME COMFORT."

MRS. ADOLPH ANDERSON

A STANDARD OF PERFECTION

Delmar, October 4th.
WROUGHT IRON RANGE Co., St. Louis, Mo.
Gentlemen:—

We have used one of your Model No. 64 "HOME COMFORT" Ranges for 30 years, and have never had to spend a cent on it for repairs. I am, today, buying one of your New Model "HOME COMFORTS," because I know it to be the Standard of Range Perfection.

CHAS. H. BLOOM, Postmaster

QUICK COOKER—LITTLE FUEL

Onawa, February 20th.
WROUGHT IRON RANGE Co., St. Louis, Mo.
Gentlemen:—

I have used a "HOME COMFORT" Range for 30 years, with the very best of satisfaction. A short time ago I purchased a new Range of a widely advertised make, which I have never been able to get satisfaction out of that I did my "HOME COMFORT." I always found a "HOME COMFORT" to be much quicker and work on a great deal less fuel than any other range I have ever seen.

MRS. FRED FANCHILD

A PERFECT RESERVOIR

Linn Grove, March 2nd.
WROUGHT IRON RANGE Co., St. Louis, Mo.
Gentlemen:—

My "HOME COMFORT" Range has now been in constant service for 10 years, and it bakes and saves fuel as well as it did when it was new. The reservoir has always been a real comfort, supplying plenty of hot water, and is so convenient. I would not want a reservoir any other place than at the front.

MRS. JOHN PETERSON

IT IS AN IMPROVEMENT

WROUGHT IRON RANGE Co., St. Louis, Mo.
Gentlemen:—

We still have a Model No. 69 "HOME COMFORT" Range we have used for over 28 years and it is in good condition and giving good service today. Our son has just bought a new Enameled Model "HOME COMFORT," which looks to us to be a great improvement in the last 28 years. They are certainly the most wonderful ranges in the world, and we never lose a chance to recommend them.

MR. and MRS. O. P. REYNOLDS

HAS PERFECT OVEN

Griswold, January 14th.
WROUGHT IRON RANGE Co., St. Louis, Mo.
Gentlemen:—

I have always been well pleased with my "HOME COMFORT" Range, which I bought in 1912. It has a perfect oven and it is very conservative in consumption of fuel. I don't believe a better range can be built unless it is your new Enameled Model.

MRS. ROSS SMITH

AN IDEAL FINISH

Humboldt, July 13th.
WROUGHT IRON RANGE Co., St. Louis, Mo.
Gentlemen:—

We are using one of your New Enamel Ranges, and find that it is exactly as it was represented to us. We consider it the greatest fuel saver and the best baker we have ever used. We would not consider a black range again at any price, and certainly not one of any make except a "HOME COMFORT."

RAY TEURMAN

DECISION REWARDED

Rembrandt, July 20th.
WROUGHT IRON RANGE Co., St. Louis, Mo.
Gentlemen:—

Since we have used a "HOME COMFORT" Range for more than 25 years, I feel qualified in saying that it is the best range money can buy. I was, perhaps, a little slow in closing the deal at the time, but I have never regretted buying it for my family. I know that I saved considerable money when I did so, as our range promises to give us good service several more years.

MR. JOHN FREDERICK

APPRECIATES DEALINGS

Prescott, September 30th.

WROUGHT IRON RANGE Co., St. Louis, Mo.

Gentlemen:—

The "HOME COMFORT" Range we bought from your salesman sometime ago is fine and satisfactory in every way, and we are all very proud of it. We thank you for making it possible for us to buy such a good range in this way, and also for your kindly favors.

AUSTIN PROCTOR

CAN'T PRAISE IT TOO HIGHLY

Wellsburg, August 1st.

WROUGHT IRON RANGE Co., St. Louis, Mo.

Gentlemen:—

Having used a "HOME COMFORT" Range for 25 years, I cannot praise it too highly. It has always been an excellent baker, and a great fuel saver, and has given us the best service of any range we ever used. A new cover for the reservoir is the only repair we have put on it during these 25 years of hard usage.

J. B. HUISMAN

WILL CONSIDER NO OTHER

Fonda, September 26th

WROUGHT IRON RANGE Co., St. Louis, Mo.

Gentlemen:—

I have used a "HOME COMFORT" Range for 25 years, and have always been perfectly satisfied with it, and will never consider buying any other range or stove if I find it necessary to replace this one.

MRS. W. H. BRADFORD

BEST MONEY CAN BUY

Fonda, November 4th.

WROUGHT IRON RANGE Co., St. Louis, Mo.

Gentlemen:—

Without doubt, the "HOME COMFORT" is the best Range that money can buy. I have now used mine since 1915 with the greatest satisfaction. I have always found it to be exactly as represented by your salesman, and I would not part with it unless I could replace it with the New Model "HOME COMFORT."

MRS. GEORGE W. FELLWOCK

C. L. Bonnett	Amboy	W. Driver	Crescent
E. R. Toop	Auburn	Henry Otte	Clarinda
J. D. Clark	Armstrong	U. R. Campbell	
E. L. Burt	Alexander		Claremont
A. E. Kinyon	Adaza	Paul Eberle	Clearfield
J. R. Lamb	Afton	W. R. Lock	Conway
J. L. Obe	Ames	W. J. Bahr	Davis City
H. R. Sturm	Albion	J. H. McDaniel	
A. Skog	Albert City		Decatur City
Chas. Stowe	Ackley	John Cox	DeKalb
H. Krafke	Alden	C. Gragort	Dows
A. C. Bowman	Brooks	Joe Stewart	Dunlap
O. A. Hammond	Beaman	Harry Kiersch	Dumfries
M. J. Burrett	Britt	H. E. Murphy	Diagonal
W. R. Legge	Belmond	Tom Robins	Dayton
O. Ellefson	Bricelyn	J. E. Jacobson	Duncombe
F. Berhow	Buffalo Center	L. Kaldenberg	Delta
H. W. Schuler	Bancroft	P. J. Menten	Eagle Lake
Wm. Kessler	Belmond	L. A. Olson	Elmore
Alta Schroeder	Bartlett	E. B. Fouser	Ellston
J. Akers	Beaconsfield	E. M. Bauer	Emerson
W. P. Whinery	Bangor	C. M. Hornby	Elliott
A. Taylor	Burnside	P. Hansel	Eagle Grove
S. L. Travis	Barnum	L. R. Cardle	Ellsworth
R. M. Dunn	Braddyville	O. A. Ryan	Eldora
C. E. Brown	Bode	M. A. Cloyd	Essex
R. Masterson	Badger	G. Warrior, Jr.	
Lloyd Braby	Bradgate		Fontanelle
A. Sorenson	Blairsburg	John Stumpf	Fonda
E. N. Drake	Blockton	B. A. Bekken	Forest City
E. I. Oxley	Bedford	J. A. Leet	Fairmont
H. Colwell	Blanchard	W. A. Livingston	
C. Retland	Carbon		Farragut
S. W. Morris	Corning	F. Evans	Fort Dodge
John Kries	Carroll	J. F. Hobbs	Farnhamville
E. G. Hartman		J. P. Hall	Fonda
	Cumberland	Carl Huss	Greenfield
Ray Miller	Clear Lake	W. F. Bin	Good Thunder
Emil Olson	Coulter	W. Dolch	Griswold
Frank White	Clarion	E. Boyd	Grand River
T. W. Bedford	Clare	C. Adair	Garden Grove
Ed. Hunt	Cromwell	T. B. Cole	
C. Still	Creston		Green Mountain
G. W. Hites	Clarion	Frank Mowery	Gladbrook
J. P. Pekin	Colo	C. C. Hatch	Granada
James Strutter	Collins	W. W. Benton	Galt
P. O. Louks	Cambridge	W. A. Bichel	Glenwood
F. J. Thomon	Clemons	David Platt	Gilman
E. R. Cain	Coin	Ray Braden	Griswold
E. A. Adams	Coburg	J. E. Swanson	Gowrie
Fred Schnoore		S. Kipper	Gilmore City
	Council Bluffs	Chris Graves	Goldfield
Tom Bakke	Callender	W. H. Howard	Gifford

Shelby Lower	Gravity	C. C. Strong	Modelia
Lewis Ramsbig	Hardy	O. Vincent	Maxwell
C. A. Imel	Hastings	E. E. Ramsey	Mo. Valley
L. W. Anderson		Ernest Dicks	Magnolia
	Henderson	C. F. Cross	Mendomin
S. E. Ramsay	Hamburg	O. T. Girton	Modale
Tony Daters	Haverhill	C. F. Mass	Mineola
A. A. Lind	Harcourt	Emil Pouton	Malvern
B. Wienold	Havelock	Mat. Hanks	Mt. Ayr
H. Reese	Honey Creek	Roy Lepley	Maloy
L. L. Lewis	Hepburn	Sara Howard	Montana
Dave Hart	Humboldt	H. Drough	Melbourne
Dan Munson	Hubbard	C. T. Loney	
D. M. Bryan	Imogene		Marshalltown
Lee Silvest	Iowa Falls	Dan Kuhn	Morton Mills
F. W. Brown	Judson	J. W. Spooner	
P. C. Macey	Jolley		Moorland
J. Brosdol	Juice	J. H. Horsman	Mallard
Jacob Sexe	Jewell	E. G. Plumb	Macedonia
Clark Luther	Kensett	P. J. Smith	McClelland
J. H. Reeve	Kent	J. C. Ryan	Mo. Valley
Severa Erickson	Kelly	T. S. Wilson	Nodaway
L. Bason	Kellerton	W. Gunderson	Northwood
H. G. Klaver	Kamrar	F. T. Hazeland	Nevada
A. Pahl	Lake Crystal	Henry Nelson	Neola
W. A. Clark	Lake City	G. Hollman	Northboro
C. T. Johnson	Lohrville	A. J. Handke	Neola
E. Sublert	Lidderdale	Fred Wise	Northboro
Z. T. Devel	Lake City	O. E. Shives	
W. S. Haake	Lewis		New Providence
Wm. Negley	Lamoni	W. E. Feese	Nodaway
G. A. Smallwood		W. G. Noble	New Market
	Linewood	Lloyd Reed	Orient
O. C. Yahler	"	A. L. Bishop	Osceola
C. St. John	"	Andy Olson	Ottosen
G. A. Hammer	Laurel	J. B. Black	Otho
Mrs. Bittner	Lake View	F. W. Friekey	Owasa
W. O. Pero	Lowell	R. V. Clark	Prescott
C. B. Harmon	Lake Mills	Nels Bjornson	
Ed. Ites	Lakota		Pemberton
A. Walker	Le Grand	Wm. Koester	Pomeroy
Jack Shadduck	Lyons	M. H. Potter	Pleasanton
P. E. Gustafson	Lanyon	Fritz Meier	Persia
C. W. Leach	Laurens	E. W. Stacey	
F. Ostertag	Loveland		Pacific Junction
G. Rentz	Luverne	B. C. Wilson	Percival
Louis Olson	Livermore	H. Baedke	Pomeroy
C. C. Miner	Lawn Hill	B. Crummer	Pocahontas
Fred Moeller	Lenox	E. Schoon	Palmer
John Gartner	Mapleton	F. H. Kay	Rembrandt
Fred Jesse	Mankota	M. E. Parker	
H. C. Kolb	Manson		Rockwell City
John Buck	Mt. Ayr	C. Stephenson	Rinard

J. J. Olsen	Rowan	P. D. Focht	Sidney	E. Strand	Thompson	C. Ziegler	Winnebago
J. Virgil Gore	Roland	C. W. Dunn	St. Anthony	Mark Shaw	Titonka	R. H. Penno	Woolstock
Hugh Shaw	Redding	S. Gilmore	State Center	W. H. Shields	Tingley	H. Hatterman	Woodbine
A. J. Black	Riverton	J. Larson	Stanton	I. F. Walker	Tabor	P. Hansen	Western
R. Sink	Rhodes	Lake Ayres	Shenandoah	Rich Bobbitt	Thurman	John Rapp	Woolstock
M. J. Conley	Red Oak	Louis Kahl	Silver City	Otto Olson	Thor	Ellis O. Bly	Williams
Wm. Gist	Rolfe	C. H. Downs	Shambaugh	M. M. Ryan	Underwood	W. J. Bohlen	
Henry Harvey	Renwick	S. Gasson	Stanton	C. A. Monroe	Union		Webster City
B. F. Neel	Rutland	Chris Hess	Shenandoah	Allem Warnaca	Villisca	S. H. Wilson	Webster
T. B. Olson	Radcliffe	Elmer Sandal	Stanhope	C. Starbuck		E. Scott	Weldon
W. Statton	Redding	C. F. Fohlin	Stratford		Vernon Center	J. H. Hussman	Wellsburg
J. Howard	Riverton	Joe Dedrick		H. D. Traypel	Van Wert	H. Tumhoffer	
F. B. Anderson	Red Oak		Steamboat Rock	W. J. Buckel	Vincent		Winnebago
Wm. Linde	St. Claire	Alva Ramsey	Sidney	R. M. Gourley	Villisca	Leo Harris	Whitten
A. A. Clymer	Somers	J. C. King	Sheridan	H. Jeanblanc	Vincent	G. H. Evans	Woolstock
O. J. Folken	Scarville	Ray Keins	Sharpsburg	H. L. Hicks	Villisca	J. M. Chambers	
G. Gorsuch	Shanon City	C. Anderson	Swea City	C. A. Carrithers	Weldon		Woodbine
H. Depue	Swea City	G. M. Johnson		W. J. Hausman		H. A. Blain	Yetty
G. Hall	Story City		Shenandoah		Wellsburg	C. W. Mitchell	Yorktown
A. E. Abel	Silver City	H. Schmidt	Tama	L. A Doege	Woden	Wm. Kneller	Yetter
J. J. Connell	Shenandoah	J. C. Young	Toledo	W. J. Wade	Montour	C. O. Lura	Zearing
J. A. Handlin	Seymour						

KANSAS

SAVED COST
Abilene, February 26th
WROUGHT IRON RANGE CO., St. Louis, Mo.
Gentlemen:—
After 16 years of perfect satisfaction, our "HOME COMFORT" Range is still giving excellent service. We have never had a cause to complain, as it has always cooked and baked well, and has more than saved its original cost in saving of fuel. It is still in good condition.
MR. AND MRS. W. J. MILLER

OUTLASTS 3 STOVES
Salina, March 31st.
WROUGHT IRON RANGE CO., St. Louis, Mo.
Gentlemen:—
My "HOME COMFORT" Range is still giving me first class service after 33 years of constant use. Some of our friends have worn out two or three ordinary stoves in the meantime and then did not get the fine satisfaction that I have had. It always has baked perfectly and has been a great fuel-saver. I would not exchange it for any stove or range except a new "HOME COMFORT".
MRS. FRANK BATTEROTY.

NO REGRETS
Miltonville, January 28th
WROUGHT IRON RANGE CO., St. Louis, Mo.
Gentlemen:—
We have used our "HOME COMFORT" Range for 21 years and expect to use it for several years yet. It is still in good, serviceable condition and has always given us complete satisfaction. We have never regretted buying it, for it heats and bakes perfectly and there is no question about the "HOME COMFORT's" durability. We prize it very highly.
JOHN MODEON

20 YEARS LONGER LIFE
Wamego, November 27th
WROUGHT IRON RANGE CO., St. Louis, Mo.
Gentlemen:—
Seven years of satisfactory service is what we have had from our "HOME COMFORT" Range. Besides always baking in the most perfect manner, we have found it to be a great fuel saver. From what I have observed, our "HOME COMFORT" should be good for a score more years without any extensive repairs or replacements.
ALLAN FULMER

BACKS OPINION WITH CASH
Tecumseh, January 15th.
WROUGHT IRON RANGE CO., St. Louis, Mo.
Gentlemen:—
We are using a "HOME COMFORT" Range that has been in constant service for about 35 years. We have built a new house and want one of your latest ranges. Please have your nearest salesman call on me, as I am ready to pay cash for a new "HOME COMFORT."
C. J. MILLIKIN

FIRM BELIEVERS
Wamego, November 27th
WROUGHT IRON RANGE CO., St. Louis, Mo.
Gentlemen:—
Our "HOME COMFORT" Range was bought from you 14 years ago and has always given perfect satisfaction. I do not think there could be a more substantial range built, for it is in practically as good condition as when new. We are certainly believers in the quality and service of "HOME COMFORT" Ranges.
A. M. HOPSOR

A "HOME COMFORT" DAUGHTER
Longton, December 27th
WROUGHT IRON RANGE CO., St. Louis, Mo.
Gentlemen:—
We have used our "HOME COMFORT" Range 16 years and have found it all that you claim for it. It is indeed a real fuel saver and a most perfect baker. My parents used their "HOME COMFORT" for 25 years and felt the same as I do about them. Any one wanting to know what a "HOME COMFORT" can do, may write me at the above address.
MRS. GEO. DUNLAP

AN ECONOMICAL PURCHASE
Clay Center, January 22nd
WROUGHT IRON RANGE CO., St. Louis, Mo.
Gentlemen:—
Just 25 years ago we bought our "HOME COMFORT" Range and I want to say that it has given us a quarter-century of complete satisfaction. It has always cooked as well as any range could and, because of its superior construction, service and fuel-saving, it has paid for itself many times. I consider it the most economical purchase we have ever made for our home.
H. P. SCHONEWEIS

31 FAITHFUL YEARS

Wamego, November 27th

WROUGHT IRON RANGE CO., St. Louis, Mo.

Gentlemen:—

I bought the "HOME COMFORT" Range we are now using 31 years ago and it is still giving us good service after all these years of duty. It has always been a fuel saver and has never failed as a perfect baker and heater. It seems to be good for many years yet.

W. J. CADER

TAKES AWAY WORRY

Clay Center, January 19th.

WROUGHT IRON RANGE CO., St. Louis, Mo.

Gentlemen:—

Our "HOME COMFORT" Range has now been in constant service for 15 years and promises to give us good service for many years to come, and it is in perfect operating condition after all this time, has always baked as no other range could bake and has taken much work and worry off Mrs. Carpenter in her kitchen duties. Its saving of work and fuel have long since paid for it.

W. J. CARPENTER

BURNS HARD COAL

Abilene, March 6th.

WROUGHT IRON RANGE CO., St. Louis, Mo.

Gentlemen:—

I have been using one of your "HOME COMFORT" Ranges in my home for 22 years. Practically all of that time, I have used hard-coal in it with the greatest satisfaction. The Range is still in excellent working condition and I do not consider that it was possible for me to have made a better selection than the "HOME COMFORT."

L. C. FENLEY

WORK MUCH LIGHTER

Onago, December 26th.

WROUGHT IRON RANGE CO., St. Louis, Mo.

Gentlemen:—

Our "HOME COMFORT" Range has cooked our meals for 26 years with the greatest satisfaction, with very little expense in fuel and no expense in repairs. It has made the burden of kitchen work much lighter on my family, and I have never regretted the day I bought it. I do not consider that there can possibly be a better range built, as ours seems good for many more years of service.

CHAS. W. COTTERMAN

RESERVOIR A REAL COMFORT

St. Marys, November 28th.

WROUGHT IRON RANGE CO., St. Louis, Mo.

Gentlemen:—

After 11 years of faithful service, our "HOME COMFORT" Range is in as good working condition as it was the first year we had it. It has done perfect baking and cooking, and the hot-water reservoir has always been a real comfort. I could not think of giving up my "HOME COMFORT".

MRS. CATHERINE PRIOR

SAVED 5 YEARS' LABOR

Wamego, December 12th.

WROUGHT IRON RANGE CO., St. Louis, Mo.

Gentlemen:—

I shall cook my Christmas turkey in the faithful oven of my "HOME COMFORT" Range which is now 35 years old. Throughout all these years it has been a "real comfort" and has saved me at least 4 or 5 years of labor out of the 35 by reducing the time and work of cooking meals. It has more than paid for itself in the saving of fuel alone. I have found it all your salesman contended it to be when we bought it off one of your mule-team wagons in 1889.

MRS. M. HOFERER

NONE BUT A "HOME COMFORT"

Howard, December 22nd.

WROUGHT IRON RANGE CO., St. Louis, Mo.

Gentlemen:—

We have had our "HOME COMFORT" Range for 28 years. It has been in constant use all that time and is in first class condition today. It is a fine baker, a great fuel saver and furnishes an abundance of hot water at the same time without extra fuel. If we ever need to replace it, it will certainly be with a new "HOME COMFORT".

MR. AND MRS. W. D. HEATER

WILL BE A "HOME COMFORT"

Frankfort, January 8th.

WROUGHT IRON RANGE CO., St. Louis, Mo.

Gentlemen:—

After 13 years of cooking on my "HOME COMFORT" Range, I can truthfully say that more service and better cooking could not be had with any other range. It has always been a perfect baker, and it is in practically as good condition as when we bought it. I believe when a better range is made, it will surely be a "HOME COMFORT" also.

MRS. ALICE CLOUD

NONE SUPERIOR

Frankfort, January 10th.

WROUGHT IRON RANGE CO., St. Louis, Mo.

Gentlemen:—

It has been 31 years since I bought our "HOME COMFORT" Range, and it is doing good work today. It heats and cooks as well as it ever did and I have never regretted buying it. If we ever need to replace it, it will certainly be with a new "HOME COMFORT" for, to my mind, there has never been a range built that can beat it.

E. F. HUXTABLE

G. A. Schoppert	Augusta	Hy. Gantembein	Dillon	F. E. Vaughn	Dexter	R. A. Carter	Eldorado
Oscar Sexton	Abilene	Eva Schmidt	"	W. M. Cruzan	Delia	M. P. Hansen	"
John Freund	Andale	F. M. Amess	Detroit	B. M. Clark	"	Chas. Facklam	Enterprise
W. M. Mitchell	Andover	J. A. Sword	"	D. D. Bartel	Durham	G. G. Morlong	"
S. Cummins	Argonia	W. O. Patteson	"	H. W. Russell	Derby	M. F. Johnson	Elk City
John Koster	Anness		Cedar Vale	J. E. Seeney	Elbing	W. B. Hagins, Jr.	
John Graham	Ark. City	I. Charpie	Clay Center	Jake Schauf	Cheney		Elk Falls
C. A. Springgate	Ashton	E. E. Tredway	Cambridge	L. Giefer	"	W. S. Taylor	Fall River
Ben Munson	Assaria	F. Hawley	"	W. H. Stover	Colwich	W. S. Fleming	Fostoria
A. H. Krebler	Bainville	A. F. Gugler	Chapman	F. D. Forward	"	Ike Braden	Frankfort
H. R. Fawning	Benton	E. E. Marts	"	J. Heitman	Clearwater	E. E. Eames	"
G. Zimmerman	Broughton	R. A. Hall	Carneiro	Leo Konecuy	"	W. D. Auchard	Green
Bertha Hofman	Bola	O. D. Johnson	Canton	E. P. Mercer	"	R. E. Dawson	"
J. V. Johnson	Burrton	B. W. Reeder	"		Conway Springs	S. H. Schmidt	Goessel
G. C. Phipps	Belle Pl.	Geo. Wood	Caldwell	J. W. Callahan	"	H. J. A. Voth	"
Joe Manley	Blaine	Roy Cottle	"	A. R. McCann	Clifton	J. H. Buller	Galva
A. Jackson	Barnard	A. J. Malloy	Centralia	M. R. Redersen	"	F. B. Wedel	"
Alma Boyd	Burns	C. N. Howes	"	J. H. Knollenberg	"	J. M. Aaron	Goddard
L. Capell	Bennington	H. Dond	Culver		Douglass	Jake Karber	Gypsum
Hy. Base	Bridgeport	E. H. Hinkle	"	W. J. Owen			

— 175 —

John B. Meyers Grenola	Theo. Liby Morganville	O. J. Walcher Perth	C. A. Percival Tescott
Loren Depew "	Nathan Black "	L. P. Fisher Peabody	W. B. Bishop "
E. F. Linnebur "	Chas. Servais Miltonvale	M. D. Allison "	F. C. Metz Talmage
Garden Plain	John Modean "	C. C. Orrell Peck	A. A. Knott "
R. E. Roberts "	H. P. Parks McPherson	C. Sargeant "	Bert Miller Turley
Geuda Springs	C. C. Ferguson "	J. C. Travnicek Rosalia	C. R. Carnahan "
J. R. Crider " "	I. D. Loonis Marquette	Wm. Erhlich "	R. L. Effner Udall
J. H. Gruber Hope	E. M. Jantz Mound Ridge	J. J. Johnston Rose Hill	Loyd Claypool "
C. Schelmer "	W. M. Huntzelman "	C. A. Randall " "	Joe Postlewait
H. Gantz Herrington	W. R. Pinkham Mentor	J. L. McDonald Roxbury	Valley Center
Thos. McRae "	Wm. Keeler "	G. F. Zech "	M. F. Liggett "
L. Bahr Halstead	Lorena Seiler Maize	Roger Harrison Riley	Tom Brown Vermillion
H. S. Akins "	Rosa Faber "	Paul Kovar Rossville	G. Jeanneret "
E. M. Wiley Havana	H. C. Hart Manchester	H. E. Honig "	O. M. Nelson Viola
C. W. Callison Howard	Wm. E. Pettit "	O. D. Perdue Sedan	Joe Simpson Whitewater
J. P. Copeland Idana	H. C. Compton Milton	Fred Yorker Smolan	C. L. White "
W. Miller Irving	Louisa Baird Milan	C. L. Peterson "	R. S. Shandy Wakefield
C. R. Beacham "	R. N. Winkle Mulvane	W. J. Hobbs Solomon	E. S. Buchanan "
C. A. Swanson Inman	J. W. Kluge Newton	Orval J. Bell "	Jack Kimanan Winfield
H. S. Catron "	F. A. Kilpatrick "	R. J. Johnston St. Marys	D. W. McDade "
Independence	George Brown Niles	Joe F. Hynek Sycamore	J. G. Hiebert Walton
J. A. Brown Junc. City	John Lyne Oak Hill	R. W. Shubbom Salina	W. S. Gilchrist "
D. A. Carter Leeds	J. A. Gunter "	L. A. Rose "	J. L. Wegman Wheaton
G. Ware Longford	G. M. Gillespie Oatville	J. F. Myall Sedgwick	R. V. Gildersleeve "
Art. Strode "	Phillip Lane "	Peter Reviert Sequin	Wiley Taylor Wamego
H. E. Murphy Longton	J. D. Taylor Onaga	W. O. Rinehart S. Haven	Caroline Hoferer "
C. F. Heart Lindsberg	George Dauin "	F. O. Robinson "	Will Burden Wellington
Earl Reed Lamar	E. A. Jacobs Potwin	W. A. Pore Towanda	Grace Holmes "
L. Hazlett Leonardville	L. L. Biggs "	H. T. Maxey "	A. B. Clark Wichita
J. C. Johnson Moline	Wm. Norris Portland	Hy. A. Jantz Tampa	C. A. Peterson "
Garrett Johnson "	Wm. Schimmel "	Isaac Dirks "	

KENTUCKY

JUST AS RECOMMENDED

Jackhorn, March 31st.

WROUGHT IRON RANGE CO., St. Louis, Mo.

Gentlemen:—

I installed one of your Enameled "HOME COMFORT" Ranges last year, and we have found it to be an ideal cooking appliance, and just what it was recommended by your salesman. I believe this Range has solved our cooking equipment problem for a long time to come. My family is certainly delighted with it, and I do not regret buying it.

R. H. WRIGHT

REAL FURNITURE

Bagdad, March 27th.

WROUGHT IRON RANGE CO., St. Louis, Mo.

Gentlemen:—

The Enameled "HOME COMFORT" Range we installed in our kitchen last year has proved to be all that it was recommended. Besides being a real article of furniture, it is certainly an ideal piece of cooking equipment. My family would not part with it if they could not get another one like it.

M. R. PUCKETT

APPRECIATES COURTESIES

Bedford, February 15th.

WROUGHT IRON RANGE CO., St. Louis, Mo.

Gentlemen:—

I want to thank you kindly for courtesies you have shown me, and tell you what I think of my "HOME COMFORT". I have found it to be and to do everything it was recommended to me by your salesman, except that I believe that it does it better. One hundred and fifty dollars would not induce me to part with my Range.

EUGENE E. GREENWOOD

A PROUD OWNER

Jeffersontown, January 12th.

WROUGHT IRON RANGE CO., St. Louis, Mo.

Gentlemen:—

I have found my "HOME COMFORT" Range more than satisfactory. I have given it 15 years of hard use without it needing repairs, and it looks almost like new—not a warp about it anywhere—and it bakes better than any stove or range I know. I have always been proud of it and always will.

MRS. F. D. MORTON

30 YEARS—NO REPAIRS

Prospect, March 16th.

WROUGHT IRON RANGE CO., St. Louis, Mo.

Gentlemen:—

I purchased a "HOME COMFORT" Range in 1886. It was in constant use for 30 years, without any repairs; but upon the death of my husband I was forced to sell it. A short time ago I saw the Range, and it is still in good condition. It always gave perfect satisfaction, was conservative on fuel, and I do not think it had an equal. I am now living with my daughter, and we are using one of your new Gray Enamel "HOME COMFORTS", and it is certainly a beauty and a perfect Range, and we would not want to do without it.

MRS. C. E. HUNT

OUT-COOKS ANY RANGE

Lancaster, January 24th.

WROUGHT IRON RANGE CO., St. Louis, Mo.

Gentlemen:—

I want to tell you how much I enjoy cooking on my "HOME COMFORT" Range. I have never seen a stove or range that will outcook it. I like it in every respect, and certainly can find no fault with it whatever. It is a perfect baker, saves much fuel, and is perfectly reliable in every way.

MRS. ELIJAH McMILLIAN

V. S. Mayhew Adolphus	J. I. Brown Bedford	Haggard King Bohon	Wm. Witt Colly
Wm. Cheek Alton	Lewis Wolf Berry	Guy Sanders Bonsville	Oscar Jones Cuzick
Curt Gains Anchorage	G. H. Kelly Blackwell	Allie Thomas Bloomfield	B. F. Jones Crestwood
W. D. Sanders Ashcamp	J. J. Noe Bethlehem	Silas Tackett Beefhide	R. C. Yager Cornishville
L. I. Perkins Ammons	Olivia Kruse Buechel	J. W. Brindley Carrollton	Ed. Lucas Constantint
Thos. Fultz Baxter	J. W. Gordon Blackey	C. Sergent Chappell	John Bennett Custer

J. T. May	Cloverport	John Garrett Hodgenville	P. Minton	Mater	Ida Webb	Sergent
L. B. Hall	Chenaultt	B. F. Irvin	Harlan	Chas. Curry	Million	W. M. Bunton	Salvisa
H. G. Garden	Cecelia	Rufus Fields	Hinton	Porter Casey	Mt. Eden	Lee Ross	Skylight
C. F. French	Colesburg	A. H. Perkins	Hattan	Joe Tackett	Monterey	S. E. Tindall	Shelbyville
J. A. Kyler	Dongola	N. J. Embry	Harrodsburg	J. E. Mitchell	Midway	M. T. Alsop	
Ben Frazier	Duncan	B. Sprowell	Hestand	J. A. Hughes	Milton		Stamping Ground
Bell Brown	Delaplane	Frank Rose	Hester	Chas. A. Shell	Naples	J. W. Collins	Tillie
Isaac Hall	Elizabethtown	Alex Moore	Hylton	R. H. Casey	New Castle	Sam Yokley	Tomkinsville
George Gray	Elliston	Stratton Evans	Irvine	J. W. Riley	Newport	A. M. True	Tackett Mill
J. W. Richards	Evarts	H. A. Cross	Irvington	R. J. Claxon	New	M. C. Feltner	Typo
B. Burkhart	Eminence	K. P. Beverly	Jonesville	C. A. Thomas	Rineyville	T. J. Tingle	Taylorsville
B. W. Howard	Eastview	H. B. Adams	Jackhorn	Floyd Tate	Rome	Wm. Terry	Tunnell Hill
T. H. Blane		R. S. Powers	Jenkins	Thomas Toole	Owenton	L. Milner	Union
	Fall of Rough	R. H. Drakeford	Keene	Mark Rose	Okolona	Elmer Elliston	Verona
W. T. Kephart	Frankfort	M. C. Carr	Lexington	G. T. Leach	Paris	J. T. Howard	
N. B. Pope		E. McMillan	Lancaster	W. C. Helton	Poor Fork		Valley View
	Fountain Run	Wm. Hogg	Lynch	W. S. Kemp	Prospects	Z. Smith	Van Arsdale
N. W. Green	Falmouth	N. B. Warren	LaGrange	G. B. Clifford	Pendleton	J. H. Haile	Vernon
J. F. Roberts	Gratz	M. E. Boulton		A. W. Steele		H. A. Owen	Versailles
Jno. C. Edwards	Gee		Long Ridge		Paynes Depot	S. M. Yates	Vine Grove
Geo. C. Taylor	Gamaliel	P. H. Snyder	Locust Hill	H. Clifford	Pendleton	Lula Black	Woodrow
R. F. Shrader	Goshen			J. H. Hogg	Roxana	W. E. Carter	Wallins
B. H. Hughes	Georgetown	C. C. Lee	Lebanon Jct.	Ray Turner	Richmond	A. B. Ewen	Willmore
D. H. Smith	Garfield	Dein McGary	McQuady	N. L. Davis	Raydure	B. G. Webster	
L. S. Morton	Glen Dean	James Campbell	Millwood	A. E. Smith	Stephensport		Whitesburg
Alvin Meers	Glendale	Ray Adams	Mason	F. M. Dixon	Sonora	J. T. Lay	Westport
A. H. Cook	Guston	Levi Saylor	Molus	M. J. Finch	Solway	Walter Coleman	
T. Vertress	Hardinsburg	James Todd	Milner	Lee Burns	Sanders		Williamstown
Ote Givan	Hudson	A. J. Arrington		G. Berkshire	Sparta	Ray Brown	Willisburg
I. S. Dupin	Hardinsburg		McRoberts	J. E. Points	Sherman	Lee Hammer	Meshack
E. A. Wiley	Henderson	K. Niece	Millstone	W. V. Jackson	Sulphur		
		B. A. Webb	Mayking				

LOUISIANA

USED ONES ARE SALEABLE

Girard, January 28th.
WROUGHT IRON RANGE CO., St. Louis, Mo.
Gentlemen:

I have bought and we have used several "HOME COMFORT" Ranges. We have moved from one part of the country to another several times, and I would sell my range, rather than move it, and buy another at the first opportunity. We have never been satisfied when forced to use a stove of any other make. "HOME COMFORT" is a real name for your range, for it has many advantages over any other cooking appliance made, especially in comfort, service, life of the range, and selling value if you desire to dispose of it. I have seen "HOME COMFORTS" that have been in use for 20 to 30 years, and in nearly every case they were almost as good as new.

MILES C. BROWN

25 YEARS—GOOD CONDITION

Tallulah, January 22nd.
WROUGHT IRON RANGE CO., St. Louis, Mo.
Gentlemne:—

Twenty-five years ago I bought one of your "HOME COMFORT" Ranges, which is still in use and in good condition today. While the range is 25 years old, I would not take the price I paid for it if I could not get a new "HOME COMFORT" promptly. I always advise my friends to buy a "HOME COMFORT" the first chance they have.

T. F. WARD

LIFE-TIME SERVICE IN IT

Mangham, January 22nd.
WROUGHT IRON RANGE CO., St. Louis, Mo.
Gentlemen:—

My "HOME COMFORT" Range has given me perfect service and satisfaction for more than 12 years. I do not believe there is any other range made that has the cooking and baking qualities and the life-time service in it that the "HOME COMFORT" has. I would not want to part with mine, except to replace it with one of your New Models.

MRS. C. R. PREWITT

MORE THAN RECOMMENDED

Delhi, December 29th.
WROUGHT IRON RANGE CO., St. Louis, Mo.
Gentlemen:—

I have been using my "HOME COMFORT" Range constantly since 1904. It has cooked an average of almost 3 meals a day in that time, and is still doing first-class service. I like the "HOME COMFORT" better than any stove or range I have ever seen or cooked on. Mine has proved to be more than it was recommended, and besides, it has doubly paid for itself in service and fuel economy. I believe the "HOME COMFORT" Range is by far the best range put out by any company.

MRS. JESSE STOUT

20 YEARS—SUPERIOR TO OTHERS

Mangham, January 20th.
WROUGHT IRON RANGE CO., St. Louis, Mo.
Gentlemen:

I have been using a "HOME COMFORT" Range for over 20 years, and I find it to be the best range I ever used. Its baking qualites, convenience and many comforts are superior to those of any other range I have ever seen. It is a great fuel saver, furnishes plenty of hot water at all times, and saves many steps about the kitchen. I certainly would not part with it except to replace it with a new "HOME COMFORT."

MRS. D. C. WRIGHT

EXACTLY AS REPRESENTED

Lucknow, January 20th.
WROUGHT IRON RANGE CO., St. Louis, Mo.
Gentlemen:—

We have one of your 1918 model "HOME COMFORT" Ranges, and we have always been well pleased with it; for we have found it exactly as it was represented to us by your salesman. It has proven to be a saver of fuel, a wonderful baker, and a perfect cooker in every respect. I would not part with my "HOME COMFORT" except to install one of your New Enameled Models.

MRS. W. R. HART

▶ID NOT MAKE MISTAKE

Start, January 19th.

Wrought Iron Range Co., St. Louis, Mo.

Gentlemen:—

I cannot say too much for the "Home Comfort" Range. I have used mine over 6 years, and still find it as perfect in every way as it was when it was new. It has saved me many steps in my kitchen work, as it has supplied, plenty of hot water, been very saving on the fuel, and quick and efficient baker. I will always recommend the "Home Comfort" Range above all others, because I know we did not make a mistake when we bought ours.

Mrs. G. H. Taylor

14 YEARS—SOLD FOR $40

Farmerville, December 24th.

Wrought Iron Range Co., St. Louis, Mo.

Gentlemen:

I bought my first "Home Comfort" Range in 1904, and used it for 14 years. I then sold it for forty dollars, and bought a new "Home Comfort" of the 1918 model and used that one until 1924. When your salesman came around with the New Enameled Model, I sold the old one for sixty-five dollars, and bought one of your Enameled Ranges, for I know it is far superior to any range that was ever built. For material, workmanship, and baking qualities, I know the "Home Comfort" cannot be equaled, and my experience with them is proof enough that I am convinced on these points, and never will buy anything but a "Home Comfort" for my family.

W. A. Futch

SOLVES KITCHEN PROBLEM

Oak Grove, January 6th.

Wrought Iron Range Co., St. Louis, Mo.

Gentlemen:—

I take great pleasure in recommending your "Home Comfort" Range as being the most economical and best baking range on the market. We used one of your older models for several years and recently bought one of your Enameled Ranges and find it to be superior to any range built. I freely advise my friends to install "Home Comforts" and solve their kitchen problem for years to come.

John L. Kelley, M. D.

WILL NOT PART WITH IT

Delhi, January 22nd.

Wrought Iron Range Co., St. Louis, Mo.

Gentlemen:—

I can gladly recommend the "Home Comfort" Range, for I have found mine to be perfect in every respect, and exactly as represented by your salesman. I would not be without one in my kitchen, and no one could induce me to part with it except to replace it with one of your New Enamel Models.

Mrs. Nellie Barker

SATISFACTORY UNDER HEAVY DUTY

Girard, January 19th.

Wrought Iron Range Co., St. Louis, Mo.

Gentlemen:—

I have been using a "Home Comfort" Range for several years, and found it entirely satisfactory under daily and heavy duty. It certainly solved our cooking problem, because of its efficiency, and I do not see how I got along without it as long as I did.

Mrs. C. Y. Bennett,
Dixie Farm.

WILL NOT TAKE A CHANCE

Delhi, January 22nd.

Wrought Iron Range Co., St. Louis, Mo.

Gentlemen:—

This is to certify that my mother, Mrs. M. J. Jones, used a "Home Comfort" Range for about 40 years, and discarded it only a few months ago. I have never seen a range of any other make that will outwear the "Home Comfort," and I certainly would not put my money into any other and take a chance.

E. J. Barker

SHE OUGHT TO KNOW

Rayville, January 20th.

Wrought Iron Range Co., St. Louis, Mo.

Gentlemen:—

My mother used "Home Comfort" Ranges from the time I was a baby, having used 2 of them in that time. I have a "Home Comfort" myself; in fact, I will never have any other, although I did wear out two stoves before I got my "Home Comfort." The "Home Comfort" is certainly all that you recommend it to be.

Mrs. W. B. Ruff

F. P. Webb	Athens	J. J. Sheley	Dubberly	J. T. Cheatham	Hartman	E. C. Gunter	Oak Grove
J. F. Dean	Arcadia	M. J. Johnson	Downsville	E. F. Parker	Ivan	Gabe Moss	Oak Ridge
S. E. Moon	Antioch	J. H. Albritton	Darnell	W. E. Brown	Ida	R. B. Murry	Oakland
J. E. Watson	Arizona	S. W. McIntosh	Delhi	Dr. Owens	Jones	M. B. Gray	Plain Dealing
W. E. Taylor	Benton	Henry Naff	Epps	H. J. Tooke	Koran	A. O. Miles	Pioneer
A. Lodato	Bethany	C. A. Curtis	Flourney	R. E. Byrd	Kilbourne	W. B. Wall	Point
John Meyers	Bastrop	J. P. Cox	Fairbanks	S. E. McMichael	Lawhon	J. S. Thomas	Robson
N. A. Burton	Belcher	H. D. Smith	Forest	Will Johnson	Lucas	R. J. Marlar	Ruston
F. A. Graham	Beckman	J. H. Noel	Gilliams	H. N. Jones	Laran	V. A. Kitchen	Ralls
S. B. Brown	Bonita	Tom Shaw	Greenwood	J. W. Nacklas	Lillie	R. M. Wood	Roosevelt
C. Lumpkins	Bernice	S. L. Rhyon	Hope	W. J. Hay	Loch Lomond	C. Burson	Sibley
W. H. Elliott	Curtis	R. H. Alexander	Heflin	I. L. Haile	Linville	S. M. Hines	Shreveport
M. J. Durham	Colquitt	P. Beard	Haughton	W. T. Graves	Mira	A. Harrison	Simsboro
Adie Kemp	Clay	A. Stanberry	Hasston	I. D. Martin	Minden	Walter Mathis	Stevenson
Sid Preston	Colsons	R. E. Banks	Haughton	J. D. Nolan	Mer Rouge	D. T. Lee	Shongaloo
M. E. Howard	Conway	R. S. Martin	Homer	C. J. Sims	Monroe	Emmett Parks	Spencer
C. Futch	Dixie	W. T. Kemp	Haynesville	E. H. Miller	Minden	J. H. Woodard	Taylor
W. McOwn	Doyline	H. C. Cole	Hilly	J. T. Tubbs	Marion	C. W. Hill	Terry

MAINE

30 YEARS AND "GOOD AS EVER"

Skowhegan, July 7th.

Wrought Iron Range Co., St. Louis, Mo.

Gentlemen:—

There isn't a stove or range in the world that can beat the "Home Comfort." I have been using mine constantly for about 30 years with absolutely no repair bill whatsoever, and it seems to be as good as it ever was. I could not ask for a better range, and, unless I bought a new model "Home Comfort," I would never be able to get a better one if I did.

Mrs. E. B. Shepardson

EMPHASIZING QUALITIES

Thorndike, August 7th.

Wrought Iron Range Co., St. Louis, Mo.

Gentlemen:—

I am using a "Home Comfort" Range that is more than 28 years old. The linings are still like new and the top has never warped nor cracked, and I wish to emphasize its splendid baking and heating qualities. With all its age and service, I would not change it even-handed, for any cast-iron stove or range I have ever seen or heard of.

Mrs. Sumner Abbott

AN OLD-TIMER GOING STRONG

Unity, August 10th.

Wrought Iron Range Co., St. Louis, Mo.

Gentlemen:—

I am using one of the first "Home Comfort" Ranges that was brought into the State of Maine. It was purchased by my grand-father, Alonzo Bacon, of Unity Plantation, before I was born. There has never been a cent paid out for repairs—even the same linings in the fire-box are still in use, with no evidence of needing renewal. The top has never warped. Today, we baked a batch of biscuits in four and one-half minutes from the time they were placed in the oven. Clyde Shorey

BURNS LESS WOOD

Hodgdon, January 27th.

Wrought Iron Range Co., St. Louis, Mo.

Gentlemen:—

We have had our "Home Comfort" Range 26 years and have used it constantly. It is practically as good as when new, and we haven't ever had any repairs for it. We do not burn nearly as much wood as we did when we had our old cast iron stove, and find the "Home Comfort" the best heater we have ever had in our home.

Mrs. George Quint

A JURY OF TWELVE

Farmington, October 15th.

Wrought Iron Range Co., St. Louis, Mo.

Gentlemen:—

We are perfectly satisfied with our purchase of "Home Comfort" Ranges, for they are exactly as represented. We believe the "Home Comfort" is the most economical and the only sensible range to buy.

Mrs. R. E. Sproule	Mrs. A. G. Staples
Mrs. A. E. Marden	Mrs. G. R. Hillman
Mrs. R. R. Stevens	Mrs. G. H. Stinchfield
Mrs. D. D. Marwick	Mrs. Chas. Davis
Mrs. O. F. Brown	Mrs. Walter Backus
Mrs. J. A. Tilton	Mrs. Arthur Thompson

DIFFICULT TO CONVINCE

Hampden Highlands, November 1st.

Wrought Iron Range Co., St. Louis, Mo.

Gentlemen:—

It took a great deal of persuasion on the part of your salesman to induce us to discard our cast-iron range for a "Home Comfort," but now that we have used our "Home Comfort" about five years, we would not change back if the old cast range was brought around free every five years and repairs delivered gratis every six months. For heating, for baking, for durability, and for fuel economy, we believe the "Home Comfort" has no equal. Mr. and Mrs. R. H. Whitney

AN EXPENSIVE EXPERIMENT

Unity, Aug. 24th.

Wrought Iron Range Co., St. Louis, Mo.

Gentlemen:—

For the past 7 years we have been using a "Home Comfort" Range, and believe it is the most practical "buy" in a cooking appliance. We got along for 9 years with a cast-iron stove by renewing the linings and grate from time to time, but at the end of that period it needed a new oven and tank, so we threw away the legs and bought another cast-iron stove of a different make. At the end of 4 years, we threw away *its* legs and bought our present "Home Comfort". Now, we never expect to have to buy another stove or range.

Mr. and Mrs. Percy Weed

A 100 PER CENT KITCHEN RANGE

St. David, May 27th.

Wrought Iron Range Co., St. Louis, Mo.

Gentlemen:—

Since 25 years ago, we have used a 100 per cent Range for our kitchen, cooking faithfully, heating in winter, and supplying an abundance of hot water all year around—it is a "Home Comfort." I consider it saved its cost in a short time in the saving of fuel alone. Hubald Cyr

COMPARED WITH OTHERS

Thorndike, August 7th.

Wrought Iron Range Co., St. Louis, Mo.

Gentlemen:—

In our home, we have a winter and a summer kitchen, using a common stove in one and our "Home Comfort" Range in the other. The "Home Comfort" is years and years older than the cast-iron stove, but is still a much better baker and a much better stove in every way.

Mrs. F. E. Gilchrist

IS MUCH OLDER BUT BETTER

Newport, September 4th.

Wrought Iron Range Co., St. Louis, Mo.

Gentlemen:—

There is a cast-iron stove at our cottage at the pond and a "Home Comfort" Range in our kitchen at home on the farm. The "Home Comfort" heats up more quickly and is so much more satisfactory in every way, although it is 23 years older than the cottage stove. There is no comparison between a cast-iron and a wrought-iron range.

Mrs. H. V. Brown

30 YEARS IN A HOTEL

Cambridge, September 2nd.

Wrought Iron Range Co., St. Louis, Mo.

Gentlemen:—

I have a 1896 "Home Comfort" Range that I am more than pleased with. This range has been used in a small hotel and it is still in first-class condition as a cooker and baker. I can't recommend it too highly, and if I should ever have to replace it, it would be with another "Home Comfort."

E. M. McCausland

WORTH 3 COMMON KIND

Stetson, August 31st.

Wrought Iron Range Co., St. Louis, Mo.

Gentlemen:—

We bought our "Home Comfort" Range several years ago and, in my opinion, it is worth three of the common kind. It has done good, perfect work always, and if we should ever need to buy another kitchen range, I hope the "Home Comfort" Range man will happen to be near, so we can get a beautiful new enameled "Home Comfort."

D. M. Blaisdell

JOKE IS ON THEM

Thorndike, August 7th.

Wrought Iron Range Co., St. Louis, Mo.

Gentlemen:—

The range man who delivered our "Home Comfort" in 1896 dropped it off a high wagon onto the frozen ground with no harm to the Range. After constant use for nearly 30 years, it is still in excellent condition. Some of my neighbors have purchased two, and a few of them three, cook stoves of other makes since I bought mine. It would appear that the joke is on those who *do not* buy a "Home Comfort" Range to begin with.

Peter Bohn

ALSO HEATS 6 ROOMS

Upper Frenchville, June 10th.
WROUGHT IRON RANGE Co., St. Louis, Mo.
Gentlemen:—

Our "HOME COMFORT" has always given supreme satisfaction. Besides cooking perfectly, it heats 3 rooms downstairs and 3 in the chamber. What more could we ask of a kitchen range?

JAMES PLOURD

SPEAKS FOR 7 RANGES

Farmington, October 15th.
WROUGHT IRON RANGE Co., St. Louis, Mo.
Gentlemen:—

I have owned and cooked over a lot of stoves, but have had more real satisfaction with my "HOME COMFORT" Range than with all the others. I live in a neighborhood where there are seven "HOME COMFORTS" in use and the owners all agree with me that it is the best range in the world.

MRS. A. L. WHITNEY

A NEVER-FAILING BAKER

Corinna, August 31st.
WROUGHT IRON RANGE Co., St. Louis, Mo.
Gentlemen:—

I find my "HOME COMFORT" the most satisfactory of all the cooking stoves and ranges I have ever used. For me, there is no comfort like the "HOME COMFORT." It heats our large kitchen nicely in winter and is a never-failing baker.

MRS. FRANK RICHARDSON

NOW HAS NEW MODEL

Athens, November 10th.
WROUGHT IRON RANGE Co., St. Louis, Mo.
Gentlemen:—

We have used a "HOME COMFORT" Range for over 30 years with the greatest comfort and satisfaction. In fact, we have always been so well pleased with it, that we have just bought one of the New Enameled Models.

MR. and MRS. H. E. SKIDMORE

JUST AS REPRESENTED

Brooks, August 20th
WROUGHT IRON RANGE Co., St. Louis, Mo.
Gentlemen:—

I bought one of your "HOME COMFORT" Ranges in 1917, and find that it is all your Company

claimed it to be. It uses about half as much wood as our old cast-iron stove did, and it is a perfect baker and a good heater. I have never spent a cent on it for repairs and the fire-box is as good as when it was new, and the top has never warped.

A. B. CURTIS

BURNT UP 3 CAST STOVES

Bangor, November 8th.
WROUGHT IRON RANGE Co., St. Louis, Mo.
Gentlemen:—

"Perfect in every way" is mild language to describe my 39 year old "HOME COMFORT" Range. My brother living in a neighboring town has bought 3 new cast-iron stoves in the meantime. Recommend it? I certainly can, with all my heart.

MRS. JOHN WELCH

KEEPS FIRE ALL NIGHT

Bethel, November 13th.
WROUGHT IRON RANGE Co., St. Louis, Mo.
Gentlemen:—

My "HOME COMFORT" Range is too far ahead of other stoves and ranges for comparison; it is a splendid baker and keeps its fire all night when properly fixed at bedtime. I would not swap it for all three of the cook stoves I had before I got it. As to fuel, I find it saves nearly half of the amount of wood consumed by the others.

MRS. CARRIE BARTLETT

30 YEARS—NO REPAIRS

Denmark, December 17th.
WROUGHT IRON RANGE Co., St. Louis, Mo.
Gentlemen:—

This year I have done the cooking for 30 summer guests beside my own family on our "HOME COMFORT" Range that is 30 years old. The man who sold us this Range said we would never have occasion to repair it and, so far, there has never been a single part replaced. The warming closet has proved especially valuable in our business, as it will keep food fresh and moist for hours. I cannot praise the "HOME COMFORT" too highly, for we have found it exactly as recommended.

MRS. GEO. L. SMALL

Dec. 23rd.—Just wish to add that we have decided to have one of your new Enameled "HOME COMFORTS" now, as "HOME COMFORT" men come around so seldom.--MRS. GEO. L. SMALL.

J. L. McGee Auburn	R. Clavette Cleveland	G. Z. Wade	L. F. Riggs Lee
H. Sinclair Ashland	A. H. Mitchell Charleston	Fort Fairfield	A. Ludden
Ray Learned Andover	Rev. A. E. Walton	D. Lachance Frenchville	Lincoln Center
O. S. York Athens	Crouseville	R. H. Preston	A. Smith Macwahoc
Levy Dows Bradbury	C. E. Jewell Canaan	Farmington	N. F. Mason Monticello
Roy Grah Blaine	C. E. Hanson Cambridge	B. I. Thompson	W. W. Jordan Mapleton
J. A. Dyer Bridgewater	L. E. Bryant Canton	Fryeburg	Walter Shaw Mars Hill
B. A. Rivers Benedicta	John Tarr Dyer Brook	B. W. Bemis Fairfield	Able Picard Madawska
H. A. Flint Bridgeton	W. F. Frost Dixfield	H. Doucette Grand Isle	A. Kelley Marcer
Mrs. J. Allen	P. E. True Denmark	C. C. Quimby Gilead	H. Webber Mt. Vernon
North Bridgeton	F. W. Knight Dexter	W. G. Stone Garland	Wm. T. Wark
C. C. Noyes Berry Mills	J. F. King	J. Taylor Guilford	E. Millinockett
E. Brooks Bethel	Dover Foxcroft	R. Moody Haynesville	Mara Gerry
Ed. Bean Bryant Pond	H. F. Shaw Easton	J. Rooney Houlton	Mattawamkeag
H. W. Lord Brownfield	H. R. Mason Eagle Lake	Loren Huchins Hiram	J. W. Moore Medway
K. R. Togg Burlington	C. P. Hamlin E. Wilton	J. Matthews Howland	H. W. Prescott Melford
Mrs. E. P. Wallin	W. N. Bridges Ellsworth	R. Leighton Harmony	R. W. White Milo
Bradley	A. Clavet East Rumford	M. A. Munn Hartland	E. G. Jones Madison
Fred Speed Bradford	R. J. Swain E. Andover	F. Martin Island Falls	J. B. Coffin Mercer
A. H. Arnold	G. A. Ewings	H. L. Dow Jay	J. W. Brown
Bradford Center	East Brownfield	F. P. Stewart Limestone	New Limerick
Dr. D. L. Harden	Chas. Porter Enfield	Geo. O'Neal Lovell	L. J. Hall North Amity
Brownville Jct.	A. A. Daigle	E. H. Witham Lincoln	J. Jacobson New Sweden
E. M. Case Carbon	Fort Kent Mills	C. P. Cyr Linneus	W. A. Newhall North Jay
M. S. Roex Chapman	A. Oullette Fort Kent	S. H. Birch LaGrange	E. L. Smith New Sharon

J. W. Foster N. Anson	G. R. Bishop Prentiss	J. H. Quinby	G. H. Deuty Sangerville
F. M. Holbrook	Linwood Lord Patton	South Bancroft	R. H. Foss Salon
New Vineyard	John Ruland Parkman	A. M. Anderson	M. Rowe Skowhegan
Ole Olson North Newry	Harry Annis Pittsfield	Stockholm	Walter McCoy Temple
R. L. Glines	W. M. Lee Perham	John J. Cyr St. David	W. Belanger
North Rumford	L. J. Lovley Presque Isle	W. H. Pomroy	Upper Frenchville
M. E. Emery	D. McCrossin Phair	Smyrna Mills	H. Trudelle
North Fryeburg	J. L. Daigle Portage	N. D. Mechard	E. Lebrun Van Buren
C. Haines Norridgewock	O. Mardin Phillips	Soldier Pond	I. M. Wortman
Ellis Dwyer Orient	J. E. Paradis Rumford	N. Boucher St. Agatha	Wytopilock
C. P. Penn Oakfield	J. A. Reed Roxbury	H. E. Oakes St. Francis	Fred Carron Wheelock
N. E. Mason Oxbrow	John Zale	E. C. Young	L. J. Williams Westfield
G. W. Crowell Oakland	Rumford Center	Sherman Mills	S. M. Tuck Washburn
Horace Wyman	Ernst Marchand	John C. Kenney Strong	R. D. Tilton Wilton
Passadumkeag	Ridlonville	Amos Ireland	H. E. Rafuse West Peru
Norman Waite	John LeBlanc Riley	South Lincoln	F. H. Davis Winn
Pattagumpus	A. O. Lilley Seldon	C. Hutchinson Starks	F. E. Wallace Waite
R. York Powersville	Guy H. Carr Spaulding	H. A. Pitman Stow	

MARYLAND

AS GOOD AS GOLD

Deer Park, July 18th.

WROUGHT IRON RANGE CO., St. Louis, Mo.

Gentlemen:—

I know your "HOME COMFORT" Ranges have proved to be as good as gold. We have had one now in our home for almost 30 years and have had repairs for it but once. I am still using it and it is yet almost as good as new.

PAUL HARVEY

APPRECIATES COURTEOUS TREATMENT

Frostburg, March 21st.

WROUGHT IRON RANGE CO., St. Louis, Mo.

Gentlemen:—

I just want to let you know that my new Enameled "HOME COMFORT" Range has been installed, and I am certainly well pleased with it. I find it a wonderful baker and everything it was recommended to be. I want to thank you for your prompt shipment, and courteous treatment in our dealings. Everything about the range is O. K.

MRS. JOSEPH B. SMITH

FINEST THING IN THE HOUSE

Sang Run, April 1st.

WROUGHT IRON RANGE CO., St. Louis, Mo.

Gentlemen:—

We are so well pleased with our "HOME COMFORT" Range that I am enclosing check to cover the full amount. We want to call it our own, for it is certainly a great range. We wouldn't know how to get along without it now, after using it for several months. My family thinks it is the finest thing we have in the house.

MARTIN L. SAVAGE

WILL REPEAT EXPERIENCE

Dameron, October 19th.

WROUGHT IRON RANGE CO., St. Louis, Mo.

Gentlemen:—

We are certainly very much pleased with our new "HOME COMFORT" Range. If it proves to be as good and as serviceable as the one we had for over 24 years, we will be more than pleased. We wish you much success.

JOS. M. GROSSBACH

Harry Cox Annapolis	T. W. Day Clarksburg	C. M. Reese Gwynnbrook	S. Snowden Mt. Airy
G. M. Ruthoin	H. S. Davis Corinth	W. F. Wise Greencastle	H. F. McCoy
Adamstown	S. W. Graham Crillin	B. B. Spalding Graceham	Mason & Dixon
J. H. Knox Accident	W. F. Scott Churchville	T. O. Warfield Glenelg	C. E. Bowman McHenry
Sid. Harvard Abingdon	F. F. McCracken	C. A. Warfield Glenwood	G. F. Sheaku
J. Mitchell Aberdeen	Cooksville	A. W. Hafe	Marriattsville
Maurice Cissel Ashton	J. P. Myers	Great Cacapon	E. E. Thomas
L. R. Osborne Boring	Clear-Springs	J. H. Dietz Hydes	New Market
J. H. Smith Bengies	W. T. Miller Detour	L. A. Martin Hampstead	C. F. Bull Owings Mills
J. J. Jones Bradshaw	J. S. Dodge Deer Park	E. L. Burdette	F. E. Gander Oakland
Irvin Wright Baldwin	C. C. Green Darlington	Hyattstown	J. E. Stiler Parkton
J. T. Carothers	C. T. Brown Dayton	D. N. Sanders Hutton	J. E. Burk Patapsco
Burkittsville	C. O. Colley Dickerson	W. S. Fender	T. J. Fields
E. S. Goodwin Barnum	H. F. Ross Emmitsburg	Havre De Grace	Point of Rocks
G. C. Murry Bel Air	A. A. Skillman Edgewood	T. W. Buchanan	John Huchon Pylesville
H. A. Jones Berkley	J. W. Rogers Ellicott City	Hampstead	R. Butler Poolesville
W. J. Dalton Baldwin	S. T. Tucker East Gulf	H. C. Gaither Highland	W. L. Green
S. A. Howes Brinklow	J. Snyder Fullerton	J. A. Grove Hagerstown	Reisterstown
C. O. Nichols Brighton	M. F. Shanklin Fort	Wm. H. Stup Ijamsville	J. F. Kline Paw Paw
J. T. Brown Brookville	E. H. Filley Forest Hill	R. Carter Jessups	C. Wacker Raspbeburg
G. A. Staubs Beallsville	F. S. Bisker Freeland	Hemp Bros. Jefferson	R. M. Fisher
J. W. Moore Boyds	J. W. Barnes Finksburg	J. J. Flickinger Keymar	Rocky Ridge
M. Michaels	C. S. Cramer Frederick	W. M. Snyder Kitzmiller	W. A. Cox Rocks
Berkeley Springs	W. Rodgers Friendsville	D. R. Cooper Knoxville	T. L. Hutchins Stoakley
C. D. Powell Berlin	N. J. Glenn Fallston	W. J. Green Lonaconing	G. R. Hook Sykesville
J. B. Seal Big Spring	W. A. Greene	G. W. Dearholt	V. M. Buhrman
O. M. Reid Brethedsville	Forest Hill	Luthersville	Smithsburg
C. H. Riley Boonsboro	J. S. Waltmeyer	J. W. Phillips	J. W. Green Swanton
E. L. Yeakle Big Pool	Fawn Grove	Long Green	F. Haye Sang Run
M. E. Grant Creasaptown	A. W. Brady Fulton	C. Buhrman Lantz	N. A. Reams Sines
C. W. Porter Chase	J. A. Trail Granite	R. S. Hyden LeGore	H. H. Moulsdale Sewell
J. I. Ensor Cockeysville	W. D. Griffith Glyndon	Wm. Loar Midland	J. D. Davis Street
M. A. Martin Carrollton	Geo. Huber Glenarm	J. E. Cursey Monkton	R. F. Canbill Sharon

W. Cecil	Walkersville	W. H. Knode		J. H. Heiser	Unionville	H. C. Krebs	Westminster
W. H. Sealing			Shepherdstown	S. R. Harvey	Vindex	C. E. Knell	Woodbine
	Simpsonville	Ed. Harris	Tuscarora	W. J. Liebro	Woodland	R. A. Daitz	Woodlawn
H. F. Flair	Silver Spring	L. E. Hess	Taneytown	H. Klahr	Woodlawn	Irving Dice	Westminster
J. W. Myers	Sellman	J. F. Rhodes	Thurmont	J. Hallands	White Marsh	C. R. Adams	Waynesboro

MASSACHUSETTS

THE FAMILY'S CHOICE
Lunenburg, October 15th.
Wrought Iron Range Co., St. Louis, Mo.
Gentlemen:—

I am desirous of getting another "Home Comfort" Range from you. Have used the one I have 30 years and have found it so very satisfactory I must have a new one. Three of my children are married and they also have "Home Comforts."
MRS. ELLEN L. IDE

OUT-WEARS 3 STOVES
Barre, January 5th.
Wrought Iron Range Co., St. Louis, Mo.
Gentlemen:—

I have used one of your "Home Comfort" Ranges for over 25 years, and it is doing good work today. During this time, it has not had a cent's worth of repairs spent on it. My sister-in-law has used three different stoves in the same length of time.
MRS. WILLIAM HARPER

MICHIGAN

A LIFETIME RANGE
Spratt, January 29th.
Wrought Iron Range Co., St. Louis, Mo.
Gentlemen:—

The "Home Comfort" Range I bought from your salesman over 21 years ago is still in good condition, and gives perfect satisfaction in every way. It surely is a lifetime Range. I always heartily recommend both the "Home Comfort" Range and your Company.
JAMES SKRAGG

12 YEARS—GOOD AS NEW
Sterling, December 31st.
Wrought Iron Range Co., St. Louis, Mo.
Gentlemen:—

I have a "Home Comfort" Range that has been in use over 12 years, and seems to be in as good condition as the day I bought it. It is a perfect baker, fuel saver, and is extremely satisfactory in every way. I certainly do not begrudge the price I paid for it.
C. LEMMER

PERFECT IN EVERY WAY
Mount Pleasant, November 13th.
Wrought Iron Range Co., St. Louis, Mo.
Gentlemen:—

We have a "Home Comfort" Range that we have used over 20 years, and I am sure it is good for many years more. It has always been a good baker and fuel saver, and is perfect in every way. I have found your Company and your salesmen honest, reliable, responsible, and courteous in all dealings.
THOMAS CLARK

THE BEST BUILT
Sterling, December 31st.
Wrought Iron Range Co., St. Louis, Mo.
Gentlemen:—

I consider the "Home Comfort" Range the best piece of kitchen equipment built. We have used ours for many years, and have never had to have repairs. It has always been the perfect baker and fuel saver it was recommended to be. I have always found your Company reliable, prompt, and courteous in my dealings with you.
ELISHA HARRIS

USES PRESSURE TANK
Pau Pau, October 19th.
Wrought Iron Range Co., St. Louis, Mo.
Gentlemen:—

We have installed the hot-water heater on our 1912 "Home Comfort", but were compelled to connect it to a 52-gallon tank instead of a 40-gallon capacity as you recommend. In an hour after building a fire in the Range, the water in the tank is hot. We have two young men rooming with us and, after they had been here a week, one of them asked how we heated the water. We explained your system and asked why he wanted to know, and he answered: "Believe me, it beats anything I've ever seen for hot water; *you sure do get it hot.*"
FRANK H. LEIGHTY

40 YEARS—GOING STRONG
Sault Ste. Marie, March 9th.
Wrought Iron Range Co., St. Louis, Mo.
Gentlemen:—

Please quote me your price on an "L" waterback, for my "Home Comfort" Range No. 1608-k. This Range has been in service for 40 years, and with the installation of this new water-back, I believe it will be good for 40 years more.
REV. T. R. EASTERDAY

33 YEARS—$3 FOR REPAIRS
Frankenmuth, September 22nd.
Wrought Iron Range Co., St. Louis, Mo.
Gentlemen:—

We have a "Home Comfort" Range, No. 64, about 33 years old, for which we need a middle firebox lining. I believe this is one of the oldest stoves in this community, yet it bakes nicely and is still a good range in every detail. We have had only $3 worth of repairs on it in all this time.
GEO. J. RUMMEL

Peter Prime	Akron	J. L. Smith	Breckenridge	Martin Rauh	Bridgeport	Ray Hales	Clare
Oscar Rosluns	Alma	C. F. Illner	Brant	Clark Briggs	Birch Run	A. J. Myers	Carson City
J. V. Beck	Ashley	Roy McIntyre	Bad Axe	John Giesler	Barryton	Robert Lott	Crystal
Wm. C. Meyer	Bay City	James Smith	Bay Port	Lewis Beyett	Care	Wm. Ward	Chesaning
W. N. Kennedy	Bath	Chas. Porter	Blanchard	C. L. Monroe	Clio	John Ball	Chesney
Geo. Burnett	Burt	H. R. Jackson		John Snyder	Carson City	Arthur Crowe	Corunna
Ernest Sims	Birch Run		Breckenridge	Wm. Horton	Caseville	Levi Snider	Chesney
S. R. Ryan	Bannister	G. B. Wilson	Butternut	Wm. Greenwall	Coleman	Bruse Brown	Cass City

William Lewis	Colling	Robt. Boyd	Harbor Beach	W. Harrington	Mecosta
Thomas Hile	Caro	I. Donahue	Hubbardston	H. Andison	Mayville
Dan Hydon	Dewitt	John Kugel	Henderson	Allen Moore	North Star
R. E. Durkee	Decker	H. R. Fox	Hemlock	A. Hodgkinson	
Louis Slickton	Deford	C. H. Kohler			North Branch
Frank Fondel	Eagle		Howard City	C. Beatty	New Lothrop
Will McIntosh	Elsie	Frank Pert	Ithaca	J. M. Wilson	Ovid
Vern Bert	Elwell	Roy Hinds	Ionia	R. J. Smith	Otisville
Thos. H. Farner	Elkton	G. B. Felton	Kingston	Hiram Huff	Owendale
D. C. May	Edmore	Carl Reinhard	Linwood	George Warner	Owasso
R. E. Hinkley	Evart	Clarence Hurd	Lansing	Frank Crane	Oakly
Wm. Ballein	Freeland	Chas. Burch	Lyons	C. Erickson	Pinconning
Lloyd Payne	Fowler	C. Boynton	Lake Odessa	Elmer Wheeler	Portland
A. Zimmerman	Flint	E. Luchenbill	Lennon	Paul Andrews	Pompeii
Frank Holser	Flushing	David Huff	Lake	Stanley Morse	Portland
Wm. Patterson	Freeland	C. E. Garner	Lakeview	S. H. Slagell	Pompeii
George Miller	Filion	J. Middleton	Munger	M. B. Townslee	
Vern Bliss	Fairgrove	Fred Bryton	Muir		Perrinton
John Pytosh	Flushing	Amos Draper	Millington	J. Wooster	Port Austin
Gust Baker	Frankenmuth	Wm. Flynn	Mt. Morris	Geo. Hiller	Port Hope
John Duncan	Farwell	Almon Hewitt	Montrose	Wm. Seiler	Portland
L. B. Tiffany	Flushing	T. Hodges	Middleton	L. Dumond	Pinconning
E. Beautord	Fostoria	H. Kreiner	Mt. Pleasant	A. J. Bower	Rosebush
F. H. Parish	Fairgrove	S. A. Thuma	Muir	P. W. Britten	Riverdale
Elson Lyon	Grand Ledge	John Garner	Middleton	Theodore Glaza	Ruth
George Dewey	Genessee	Oscar Marr	Marlette	J. E. Small	Rosebush
Frank Shearer	Gladwin	Otto Leideke	Merrill	T. D. Lyon	Remus
Joe Loba	Grindstone	Elmer Case	Millington	Gilbert Olson	Rodney
R. L. Havens	Gagetown	Roy Moore	Montrose	B. J. Kerns	Reese
F. A. Jensen	Greenville	G. Smith	Mt. Pleasant	A. F. Henning	St. Johns
Wm. Johnson	Gagetown	Wm. Newman	McBrides	A. Johnson	St. Louis

Chas. Richards	St. Johns
F. E. Cahoon	Sarnac
E. Truckle	Swan Creek
Rebecca Campbell	Shiloh
Ray Green	St. Johns
F. G. Walter	Sarnac
Ray Sears	Sunfield
Wm. Friedman	Sandusky
Millard White	Sterling
S. Schwartz	Standich
G. Pietcher	St. Louis
F. Schinger	Saginaw
Fred Schaarr	
	Saginaw W. Side
J. Rehman	St. Charles
H. L. Post	Shephard
Robt. Gibson	Stanton
E. S. Wilson	Sheridan
G. H. Minard	Sidney
E. S. Rose	Six Lakes
Frank Cutler	Sears
Chas. Nicolai	Snover
Gilbert Smith	Silverwood
Peter Murray	Ubly
Elmer Hahn	Unionville
Fred Sinclair	Vestaburg
L. B. Furman	Vassar
D. C. Hill	Wheeler
Thomas Mead	Weidman
John W. Roberts	Wilmot

MINNESOTA

HAS TWO IN DAILY USE
Austin, October 4th.
WROUGHT IRON RANGE CO., St. Louis, Mo.
Gentlemen:—
We have two "HOME COMFORT" Ranges. One is 33 years old, and is still in use in our summer kitchen. The other is 8 years old, and is in constant daily service. Both give splendid satisfaction, being perfect bakers and fuel savers.
TOM EMERSON

SAVES MANY STEPS
Dodge Center, March 6th.
WROUGHT IRON RANGE CO., St. Louis, Mo.
Gentlemen:—
I think my "HOME COMFORT" Range is the finest stove made when it comes to construction and cooking qualities. It has always baked well, with a regular even heat that is fast and uniform. I have always found the reservoir hot water supply a most convenient feature, saving a great many steps in doing my work.
MRS. E. D. HARDING

CONSIDERS IT PERFECT
Dodge Center, March 2nd.
WROUGHT IRON RANGE CO., St. Louis, Mo.
Gentlemen:—
My "HOME COMFORT" Range has now been in use since 1917, and I find that it is all that it was recommended to be and more. Its cooking and baking has always been satisfactory, and cannot be excelled by any range. I consider my range perfect in its construction and cooking qualities.
MRS. F. H. WARNER

40 YEARS—STILL GOING
Austin, March 5th.
WROUGHT IRON RANGE CO., St. Louis, Mo.
Gentlemen:—
We have a "HOME COMFORT" Range that has been in use for nearly 40 years, and is still giving perfect satisfaction in every way. It has never had a repair, and is still the wonderful baker and fuel saver that it has always been.
MRS. W. A. MADDEN

GRANDMOTHER'S RANGE—41 YEARS OLD
Dodge Center, March 2nd.
WROUGHT IRON RANGE CO., St. Louis, Mo.
Gentlemen:—
For 6 years I have been using a "HOME COMFORT" Range that my grandmother used for 35 years. It has given perfect satisfaction, and bakes as well as it ever did. You will note this range is 41 years old, and that speaks for itself.
MRS. WM. G. HOUSE

A QUICK COOKER
Austin, January 19th.
WROUGHT IRON RANGE CO., St. Louis, Mo.
Gentlemen:—
The "HOME COMFORT" Range I bought in 1918 is still giving the very best of service. It is a quick baker and cooker, supplies plenty of hot water at all times, and is very economical in the amount of fuel it requires. I never hesitate to recommend it very highly.
MRS. J. RISINS

APPRECIATES SERVICE
West Concord, February 14th.
WROUGHT IRON RANGE CO., St. Louis, Mo.
Gentlemen:—
Parts for our "HOME COMFORT" arrived today, and we wish to thank you for your promtpness in taking care of our order. It is the first time we have ever had service on our range, and we sure want you to know that we take pleasure in recognizing treatment of this kind.
W. J. BARR

RETAINS QUALITIES
West Concord, March 2nd.
WROUGHT IRON RANGE CO., St. Louis, Mo.
Gentlemen:—
My "HOME COMFORT" Range has given me splendid service for 14 years. It is in good condition at this time, and still retains its heating and cooking qualities. I have been well satisfied with it in every particular from the day it was purchased to the present, and I think there are several years of service and satisfaction in it yet.
MRS. JAKE AGERTER

RESERVOIR A REAL COMFORT
Dodge Center, February 17th.
Wrought Iron Range Co., St. Louis, Mo.
Gentlemen:—

I have used my "Home Comfort" Range constantly since 1911, and it is still in good condition. As a perfect baker and a fuel saver, I do not believe it can be beat. It is a real comfort to have a reservoir of hot water handy at all times. I expect my range to last for many years, and always do perfect work.

Mrs. Lottie Bennett

KNOWS THEIR REAL WORTH
Austin, March 3rd.
Wrought Iron Range Co., St. Louis, Mo.
Gentlemen:—

After using a "Home Comfort" Range for 33 years with perfect satisfaction in every way, we have just bought one of your New Enamel Models with which to replace it. We could not think of using any but a "Home Comfort" Range, for we certainly know their real worth.

Mr. and Mrs. E. D. Nelsen

PRIZES IT VERY HIGHLY
Sargeant, January 20th.
Wrought Iron Range Co., St. Louis, Mo.
Gentlemen:—

I have used my "Home Comfort" Range for 15 years, and have found it to be satisfactory in every way, and exactly as it was represented to me when I bought it. It is still in good usable condition; however, I have just ordered one of your New Enamel Models because of its beauty and improvements; and I know I shall prize it very highly.

Mrs. F. A. Pick

NEXT—THE NEW MODEL
Adams, March 9th.
Wrought Iron Range Co., St. Louis, Mo.
Gentlemen:—

We have had our "Home Comfort" Range nearly 25 years, and can say that it has given the best results, and has been all anyone could ask of a kitchen range. We certainly do not regret buying it, and if we ever replace it with a new one, it will surely be a New Enamel "Home Comfort."

Mrs. James Thelen

DOES NOT REGRET BUYING
Brounsdale, January 19th.
Wrought Iron Range Co., St. Louis, Mo.
Gentlemen:—

I bought a "Home Comfort" Range 7 years ago and we have always found it satisfactory, and exactly as it was represented. It has been a source of real comfort to my family, and has solved the cooking problem completely. It has always been a reliable baker, and very economical as to fuel, and I certainly do not regret my investment.

J. L. Lewis

GOOD FOR MANY YEARS
Renova, January 22nd.
Wrought Iron Range Co., St. Louis, Mo.
Gentlemen:—

I have used my "Home Comfort" Range since 1910, and have had plenty of success in using it. It bakes well and cooks good, and has never needed any repairs. It will doubtless continue to be in good condition, and give me good service for many years to come.

Mrs. C. Largervall

A PERFECT BAKER
Brounsdale, January 21st.
Wrought Iron Range Co., St. Louis, Mo.
Gentlemen:—

For 15 years, we have used a "Home Comfort" Range with perfect satisfaction. It is a good fuel saver, and it certainly is a perfect baker.

Mrs. B. E. Tucker

GREAT FUEL SAVER
Lyle, January 15th.
Wrought Iron Range Co., St. Louis, Mo.
Gentlemen:—

I have been using my "Home Comfort" Range since 1917, and have always found it satisfactory in every way, especially when it comes to baking. It is a great fuel saver, and I find the hot water reservoir a great convenience and step saver.

Mrs. T. L. Searles

PRACTICALLY NO REPAIRS
Elkton, January 21st.
Wrought Iron Range Co., St. Louis, Mo.
Gentlemen:—

I have used a "Home Comfort" Range for over 27 years, and it is still giving us splendid service. It has always baked good, using very little fuel, and has needed practically no repairs. I could not think of using any but a "Home Comfort" Range.

Mrs. Bertha Dammam

BEST RECOMMENDATION
Dexter, January 23rd.
Wrought Iron Range Co., St. Louis, Mo.
Gentlemen:—

For the past 7 years, I have used a "Home Comfort" Range with perfect satisfaction. It is a good baker, and a great fuel saver. I give my best recommendation for the "Home Comfort" Range.

Mrs. Fred Tiedemann

"IN EVERY RESPECT"
Brounsdale, January 15th.
Wrought Iron Range Co., St. Louis, Mo.
Gentlemen:—

My "Home Comfort" Range has been doing daily service in my kitchen since 1912. I have always found it satisfactory in every respect, and have had the very best of service from it.

Mrs. N. E. Scott

B. H. Haak Guckeen	W. F. Kirby Kasota	W. Radke Minnesota Lake	A. J. Anderson Otisco
Frank Vanek Glenville	W. F. Wilder "	Wm. Talzman "	Max Fitzke Ottawa
Adiers Westrum "	Chas. Rodell "	Adolph Brandt " "	A. M. Simorett "
Edw. Schradle "	Dorothy Teubke Kenyon	A. J. Dezell Matawan	G. F. Steinberg "
G. S. Olson Hayward	G. A. Dahn LeSuer Center	John E. Conner	Ernie Brandenburg
Oscar Arlison "	Rev. Wagner "	Madison Lake	Pemberton
Ernst H. Peterson "	H. R. Snow " "	Anton Weber Nicollet	Frank Weber St. Weber
O. Sandvold Hartland	V. J. Jeno Longsdale	R. D. Gleason "	P. J. Weber " "
W. C. Robinson "	Adolph Shamby "	Gustave Dallman "	J. T. Ballman " "
J. O. Kvenvold "	August Witt Morristown	May Brick New Richland	Emil Abraham Smith Mill
C. F. Craven Huntley	A. F. Schmichtenberg "	Irvin Kast "	H. Olhaft Waseca
A. L. Lieska Henderson	J. H. Pope "	C. L. Herbert " "	A. F. Hubbard Lineville
John Ryon Janesville	C. J. Wolle Modelia	Arthur Kester Northfield	M. M. Painter Leon
L. H. Britton "	Theodore Arndt "	F. DeWolfe "	H. Dagner Waldorf
Ernst Rocker "	Lesle H. Thurston "	Ed. DeWolfe "	John Mille Wells
Peter Gilleske Kilkenny	Horace Ray Medford	John Prochaska "	T. R. Markey "
Peter E. Crosby "	E. R. Webster "	New Prague	C. W. Johnson "
Adolph Staska "	Albert L. Webb "	Otto Oakes New Ulm	R. Schulz Waterville
F. Velishek "	J. P. Gold Manchester	Hugo Gieseke " "	J. R. Greaves "
W. I. Teubener Granada	Al. Severson "	James Larson Owatonna	
Julius Jelle Kiester	Louis Graedalen "	Clarence Young "	
H. P. Peterson "		C. M. Coulter "	

MISSISSIPPI

KEEPS WATER HOT
Blue Mountain, December 29th.
WROUGHT IRON RANGE CO., St. Louis, Mo.
Gentlemen:—
We have been using our new Enameled "HOME COMFORT" Range for several weeks and have found it exactly as your salesman represented it to be. It is a perfect baker, the reservoir keeps the water hot, and the enamel easy to keep clean and beautiful.
MRS. BLANCH SHANKLES

OLD RANGE HAS VALUE
Independence, December 22nd.
WROUGHT IRON RANGE CO., St. Louis, Mo.
Gentlemen:—
I used my first "HOME COMFORT" Range for 32 years and at the expiration of that time, sold it for $20 and bought your 1916 Model, which I am using today. Your "HOME COMFORT" Range is, in my estimation, based on my experience with it and others, the best range ever made.
MRS. H. L. BLEDSOE

SUPERIOR TO OTHERS
Wheeler, December 22nd.
WROUGHT IRON RANGE CO., St. Louis, Mo.
Gentlemen:—
I have been using a "HOME COMFORT" Range for the past 13 years, and it is now doing first-class work. It bids fair to last 13, or more, years longer. I am greatly pleased to say that your Range is much superior to any range I have ever used or seen. With best wishes, I am,
MRS. C. G. KIZER

THEY'RE GREAT FRIENDS
Repley, September 29th.
WROUGHT IRON RANGE CO., St. Louis, Mo.
Gentlemen:—
My "HOME COMFORT" Range and I are great friends and I would hate to think that I would ever have to do without it. I can certainly recommend it very highly.
MRS. CALLIE PORTER

G. M. Rowland Ashland	T. L. Alford Cheraw	A. E. Harper Florence	P. H. Lyles Lawrence
Bob Bagwell Ackerman	J. M. Mallard Chunky	C. E. Jones Forest	E. P. Brown Lockheart
J. Polk Agricola	Joe H. Clark Complete	W. Allen Georgetown	J. F. Earhart Louisville
F. M. Buckley Arm	A. N. McDunas Chicora	H. A. Simmons Gholson	G. C. McClain Laurel
J. W. Halbert Artesia	N. L. Hutts Clara	L. G. Hood Gass	N. A. Dickson
Abe Dukes Abbeville	M. V. Perkins Coldwater	H. G. Coner Hesterville	Looxahama
W. M. Eubanks Bexley	N. M. Flowers Cockrum	F. L. Wright Horn Lake	Frank Emmons Lake
Jack Agee Bay Springs	J. B. Gibbon Chunky	J. L. Holder Hurley	J. A. Smith McCool
F. U. Wilson Bailey	D. T. Rye Cliftonville	J. S. Millis Hathorn	D. B. McKenzie Michigan
B. N. Martin Bossfield	T. J. Jackson Crawford	Solomon Ford Hub	W. W. Hunt McCool
John Chisolm Bailey	J. J. Raley De Soto	Dr. J. H. Moore	O. J. Byrd Mt. Olive
J. C. Williams Byhalia	T. J. McCoy Daleville	Holly Springs	J. J. McClune Moss Point
C. S. Lackey Bailey	T. S. McKee DeKalb	Ben Bean Hudsonville	T. C. Kinard Marion
W. H. Dyess Bucatunna	Lewis George Duffee	W. W. Harris Harrisville	U. L. Freeman
G. C. Jennings	E. J. Johnson Dixon	Joe McLendon Hillsboro	Mendenhall
Blue Mountain	R. L. Shackeford Deemer	Ed. B. Bowie	R. H. Sullivan Mize
A. C. Manning Braxton	J. M. Thomas Decatur	Harpersville	W. O. Bush Moselle
L. Young Bigbee Valley	W. P. Searcy Drew	Henry Taller Jayess	W. J. Clark Meridan
G. H. Hinton Brookville	Swip Bracey Darbun	A. J. Polk Johns	O. L. Russell Monticello
H. H. Johnson Center	W. A. Thompson Ethel	J. S. Gilbert Koscusko	C. J. Joyner
John McRae Crandall	W. B. Moffitt Enterprise	E. D. Adams Kreole	Mt. Pleasant
J. W. Stewart Collins	E. L. Lematre Escatawpa	G. B. Ingram Kewanee	C. N. Studay Meridan
I. S. Cooksey "	T. R. Beech Elliville	Oscar Conerley Kokomo	N. Evans Matherville
Walter Rogers Conehatta	S. P. Moore Enterprise	Mat. Shaw Langsdale	John Fuller Myrtle
J. M. Hodge Complete	M. I. Cook	C. S. Barr Lucedale	C. H. Sullivan Mize
S. J. Garner Carson	French Camps	Jim King Lockheart	W. J. Odom Magee
R. L. Davis Columbus	A. B. Rogers "	E. H. Hill Lauderdale	J. R. Cooper Mendenhall
J. L. Smith Caledonia	Fearns Springs	J. D. Shelton Lamar	J. A. Shields Morton
E. J. Singley Columbia	N. E. Warrell Fentress	F. O. Roberts Lewisburg	W. L. Young Macon

R. C. Conner McLeod
R. Short Mashulaville
W. M. Parker Newton
C. V. Sills New Hebron
John C. Lloyd Nesbitt
M. E. Ferguson Noxapater
J. R. Woodham Newton
T. L. McNull Olive
J. H. Morris Oxford
A. J. Price Oakvale
Col. J. Smith Plum Point
Ed. J. Simrna Pecan
J. H. Rodgers Pachuta
Robt. E. Tyrone Prentiss
P. S. Scott Preston
W. E. Palmer Portersville
John Sayles Potts Camp
J. T. Daws Philadelphia
T. R. Woodruff Pachuta

L. J. Stockstill Picayene
R. N. Parker Puckett
M. Walker Pinola
Bob Miles Pulaski
J. L. Robbins Paulette
F. M. Hays Quitman
W. G. Bradley Rounsaville
T. F. Graham Rose Hill
Lee A. Clay Rio
L. S. Berkley Red Banks
W. E. Foley Rose Hill
A. J. Ward Ripley
W. M. Walker Raleigh
T. B. Barnett Ravine
D. C. Wigley Sallis
C. D. Bodie Shubutta
W. V. Morgan Sanford
J. W. Ward Shipman
S. F. Hillburn Soso

J. M. Walters Seminary
J. B. Pickering Summerland
A. G. Boyd Scooba
Alex Loveless Sunirall
M. E. Clark Schanberville
H. H. Bozeman Silver Creek
S. L. Holley Steens
E. W. Foxworth Sandy Hook
M. A. Eubanks Stallo
A. R. Fowler Samneville
J. A. Randle Starkville
T. C. Grave Soso
L. O. King Summerland
C. W. Black Shivers
U. M. Long Sebastpool
J. S. Catlett Toomsuba
C. C. Wilson Ted

Bob Shelton Toomsuba
Hardy Brown Tyro
W. J. Garner Taylorsville
R. S. Craft Traxler
J. O. Walter Union
D. L. Goodwin Vashurg
Rodney Ford West
J. W. Briscoe Winborn
E. Y. Pickle Weir
M. G. Johnson Wade
J. B. Hartley Waterford
James Smith Wanilla
J. A. Tatum Walnut Grove
J. E. Naylor Waterford
A. G. Bushy Waynesboro
J. C. Meeks Walnut
G. B. Floate Wyatte
R. T. Layton Weathersby
S. P. Casey Zama

MISSOURI

THIRTY-FIVE YEARS IN HOTEL
Gibbs, Sept. 15th.
WROUGHT IRON RANGE Co., St. Louis, Mo.
Gentlemen:—
I have used a "HOME COMFORT" in my hotel constantly for 35 years, and 6 months ago I bought and added another one, for I find them to be the best range made. No other range in the world would have stood the heavy duty I have put on my old "HOME COMFORT." MRS. BERT BAROWS

LIKES DEALINGS
Jamesport, June 15th
WROUGHT IRON RANGE Co., St. Louis, Mo.
Gentlemen:—
I consider the purchase of my "HOME COMFORT" Range the best investment I have ever made. It cooks quickly and perfectly, and with so little fuel. It is a great comfort to any housekeeper. Also, I wish to commend both your company and your salesmen for your honorable dealings and methods. I find your representatives very gentlemanly and courteous. MRS. W. K. WYNNE

FOR PEOPLE WHO CARE
Gilman City, June 30th.
WROUGHT IRON RANGE Co., St. Louis, Mo.
Gentlemen:—
After 30 years of married life, and having burned up four "supposed to be" standard stoves, I purchased one of the new "HOME COMFORT" Ranges, enameled inside and out. We find it just as represented and recommended—a real range for people who care. MR. and MRS. W. D. SMITH

HIS SON KNOWS
Novelty, October 22nd.
WROUGHT IRON RANGE Co., St. Louis, Mo.
Gentlemen:—
Our old faithful "HOME COMFORT" Range is now 25 years old and is still doing good work. My son has just bought one of your new Enameled Ranges because he knows what our "HOME COMFORT" has meant to us and how it has proved its durability. There can be no better range made for long service. LEE GREENLEY

THE ONLY RANGE
Maywood, October 27th.
WROUGHT IRON RANGE Co.,
Gentlemen:—
We have had our HOME COMFORT range 5 years and we think it is "the only range." MRS. BERT M. JOHNSON

FAITHFUL FOR 36 YEARS
Jamesport, June 12th.
WROUGHT IRON RANGE Co., St. Louis, Mo.
Gentlemen:—
Today we are using a No. 96 "HOME COMFORT" Range which I bought at a public sale and which has been in use for 36 years. Even with all its age, it still bakes perfectly and consumes less than half the fuel of any ordinary stove. MR. and MRS. FRANK ELDER

PROTECTS GOOD MONEY
Jamesport, June 10th.
WROUGHT IRON RANGE Co., St. Louis, Mo.
Gentlemen:—
We have used a "HOME COMFORT" Range constantly for 30 years. We certainly would never think of putting our good money into any other range made. JOHN McATEE

FAITHFUL FOR 40 YEARS
Edina, October 20th.
WROUGHT IRON RANGE Co., St. Louis, Mo.
Gentlemen:—
I have used my "HOME COMFORT" Range 40 years and it still is in good condition for its age and bakes as well as ever. I do not think there is another range made that could have done nearly half as well as my old faithful "HOME COMFORT." MRS. ALICE MURPHY

FAITHFUL FOR 46 YEARS
Jamesport, June 12th.
WROUGHT IRON RANGE Co., St. Louis, Mo.
Gentlemen:—
Forty-six years ago we bought a "HOME COMFORT" Range from off one of your mule-team wagons. This old faithful has been in constant use ever since then and is still doing its duty today as well as ever. No one should spend their good money for any other kind of a range. DAN KEHLER

THREE IN ONE FAMILY
Wyconda, December 15th.
WROUGHT IRON RANGE Co., St. Louis, Mo.
Gentlemen:—
Our HOME COMFORT range has been in constant use for over 20 years and it is in excellent condition today. There are two more "HOME COMFORTS" in our family. We would not think of buying any other. J. B. CAMERON

EASILY KEPT CLEAN

Maysville, October 28th.

WROUGHT IRON RANGE CO., St. Louis, Mo.

Gentlemen:—

We are well pleased with our "HOME COMFORT" Range. It is so easily kept clean and bakes so nicely. We are glad to recommend it always.

CHAS. W. MCCREA

STANDS BACK OF GOODS

Kahoka, December 12th.

WROUGHT IRON RANGE CO., St. Louis, Mo.

Gentlemen:—

We have used our "HOME COMFORT" Range for 20 years and we are positive there is no better range made anywhere. We have never been out one cent for repairs. Both our brother and our daughter have just bought new Enameled Model AB "HOME COMFORTS." We like to deal with people who stand back of their goods and come back to see you after you have bought.

MR. and MRS. JOHN TAYLOR

OUTLASTS THREE OTHERS

Wyconda, Dec. 15th.

WROUGHT IRON RANGE CO., St. Louis, Mo.

Gentlemen:—

We have used our "HOME COMFORT" Range for 28 years and it is still the great baker and fuel saver it always has been. We have used several common stoves, but none ever compared with our "HOME COMFORT." Several of my neighbors have bought three stoves and ranges since we bought our "HOME COMFORT," but they are all gone. We have just bought one of your new Model AB Enameled Ranges, for we would use no other kind but a "HOME COMFORT."

EMMETT ROBERTSON

GOOD FOR LIFETIME

Mayfield, January 1st.

WROUGHT IRON RANGE CO., St. Louis, Mo.

Gentlemen:—

It gives me great pleasure to recommend your "HOME COMFORT" Range. We have had one in constant use for the last 36 years and I think it is good for the rest of my life which I anticipate will be many more years yet. I have never made an investment in anything that has given me the returns of the one I made in my "HOME COMFORT" Range.

H. L. BOLLINGER

SAVING ITS PRICE

Mayfield, December 5th.

WROUGHT IRON RANGE CO., St. Louis, Mo.

Gentlemen:—

While we have had our new "HOME COMFORT" Range but about a month, it has already proven to be exactly as you represented it. It is an excellent baker and heater, and will run on the least amount of fuel of any stove we have ever had and it looks like it is going to save its price in fuel consumption alone. I cannot recommend it too highly to my neighbors and friends.

MRS. C. F. BOLLINGER

HER DAUGHTER KNOWS

Jamesport, June 14th.

WROUGHT IRON RANGE CO., St. Louis, Mo.

Gentlemen:—

I have been using my "HOME COMFORT" Range constantly since 1912 and it is in perfect condition today and bakes as good as ever. Mother used her "HOME COMFORT" over 30 years with the same satisfaction. I never fail to give the "HOME COMFORT" a recommendation as a Real Range.

MRS. WILL MANN

SPOKEN FROM THE HEART

Jamesport, May 19th.

WROUGHT IRON RANGE CO., St. Louis, Mo.

Gentlemen:—

I feel that I cannot say enough for the "HOME COMFORT" Range, for I think it is the Greatest Range on Earth. My mother bought one before I was large enough to cook—I learned to cook on it—and she is still using it. When I married and started housekeeping, we bought a cheaper range—it is gone. Today we purchased from your salesman a "HOME COMFORT" Model "AB" with its beautiful enamel finish and everything. It is certainly the most beautiful and most perfect range I have ever seen.

MRS. FRED FORTH

LIKE MOTHER—LIKE SONS

Milan, September 1st

WROUGHT IRON RANGE CO., St. Louis, Mo.

Gentlemen:—

Our mother bought a "HOME COMFORT" Range 36 years ago and has used it ever since. Each of us is buying a new Enameled "HOME COMFORT" today, for we know positively that they are the very best kitchen range made.

JOHN and MIKE LEE

36 YEARS—THEN MODEL "AB"

Patton, December 4th.

WROUGHT IRON RANGE CO., St. Louis, Mo.

Gentlemen:—

I purchased a "HOME COMFORT" Range from you 36 years ago and have just replaced it with your new Enameled Model "AB" Range. We would not be without a "HOME COMFORT" in our kitchen. It has always been a perfect baker and a great fuel saver.

H. F. BOLLINGER

A. C. Smith	Amity	E. M. Powell	Benton	B. Mattson	Conception	L. B. McCall	Downing
R. S. Parks	Anove	J. M. Breeze	Breckenridge	George Swinford	"	L. B. Russell	Elmo
Edward Todd	Albany	B. Alexander	Boynton	J. E. Finnell	Clearmont	Jas. W. Day	Edina
Ed. Campbell	Allendale	S. A. Harrison	Bethany	L. G. Taylor	Cora	Horace Johnson	"
Ray Murray	Albany	Laura Meilike	Baring	Josie Vandyke	Cardwell	E. P. Brown	Ewing
W. F. Holton	Arbela	J. B. Meek	Brimson	R. H. Hanse	Crowder	E. H. Couch	Emden
J. W. Duffey	Advance	Wm. Beattie	Barnard	H. H. Minner	Catron	T. L. Moore	East Prairie
C. H. Croy	Arbor	R. R. Staples		L. L. Roder	Charleston	E. R. Colborn	Essex
L. Croy	Allenville		Burlington Jct.	T. L. Middleton		G. T. Teaford	Ellington
J. G. Hartle	Advance	B. Smith	Center		Commerce	R. L. Neely	Fremont
Curtis Strong	Arbyrd	J. H. Ramsey	Craig	A. C. Miller	Daisy	J. M. Shrum	
J. D. McCormack		Frank Collins	Clarksdale	Philip Seabaugh	Deta		Fredericktown
	Annapolis	Thomas McManus	"	C. S. Evans	Des Arc	Cave Currie	Fairfax
Oscar Funk	Advance	F. Shimeman	Chillicothe	Geo. W. Luna	Dexter	L. B. Dochterman	
J. J. Sims	Acorn	Warren Meservey	Chula	Harve Temple	Doniphan		Farmington
W. M. Smith	Bertrand	Jud Craig	Cainsville	E. Jackson	Darlington	Polar Wave Ice Co.	Foley
W. L. Presson	Bernie	Mrs. J. B. Thompson		M. Garrett	Denver	G. P. Webb	Grain Valley
R. W. Cross	Bell City		Canton	Lee Decker	Dawn	Jasper Barber	Gentry
T. L. Wood	Biggers	Martin Boyer	Cantwell	C. W. Douglass	Dunlap	L. Davis	Grant City

John Stretch Gilman City	P. H. Potter McFall	G. Hesse Neelys Landing	Leslie Hobb Saline
Byron Maharg Gallatin	L. B. Eichelberger	Wm. Shy New Madrid	H. B. McDowell
Dan Ward Granger	Mt. Sterling	W. B. Grice Oran	Skidmore
Alta Blaine Greensburg	A. L. Adams Memphis	J. W. Meyer Oregon	B. Winemiler Sheridan
Dennis Kettle Gorin	O. E. Mankoff "	Clyde Hatcher Osgood	F. H. Squire Savannah
Fred Lindquist Green Top	Mrs. C. E. Thompson	U. S. Brassfield "	George Courtney "
H. A. Crosby Gibbs	Mark	Cal Rockey Princeton	J. H. Elsworth Stahl
S. F. Davis Graham	Wm. D. Baker Mill Grove	Alvin Hughes Parnell	J. D. Wells Stanberry
F. S. Coffman	H. Rutherford " "	Walter Walker "	G. R. Kiser Skidmore
Green Castle	John Hunter Martinsville	C. J. Miller Pattonsburg	Chas. McDaniel "
J. W. Welker Greenbrier	Jake Samer "	A. W. Canfield "	Tom Breeze Sampsel
W. W. Ford Gordonville	J. D. Pilcher Mt. Moriah	W. H. Banks Palmyra	Ira Cooper "
Scott Watson Greenville	Roy Hinton Monticello	Mrs. J. O. Shuford "	T. L. Adams Spickarc
N. Myers Hadley	Homer Wallace "	C. H. Doscher, Phila.	A. R. Browning "
W. F. Scott Hurdland	L. E. Terry Melbourne	J. O. Shuford "	Jasper Seabaugh
Claude Thomas Hannibal	I. E. Patterson Maitland	Jesse P. Carter Pickering	Sedgewickville
P. C. Currey Hopkins	C. A. McCooper	John Garrard Parnell	G. T. McDonald Senath
C. F. Russell Humphreys	Maryville	P. E. Candle "	R. W. Barnes Sikeston
Oran M. Fairley Harris	Harry McDowell "	H. E. Wilson Pollock	Russell Burke Rockport
John Adams Hatfield	L. C. Smith Milan	W. J. Rodgers "	Will Taylor "
J. K. Mills Jameson	S. H. Simpson "	Geo. Kimble Phelps City	Harry Shelby Tarkio
F. Thompson Jamesport	C. E. Corbin Lutesville	C. C. Seabaugh Patton	James Showalter "
J. H. Gordon Jackson	E. E. Harrell Lilburn	J. E. Stucker "	R. M. Baker Trenton
W. W. Meyers Kewanee	Louis Shields LeForge	Poplar Bluff	L. D. Dennis "
I. Bacon Kidder	T. B. Blount Lesterville	C. A. Allen Parma	Mrs. Osjong Tower
Homer Schultz King City	W. A. Roberts Liebig	Lee Atwell Portageville	J. M. Scott Taylor
Wm. Bradley Knox City	E. L. Raglin Lodi	T. A. Walker Paynor	Mrs. C. H. Stratton "
J. H. Kittle Kahoka	R. H. Duncan Leeper	I. N. Gill Patterson	Frank Veale Union Star
C. A. Waters Kirksville	Grace Sorrell Marble Hill	Harry Ross Piedmont	R. L. Cullor Unionville
Clyde I. Douglass "	R. M. Hahn Millersville	Val Marschino Perkins	A. E. Hackathorn "
C. A. Noland Lucerne	J. T. Wilferth Mayfield	W. F. Shawver Quitman	E. F. Koger Van Buren
B. J. Gilworth "	Oscar Pippins Malden	Glen Anderson "	Bill Ruhl Vanduser
Otis Schnelle Lemons	E. G. Ford Morehouse	A. A. Erwin Queen City	C. E. Henson
John Gibson Lock Springs	A. B. Lovins Marston	A. D. Ferguson " "	Williamsville
Samuel Denney LaBelle	Uriah Husk Matthews	J. B. Polley Ridgeway	C. M. Wood Winston
Noah Morgan Lewistown	W. M. Kenser Morley	Ed. F. Edson "	J. B. Caldwell "
J. B. Crandall "	J. G. Bone Mill Spring	Monroe Parrish Rutledge	E. H. Lipper Wyaconda
Roy Jennings LaGrange	Robert Minner Morley	R. R. Arehart "	Emmett Robertson "
Fred W. Maiers "	W. R. Boswell New Point	J. H. Miller "	E. P. Mitts Williamstown
W. E. Lee Luray	W. O. Myers Newark	Bob Johnson Randles	W. E. Bailey Winigan
C. L. Browning Laredo	Wm. Lake Nelsonville	E. Z. Mann Redford	S. T. Branch Warren
H. F. Anderson "	R. A. Wharton "	Elmer Best Revere	C. K. Eggers
F. Kendrick Monroe City	E. O. Patterson Norwood	W. H. Ehrhart "	Wilmathsville
C. F. Lahnenbauer " "	W. H. DeVaald Novinger	A. H. Hunt Ravenwood	G. C. Yowell Yarrow
J. R. Warren Maysville	J. T. Stout Newtown	W. H. Burr "	W. F. Hays Youngstown
Basil Winslow "	T. V. McClanahan "	S. R. Breeding Reger	

NEBRASKA

DOESN'T REGRET INVESTMENT

Sargent, January 27th.

Wrought Iron Range Co., St. Louis, Mo.

Gentlemen:—

We are now using our second "Home Comfort" Range, and I can truthfully say that I have never seen any stove or range that can beat them when it comes to cooking and baking. I certainly would not think of spending money for any other make when I can get a "Home Comfort" for the price at which they are sold. I recommend the "Home Comfort" to my friends and neighbors, for I know they will not make a mistake and will never regret the investment.

J. E. Grint

27 YEARS—NO REPAIRS

Wakefield, May 17th.

Wrought Iron Range Co., St. Louis, Mo.

Gentlemen:—

We are today cooking on a Model No. 96 "Home Comfort" Range which has seen 27 years of continuous service. It has the same grates, firebox linings, and the same pipe and elbows that came with the Range when new. It has always been a good fuel saver and a perfect heater and baker. I advise anyone who is in the market for a Range to examine the "Home Comfort" before spending their money for another.

Mrs. J. O. Felt

KNOWS WHAT SHE'S BUYING

Stanton, December 15th.

Wrought Iron Range Co., St. Louis, Mo.

Gentlemen:—

I have used a No. 99 "Home Comfort" Range in my home for twenty-two years. Unquestionably, it is a perfect baker and a great fuel saver. I am today purchasing a new "Home Comfort" from your salesman, because I know just what I am buying.

Mrs. J. N. Kern

GIVES PERFECT SATISFACTION

Wausau, May 5th.

Wrought Iron Range Co., St. Louis, Mo.

Gentlemen:—

We have used our Model No. 99 "Home Comfort" Range 24 years. It has stood the test of time and has given excellent service and perfect satisfaction.

Mrs. Emma Baggstrom

34 YEARS—NO REPAIRS

Leigh, January 16th.

Wrought Iron Range Co., St. Louis, Mo.

Gentlemen:—

We have now used one of your No. 69 "Home Comfort" Ranges 34 years, and it is still doing perfect work today, baking as well as it ever did. It has the same base-pipe joint, the same grates and fire-linings, in fact, it has never been repaired in all that time.

E. F. Lee

Henry Philleo Ayr	Harry H. Smith Cowles	Will Kennard Geneva
Tom Meyer Aurora	Norman Coulter Crete	J. S. Delaney "
Glen Archer "	Pete Isley Cortland	Harry P. Gohel Grafton
Geo. Busing Alexandria	Siebert Fissen "	S. C. Wilson "
Andrew Loetscher "	Jack Dehart Deweese	H. H. Dieckman Giltner
Everett North Armour	Albert J. Roth "	J. A. Kingston "
Chas. Barnes "	C. W. Stern Denton	H. W. Graham Gresham
C. L. Cherry Adams	Lloyd A. Johnson "	J. D. Lauer "
Mrs. Heiko Cooper "	Roy A. Foelfs Diller	Louis Gehl Garland
R. W. Simpson Auburn	D. N. Gridley "	James Adams "
A. P. Whitwell "	Will Foz Daykin	Wm. V. Harms Gileod
Wm. Oldenberg Avoca	Ira E. Baker "	Wm. Naiman, Jr. "
James Blaker Barnston	M. D. Rhodes Doniphan	R. F. Bangert Guide Rock
J. H. Wayman "	E. E. Spaulding "	Wm. Markland Glenrock
Bennett Essex Beatrice	Paul Virus Deshler	C.O.Swanson Greenwood
John Engler, Jr. "	H. W. G. Hoffmeyer "	W. D. Miller "
H. L. Raney Blue Spgs.	F. C. Pittman Davenport	O. W. Lukow Holstein
G. D. Hevelone "	Chris. Jorgenson "	John Kothe Hastings
Soren Olson Bostwick	Carl Buss Dewitt	Chas. Whittlake Harvard
S. M. Southerland "	W. M. Buss "	R. C. Gish Holmesville
C. J. Carlson Bertrand	A. F. Lutzenhusen "	C. E. Bowers Hampton
W. R. Borin Bloomington	Dorchester	Thos. Timmens Hardville
J. Meyer Beaver Crossing	A. Baunberger Dawson	B. F. Sloan Huntley
H. Wagenkneoht Bee	A. H. Utermohlen "	Julius Hirtzel Harbine
J. J. Vrana	W. A. Decker Elwood	Chas. E. Emily Helvey
Frank West Bruning	H. Schilling Eustis	Lars Anderson Hardy
H. A. Hulse	Ev. Johnson Eldorado	G. W. Hanson Holdrege
W. H. Carlson Belvidere	M. E. Lingren Edgar	F. C. Craig Hebron
L. B. Bloomfield "	H. M. W. Smith "	A. W. Friesen Henderson
Leroy Anderson Benedict	H. A. Miner Exeter	A. J. Heble Hebron
O. B. Waterbury "	John Christiansen "	G. W. Slater Humboldt
H. H. Bentz Blue Hill	C. E. Fairchild Endicott	W. E. L. Jones Invale
E. R. Hendrickson "	F. B. Edlund Elm Creek	Walt Felzien Juniata
L. J. Gartner Burchard	Dan Munchaw Eagle	L. C. Wilhems Jensen
Walter Graham "	B. A. Munchaw "	Herman Burr Julian
L. J. Wagner Bradshaw	Bryan Smith Elmwood	J. F. Goering Johnson
Geo. Beoning Bladen	F. M. Snavely "	H. R. Hauptman Julian
G. M. Jewell Brock	H. A. Sheets Fairfield	E. D. Ernst Kensaw
B. I. McInish Brounsville	R. J. Houch Fairmont	M. C. Durland Lexington
J. H. Mueller Clearwater	Frank Jackson "	W. E. Mitchell Liberty
V. F. Dawson Clay Center	C. R. Gingery Filley	R. J. Black Lincoln
J. H. Bradney "	P. W. Graves "	Jess Dunn Lawrence
Ray Hines Cozad	H. N. Darrow Fairbury	V. B. Humphreys Loomis
K. F. Mara Ceresco	H. N. Darrow Franklin	John Reining Lawrence
C. J. Rodeman Cordova	Jerry Wallman Filley	I. F. Martin Liberty
C. E. Bentebaugh "	Henry Backer Friend	Arch G. McCoy Lewiston
J. N. Calhoun Chester	Frank Kanzak Glenvil	N. F. Hennings Louisville
Carl Effenbeck "	John Hamburger "	F. Bennett Mason City
C. F. Golter Campbell	E. Hozberg Gothenberg	John McIntosh Marquette
Jimmie Madsen "	Gerald Covett Gibbon	

C. E. Nelson Malcolm
John Wyman, Jr. Milford
W. R. Anderson McCool
Louis Schmidt Murdock
G. L. Kraeger Mynard
U. S. Dillon Nora
Andrew Theosen Norman
C. E. Allison Newark
John Akinso Nehawka
G. P. Pflasterer Overton
Miles Hurley Ohiowa
Wm. Kunecke O'Dell
F. A. Selby Oak City
W. H. Palmer Pauline
Wm. Gruhn Poole
K. Fisher Pickrell
A. C. Anderson Phillips
Wm. G. Pimps Plymouth
O. P. Helvey Powell
James Gilbron Prosser
A. F. Nobbman
Pleasant Dale
F. Boren Pawnee City
Wm. Gartner Roseland
Claude Rhoades Ravenna
M. W. Seckler Ragan
G. M. Clark Raymond
A. A. McKennan Roca
Elmer Thrasher Reynolds
Jerry Petersen Ruskin
L. L. Lasimer Raymond
A. Hackett Riverton
Johann Rose Rosemont
E. R. Rife Red Cloud
M. L. Moore Shelton
Ole Hansen Sutton
Chas. Krug Strang
C. F. Sissel Sheckley
E. D. Risden Stockham
John Godden Steele City
H. L. Conn Superior
John Zimmer Sweetwater
Hugh Pichrel Seward
Thos. Jelinek Wilber
A. T. Hutchinson
Waverly
A. T. Hansen
Weeping Water
Robert Preston York

NEW JERSEY

TAKES ADVANTAGE OF CHANCE

Pattersville, October 16th.

WROUGHT IRON RANGE CO., St. Louis, Mo.

Gentlemen:—

The "HOME COMFORT" Range I bought from you sometime ago is giving capital service. I was using one I bought from you 16 years ago and sold it to my son, and it is good for at least 25 years more. I bought this new one from your salesman when he was here, for I knew we don't get a chance to get them very often. I would be safe in saying that your "HOME COMFORT" is the best range in the world.

HORACE ULMER

PRESSURE TANK PROBLEM SOLVED

Woodstown, November 7th.

WROUGHT IRON RANGE CO., St. Louis, Mo.

Gentlemen:—

We have had our "HOME COMFORT" Range since 1914, and have been using it constantly since that time. Our oven is a most wonderful baker and the range-top has never warped a bit. The water system is the best we have ever used for our tank is always hot and ready. We will never use any other range.

MRS. W. A. COMBS

NO OTHER AT ANY PRICE

Woodstown, November 7th.

WROUGHT IRON RANGE CO., St. Louis, Mo.

Gentlemen:—

I just want to say that I have been using my "HOME COMFORT" Range for ten years, and I know it is all you claimed for it. I cannot say too much for it, for I have found it to be economical in fuel, a most splendid baker, and, in fact, a perfect range in every respect. Were I buying a new range today, it would be a "HOME COMFORT" and no other at any price.

MRS. N. STOKES EVANS

WORDS CANNOT EXPRESS IT

Yorktown, November 1st.

WROUGHT IRON RANGE CO., St. Louis, Mo.

Gentlemen:—

We bought our "HOME COMFORT" Range in 1914. Although we have used it constantly all this time, we haven't paid out a cent on it for repairs, and it is practically as good as new today. If we ever have to buy another range, it will certainly be another "HOME COMFORT," but words cannot express what we think of ours.

MRS. WM. HILES

NO REPAIRING NEEDED

Woodstown, October 31st.
WROUGHT IRON RANGE CO., St. Louis, Mo.
Gentlemen:—

I have been using my "HOME COMFORT" Range for 10 years, and it has proved satisfactory in every way. It has never cost me a penny for repairs.

MRS. E. A. LIPPENCOTT

DOUBLE PRICE WON'T BUY IT

Phalanz, January 23rd.
WROUGHT IRON RANGE CO., St. Louis, Mo.
Gentlemen:—

We have been using our "HOME COMFORT" Range since 1914. It heats, cooks and bakes perfectly, and we would not part with it for twice what we paid for it if we couldn't get another one like it.

DANIEL McCORMICK

SATISFIED IN EVERY WAY

East Vineland, November 10th.
WROUGHT IRON RANGE CO., St. Louis, Mo.
Gentlemen:—

Its 4 year we have the Range Stove and we find that it is very good. It satisfied me in every way. We nevery find anything wrong with it.

PETER DEL CONTE

THE ENVY OF THE NEIGHBORS

Juliustown, June 16th.
WROUGHT IRON RANGE CO., St. Louis, Mo.
Gentlemen:—

We think we have a beautiful range, for our "HOME COMFORT" is the envy of the neighbors. It is certainly a fine cooker, and is an ornament to any home.

F. C. ASHBOLT

Pavlo Masetto	Absecon	Fred Wolfe	Eaton Town	Ed. Bailey	Keyport	H. Fliender	Oakhurst
C. Giberson	Atsion	F. Smith	English Town	J. Meigt	Linecroft	J. Wildrick	Oxford
Angelo Cozzi	Atco	A. B. McMullen		C. Brown	Long Branch	A. Jencoll	Pomerania
Geo. Salts	Asbury		Egg Harbor City	P. Hunger	Long Valley	C. W. Howe	Pleasantville
K. Schanck	Adelphia	H. Grouser	E. Millstone	W. M. Strowbridge		Wm. Myers	Pittstown
A. Dubois	Andover	H. F. Bouchell			Liberty Corner	C. McPherson	Pemberton
W. L. Decker	Allamuchy		E. Stroudsburg	E. B. Phillips	Lakewood	E. Carror	Plainfield
F. G. Lucas	Browns Mills	B. Marks	Farmingdale	G. W. Burd	Lafayette	B. Sinkway	Port Murray
R. Boccello	Berlin	G. Makowski	Freehold	Wm. Spink	Mays Landing	J. H. Plummer	Quinton
Wm. N. Tilton	Belmar	R. Hartt	Fairhaven	A. King	Manasquan	John Kardis	Roebling
E. P. Bryan, Jr.		J. C. Conrad	Far Hills	J. Ravattini	Matawan	K. C. Taylor	Red Bank
	Boundbrook	J. C. Ackerman		Wm. Conway	Marlboro	Wm. Jenkins	Rockway
Frank Tiger	Brookside		Farmingdale	F. Huff	Morris Plains	K. Loeser	Rahway
Eunice DeHart	Bartley	Chas. Cornish	Gillette	John Nenham	Morristown	T. Desilvso	Sicklerville
M. Appallo	Bernardsville	F. Weber	Green Village	J. Paprillo	Mendham	Alek Kulesa	Sayreville
Steve Kerekes	Bridgeville	F. S. Anthony	Gladstone	A. Haverlick	Millington	J. Gubernat	S. Plainfield
Wm. Liepe	Cologne	G. Barabas	Gr. Meadows	H. A. Moore	Millington	Gus Quenzer	Springlake
Joe Graham	Cedar Brook	J. Deluca	Hammonton	L. Afgar	Middle Valley	D. Reevey	Shrewsberry
Geo. Bean	Califon	P. Curly	Holmdel	Wm. Wood	New Vernon	Walter Burdge	Stanhope
Laura Horton	Chester	Wm. Burdge		H. Mechkouchi		Odes Steele	Waterford
L. D. Gano			Herbertsville		New Brunswick	Regie Janto	Winslow
	Center Valley	C. Ervine	Hope	Hall Oder	Naughtright	Alb. Naabe	Williamstown
L. Traficante	Deans	Albert Drake		J. W. Heuse	Newton		
John Nagle	Dover		Hackettstown	H. E. Siebert		F. J. Howell	Wharton
Earl Smith	Delaware	G. Fuches	Ironia		New Providence	M. Crine	Wicatunk
R. Grasso	Elm	Louis Vogel	Jamesburg	J. Bohm	Old Bridge	M. Will	Westfield

NEW YORK

DROVE 17 MILES FOR HIS

Lyndonville, April 20th.
WROUGHT IRON RANGE CO., St. Louis, Mo.
Gentlemen:—

We recently bought a "HOME COMFORT" Range from your salesman, and it is giving perfect satisfaction. It is a good baker and certainly is a fuel saver. We had one neighbor drive 17 miles to get one of your Ranges, because he knew he would not be able to get a "HOME COMFORT" after your salesmen left this county.

MRS. WM. GEIGER

35 YEARS—GOOD FOR 20 MORE

Cedarhurst Farm, Ashville, October 28th.
WROUGHT IRON RANGE CO., St. Louis, Mo.
Gentlemen:—

I have and am using a "HOME COMFORT" Range that my grandfather purchased of your salesmen over 35 years ago, it being a No. CI. You may be interested in knowing that the only expense required to put this old-timer in good working order was a new copper cover for the reservoir and the renickeling of the fittings, a total cost of less than $5 for repairs for 35 years. The range now gives every indication of being good for at least 20 years longer.

EARLE W. GAGE

33 YEARS—CONDITION PERFECT

Clover Hill Fruit Farm, Penn Yan, April 12th.
WROUGHT IRON RANGE CO., St. Louis, Mo.
Gentlemen:—

I have a "HOME COMFORT" Range No. 65 which has been in constant use for 33 years, and it is still in perfect condition. We have needed almost no repairs for it in that entire time, and the work done by it has always been satisfactory. I never fail to recommend it.

R. LEE EDMONDS

NONE OTHER WOULD FILL BILL

Cedarhurst Farm, Stanfordville, October 15th.
WROUGHT IRON RANGE CO., St. Louis, Mo.
Gentlemen:—

The Range shipped by you has arrived in fine shape, is set up, been tested as to baking, etc., and is entirely satisfactory, as I expected it would be. All the parts were with it and fitted exactly. I am delighted with it and thank you for prompt service as well as it being exactly as advertised. I have used up one "HOME COMFORT" Range—not exactly, either, for it is still doing business—and when I thought of a new one, I could think of none that I thought would fill the bill, with this result. Thank you for your courtesy and service.

MRS. FLORENCE HOAG

"OLD TIME WONDER"

Cazenovia, January 1st.

Wrought Iron Range Co., St. Louis, Mo.

Gentlemen:—

I have installed the few repairs for our old "Home Comfort" Range and it is again the "old time wonder" that it has always been. Many thanks for shipping my order promptly.

Irv. T. Loveland

43 YEARS' FAITHFUL SERVICE

Lagrangeville, November 30th.

Wrought Iron Range Co., St. Louis, Mo.

Gentlemen:—

Some 10 years ago one of your salesmen stopped overnight with us and wanted us to buy a new "Home Comfort" Range, but as we had a "Home Comfort" of an early model, we could not think of making a change at that time. Our old Range has now seen 43 years of faithful service and still does good work, but we would like to get in touch with your salesman about a "Home Comfort" of latest model.

C. V. Brinkerhoff

WORTH TWICE ITS PRICE

New Hampton, April 2nd.

Wrought Iron Range Co., St. Louis, Mo.

Gentlemen:—

I would not part with my "Home Comfort" Range for twice the amount I paid for it.

Mrs. Albert Hawkins

Frank Baity Auburn	C. G. Simons Genesee	H. Thurston Moravia	Salem Deuel Stanley
Thos. Cullen Aurora	G. A. DeForest Genoa	T. Higgins McGraw	Floyd Morris Shortsville
Harry Lyons Avoca	Frank Woodard	Fred Boldt Marathon	T. M. Hagan Savannah
F. E. Hurd Belmont	Great Valley	Leland Gardner	E. Yates South Butler
Will Baldwin Bolivar	C. Davenport Groton	Mt. Morris	Mrs. P. May Savannah
W. Kostyshak	Joseph Huber Geneseo	S. B. Smith Mehoopany	V. O. Snover
Binghamton	J. Hobart Gorham	G. M. Burr Meshappen	Skinners Eddy
Hilson Brothers	Ray Van Fleet	Algia Shaw Nunda	C. Williams Sicklerville
Bovina Center	Greenwood	E. Graff Naples	L. Spencer Towanda
E. M. Fox Beaver Dams	J. F. Wallace Hornell	H. E. Judson Newport	E. C. Lincoln Taylor
H. A. Conley Branchport	B. Bowen	J. Hewitt Olean	D. A. Cruver
H. F. Boggs	Honeoye Falls	L. H. Stone Powell	Tunkhannock
Bristol Center	R. L. Redfield Homer	W. A. Powner	Webber Kamp Tuscarora
Geo. La Fever Cuba	Peter Barbacki	Princeton Jct.	J. F. Morey Troupsburg
Mark Abbey	Hamburg	B. Doran Portville	Earl Weed Ulster
Columbia Cr. Rds.	C. B. Jones Holcomb	M. R. McNair	Allen Cass Union Valley
Mrs. A. Scofield Conklin	Arthur Daggett Hall	Port Byron	H. Green Victor
A. C. Bash	F. A. Carlson	Chas. Wilde Pittsford	John Ordiway Willsville
Conewago Valley	Hammondsport	C. E. Tears Pennyan	Alin Cobb Wyalusing
Lucy Jones Cayuga	Harry Stevens	M. Kammer Palmyra	S. W. May Wellersburg
J. F. Ford Cato	Hopewell Junction	C. G. Taylor Quakertown	P. L. Ransom Wysox
L. D. Rowe Cincinnatus	Albert Elder Nimrod	O. S. Lawrence Richburg	C. O. Parish Weedsport
J. Leonard Carbondale	Clayton Marlatt Jasper	L. E. Cannon Rome	A. C. Ransford
Earl Stones Conesus	F. V. Edson Jordan	Allen O'Bryan Red Creek	Whitney Point
J. March Canandaigua	F. N. Thurston	Elmer Ferguson Rush	D. D. Donavon
C. L. Maslyn	Kirkwood	R. A. Clark Rushville	Webster's Crossing
Clifton Springs	H. Rafferty King Ferry	W. Hardenrider	Geo. Bill Wayland
George Miller Cohocton	R. Cruthers Locke	Rexville	A. R. Steele W. Henrietta
T. Noble Clyde	Thos. B. O'Neal	C. W. Howe Rome	Elmer Schlottman
F. H. Palmer Dryden	Lake Clear Jct.	David Bell Rushville	W. Henrietta
Chas. Acombe Dansville	J. J. Farron Lima	E. J. Baker Scio	James Davis Wolcott
M. C. Rose Dundee	C. Vandius Lodus	C. A. Pennay Stevensville	Cornich DeMinck
E. M. Bishop Ensenore	E. Zegers Lyons	E. Switzer Sennett	Wolworth
C. Persins E. Palmyra	J. G. Carter Laceville	Aden Gilbert Solon	Howard Crosby Wayne
Geo. Elston Friendship	A. E. Wright	P. Fisher Springwater	Ray Perry Watkins
P. G. Strong	Machias Jct.	G. E. Meyer	J. G. Clark Waterloo
Franklinville	H. D. Slade Moravia	Skaneateless	S. E. Iraman Wayland
J. Putkowski Florida	E. Thurston Montezuma	E. Milliman Scottsburg	

NORTH CAROLINA

GREAT FUEL SAVER

Forest City, April 3rd.

Wrought Iron Range Co., St. Louis, Mo.

Gentlemen:—

The new Enameled "Home Comfort" Range we purchased last fall has given the best of satisfaction. We find it to be a great fuel saver, a perfect baker, and the best Range we have ever used.

Joe L. Doggett

HE COULD HAVE SAVED MONEY

Selma, May 3rd.

Wrought Iron Range Co., St. Louis, Mo.

Gentlemen:—

We purchased a "Home Comfort" Range from you several years ago and can say that it has not cost us one cent for repairs during all this time and has given perfect satisfaction in every respect. It is in good condition today. In the past, we have spent a considerable sum of money for other stoves and repairs, but never owned one that gave us the satisfaction of our "Home Comfort." We cheerfully recommend the "Home Comfort" as being a great labor saver as well as a fuel saver to anyone needing a range.

S. T. Thorn

NO BETTER PURCHASE

Merrill, April 9th.

Wrought Iron Range Co., St. Louis, Mo.

Gentlemen:—

Nearly a year ago we installed one of your Enameled Model "Home Comfort" Ranges. We have found it to be exactly as represented, and one of the most valuable pieces of furniture we have in our house. It has certainly solved the cooking problem for my family, and I am sure I could not have made a better purchase in a cooking appliance.

George Schultheis

EXACTLY AS REPRESENTED

Wrought Iron Range Co., St. Louis, Mo.
Gentlemen:—

Several months ago I bought one of your Enameled "Home Comfort" Ranges, which has been in constant daily use in our kitchen. We find it to be exactly as represented, and besides being very beautiful, it has proved to be a perfect baker as recommended. We certainly do not regret having installed it.　　　　　　　　　Mike L. Borders

SAVES MANY STEPS

Rutherfordton, March 26th.
Wrought Iron Range Co., St. Louis, Mo.
Gentlemen:—

I am more than pleased with my Enameled Model "Home Comfort" Range, which I bought from your salesman last September. It is so easy to keep clean, bakes to perfection, and saves quite a little fuel in cooking. The hot water reservoir is one of the most convenient features of the Range and saves a great many steps. I would not want to give my range up.　　　Mrs. Stella Culbreth

$85 FOR EXPERIENCE

Dunn, March 3rd.
Wrought Iron Range Co., St. Louis, Mo.
Gentlemen:—

I bought one of your "Home Comfort" Ranges in 1900, and used it 22 years with perfect satisfaction. At the end of that time, we decided to have a new range in our kitchen, bu: your salesmen were not in this territory, so we bought a range of another make, paying $85.00 for it. We used it only 1 year. We now have one of your Enameled "Home Comfort" Ranges, and I am sure that it is the best range made for efficiency and economy, and has no equal on earth.

G. J. Hodges

BEST MONEY CAN BUY

Dunn, February 26.
Wrought Iron Range Co., St. Louis, Mo.
Gentlemen:—

I have a 1915 Model "Home Comfort" Range. It has been in daily use, and I have found it to be perfect in every respect, and exactly as it was represented to us. While it is still in good condition, I could not resist buying one of your New Enameled Ranges from your salesman when he recently called. I know that it is the very best range that money can buy.　　　　　　Mrs. Annie Dunn

NOT CONTENTED WITHOUT ONE

Windsor, April 16.
Wrought Iron Range Co., St. Louis, Mo.
Gentlemen:—

After using a "Home Comfort" Range for many years, we bought a 1919 Model on account of its improvements. Both Ranges have always proved to be exactly as your salesman represented them to us, both being fine bakers, great fuel savers, to say nothing of the convenience of hot water supply and other features. I could not be without a "Home Comfort" Range in my kichen, and be contented.

Mrs. Frank Parker

40 YEARS—NO SUBSTITUTE GOES

Brandywine, March 18.
Wrought Iron Range Co., St. Louis, Mo.
Gentlemen:—

The "Home Comfort" Range we bought from you about 40 years ago has at last given up its useful life, and we must have another "Home Comfort," or eat our food raw; for there is no other range made that can take its place. Please have your salesman, if he is near this vicinity, call and take our order. We want one of your new Model Enameled Ranges, and when we get it, we will consider that our cooking problem is solved for another 40 years.

John D. Keister

THE MOST SUCCESSFUL

Uree, March 22nd.
Wrought Iron Range Co., St. Louis, Mo.
Gentlemen:—

We have now had our Enameled "Home Comfort" Range nearly a year, and it is certainly proving well worth the price I paid for it. My family thinks it is a real comfort, for it is the most successful cooker and baker we have ever owned.

George Whiteside

HE NOW KNOWS WHY

Dunn, March 13th.
Wrought Iron Range Co., St. Louis, Mo.
Gentlemen:—

I bought a "Home Comfort" Range in 1919, and it has given perfect satisfaction in every way. We now know why they are called the best range, and we would have no other make. I expect this range to last us for many, many years.

Y. E. Irey

SOLVES COOKING PROBLEM

Tawas City, April 1st.
Wrought Iron Range Co., St. Louis, Mo.
Gentlemen:—

The new Enameled Model "Home Comfort" Range I bought from your salesman in February is now giving perfect satisfaction in our kitchen. It has certainly proved a great comfort to my family as well as justifying the recommendation that was given it. I do not think that I could have made a better investment in a piece of cooking equipment, and I believe that our cooking problem is solved for many years to come.

Robert Watts

30 YEARS—CONSTANT USE

Cary, April 10th.
Wrought Iron Range Co., St. Louis, Mo.
Gentlemen:—

I am now using a "Home Comfort" Range that has been in constant use for over 30 years. It has always been a perfect baker and cooker, and has always proved to be as it was recommended to us in the beginning. I think this is ample proof that it is the very best kitchen range made, for I know of no other that would ever equal this record.

Mary J. Woodward

A PROUD FAMILY

Posen, April 21st.
Wrought Iron Range Co., St. Louis, Mo.
Gentlemen:—

We are certainly well pleased with our Enameled "Home Comfort" Range. It is certainly a beauty, and my family is very proud of it. I know I shall receive many years of perfect cooking service from it, for the "Home Comfort" Range has always borne a reputation for long service and perfect work.

William Christopenson

COMPLETE SATISFACTION

Pageland, April 10th.
Wrought Iron Range Co., St. Louis, Mo.
Gentlemen:—

I have had my Enameled "Home Comfort" over a year, and I want to say that it has certainly been a source of much satisfaction. Its beauty, economy, and service have been all that they were represented to be, and I certainly do not regret buying it. It is a wonderful baker, and surely saves many steps in the kitchen.

Mrs. N. D. Terry

NO BETTER CHOICE

Spratt, March 22nd.

Wrought Iron Range Co., St. Louis, Mo.

Gentlemen:—

I wish to say that the new Enameled Model "Home Comfort" Range which we are now using, is giving perfect satisfaction, and we have found it to be as represented by your salesman. I do not believe I could have made a better choice in buying a Range, and certainly do not regret having done so.

W. E. Barlow

50 YEARS—SAME PIPE

Denim, January 15.

Wrought Iron Range Co., St. Louis, Mo.

Gentlemen:—

I have used one of your "Home Comfort" Ranges for over 50 years, and have never paid out anything for repairs; in fact, the same pipe that came with it was still on it when we replaced it with a new one a short time ago. I can certainly recommend the "Home Comfort," and will not have any other make.

Mrs. Mary Galend

25 YEARS—NONE SUPERIOR

Woodville, April 9th.

Wrought Iron Range Co., St. Louis, Mo.

Gentlemen:—

In 1909 I bought a "Home Comfort" Range from your salesman, and it has always proved very highly satisfactory, and is still in usable condition. However, when your salesman recently showed us the New Enamel "Home Comfort" we bought one so that we might possess the very best range on the market today. I am sure there is no superior range made.

T. I. Phelps

40 YEARS—STILL GOING

Lurinburg, February 5th.

Wrought Iron Range Co., St. Louis, Mo.

Gentlemen:—

In the year of 1884 we bought one of your "Home Comfort" Ranges from one of your salesmen. Three meals a day have been cooked on it ever since we bought it, and it is in splendid condition now. I feel that several sales have been made in this neighborhood by seeing it and hearing us explain what a wonder it is.

A. A. Leitch

20 YEARS—STILL FAITHFUL

Dunn, March 7th.

Wrought Iron Range Co., St. Louis, Mo.

Gentlemen:—

I used my "Home Comfort" Range since 1905, and I would not part with it today for the price we paid for it. I know it is certainly the best range ever made, for it has always given faithful service, being an ideal baker and great fuel saver, and perfect in every respect. If I ever replace this one, it will surely be with a New "Home Comfort."

Mrs. J. H. Sorrell

NO KITCHEN COMPLETE WITHOUT IT

Unionville, March 27th.

Wrought Iron Range Co., St. Louis, Mo.

Gentlemen:—

I bought one of your Enamel "Home Comfort" Ranges in January, 1924, and have found it to be as represented. It has proved a great comfort to my family, and we do not consider any kitchen complete without a "Home Comfort" Range. I certainly do not regret buying it.

J. A. Rushing

GIVING ENTIRE SATISFACTION

Rocky Mount, October 26th.

Wrought Iron Range Co., St. Louis, Mo.

Gentlemen:—

I bought a "Home Comfort" Range from one of your traveling salesmen 8 years ago and it has given entire satisfaction. I found the range as represented and would advise anyone who needs a range to look into the merits of the "Home Comfort" before purchasing another make.

Joseph Murry

MORE PROOF

Benson, March 3.

Wrought Iron Range Co., St. Louis, Mo.

Gentlemen:—

We have used one of your "Home Comfort" Ranges for the past 6 years, and take great pleasure in recommending it as the best cooking appliance we have ever used. It has always given perfect satisfaction in every way, and we have found it to be exactly as it was recommended to us.

Mr. and Mrs. J. H. Hodges

"NO BETTER RANGE BUILT"

Dunn, March 12th.

Wrought Iron Range Co., St. Louis, Mo.

Gentlemen:—

We are using the "Home Comfort" Range I bought in 1904, and I can cheerfully say that the "Home Comfort" is the greatest range made for comfort, convenience, and wearing qualities. I am sure there is no better range built, and for that reason I recently gave your salesman an order for one of your New Enamel Models. Our old range proved to be everything a range should be, and exactly as represented to us, and I am sure there cannot be a better range than your New Model "Home Comfort" made by any one.

J. P. Jackson

31 YEARS—NO REPAIRS

Selica, May 24th

Wrought Iron Range Co., St. Louis, Mo.

Gentlemen:—

The "Home Comfort" Range is what your company represents it to be. I say this after 5 years' personal use of one and seeing my family use one for 31 years before I got mine. They have never spent a penny for repairs.

Mrs. W. C. McCod

CANNOT BE EQUALED

Dunn, April 14.

Wrought Iron Range Co., St. Louis, Mo.

Gentlemen:—

We have a 1918 model "Home Comfort" Range. For efficiency, economy, and convenience in the kitchen, it certainly cannot be equaled. We would not use another unless it were impossible to get a "Home Comfort."

Mr. and Mrs. W. A. West

WOULD NOT DENY FAMILY

Duke, March 2.

Wrought Iron Range Co., St. Louis, Mo.

Gentlemen:—

My 1918 Model "Home Comfort" Range has always given perfect service in every way. It has been a faithful baker, and heater, supplying plenty of hot water in the reservoir; and I honestly would not take what I gave for it and force my family to use some other range.

N. A. Sawyer

J. A. Rawls	Aulander	I. V. Outlaw	Goldsboro	W. L. Hill	Marshville	T. Ramsey	Seaboard
H. McCowan	Ayden	P. D. Butler	Gates	J. N. Barbee		J. E. Hagwood	
Newitt Allen	Angier	J. H. Hall	Gatesville		Mt. Croughan		Spring Hope
Geo. Hall	Akaskie	L. D. Wood	Garner	C. J. Jones	Mt. Holly	E. Oneal	Speed
F. F. Lee	Ansonville	W. H. Olds	Grifton	Andrew Fowler	Monroe	W. H. Wynne	Stokes
J. C. Bowen	Ashville	J. L. Camp	Garysburg	D. J. Doleson	Marion	W. H. Heath	Snow Hill
G. A. Cox	Blounts Creek	W. Edmond	Gumberry	W. S. Waters	Mooresboro	C. D. Whitley	
E. H. Shepherd	Bath	Lane Lovick	Grimesland	R. Williams	Nealsville		Red Boiling Springs
M. C. Mullen	Bunn	C. C. Quick	Ghio	H. G. Gragg	North Cove	Albert Cherry	"
A. C. Johnson	Benson	W. H. Norton	Gibson	W. J. Warren	Neuse	W. W. Gray	Ruth
A. K. Boykin	Bailey	W. T. Bowen	Grover	G. W. Hardee	Ogden	J. C. Buff	"
J. L. Lewis	Blounts	H. C. McGinnis	Henrietta	O. G. Lewpelton	Olin	A. H. Early	"
W. J. Perry	Bailey	L. C. Price	Hollis	E. C. Chews	Osborne		Rutherfordton
R. M. Cracker	Bethel	R. Logan	Harris	W. O. Stubbs		T. D. Keeter	"
D. P. O'Neil	Bridgewater	A. L. Oakes	Hookerton		Old Hundred	Fred McCloud	
Paul Klutz	Blowing Rock	J. H. Boyd	Halifax	W. W. Parker	Old Fort		Sherrills Ford
S. J. White	Bessemer City	W. I. Porter	Hollister	C. W. Gaddy	Peachland	J. H. Godfrey	Sevier
Joe Sain	Bellwood	J. B. Watson		W. E. Davis	Polkton	G. T. Wright	Shelby
W. Wray	Boiling Springs		Harrellsville	W. H. Parker	"	H. L. Roberts	"
I. B. Lovelace	Bostic	H. T. Hopewell	Hassell	L. H. Morris	Pinetown	D. D. Dixon	Tarboro
W. F. Edwards	Colerain	O. T. Everett	Hamilton	D. R. Tucker	Pee Dee	J. A. House	Thelma
T. C. Cox	Cove City	L. Deloatch	Henrico	Andrew Tillman	" "	O. McDaniel	Trenton
J. A. Walker	Conetoe	J. F. Peek	Ingalls	P. Peacock	Princeton	W. E. Britton	Tunis
M. J. Riley	Como	Chas. Simpson	Jamesville	E. Chesson	Plymouth	J. A. York	Unionville
G. C. Dove	Cary	Mrs. M. B. DeLoach		G. Carter	Pink Hill	J. R. Little	"
R. C. Chaplin	Conway		Jackson	G. N. Parks	Pikeville	D. D. Davis	Union Mills
Glenn Morrow	Claremont	John Earp	Kenly	H. Wadford	Princeton	T. W. Geer	" "
W. J. Head	Center Point	P. B. Worley	Kinston	E. N. Edwards		J. W. Conner	Uree
S. J. Self	Casar	C. A. Smith	Kelford		Pleasant Hill	T. R. Searcy	"
I. Lancaster	Caroleen	R. B. Waterson		A. E. Bridges	Potecasi	R. E. Cleaton	Vultari
C. B. Honeycutt	Davidson		Kings Mountain	B. E. Jenkins	Parmele	J. H. Harris	Vanceboro
John Perry	Charlotte	W. S. Jernigan	Lewiston	E. F. Smoot	Rosemary	W. J. Paul	Wadesboro
W. A. Eubanks	Dover	W. S. Bell	Louisburg	C. T. Harrell	Roxobel	T. A. Gaudy	"
W. E. Cross	Drum Hall	S. F. Howell	Lilesville	C. E. Philps	Roduco	L. L. Wakefield	Willette
L. Outlaw	Deep Run	L. Smith	Lincolnton	J. W. Mills	Richlands	C. E. Griffin	Wingate
T. N. Eure	Eure	G. B. Brown	Lafayette	G. T. Roebucks		F. N. Shepard	
G. W. Harper	Enfield	A. M. Dove	Lattimore		Robersonville		Washington
A. H. Clayton	Edwards	R. A. White	Lawndale	J. N. Small	Raleigh	David Smith	Winterville
Sam Stulls	Edgemont	W. E. Carson	Littleton	Col. K. R. Davis		L. T. Bond	Windsor
W. D. Earl	Earl	J. Braxton	LaGrange		Seven Springs	J. E. Britton	Woodville
D. C. Waters	Ellenboro	C. C. Parker	Lasker	R. E. Parker	Rich Square	W. A. Todlach	Woodard
J. S. Mallory	Fletcher	W. S. Murray	Mebane	E. T. Welsh	Speed	S. J. Smith	Whitakers
Lem Williams	Fallston	James Lee	Merry Hill	J. P. Massey	Spring Hope	Lee Jones	Wakefield
W. L. Hunt	Forest City	W. V. Sanders	McCullers	Geo. Perry	Snow Hill	M. Turner	Weldon
W. S. Tugwill	Farmville	J. B. Creech	Middlesex	C. L. Garner	Selma	A. L. Weaver	Winton
B. L. Townsend		R. J. Jones	Mt. Olive	C. L. Sanders		G. W. White	Williamston
	Fair Bluff	A. Faison			Smithfield	Mrs. D. T. Lee	Wendell
W. N. Lee	Four Oaks		Margarettsville	W. F. Kirby	Sims	J. I. Adams	Winterville
S. E. Sasser	Fremont	P. L. Teal	Morven	B. W. Smith	Saulston	G. R. Barnes	Zebulon

NORTH DAKOTA

32 YEARS—NO REPAIRS

Blanchard, May 26th.

Wrought Iron Range Co., St. Louis, Mo.

Gentlemen:—

I have a "Home Comfort" Range that I think has a record. I have had it in daily use for 32 years now, and it still has the first reservoir, first grate and the first lids just like we bought it from your salesman. If there is another stove or range that can beat my old faithful "Home Comfort", please let me know.

Mrs. Emil Holzkamm

KNOWS THEY'RE UNBEATABLE

Sherwood, March 2nd.

Wrought Iron Range Co., St. Louis, Mo.

Gentlemen:—

With this letter is my order for a few repairs for my "Home Comfort" Range. I have now used my range 19 years, and this is the first cent I have been out for repairs. Some of my neighbors have bought new stoves of other makes which have been repeatedly repaired since I bought my "Home Comfort".

My son wants to see your salesman at first opportunity, as he is now ready for a new range and will have nothing but a "Home Comfort". Like me, he knows they cannot be beat.

John Wallstrum

OHIO

THERE'S NO SUBSTITUTE

Lancaster, July 27th.

Wrought Iron Range Co., St. Louis, Mo.

Gentlemen:—

I purchased a "Home Comfort" Range 22 years ago and it is about as good today as the day it was bought, and for boiling and baking it has no equal. I would say to my neighbors and friends, and those who are thinking of buying a stove or Range they will make no mistake by buying a "Home Comfort". I would not take $150.00 in cash if I could not get another one like it.

S. B. Halderman

HE KNEW ITS WORTH

Batavia, October 15th.

Wrought Iron Range Co., St. Louis, Mo.

Gentlemen:—

I have bought out Mr. Lester and am assuming his contract with you for a "Home Comfort" Range. My mother has one of your ranges and has used it 18 years and it is a good range today. That is why I am glad to take it.

Roy Franks

HAS ORIGINAL GRATE

Aberdeen, September 20th.

Wrought Iron Range Co., St. Louis, Mo.

Gentlemen:—

I have used a "Home Comfort" Range for nearly 30 years; it has been in constant use all these years. The same grate and back wall are in it that was bought with it. I have this day bought a new one for the improvements and will say they save fuel and are a great comfort to the housewife. I can recommend them to my friends and neighbors.

Thos. S. Shelton

WILL HAVE NO OTHER

Manchester, April 10th.

Wrought Iron Range Co., St. Louis, Mo.

Gentlemen:—

I have a "Home Comfort" Range that I have used 10 years and can say it is perfect in every way and as good as new today. I would not have it taken out of my kitchen for the price I paid for it. If it was worn out I would buy a new "Home Comfort".

Mrs. Della Pense

"CAN DEPEND UPON THEM"

Gambier, May 1st.

Wrought Iron Range Co., St. Louis, Mo.

Gentlemen:—

I am glad that there is a firm in this country of ours that sells a Range that we can depend upon. The "Home Comfort" does all you say it will do, and more. We are certainly pleased with ours and we never fail to praise it.

Chas. Benedict

BURNS WOOD AND COAL

Newark, June 23rd.

Wrought Iron Range Co., St. Louis, Mo.

Gentlemen:—

I have had in constant use in my home since October, 1889, one of your "Home Comfort" Ranges purchased from one of your wagons and can cheerfully say it has given perfect satisfaction. I burn wood through the summer and coal during the winter months. Anyone that wants the best, don't hesitate to buy the "Home Comfort" Range, for it is second to none.

Elizabeth Allison

HIS MONEY IS SAFER

Keene, January 15th.

Wrought Iron Range Co., St. Louis, Mo.

Gentlemen:—

Twenty-seven years ago, I purchased one of your "Home Comfort" Ranges which has always been entirely satisfactory and exactly as it was represented. My family wants a new range, and I have decided to buy them one. Local hardware merchants handle ranges of advertised retail makes, and have tried to sell me one; but my family wants a new "Home Comfort", and I certainly feel safer in putting my money into the "Home Comfort" than any other range, for I know I will not make a mistake. Please have your nearest salesman call on me as soon as possible.

James Layman

A FIRM BELIEVER

Walhonding, January 9th.

Wrought Iron Range Co., St. Louis, Mo.

Gentlemen:—

I bought a "Home Comfort" Range from your salesman some time ago and we are more than satisfied with it. I would not take the price I paid for it and do without its conveniences, baking and fuel saving. If I ever give up farming, I want to sell "Home Comfort" Ranges for you, for I believe anyone who believes in them as I do, can surely sell them.

J. E. Hagans

15 YEARS—NO REPAIRS

New London, March 10th.

Wrought Iron Range Co., St. Louis, Mo.

Gentlemen:—

A few days ago one of your salesmen working shape regardless of heat or cold; good worked "Home Comfort" Model. I would certainly like to have your new Range, but I have a "Home Comfort" bought 15 years ago from one of your wagons. It is still in fine shape, although we have never done a thing to it since we owned it in the way of repairs. It promises to last us for several years yet, and when we replace this one, it will surely be with a New Enameled "Home Comfort" Range.

Mrs. P. Brewster

GRANDFATHER'S RANGE

Gallipolis, January 19th.

Wrought Iron Range Co., St. Louis, Mo.

Gentlemen:—

I would like to know if you can furnish me a few repairs for my "Home Comfort" Range which is one of the earliest ranges you made. It was originally bought by my grandfather when I was a little girl, over 40 years ago, and was given to me when I was married, 20 years ago. I have never cooked a meal on any other range except this one, and with a few repairs it will last for several years yet. When your salesman visits this territory the next time, I wish you would have him call on me and show me the "Home Comfort" with its latest improvements. I expect to keep my old range always but it would be nice to have a new range also.

Mrs. Allen Jones

DOES NOT CHANGE

Pickerington, June 20th.

Wrought Iron Range Co., St. Louis, Mo.

Gentlemen:—

I hereby certify that I purchased from one of your traveling salesmen one of your "Home Comforts" and I am glad to say that this range has been in service for the past 23 years, cooking three meals per day during that time. I can recommend them in the highest terms for always retaining shape regardless of heat or cold. Good workmanship, material and longevity. My stove is practically in as good condition as when taken from wagon.

Mrs. Frank Taylor

LASTS A LIFETIME

Cheshire, March 16th.

Wrought Iron Range Co., St. Louis, Mo.

Gentlemen:—

This is to certify that I have been using a "Home Comfort" Range for about 10 years. It gives entire satisfaction in all respects. If this one that I now have does not outlast me, I will have another. But, from all indications, it will outlast me. I would advise anyone that needs a stove to buy a "Home Comfort" Range, as there is none better.

Mrs. W. C. Reed

USED TWO GENERATIONS

Jefferson, June 29th.

WROUGHT IRON RANGE CO., St. Louis, Mo.

Gentlemen:—

Meeting your representative here today, I had to tell him my experience with one of your "HOME COMFORT" Ranges I traded for in 1892. I bought a new cast iron range in the year 1890. I will not mention name, but paid $45.00 for same, and it was considered first-class; used it two years burning wood, coal and coke, and at the end of two years it was badly cracked and warped on top and the grate burned out. I then had a chance to trade for one of your "HOME COMFORTS". I used this stove for several years burning wood, coal and coke in it. I later moved to Buffalo, N. Y., and used gas for fuel there and after that moved to Ohio and used coal and wood until 1908. In 1906 my son was married and his wife had a favorite stove she thought she wanted. They bought same, paying fifty dollars for it (cast iron) in 1907. They came to live with me and his wife used our old "HOME COMFORT" for a while and said she would give up, it was the best stove she ever saw. In 1908 I held an auction and was to sell everything. My son's wife asked me if I would trade stoves with her and let her sells hers in place of the old "HOME COMFORT". Of course I said "yes" and they have the stove today and you could not get it for any other make in the world.

H. R. WEBSTER

George Stauffer Ashland	S. J. Buler E. Claridon	A. G. Sheldon Mantua	M. A. Brown Rock Creek
Leo Mote Austinburg	A. L. Bastian E. Sparta	Harvey Sherer Magnolia	H. M. Hubbard "
F. D. Smith Ashtabula	Lenard Mark E. Canton	G. E. Morison	C. H. Hutton Ravenna
James Conley Amelia	Chas. Brown Freedom	Marshallville	Fayette Clark Rome
Tom Kinsey Augusta	Lewis Craft Farmdale	O. H. Irwin Middlefield	Howard Haskins "
S. M. Faloon Alliance	Geo. Stoltz Geneva	F. C. Hosmer "	M. C. Bemer Shenodville
Homer Buchanan	C. Benedict Gambier	L. E. Rhodes Montville	Lloyd W. Stratton
Amsterdam	B. F. Thrasher	H. Korntzky Madison	Springfield
W. H. Heckman Atwater	Garrettsville	H. E. Shrader Massillon	Fred Weingart Salem
A. Maurer Apple Creek	Mike Surak Garard	Thomas Edgar New Lyme	W. E. Frederick "
L. H. Critchfield	W. P. Coy Greenford	Geo. W. Crook	W. C. Harvis Salineville
Big Prarie	Bertram Dale Harrison	New Waterford	L. E. Broods Andover
W. E. Uhler Burbank	Ira Gohley Homeworth	Leonel Smith Neward	Hershel M. Bell Signal
C. R. Stanley Beloit	E. E. Reeder Hanoverton	James M. Romig	James Ingram Shilog
A. J. Cormany	Robt. Brown Homerville	New Cumberland	J. T. Arnold Seville
Barberton	N. W. Dayton Hiren	Ray Snyder N. London	J. S. Hartman
R. S. Hawkins	G. F. Carson Hubbard	O. C. Coure "	Sharon Center
Berlin Center	C. E. Roberts Huntsburg	R. H. Wilson	O. E. Thompson Spencer
W. Stafford Burton	J. S. Brunbaugh	Newton Falls	W. R. Wilkin Suffield
T. J. Holmes Barton	Hartville	P. T. Bender N. Benton	W. A. Boreman Shreve
Cyrus Singer Bowdil	D. R. Aber Jeromeville	C. D. Bailey "	S. E. Conrad Sterling
W. A. Lewis Conneaut	T. B. Mead Jefferson	Mrs. M. A. Schulz	P. R. Musser Smithville
E. J. Swape Carrollton	J. A. Waugh Kensington	North Jackson	S. A. Smith Tyrell
W. E. Brown Columbiana	Samuel Telfer Kilfore	Floyd Johnson	A. Brockway Thompson
E. F. Selsor Camden	Ed. Esinger Kent	New Springfield	C. D. Nilber "
A. Bender College Corner	Emerson Burr Kinsman	Perry C. Jones Niles	R. M. Adams Uniontown
L. F. Duecker Copely	C. C. Strine Laudonville	H. Shew North Industry	A. L. Ogram
Wm. Ruddy	Lute Lodge Leetonia	P. H. Nelker	Williamsfield
Chippewa Lake	W. H. Craig Lisbon	New Middleton	E. J. Dodge "
Cliff Bauman Cortland	R. E. Richards Lodi	M. A. Woods Navarre	R. W. Wilson Windsor
J. L. Smith Croton	B. W. Sly Lockwood	Bert Wiswell Oakfield	J. A. McIntosh Wellsville
Emery Lawrence Copely	J. W. Snyder Louisville	B. F. Brock Oxford	J. E. Bunfield "
J. McDonald Canfield	F. Wheadon Magnolia	G. W. Venousdale "	Wm. Little Willoughby
Wm. Kempe Chardon	Don Manfull	B. F. Geiser Orville	F. J. Ebeling "
H. E. Little Chagrin Falls	Mechanicstown	L. E. Parrott Perryville	C. J. Moore Wadsworth
Ray F. Gill Canton	Harry Masters Malvern	C. H. VanCopper "	A. Fleming Windham
T. Arcaro Canal Fulton	Fred Rukenbrod "	T. M. Huntley Pierpont	W. N. Hileman W. Salem
L. T. Harklers Dorset	C. E. Hartman Maximo	John Blank "	W. D. Boothe Wayland
J. H. Martin Dellroy	Russell Haidet "	Frank Bener Portsmouth	Albert Ernest Warren
Ed. Thomas Dalton	W. Smith Mt. Sterling	C. Hladik Painsville	A. Henry W. Farmington
L. Roudebush Doylestown	G. Purdy Mansfield	Christ Parry "	L. A. Henshaw Wooster
B. B. Faust E. Orwell	J. B. Stull Mt. Vernon	D. L. Kneisly Perry	Evan W. Jones
C. E. Elliott Eagleville	Fk. Flecknoe " "	John Deckleman "	Waynesburg
W. D. Hart Eaton	A. Lee Madison	D. T. Morris Phalanx Sta.	R. E. Wilson
Willis Burt E. Palestine	R. T. McCune "	C. H. Cunningham	Youngstown
Arlie B. Miller	Jacob Munz Montor	Rochester	W. A. Chubb "
Ellsworth Sta.	J. C. Burnett "	L. L. Porter Poland	
L. T. Byers Eaton	D. L. Dressler Medina	Herm. Bader Petersburg	

OKLAHOMA

HAS NEW ENAMEL MODEL

McAlester, December 29th.

WROUGHT IRON RANGE CO., St. Louis, Mo.

Gentlemen:—

My New Enameled "HOME COMFORT" Range is giving such good satisfaction that I am delighted. It is such a fuel saver and does such good baking. Everything your salesman told me about it has proved to be just that way.

MRS. T. W. BROWN

TWENTY YEARS UNDER HEAVY DUTY

Kingfisher, January 3rd.

WROUGHT IRON RANGE CO., St. Louis, Mo.

Gentlemen:—

We have used our "HOME COMFORT" Range for over 20 years. While our range has always been under heavy duty, it has always given us complete satisfaction. If there is a better range built, I'll insure it has a "HOME COMFORT" trade-mark on it.

F. GUINN

TEN YEARS—LIKE NEW

Kingfisher, January 3rd.
WROUGHT IRON RANGE Co., St. Louis, Mo.
Gentlemen:—
We have had our "HOME COMFORT" Range for 10 years and it seems to be as good as the day we bought it. It has given us perfect satisfaction in every way and we would not think of doing without it.

F. M. McMILLAN

A BETTER RANGE NOT MADE

Union City, January 6th.
WROUGHT IRON RANGE Co., St. Louis, Mo.
Gentlemen:—
I bought our "HOME COMFORT" Range in 1890 and it always gave us perfect satisfaction in every way. I have this day given your salesman my order for one of your new Enameled Model "HOME COMFORTS" because my experience has taught me that money cannot buy a better range, for a better range is not made. We look forward to the many, many years of satisfied service we got from our first one.

H. F. ALBERTS

WOULD NOT PART WITH IT

Banner, January 9th.
WROUGHT IRON RANGE Co., St. Louis, Mo.
Gentlemen:—
I have used my "HOME COMFORT" Range 10 years and I have always found it to be a perfect baker and a great fuel saver. Its many conveniences, such as the warming closets, hot-water reservoir, and the even heat of its level top, have given me much comfort and satisfaction and made my work so much lighter. I would part with almost anything in my house before I would separate from my "HOME COMFORT" Range.

MRS. W. V. HAVERLY

THEY KNOW BEYOND DOUBT

Calumet, January 8th.
WROUGHT IRON RANGE Co., St. Louis, Mo.
Gentlemen:—
Our folks at home having used a "HOME COMFORT" Range for many, many years, and knowing beyond doubt of its superior quality and long term of service, we have recently installed the new Enameled Range bought from your salesman and find it all you claim for it. We do not believe there is a range in the world that is superior to the "HOME COMFORT" or can even begin to match it.

MR. and MRS. C. J. HANSEN

SAVED COST IN FUEL

Geary, January 5th.
WROUGHT IRON RANGE Co., St. Louis, Mo.
Gentlemen:—
The "HOME COMFORT" Range I bought from your salesman in 1905 is still going strong and has always given us the best of satisfaction. Cooks well, hot water all the time, and has saved its cost in economy of fuel. I doubt that this can be said of any other range made after 20 years of constant service.

S. J. JACKSON

SAVED COUNTLESS HOURS

Hitchcock, January 10th.
WROUGHT IRON RANGE Co., St. Louis, Mo.
Gentlemen:—
I bought one of your "HOME COMFORT" Ranges in 1900 and have not spent a cent on it for repairs in all these 25 years. I do not believe any other range made can show such a record. We have always had good service from it and its many features of economy have certainly saved countless hours of kitchen work for my family.

JAKE NOEL

HOT WATER ALWAYS HANDY

Cashion, December 31st.
WROUGHT IRON RANGE Co., St. Louis, Mo.
Gentlemen:—
For 15 years, our old faithful "HOME COMFORT" Range has given me the best of service. There is a lot of satisfaction in cooking on a range that is such a fine baker and heater, with hot water always handy and the warming closets warm and ready.

MRS. GEORGE HESSLER

NO MORE POLISHING TO DO

Banner, January 7th.
WROUGHT IRON RANGE Co., St. Louis, Mo.
Gentlemen:—
I have used my "HOME COMFORT" Range 2 years and am perfectly satisfied with it in every way. It has proved to be a wonderful fuel saver and a perfect cooker and baker just as you recommended it to be. The Enamel Finish is so easily kept clean, no more polishing to do—just rub it off with a damp cloth and it always looks nice and clean. I would not give it up.

MRS. THEO. WILLIAMS

PERFECT OVEN BAKES QUICKLY

Omega, January 9th.
WROUGHT IRON RANGE Co., St. Louis, Mo.
Gentlemen:—
I have used my "HOME COMFORT" Range 20 years and cannot say too much in its praise. It has saved me many, many hours and days of kitchen work—walking and standing, feeding in the fuel and waiting for something to cook, as must be done with most common stoves. Then, too, with plenty of hot water at my elbow, a nice warming closet within easy reach, and, best of all, a perfect oven that bakes quickly and properly—I don't see how anyone can get along without one.

MRS. SAM LAWRER

WOULD NOT TAKE $200

Watts, September 14th.
WROUGHT IRON RANGE Co., St. Louis, Mo.
Gentlemen:—
I bought a "HOME COMFORT" Range from your salesman last fall. I am moving to Newton, Kas., Route 5, and am taking my range with me. If I could not buy another one like it, it would take over $200 to buy it from me.

HENRY LEE

BEST INVESTMENT EVER MADE

Okache, January 12th.
WROUGHT IRON RANGE Co., St. Louis, Mo.
Gentlemen:—
We bought our "HOME COMFORT" Range 10 years ago and it has proved to be one of the very best investments we have ever made. It has always baked and cooked perfectly, has saved us a lot of fuel, and I don't think there is another range built that will stand the use our "HOME COMFORT" has and come through with not even a cracked or warped lid. Every farm-wife should have a "HOME COMFORT" Range and be happy.

C. H. MOELLER

OLD RANGES IN DEMAND

Kingfisher, January 2nd.
WROUGHT IRON RANGE Co., St. Louis, Mo.
Gentlemen:—
Seven years ago I bought one of your "HOME COMFORT" Ranges "second-handed" and we used it with perfect satisfaction until just recently, when I sold it for as much as I paid for it. We now have one of your new Enameled "HOME COMFORTS" and expect it to last us for many, many years. There is no range on the market that cooks, heats, and saves fuel like your "HOME COMFORT."

J. F. McMILLAN

TWENTY YEARS—SAVED ITS COST

Calumet, January 7th.

WROUGHT IRON RANGE CO., St. Louis, Mo.

Gentlemen:—

I have used one of your "HOME COMFORT" Ranges since 1905 and it looks and cooks as good as new. It always has baked perfectly, has more than saved its cost in these 20 years in the saving of fuel. I heartily recommend it as the most economical range one can buy. MRS. PAT MANSFIELD

S. S. Mann	Arnett	L. S. Smith	Grand Valley	M. T. Porter	Medford	D. E. Dean	Range

S. S. Mann	Arnett	L. S. Smith	Grand Valley	M. T. Porter	Medford	D. E. Dean	Range
E. Crawford	Ames	Mrs. John Gill	Guymon	J. J. Hallow	Lamont	A. H. Riffel	Shattuck
J. E. Lewis	Adamson	L. Harris	Hughes	M. Wilson	Manchester	C. A. Osborn	Saltfork
F. A. Hays	Byron	J. Williams	Heavenor	R. E. Mecom	McCurtain	R. Brown	Speermore
R. P. Tucker	Beichert	G. C. Gatlin	Howe	J. Chambers	Monroe	T. N. Gough	Stuart
W. M. Belcher	Braden	E. C. Keffer	Hill	G. B. Ely	McAlester	A. E. Boyd	Spiro
O. H. Duff	Blacker	P. C. Conser	Hodgen	C. R. Mott	Nash	W. C. Pierce	Shady Point
C. J. Hansen	Calumet	J. W. Elliott	Haywood	J. N. Bech	Navina	L. H. Bowen	Scipio
G. Northcroft	Caldwell	M. Clarke	Hartshorne	J. Palmer	N. McAlester	J. C. Bell	Savanna
S. L. Palmer	Cowlington	J. L. Muckels	Hadler	E. Gibler	Optima	John Adams	Stewart
J. N. Norris	Cameron	H. J. Klassen	Hooker	W. A. Morris	Pondcreek	S. O. Deney	Talihina
G. L. Coffee	Canadian	W. Barnes	Hardesty	F. J. Koch	Perryton	C. M. Pain	Tuckahoma
John Guess	Crowder	Tom Lewis	Indianaola	W. T. Mankin	Panola	T. E. Lute	Tyrone
Philip Keith	Carbon	S. P. Lance	Jet	T. R. Scott	Poteau	L. Beadman	Vining
R. B. Rolls	Damon	L. M. Bowling	Jefferson	E. A. Miser	Panama	H. J. Locke	Wakita
S. Showalter	Drummond	F. M. Driver	Keota	R. J. Pickett	Renfrow	E. Perisot	Wilburton
F. F. Steben	Dombey	J. W. Cox	Kintar	F. P. Norris	Red Oak	W. A. Gardner	Wister
J. E. Johnson	Goltry	J. C. Cordell	Kiowa	C. M. Lessel	Rock Island	W. S. Ray	Williams
T. J. Kenny	Gibbon	J. P. Bone	Krebs	J. H. Mills	Russellville	Theo. Williams	Yukon

FIFTEEN YEARS—BEST BAKER

Okarche, January 2nd.

WROUGHT IRON RANGE CO., St. Louis, Mo.

Gentlemen:—

Our "HOME COMFORT" Range is now 15 years old and is still the best baker we have ever used. We would never have any other but a "HOME COMFORT" in our home.

A. J. THOMPSON

PENNSYLVANIA

WHAT MORE COULD BE SAID?

Wellsboro, January 31st.

WROUGHT IRON RANGE CO., St. Louis, Mo.

Gentlemen:—

After using two "HOME COMFORT" Ranges for the past 32 years, we are so well pleased with them that we are today buying from your salesman two of your new enameled ones. What more could we say to recommend the "HOME COMFORT?"

FRANCIS J. CLEMENS
ERA CLEMENS

$2.00 REPAIRS IN 31 YEARS

Swiftwater, June 23rd.

WROUGHT IRON RANGE CO., St. Louis, Mo.

Gentlemen:—

We have a "HOME COMFORT" Range No. 67 which is nearly 31 years old and has been used all these years without a cent's worth of repairs. We now need the two middle sections of the firebox lining, that is all. Please send them to us.

SIMON WARNER

USES MUCH LESS FUEL

Hallstead, November 20th.

WROUGHT IRON RANGE CO., St. Louis, Mo.

Gentlemen:—

We are certainly pleased with our "HOME COMFORT" Range. It is such a good baker and heater, and we don't use nearly as much wood as we did with our old stove. If we couldn't get another one, we would not part with our "HOME COMFORT" for any price.

MRS. G. A. WATSON

SIX IN ONE FAMILY

Crooked Creek, February 2nd.

WROUGHT IRON RANGE CO., St. Louis, Mo.

Gentlemen:—

I wish to express my appreciation of the "HOME COMFORT" Range. There has been six "HOME COMFORTS" placed in my father's family since 1892, and they are all there to stay.

MRS. FRED SCHEELEY

EXACTLY AS REPRESENTED

Mahaffey, March 9th.

WROUGHT IRON RANGE CO., St. Louis, Mo.

Gentlemen:—

I bought a "HOME COMFORT" Range over 12 years ago, and found it to be exactly as represented. We like it fine in every respect. If it ever wears out—and I don't think it will for a great many years—I want another "HOME COMFORT."

CRAIG McGEE

SAFEGUARDS MONEY

Dalmatia, December 27th.

WROUGHT IRON RANGE CO., St. Louis, Mo.

Gentlemen:—

We have had a "HOME COMFORT" Range for over 20 years, and never have spent one cent on it for repairs, because it hasn't needed them. My family would not part with it for any other range made, unless it were another "HOME COMFORT," and I certainly would not want to put my money in any other make. It has always been exactly as represented, and I have always found your Company courteous and pleasant to deal with.

E. D. WITMER

SHE WANTED THE VERY BEST

Potts Grove, December 30th.

WROUGHT IRON RANGE CO., St. Louis, Mo.

Gentlemen:—

I want you to know that I think there is no Range like the "HOME COMFORT," or I would not have bought one of your New Models in July of 1924. At that time I was using a "HOME COMFORT" which had been in use for over 30 years. It is still in good condition as far as baking and cooking is concerned, but when we saw one of your New Enameled Ranges, and how beautiful it is, we could not resist buying a new one. This new Range is as perfect as it looks, and is all that you rerpesent it to be and more. I think it is the most beneficial addition to our kitchen we could have made, for it is a real piece of furniture.

MRS. F. S. TIFFANY

HAS TWO IN DAILY USE

Loganton, October 14th.

Wrought Iron Range Co., St. Louis, Mo.

Gentlemen:—

I bought our first "Home Comfort" Range over 30 years ago, and another one in 1914. Both are in use, and in good condition, and promise to last for many years. I would not have any other stove or range in my kitchen.

Daniel Barner

IS A PERFECT BAKER

Hillsdale, December 29th.

Wrought Iron Range Co., St. Louis, Mo.

Gentlemen:—

I have used my "Home Comfort" Range for the past 11 years and have always been well satisfied with it. It has always been a perfect bake and used very little fuel compared with other ranges. I would not part with it for any other range I have ever heard of.

Mrs. H. C. Schuengost

SHE OUGHT TO KNOW

Mahaffey, March 6th.

Wrought Iron Range Co., St. Louis, Mo.

Gentlemen:—

I have used a "Home Comfort" Range for 35 years, and will say it certainly was a good Range in every way. No one can convince me that the "Home Comfort" is not the best kitchen Range ever made.

Mrs. Mary E. Shields

$200 WILL NOT BUY IT

Solona, December 25th.

Wrought Iron Range Co., St. Louis, Mo.

Gentlemen:—

My "Home Comfort" Range has always given me more satisfaction than any other stove or range I have used. It bakes evenly and quickly, and takes half as much fuel as an ordinary stove. I must say that the "Home Comfort" is far superior to any Range I have ever seen. I would not take $200 if I could not get another "Home Comfort."

Mrs. I. E. Weaver

SAVES FAMILY WORK AND WORRY

Moshannon, November 24th.

Wrought Iron Range Co., St. Louis, Mo.

Gentlemen:—

I bought a "Home Comfort" Range from your salesman nearly 20 years ago. It has always given the best of satisfaction and has certainly saved my family a lot of work and worry. I surely do not regret buying it, and if I ever have to replace this one, it will certainly be with your latest Model Range.

C. A. Schmart

IT IS A "HUM-DINGER"

Creekside, November 5th.

Wrought Iron Range Co., St. Louis, Mo.

Gentlemen:—

We received our new "Home Comfort" Range long ago and have it going in the kitchen. It is a "hum-dinger," and everybody says so.

W. R. Spence

J. W. Carson Aaronsburg
W. Halteman Analomink
W. E. Tennant Alford
Ed. Horton Ansonia
H. P. Welch Allenwood
H. R. Antis Bellefonte
R. J. Albright Boalsburg
J. Kleckner Booneville
J. A. Kinney Bodines
S. W. Adams Berwick
J. T. Kline Bloomsburg
F. Pensyl Bangor
Wm. Wolbert Bartonsville
Beaver Springs
L. K. Fisk Brooklyn
Vincent Carros
Brackney
L. Workman Bloosburg
W. W. Oliver Beach Lake
Russell Druck Brogueville
W. F. Rishel Center Hall
O. K. Fry Charhams Run
Frank Uhl Catawissa
L. Bower Calvert
C. W. Matts Cogan Sta.
C. Kresge Cresco
Martin Kutch Carbondale
W. C. Baldwin Clifford
R. H. Gager Cold Springs
H. C. Shultz Danville
Ed. Frey Dewart
G. G. Bunting Dyberry
W. E. Smith Delta
R. E. Doyle
E. Stroudsburg
J. F. Holt Fleming
R. A. Ludlow
Farrandsville
G. T. Garfield Fields
I. P. Fregley
Fishers Ferry
Z. C. Bell Forest City
W. H. Stabley Felton
L. M. Brown Fawn Grove

John Preston Grover
B. L. Bedford Gelatt
W. M. Mason Gains
R. A. Wagner
Glen Rock
W. G. Pletcher
Hepburnville
C. Forest Hughesville
T. W. Banks Henryville
John Munger Honesdale
J. A. Benedick
Herrick Center
L. A. King Hop Bottom
L. J. Lone Hartford
G. A. Watson Hallstead
F. Kruel Hoadleys
H. J. Mantz Hawley
A. Green Jersey Shore
J. E. Werman Jerseytown
W. H. Burdick Jackson
Mrs. F. Barnat Karthaus
Wm. Frabel
Krumkletown
V. Hoffman Kresgeville
J. P. Williams Kremis
C. A. Mull Kreamer
M. E. Pennay Kingsburg
B. L. Mosher Kingsley
C. C. Workman
Mingoville
O. B. Barger Moshannon
Boaz Stewart Modena
D. O. Swinehart
McElhatton
E. F. Downs Mill Hall
J. G. Worthington
Montoursville
J. W. Kilmer
Montgomery
G. W. Harris Muncy
W. McClemons
Muncy Valley
W. H. Montague
Mawrglen

M. D. White Mansfield
J. C. Hay Milton
C. F. Gill McClure
H. Jordan Middleburg
J. E. Rick Montrose
Joe Cooper
Middlebury Center
R. Campbell Morris
G. A. Smith Mifflinburg
M. C. Jolly Millmont
T. Wilcox Milanville
W. F. Sinclair
Muddy Cr. Fk.
C. F. Lutz Nescopeck
P. H. Sewald Nisbet
R. M. Kohl
Northumberland
F. U. LaBarr
New Milford
H. D. Maurer
New Berlin
Chas. Nogle
New Columbia
E. A. Warwick
Narrowsburg
R. C. Roberts Nicholson
D. F. Harrigan
New Freedom
M. Gelty Orangeville
E. Wighaman
Port Matilda
J. B. Croman
Picture Rocks
W. Kostenbander
Pottsgrove
L. G. Confer Pottersdale
H. Frey Pensdale
W. H. Knapp
Penns Creek
Roy Perry Snedkerville
J. F. Myers Spring Mills
W. H. Meyer
State College

I. A. Weaver Salona
J. O'Neil Stroudsburg
Earl Deechalka Scot Run
A. D. Mofler
Strawberry Ridge
F. W. Gass Sunbury
G. Tripp South Gibson
R. L. Place S. Auburn
A. Schmoll Springville
C. Ramey Susquehanna
J. K. Prentick
Stevens Point
E. Getz Saylorsburg
G. E. Harkins Street
A. M. Miles
Stewartstown
Mrs. C. Gakle Tylersville
Jessie Steige Trout Run
F. A. Kleeman
Turbotville
Bruce Belcher Thompson
R. H. Cole Tioga
Dora Lyons Unityville
W. M. Mock Uniondale
S. H. Orndorff
Woodward
L. Carson White Pine
W. Weaver Williamsport
R. A. Perry Waterville
G. W. Root
Washingtonville
Daniel Blue Wilton
D. H. Trutt Watsontown
P. Haggerty
White Valley
Wm. Rose Wellsboro
N. Baker White Deer
H. W. Predix Winfield
E. T. Jolly Weikert
T. P. Sauky Waymart
Ira Fishell Woodbine

SOUTH CAROLINA

MANY IMPORTANT FEATURES

Jefferson, March 23rd.
Wrought Iron Range Co., St. Louis, Mo.
Gentlemen:—

I wish to say that the Enameled "Home Comfort" Range I installed more than a year ago is giving perfect satisfaction. It is a wonderful baker and fuel saver, and has many other conveniences and features equally important. It has certainly proved a great comfort to my family.

W. A. Plyler

KNOWS FROM EXPERIENCE

Nichols, January 29th.
Wrought Iron Range Co., St. Louis, Mo.
Gentlemen:—

I bought a "Home Comfort" Range over 26 years ago, and it has always given entire satisfaction in every way. Knowing its worth, I have just bought one of your New Enamel Models from your salesman and consider it with its improvements far superior to any range I have ever seen.

W. E. Baker

KNOWS ITS WORTH

Marion, January 29th.
Wrought Iron Range Co., St. Louis, Mo.
Gentlemen:—

I bought a "Home Comfort" Range from your salesman in 1905 which has always given us the best of satisfaction, and been a real comfort in our home. Knowing the worth of the "Home Comfort" I have today bought one of your New Enamel Models from your salesman, and am sure of the extreme satisfaction we shall receive from it. I am sure it is the very best Range on the market.

J. A. Atkinson

MADE BEST SELECTION

Bingham, April 2nd.
Wrought Iron Range Co., St. Louis, Mo.
Gentlemen:—

We have been using our Enamel "Home Comfort" Range for over a year with real comfort and satisfaction. We have found it to be all that it was represented to us, and certainly do not regret installing it. I know I could not have made a better selection in the matter of a kitchen Range for my family.

R. L. Alford

WORTH THE PRICE

Pageland, March 31st.
Wrought Iron Range Co., St. Louis, Mo.
Gentlemen:—

Over a year ago, I had one of your improved Enamel "Home Comfort" Ranges installed in our kitchen. It has been giving faithful service since that time, and has proved to be the wonderful Range it was recommended to us. My family is certainly proud of it, and we consider it well worth the price we paid for it.

F. A. Gulledge

CAN'T BE EQUALED

Fort Mills, April 3rd.
Wrought Iron Range Co., St. Louis, Mo.
Gentlemen:—

We installed one of your new Enameled "Home Comfort" Ranges several months ago when your salesmen were in this county. I desire to say that it is giving perfect satisfaction, and find it to be exactly as it was represented. I do not believe the baking qualities of the "Home Comfort" can be equaled by any other Range made, for it certainly does its work perfectly. It is indeed a great comfort and convenience, besides being a great fuel saver.

A. N. Hall

SUPERIOR SERVICE

Clio, March 24th.
Wrought Iron Range Co., St. Louis, Mo.
Gentlemen:—

We have been using one of your Enameled Model "Home Comfort" Ranges in our home kitchen for more than a year. We have found it to be all that it was represented to us and more. It is certainly an ornament to any kitchen, and its superior service is equal to its appearance.

W. L. McQuage

SAVES FUEL

Blacksburg, March 26th.
Wrought Iron Range Co., St. Louis, Mo.
Gentlemen:—

I bought one of your Enameled "Home Comfort" Ranges about a year ago when your salesmen were in this county. The Range is doing perfect work, and has proved all it was recommended to be. The "Home Comfort" is certainly a wonderful kitchen Range, is an excellent baker, a quick heater, and very saving on fuel. We are well pleased with it.

J. H. Austell

WILL HAVE NO OTHER

Dillon, January 1st.
Wrought Iron Range Co., St. Louis, Mo.
Gentlemen:—

I purchased from your salesman, a few days ago, one of your New Enamel Ranges, with which we are very highly pleased. Since using a "Home Comfort" Range for over 20 years, and finding it to be all that it was represented to us in the beginning, it did not take long for me to decide to install one of your New Enamel Models.

Tom Carter

MOST PERFECT BAKER

Taxahaw, March 30th.
Wrought Iron Range Co., St. Louis, Mo.
Gentlemen:—

The Enameled "Home Comfort" Range I bought from your salesman over a year ago has been giving faithful service and has proven to be all that it was represented to us and more. My family thinks it is a wonderful Range, since it is the most perfect baker we have ever owned, a quick heater, and a great fuel and labor saver. Every housewife deserves to own one.

U. A. McManus

WORK IS LIGHTENED

Green Sea, January 15th.
Wrought Iron Range Co., St. Louis, Mo.
Gentlemen:—

My "Home Comfort" Range has given me constant service for over 23 years, and it is still in perfect cooking condition. It cooks with less fuel than any other range I have ever seen. It has been a source of great satisfaction in my home, and it has certainly lightened my work very much during these years of service.

Mrs. A. G. Strickland

COOKING PROBLEM SOLVED

Kollocks, April 1st.
Wrought Iron Range Co., St. Louis, Mo.
Gentlemen:—

I desire to state that the "Home Comfort" Range we bought from you more than a year ago is giving perfect satisfaction. It cooks better than any stove or range we have ever owned, and is certainly a big asset to our kitchen. Our cooking problem is solved for many years to come, for "Home Comfort" Ranges have always had a reputation for long life and durability.

S. O. Peynes

PLEASURABLE DEALINGS

Bishopville, January 23rd.

Wrought Iron Range Co., St. Louis, Mo.

Gentlemen:—

I have used one of your "Home Comfort" Ranges for over 8 years, and since I need to install a second range, I have just bought one of your new models. I find the "Home Comfort" superior to any range I have ever used, it being economical as to fuel, and very durable. I have always found it a pleasure to deal with your company.

L. H. Jennings
Pres., S. Carolina Federation of Women's Clubs

SAVES TIME

Kershaw, April 2nd.

Wrought Iron Range Co., St. Louis, Mo.

Gentlemen:—

My "Home Comfort" Range which I purchased from your salesman last year has been giving excellent service and has proved to be all that it was represented to me. It is a wonderful baker, and because of its quick and even heat, saves me much time that I would otherwise be spending in the kitchen. I would not want to part with it.

Mrs. Helen C. Estridge

A PERMANENT INVESTMENT

McCall, March 25th.

Wrought Iron Range Co., St. Louis, Mo.

Gentlemen:—

We have one of your Enameled Ranges, which I bought from your salesman in March, 1924. It has proved to be a source of real comfort and satisfaction in our home kitchen, and exactly as it was represented to us. It certainly does perfect cooking, is easy to keep clean, and has many little conveniences that have saved many kitchen steps in my household. I consider it a permanent investment, and certainly do not regret buying it.

N. W. Adams

JUST AS REPRESENTED

McCall, March 28th.

Wrought Iron Range Co., St. Louis, Mo.

Gentlemen:—

The first year of service of our Enamel "Home Comfort" Range has been more than satisfactory, and has proved that it is as it was represented to us. From the records and reputation of "Home Comfort" Ranges I have known, I think this one will solve our cooking problem for many years. It is certainly a beautiful product and a wonderful cooker.

H. G. McCall

F. S. Stevens	Angulus	Ed. Taylor	Patrick	Ben. Mullins	Marion	J. W. Lowery	Ruby
W. J. Kirby	Atlanta	M. L. Brown	"	J. P. Gay	Maggett	J. W. Ratliff	"
A. McKinnon	Bethune	J. M. Hyman	Pamplico	H. G. McCall	McCall	W. F. Howle	Society Hill
J. J. Mathis	Bishopville	L. W. Hyman	"	J. W. Leonard		J. C. Griggs	" "
J. M. Thornton	Blaney	E. L. Gandy	Dovesville		Mt. Croughan	S. J. Kirby	Scranton
J. B. Heins	Blythewood	J. D. Brown	Effingham	J. T. Wilhelm		J. J. Daniels	"
V. Thomason	Blacksburg	F. W. Dickson	Fort Mill		Middendorf	A. A. Knight	Taxahaw
A. C. Green	Bennettsville	L. C. Baker	Florence	R. L. Hart	Mars Bluff	W. A. McManus	"
W. N. Dial	Blenheim	J. A. Kister	Gastonia	Ed. Wilson	" "	E. Kirby	Timmonsville
H. A. Huffman		D. E. Couch		J. M. McDonald	McBee	G. C. Hatchell	"
	Connellys Springs		Heath Springs	R. M. Wilson	Osceola	Ed. C. Newton	Tatum
F. H. Hall	Cowpens	G. R. Brown	Hartsville	E. Willis	Olanta	T. L. Willid	Vale
D. A. Pendleton	Clover	O. P. Taylor	Hyman	M. W. Hinds	Orum	J. B. Leatherman	"
B. N. Craft	Cherryville	O. W. Baker	Jefferson	Jim Starnes	Pageland	W. D. Westmoreland	
J. S. McQuage	Clio	B. M. Driggins	Kollock	K. P. Stewart	"		Woodruff
J. E. Adams	Chesterfield	J. S. Rowell	Lancaster	L. C. King	Darlington	B. S. Funderburg	
G. R. Spincer	Cheraw	B. F. Craft	Lydia	S. Branham, Jr.			Yonges Island
W. R. Lee	Cowards	J. S. Watford	Lamar		Ridgeway	Milton Watson	York
D. McQueen	Dunbar	D. D. McRae	Minturn	H. S. Ferguson	Riverside	Wm. McCarter	"

TENNESSEE

EVERY WIFE DESERVES ONE

Brunswick, September 11th.

Wrought Iron Range Co., St. Louis, Mo.

Gentlemen:—

We have been a user of a "Home Comfort" Range since 1903. After 22 years of continual service, it is still in good condition and will be for many years to come. No one can make a mistake by buying a "Home Comfort" Range, and every wife deserves one.

A. M. Bledsoe

35 YEARS—BUYS ANOTHER

Oakland, August 20th.

Wrought Iron Range Co., St. Louis, Mo.

Gentlemen:—

I have been cooking on one "Home Comfort" Range for 35 years, and it has always given perfect satisfaction. About 30 days ago, I bought one of your new Model Enameled 22 Ranges from your salesman and it sure is a beauty. I really don't believe I could keep house without a "Home Comfort" Range. Anyone who has tried it will always be a "Home Comfort" booster.

Miss Gertrude Stafford

BEST RANGE EVER BUILT

Germantown, October 23rd.

Wrought Iron Range Co., St. Louis, Mo.

Gentlemen:—

I am so proud of my new Enameled "Home Comfort" Range that I want to tell you that I think it is the best cooking and baking range ever built by any company. I also find it to be a great fuel saver—in fact, I never had imagined that a range could be built that would require such a small amount to cook a meal. But, the "Home Comfort" is so easily regulated when properly done.

Mrs. Mary Sandridge

USING SECOND ONE

Capleville, December 1st.

Wrought Iron Range Co., St. Louis, Mo.

Gentlemen:—

We have a new "Home Comfort" Range that we recently bought through your salesman. This is our second "Home Comfort" and we are very much pleased with it. We have used your range for many years and wife thinks there is none other nearly as good.

F. M. Malone

"HOME COMFORT" A TREASURE

Martha, February 10th.

WROUGHT IRON RANGE CO., St. Louis, Mo.

Gentlemen:—

Our "HOME COMFORT" Range is certainly a t easure. It has given perfect satisfaction in every way, and our one regret is that we did not buy one years ago. We hope we will never be forced by any circumstances to use any other range.

ROBERT GUISON

WHY HE BOUGHT IT

Morristown, September 23rd.

WROUGHT IRON RANGE CO., St. Louis, Mo.

Gentlemen:—

We are certainly well pleased with our "HOME COMFORT" Range and consider it the best cooking range on the market—that is why we bought it. Please accept our best regards.

G. W. MORELOCK

G. L. Maynard	Allons	A. F. Smith	Crawford	R. T. Wills	Luther	S. R. Williams	Pallmall
W. W. Moran	Antioch	Jasper Terry	Cokeville	G. D. Leamons	Lee Valley	Sam Kite	Persia
J. N. Hobbs	Alexandria	C. C. Davis	Carthage	Fred Cox	Lancing	A. W. Evans	Petros
H. J. Guffey	Allardt	W. H. Lee	Del Rio	J. A. Hunter	Livingston	Minnie Savage	Quebec
A. F. McFarlan	Ashland	W. A. Ryon	Deer Lodge	F. C. Howe	Lascassas	R. L. Henry	Rutledge
Bill Lane	Afton	F. W. Richmon		Ray Close	Liberty	J. D. Hash	Rock Island
Tom Hooks	Annadel		Dixon Springs	C. B. Carson	Limestone	M. J. Howe	Rogersville
Milton Smith	Alpine	Van Gaither	Eads	M. V. Adams	Leeville	Geo. Crisp	Rose
J. W. Carr	Allred	J. T. Higgins	Erwin	J. T. Patrick	Lenow	M. V. Calahan	Rickman
D. M. Morris	Allgood	H. T. Lawson	Eidson	C. L. Barrom	Lucy	J. D. Nichols	Roma
R. H. Chipman	Ashport	W. Blaylock	Eastland	J. W. Barnes	Medina	J. S. Killer	Rockwood
J. F. Smith	Atoko	W. K. Manis	Forbus	Dennis Hall	Macon	Bob Risden	Riddleton
W. C. Webb	Arlington	S. P. Mills	Greenville	W. A. Adair	Moscow	W. D. Taft	Ravenscroft
O. H. Hembree	Bells	Jordon Jones	Grand Jct.	Joe Dodd	Medon	Will Harlin	Roam
H. Wallace	Brownsville	Chas. Shepard	Gold Dust	B. A. Johnson	Malesuo	J. S. Pulliam	Rossville
E. M. Richards	Bells	C. E. Callis	Germantown	J. J. Maners	Mercer	W. W. Harrison	Ripley
C. W. Saulin	Beechbluff	Tom Brown	Gainsboro	P. M. Mashburn	Mason	O. H. Thomas	Raleigh
J. P. Sasser	Brighton	J. O. Hamilton	Granville	J. B. Mathew	Martin	J. S. Taylor	Somerville
A. J. Baskin	Burlison	H. E. Swain	Gladesville	Wilbur Wright	Mosheim	J. T. Smith	Stanton
S. P. McGowan	Byhalia	O. P. Campbell	Gazaway	J. D. Lody	Morristown	C. P. Waynick	
J. C. Keller	Buntyn	W. H. Hinson		A. J. Rader	Midway		Spring Creek
E. E. Ellis	Brunswick		Huntington	R. F. Brewer	Mooresburg	G. B. Davis	Sneedville
C. Branton	Bryson City	G. T. Goodrich		M. G. Clark	Mt. Juliet	A. Tinch	Sunbright
John H. Halt	Bybee		Humboldt	E. D. Reagan	Monroe	C. Medley	Silver Point
J. E. Cook	Baileyton	J. T. Watson	Henning	W. P. Hicks	Monterey	R. Scott	Sparta
J. H. Long	Bulls Gap	A. Simons	Hartford	J. A. Cothern	Monoville	W. A. Hill	Townsend
B. L. Hunley	Burem	George Long	Hermitage	D. M. Draper	Martho	H. W. Woody	Telford
J. J. Jones	Brotherton	Sam Wright	Helena	J. C. Wright	Mt. Juliet	B. B. Bird	Vanhill
J. H. Sells	Byrdstown	Walter Burris	Hilham	H. M. Dill	Milton	T. E. Short	Vildo
O. F. Hunter	Bethpage	J. F. Duncan	Hartsville	J. H. Woody	Newport	Lee Person	Warren
H. W. Cole	Baxter	Mac Stewart	Hermitage	W. A. Bond	Norene	J. L. Deaton	Whiteville
A. M. Ray	Covington	J. Conatser	Jamestown	J. H. Washam	New River	G. R. Tunnell	White Pine
I. W. Lowrey	Collierville	T. J. Ervin	Jonesboro	P. G. Gentry	Norene Star	J. W. Bell	Willett
E. R. Stone	Capleville	J. H. Duffy	Juno	M. V. Stover	Oakley	J. E. Home	Whitesburg
W. G. Harris	Capleville	L. A. Callis	Jackson	John Cotton	Oneida	Martin Lyons	Wartburg
Trueman Wallace	Clinton	C. E. Stewart		D. R. Rich	Oakland	Wm. H. Browder	Wheat
J. E. Nix	Clermont		Kerryville	H. H. Meaks	Oakfield	W. R. Chambers	Winona
Thos. Styles	Cosby	D. Manning	Lebanon	R. Smith	Oakville	P. F. Burnley	Willard
J. M. Beard	Chuckey	S. L. Gregory	La Fayette	R. J. Reviere	Prestige	J. W. Chisan	Walling
R. L. Long	Church Hill	E. Fields	Lantana	Wm. Neal	Pioneer	Bird Smith	Watertown

TEXAS

USED SINCE 1908

Salesville, January 3rd.

WROUGHT IRON RANGE CO., St. Louis, Mo.

Gentlemen:—

I bought a "HOME COMFORT" Range from your salesman in 1908 and it is still in good condition after its 27 years of service. It cooks and bakes as well as it ever did and I think it will last us several years yet. If we ever discard it, we will buy one of your new ones.

C. D. WALKER

WELL WORTH THE PRICE

Springtown, January 6th.

WROUGHT IRON RANGE CO., St. Louis, Mo.

Gentlemen:—

We are certainly highly delighted with our new Enameled "HOME COMFORT" Range, for it is all you claim it to be. It is well worth its price; in fact, we would not take $200 for it and be forced to be without a "HOME COMFORT."

MR. AND MRS. R. R. SHOWN

WOULDN'T SELL FOR $300

Wetherford, December 22nd.

WROUGHT IRON RANGE CO., St. Louis, Mo.

Gentlemen:—

I am highly pleased with my "HOME COMFORT" Range. I would not take $300 for it if I couldn't get another one like it.

MRS. HENRY McFARLAND

SAVING IN FUEL PAYS FOR IT

Dublin, January 5th.

WROUGHT IRON RANGE CO., St. Louis, Mo.

Gentlemen:—

Our new Enameled "HOME COMFORT" Range has proved to be all your salesman represented it to us. We can truthfully recommend it as a perfect baker and a fuel saver. We are burning coal and find that our saving in fuel alone will pay for the range in a comparatively short time. We certainly would not take twice the price we paid for it, if we could not get another.

MR. AND MRS. LEONARD HANCOCK

BIG SUCCESS WITH GAS
Weatherford, December 27th.
Wrought Iron Range Co., St. Louis, Mo.
Gentlemen:—

We bought a "Home Comfort" Range in 1911 from your salesman who worked in this territory. We have always been so well pleased with it that we bought one of your new enameled ones when your salesman was around this year. We have attached gas to the new one, and am glad to say that it is a big success in every particular.
Mr. and Mrs. H. Lowery

KNOCKS OUT OIL STOVE
Perrin, December 30th.
Wrought Iron Range Co., St. Louis, Mo.
Gentlemen:—

We very recently bought a new Enameled Model AB. "Home Comfort" Range from your traveling salesman, and I think it is just wonderful. I cooked on an oil stove five years because I considered it the only stove for quick cooking—until I got my new "Home Comfort." I find it beats my oil stove so badly that I won't ever fool with an oil stove any more. Now, I will never have anything but a "Home Comfort" in my home, for I find it to be the perfect range you say it is.
Mrs. H. R. Ramsey

TWO IN HOTEL KITCHEN
Linden, December 27th.
Wrought Iron Range Co., St. Louis, Mo.
Gentlemen:—

Since 1911, I have been cooking on a "Home Comfort" Range here in my hotel. I have been so well pleased with it in every way, that I bought your 1921 Model "Home Comfort" and installed it beside the older one. The old one still cooks just as good as the newer one, in fact there is no difference between the two when it comes to good cooking, with which I have built up my hotel business. I believe this reputation is due to my "Home Comfort" Ranges. I am sure they are superior to any other range one may purchase for their durability and fuel saving, to say nothing of their superior cooking qualities, and many conveniences.
Mrs. Mattie Jackson

FITS BILL EXACTLY
Kempner, September 20th.
Wrought Iron Range Co., St. Louis, Mo.
Gentlemen:—

We are certainly delighted with our "Home Comfort" Range. It fits the bill exactly in the way of being a perfect cooker.
Charlie W. Taylor

"A RATHER FAST LIFE"
Bivins, January 2nd.
Wrought Iron Range Co., St. Louis, Mo.
Gentlemen:—

We have a "Home Comfort" Range that we have used 15 years which has led a rather fast life. It was blown away in a cyclone, set out in the rain, and kept in a leaky house 4 years, but it still heats and cooks well. I have expressed my opinion of the "Home Comfort" today by buying one of your latest models, the new enameled "Home Comfort," and I fully believe it will last us 25 or 30 years under constant duty. Could I express my faith in it and your company in any better way?
S. M. Hall

NO ROOM FOR REGRET
Hooks, January 16th.
Wrought Iron Range Co., St. Louis, Mo.
Gentlemen:—

When we began keeping house, one of the first things I bought was a "Home Comfort" Range, because I knew their quality, their worth, and the reputation of your Company back of your guarantee. The superiority of the "Home Comfort" Range is not debatable, because of the material, workmanship and lifetime service you build into them. I will never have anything in my kitchen but a "Home Comfort," for when they are installed, there is no room left for regret.
W. L. Gibson

WOULD BUY IF COST MORE
Granbury, December 27th.
Wrought Iron Range Co., St. Louis, Mo.
Gentlemen:—

I am now in my 86th year and am cooking on my third "Home Comfort" Range, for I have lately bought one of your new enameled ones. I used my first "Home Comfort" 22 years, from 1877 to 1899, then I used my second one 25 years. I think my new enameled range, for which I was glad to pay cash, is superior to any range on the market and I wouldn't be without it if it cost more than the present price, for I don't think I could get along without my "Home Comfort." I am sure I won't have to buy another one. I wish your company the greatest success.
Mrs. Susan Brady

THERE'S A BIG DIFFERENCE
Garner, January 2nd.
Wrought Iron Range Co., St. Louis, Mo.
Gentlemen:—

I don't see how I ever got along with our old cast-iron stove. My new "Home Comfort" bakes perfectly and I can now cook a meal with half the wood the old stove required. I am sure no one will ever regret buying a "Home Comfort," it is so beautiful and easy to keep clean.
Mrs. W. F. Murphy

RAISED ON A "HOME COMFORT"
Salesville, January 2nd.
Wrought Iron Range Co., St. Louis, Mo.
Gentlemen:—

My mother has had her "Home Comfort" Range since I was a child—I was practically raised on "Home Comfort" cooking. At first opportunity to buy one from your salesman, I bought without solicitation, for I already knew just what they were—all that your company claims for them in cooking, fuel saving and other features. Mrs. Sweet joins me in best wishes.
J. C. Sweet

Note: Mr. Sweet not only bought without solicitation, but insisted on paying cash with order.—C. C. G., Div. Supt.

IT IS FREE FROM RUST
Carbon, January 1st.
Wrought Iron Range Co., St. Louis, Mo.
Gentlemen:—

We bought a "Home Comfort" Model AB Range last May and we think it is a dandy. Now that we have had it a few months, we could never think of giving it up, for no other range or stove could cook nearly as well on such little fuel. It is as free from rust as one could possibly be made. We are delighted with it, and wish your Company and your salesmen the best of success.
Mr. and Mrs. W. R. Garrett

IT'S A "HOUSE-WIFE'S REAL FRIEND"
Springtown, January 1st.
Wrought Iron Range Co., St. Louis, Mo.
Gentlemen:—

Now that we have amply tried out our new Model AB "Home Comfort" Range, we do not hesitate to say that we will never be without one in our kitchen. It is certainly a "house-wife's real friend" and we prize it very highly.
Mr. and Mrs. S. T. Woody

ITS REAL VALUE

Thornton, January 18th.

WROUGHT IRON RANGE Co., St. Louis, Mo.

Gentlemen:—

I have one of your New Enamel Model "HOME COMFORT" Ranges, installed a few months ago, and it is giving perfect satisfaction in every way. Your salesman recommended it very highly, but I find it to be more than he claimed for it. The "HOME COMFORT" Range wasn't a stranger to me, however, for I baked my first biscuits over 25 years ago on one of your earlier models in my father's home. So you see I know the real value of the "HOME COMFORT" Range.

MRS. W. T. KILPATRICK

SAYS THIS MERCHANT

Talty, December 18th.

WROUGHT IRON RANGE Co., St. Louis, Mo.

Gentlemen:—

I am a merchant here in Talty. We are now using a "HOME COMFORT" Range which I bought from your salesman 20 years ago. It is, and always has been, in perfect condition, and I consider them the best range made. It is certainly a fuel saver and a fine cooker and baker.

M. F. TALTY

MORE THAN REPRESENTED

Springtown, January 5th.

WROUGHT IRON RANGE Co., St. Louis, Mo.

Gentlemen:—

We recently bought from your salesman a new Model AB "HOME COMFORT" Range which has now been installed in our kitchen about five weeks. After a thorough test, we are pleased to say that it is exactly as your salesman represented it and more. It is the most even baker and fuel saver we have ever seen. If every family knew what we know now, they would sure have a beautiful Enameled "HOME COMFORT" in their home. With best wishes, we are,

MR. AND MRS. J. A. WOODY

ENAMELED RANGE A MASTERPIECE

Linden, January 4th.

WROUGHT IRON RANGE Co., St. Louis, Mo.

Gentlemen:—

We bought our "HOME COMFORT" Range in 1909 and it has been in continuous use ever since that time and still has many years of service left in it. I have just sold it for a fair price after installing one of your new Enameled Model AB Ranges. This should show you my attitude toward the "HOME COMFORT" Range which I think is a masterpiece.

MRS. G. E. BURNS

WONDERFULLY PERFECT

Weatherford, December 29th.

WROUGHT IRON RANGE Co., St. Louis, Mo.

Gentlemen:—

After cooking on our new "HOME COMFORT" for several days, we are pleased to say that it is a wonderfully perfect baker and a great fuel saver; in fact, we feel that it has no equal anywhere. We are certainly pleased with it and do not hesitate to recommend it over all other ranges.

MRS. M. E. HARRISON

SHE'S GLAD 1095 TIMES A YEAR

Novice, August 2nd.

WROUGHT IRON RANGE Co., St. Louis, Mo.

Gentlemen:—

I want to say that the "HOME COMFORT" Range is the best in the world. This is my second one and if my house hadn't burned and the chimney fallen on it, of course I would be using the first one yet. If ever I have to sell something for a living, please let me sell the "HOME COMFORT" Range, for it is the only thing I know of that I could sell without telling a story to sell it. You may guess that I am made glad 1095 times a year by having my "HOME COMFORT" to cook on.

MRS. J. M. BARNETT

BAKES BISCUITS "OUT DOORS"

Rotan, January 15th.

WROUGHT IRON RANGE Co., St. Louis, Mo.

Gentlemen:—

We bought our first "HOME COMFORT" Range 19 years ago—used it almost three times a day for 18 years. We did not pay out a cent for repairs in this length of time. While we were having our kitchen repaired before putting up a new Enameled "HOME COMFORT," we set this old range out in the yard and used it for a few days longer. It still cooked perfectly well, even out in the open—browned the biscuit a beautiful brown when the wind was blowing a gale.

I suppose I would still be using this same range, but your salesman happened to call with his Enameled Model, and we had to place our order with him for a new one before we could get rid of him. I want to say right here that your Company will certainly do well to keep him—can't understand how you did without him so long—he isn't so good looking, but he's certainly a "No. 1" "HOME COMFORT" Range salesman.

I have been using my new Enameled Range about 18 months and it is a peach. I can recommend it to the public as a "Perfect Range" and the cheapest one in the end that one can buy. I would not part with my "HOME COMFORT" for the price I paid if I could not buy another of the same kind. I want to add that my old range has been transferred to another home and is still cooking "three squares a day." only wish that every woman could have a "HOME COMFORT" Range installed in her kitchen.

MRS. W. B. WILLINGHAM

25 YEARS—GOOD FOR 40

Atlanta, January 23rd.

WROUGHT IRON RANGE Co., St. Louis, Mo.

Gentlemen:—

I have a number 1900 "HOME COMFORT" Range which I bought from your salesman 25 years ago. It has been in constant use all these years, and I can truly say that I think it will last 15 years more. It has always been a perfect baker, and a great fuel saver, and I cannot understand why any one who wants a lifetime kitchen range does not install a "HOME COMFORT." I consider that the "HOME COMFORT" Range leaves absolutely no room for regret.

B. L. M. BANTHIM

MORE PROOF

Gorman, December 26th.

WROUGHT IRON RANGE Co., St. Louis, Mo.

Gentlemen:—

We are using one of your new enameled "HOME COMFORT" Ranges and are certainly well pleased with it. We would not take $200 for it if we could not get another one just like it. It certainly is a great fuel saver and a good baker.

MR. AND MRS. F. A. NEWELL

22 YEARS—NO REPAIRS

Linden, December 15th.

WROUGHT IRON RANGE Co., St. Louis, Mo.

Gentlemen:—

I have a "HOME COMFORT" Range which I have used 22 years and I have not spent one penny on it for repairs during that time. It cooks and bakes as well as it ever did and looks like it will give first-class service several years longer.

MRS. ANNIE ANDERSON

25 YEARS—"SAME GOOD SERVICE"

Linden, January 2nd.

WROUGHT IRON RANGE CO., St. Louis, Mo.

Gentlemen:—

I have been using one of your 1900 Model "HOME COMFORT" Ranges since February of that year. I am sure it is the very best range on the market. It is still giving the same good service it did 25 years ago, and I would not exchange it for any other kitchen stove or range made.

MRS. G. P. McMIHAEL

EVERY WIFE SHOULD HAVE ONE

Garner, December 31st.

WROUGHT IRON RANGE CO., St. Louis, Mo.

Gentlemen:—

We are certainly proud of our New Enameled "HOME COMFORT" Range. After cooking on it for several days, we would not think of parting with it. It is such a wonderful baker, wood-saver and labor-saver. Every housewife should certainly have one.

MRS. P. J. BIELSS

F. W. Becker Anderson	H. R. Cook Celeste	I. M. Walker Eolian	W. Norris Hennessey
F. F. Humphrey Abilene	A. Sparks Clarksville	C. A. Kinsey Easterly	R. F. Crumley High
A. O. Sweat Aberdeen	I. E. Weaver Crowell	A. T. White Eliasville	T. D. Wood Hempstead
G. W. Taylor Alma	J. P. Adams Carrier	John Gowan Emhouse	J. W. Honner Howth
F. T. Todd Ambrose	J. M. Bean Collinsville	Oce Lloyd Folette	J. P. Ballinger Huntoon
C. S. Lamar Afton	J. M. Holderby Courtney	F. A. Dickert Floydada	E. D. Byrd Higgins
Ed. Hobbs Anderson	P. Henry Chillicothe	Wm. Godwin Ford City	J. M. Koch Huntsville
H. C. Adams Augusta	S. M. Liles Canadian	J. W. Moore Fairfield	J. M. Rodgers
J. J. Meadows Anson	W. P. Fauer Centralias	I. H. Bandy Ft. Spunky	Harpersville
W. A. Looney Axtell	W. T. Chapman Crecy	W. P. Newton Forney	A. Roley Hubbard
B. G. Leggett Azle	N. H. Buller Crockett	H. W. Ediger	J. T. Tucker Italy
N. C. Joyner Annona	F. A. Kirby Crandall	Farnsworth	B. F. Eidson Ivanhoe
W. R. Hicks Avery	A. R. Koch Crescent	W. D. Johnson Frosa	W. B. Burns Iola
E. D. Ashley Albion	J. F. Young Caviness	C. F. Meyer Flomot	H. H. Murry Idalou
J. D. Parks Acworth	T. J. Shipman Chicota	G. M. Borth Follett	R. M. Ford Johnsville
W. Davis Apple Spgs.	T. N. Raines	J. D. White Franklin	T. E. Craig Jacksboro
O. M. Gilstrap Bomarton	Cunningham	H. S. McAdams Frost	F. F. Miller Jiba
B. C. Wright Balco	W. H. Robeson	R. S. Maddox Fulbright	T. C. Deck Jewett
R. A. Parker Beaver	Centerville	W. T. Dave Friday	W. C. Montgomery
H. S. Dowers Boyd	J. A. Sanders Cooledge	B. L. Kimbell Gasoline	Joseph
Chas. Merka Bryan	B. P. Horne Chillicothe	John Gill Guymon	M. R. Bigers Jean
J. F. Browning Baird	W. A. Sweeney Caddo	G. H. Gaskin Gray	J. M. Moore Kurten
J. H. Sides Blanket	D. D. Hale Corsicana	H. H. Symons Graham	S. E. Jackson Kirkland
W. W. Rhodes Bluff Dale	J. F. Sheets Chatfield	C. F. Cornwell Gorman	H. H. Janzen Kremlin
W. G. Jenkins Bonham	M. V. Evans Currie	E. P. Young Gustine	M. L. Shumate Kirvin
B. B. Baxter Blossom	Mrs. A. J. Martin	Ed. Golladay Giles	W. J. Taylor Kennard
John Mastry Bison	Clarksville	I. P. Smith Gap	T. M. Yant Kaufman
C. Walters Bells	R. L. Linton Carlisle	W. T. Dillon Gorman	N. F. Rodgers Kemp
G. A. Bishop Bedias	J. J. McCrary De Kalb	H. L. Anderson Gordon	C. C. Wells Kingfisher
W. A. Noland Buffalo	J. M. Murphy	J. M. Wayman Goltry	M. C. Livingston
A. R. Nash Bryson	Dalby Springs	A. R. Boles Gordonville	Knox City
J. Taylor Biardstown	H. F. Mahlmann	J. T. Goodman Gunter	E. A. Penland Keechi
W. H. Moore Brookston	Deanville	C. E. Webb Goodlett	J. H. Brooks Kosse
A. C. Rogers Bremond	J. A. Coleman DeLeon	B. W. Brown Glazier	L. M. Dosser Kerens
A. F. Gilbert Brazos	E. Barnes Dozier	J. O. Kesler Gageby	M. T. Smith Logan
G. F. Hamilton Brad	E. D. Teague Duster	W. J. Ertes Gem	Fred Littau, Jr. Lipscomb
C. S. Hummer Bagwell	W. L. Cantrell Dunlap	W. G. Carter Granbury	Jack Keeling Leary
S. Woodson Booker	B. J. Camp Dothon	T. E. Parks	Chas. Lewis Lyons
R. H. Wright	W. W. Martin Dublin	Georges Creek	J. E. Purvis Lamkin
Breckenridge	J. P. Callahan Dodd City	W. S. Tyer Grapeland	T. H. Jackson Lorenzo
G. H. Crisp	P. O. Brack Denison	J. T. Gibson Grow	C. E. Meyers Lelia Lake
Bald Prairie	S. S. Terrell Detroit	C. M. Rhodes Groesbeck	J. C. Borgley Lacasa
F. H. Newby Bunger	W. F. Zieber Drummond	R. S. Cupp Gause	M. J. Lawrence Lipan
J. B. Ragan Barry	T. C. Eggleston Dexter	M. D. May Granbury	Claude Leach Lockney
F. C. Bell Bogata	F. M. Adams Duke	V. E. May Glen Rose	T. E. Walls Lakeview
J. D. Roach Catesby	R. E. Grape Dover	B. D. Moore Graham	D. C. Pope Lipan
C. C. Wyatt Caldwell	D. L. Noser Deport	L. J. Noeman Garner	J. N. Dean Lovelady
C. M. Mitchell	G. C. Wilson Dodd City	R. Rushing Groveton	T. B. Coleman Louise
College Station	P. F. Scott Dime Box	R. Kline Higgins	J. M. Stubbs Lexington
J. B. Warren Chriesman	J. H. Oakes Donie	H. J. Klassen Hooker	R. G. Gibson Leona
F. Langletz Caldwell	J. A. Nichols Dawson	J. A. Autrey Hooks	T. D. Station Lubrock
T. C. Clearman Clyde	E. P. Putnam Dobbin	W. E. Mullins Hedley	S. Walton Lipscomb
A. J. Moore Childress	J. Redman Darrouzett	S. I. Grissett Hico	T. T. Huffman Loving
R. C. McGinnis	Mrs. B. Swink Dawson	S. S. Ragsdale	O. O. Rachel Maud
Comanche	A. Parke Dicey	Huckabay	M. Dunlap Millican
J. W. Carter Carlton	H. H. Luke Dennis	W. Rutherford Howe	A. N. McDonald
N. E. Sweeden Comyn	C. A. Blosser Elmwood	G. T. Barnett	McAdos
C. S. Lewis Chalk	B. H. Green Eastwood	Honey Grove	W. Z. Mauldin Milford
O. C. Hulme Crosbyton	Mrs. R. N. Champion	H. A. Wessenger	J. T. Thomas Mertens
J. B. Estes Clarendon	Ennis	Hillsdale	A. L. Wilson Midlothian
H. Wernette Can Raub	W. J. Beasly Ector	Dr. R. W. Saddler Howe	J. P. Moody Morgan Mill
W. L. Yeager Cisco	T. H. Janett Estelline	B. C. Lewis Hagerman	J. E. Tole Margaret
W. I. Lovell Carbon	W. J. Steen Edam	W. N. Tuqua Hamilton	W. N. Holmes McLean
John Polak Crisp	F. C. Gregory Elbert	W. A. Guinn Hico	Philip Baty Mexia
C. H. Dowdy Clairette	W. R. Rodgers Elmina	Henry Ford Hollis	E. D. Abney Memphis
A. L. Fisher Carlton	G. W. Balman Elmwood	Terry Cooper Hamlin	C. W. Young Marshall

W. M. Landers	Medillo	M. D. Hornsby	Procter	L. C. Barrow	Rainbow	G. H. Currie	Turkey
T. H. Oglesby	Minter	J. L. Blount	Paducah	J. L. Horne	Rosser	J. W. Casper	Tell
W. E. Coker	Marquez	E. L. Lamb	Pioneer	C. C. Clark	Roxton	J. T. Robinson	Trinton
J. L. Cohen	Mt. Calm	T. B. Savage	Petty	B. T. Pullen	Rockwall	C. N. Davis	Thalia
C. C. Cask	Marlin	G. O. Gibson	Paris	G. W. Ray	Rockdale	J. L. Wright	Turkey
E. D. Wilson	Mexia	J. H. Parker	Pattonville	W. W. Small	Ramsdel	J. Cherry	Talor
W. E. Kirkman	Moran	G. E. Barnes	Pottsboro	W. L. Marshall		M. A. Wilhoir	
C. E. Burnett	Miami	W. Maywald	Plantersville		Roaring Sprgs.		Thorp Spg.
B. L. Webb	Mobeetie	Willis Fuqua	Piedmont	N. C. Martin	Riverside	G. W. Ayers	Terrell
J. H. Smith		Pet Dahl	Pettus	V. E. Veale	Ranger	M. L. Henson	Thornton
	Mineral Wells	M. A. Bennett	Parnell	J. A. Hall	Richland	B. Calome	Tehuacana
J. A. Gibbs	Madisonville	H. W. Clifton	Poluxy	Mike Nagy	Rice	A. J. Kirby	Texarkana
J. B. Knight	Midway	A. F. Pierce	Percilla	S. J. Willingham	Rotan	J. S. Arche	Tolbert
J. W. Booth	Moran	J. W. Buster	Paris	Gordan Cumming		J. H. Dunlap	Trinity
J. L. Callaway	Mumford	W. H. White	Petty		Sherman	R. W. Gill	Trevat
I. W. Cox	Markly	J. H. Counts	Pointblank	J. H. Berry	Seymour	R. N. Beatty	Vivian
A. W. Hunter	Merkel	J. D. Litton	Palo Pinto	W. J. Brown	Speermore	L. Morgan	Van Alstyne
S. P. Wootton	Murray	W. R. Goss	Paducah	F. D. Jennings	Simons	J. B. Blackburn	Vera
R. T. Pope	Millsap	J. A. Russell	Perryton	T. W. Brown	Shamrock	A. W. Cris	Vernon
A. A. Walker	Manchester	W. D. Mitchell	Phelps	W. E. Armstrong		John Price	Vesey
W. C. Pierce	New Boston	R. E. Durham	Padgett		Somerville	R. S. Williams	Westover
B. F. Sandel	Nimrod	D. T. Holbart	Proffitt	A. T. Fish	Swearingen	D. R. Royder	Wellborn
N. Thompson	Nayasota	J. M. Abbott	Padgett	W. L. Curtis	Seagoville	E. E. Brown	Waukomis
W. B. Hamilton	Newlin	J. A. Putnam	Purdon	J. T. Reid	Sparenburg	S. Cadwell	Whitesboro
R. Lawson	Normangee	S. L. Heath	Poolville	A. T. Allison	Stephenville	G. G. Wade	Whitewright
J. B. Hariss	N. Zulch	W. R. Ramsey	Perrin	H. Martin	Sumner	J. E. Knight	Winkler
W. M. Good	Notla	C. W. McCarty	Peaster	Gavlin Adams	Sadler	B. E. Goodrun	Weldor
R. F. Jones		S. J. Jones	Pennington	T. B. Stoneham		A. E. Duke	Wortham
	New Waverly	L. V. Pointer	Quitaque		Stoneham	Julius Roese	Washington
W. T. McBride		W. A. Atkinson	Quail	T. E. Lucas	Singleton	M. Varley	Whitehouse
	New Baden	W. E. Holley	Quanah	G. F. Brooks	Shiro	C. Burnett	Wills Point
J. B. Hulse	New Castle	J. T. Baldwin		J. H. Gabriel	Streetman	G. J. Heflen	Waller
I. A. Joplin	Negley		Red Springs	W. D. Harvey	Scurry	J. C. Moore	Wheeler
B. Ayers	Nighton	J. G. Hamilton	Riverside	W. E. Ditto	Sumner	J. J. Webb	Wellington
J. O. Williams	Oplin	J. O. Spencer	Redwater	J. A. Moore	Shamrock	H. L. Parsley	Willis
C. B. Goodwin	Okra	W. O'Dell	Rowden	D. I. Barnett	Staley	C. A. Martin	Whiteflat
J. R. Howe	Okarthe	E. G. Rone	Rucker	J. C. Smith	Salesville	L. T. Taylor	Woodson
A. P. Goodwin	Omega	J. N. Bowen	Rector	W. T. Gentry	Slaton	W. M. Spicer	Wayland
W. L. Oakwood		D. J. Blanton	Ralls	R. H. Adams		W. G. Currey	Wheelock
	Oakwood	J. J. Tucker	Ranger		Spring Creek	J. V. Ellis	Weatherford
C. W. Adams	Oakhurst	J. W. Earp	Romney	L. N. Thomas	S. Bend	T. J. Wells	Whitt
W. E. Turner	Odell	J. L. Clark	Rising Star	Clark DuBose	Streetman	C. L. Lunsford	
J. B. Railey	Oletha	W. C. Rockett	Red Oak	G. C. Craig	Springtown		Woodland
C. B. Carter	Olney	J. H. Harris	Ravenna	C. L. Liggins	Scrap	J. T. McGuire	Wawaka
P. J. Keester	Orth	J. McCloskey		O. Z. Lott	Saron	G. C. Stoneham	Yarboro
J. W. Johnson	Perryton		Roans Prairie	C. F. Teague	Texarkana	C. Shields	Young
T. M. Ledbetter	Putnam	J. K. Hoke	Richards	R. H. Holiday	Tabor	R. N. Batten	Zach

VIRGINIA

GIVES NEW INTEREST

Ibex, April 3rd.

WROUGHT IRON RANGE CO., St. Louis, Mo.

Gentlemen:—

The Enameled "HOME COMFORT" Range I had installed several months ago is giving us excellent service, and is giving my family a new interest in their kitchen work. It is very saving with fuel, and does its work in a very superior manner. Its baking and cooking are perfect. I certainly do not regret its installation.

E. P. DAVIS

A REMARKABLE PRODUCT

Wise, April 7th.

WROUGHT IRON RANGE CO., St. Louis, Mo.

Gentlemen:—

We have not been disappointed with our new Enameled "HOME COMFORT" Range which has now been in use for nearly a year. The "HOME COMFORT" is certainly a remarkable product, and has had for years the reputation of being the very best kitchen Range on the market. I expect this Range to last for many years, but if I am ever called upon to replace it, it will certainly be with another "HOME COMFORT".

L. V. FULTON
(Deputy Sheriff)

HE KNOWS

Wise, April 6th.

WROUGHT IRON RANGE CO., St. Louis, Mo.

Gentlemen:—

I want to say that the Enameled "HOME COMFORT" Range we are using is all that I expected it to be from your salesman's representation. I did not have to depend upon his recommendations, however, for this is the third "HOME COMFORT" Range I have bought. I know their real quality and worth; therefore, I would not put my money into any other Range made.

J. E. C. HYLTON

SAVES MANY STEPS

Pound, April 8th.

WROUGHT IRON RANGE CO., St. Louis, Mo.

Gentlemen:—

We are using one of your Enameled "HOME COMFORT" Ranges, which I bought from your salesman last fall. We have found it to be all it was recommended and more. Besides being a perfect baker and fuel saver, it is also a step saver in the kitchen, and makes the kitchen work a great deal easier because of its many conveniences. My family is very proud of it.

ORLEIN MULLINS

HE MADE BEST CHOICE

Norton, April 4th.

Wrought Iron Range Co., St. Louis, Mo.

Gentlemen:—

I desire to say that the new Enameled "Home Comfort" Range which I bought from you several months ago is giving excellent service and satisfaction. It is a real comfort to our home, and I do not believe I could have made a better choice. I certainly do not regret buying it.

R. M. Arnold

QUALITY AND APPEARANCE

Big Stone Gap, April 2nd.

Wrought Iron Range Co., St. Louis, Mo.

Gentlemen:—

Last summer I bought one of your Enameled "Home Comfort" Ranges from your salesman. It is giving the best of satisfaction, and we are well pleased with the quality of its cooking, as well as its beautiful appearance. I believe we have a Range that will last us for a great many years.

L. M. Collier

EASY TO KEEP CLEAN

Big Stone Gap, April 1st.

Wrought Iron Range Co., St. Louis, Mo.

Gentlemen:—

We have one of your Enameled Model "Home Comfort" Ranges, which I purchased from your salesman last July. We have found it to be a perfect baker and an ideal cooker in every respect. My family like it, especially because it is so easy to keep clean.

John Gilley

LIGHTENS FARM-WIFE'S WORK

Lovettsville, October 16th.

Wrought Iron Range Co., St. Louis, Mo.

Gentlemen:—

I have used my "Home Comfort" Range 10 years and find it to be satisfactory in every way. It has always baked well and has paid for itself in the saving of fuel and labor a long time ago. It is the only really economical range for anyone to buy, and every farm-wife should have one to help lighten her work, for the "Home Comfort" will certainly do it.

Mrs. S. Henry George

PERFECTLY SATISFIED

Roanoke, November 1st.

Wrought Iron Range Co., St. Louis, Mo.

Gentlemen:—

Our "Home Comfort" Range is the best one we have ever seen and we are perfectly satisfied with it in every way. We do not believe there can be a better range made.

Mack Smith

NO SHADOW OF REGRET

Dante, January 26th.

Wrought Iron Range Co., St. Louis, Mo.

Gentlemen:—

We consider our "Home Comfort" Range the best stove we have ever had in our house. We are certainly glad we have it and do not regret buying it for one minute.

D. C. Frazier

LIKES GOOD TREATMENT

Buena Vista, October 20th.

Wrought Iron Range Co., St. Louis, Mo.

Gentlemen:—

I must say that we are well pleased with our "Home Comfort" Range, and we don't think it can be surpassed by any other. It is easily and quickly heated and we find a great saving in time. It cooks a meal so quick that it doesn't give me time to attend to my stock in the morning before the bell is ringing for breakfast. I don't think there is one made that can beat it. Please accept my thanks for good treatment.

Joe S. Richeson

APPRECIATES COURTESIES

Baskerville, October 16th.

Wrought Iron Range Co., St. Louis, Mo.

Gentlemen:—

We want to thank you for courtesies extended to us, and wish to say our "Home Comfort" Range is very fine.

S. W. Alexander

WOULDN'T PART WITH IT

Alberta, October 7th.

Wrought Iron Range Co., St. Louis, Mo.

Gentlemen:—

Many thanks for your kindness and much success for your future. We would not think of parting with our "Home Comfort" Range.

J. B. Clark

W. E. Wood Alexandria	C. B. Lee Clifton	W. E. Lucus Gaylord	W. Hepson Merrifield
S. Pettit Accotink	T. F. Moler	M. C. Calvert Gainesville	J. Rector McLean
H. F. Brent Amissville	Clifton Station	J. C. Goodloe Gordonville	W. Smith Middleburg
T. C. McIntosh Arcola	W. T. Gray Catlett	W. L. Batts Glendie	W. Houghton Markham
Will Russ Ashburn	Arch Sinclair Casanova	M. A. Randolph Hamilton	J. W. Moore Midland
Milton Chinn Agnesville	F. H. Rhodes Calverton	S. F. Reed Herndon	Clay Leach Marshall
W. T. Gibson Burnleys	H. T. Jones Clarksville	D. H. Polen Hay Market	C. E. Arnott Mountville
W. T. Bracey Brodnax	E. J. Hasenbuhler	R. B. Payne Hoadley	H. T. Kirby Middleburg
J. F. Human Burdis	Cherry Run	W. E. Fisher Hawling	R. Wells Manassas
C. Willmars Boston	J. W. Harrison	B. W. Hitt Hughes River	T. V. Overby Macon
John Walker Batna	Clifton Station	W. Reach Heflin	N. Ball Nokesville
W. H. Kusper Brandy	Kemp Shaffer Delaplane	G. W. Jones Jones Store	T. Peryear Nelson
D. Shephard Berryville	J. E. Bowman	C. B. Chilton Ladota	A. C. Posey Nabsco
S. Ball Boyce	Dawsonville	Henry Cottoms Lignum	David White Orlean
A. W. Teates Bealton	Wm. D. Peale Dumfries	Clia Brown LaGrange	J. M. Walker Ogburn
M. Russell Bristow	A. E. Groff East Falls Ch.	C. P. Redmond Leesburg	R. L. Lahr Orange
G. T. White Bealeton	King Warner Eckington	C. L. Dixon Lorton	J. S. Powell Occoquan
G. Lee Bluemont	D. S. Childress Elkwood	W. V. Thorn Lois	L. B. Payne Purcellville
John Bunk Berryville	W. E. Sykes Emporia	T. A. Belt Lincoln	E. G. Rust Philmont
J. J. Burke Brightwood	John Anderson Fairfax	H. Sanbower Lovettsville	J. A. Miller Quinton
A. Harris Bracey	Ed. Gutridge	J. H. Harener Leesburg	S. G. Bettin Quantico
H. T. Mason Baskerville	Fairfield Station	A. E. Wilt Luckets	R. S. Gallihugh Rapidan
Huff Harris Blackridge	E. B. Walker Forksville	R. L. Broyles Leon	H. C. Priest Rapidan
D. A. Hite Buffalo Jct.	Thos. Thurston	L. E. Fry Locust Dale	J. H. Golay Rhoadsville
T. H. Blanks Blackburg	Front Royal	Wm. Barzd Lacrosse	O. Fritter Roseville
J. E. Ham Barboursville	A. Porks Fredericksburg	H. Dickinson Lahore	W. M. Maddox Ruby
Mark Thomas Bristow	Keith Wine Falmouth	G. T. Foster Lahn	F. H. McGuire Shipman
J. D. Dodson Culpepper	M. Aylor Griffinsburg	A. K. Finney Logan	J. H. Epps Skippers

<table>
<tbody>
<tr><td>A. D. Bullock</td><td>Sealston</td></tr>
<tr><td>Jos. Brooks</td><td>Sterling</td></tr>
<tr><td>B. G. Rainey</td><td>South Hill</td></tr>
<tr><td>R. N. Roberts</td><td>Somerset</td></tr>
<tr><td>C. J. Brooking</td><td>Summitt</td></tr>
<tr><td>E. F. Furgerson</td><td>Storck</td></tr>
<tr><td>Geo. Storck</td><td>Stafford</td></tr>
<tr><td>H. B. Kerns</td><td>Trone</td></tr>
<tr><td>S. S. Fawley</td><td>The Plains</td></tr>
<tr><td>J. M. Carter</td><td>Uni</td></tr>
<tr><td>H. M. Lohr</td><td>Union Level</td></tr>
<tr><td>H. M. Roberts</td><td>Vienna</td></tr>
<tr><td>Wm. Winston</td><td>Vaughan</td></tr>
<tr><td>G. S. Brown</td><td>Warrenton</td></tr>
<tr><td>J. M. Riley</td><td>Waterloo</td></tr>
<tr><td>S. G. Mills</td><td>Waterford</td></tr>
<tr><td>F. Dabney</td><td>Waterloo</td></tr>
<tr><td>D. O. Coughlin</td><td>Woodville</td></tr>
</tbody>
</table>

A. D. Bullock Sealston
Jos. Brooks Sterling
B. G. Rainey South Hill
R. N. Roberts Somerset
C. J. Brooking Summitt
E. F. Furgerson Storck
Geo. Storck Stafford
H. B. Kerns Trone
S. S. Fawley The Plains
J. M. Carter Uni
H. M. Lohr Union Level
H. M. Roberts Vienna
Wm. Winston Vaughan
G. S. Brown Warrenton
J. M. Riley Waterloo
S. G. Mills Waterford
F. Dabney Waterloo
D. O. Coughlin Woodville

Ed. Moss Warren Plains
L. H. Olinger Winchester
J. H. Jarvis Andover
E. L. McCracken "
H. A. Ward Appalachia
J. W. Miller "
Baxter Qualls
Big Stone Gap
M. H. Garrison " "
E. V. Frazer Blackwood
Baxter Skeen Ben Hur
H. A. Sprinkle " "
Julia Dotson Coeburn
Gella Holbrook "
J. S. Willis Caylor
H. C. Napier Dooley
Mode Poteet Dot
P. R. Hinkle "
C. M. Barker Duffield

Lon Chadwell Ewing
Dan Richmond "
B. C. Tate E. Stone Gap
G. E. Graham " "
Mary Mitchell Esserville
J. H. Clark "
Roy Burnett Golden
Emory Gardner Graden
D. W. Ely Hagan
Anthony Ely "
W. J. Gibson Jonesville
I. V. Redwine "
M. W. Keestuson "
J. E. Thomas Keokee
H. W. Woodard "
D. S. Woodard
Leona Mines
W. E. Woodard "
Robt. E. Kirk Sallann

W. P. Hupp Norton
E. M. Taylor "
Walker Cowden "
Jim Reasor Olinger
L. M. Hart "
Palmer Pugh
Pennington Gap
Elias Harber " "
Orben Mullins Pound
Dewey Lee Rose Hill
L. J. Ramsay "
B. L. Ramsey Saint Paul
F. J. Hale St. Charles
Joe Osbourne " "
Lizzie Moneyhun
Toms Creek
Annie Phillips
Virginia City
Jocy Dotson Wise

WEST VIRGINIA

DID NOT MAKE A MISTAKE
Morgantown, March 6th.
WROUGHT IRON RANGE CO., St. Louis, Mo.
Gentlemen:—

I have just purchased from your salesman one of your New Enameled Model "HOME COMFORT" Ranges, and know that I have not made a mistake in buying it. This range is replacing in our kitchen a "HOME COMFORT" that we have used for over 25 years, and have only paid out five dollars for repairs in all that time. However, while it is in fairly good condition yet, I wanted to install one of your new ranges while your salesman was in this community, and not have to wait 2 or 3 years till he came back again.

HARRY BEAL

MUST HAVE VERY BEST
Cuzzart, January 13th.
WROUGHT IRON RANGE CO., St. Louis, Mo.
Gentlemen:—

We have used our "HOME COMFORT" Range for 16 years, and it is a good one yet; however, when your salesman showed me your New Enamel Range, I liked it so well that I bought one. I feel that it is the very best range that can be made, and I would not think of putting my money into any other kind. They are perfect bakers, great fuel savers, and an ornament to any home.

A. K. LIVENGOOD

"TAKE PIANO—LEAVE RANGE"
Meadow Creek, March 16th.
WROUGHT IRON RANGE CO., St. Louis, Mo.
Gentlemen:—

I am perfectly satisfied with my "HOME COMFORT" Range, and really could not get along without it. Everyone coming to my house admires it. I have had a piano in my home for years, and if anything should happen, and I would be forced to give up one or the other, I would say, "Take the piano, and leave my 'HOME COMFORT' Range." Before I got it, I had to brown my bread on top of the stove, but my "HOME COMFORT" browns everything I put into its oven. I must say the "HOME COMFORT" is worth every dollar I have paid for it.

MRS. JESSE WADDY

IT IS A MASTERPIECE
Valley Point, February 11th.
WROUGHT IRON RANGE CO., St. Louis, Mo.
Gentlemen:—

For 15 years our "HOME COMFORT" Range has given us the best of service, and has been all that could be asked of any range. We viewed several stoves in the past, but we think the "HOME COMFORT" is a masterpiece and cannot be beat.

MR. AND MRS. ASBURY LISTON

30 YEARS—STILL FAITHFUL
WROUGHT IRON RANGE CO., St. Louis, Mo.
Gentlemen:—

I have used my "HOME COMFORT" Range for 30 years, and it is yet in good condition, and does its work as faithfully as when it was practically new. It has been a real comfort to me, and I do not feel I could get along without it. If I must ever replace it with another, it will certainly be with a new "HOME COMFORT."

MRS. EVELYN RILEY

HAS NEEDED NO REPAIRS
Tunnelton, February 6th.
WROUGHT IRON RANGE CO., St. Louis, Mo.
Gentlemen:—

I bought a "HOME COMFORT" Range in 1901, —we are still using it—it still gives perfect satisfaction. I have never spent one cent for repairs, and I do not believe there is another range that could equal this record.

A. G. BIGGINS

A LIFE-TIME RANGE
Sisterville, April 18th
WROUGHT IRON RANGE CO., St. Louis, Mo.
Gentlemen:—

The "HOME COMFORT" Range I bought over 20 years ago is still in daily service, and has never cost me a dollar for repairs. It is certainly a lifetime range, and no one will make a mistake when they buy a "HOME COMFORT." The first cost is practically the only cost, and they work faithfully for years.

ARCH T. LEWIS

ONLY COST IS FIRST COST
New Martinsville, April 15th.
WROUGHT IRON RANGE CO., St. Louis, Mo.

Gentlemen:—

Twenty-eight years ago I bought a "HOME COMFORT" Range which has always given us complete satisfaction, notwithstanding the fact it went through one fire. While it experienced some slight damage, we have been able to use it since, and it is still doing duty today. I can say the "HOME COMFORT" is a remarkable range, and do not believe there is another range made that possesses the durability or so many years of service as it does, and I am sure that it is the cheapest range in the long run, for the only cost I have been out is what I first paid for it.

JOHN CHRISTIN

IT BAKES TO PERFECTION
Morgantown, March 4th.
WROUGHT IRON RANGE CO., St. Louis, Mo.

Gentlemen:—

Our "HOME COMFORT" Range is now 25 years old, and it bakes to perfection in the same way that it has always done. It is practically as good as when new, and we certainly would not think of exchanging for a new one of any make unless it were a New "HOME COMFORT."

MR. AND MRS. C. B. SHRIVER

DOING TWICE THE BAKING
Cassville, March 2nd.
WROUGHT IRON RANGE CO., St. Louis, Mo.

Gentlemen:—

For the past 25 years, our "HOME COMFORT" Range has supplied us with three meals daily, and I am confident that it has done twice as much baking and cooking as any other range in this community. It is still in good condition for service, and I think it will last for several years to come. If I were buying a new range today, I would not consider any other but one of your New Model "HOME COMFORTS."

W. L. SUTTON

BEST "BUY" ON MARKET
White Sulphur Springs, April 10th.
WROUGHT IRON RANGE CO., St. Louis, Mo.

Gentlemen:—

I wish to say that after using my "HOME COMFORT" Range more than a year, I am more than pleased with it, and consider it by far the best buy on the market. I do not consider that any home kitchen is complete without a "HOME COMFORT" Range, and I never lose an opportunity to recommend it.

A. W. HIPPERT

JUST AS RECOMMENDED
Morgantown, March 4th
WROUGHT IRON RANGE CO., St. Louis, Mo.

Gentlemen:—

We are using one of your 1922 Model "HOME COMFORT" Ranges, that we bought when your men were working in this county. It has always given us the satisfaction we had a right to expect from the way the range was recommended to us, and have never regretted our investment. I know that I got more than my money's worth, and my family think they have the best range made.

W. E. SHRIVER

APPRECIATES DEALINGS
Flattop, October 18th.
WROUGHT IRON RANGE CO., St. Louis, Mo.

Gentlemen:

We thank you very much for your good treatment of us in our dealings with you, as well as for the good "HOME COMFORT" Range. We are surely well pleased.

J. N. LILLY

HAS SAVED MANY DOLLARS
New Martinsville, April 17th.
WROUGHT IRON RANGE CO., St. Louis, Mo.

Gentlemen:—

We have used our "HOME COMFORT" Range for over 35 years, and it has never cost us anything for repairs. It has always done its work faithfully and has certainly been a great comfort to our home, and I know that it has saved me many dollars that I could have spent replacing and repairing stoves or ranges of other makes.

ALFERD NUTEN

H. C. Reed	Auto	H. S. Burr	Burr	W. J. Mitchell	Engle	O. B. Owen	Henning
O. G. Weaver	Arden	W. M. Hoover	Bartow	S. W. Harper	Elkins	I. H. Haines	Higginsville
B. Gladden	Anthony	D. L. Reed	Bertha	C. E. Holden	Elgwood	A. S. Wolford	Hay
F. Pyles	Augusta	I. B. Finks	Coalton	F. Streets	Elks Garden	C. Gidwell	Harpers Ferry
J. A. Cooper	Athens	M. Collins	Cecil	W. S. Gibson	Edray	A. L. Hyre	Harner
N. V. Wagoner	Alaska	M. E. Johnson	Clay	G. W. Jenkins	Evansville	H. C. Spencer	Hillsboro
A. L. Taylor	Arbovale	A. J. McKenny	Carlisle	J. D. Vandall	Elton	B. W. Carney	Hinton
W. E. Erwin	Alderson	J. H. Miller	Caldwell	C. Crouch	Elkwater	A. Metzner	Helvetia
P. Newman	Arden	W. D. Crane	Clintonville	W. L. Pharis	Elkins	A. F. Buckland	Hinton
D. T. Smith	Aurora	E. E. Crane	Crawley	O. L. Gower	Ellamore	S. B. Turner	Inwood
Wm. Murphy	Adolph	A. Elsea	Charlestown	E. M. Lilly	Ellison	H. Kimmel	Independence
C. A. Boyles	Alexander	G. B. Drake	Crawford	E. G. Baldwin	Frankford	R. L. Nester	Junior
J. W. Reger	Alton	H. J. Weeks	Clover Lick	W. B. Burns	Ft. Springs	S. M. Ball	Johnson
S. J. Bragg	Brooks	L. B. Hamrick	Cass	Clyde Ours	Fisher	B. Grimmett	Judson
B. D. Hill	Belington	T. L. Lynch	Countsville	R. R. Byrd	Franklin	F. C. Poling	Karson
H. G. Glass	Buckhannon	J. T. Richmond	Clayton	Walter Fink	Flat Top	H. J. Combs	Kirby
J. L. Williams	Beckley	Wm. George	Coalton	J. R. Garten	Forest Hill	W. H. Smith	Keyser
John Gragg	Bridgeport	A. J. Snyder	Czar	C. Boyles	Galoway	J. F. Sibold	Keenan
L. J. Lewis	Bunker Hill	A. H. Bryant	Dawson	S. S. Shriver	Grafton	J. S. Bright	Kerens
Ross Sims	Blue Sulphur	J. Hallandsworth	Droop	Tom Bramar	Glengary	J. E. Ratcliff	Landes
H. J. Walkup	Beard	J. Handyshell	Delray	K. M. Masters	Ganotown	S. Arbogast	Laurel Dale
C. M. Cullins	Brake	Allen Lodge	Dorr	E. Shroader	Gerardstown	F. H. Coler	Lahmarsville
J. J. Young	Boliver	J. A. Hively	Dunmore	C. Lyon	Greenland	J. M. Gilkerson	Lawn
G. L. Mills	Bakerton	C. M. Gratehouse	Durbin	H. Adams	Green Spring	W. E. Grabill	Levels
E. R. Conrad	Bowden	L. B. Lemon	Dorothy	Fred Vance	Glace	R. A. Whitacre	Loom
P. C. Weese	Beverly	S. F. Davis	Dry Fork	C. W. Bartlett	Grafton	E. A. Ludwick	
L. A. Iser	Blaine	J. E. Graham	Davis	W. E. Grogg	Gaines		Laurel Dale
J. Hedrick	Brood	Robt. Crigler	Ellamore	D. D. Morple	Hall	E. R. Morgan	Lobelia
G. C. Beard	Beard	W. L. Huffman	Esty	E. S. Spinks	Hughart	L. W. Bradford	Lester

A. J. Shaffer — Lead Mine
I. E. Gainor — Montrose
J. A. Corley — Mabie
Coy Poling — Moatsville
J. F. Mathias — Mathias
Lee Mitchell — Mt. Clair
Sam Bagen — Millville
E. H. Hamrick — Marlinton
W. L. Herold — Minnehaha
Q. McMillian — Mabscott
John Phipps — Maynor
Harl Taylor — Mill Creek
H. R. Meadows — Montrose
Chas. Ullery — Mabie
J. Bowles — Meadow Creek
M. O. Conner — Norton
J. W. Marsh — Nestorville
C. V. Gardner — New Creek
D. W. Alderman — Neola

Clint Wolfe — Newbury
A. Arbogast — Norton
E. B. Hoover — Organ Cave
A. J. Klein — Okanoko
E. S. Merritt — Old Fields
A. C. Barlow — Onoto
T. L. Boyles — Phillips
L. D. Veach — Purgitsville
L. P. May — Peru
C. F. Cook — Pickaway
F. R. Combs — Posey
J. H. Beckner — Parsons
J. Blankenship — Pipestem
C. W. DePay — Pickins
A. M. Reed — Queens
J. E. Lipps — Ronceverte
D. H. Simms — Rainelle
D. S. Rapp — Romney
E. B. Brofford — Rockoak

J. D. Clipp — Rippon
Homer Lee — Rada
I. P. Vance — Roaring
L. Simmons — Riverton
J. M. Asbury — Renick
B. L. Kincaid — Rock Cave
Will Smith — Sago
A. B. Shipman — Stroder
A. H. Kincaid — Sewell
F. E. Halliday — Smoat
M. C. Dalton — Sinks Grove
E. F. Taylor — Springfield
L. A. Duke — Sabraton
A. G. Lilly — Streeter
S. Reed — Second Creek
M. J. McCoy — Spice
Sherman Pyles — Seebert
J. L. Walkup — Spruce
S. L. Lilly — Sylvia

Bailey Mills — Sprague
P. S. Little — Stover
J. J. Cattle — Surveyor
T. C. Talbott — Simpson
E. H. Snider — St. George
F. N. Rader — Silica
L. E. Scott — Sandstone
W. T. Jamison — Union
R. Martin — Volga
B. Shiflett — Valley Bend
W. Arbogast — Valley Head
J. R. Snapp — Winchester
W. O. Bonnett — Weston
J. A. Arbogast — Woodrow
J. L. Tennant — Watson
C. E. Holden — Warford
G. C. Freeman — Weaver
B. Adams — Yantus

WISCONSIN

JOKE WAS ON THEM

Chippewa Falls, October 2nd.
Wrought Iron Range Co., St. Louis, Mo.
Gentlemen:—

Your letter of reply received. I surely appreciate the prompt attention given the oven-door frame which I wrote about. The break which we were positive that we had discovered, proved to be a mere mith. My daughter applied a few vigorous strokes with steel wool, and erased the supposed "break" which proved to be a thread of paint or something similar appearing like a break or crack. The joke is on us, we frankly confess. We are pleased to say that our "Home Comfort" is all your salesman represented it to be.

Mrs. Wm. Johnson

Jas. Boland — Arcadia
Bert Olson — Albertville
J. P. Nevens — Athens
P. A. Wilger — "
J. Sobatta — Arcadia
Laura York — Arkansaw
R. B. Ganoe — "
Fred Boers — Antigo
C. F. Johnson — "
W. Wagner — Boyd
Raymond Keople — "
P. Gesler — Bloomer
John Baranek — "
F. Olszewski — Birnamwood
H. R. Kosbob — "
Ole Moen — Baldwin
C. Klinderson — "
B. M. Olson — Boyceville
O. T. Thompson — "
R. Norman — Bay City
Ed. Rabel — "
L. Larson — Beldenville
A. Stewart — "
C. Clark — Boyceville
J. Hutchinson — Bloomer
Paul Manke — Bangor
H. W. McDougall — Bryant
J. Kaufman — Birnamwood
C. B. Seifert — "
George Vixer — Boyd
Chas. Moser — Cochrane
Ray Libbey — "
Chippewa Falls
G. B. Kneeland — " "
Anson Heagle — Cadott
John Peterson — "
Helmer Hanson — Curtiss
A. Knight — "
M. Gilbertson — Colfax
Louis Sather — Corn Valley
Anton Von Dreel — Colby
Ollie Brooks — Caryville

M. N. Olson — Colfax
Carlyton Gansing — "
Rudolph Bekkum — Caston
Iver Quinn — "
H. Krase — Dorchester
Frank Heitz — Durand
Gust Ullman — Deerbrook
G. Hotchkiss — "
L. A. Larson — Eleva
John Rauen — Edgar
H. Ameling — "
John Morew — Eau Claire
Lynn Falcon — "
P. Noll — Ellsworth
S. Johnson — "
Sam Hathway — Elk Mound
A. Christinson — " "
Sam Ulness — Eleva
Oscar Iverson — "
John Carroll — Eland
R. S. Meverden — "
A. Hund — Fountain City
Otto Kennebeck — " "
F. W. Mueller — "
A. Gust — Fallcreek
Abraham Muhr — "
Orin Guenderson — "
Gilmanton
G. Sumner — Greenwood
A. A. Brecker — "
E. Brandt — Glenwood City
M. Mortensen — " "
G. Drew — Gleason
Chas. Kruming — "
Wm. Watler — Hatley
P. Milanoski — "
Frank Buggs — Hamburg
Wm. Langhoff — "
R. A. Moen — Hammond
E. W. Douglas — "
John Rybold — Holmen
Ed. Burrows — "

And. Winsand — Independence
Elmer Hestkind — "
Dellie Street — Knapp
V. Johnson — "
P. Fenk — Kenosha
F. Johnel — LaCrosse
W. J. Miller — "
A. Frederickson — Loyal
R. Lubanski — "
Marshalltown
Thos. Ede — Mondovi
J. I. Wulff — "
T. Thorpe — Mendora
D. Nicks — Millston
J. Sicklinger — Marathon
T. Sulzer — "
John Kalasek — Mosinee
Aug. Steffen — "
A. Jaeger — Merrill
Ed. Gieger — "
Mrs. C. Londerville — "
Peter Vrieze — Maiden Rock
Chas. Baggie — " "
Chris Peterson — " "
E. G. Johnson — "
Menomonie
Thos. Lackner — "
John Shellhouse — "
Ole Hoode — Meridan
E. E. Rossman — Mondovia
T. C. Thorson — "
Wm. Bartlett — Naugart
R. W. Geise — "
Gustav Longbecker — "
Elmer Oelstrom — Owen
W. M. Cammers — "
Edw. Kleming — "
R. Tanten — Pigeon Falls
E. A. Hegge — " "
C. Wakefield — Pepin
Clarence Reed — "
Matt Pias — Ringle

Fred Burgoyne — "
S. H. Lewis — Roberts
E. Frey — River Falls
Ed. Stock — " "
Carl Phillips — " "
P. Mulholland — Rock Elm
M. E. O'Connell — "
J. Enge — Rock Falls
Ira Isham — " "
P. C. Peterson — " "
Harry Mason — Rockland
Adolph Olson — "
J. L. Hesselberg — "
C. F. Neuman — Spencer
W. Sakach — Stanley
John Kastle — "
Mike Jordan — "
I. A. Reiton — "
Spring Valley
A. J. Swenson — " "
T. Ellefson — "
C. Edminson — "
H. W. Schmitz — Sparta
Louis Haas — "
John Zimmer — Thorp
F. Boyaski — "
Edward Deitman — Unity
H. Burt — West DePere
W. F. Watts — Wither
Constant Petit — Winter
W. Grebe — Wausau
A. Dennis — "
F. E. Boerner — "
F. Meredith — Wilson
S. N. Swanson — "
Ed. Dale — Woodville
Frank Colburn — "
W. L. Kalbrenner — "
Tom Everson — White Hall
J. F. Peterson — " "
Anderson Bros. — "
F. F. Miller — West Salem
E. L. Marking — " "

A Few Testimonials From Hotels and Institutions

OFFICE UNION STATION CAFE COMPANY St. Louis, Mo.

Wrought Iron Range Co., St. Louis, Mo.

Gentlemen:—

It is due your Company that I should bear my testimonial to the service of the complete kitchen outfit furnished me by your Company, and which has been in service and under the management of four different chefs and kitchen crews; each of these has pronounced your ranges and other apparatus the most complete in point of durability, convenience and economy that it had ever been their good fortune to work over. Respectfully yours,

President and Manager Union Station Cafe Co. S. O. Hemenway,

HOTEL JEFFERSON St. Louis, Mo.

Wrought Iron Range Co., St. Louis, Mo.

Dear Sirs:—

Since March, 1904, we have had one of your gas ranges in use at the Jefferson, and it has given us satisfaction in every respect, and is now being used in our kitchen. We have used several of your coal ranges in the Arlington and Eastman Hotels at Hot Springs, and they have always given excellent satisfaction, so much so that I had you replace the Eastman range last fall, the old one having been in use for ten years. I would recommend your goods highly to anyone you might refer to me.

Very truly yours, (Signed) Lyman T. Hay, General Manager

LACLEDE HOTEL St. Louis, Mo.

J. L. Griswold, proprietor Laclede Hotel, St. Louis, endorses what his steward, A. C. Howard, says of our range: "The range furnished our hotel by your Company is giving the most perfect satisfaction. I consider it in many respects the best I have ever seen in twenty years' experience."

THE AMERICAN HOTEL St. Louis, Mo.

Wrought Iron Range Co., St. Louis, Mo.

Gentlemen:—

It gives me pleasure to recommend your house to anyone looking for a complete kitchen outfit. All the goods you placed in our kitchen at the opening of this house have proved to be most satisfactory and we take pleasure in showing our guests through our kitchen as we consider it one of the best and most up-to-date kitchens in this city. We can most highly recommend our gas range which you installed for us, as we feel it to be economical in the use of gas and it has been most satisfactory in every way. We consider the gas range to be as near perfect as any we have ever seen.

Yours truly, (Signed) C. C. Butler, Manager

FAIRMONT HOTEL
Under Management of the Palace Hotel Company San Francisco, California

Wrought Iron Range Co., St. Louis, Mo. San Francisco, October 22nd.

Gentlemen:—

It affords me great pleasure to say to anybody contemplating the fitting up of kitchen of any hotel or restaurant, that I have used the Wrought Iron Range Co.'s goods for a long time. Having found them to be so satisfactory, I am pleased to say, we have installed the same in the new kitchen of the Palace Hotel and expect great results therefrom. Very respectfully yours,

Fairmont Hotel (Signed) E. D. Arbogast, Chef de Cuisine, of Fairmont and Palace Kitchens

LOUISVILLE HOTEL Louisville, Kentucky

Wrought Iron Range Co., St. Louis, Mo.

Gentlemen:—

I have been using your Wrought Iron Range for a number of years and I want to say that the castings are far superior to any I ever used. I have been using a range of another make and one of Wrought Iron Range Company in our kitchen for seventeen months. I have not purchased any extra pieces for the "Home Comfort" stove while I have replaced castings several times on the other one.

Wishing you success with your range, Yours truly, (Signed) Bert DeVault, Steward

HOTEL BENTLEY Alexandria, Louisiana

Wrought Iron Range Co., St. Louis, Mo.

Gentlemen:—

Replying to yours of October 13th, I will state that it affords me a great deal of pleasure to recommend the cooking apparatus, which we purchased of you in the outfit we bought for the Hotel Bentley. This is the third one that I have purchased of you for three different hotels, all of which give perfect satisfaction, and I do not believe there is anything better on the market, or the equal of this one, and I assure you that I believe that after any hotel men use one, that they would not be without it.

With best wishes, I beg to remain, Yours very truly, (Signed) J. F. Letton, Manager

NEW CAPITOL HOTEL Little Rock, Arkansas

Wrought Iron Range Co., St. Louis, Mo.

Dear Sirs:—

The kitchen outfit we purchased from you for the New Capitol Hotel is entirely satisfactory, and doing good work. We do not hesitate to recommend your goods to anyone because we know they will give satisfaction. Yours truly, E. Belaire, Manager

"THE GEORGIAN" Athens, Georgia

Wrought Iron Range Co., St. Louis, Mo.

Dear Sirs:—

The kitchen, pantry and bakeshop outfit bought from your company, for this hotel, and installed almost a year ago has given perfect satisfaction, and the owners of the hotel and myself are well pleased with the results. I should not wonder if you get some good business this winter on account of it, as several hotel men have been through the culinary department and all expressed admiration for the plan and equipment. Very truly yours, (Signed) M. P. O'Callahan, Manager

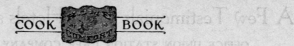

A Few of the Large Kitchens Using "Home Comfort" Ranges

U. S. GOVERNMENT

Aviation Repair Dept.	Dallas, Texas
Denver Tubercular Hospital	Denver, Colo.
Walter Reed Hospital	Washington, D. C.
Balloon School Hospital	Ft. Omaha, Neb.
Bergs Sanitarium	San Antonio, Texas
Quartermaster	Jeffersonville, Ind.
Quartermaster	Jefferson Bar., Mo.
U. S. Engineer's Office	Kansas City, Mo.
U. S. Engineer's Office	Memphis, Tenn.
U. S. Engineer's Office	Montgomery, Ala.
U. S. Engineer's Office	Rock Island, Ill.
U. S. Engineer's Office	St. Louis, Mo.
Marine Corps	Puget Sound, Wash.
Marine Corps	San Francisco, Calif.
Marine Barracks	Mare Island, Calif.
Post Exchange	Ava, Ill.
Post Hospital	Ft. Sill, Okla.
Quartermaster	Ft. Slocum, N. Y.
Depot Quartermaster	St. Louis, Mo.
Post Mess	Jefferson Bar., Mo.
Wisconsin State Camp	Union Grove, Wis.
U. S. Navy Yard	Portsmouth, N. H.
U. S. Navy Yard	Boston, Mass.
U. S. Navy Yard	Charlestown, Mass.
U. S. Navy Yard	New London, Mass.
U. S. Navy Hospital	Newport, R. I.
U. S. Coast Guard Academy	New London, Conn.
U. S. Veterans Hospital	San Fernando, Calif.
U. S. Veterans Hospital	Minnehaha, Minn.
U. S. Veterans Hospital	Sheridan, Wyo.
U. S. Veterans Hospital	Hot Springs, S. Dak.
U. S. Veterans Hospital	Dwight, Ill.
U. S. Veterans Hospital	Tucson, Ariz.
U. S. Trachoma Hospital	Richmond, Ky.
Pipestone Indian School	Pipestone, Minn.
Indian Day Schools	Elks, Nev.
Tohatchi Indian School	Gallup, New Mex.
Indian School	Concho, Okla.
U. S. Forest Service	East Tawas, Mich.
Scott Field	Belleville, Ill.
Coast Defenses of Portland	Ft. Preble, Me.
Army Medical Supply Depot	St. Louis, Mo.
Naval Detention Camp, Deer Island	Boston, Mass.
Naval Hospital	Ft. Lyon, Colo.
U. S. Marine Hospital	Staten Island, N. J.
Whipple Barracks	Phoenix, Ariz.
Brunswick Plant	Brunswick, Ga.
Navy Yard	Quincy, Mass.
U. S. General Hospital	Denver, Colo.
Jefferson Barracks Hospital	Jefferson Bar., Mo.
Camp Bragg	Fayetteville, N. C.
Valparaiso U. Army Depot	Valparaiso, Ind.
Westminster College (for Govt. Service)	Fulton, Mo.
S. A. T. C. Mess, University California	San Francisco, Calif.
Camp Abraham Eustis	Virginia
Camp Wheeler	Macon, Ga.
Naval Air Station	Chatham, Mass.
New Post	Ft. Sill, Okla.
Camp Sevier	Greenville, S. C.
Camp North Jackson	Dent Stations, S. C.
U. S. C. Q. M.	Ft. Rosecrans, Calif.
U. S. Q. M.	Galveston, Texas
Fort Douglas	Utah
U. S. Engineers	Florence, Ala.
U. S. Marine Barracks No. 4	Philadelphia, Pa.
U. S. Marine Hospital	St. Louis, Mo.
General Hospital No. 2	Ft. McHenry, Md.
Stephen Henry Gale Hospital	Haverhill, Mass.
U. S. Naval Hos. Reservation	Brooklyn, N. Y.
Marine Guard Barracks	Quantico, Va.

U. S. A. Hospital No. 10	Roxbury, Mass.
U. S. Public Health Service	Philippine Islands

We also furnished 5,756 army ranges, each having a capacity to cook for 100 men, and approximately 1000 army ranges with capacity to cook for 25 men. A great many of the larger ranges were shipped to France, the smaller ranges being used in officers' quarters in U. S.

DISTRICT OF COLUMBIA

St. Elizabeth's Hospital	Anacosta

ALABAMA

Arlington Hotel	Oxford
Rusco Hotel	Alexandria
Hervey Hotel	Birmingham
Ridgway Hotel	Danville
Athens Female College	Athens
Talladega College	Talladega

ARIZONA

North Arizona Normal School	Flagstaff
Pioneers' Home	Prescott
Y. M. C. A.	Phoenix
Fred Harvey	Ashforks
St. Mary's Hospital	Tucson
Sisters of St. Joseph	"
Arizona State Prison	Florence
Y. M. C. A.	Phoenix

ARKANSAS

New Moody Hotel	Hot Springs
Hoxie Cafe	Hoxie
Gus Blass Co.	Little Rock
New Subiaco	Subiaco
Arlington Hotel	Hot Springs
Arkansas State Penitentiary	Little Rock
Eastman Hotel	Hot Springs
Grand Central Hotel	Fort Smith
St. Scholasticus Convent	Shoal Creek

CALIFORNIA

Palace Hotel	San Francisco
City Hospital	"
Ft. McPherson	Angel Island
San Quinton Prison	Sacramento
Los Angeles' Athletic Club	Los Angeles
St. Francis Hotel	San Francisco
Hotel Oakland	"
Pilgrims' Club	Catalina Islands
Angeles Hospital	Los Angeles
Scottish Rite Cathedral	" "

COLORADO

Y. M. C. A.	Denver
El Jebel Temple	"
Mozart Cafe	"
Gloeckner Sanitarium	Colorado Springs
Andlers Hotel	" "
Boulderado Hotel	Boulder
State Penitentiary	Canon City
State Industrial School	Golden
Great Western Sugar Co.	Ault
Union Printers' Home	Colorado Springs
Cragmoor Sanitarium	" "
Children's Hospital Assn.	Denver
Denver County Jail	"
Y. M. C. A.	Estes Park
U. S. Naval Hospital	Fort Lyon
Hotel Colorado	Fort Collins
Woodcroft Hospital	Pueblo
Denver Tubercular Hospital	Sable
Denver Public Schools	Denver

Hotel Colorado..............Glenwood Springs
La Court Hotel..................Grand Junction
Edinger Cafeteria................Manitou
Dunnigans Cafe.................Fort Collins
Busy Bee Cafe..................Fort Morgan
Acacia Hotel..............Colorado Springs
Myron Stratton Home........... "   "
Phelp's Cafeteria.................... "
Bachelor Consolidated Mines Co...Ouray

CONNECTICUT

Waldorf System, Inc. (4 stores)..Hartford
Longley Lunch Co. (3 stores).....
Middlesex Hospital..............Middletown
Psychopathic Hospital..........Norwich
California Lunch Co..............Hartford
Robbins, Inc...................... "
W. W. Walker Co................. "
Mystic Oral School for Deaf......Mystic
Odd Fellows Home.................Groton

FLORIDA

Benedictine Sisters...............San Antonio
Holy Name Convent............... "   "
New Duvall Hotel................Jacksonville
Aragon Hotel.................... "
The Placide.....................Rockledge
Fountain City House..............Daytona
San Carlos Hotel................Pensacola
Cattaneos Grill..................Daytona

GEORGIA

Southern Military Academy.......Greensboro
U. S. Penitentiary...............Atlanta
Base Hospital................Fort Oglethorpe
Confederate Veterans' Home......Atlanta
Jackson Hotel Co................ "
Southern Hotel..................Vienna
The Georgian Hotel..............Athens
Oriental Hotel..................Atlanta

ILLINOIS

Y. W. C. A.....................Springfield
Springfield Cafeteria..............
International Shoe Co.............Wood River
International Shoe Co.............Belleville
Anna State Hospital.............Anna
Elgin State Hospital.............Elgin
Watertown State Hospital........Watertown
Dixon State School..............Dixon
McKendree College...............Lebanon
Pittenger Hotel.................Centralia
LeClair Hotel...................Moline
Western Military Academy........Alton
Chicago University..............Chicago
Auditorium Hotel................ "
State Training School for Girls....Geneva
University of Illinois............Urbana
Alton State Hospital.............Alton
U. S. Marine Hospital...........Chicago
Dixon State Hospital.............Dixon
Watertown State Hospital........E. Moline
Immaculate Conception Academy.Belleville
Illinois Hotel..................Bloomington
Camp Grant.....................Rockford
C. B. & Q. R. R. Co..............Chicago
Hotel Delite....................Casey
Memorial Methodist Hospital.....Mattoon
St. Charles School for Boys......St. Charles
Greenville College...............Greenville
Parkside Hotel..................Kewanee
Lincoln State School & Colony....Lincoln
Lincoln Field Jockey Club........ "
St. Francis Hospital.............Quincy

INDIANA

Culver Military Academy........Culver
Indian Day School...............Fort Wayne
DePauw University..............Greencastle
Indiana Reformatory.............Jeffersonville
U. S. Marine Hospital...........Evansville
Aged Persons' Home.............Honey Creek

Van Camp Packing Co..........Indianapolis
Severin Hotel..................Indianapolis
Claypool Hotel................. "
Sherman Hotel.................. "
Feeble Minded Institute.........Ft. Wayne
Boy Scouts of America..........Terre Haute
Robertson Bros. Store..........South Bend

IOWA

Iowa State College..............Ames
Davenport High School..........Davenport
Industrial School for Boys.......Eldira
State Hospital & Colony.........Woodward
Mercy Hospital.................Cedar Rapids
St. Joseph Sanatorium...........Dubuque
Central Holiness University......University Park
Iowa Hospital for the Insane......Independence
St. Bernard Hospital............Council Bluffs
St. Joseph's Hospital............Keokuk

KANSAS

Girls' Industrial School..........Beloit
Union Pac. R. R.................Armstrong
Security Benefit Home...........Topeka
Soldiers' Home.................Leavenworth
Mt. St. Joseph's College.........Concordia
Mt. St. Joseph's College.........Abilene
St. Margaret Hospital...........Wyandotte
Gladstone Hotel.................Arkansas City
Salina Normal University........Salina
Fred Harvey...................Emporia

KENTUCKY

Y. M. C. A. & Y. W. C. A.......Louisville
Girls' High School............... "
Boys' High School............... "
Western Insane Hospital.........Hopkinsville
Rauscher Hotel.................Bowling Green
House of Reform................Glendale
Millersburg Female Hospital......Millersburg
Branch Penitentiary.............Eddyville
State College..................Lexington

LOUISIANA

U. S. Marine Hospital...........New Orleans
Standard Oil Co................Shreveport
Holy Rosary Inst...............Lafayette
Louisiana State Hospital.........Pineville
St. Joseph's Abbey..............Covington
La. State Normal School.........Natchitoches
Deaf and Dumb Institute........Baton Rouge
Hotel Gruenwald...............New Orleans
Academy Sacred Heart.......... "   "
De La Salle Normal School......La Fayette

MAINE

Maine State Prison.............Thomaston
College Du St. Nom de Marie.....Van Buren
Coast Defenses of Portland......Ft. Preble
Technology Summer Camp........East Machias
Camp O-At-Ka.................East Sebago
Central Institute...............Pittsfield
Madawaska Training School......Kent

MASSACHUSETTS

Long Island Hospital...........Boston
City Hospital................... "
Waldorf Lunch Co. (20 stores)... "
Chas. Weegham Corp. (2 stores).. "
Boston State Hospital..........Matapan
Belchertown State Hospital......Belchertown
Waldorf System Inc. (6 stores)...Springfield
State Sanitarium...............Westfield
Mass. Reformatory for Women....Farmington
Naval Air Station..............Chatham
Foxboro State Hospital.........Foxboro
Gardner State Colony...........Gardner
Medfield State Hospital.........Medfield
Westboro State Hospital.........Westboro
Westborough State Hospital......Westborough
State Infirmary................Tewksbury

Worcester State Hospital.........Worcester
Levi Warren Junior High School..West Newton
Majestic Grill....................Pittsfield
Berkshire Lunch................. "

MICHIGAN

Berghoff Hotel....................Detroit
Edelweiss Hotel................. "
Wequetonsing Golf Club..........Harbor Springs
Woman's Benefit Ass'n...........Port Huron
Jackson Penitentiary............Jackson
Eastern Michigan Asylum.........Pontiac
Murray Hill Hotel...............Sault Ste. Marie

MINNESOTA

Women's Reformatory............Shakopee
State Hospital..................St. Peter
State Asylum....................Hastings
State Prison....................Stillwater
Soldier's Home.................Minneapolis
Minnesota Soldiers' Home.......Minnehaha

MISSISSIPPI

Miss. State Charity Hospital......Vicksburg
Miss. Agricultural and Mechanical
    College....................Starkville
State Lunatic Asylum............ackson
Vicksburg Hotel Co.............Vicksburg
Illinois Central Eating House.....Jackson

MISSOURI

City Hospital...................St. Louis
Hospital for Insane............. "   "
St. Louis High Schools.......... "   "
Mt. St. Rose Hospital........... "   "
St. John's Hospital............. "   "
Masonic Hospital................ "   "
Moolah Temple................... "   "
Jefferson Hotel................. "   "
American Hotel.................. "   "
Maryland Hotel.................. "   "
Y. M. C. A. & Y. W. C. A........ "   "
Missouri Athletic Assn.......... "   "
Internat'l Shoe Co. (7 factories)... "   "
Brown Shoe Co. (2 factories).... "   "
Catholic Women's Assn........... "   "
Bell Telephone Co............... "   "
Scottish Rite Cathedral......... "   "
Sansone Hotel..................Springfield
Scottish Rite Cathedral........Joplin
State Insane Hospital...........Farmington
State Insane Hospital...........Fulton
Greers R. R. System............Kansas City
Central Wesleyan College.......Warrenton
Kemper Military Academy........Boonville
State Teacher's College........Springfield
Southeast Mo. Teachers' College..Cape Girardeau
Mo. State Hospital.............Nevada
Mo. State Penitentiary.........Jefferson City
Mo. State Sanitarium...........Mt. Vernon
Industrial Home for Girls......Chillicothe
Central Wesleyan Orphan Home...Warrenton
Colony for Feeble Minded and
    Epileptic..................Marshall

NEBRASKA

Girls' Industrial School........Geneva
Indian School..................Rushville
Martin Luther Academy..........Sterling
U. S. Veterans' Bureau.........Bellevue
Lincoln State Hospital.........Lincoln
Soldiers' and Sailors' Home....Milford
Great Western Sugar Co.........Gering
Institution for the Blind......Nebraska City
Paddock Hotel..................Beatrice
Home for the Friendless........Lincoln
S. Shindo......................Grand Island
N. A. Darling..................Kimball

NEVADA

Nevada Consolidated Copper Co...McGill

NEW JERSEY

State Hospital..................Morris Plains

NEW MEXICO

St. Vincent Sanitarium ....Santa Fe
Amsden Lumber Company ......Farmington
Continental Oil Co..............Gallup

NEW YORK

General Electric Co.............Schenectady
Ellis Hospital................. "
U. S. Military Academy.........West Point
State Hospital.................Rochester
U. S. Recruit Station..........Ft. Slocum
Albion State Training School....Albion
State Agricultural School......Industry
Utica State Hospital...........Marcy
St. Agatha's Hospital..........Nanuet
Hotel Statler..................Buffalo
Hudson State Hospital..........Poughkeepsie
Skidmore College...............Saratoga Springs
Nathan Littauer Hospital.......Gloversville

NORTH CAROLINA

Golden Industrial Inst..........Bostic
Indian School.................Ellamore
Great Eastern R. W. C..........Kingston
Guildford House...............Greensboro
Highland Lane Club............Hendersonville
Blue Ridge Ass'n..............Asheville
McCless Hotel.................Lake Jonaluska
Moore's Spring Hotel..........Rural Hall
Mars Hill College.............Marshall

NORTH DAKOTA

U. S. Indian Service............Narrows
Jamestown College..............Jamestown

OHIO

Adams County Infirmary.........Winchester
National Soldiers' Home........Dayton
National Cash Register......... "
Sisters of Precious Blood......Frank
Asylum for Insane.............Toledo
St. Anthony's Orphanage....... "
Hocking Valley R. R. Co........Columbus
Proctor & Gamble Mfg. Co.......Cincinnati

OKLAHOMA

Osla College for Women.........Chickasha
Indian School..................Concho
Indian School..................Millerton
State Training School..........Paul's Valley
Oklahoma State Hospital........Norman
Soldiers' Tubercular Sanitarium..Sulphur
Y. W. C. A.....................Tulsa
Oklahoma Hospital..............Vinita
Eastern Oklahoma Hospital...... "
Oklahoma School for Deaf.......Sulphur
Deaf and Blind State Inst......Taft
University State Hospital...... "

PENNSYLVANIA

State Normal School............Indiana
State Normal School............Mansfield
International Navigation Co......Philadelphia
Lafayette Hotel................Uniontown
Morrison House.................Reedsville
Pennsylvania R. R. Co..........Philadelphia
Fry Bros......................Williamsport
McCann's Restaurant...........Pittsburgh
Torrance State Hospital........Torrance

RHODE ISLAND

State Hospital for Insane.......Howard
State Infirmary................ "
State Sanitarium.............. "

COOK BOOK

SOUTH DAKOTA

Indian School..................Flandreau
State Normal School..........Springfield
Battle Mountain Sanitarium.....Hot Springs
Insane Asylum..................Aberdeen
Soldiers' Home.................Hot Springs
St. Martin's Convent...........Sturgis

TENNESSEE

Chisca Hotel...................Memphis
Peabody Hotel..................   "
Insane Hospital................Nashville
Appalachian Mills..............Knoxville
Presbyterian Hospital..........Jackson
Western Hospital...............Boliver
St. Joseph's Hospital..........Memphis
Sisters Charity Hospital.......Nashville

TEXAS

Deaf, Dumb and Blind School.....Austin
U. S. School of Radio Operators... "
St. Paul's College.............San Antonio
St. Louis and S. W. R. R.......Mount Pleasant
Bishop College.................Marshall
Seton Infirmary................Austin
Insane Asylum..................Eula
State Blind Asylum.............Corsicana
Confederate Home...............Austin
St. Joseph Orphanage...........San Antonio
Denison Hotel..................Denison

UTAH

Hotel Utah.....................Salt Lake City
Indian School..................Ft. Duchesne
Wasatch Academy................Mt. Pleasant
St. Mary's Academy.............Salt Lake City

VERMONT

State Prison...................Windsor
State Normal School............Castleton

VIRGINIA

Richmond Hotel.................Richmond
State Normal School............Hampton
Staunton Military Academy......Staunton
State Teachers' College........Farmville
Virginia Hotel.................Bristol
St. Paul Normal and Ind. School..Lawrenceville
Augusta Co. Welfare Home.......Staunton
Jefferson Hotel................Richmond
Colonial Hotel.................Norfolk

WASHINGTON

Columbia Co. Farmers' Corp.....Dayton
True Hotel.....................Pullman
Ranier Grand Hotel.............Seattle
Tacoma Hotel...................Tacoma
Hotel Spokane..................Spokane

WISCONSIN

Wisconsin Zinc Co..............Benton
Cathedral Choir School.........Fon du Lac
St. Agnes Convent.............. "   "
Secretariat Institute..........Beloit
Hotel Racine...................Racine
St. Elizabeth Hospital.........Appleton
St. Mary's Hospital............Milwaukee
St. Mary's Hospital............Racine

WYOMING

Wyoming Industrial Institute.....Colter
Plains Hotel...................Cheyenne
Midwest Refining Co............Casper

FOREIGN

Afro-American Co...............Capetown,
Royal Arms Hotel...............S. Africa
B. J. Hannon...................Carlow, Ireland
                              Goresbridge
                              County,
                              Kilkenny,
                              Ireland

Dr. H. N. Allen................Chemulpo,
                              Corea, Asia
Phra Suriya....................Bangkok, Siam, Asia
Salvador Franco................Bogota, S. A.
S. J. Christen.................Santiago, Chili, S. A.
Henreaux, Gen'l U.
  Prest. de la Republica
  Dominicana...................San Domingo
Chas. Jefferson Clark..........Buluwayo Meta-
                              beleland, S. Africa
Pentitentiary, Fed. Dist.
  of Mexico....................Mexico City, Mex.
Secretaria de Guerr y
Marina.........................Mexico City, Mex.
Geo. D. Barron.................Monterey, Mex.
Foundling Home.................Mexico City, Mex.
School of Arts.................Guadalajara
Winnipeg Gen'l Hospital........Winnipeg
Board of Foregin Missions......Chili
Foundlings' Home...............Guadalajara
Military Hospital..............Guadalajara
City Jail......................Guadalajara
Hospital Malibar...............Mexico
Hospital Genill................Mexico
Military Hospital..............Monterey
Manuel Garcia..................Tela, Honduras
Internacional Minera S. A......Guadalupe, Mex.

INDIA

Savoy Hotel....................Kandy, Ceylon

MEXICO

Restaurant Weber...............Mexico
Lic. Francisco Mancera.........Mexico
Hotel Pomeroy..................Guadalajara
R. & W. J. Wilson & Co.........El Oro
J. M. Mendoza..................Gomez Palacio
Modesto Ugaldo.................Oaxaca
Hotel Victoria.................Durango
Hotel Torreon..................Torreon
Hotel Iberia................... "

NOVA SCOTIA

Norfolk House..................New Glasgow
Pictou County Insane Asylum....Stallarton
Pictou Marine Railway..........Pictou
Vendome Hotel..................New Glasgow
Windsor Hotel.................. "   "

ONTARIO, CANADA

Bodega Cafe....................Toronto
Bowman House...................Waterloo
Clarendon Hotel................Toronto
Clemes House...................Spences Bridge
Daisy Restaurant...............Toronto
Empire Restaurant and Hotel.... "
Garner House...................Chatham
Graham's Hotel.................Allandale
Graham House...................Barrie
Grand Central Hotel............Collingwood
Grand Central Hotel............St. Catherine
G. N. Transit Co...............Collingwood
Hayden House...................Toronto Jct.
Homewood Retreat...............Guelph
Hotel Quinte...................Belleville
Insane Asylum..................Guelph
McKellar House.................Glenco
Moulton College................Toronto
Red Lion Hotel................. "
St. John Industrial School.....East Toronto
St. Lawrence Hall..............Morrisburg
Trinity College................Port Hop
Union Station..................Toronto
Victoria Industrial School for
  Boys.........................Mimico
Walker House...................Toronto
Zimmerman House................Waterloo
King Edwards Hotel.............Toronto
Northern Navigation Co.........Collingwood

PHILIPPINE ISLANDS

Governor General's Palace......Manila

— 215 —

General Index

Comments and References

Classification of Recipes

CULVER MILITARY ACADEMY

A UNIQUE WORK CONDUCTED UNDER THE SUPPORT AND MANAGEMENT OF
THE CULVER BROTHERS, OWNERS OF WROUGHT IRON RANGE COMPANY,
ST. LOUIS, MO.

The Culver Military Academy, located on Lake Maxinkuckee, Culver, Indiana, is a Preparatory School for boys between the ages of 10 and 18. It has achieved the highest standards of excellence as an educational institution, drawing patronage not only from every section of America, but from many foreign countries.

CULVER has been designated by the U. S. Government for twenty-seven consecutive years as one of the "distinguished" or "Honor" institutions in the country. Its investment has grown from a small one to an estate of a thousand acres containing scores of buildings valued at several million dollars; is in operation practically all year in the conduct of its many branches—

Culver Military Academy,

Culver Black Horse Troop,

Culver Artillery,

Culver Summer Naval School,

Culver Woodcraft School.

In 1932 there were 480 graduates of Culver, (among 136 colleges) most of whom distinguished themselves in scholastic and athletic achievements.

This institution has always been operated as a non-profit sharing corporation—no earnings nor profits have inured to the benefit of the stockholders, trustees or officers.

On June 9, 1932, to insure the perpetuity of this institution, the stockholders, under the "Culver Covenant," transferred their ownership to a Trust Foundation.

Space here does not permit calling attention to the many advantages of a training at Culver Military Academy; but to anyone interested, literature will be gladly sent upon request.

CULVER CADETS MARCHING TO PARADE

Memoranda for New Recipes

Memoranda for New Recipes

Memoranda for New Recipes

NAME OF PARENT...

STREET ADDRESS..

CITY..STATE..

NAME OF SON..AGE...............................

PRESENT GRADE IN SCHOOL...

You may use my name in writing the above parent or boy. Yes No
                                                   ☐   ☐

- -

NAME OF PARENT...

STREET ADDRESS..

CITY..STATE..

NAME OF SON..AGE...............................

PRESENT GRADE IN SCHOOL...

You may use my name in writing the above parent or boy. Yes No
                                                   ☐   ☐

- -

NAME OF PARENT...

STREET ADDRESS..

CITY..STATE..

NAME OF SON..AGE...............................

PRESENT GRADE IN SCHOOL...

You may use my name in writing the above parent or boy. Yes No
                                                   ☐   ☐

- -

NAME OF PARENT...

STREET ADDRESS..

CITY..STATE..

NAME OF SON..AGE...............................

PRESENT GRADE IN SCHOOL...

You may use my name in writing the above parent or boy. Yes No
                                                   ☐   ☐

- -

NAME OF PARENT...

STREET ADDRESS..

CITY..STATE..

NAME OF SON..AGE...............................

PRESENT GRADE IN SCHOOL...

You may use my name in writing the above parent or boy. Yes No
                                                   ☐   ☐

NAME OF PARENT

STREET ADDRESS

CITY _____ STATE

NAME OF SON _____ AGE

PRESENT GRADE IN SCHOOL

You may use my name in writing the above parent or boy.   Yes ☐   No ☐

NAME OF PARENT

STREET ADDRESS

CITY _____ STATE

NAME OF SON _____ AGE

PRESENT GRADE IN SCHOOL

You may use my name in writing the above parent or boy.   Yes ☐   No ☐

NAME OF PARENT

STREET ADDRESS

CITY _____ STATE

NAME OF SON _____ AGE

PRESENT GRADE IN SCHOOL

You may use my name in writing the above parent or boy.   Yes ☐   No ☐

NAME OF PARENT

STREET ADDRESS

CITY _____ STATE

NAME OF SON _____ AGE

PRESENT GRADE IN SCHOOL

You may use my name in writing the above parent or boy.   Yes ☐   No ☐

NAME OF PARENT

STREET ADDRESS

CITY _____ STATE

NAME OF SON _____ AGE

PRESENT GRADE IN SCHOOL

You may use my name in writing the above parent or boy.   Yes ☐   No ☐